DATA STRUCTURES AND PROBLEM SOLVING WITH TURBO PASCAL

WALLS AND MIRRORS

Frank M. Carrano
University of Rhode Island

Paul Helman
Robert Veroff
University of New Mexico

Addison-Wesley Publishing Company
Menlo Park, California ▪ Reading, Massachusetts ▪ New York ▪ Don Mills, Ontario
Wokingham, U.K. ▪ Amsterdam ▪ Bonn ▪ Paris ▪ Milan ▪ Seoul ▪ Taipei ▪ Sydney
Singapore ▪ Tokyo ▪ Madrid ▪ San Juan, Puerto Rico ▪ Mexico City

Sponsoring Editor: J. Carter Shanklin
Production Editor: Jean Lake
Design: The Book Company
Copy Editor: Rebecca Pepper
Cover Design: Yvo Riezebos
Composition: GTS Graphics

Library of Congress Cataloging-in-Publication Data

Carrano, Frank M.
Data structures and problem solving with Turbo Pascal : walls and mirrors / Frank M. Carrano, Paul Helman, Robert Veroff.
p. cm.
Includes index.
ISBN 0-8053-1217-X
1. Pascal (Computer program language) 2. Turbo Pascal (Computer file) 3. Data structures (Computer science) I. Helman, Paul. II. Veroff, Robert. III. Title.
QA76.73.P2C3665 1993
005.7′3—dc20 92-29450
CIP

4 5 6 7 8 9 10-RNT-98 97 96 95

Addison-Wesley Publishing Company
2725 Sand Hill Road
Menlo Park, CA 94025

```
      sortedListType = object(listType)     { descendent }
         { the constructor is inherited }
         destructor Done; virtual;          { virtual method }
         procedure ListInsert(Item: integer);      { method }
      end;  { object }
```

procedure definition

```
procedure One(Y : real; var C : arrayType; var F : text);
{ Sample procedure definition. Y is a value parameter;
  C and F are variable parameters. }
var Index : integer;                          { local variable }
begin
   <procedure body>
end;  { One }
```

function definition

```
function Max(A, B : integer) : integer;
{ Sample function definition. }
begin
   Max := A;
   if A < B
      then Max := B
end;  { Max }
   .
   .
   .
```

variable declarations

```
var   Size : integer;                         { integer }
      Average : real;                         { real }
      Ch : char;                              { character }
      Done : boolean;                         { boolean }
      Values : arrayType;                     { array }
      Heading : nameType;                     { string }
      DataFile : fileType;                    { general file }
      MyFile : text;                          { textfile }
      LetterSet: setType;                     { set }
      Head : ptrType;                         { pointer }
      Person : personType;                    { record }
      SL: sortedListType;                     { object }
      S: stackType;                           { type from unit }
```

program body

```
begin  { Main Program }
   .
   .
   .
   One(Average + 5.1, Values, MyFile);        { procedure call }
   Size := Max(5, Size);                      { function call }
   .
   .
   .
end.  { Program }
```

PREFACE

In a field as dynamic as computer science, it is common to see great diversity in undergraduate computer science curricula. This book includes comprehensive coverage of enough topics to make it appropriate for several kinds of courses. The focus on problem-solving tools, such as data abstraction, makes this book suitable for a second course in computer science. In addition, you can use this book in other courses such as introductory data structures, elementary software engineering, or advanced programming and problem solving. The goal remains to give students a superior foundation in data structures and modern problem-solving techniques.

APPROACH

As I set out to transform *Walls and Mirrors* into a book that you could use with Turbo Pascal, my goal was to do more than simply translate the programming examples from one version of Pascal to another. Unlike Standard Pascal, Turbo Pascal provides both units and object-oriented programming (OOP), features that enhance our main theme, data abstraction. Object-oriented programming is presented in a way that allows you to cover as much or as little of this new technique as desired.

In addition to extensively treating these additional topics, this edition improves all programming examples by adopting a consistent style for Pascal identifiers and by improving modularity. Finally, I have fine-tuned the presentation by rewriting and rearranging material to make the book more readable and by redrawing all illustrations.

Flexibility

The extensive coverage of this book should provide you with the material that you want for your course. You can select the topics you desire and present them in a flexible order. In Part I, you can choose among Pascal review topics according to your students' background. In Part II, three chapters provide an extensive introduction to data abstraction and recursion. Both topics are important, and there are various opinions about which should be taught first. Although in this book the chapter on data abstraction precedes the chapters on recursion, you can simply reverse this order. As I mentioned already, you can cover as much or as little of the new sections on object-oriented programming as you desire without affecting the continuity of instruction.

Parts III and IV treat topics that you can cover in a flexible order. For example, you can introduce tables before queues or cover hashing, 2-3 trees, graphs, or priority queues any time after tables and in any order. You can also cover topics from the last chapter earlier. For example, you can cover external sorting after you cover mergesort. The *Instructor's Guide* suggests other ways to order the topics in this book.

Data Abstraction and Object-Oriented Programming

The design and use of abstract data types (ADT's) permeate our problem-solving approach. Several examples demonstrate how to design an ADT as part of the overall design of a solution. The distinction between an ADT and the data structure that is used to implement it remains in the forefront throughout the discussion. We show how to prevent direct user access to this data structure by implementing the ADT as a unit. The importance of weighing trade-offs when selecting a data structure for a particular application is also emphasized.

Recognizing the evolution toward object-oriented programming, this book provides a new optional section in Chapter 4 that covers the fundamentals of OOP with many examples of Turbo Pascal objects. Subsequent chapters demonstrate how to write each abstract data type as an object. This material enables you to make the transition to OOP at whatever level is comfortable. You can even choose to omit coverage of object-oriented programming in your course now, leaving the material for future reference.

Problem Solving

This book helps students to learn to integrate problem-solving and programming abilities by emphasizing both the thought processes and the methods that computer scientists use. Learning how a computer scientist develops, analyzes, and implements a method is just as important as learning the mechanics of the method; a cookbook approach to the material is insufficient.

We present analytical tools for the development of solutions within the context of example problems. Procedural abstraction, data abstraction, the successive refinement of both algorithms and data structures, and recursion are used to design solutions to problems throughout the book, including two large case studies.

We introduce Pascal pointers and linked list processing early and use the techniques in building data structures. We also introduce at an elementary level the order-of-magnitude analysis of algorithms. This approach allows the consideration—first at an informal level, then more quantitatively—of the advantages and disadvantages of array-based and pointer-based data structures.

This comparative approach continues with an analysis of the classic information storage and retrieval operations that the ADT table provides. Our exploration of various implementations of a table leads us to consider issues of efficiency and motivates the need for the binary search tree implementation. Thus, we continually emphasize the trade-offs between potential solutions, and this emphasis becomes a central problem-solving theme.

Finally, programming style, documentation, debugging aids, and loop invariants are important parts of our problem-solving methodology to implement and verify solutions.

Applications

Classic application areas arise in the context of the major topics of this book. For example, searching and sorting are discussed in the context of both recursion and the abstract data type table. Binary search, quicksort, and mergesort, being naturally recursive algorithms, appear early and are used to introduce order-of-magnitude analysis. In the context of the ADT table, later parts of the book introduce such topics as binary search trees, 2-3 trees, hashing, and file indexing. Searching and sorting is again considered in the context of external files.

Algorithms for recognizing and evaluating algebraic expressions are first introduced in the context of recursion, and are considered again later as an application of stacks. Other applications include, for example, the Eight Queens problem as an example of backtracking, event-driven simulation as an application of queues, and graph searching and traversals as other important applications of stacks and queues.

NEW AND REVISED MATERIAL

This book contains much new or revised material as follows:

- **Additional topics in Turbo Pascal.** Coverage of strings and short-circuit evaluation of boolean expressions, revised reviews of arrays, records, files, and sets, as well as new appendixes that summarize Turbo Pascal, all facilitate the transition from the introductory course to this one.
- **Units.** Turbo Pascal units are introduced formally in Chapter 2, while their significance and relationship to data abstraction are illustrated in Chapter 4. All ADT's that are presented in subsequent chapters are implemented as units.
- **Object-oriented programming (OOP).** Chapter 4 includes an extensive new section that describes the underlying principles of object-oriented programming—encapsulation, inheritance, and polymorphism—and includes many Turbo Pascal examples of objects. Subsequent chapters provide an object version of each new ADT discussed. Those who do not wish to cover OOP at this time can skip these sections without loss of continuity.
- **Improved programming style.** All programming examples use a consistent style for Pascal identifiers. All ADT's are implemented as units, and programs use these units whenever possible. All main programs declare their variables immediately prior to their start—a feature that Turbo Pascal provides—instead of prior to the first subprogram definition, as required by Standard Pascal. Thus, such programs enforce the stylistic ban on passing variables globally to procedures and functions.
- **Improved figures.** All figures have been redrawn and edited for clarity and consistency.
- **New and revised appendixes.** A new appendix describes all available Turbo Pascal compiler directives. Other appendixes and the inside covers conveniently summarize Turbo Pascal in a form that students will find useful while writing programs.

OVERVIEW

The pedagogical features and organization of this book were carefully designed to facilitate learning and to allow instructors to easily tailor the material to a particular course. Acknowledged later in this preface are the numerous people who used previous editions of *Walls and Mirrors* in their courses and provided many useful suggestions that were incorporated into the present work.

Pedagogical Features

This book contains the following features that help students not only during their first reading of the material, but also during subsequent review:

- Chapter outlines and previews
- Key Concept boxes
- Margin notes
- Chapter summaries
- Common Pitfalls/Debugging sections
- Self-test exercises with answers
- Chapter exercises and projects. The most challenging exercises are labeled with asterisks. Answers to most of these additional exercises appear in the *Instructor's Guide.*
- Case studies. In an attempt to illustrate "real-world programming," two major case studies develop and later modify a large interactive inventory program. The goal is to demonstrate that top-down design and modularity are invaluable aids in the development and modification of a large program. Other complete programs illustrate the role of units and ADT's in the problem-solving process.
- Appendixes
- Glossary of terms

Organization

The chapters in this book are organized into four parts. In most cases, Parts II and III will form the core of a one-semester course. The coverage given to Parts I and IV will depend on what role the course plays in your curriculum. More detailed suggestions for using this book with different courses appear in the *Instructor's Guide.*

Part I: Programming and Software Engineering. Much of Part I resembles an extension of an introductory course in that its emphasis is more on programming than on the earlier stages of the problem-solving process. The topics in this part include structured programming with Turbo Pascal; major issues in software engineering; Turbo Pascal arrays, strings, records, files, sets, units, and pointer variables; and linked lists. Part I concludes with a case study in which we design and implement an interactive inventory system. You can choose among the topics in Part I according to the background of your students.

Part II: Problem-Solving Tools. We begin Part II with a lengthy discussion of data abstraction and the main concepts of object-oriented programming—encapsulation, inheritance, and polymorphism—and provide several Turbo Pascal examples of these ideas. As was mentioned earlier, the new sections on object-oriented programming offer you the opportunity to include this topic in your course without requiring that you do so immediately.

The ability to think recursively is one of the most useful skills that a computer scientist can possess and is often of great value in helping one to better understand the nature of a problem. We discuss recursion extensively and include examples that range from simple recursive definitions to recursive algorithms for searching and sorting.

The final chapter in Part II introduces the student to order-of-magnitude analysis and Big O notation by examining the efficiency of several searching and sorting algorithms, including the recursive mergesort and quicksort.

We have chosen to discuss data abstraction (Chapter 4) before recursion (Chapters 5 and 6). If you prefer to present recursion first, you can cover Chapter 5 or both Chapters 5 and 6 before you cover Chapter 4.

Part III: Problem Solving with Abstract Data Types. Part III continues the use of data abstraction as a problem-solving tool. We present such basic abstract data types as the stack, queue, table, and priority queue along with the data structures used to implement them. Each ADT is implemented as a unit; optional sections show each ADT implemented as an object. We note that these abstract data types fall into two categories: those that organize their data by position (stacks and queues) and those that organize their data by value (tables and priority queues). Also included in Part III is extensive coverage of binary trees, graphs, and heaps.

Note that if you want to develop the ADT table even further before you cover the other topics in this part, you can skip or postpone Chapters 11 and 12 and move directly to the advanced techniques in Part IV.

Part IV: Advanced Techniques for the Management of Data. Part IV presents more-complex data structures and advanced algorithms for searching and sorting. We develop 2-3 trees and hashed table implementations and analyze which operations each supports best. We then consider the problem of sorting and indexing data stored in external direct access files. We apply mergesort to external direct access files and show how external hashing and B-tree indexes are generalizations of the internal hashing schemes and 2-3 trees already developed.

TO THE STUDENT

As former college students and as educators who are constantly learning, we wrote this book with you in mind. You will find such learning aids as margin notes, chapter summaries, self-test exercises with answers, a glossary, and Turbo Pascal reference material in the appendixes and inside the covers. If you have not already done so, you should review the list of this book's features given earlier in this preface in the section "Pedagogical Features."

Our presentation makes some basic assumptions about your knowledge of Turbo Pascal. Some of you may need to review this material or learn it for the first time by consulting, for example, the book you used in your Pascal course and Chapter 2 of this book. You will need to know about arrays, strings, records, files, and—to a lesser extent—sets. Although Chapter 2 presents these topics, your instructor might not cover them in class.

Realize that this book will expand your knowledge of Turbo Pascal. Although you should be able to use the four simple data types integer, real, character, and boolean, as well as subrange types and one-dimensional arrays of each of these types, we recognize that many of you will need to develop the ability to sense which types are appropriate in a particular situation. This book will help you by answering the following kinds of questions: When does the use of a subrange add to the readability of a program, when does it detract from it, and how does it interact with program debugging? When is an array the most efficient data structure as opposed to, say, a linked list—a structure you will encounter soon.

We also assume that you are familiar with the way Turbo Pascal evaluates expressions and executes statements. Moreover, you should have good judgment in choosing between control structures: *while* versus *for* versus *repeat*; *if-then* versus *if-then-else* versus *case*. You should appreciate the evils of the *goto*. There are, however, some subtleties in these matters that we shall explore. Similarly, we assume that you can write procedures and functions and are well versed in such matters as parameter passing and scope rules for variables. However, we shall continually demonstrate the role of modularity as perhaps the single most important factor that contributes to good program development, readability, and modifiability. We assume no experience with recursive subprograms, which are included in Part II of this book.

SUPPLEMENTARY MATERIALS

The following items are available to help instructors:

- *Instructor's Guide.* This guide contains teaching notes and suggestions, solutions to most exercises and programming projects, additional material that you may want to include in your course, several large software development projects, and transparency masters.
- Test Bank. A collection of questions and problems suitable for examinations and quizzes is available to instructors.

- Student's Program Disk. All the programs, units, procedures, and functions that appear in the book are available on a Turbo Pascal disk for student use.
- Instructor's Disk. In addition to all the material that appears on the Student's Program Disk, the Instructor's Disk contains the programs for the case studies, selected exercises, and supplementary projects described in the *Instructor's Guide*.

ACKNOWLEDGMENTS

It is a pleasure to acknowledge the outstanding work of Paul Helman and Robert Veroff, the authors of the first edition of *Walls and Mirrors*. As one who has taught from this innovative work, I am pleased to continue my contribution to its evolution.

Many wonderful people have helped create this book. At Addison-Wesley, Dan Joraanstad, Carter Shanklin, Vivian McDougal, Jean Lake, Mary Tudor, Colleen Dunn, and John Thompson provided invaluable guidance and assistance. Special thanks to Rebecca Pepper, an outstanding copy editor.

Others were always there for help and support. Among them are Doug McCreadie, Ted Emmott, John Cardin, Irene Azzinaro, Jim Abreu, Bill Harding, Maybeth Cassidy, Gail Armstrong, Ed Lamagna, Lorraine Berube, Marge White, Jim LaBonte, and Janet Prichard.

My sincere appreciation goes to many others who were involved in earlier versions of this book: Alan Apt (who initiated *Walls and Mirrors*), Mark McCormick, Jean Foltz, Mary Ann Telatnik, Shirley McGuire, John Turner, David Clayton, David Tetreault, Mike Hayden, Laura Kenney, Mary Shields, George Calmenson, Wendy Calmenson, Chris Spannabel, Manisha Mande, John O'Donnell, and Guy Mills.

The suggestions from outstanding reviewers contributed greatly to this book's present form. In alphabetical order they are

James Ames—*Virginia Commonwealth University*

George Hamer—*South Dakota State University*

Urban LeJeune—*Stockton State College*

Keith Pierce—*University of Minnesota*

J. D. Robertson—*Bentley College*

Charles Saxon—*Eastern Michigan University*

Many other people provided input for the previous editions of *Walls and Mirrors* at various stages of its development. All of their comments were useful and greatly appreciated. In alphabetical order they are: Sto Bell, Richard Botting, Wolfin Brumley, Philip Carrigan, Michael Clancy,

Michael Cleron, Shaun Cooper, Charles Denault, Stephanie Horoschak, Kris Jensen, Ken Lord, Jane Wallace Mayo, Sue Medeiros, Cleve Moler, Rayno Niemi, Andrew Oldroyd, Larry Olsen, Roy Pargas, Keith Pierce, David Radford, Stuart Regis, John Rowe, Sharon Salveter, Linda Shapiro, Richard Snodgrass, Neil Snyder, Paul Spirakis, Clinton Staley, Mark Stehlick, Harriet Taylor, Susan Wallace, and Brad Wilson.

Thank you all.

F. M. C.

BRIEF CONTENTS

CONTENTS

APPLICATIONS

I

Programming and Software Engineering

CHAPTER 1

Principles of Programming and Software Engineering

PREVIEW This chapter summarizes several fundamental principles that serve as the basis for dealing with the complexities of large programs. The discussion both reinforces the basic principles of structured programming, which are further illustrated by the case study in Chapter 3, and demonstrates that writing well-structured and well-documented programs is cost-effective. The chapter also presents a brief discussion of algorithms and data abstraction, and indicates how these topics relate to the book's main theme of developing problem-solving and programming skills. Later, in Parts II, III, and IV of the book, the focus will shift from discussions of programming principles to the development and use of new problem-solving tools. Even when the focus of discussion is on these new tools, you should note how all solutions adhere to the basic principles discussed in this chapter.

PROBLEM SOLVING AND SOFTWARE ENGINEERING

Where did you begin when you wrote your last Pascal program? After reading the problem specifications and after the requisite amount of procrastination, most novice programmers simply begin to write Pascal statements. Obviously, their goal is to get their programs to execute, preferably with correct results. Therefore, they run their programs, examine error messages, insert semicolons, change the logic, delete semicolons, pray, and otherwise torture their programs until they work. Most of their time is probably spent debugging both syntax and program logic. Certainly, your programming skills are better now than when you wrote your first program, but will you be able to write a really large program by using the approach just described? Maybe, but there are better ways.

Coding without a solution design increases debugging time

Realize that an extremely large software development project generally requires a team of programmers rather than a single individual. Teamwork requires an overall plan, organization, and communication. A haphazard approach to programming will not serve a team programmer well and will not be cost-effective. Fortunately, there is a branch of computer science—**software engineering**—that provides techniques to facilitate the development of computer programs.

Software engineering facilitates development of programs

Whereas a first course in computer science typically emphasizes programming issues, the focus in this book will be on the broader issues of problem solving. This chapter begins with an overview of the problem-solving and programming processes and their close relationship.

What Is Problem Solving?

Here the term **problem solving** refers to the entire process of taking the statement of a problem and developing a computer program that solves that problem. This process requires you to pass through many phases, from gaining an understanding of the problem to be solved, through designing a conceptual solution, to implementing the solution with a computer program.

A solution specifies algorithms and ways to store data

Exactly what is a solution? Typically, a **solution** consists of two components: algorithms and ways to store data. An **algorithm** is a concise specification of a method to solve a problem. One action that an algorithm often performs is to operate on a collection of data. For example, an algorithm may have to put new data into a collection, remove data from a collection, or ask questions about a collection of data. When constructing a solution, you must organize your data collection so that you can operate on the data easily in the manner that the algorithm requires.

An ADT is a collection of data and a set of operations on that data

Perhaps this description of a solution leaves the false impression that all the cleverness in problem solving goes into developing the algorithm and that how you store your data plays only a supporting role. This is far from the truth. You need to do much more than store your data; you also need to operate on the data. In Chapter 4, you will learn that an **abstract data type,** or ADT, is a collection of data *and* a set of operations on that data. For example, suppose that you need to store a collection of names in a manner that allows you to search rapidly for a given name. The binary search algorithm, which is described in Chapter 5, enables you to search an array efficiently, if the array is sorted. Thus, one solution to this problem is to store the names sorted in an array and to use a binary search algorithm to search the array for a specified name. You can view the *sorted array together with the binary search algorithm* as an ADT that solves this problem.

Problem-Solving Tools: Top-Down Design, Procedural and Data Abstraction, Information Hiding, Object-Oriented Programming, and Recursion

Several tools will help you to design a solution to a given problem. Some of these tools are top-down design, procedural abstraction, data abstraction, information hiding, object-oriented programming, and recursion.

Top-down design. When you begin to write programs of moderate size and complexity, you will find it difficult to cope with the entire program at once. Most people who write programs and most people who read programs are similarly limited. Modularity through top-down design is a solution to this and other problems associated with large programs. What is meant by top-down design and modularity? The philosophy of top-down design is that you should address a task at successively lower levels of detail. You should partition a program into independent **modules**—procedures, functions, and other blocks of code—as Figure 1-1 depicts.

To understand the concept of a modular solution, consider a simple example. Suppose that you wanted to find the median among a collection of test scores. Figure 1-2 uses a **structure chart** to illustrate the hierarchy of modules that solve this problem. At first, each module is little more than a statement of *what* it needs to solve and is devoid of detail. You refine

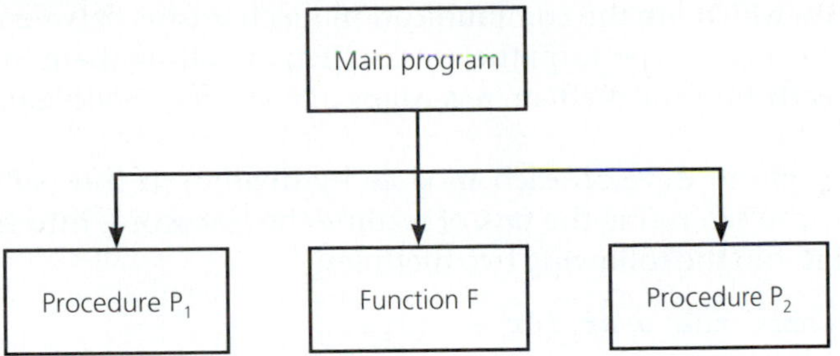

Figure 1-1

A program partitioned into independent modules

each module, in turn, by partitioning it into additional smaller modules. The result is a hierarchy of modules; each module is refined by its successors, which solve smaller problems and contain more detail about *how* to solve the problem than their predecessors. The refinement process continues until the modules at the bottom of the hierarchy are simple enough for you to translate directly into Pascal procedures, functions, and isolated blocks of code that solve very small, independent problems. In fact, each lowest-level module should perform one well-defined task. Software engineers call such modules **highly cohesive.** This strategy of dividing a program into isolated components should be fairly familiar to you.

Notice from Figure 1-2 that you can break the solution into three independent tasks:

A solution consisting of independent tasks

```
Read the test scores into an array
Sort the array
Get the "middle" element of the array
```

You can develop the module that solves each of these tasks in virtual isolation from the other modules. In fact, you should design modules that are as independent, or **loosely coupled**, as possible, except of course for their

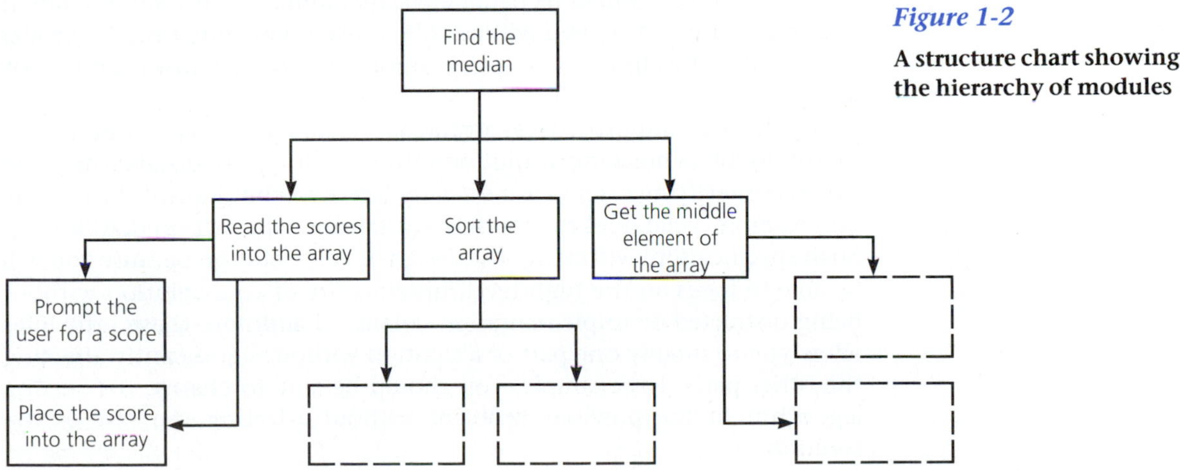

Figure 1-2

A structure chart showing the hierarchy of modules

interfaces, which are the communication mechanisms between modules. If the three modules perform their tasks, then by calling them in order you will correctly find the median, regardless of *how* each module performs its task.

You begin to develop each module by dividing it into subtasks. For example, you can refine the task of reading the test scores into an array by dividing it into the following two modules:

Subtasks

```
Prompt the user for a score
Place the score into the array
```

You continue the solution process by developing, in a similar manner, modules for each of these two tasks.

A modular program has many advantages, several of which are discussed in the following sections. In general, modularity and top-down design help to simplify the problem-solving process. Thus, you should practice modularity at all points of the problem-solving process.

Specify what to do, not how to do it

Procedural abstraction. When you use top-down design and modularity to solve a problem, each algorithm begins as a "black box." As the problem-solving process proceeds, you gradually refine the black boxes until eventually you implement their actions by writing Pascal code. Each black box specifies *what* it does, but not *how* it does it. No one black box may "know" how any other black box performs its task—it may know only what that task is. For example, if one part of a solution is to sort some data, one of the black boxes will be a sorting algorithm. The other black boxes will know that the sorting black box sorts, but they will not know how it sorts. In this way the various components of a solution are kept isolated from one another.

Typically, these black boxes are implemented as subprograms. **Procedural abstraction** separates the purpose of a subprogram from its implementation. Once a subprogram is written, you can use it without knowing the particulars of its algorithm as long as you have a statement of its purpose and a description of its parameters. Assuming that the subprogram is documented properly, you will be able to use it knowing only its header statement and its initial descriptive comments; you will not need to look at its code.

Modularity and procedural abstraction complement each other. Modularity involves breaking a solution into modules; procedural abstraction involves specifying each module clearly *before* you implement it in Pascal. For example, what does the module assume and what action does it take? Such specifications will clarify the design of your solution because you will be able to focus on the high-level functionality of your solution without being distracted by implementation details. In addition, these principles allow you to modify one part of a solution without significantly affecting the other parts. For example, you should be able to change the sorting algorithm in the previous problem without affecting the rest of the solution.

Procedural abstraction is essential to team projects. After all, in a team situation, you will have to use subprograms written by others, frequently without knowledge of their algorithms. Will you actually be able to use such a subprogram without studying its code? In fact, you do each time you use a Pascal standard procedure such as *writeln* or a standard function such as *sqrt*.

Data abstraction. Most introductory courses stress the modular development of algorithms, and you will see many more examples that illustrate this technique further. For most of you, however, the application of modular development to data is a new concept. Procedural abstraction means focusing on what a module does instead of the details of its algorithm. Similarly, with **data abstraction** you focus on the operations that you will perform on the data instead of on how you will implement the operations. Clearly, you will eventually be concerned about programming detail. However, the principle of abstraction asks that you suppress your implementation concerns—for both algorithms and data structures—while you design the high-level functional aspects of the solution.

Specify what you will do to data, not how to do it

As was mentioned previously, an **abstract data type**, or ADT, is a collection of data and a set of operations on that data. Such operations might add new data to the collection, remove data from the collection, or search for some data. The other modules of the solution will "know" *what* operations the ADT can perform. However, they will not know *how* the data is stored or *how* the operations are performed.

For example, you have used a Pascal array, but have you ever stopped to think about what an array actually is? You will see many pictures of arrays throughout this book. The artist's conception of an array may resemble the way a Pascal array is implemented on a computer, and then again it may not. The point is that you are able to use an array without knowing what it "looks like"—that is, how it is implemented. Although different systems may implement Pascal arrays in different ways, the differences are transparent to the programmer. For instance, regardless of how the array *Years* is implemented, you can always store the value 1492 in location *Index* of the array by using the statement

```
Years[Index] := 1492
```

and later write out that value by using the statement

```
writeln(Years[Index])
```

Thus, you can use an array without knowing the details of its implementation, just as you can use the function *sqrt* without knowing the details of its implementation.

Likewise, you can perform operations on the data in an ADT without knowing the details of the ADT's implementation. Ultimately, you will implement each ADT by using **data structures.** A data structure is a construct that you can define within a programming language to store a col-

An ADT is not a fancy name for a data structure

lection of data. For instance, you might store some data in a Pascal array of integers, or in an array of records, or in a record of arrays. You will learn much more about abstract data types and data structures in Chapter 4.

Within problem solving, abstract data types support algorithms, and algorithms are part of what constitutes an abstract data type. As you design a solution, you should develop algorithms and ADT's in tandem. The global algorithm that solves a problem suggests operations that you need to perform on the data, which in turn suggest ADT's and algorithms for performing the operations on the data. However, the development of the solution may proceed in the opposite direction as well. The kinds of ADT's that you are able to design can influence the strategy of your global algorithm for solving a problem. That is, your knowledge of which data operations are easy to perform and which are difficult can have a large effect on how you approach a problem.

As you probably have surmised from this discussion, there frequently is not a sharp distinction between an "algorithms problem" and a "data structures problem." It is often possible to look at a program from one perspective and feel that the data structures support a clever algorithm and then to look at the same program from another perspective and feel that the algorithms support a clever data structure.

Information hiding. As you have seen, abstraction identifies the essential aspects of both modules and data structures, which you can treat as black boxes. Abstraction tells you to write functional specifications for each black box; it is responsible for their outside, or **public**, views. However, abstraction also helps you to identify details that you should *hide* from public view—details that should not be in the specifications but should be **private.** The principle of **information hiding** not only hides such details within the black box, it also ensures that no other black box can access these hidden details. Thus, you should hide certain details within your modules and ADT's and make them inaccessible to all other modules and ADT's.

All modules and ADT's should hide something

Information hiding limits the ways that you need to deal with modules and ADT's. As a user of a module or ADT, you do not worry about implementation details. As an implementer of a module or ADT, you do not worry about their uses.

Object-oriented programming. The concepts of modularity, procedural abstraction, data abstraction, and information hiding are embodied in **object-oriented programming**, or OOP. Three basic principles characterize this approach to problem solving. **Encapsulation** is the combination of data and the operations that you can perform on that data into an **object.** Although an abstract data type is a collection of data and operations, Pascal does not provide a special way to identify the ADT or to associate the data with the operations. OOP, however, actually defines objects within the pro-

Objects encapsulate data and operations

gramming language. In addition, an ADT's operations act on a data structure, whereas an object acts on itself.

The other principles of OOP are much more than simple packaging devices and provide its power. **Inheritance**, whereby objects inherit properties from other objects, allows you to reuse objects that you defined earlier—perhaps for different purposes—with appropriate modification. Inheritance may make it impossible for the compiler to determine which operation you require in a particular situation. However, **polymorphism** enables this determination to be made at execution time. That is, the outcome of a particular operation depends upon the objects on which the operation acts. For example, if you use the + operator with numeric operands in Turbo Pascal, addition occurs, but if you use it with string operands, concatenation occurs. Although in this simple example, the compiler can determine the correct meaning of +, polymorphism allows situations whereby the meaning of an operation is unknown until execution time.

Objects can inherit properties of other objects

Note that OOP is not a part of Standard Pascal, but under Turbo Pascal,[1] the object is another data type. Chapter 4 discusses OOP in Turbo Pascal further.

Recursion. Recursion is another extremely powerful problem-solving tool. Problems that at first appear to be quite difficult often have simple recursive solutions. Like top-down design, recursion breaks a problem into several smaller problems. What is striking about recursion is that these smaller problems are of *exactly the same type* as the original problem. That is, a recursive solution solves a problem by solving a smaller instance of the same problem! It solves this new problem by solving an even smaller instance of the same problem. Eventually, the new problem will be so small that its solution will be either obvious or known. This solution will lead to the solution of the original problem.

For example, suppose that you could solve problem P_1 if you had the solution to problem P_2, which is a smaller instance of P_1. Suppose further that you could solve problem P_2 if you had the solution to problem P_3, which is a smaller instance of P_2. If you knew the solution to P_3 because it was small enough to be trivial, you would be able to solve P_2. You could then use the solution to P_2 to solve the original problem P_1.

Recursion can seem like magic, especially at first, but as you will see in Chapters 5 and 6, recursion is a very real and important problem-solving tool that is an alternative to **iteration.** An iterative solution involves loops, a concept with which you are undoubtedly quite familiar. Although not all recursive solutions are better than iterative solutions, recursion can provide straightforward solutions to problems that have complex iterative solutions.

Recursion can provide simple solutions to difficult problems

---

[1]Beginning with version 5.0.

The Life Cycle of Software

The development of good software involves a lengthy and continuing process known as the software's **life cycle.** This process begins with an initial idea, includes the writing and debugging of programs, and continues for years to involve corrections and enhancements to the original software. Here is a list of the phases in the life cycle of typical software:

Phase 1: Specification. Given an initial statement of the software's purpose, you must specify clearly all aspects of the problem. Note that often the people who describe the problem are not programmers and that the initial problem statement might be imprecise. The specification phase, then, requires that you bring precision and detail to the original problem statement and that you communicate with both programmers and nonprogrammers.

Make the problem statement precise and detailed

Here are some questions that you must answer as you write the specifications for the software. What is the input data? What data is valid and what data is invalid? Who will use the software, and what user interface should be used? What error detection and error messages are desirable? What assumptions are possible? Are there special cases? What is the form of the output? What documentation is necessary? What enhancements to the program are likely in the future?

Prototype programs can clarify the problem

One way to improve communication between people and to clarify the software specifications is to write a prototype program that simulates the behavior of portions of the desired software product. For example, a simple—even inefficient—program could demonstrate the proposed user interface for analysis. It is better to discover any difficulties or to change your mind now than after programming is underway or even complete.

Realize that your previous programming assignments included program specifications. Perhaps aspects of these specifications were unclear and you had to seek clarification, but most likely you have had little practice in writing your own program specifications.

Phase 2: Design. Once you have completed the specification phase, you must design the algorithms that will accomplish the required tasks. Determine whether you can use programs or subprograms that already exist to perform some of the work. By using top-down design principles, divide the project into modules. Next, indicate the interaction between modules; a structure chart provides a clear picture of these relationships.

A structure chart shows the relationship between modules

At this point, it is important that you clearly specify not only the purpose of each module but also the **data flow** between modules. For example, you should provide answers to these questions for each module: What data is available to the module before its execution? What does the module assume? What does the data look like after the module executes? Thus, you should specify in detail the assumptions, input, and output for each module. One way to make these specifications is by writing both a **precondition**, which is a statement of the conditions that must exist at the beginning of a module, and a **postcondition**, which is a statement of the conditions at the end of a module. For example, you might describe a procedure that sorts an array as follows:

Subprogram specifications include preconditions and postconditions

```
procedure Sort(A, N)
{ Sorts an array into ascending order.
  Precondition: A is an array of N integers, 1 <= N <= Max.
  Postcondition: A[1] <= A[2] <= ... <= A[N], N is
  unchanged. }
```

Finally, you can use pseudocode to specify the details of the algorithms.

It is likely that you have spent little or no time in the design phase for your programs. It is imperative that you change this habit! The end result of top-down design is a solution that is easy to translate into the control structures and data structures of a particular programming language. By spending adequate time in the design phase, you will spend less time when you write and debug your program.

Phase 3: Verification. There are formal, theoretical methods for proving properties about an algorithm that you could use to establish that an algorithm is correct. Although research in this area is incomplete, it is useful to mention some aspects of the verification process.

An **assertion** is a statement about a particular condition at a certain point in an algorithm. Preconditions and postconditions are simply assertions about conditions at the beginning and end of modules. An **invariant** is a condition that is always true at a particular point in an algorithm. A **loop invariant** is a condition that is true before and after each execution of an algorithm's loop. Later in this chapter, you will see how to use loop invariants to write correct loops.

There are theoretical ways to prove that some algorithms are correct

Proving that an algorithm is correct is like proving a theorem in geometry. For example, to prove that a module is correct, you would start with the preconditions (the axioms and assumptions in geometry) and demonstrate that the steps of the algorithm lead to the postconditions. To do so, you would consider each step in the algorithm and show that an assertion before the step leads to a particular assertion after the step. There are formal ways to make these demonstrations for various constructs such as `if` statements, `while` loops, and assignment statements.

As you prove that individual statements are correct, you need to collect them together to prove that sequences of statements, and then modules, and finally the program is correct. For example, suppose that you show that if assertion A_1 is true and statement S_1 executes, then assertion A_2 is true. Also, suppose that you have shown that assertion A_2 and statement S_2 lead to assertion A_3. You can then conclude that if assertion A_1 is true, executing the sequence of statements S_1 and S_2 will lead to assertion A_3. By continuing in this manner, you eventually will be able to show that the module is correct.

Clearly, if you discovered an error during the verification process, you would correct your algorithm and possibly modify the problem specifications. Thus, by using invariants, it is likely that your algorithm will contain fewer errors *before* you begin coding. As a result, you will spend less time debugging your program.

Coding is a relatively minor phase in the software life cycle

Phase 4: Coding. Next, you must translate the algorithms into a particular programming language and remove the syntax errors. Although this phase is probably your concept of programming, realize that the coding phase is not the major part of the life cycle for most software—actually, it is a relatively minor part.

The solution that a top-down design produces is a hierarchy of subproblems, which will correspond to modules in a program. In Figure 1-3, the solution to problem A is defined in terms of subproblems S_1, S_2, and S_3. Before you begin to code the module that solves problem A, it seems reasonable that you should first implement the solutions to subproblems S_1, S_2, and S_3. This is a **bottom-up implementation**. Once you are confident that the modules for S_1, S_2, and S_3 are working, you can use them to continue to implement the solution to problem A.

In some situations it might be reasonable to implement a module before implementing some of its submodules—that is, to work in a top-down fashion. For example, in Figure 1-3, you might choose to implement module A before module S_3. In this case you would write a dummy procedure for S_3 that does nothing but report that it has been called. These dummy procedures, which are often called **stubs**, allow you to focus your attention on the central parts of the solution.

You also can implement a certain module at various levels of refinement. For example, suppose that you want to implement S_3 before you implement S_1, but S_3 needs the data that S_1 reads. You could use assignment statements in S_1 that define some typical values for S_3 to use. In this way you can concentrate on S_3 without the distraction of entering input. Alternatively, you could implement S_3 by itself in its own special main program that thoroughly tests S_3. Your approach will depend in part on the complexity of the module in question.

Design a set of test data to test your program

Phase 5: Testing. During the testing phase, you need to remove as many logical errors as you can. At first, test the program with valid input data that leads to a known solution. If certain data must lie within a range, include values at the endpoints of the range. For example, if the input

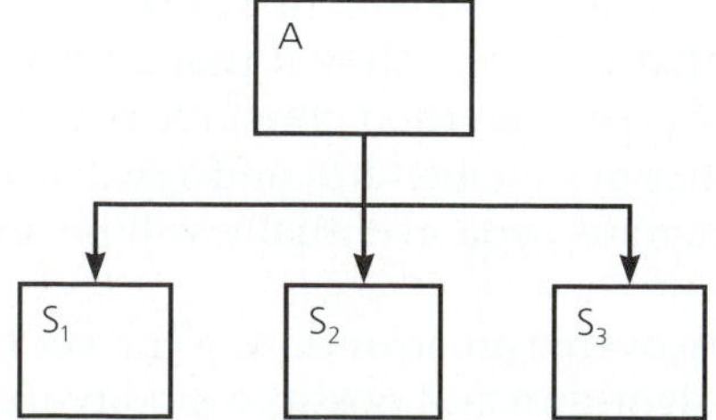

Figure 1-3

Top-down design, bottom-up implementation

value for *N* can range from 1 to 10, be sure to include test cases in which *N* is 1 and 10. Also, include invalid data to test the error-detection capability of the program. Try some random data, and finally try some actual data.

Phase 6: Refining the solution. The result of the previous steps of the solution process is a correct program, which you have tested extensively and debugged as necessary. If you have a program that solves your original problem, you might wonder about the significance of this step of the solution process.

Develop a working program under simplifying assumptions, then add refining sophistication

Often the best approach to solving a problem is first to make some simplifying assumptions during the top-down design of the solution—for example, you could assume that the input will be in a certain format and will be correct—and next to develop a complete working program under these assumptions. You can then add more sophisticated input and output routines, additional features, and more error checks to the working program. Of course, you must take care to ensure that the final refinements do not require a complete redesign of the solution. You can usually make these additions cleanly, however, particularly when you have used a modular design. In fact, the ability to proceed in this manner is one of the key advantages of having a modular design! Thus, the approach of simplifying the problem initially makes a refinement step necessary in the solution process.

Here is a good example of the fact that the phases within this life cycle—or alternatively, the steps within a solution process—are not completely isolated from one another. To make realistic simplifying assumptions early in the design process, it is necessary to have some idea of how you will account for those assumptions later on.

Phase 7: Production. When the software product is complete, it is distributed to its intended users, installed on their computers, and used.

Phase 8: Maintenance. Maintaining a program is not like maintaining a car. Software does not wear out if you neglect it. However, users of your software invariably will detect errors that you did not discover during the testing phase. Correcting these errors is part of maintaining the software. Another aspect of the maintenance phase is the enhancement of the software by adding more features or by modifying existing portions to better suit the users.

Figure 1-4 pictures the eight phases of the software life cycle. The circular arrangement suggests that the phases are part of a cycle and are not simply a linear list. It is likely, for example, that during the maintenance phase you will have to return to the problem specifications to verify or modify them. Also notice that the eight phases surround a documentation core in the figure. Documentation is not a separate phase, as you might expect. Rather, it is integrated into all phases of the software life cycle.

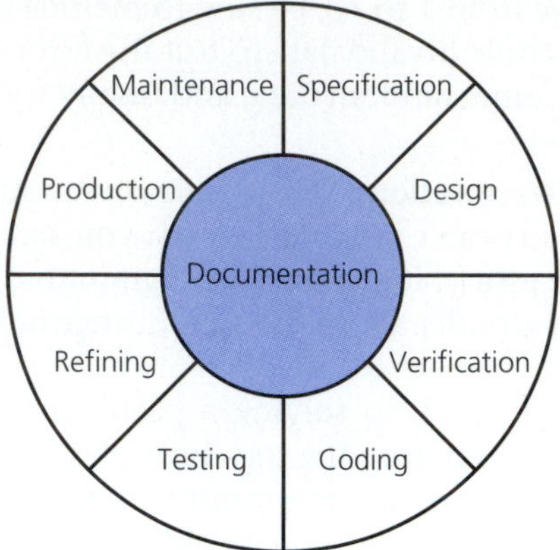

Figure 1-4
The life cycle of software

Is a program's life cycle relevant to *your* life? It definitely should be! You should view Phases 1 through 6 as the steps in a problem-solving process. Using this strategy, you first design and implement a solution (Phases 1 through 5) based on some initial simplifying assumptions. The outcome is a well-structured program that solves a somewhat simplified problem. The last step of the solution process (Phase 6) refines your work into a sophisticated program that meets the original problem specifications.

Loop Invariants

As was mentioned earlier, a loop invariant is a condition that is true both before and after the execution of a loop. This section discusses loop invariants further and shows you how to use them to demonstrate the correctness of iterative algorithms. By using invariants, you can detect errors before you begin coding and thereby reduce your debugging and testing time. Overall, invariants can save you time.

Consider this simple example of a loop that computes the sum of the first *N* elements in the array *A*:

```
{ Compute the sum of A[1], A[2], . . ., A[N] }
Sum := 0;
j := 1;
while j <= N do
begin
   Sum := Sum + A[j];
   j := succ(j)
end
```

Before this loop begins execution, *Sum* is 0 and *j* is 1. After the loop executes once, *Sum* is *A[1]* and *j* is 2. In general,

Loop invariant

Sum is the sum of the elements A[1] through A[j - 1]

This statement is the invariant for this loop.

You can use invariants to establish the correctness of an iterative algorithm by showing that each of the following four points is true:

Steps to establish the correctness of an algorithm

- **The invariant must be true initially**, before the loop begins execution for the first time. In the previous example, *Sum* is 0 and *j* is 1 initially. In this case, the invariant states that *Sum* contains the sum of the elements *A[1]* through *A[0]*, which is true because there are no elements in this range.
- **An execution of the loop must preserve the invariant.** That is, if the invariant is true before any given iteration of the loop, then you must show that it is true after the iteration. In the example, the loop adds *A[j]* to *Sum* and then increments *j* by 1. Thus, after an execution of the loop, the most recent element added to *Sum* is *A[j - 1]*; that is, the invariant is true after the iteration.
- **The invariant must capture the correctness of the algorithm.** That is, you must show that if the invariant is true when the loop terminates, the algorithm is correct. When the loop in the previous example terminates, *j* contains *N* + 1 and the invariant is true: *Sum* contains the sum of the elements *A[1]* through *A[(N + 1) - 1]*, which is the sum that you intended to compute.
- **The loop must terminate.** That is, you must show that the loop will terminate after a finite number of iterations. In the example, *j* begins at 1 and then increases by 1 at each execution of the loop. Thus, *j* eventually will exceed *N* regardless of *N*'s value. This fact and the nature of the *while* statement guarantees that the loop will terminate.

Notice the clear connection between the previous demonstration and **mathematical induction.**[2] Showing the invariant to be true initially, which establishes the **base case**, is analogous to establishing that a property of the natural numbers is true for 0. Showing that each iteration of the loop preserves the invariant, which is the **inductive step**, is analogous to showing that if a property is true for an arbitrary natural number k, then the property is true for the natural number $k + 1$. After performing the previous four steps, you can conclude that the invariant is true after every iteration of the loop—just as mathematical induction allows you to conclude that a property is true for every natural number.

Identifying loop invariants will help you to write correct loops. You should state the invariant as a comment that precedes each loop. For example, in the previous example, you might write the following:

State loop invariants in your programs

```
{ Invariant: 1 <= j <= N + 1 and Sum = A[1] + . . . + A[j-1] }
while j <= N do
   . . .
```

[2]A review of mathematical induction appears in Appendix A.

What Is a Good Solution?

Before you devote your time and energy to the study of problem-solving tools, it seems only fair that you see at the outset why mastery of these tools will help to make you a good problem solver. An obvious statement is that the use of these tools will produce good solutions. This statement, however, leads to the more fundamental question, what *is* a good solution? A brief attempt at answering this question concludes this section.

Because a computer program is the final form your solutions will take, consider what constitutes a good computer program. Presumably, you write a program to perform some task. In the course of performing that task, there is a real and tangible **cost**. This cost includes such factors as the computer resources (computing time and memory) the program consumes, the difficulties encountered by those who use the program, and the consequences of a program that does not behave correctly.

However, the costs just mentioned do not give the whole picture. They pertain to only one phase of the life cycle of a solution—the phase in which it is an operational program. In assessing whether or not a solution is good, you also must consider the phases during which you developed the solution and the phases after you wrote the initial program that implemented the solution. Each of these phases incurs costs, too. The total cost of a solution must take into account the value of the time of the people who developed, refined, coded, debugged, and tested it. A solution's cost must also include the cost of maintaining, modifying, and expanding it.

Thus, when calculating the overall cost of a solution, you must include a diverse set of factors. If you adopt such a multidimensional view of cost, it is reasonable to evaluate a solution against the following criterion:

A multidimensional view of a solution's cost

> *A solution is good if the total cost it incurs over all phases of its life cycle is minimal.*

It is interesting to consider how the relative importance of the various components of this cost has changed since the early days of computing. In the beginning, the cost of computer time relative to human time was extremely high. In addition, people tended to write programs to perform very specific, narrowly defined tasks. If the task changed somewhat, a new program was written. Program maintenance was probably not much of an issue, and there was thus little concern if a program was hard to read. It was common for a program to have only one user, its author. As a consequence, programmers tended not to worry about misuse or ease of use of their programs; a program's interface generally was not considered important.

In this type of environment, one cost clearly overshadowed all others: computer resources. If two programs performed the same task, the one that required less time and memory was better. How things have changed! Since the early days of computers, computing costs have dropped dramatically, thus making the value of the problem solver's and programmer's time a much more significant factor in the cost of a solution. Another consequence of the drop in computing costs is that computers now are used to perform tasks in a wide variety of areas, many of them nonscientific. People who interact with computers often have no technical expertise and no knowledge of the workings of programs. People want their software to be easy to use.

Today, programs are larger and more complex than ever before. They are often so large that many people are involved in their design, use, and maintenance. Good structure and documentation are thus of the utmost importance. As programs perform more highly critical tasks, the prices for malfunctions will soar. Thus, society needs both well-structured programs and techniques for formally verifying their correctness. People will not and should not entrust their livelihoods—or their lives—to a program that only its authors can understand and maintain.

Programs must be well structured and documented

These developments have made obsolete the notion that the most efficient solution is always the best. If two programs perform the same task, it is no longer true that the faster one is necessarily better. Programmers who use every trick in the book to save a few microseconds of computing time at the expense of clarity are not in tune with the cost structure of today's world. You must write programs with people as well as computers in mind.

At the same time, do not get the false impression that the efficiency of a solution is no longer important. To the contrary, there are many situations in which efficiency is the prime determinant of whether or not a solution is even usable. The point is that a solution's efficiency is only one of many factors that you must consider. If two solutions have approximately the same efficiency, then other factors should dominate the comparison. However, when the efficiencies of solutions differ *significantly,* this difference can be the overriding concern. The stages of the problem-solving process at which you should be most concerned about efficiency are those during which you develop the underlying methods of solution—the algorithms and the data structures. It is the choice of the algorithms and data structures, far more than the manner in which you code them, that leads to significant differences in efficiency.

Efficiency is only one aspect of a solution's cost

The problem-solving philosophy that we advocate in this book reflects our view of the multidimensional cost of a solution. We believe that this philosophy is reasonable in today's world and that it will be reasonable in the years to come.

A SUMMARY OF KEY ISSUES IN PROGRAMMING

Given that a good solution is one that, in the course of its life cycle, incurs a small cost, the next questions to ask are, what are the characteristics of good solutions, and how can you construct good solutions? This section summarizes the answers to these very difficult questions. You will find more complete answers by observing the principles of problem solving that are practiced throughout the book. For example, Chapter 3 presents a large case study. A major goal of this case study is to demonstrate how you can solve a formidable problem by carefully following a few key programming principles. Throughout the remainder of the book, even as the emphasis shifts from programming to the earlier stages of the design of a solution, you should note how the programs attempt to adhere to these principles.

The programming issues that this section discusses should be familiar to you. However, it is usually the case that the beginning student does not truly appreciate their importance. After the first course in programming, many students still simply want to "get the thing to run." We hope that the discussion to follow and the case study in Chapter 3 will help to emphasize just how important these issues really are.

One of the most widespread misconceptions held by beginning students is that a computer program is "read" only by a computer. As a consequence, the beginning student tends to consider only whether or not the *computer* will be able to "understand" the program—that is, will the program compile, execute, and produce the correct output? The truth is, of course, that other people often must read and modify programs. In a typical programming environment, many individuals share a program. One person may write a program, which other people use in conjunction with other programs written by other people, and a year later, a different person may modify the program. It is therefore essential that you take great care to design a program that is easy to read and understand.

People read programs, too

You should always keep in mind the following six issues of program structure and design:

KEY CONCEPTS

Six Key Programming Issues

1. Modularity through top-down design
2. Modifiability
3. User interface
4. Fail-safe programming
5. Style
6. Debugging

Modularity Through Top-Down Design

As will be continually emphasized, you should practice modularity through top-down design at all phases of the problem-solving process, beginning with the initial design of a solution. A modular implementation generally follows naturally from a solution that you have developed through top-down design. Our earlier discussion of top-down design indicated that modules at the top level of a solution specify *what* major tasks are necessary to solve the problem. Further refinement of each of these modules produces other modules that specify smaller problems. Ultimately, each bottom-level module performs one well-defined task and discloses by its implementation *how* the task is performed.

As was noted earlier, a modular program has several advantages. As the size of a program grows, many programming tasks become more difficult. Modularity is a means of slowing down the rate at which the level of difficulty grows. The primary difference between a small modular program and a large modular program is simply the number of modules each contains. Because the modules are independent, working on one large modular program is not very different from working on many small, independent programs. On the other hand, working on a large nonmodular program is more like working on many interrelated programs simultaneously.

More specifically, modularity has a favorable impact on the following aspects of programming:

Modularity facilitates programming

- **Constructing the program.** Keeping track of what is going on in a large, complex program can quickly become very difficult. By restricting attention to small, independent modules, *the task of writing a large program is reduced to one of writing many small programs*. This approach also permits team programming, where several programmers work independently on their own modules.
- **Debugging the program.** Debugging a large program can be a monstrous task. Imagine that you type a 10,000-line program and eventually get it to compile. Neither of these tasks would be very much fun. Now imagine that you execute your program and, after a few hundred lines of output, you get the message

  ```
  range check error
  ```

  at the assignment statement

  ```
  A[Place] := 0
  ```

  How did `Place` get out of range? You should anticipate spending the next day or so tracing through the intricacies of your program before discovering what has gone wrong.

  A great advantage of modularity is that the task of debugging a large program is reduced to one of debugging many small programs. When you begin to code a module, you should be almost certain that all other modules coded so far are correct. That is, before you consider a module finished, you should test it extensively, both separately and in context with the other modules, by calling it with actual parameters carefully chosen to induce all possible behaviors of the modules. If this testing is done thoroughly, you can have a high degree of certainty that any problem is a result of an error in the last module added. *Modularity isolates errors.*

Modularity isolates errors

More theoretically, as was mentioned before, there are formal methods for proving properties of programs that you can use to establish the correctness of a program. Modular programs are amenable to this verification process.

Modular programs are easy to read

- **Reading the program.** A person reading a large program may have trouble seeing the forest for the trees. Just as a top-down design helps the programmer cope with the complexities of solving a problem, so too will it help the reader of a program to understand how a program works. A modular program is easy to follow because the reader can get a good idea of what is going on without reading any of the code. A well-written module can be understood fairly well from only its name, header comment, and the names of the other modules that it calls. The reader of a program needs to study actual code only if he or she requires a detailed understanding of how the program operates. This is discussed further in the section on style later in this chapter.

Modularity isolates modifications

- **Modifying the program.** Modifiability is the topic of the next section, but as the modularity of a program has a direct bearing on its modifiability, it is briefly mentioned here. A small change in the requirements of a program should require only a small change in the code. If this is not the case, it is likely that the program is poorly written and, in particular, that it is not modular. To accommodate a small change in the requirements, a modular program usually requires a change in only a few of its modules, particularly when the modules are independent (that is, loosely coupled) and each module performs a single well-defined task (that is, is highly cohesive). *Modularity isolates modifications.* A simple example is presented in the discussion of modifiability in the next section.

Modularity eliminates redundancies

- **Eliminating redundant code.** Another advantage of modular design is that you can identify operations that occur in many different parts of the program and implement them as subprograms. This means that the code for an operation will appear only once, resulting in an increase in both readability and modifiability. The example in the next section demonstrates this point.

Modifiability

Imagine that the specification for a program changes after some period of time. Frequently, people require that a program do something differently than they specified originally, or they ask that it do more than they requested originally. This section examines two techniques that make a program easy to modify: the use of subprograms and the use of user-defined constants.

Subprograms. Suppose, for instance, that a library has a large program to catalog its books. The program represents a book with a record,[3] which the following statements define:

```
const StringSize = 30;

type  nameType = string[StringSize];
      bookType = record
         CallNumber : real;
         Author     : nameType;
         Title      : nameType
      end;  { record }

var   Request : bookType;
```

Suppose that at several points the program needs to print out the information about a requested book. At each of these points, the program could include this sequence of statements:

```
with Request do
begin
   writeln('Call number : ', CallNumber:6:2);
   writeln('Author : ', Author);
   writeln('Title : ', Title)
end; { with }
```

Alternatively, you could replace this sequence with a call to the following procedure, *PrintInfo*:

```
procedure PrintInfo(Request : bookType);
begin
   with Request do
   begin
      writeln('Call number : ', CallNumber:6:2);
      writeln('Author : ', Author);
      writeln('Title : ', Title)
   end { with }
end;  { PrintInfo }
```

Subprograms make a program easier to modify

Not only does the use of the procedure have the obvious advantage of eliminating redundant code, it also makes the resulting program more modifiable. Suppose that, after the library's program has been running for a year, the library's staff notices that their patrons often wish to know the

[3]Do not worry if you have not studied records or if you do not remember them. You still should be able to understand the point of this example. Note that Chapter 2 reviews records.

length of a given book. This addition requires changing only the type definition of *bookType* to

```
bookType = record
   CallNumber : real;
   Author     : nameType;
   Title      : nameType;
   Pages      : posIntType { new field, where }
end;  { record }          { posIntType = 1..maxint }
```

and adding the statement

```
writeln('Length : ', Pages:5, ' pages')
```

to the *writeln* statements in the definition of the procedure *PrintInfo*. If you had not used a procedure, the modification would have required you to insert the *writeln* statement at each point where the program prints the information. Merely finding each of these points could be difficult, and you probably would overlook a few. In this simple example, the advantages of using subprograms should be clear.

For a slightly more subtle illustration, recall the earlier example of a solution that, as one of its tasks, sorted some data. Developing the sorting algorithm as an independent module and eventually implementing it as a procedure would make the program easier to modify. For instance, if you found that the sorting algorithm was too slow, you could replace the sort procedure without even looking at the rest of the program. You simply could "cut out" the old procedure and "paste in" the new one. If instead the sort was integrated into the program, the required surgery might be quite intricate.

In general, it is a very bad sign if you need to rewrite a program to accommodate small modifications. Usually, it is easy to modify a well-structured program slightly: Because each module solves only a small part of the overall problem, a small change in problem specifications usually affects only a few of the modules.

User-defined constants make a program easier to modify

User-defined constants. The use of user-defined, or named, constants is another way to enhance the modifiability of a program. For example, Pascal's restriction that an array must be of a predefined, fixed size causes a bit of difficulty. Suppose that a program used an array to process the SAT scores of the computer science majors at your university. When the program was written, there were 202 computer science majors, so the array was defined by

```
type scoresType = array[1..202] of integer;
```

The program processes the array in several ways: For example, it reads the scores, prints the scores, and averages the scores by using a construct such as

```
for Index := 1 to 202 do
    Process the score
```

If the number of majors should change, not only do you need to redefine the type *scoresType*, but you must also change each loop that processes the array to reflect the new array size. In addition, there may be other references in the code that depend on the size of the array. A 202 here, a 201 there—which to change?

On the other hand, if you use a named constant such as

```
const NumberOfMajors = 202
```

you can define the array by using

```
type scoresType = array[1..NumberOfMajors] of integer;
```

and write the processing loops in this form:

```
for Index := 1 to NumberOfMajors do
    Process the score
```

If you write references that depend on the size of the array in terms of the constant *NumberOfMajors* (such as *NumberOfMajors - 1*), you can change the array size simply by changing the definition of the constant and then compiling the program again.

User Interface

Another area in which you need to keep people in mind is the design of the user interface. Humans often process a program's input and output. Here are a few obvious points:

- *Prompt the user for input* In an interactive environment, the program should always prompt the user for input in a manner that makes it quite clear what it expects. For example, the prompt "?" is not nearly as enlightening as the prompt "Enter account number for deposit." You should never assume that the users of your program will know what response the program requires.
- *Echo the input* A program should always echo its input. Whenever a program reads data, either from a user at a terminal or from a file, the program should include the values it reads in its output. This inclusion serves two purposes: First, it gives the user a check on the data entered—a guard against typos and errors in data transmission. This check is particularly useful in the case of interactive input. Second, the output is more meaningful and self-explanatory when there is a record of what input generated the output.
- *Label the output* The output should be well labeled and easy to read. An output of

```
1800  6  1
Jones, Q.  223 2234.00 1088.19  X, Y  Smith, T. 111
110.23 L,  Harris, V.  44  44000.00 22222.22
```

is more prone to misinterpretation than is

```
CUSTOMER ACCOUNTS AS OF 1800 HOURS ON JUNE 1
Status codes:
X = new account, Y = joint account, L = inactive account

NAME           ACC#     CHECKING      SAVINGS       STATUS

Jones, Q.      223      $ 2234.00     $ 1088.19     X, Y
Smith, T.      111      $  110.23     ---------     L
Harris, V.      44      $44000.00     $22222.22     ------
```

These characteristics of a good user interface are only the basics. Several more subtle points separate a program that is merely usable from one that is user friendly. Students tend to ignore a good user interface, but by investing a little extra time here, you can make a big difference: the difference between a good program and one that only solves the problem. For example, consider a program that requires a user to enter a line of data in some fixed format, with exactly one blank between the fields. A free-form input that allows any number of blanks between the fields would be much more convenient for the user. It takes so little time to add a loop that skips blanks, so why require the user to follow an exact format? Once you make this small additional effort, it is a permanent part of both your program and your library of techniques. The user of your program never has to think about input format. Contrast this with having all users worry about input format every time they use your program.

Fail-Safe Programming

A fail-safe program is one that will perform reasonably no matter how anyone uses it. Unfortunately, this goal is usually unattainable. A more realistic goal is to anticipate the ways that people might misuse the program and to guard carefully against these abuses.

Check for errors in input

This discussion considers two types of errors. The first type is an *error in input data*. For example, suppose that a program expects a nonnegative integer but reads −12. When a program encounters this type of problem, it should not abort without displaying some sort of useful message. The message

```
range check error
```

is not as useful as the message

```
-12 is not a valid number of children.
Please reenter this number.
```

The second type of error is an *error in the program logic*. Although a discussion of this type of error belongs in the debugging section at the end of this chapter, detecting errors in program logic is also an issue of fail-safe programming. A program that appears to have been running correctly may at some point behave unexpectedly, even if the data that it reads is valid. For example, the program may not have accounted for the particular data that elicited the surprise behavior, even though you tried your best to test the program's logic. Or perhaps you modified the program and that modification invalidated an assumption that you made in some other part of the program. Whatever the difficulty, a program should have built-in safeguards against these kinds of errors. It should monitor itself and be able to indicate that *there is something wrong with me and you should not trust my results*.

Check for errors in logic

Guarding against errors in input data. Suppose that you are computing statistics about the people in income brackets between $10,000 and $100,000. The brackets are rounded to the nearest thousand dollars: $10,000, $11,000, and so on to $100,000. The raw data is a file of zero or more lines of the form

```
<G> <N>
```

where *N* is the number of people with an income that falls into the *G*-thousand-dollar group. Several people have compiled the data, so there may be several entries for the same value of *G*. As the user enters data, the program must add up and record the number of people for each value of *G*. From the problem's context, it is clear that *G* is an integer in the range 10 to 100 inclusive, and *N* is a nonnegative integer.

As an example of how to guard against errors in input, we will consider the input procedure for this problem. The first attempt at writing this procedure will illustrate several common ways in which a program can fall short of the fail-safe ideal. Consideration of several possible modifications to the procedure will lead to some dos and don'ts about fail-safe programming in general and for the use of subrange types in particular. Eventually you will see an input procedure that is much closer to the fail-safe ideal than the original solution.

Many of the points here specifically concern Pascal, so actual code rather than pseudocode will be used. A first attempt at the procedure might be

```
const Low = 10;              { low end of incomes considered }
      High = 100;            { high end of incomes considered }

type  thousandsType = Low..High;
      tableType     = array[thousandsType] of integer;

procedure ReadData(var IncomeData : tableType);
{ ------------------------------------------------------
  Reads and organizes income statistics.
  Precondition: The calling module prompts user and gives
  directions. Input data is error-free and each input line
  is in the form <G> <N> where N is the number of people
  with an income in the G-thousand-dollar group. Ctrl-Z
  followed by a carriage return terminates input.
  Postcondition: IncomeData[G] = total number of people with
  an income in the G-thousand-dollar group.
  ------------------------------------------------------ }
```

This procedure is not fail-safe

```
var  Group, Number : integer;              { input values }
     Index : thousandsType;                { loop control }

begin
   for Index := Low to High do             { zero out the array }
      IncomeData[Index] := 0;

   while not eof do                        { while not Ctrl-Z }
   begin
      readln(Group, Number);                         {read data}
      writeln('Income group = ', Group:3,
              ' and Number = ', Number:7);    {echo print}

      IncomeData[Group] := IncomeData[Group] + Number
   end  { while }
end;  {ReadData}
```

This procedure has some problems. If an input line contains unexpected data, the program will not behave reasonably. Consider two specific possibilities:

- The program accepts a negative value for *Number*. Although a negative value for *Number* is invalid because you cannot have a negative number of people in an income group, the program will add *Number* to the group's array entry. Thus, the statistics that other parts of the program produce will not be valid.
- The first integer on the line is not in the range *Low..High*. The reference *IncomeData[Group]* will then cause execution to terminate with the message

  ```
  range check error
  ```

  if you used the *$R+* compiler directive.[4]

Do not use subrange types to detect invalid input data

A first attempt at addressing these two problems uses Pascal's facility for subrange types. As you will see, however, *it is not appropriate to use subrange types as the only mechanism for catching errors in input.* For example, because the number of people in any income group should never be negative, you might change the global type definitions to

```
type nonnegType     = 0..maxint;       { new type }
     thousandsType = Low..High;       { remains the same }
     tableType = array[thousandsType] of nonnegType; {an array
           of this type can contain only nonnegative integers}
```

Does this change really address the concern about a negative input value for *Number*? First, notice that it is possible to add a negative value to an

[4]See Appendix H for a description of Turbo Pascal's compiler directives.

entry of `IncomeData` without that entry becoming negative. For example, if `Number` is −4,000 and `IncomeData[Group]` is 10,000, then `IncomeData[Group] + Number` is 6,000. Thus, a negative value for `Number` could remain undetected and invalidate the results of the rest of the program.

Not only would the subrange fail to catch many input errors, but also when it did catch errors, the errors might not be obvious. For example, suppose that `Number` is −4,000 and `IncomeData[Group]` is 2,143. When the program computed `IncomeData[Group] + Number`, it would terminate with a range check error message because `IncomeData[Group]` is negative. This message is not particularly useful! It does not specifically tell you that `Number` was negative. This ungraceful termination caused by an error in input is not consistent with the desire for a fail-safe program.

Thus, making `IncomeData` an array over the subrange `nonnegType` does not adequately address the problem of invalid input values for `Number`. However, there is another reason for wanting `IncomeData` to be an array of this type, as you will see in the next section, "Guarding Against Errors in Program Logic."

The next attempt at solving the problem of invalid input might be to declare the variable `Number` to be type `nonnegType`. However, this idea is not adequate either. If the data contains a negative value for `Number`, the program will terminate with a range check error message. A fail-safe program should detect the invalid data but not abort. A better solution is to leave `Number` as an integer, but always to check its value before storing it in the array, as this pseudocode indicates:

Test for invalid input data

```
readln(Group, Number)
. . .
if Number >= 0
    then add Number to IncomeData
    else handle the error
```

Notice that Pascal allows you to assign a variable of type *T* (in this case, `integer`) to a variable whose type is a subrange of *T* (in this case, `nonnegType`), as long as the value of the first variable is within the specified range.

Now that you have seen a satisfactory solution to the problem of an invalid input value for `Number`, it is clear how you can solve the problem of an invalid input value for `Group`. After the program reads a value for `Group`, it must check to see if it is in the range `Low..High`. If the value is in range, you may use `Group` to subscript the array `IncomeData`. However, if it is not in range, you must handle the input error.

There are several reasonable courses of action for the program to take after it has encountered an error in the input. One possibility is for the program to print out an informative message, such as

```
The value 9 supplied for the income group
is not in the required range of 10..100
```

and terminate. Another possibility is to print out a similar message, ignore the bad input line, and continue. Which action is correct really depends on how the program uses the data once it is read.

These points are illustrated with a solution that attempts both to make the input procedure as universally applicable as possible and to make the program that uses it as modifiable as possible. In the following solution, when the input procedure encounters an error in input, it will print out a message, set a flag, ignore the data line, and continue. By setting a flag, the procedure leaves it to the calling routine to determine the appropriate action—such as abort or continue—when there is an input error. Thus, you can use the same input procedure in many contexts and can easily modify the action taken upon encountering an error. Error handling is discussed further in the section on style later in this chapter.

```
const Low = 10;          { low end of incomes considered }
      High = 100;        { high end of incomes considered }

type  nonnegType     = 0..maxint;
      thousandsType  = Low..High;
      tableType      = array[thousandsType] of nonnegType;
```

A procedure that includes fail-safe programming

```
procedure ReadData(var IncomeData : tableType;
                   var DataError : boolean);
{ ---------------------------------------------------------
  Reads and organizes income statistics.
  Precondition: The calling module prompts user and gives
  directions. Each input line contains exactly 2 integers in
  the form <G> <N> where N is the number of people with an
  income in the G-thousand-dollar group. Ctrl-Z followed by
  a carriage return terminates input.
  Postcondition: IncomeData[G] = total number of people with
  an income in the G-thousand-dollar group. If either G or N
  is erroneous (G not in the range [Low..High] or N
  negative), the program ignores the data line, prints a
  message, sets the flag DataError to true, and continues.
  In this case, the calling routine should take action.
  DataError is false if there are no data errors.
  --------------------------------------------------------- }
var  Group, Number : integer;     { input values }
     Index : thousandsType;       { loop control }

begin
   DataError := false;            { no data error found yet }

   for Index := Low to High do    { zero out the array }
      IncomeData[Index] := 0;
```

```
   while not eof do                    { while not Ctrl-Z }
   begin
      readln(Group, Number);
      writeln('Input line contains income group  ',
             Group:3, '  and  Number  ', Number:7);
      if ( (Group >= Low) and (Group <= High) )
                                     and (Number >= 0)
         then     { the input is valid - add it to the tally }
            IncomeData[Group] := IncomeData[Group] + Number
         else    { error in input data }
         begin
            writeln('Error in input:');
            if ( Group < Low ) or ( Group > High )
               then writeln('Income group not',
                                 ' in range 10..100.');

            if ( Number < 0 )
               then writeln('Number is negative.');
            writeln('This input line will be ignored.');
            writeln;
            DataError := true { set error flag }
         end  { else }
   end  { while }
end; { ReadData }
```

This input procedure will behave gracefully in the face of most common input errors. However, it is not completely fail-safe. What happens if an input line contains only one integer? What happens if an input line contains a noninteger? The procedure would be more fail-safe if it read its input character by character, converted the characters to integer, and checked for end of line. In most contexts, this processing would be a bit extreme. However, if the people who enter the data frequently err by typing nonintegers, you could alter the input procedure easily because the procedure is an isolated module. In any case, the procedure's header comment should include any assumptions it makes about the data and an indication of what might make the program abort abnormally.

Guarding against errors in program logic. Now consider the second type of error that a program should guard against: errors in its own logic. These are errors that you may not have caught when you debugged the program, or that you may have introduced through program modification.

Unfortunately, there is no reliable way for a program to let you know when something is wrong with it. (Could you rely on a program to tell you that something was wrong with its mechanism for telling you that there is something wrong?) However, you can build checks into a program that ensure that certain conditions always hold when the program is correctly implementing its algorithm. As was mentioned earlier, such conditions are called invariants.

As a simple example of an invariant, consider again the array `IncomeData` from the previous example. *All integers in this array must be greater than or equal to zero.* Recall that `IncomeData` was left as an array of `nonnegType` values. Although this choice does not help to guard against input errors, to some extent it does guard against errors in the program's logic when you use *$R+*. For example, if at any time the program attempts to store a negative value in the array, the program terminates. The termination is not very graceful, but it is far better for a program to terminate ungracefully than it is for it to continue to produce output that—unbeknownst to the users—is incorrect.

Pascal's range checking should really be your last line of defense against errors in a program's logic. If, for example, the program computes a value to add to an entry of the array `IncomeData`, it might be reasonable for the program to check first that this computed value is within some range of believability. If the value is outside such a range, the program can terminate with a message that alerts its users to a potential problem and requests that debuggers be called in.

Subprograms should check the values of their parameters

Another general way in which you should make a program fail-safe is to make each subprogram check the values of its parameters. For example, consider the following function, *SumBetween*, which returns the sum of all the integers between integers *X* and *Y*.

```
function SumBetween(X, Y : integer) : integer;
{ ---------------------------------------------------------
  Returns the sum of all the integers between X and Y.
  Precondition: X and Y are integers such that X <= Y.
  Postcondition: Returns SumBetween = X + (X + 1) + ... + Y.
  X and Y are unchanged.
  --------------------------------------------------------- }
var Sum, Index : integer;
begin
   Sum := 0;
   for Index := X to Y do
      Sum := Sum + Index;
   SumBetween := Sum
end;  { SumBetween }
```

The header comment of this function contains a precondition—information about what assumptions are made—*as should always be the case.* The value that this function returns is valid only if the precondition is met. If *X* is greater than *Y*, then the function will return the incorrect value of zero.

In the context of the program for which this function was written, it may be reasonable to make the assumption that *X* will be less than or equal to *Y*. That is, if the rest of the program is working correctly, then it will call *SumBetween* only with correct values of *X* and *Y*. Ironically, this last observation gives you a good reason for *SumBetween* to check the relationship between the values of *X* and *Y*: If it turns out that *X* is greater than *Y*, then the warning that results from the check indicates that something may be wrong elsewhere in the program.

Another reason the function `SumBetween` should check whether `X` is less than or equal to `Y` is that the function should be correct outside the context of its program. That is, if you borrow the function for use in another program, the function should warn you if you use it incorrectly by passing it an `X` that is greater than `Y`. A stronger check than simply the statement of the assumptions in the header comment is desirable. Thus, *a subprogram should state its assumptions and, when possible, check that its parameters conform to these assumptions.*

Style

The following eight issues of personal style in programming are considered here:

Eight Issues of Style

KEY CONCEPTS

1. Extensive use of subprograms
2. Avoidance of global variables in subprograms
3. Proper use of variable parameters
4. Proper use of functions
5. Avoidance of *goto*
6. Error handling
7. Readability
8. Documentation

Admittedly, much of the following discussion reflects the personal taste of the authors; there certainly are other good programming styles.

It is difficult to overuse subprograms

Extensive use of subprograms. You should use subprograms extensively; it is very difficult to overuse them. If a set of statements performs an identifiable, recurring task, it should be a subprogram. However, a task need not be recurrent to justify the use of a subprogram.

There are two arguments against the extensive use of subprograms. First, subprograms may incur a large overhead. A program with all its code in line runs faster than one that calls subprograms to execute the same statements. However, it is false to infer from this fact that it is cheaper to use programs that do not contain subprograms. The use of subprograms is cost-effective if you consider human time as a significant component of the program's cost. In addition to the consideration of the cost of human time, current research trends support extensive use of subprograms. Compilers can reduce the penalties for subprogram calls. Transformation tools take a program with subprograms and transform it for execution into an equivalent program with the subprograms represented in line.

A second objection to the extensive use of subprograms is that they can be difficult to read. *Perhaps* you have overused subprograms if they cause a reader to move back and forth constantly through the program. However, if the subprograms implement recurring tasks, the distraction they may cause is made up for by the increase in the program's modifiability. In short, it is possible to overuse subprograms, but it is far easier to underuse them.

Avoidance of global variables in subprograms. One of the main advantages of subprograms is that they can implement the concept of an isolated module. This isolation is sacrificed when a subprogram accesses a global variable, because the effects of a subprogram's action are no longer self-contained or limited to variable parameters. Hence, the isolation of both errors and modifications is greatly compromised when global variables appear in subprograms.

Use global variables sparingly

Should a subprogram ever access global variables? Sometimes, but only if the sacrifice of isolation is justifiable. *If some piece of data is so inherently important to a program that almost every subprogram must access it, then the data is global in nature.* Allowing the subprograms global access to the variables that contain this data best reflects the relationship between the data and the program as a whole.

Proper use of variable parameters. A subprogram does interact, in a controlled fashion, with the rest of the program via the use of parameters.

Value parameters

Value parameters, which are the default when you do not specify the keyword `var`, pass values into the subprogram, but any change that the subprogram makes to these parameters is not reflected in the actual parameters back in the calling routine. The communication between the calling routine and the subprogram is one-way. Because the restriction to one-way communication supports the notion of an isolated module, *you should use value parameters when possible.*

Variable parameters

When is it appropriate to use **variable parameters**? The obvious situation is when a procedure needs to return values to the calling routine. However, if the procedure needs to return only a single value, it may be more appropriate to use a function. If a function is not appropriate, then variable parameters are probably in order.

There is another situation in which variable parameters might be desirable, but the issues are very subtle. Suppose that a subprogram has a parameter `X` whose value it does not alter. The natural choice is for `X` to be a value parameter. However, invoking a subprogram with a value parameter `X` causes the subprogram to copy the value of the actual parameter that corresponds to `X` into temporary storage that is local to the subprogram. This copying incurs very little overhead if `X` is a simple variable, but the computing time and storage required to copy a large array might be significant. However, if `x` were a variable parameter, no copy of it would be made, which could lead to significant savings in computer resources.

The problem with making `x` a variable parameter is that it conveys misinformation about the subprogram's relation to the rest of the program. By convention, you use a variable parameter to communicate a value from the subprogram back to the calling routine. However, variable parameters whose values remain unchanged make the program more difficult to read and more prone to errors if modifications are required. The situation is analogous to using a constant instead of a variable whose value never changes. Thus, there is a trade-off between readability and modifiability on the one hand and efficiency on the other. Unless there is a significant difference in efficiency, we generally take the side of readability and modifiability. Later, this book explores such trade-offs more fully.

Proper use of functions. Because Pascal could not possibly include all potentially useful statements in its set of primitive statements, it provides the programmer with procedures, a mechanism for writing new statements out of the built-in primitives. You can call a procedure from any point in a program at which you need the user-defined statement. Similarly, a function is a mechanism by which the programmer can write new *expressions.* Any time you need to calculate a value, you can call a user-defined function as if it were part of the language.

Functions should not have side effects

Because you use a function as an expression, you should use it, as you would any other expression, only to compute a simple value. This use corresponds to the mathematical notion of a function. Therefore, it would be strange indeed if a function did *anything* other than return the required value. Imagine evaluating the expression `2 * x` and having the values of five other variables change! *A function should never do anything but return the required value.* That is, a function should never have a **side effect.**

What functions have potential for side effects?

Functions with the potential for side effects

- **Functions with global variables.** If a function references a global variable, it has the potential for a side effect. *In general, functions should not assign values to global variables.*
- **Functions with variable parameters.** A variable parameter indicates that its values will change within the function. (However, recall the previous discussion on the use of variable parameters.) This is a side effect. *In general, functions should not use variable parameters.* If you need variable parameters, use a procedure.
- **Functions that perform I/O.** Input and output (I/O) are side effects. *In general, functions should not perform I/O.*

Avoidance of `goto`. One of the most important factors contributing to well-structured programs is an orderly flow of control. An orderly flow of control implies the following:

KEY CONCEPTS

Orderly Flow of Control

1. The general flow of a program is forward.
2. A module is entered only at its beginning and exited only at its end.
3. The conditions for terminating loops are clear and uniform.
4. The alternative cases of conditional statements are clear and uniform.

The use of a `goto` almost always violates at least one of these conditions. In addition, it is very difficult to verify the correctness of a program that contains a `goto`. Therefore, in general, you should avoid the `goto`. There are, however, *rare* situations where you will need an exceptional flow of control. Such cases include those requiring either that a program terminate execution when an error occurs, or that a subprogram return control to its calling module. The inclusion in Turbo Pascal of both `halt` and `exit` makes the use of `goto` unnecessary.

Error handling. A fail-safe program checks for errors in both its input and its logic, and attempts to behave gracefully when it encounters them. Error handling often necessitates exceptional actions that would constitute bad style in normal program execution. For example, error handling may involve the use of functions with side effects. You often must choose between several courses of action, no single one of which is completely satisfactory.

A subprogram should check for certain types of errors, such as invalid input or parameter values. What action should a subprogram take when it encounters an error? The procedure `ReadData` in the income statistics program earlier in this chapter printed an error message and returned a boolean flag to the calling routine to indicate that it had encountered an invalid line of data. Thus, the procedure left it to the calling routine to decide on the appropriate action. In some situations, however, it is more appropriate for the subprogram itself to take the action—for example, when the required action does not depend on the point from which the subprogram is called.

If a *function* handles errors by printing an error message or returning a flag, it violates the rule against functions with side effects. Despite this fact, these actions seem reasonable for functions as well as procedures.

Depending on context, the appropriate action in the face of an error can range from ignoring erroneous data and continuing execution to terminating the program. In the case of a fatal error that calls for termination, a `halt` might be the cleanest way to abort. Suppose that you are nested deep within procedure calls, `while` loops, and `if-then-else` statements when you encounter a fatal error. The first course of action could be to call a diagnostics procedure, which would print out as much information as possible to help the user determine why the program had to abort—including, for example, current values of variables and an echo of erroneous data. After the procedure has reported all this information, the program should terminate. However, if the diagnostic procedure returns control to the point from which it was called, you still must exit from many layers of nested control structures. A cleaner solution is for the last statement of the diagnostic procedure to be *halt*.

Readability. For a program to be easy to follow, it should have a good structure and design, a good choice of identifiers, good indentation and use of blank lines, and good documentation. You should avoid clever programming tricks that save a little computer time at the expense of much human time. You will see examples of these points in the programs throughout the book.

Choose identifiers that describe their purpose, that is, are self-documenting. Distinguish between reserved words,[5] such as *while*, standard identifiers, such as *integer*, and user-defined identifiers. We use the following conventions:

- Reserved words are lowercase and appear in boldface.
- Standard identifiers, standard functions, and standard procedures are lowercase.
- User-defined identifiers are both upper- and lowercase. When an identifier consists of two or more words, the words each begin with a capital letter. An exception is user-defined data types, which begin with a lowercase letter and end in *Type*.

Use a good indentation style to enhance the readability of a program. The layout of a program should make it easy for a reader to identify the program's modules. Use blank lines to offset each subprogram. Also, within both subprograms and the main program, you should offset with blank lines and indent individual blocks of code visibly. These blocks are generally—but are not limited to—the actions performed within a control structure, such as a *while* loop or an *if-then-else* statement.

There are several good indentation styles to choose from. The four most important general requirements of an indentation style are that

Guidelines for indentation style

- Blocks should be indented sufficiently so that they stand out clearly.
- In a compound statement, the *begin* and the *end* should line up:

```
begin
  <statement1>
  <statement2>
       .
       .
       .
  <statementN>
end
```

[5]See Appendix C for a list of reserved words and standard identifiers.

- Indentation should be consistent: Always indent the same type of construct in the same manner.
- The indentation style should provide a reasonable way to handle the problem of **rightward drift**, the problem of nested blocks bumping against the right-hand margin of the page.

Within these guidelines there is room for personal taste. Here is a summary of the style you will see in this book.

Indentation style in this book

- A *while* or *for* loop is indented for a simple action as

```
while <cond> do
  <statement>
```

  and for a compound action as

```
while <cond> do
begin
  <statements>
end
```

- An *if-then-else* statement is indented for simple actions as

```
if <cond>
  then <statement1>
  else <statement2>
```

  and for compound actions as

```
if <cond>
  then
  begin
     <statements>
  end

  else
  begin
     <statements>
  end
```

  There is one special use of the *if-then-else* statement for which another style is used: when cascading *if-then-else-if*'s choose among three or more different courses of action. Instead of writing

```
if <cond1>
  then <action1>
  else if <cond2>
    then <action2>
    else if <cond3>
      then <action3>
```

we write

```
if <cond1> then
  <action1>
else if <cond2> then
  <action2>
else if <cond3> then
  <action3>
```

This indentation style better reflects the nature of the construct, which is like a generalized *case* statement:

```
<cond1> : <action1>
<cond2> : <action2>
<cond3> : <action3>
```

- We often use *begin/end*'s to increase readability, even when they are not a syntactic necessity. For example, in the construct

```
while <cond1> do
begin
  if <cond2>
     then <action1>
     else <action2>
end
```

the *begin/end* is syntactically unnecessary because an *if-then-else* is a single statement. However, the *begin/end* highlights the scope of the *while* loop.

Documentation. A program should be well documented so that others can read, use, and modify it easily. There are many acceptable styles for documentation, and exactly what you should include often depends on the particular program. The following are the essential features of any program's documentation:

KEY CONCEPTS

Documentation

1. A header comment for the program that includes

   a. Statement of purpose
   b. Author and date
   c. Description of the program's input and output
   d. Description of how to use the program
   e. Assumptions such as the type of data expected and what could go wrong. *This is very important!*
   f. Brief description of the global algorithms and data structures
   g. Description of the key variables

2. A "miniheader" comment in each module, similar to the program's header, that contains information pertinent to that module, including its preconditions and postconditions
3. Comments in the body of each module to explain important and confusing parts of the program

Beginning programmers tend to downplay the importance of documentation because the computer does not read comments. By now, you should realize that people do read programs. There is also a tendency for beginners to document programs as a last step. However, you should write documentation as you develop the program. The task of writing a large program might extend over a period of several weeks. You may find that the procedure that seemed so obvious when you wrote it last week will seem confusing when you try to debug it next week.

Debugging

No matter how much care you take in writing a program, there inevitably will be bugs that you need to track down. Fortunately, programs developed under the guidelines presented in the previous sections are generally amenable to debugging. Programs that are modular, clear, and well documented are certainly easier to debug than those that are not. Fail-safe techniques, which guard against certain errors and report them when they are encountered, are also a great aid in debugging.

Many students seem to be totally baffled by bugs in their programs and have no idea how to proceed. These students simply have not learned to track down a bug systematically. Without a systematic approach, finding a small bug in a large program can indeed be a difficult task.

The difficulty that many people have in debugging a program is perhaps due in part to a desire to believe that their program is really doing what it is supposed to do. For example, on receiving a range check error message at line 1098, a student might say, "That's impossible. The statement at line 1098 was not even executed, because it is in the *else* clause, and I am positive that the *then* clause was executed." This student must do more than simply protest. The proper approach is either to trace the program's execution by using Turbo Pascal's debugging facilities or to add *write* statements that show which clause was executed. Thus, you verify the value of the boolean condition. If the condition is false when you expect it to be true—as the error message indicates—then the next step is to determine how it became false.

Use temporary ***write*** *statements to find bugs*

How, then, can you find the point in a program where something becomes other than what it should be? In Turbo Pascal, you can trace a program's execution either by single-stepping through the statements in the program or by setting **breakpoints**. You also can examine the contents of particular variables by either establishing **watches** or inserting temporary *write* statements. The key to debugging is simply to use these tools to tell you what is going on. This may sound pretty mundane, but the real trick is to use these tools in an effective manner. After all, you do not simply put breakpoints, watches, and *write* statements at random points in the program and have them report random information.

Systematically verify a program's logic to determine where an error occurs

The main idea is to systematically locate the points of the program that cause the problem. A program's logic implies that certain conditions should be true at various points in the program. (Recall that these conditions are called invariants.) A bug means that a condition that you think ought to be true is not. To correct the bug, you must find the first point in the program at which one of these conditions differs from expectation. By inserting either breakpoints and watches or *write* statements at strategic locations of a program—such as at the entry and departure points of loops and subprograms—you can systematically isolate the bug.

These diagnostic tools should inform you whether things start going wrong before or after a given point in the program. Thus, after you run the program with an initial set of diagnostics, you should be able to trap the bug between two points. For example, suppose that things are fine before you call procedure P_1, but something is wrong by the time you call P_2. This kind of information allows you to focus your attention between these two points. You continue the process until eventually the search is limited to only a few statements. There is really no place in a program for a bug to hide.

The ability to place breakpoints, watches, and *write* statements in appropriate locations and to have them report appropriate information comes in part from thinking logically about the problem and in part from experience. Here are a few general guidelines.

Debugging subprograms. Two key locations to place breakpoints are at the beginning and end of a subprogram. You should examine the values of the parameters at these two locations by using either watches or *write* statements.

Debugging loops. You should place breakpoints at the beginnings and ends of loops and examine the values of key variables, as the comments in this example indicate:

```
{ Examine values of Start and Stop before entering loop. }

for Index := Start to Stop do
begin
   { Examine the values of Index and key }
   { variables at the beginning of iteration. }
         .
         .
         .
   { Examine the values of Index and key }
   { variables at the end of iteration. }
end;

{ Examine values of Start and Stop after exiting loop. }
```

Debugging *if-then-else* statements. You should place a breakpoint before an *if-then-else* statement and examine the values of both the boolean expression and its variables. You can use either breakpoints or *write* statements to determine which branch the *if* statement takes, as this example indicates:

```
{ Examine the values of <condition> and the }
{ variables in <condition> before the if-then-else. }

if <condition>
   then
   begin
      writeln('Condition is true, ',
                       'so follow the then branch.');
      .
      .
      .
   end

   else
   begin
      writeln('Condition is false, ',
                      'so follow the else branch.');
      .
      .
      .
   end;
```

Using *write* statements. Sometimes *write* statements can be more convenient than watches. Such *write* statements should report both the values of key variables and the location in the program at which the variables have those values. You can use a comment to label the location, as follows:

```
{ This is point A }
writeln('At point A in the procedure Compute:');
writeln('X=', X, ' Y=', Y, ' Z=', Z)
```

Using special dump routines. Often the variables whose values you wish to examine are arrays or other, more complex data structures. If so, you should write dump routines to accomplish the task. You can easily move the single statement that calls each dump routine from one point in the program to another as you track down a bug. The routines should display the data structures in a highly readable manner. The time that you spend on these routines often proves to be worthwhile, as you can call them repeatedly while debugging different parts of the program.

Hopefully, this discussion has conveyed the importance of the *effective use of diagnostic tools in debugging.* Even the best programmers have to spend some time debugging. Thus, to be a truly good programmer, you must be a good debugger.

SUMMARY

1. Software engineering is a branch of computer science that studies ways to facilitate the development of computer programs.
2. The life cycle of software consists of eight phases: specifying the problem, designing the algorithm, verifying the algorithm, coding the programs, testing them, refining the solution, using the software, and maintaining the software.
3. A loop invariant is a property of an algorithm that is true before and after each iteration of a loop. Loop invariants are useful in developing iterative algorithms and establishing their correctness.
4. When evaluating the quality of a solution, you must consider a diverse set of factors: the solution's correctness, its efficiency, the time that went into its development, its ease of use, and the cost of modifying and expanding it.
5. When designing a solution, you should proceed in a top-down fashion and break the tasks into independent modules, which you gradually refine. Some of these modules perform algorithmic-type tasks, such as sorting an array, and others perform data-management-type tasks, such as retrieving a data item. In either case, each module should be a "black box" from the perspective of the rest of the program.
6. Take great care to ensure that the final solution is as easy to modify as possible. Generally, a modular program is easy to modify because changes in the problem's requirements frequently affect only a handful of the modules. The use of user-defined (named) constants—for example, in the declarations of array bounds—is another factor that can greatly enhance a program's modifiability.
7. A program should be as fail-safe as possible. For example, a program should guard against errors in input and errors in its own logic. By checking invariants—which are conditions that are true at certain points in a program—you can monitor correct program execution.
8. A subprogram should correspond as much as possible to the notion of an isolated module. To this end, do not overuse global variables, and avoid functions with side effects whenever possible.
9. A subprogram should always include a header comment that states its purpose, its precondition—that is, the conditions that must exist at the beginning of a module—and its postcondition—the conditions at the end of a module.

COMMON PITFALLS/DEBUGGING

1. **The effective use of available diagnostic tools is one of the keys to debugging. You should use Turbo watches or `write` statements to report the values of key variables at key locations. These locations include the beginnings and ends of procedures and loops and the branches of conditional statements.**

2. **To make it easier to examine the contents of arrays and other, more complex data structures while debugging, you should write dump routines that display the contents of the data structures. You can easily move calls to such routines as you track down a bug.**

3. **Your programs should guard against errors. A fail-safe program checks that an input value is within some acceptable range and reports if it is not. An error in input should not cause a program to terminate before it clearly reports what the error was. A fail-safe program also attempts to detect errors in its own logic. For example, in many situations subprograms should check that the parameters have valid values.**

4. **You should use subrange types only as a last line of defense against errors and not in general to guard against errors in input. A variable into which data is read should not be of a subrange type, because an out-of-range value causes an ungraceful termination, if *$R+* is specified. However, subrange types help to enforce a condition in the program's logic.**

SELF-TEST EXERCISES

The answers to all Self-Test Exercises are at the back of this book.

1. What is the loop invariant for the following?

```
Index := 1;
Sum := A[1];
while Index < N do
begin
   Index := succ(Index);
   Sum := Sum + A[Index]
end
```

2. Write specifications for a procedure that computes the sum of the first five positive integers in an array of *N* arbitrary integers.

EXERCISES

1. Consider the following program, which interactively reads and writes the identification number, name, age, and salary (in thousands of dollars) of a group of employees. How can you improve the program? Some of the issues are obvious, while others are more subtle. Try to keep in mind all the topics discussed in this chapter.

```
program Stats;

var X1, X2, X3, I : integer;
     Name : array[1..8] of char;

begin
   while not eof do
   begin
      read(X1);
      for I := 1 to 8 do
         read(Name[I]);
      readln(X2, X3);
      writeln(X1, Name, X2, X3)
   end
end.
```

2. This chapter stressed the importance of adding fail-safe checks to a program wherever possible. What can go wrong with the following function? How can you protect yourself?

```
function Tangent(X : real) : real;
begin
   Tangent := sin(X)/cos(X)
end
```

3. Modify the function *SumBetween*, which appears in the section "Fail-Safe Programming," to ensure that *X* <= *Y*.

4. Consider a program that will read employee information into an array of records, sort the array by employee identification number, write out the sorted array, and compute various statistics on the data, such as the average age of an employee. Write complete specifications for this problem and design a modular solution. What subprograms did you identify during the design of your solution? Write specifications, including preconditions and postconditions, for each subprogram. Implement your solution by using stubs.

5. Write the procedure that Self-Test Exercise 2 describes, and state the loop invariants.

6. Write the loop invariants for the function *SumBetween* that appears in this chapter.

7. Demonstrate that the algorithm in Self-Test Exercise 1 correctly computes *A[1]* + *A[2]* + ··· + *A[N]* by using loop invariants.

8. The following program is supposed to compute the **floor** of the square root of its input value *X*. (The floor of a number *n* is the largest integer less than or equal to *n*.)

```
program SquareRoot;
{ Computes and prints floor(sqrt(X)) for an input value
  X >= 0}

var X, Result, Temp1, Temp2 : integer;

begin
   { initialize }
   readln(X);
   Result := 0;
   Temp1 := 1;
   Temp2 := 1;
   { compute floor }
   while Temp1 < X do
   begin
      Result := succ(Result);
      Temp2 := Temp2 + 2;
      Temp1 := Temp1 + Temp2
   end;

   writeln('The floor of the square root of ',
               X:1, ' is ', Result:1)
end.
```

There is a bug in this program.

a. What output does the program produce when *X* = 64?

b. Debug the program on the computer. Describe the steps that you took to find the error.

c. How can you make the program more user friendly and fail-safe?

9. Suppose that due to some severe error, you must abort a program from a location deep inside nested procedure calls, *while* loops, and *if-then-else* statements. Write a diagnostic procedure that you can call from anywhere in a program. This procedure should take an error code as an argument (some mnemonic enumerated type), print an appropriate error message, and terminate program execution.

PROJECTS

10. Write a program that sorts and evaluates bridge hands.

INPUT

The input is a stream of character pairs, which represent playing cards. For example,

```
2C QD TC AD 6C 3D TD 3H 5H 7H AS JH KH
```

represents the 2 of clubs, queen of diamonds, 10 of clubs, ace of diamonds, and so on. Each pair consists of a rank followed by a suit, where rank is A, 2, ..., 9, T, J, Q, or K, and suit is C, D, H, or S. You can assume that there will be no errors in the input and that exactly 13 cards will be represented on each input line. Input is terminated by an end of file. For this problem you are to form a hand of 13 cards from each input line.

OUTPUT

Print each hand of 13 cards in a readable form arranged both by suits and by rank within suit (aces are high). Then evaluate the hand by using the following standard bridge values:

Aces count 4

Kings count 3

Queens count 2

Jacks count 1

Voids (no cards in a suit) count 3

Singletons (one card in a suit) count 2

Doubletons (two cards in a suit) count 1

Long suits with more than 5 cards in the suit count 1 for each card over 5 in number

For example, for the previous sample input line, the program should produce the output

```
CLUBS          10    6     2
DIAMONDS       A     Q    10    3
HEARTS         K     J     7    5    3
SPADES         A
Points = 16
```

because there are 2 aces, 1 king, 1 queen, 1 jack, 1 singleton, no doubletons, and no long suits. (The singleton ace of spades counts as both an ace and a singleton.)

Optional: See how much more flexible and fail-safe you can make your program. That is, try to remove as many of the previous assumptions in input as you can.

11. Write a program that will act as an interactive calculator capable of handling very large (larger than *maxlongint*) nonnegative integers. This calculator need perform only the operations of addition and multiplication.

In this program each input line is of the form

```
<num1> <op> <num2>
```

and should produce output such as

```
      <num1>
<op>  <num2>
-----------
      <num3>
```

where <*num1*> and <*num2*> are (possibly very large) nonnegative integers, <*op*> is the single character + or *, and <*num3*> is the integer that results from the desired calculation.

Design your program carefully. You will need the following:

a. A data structure to represent large numbers; for example,

```
array[1..MaxSize] of 0..9
```

b. A procedure to read in numbers. Skip leading zeros. Do not forget that zero is a valid number.

c. A procedure to write numbers. Do not print leading zeros, but if the number consists of all zeros, print a single zero.

d. A procedure to add two numbers.

e. A procedure to multiply two numbers.

In addition, you should

f. Check for overflow (numbers with more than *MaxSize* digits) when reading, adding, and multiplying numbers.

g. Have a good user interface.

Optional: Allow signed integers (negative as well as positive integers) and write a procedure for subtraction.

CHAPTER 2

Review of Advanced Pascal

PREVIEW Most of this chapter reviews the Turbo Pascal structured data types: arrays, strings, records, files, and sets. Even if you choose not to read this review material, you should not skip the section that discusses separately compiled units.

Every high-level programming language provides a collection of built-in data types, which are called the language's **primitive data types**. Integers, reals, characters, and arrays are primitive data types that almost all high-level languages support. Pascal is unusually rich in the data types it allows. The **simple data types** are integer, real, character, boolean, enumerated types, and subrange types. To this list, Turbo Pascal adds the types *shortint*, *longint*, *single*, *double*, *extended*, *comp*, *byte*, and *word*. This chapter reviews the **structured data types** *array*, *string*, *record*, *file*, and *set*. Chapter 3 introduces pointers, and Chapter 4 presents objects.

ARRAYS

An array has a fixed size: do not exceed it

Recall that an array is a collection of **elements**, or **components**, that have the same data type. An array contains a finite, fixed number of elements, which have an order. Thus, there is a first element, a second element, and so on, as well as a last element. You must know the maximum number of elements possible in a particular array when you write your program, *before* you execute it. Because you can access the array elements directly and in any order, an array is a **direct access**, or a **random access**, data structure.

Although you are probably comfortable with **one-dimensional arrays**, a brief review will set the stage for multidimensional arrays and arrays of arrays.

One-Dimensional Arrays

When you decide to use an array in your program, you must declare it and, in doing so, indicate its maximum size. The following statements declare a one-dimensional array, *MaxTemps*, which contains the daily maximum temperatures for a given week:

An array with integer subscripts

```
const DaysPerWeek = 7;
type  arrayType = array[1..DaysPerWeek] of real;
var   MaxTemps : arrayType;
```

You can refer to any of the real elements in this array directly by using an expression, which is called the **index**, or **subscript**, enclosed in square brackets. The array's type definition indicates the type and range of valid indexes. For *MaxTemps*, indexes must have integer values in the range 1 to 7. For example, *MaxTemps[5]* is the fifth element in the array. Also, if *K* is

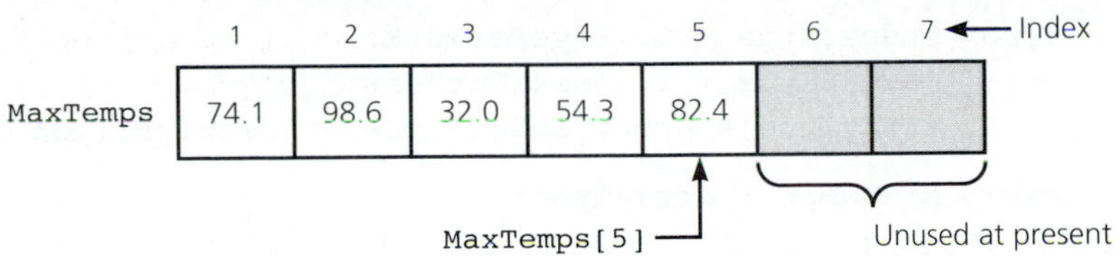

Figure 2-1

A one-dimensional array of at most seven elements

an integer variable whose value is 5, then *MaxTemps[K]* is the fifth element in the array, and *MaxTemps[K + 1]* is the sixth element. Figure 2-1 illustrates the array *MaxTemps*, which at present contains only five temperatures. *MaxTemps[5]* is the last value in the array and *MaxTemps[6]*, for example, is undefined. (Turbo Pascal does not check the range of array indexes unless you specify the *$R+* compiler directive. See Appendix H for information about compiler directives.)

Clearly, before you can retrieve an element of an array, you must assign it a value. You can assign or retrieve element values either one element at a time by using the previously described notation or all at once. That is, if *X* and *Y* are arrays of the same type, the statement

```
X := Y
```

assigns to each element of *X* the value in the corresponding element of *Y*.

Although the indexes for *MaxTemps* must be integer valued, indexes in general can be of other ordinal data types as well. For example, consider the following type definitions and variable declarations:

Arrays with enumerated subscripts

```
type  dayType = (Sun, Mon, Tues, Wed, Thurs, Fri, Sat);
      tempArrayType = array[dayType] of real;
      codeArrayType = array['A'..'Z'] of integer;

var   Temps : tempArrayType;
      Codes : codeArrayType;
```

Temps is another array of seven real elements, but it does not have integer indexes. Instead, *Temps[Thurs]* is the fifth element in the array. Similarly, the 5th integer of the 26 integers in the array *Codes* is *Codes['E']*.

You can use one-dimensional arrays for simple lists: for example, a list of at most 7 temperatures or a list of at most 50 exam scores. Note that you refer to the elements in a one-dimensional array by using one index. However, you can also declare **multidimensional arrays**, which have more than one index.

Multidimensional Arrays

Suppose that you wanted to represent the minimum temperature for each day during 52 weeks. The following statements declare a **two-dimensional array**, *MinTemps*:

```
const DaysPerWeek = 7;
      WeeksPerYear = 52;
```

```
type  index1Type = 1..DaysPerWeek;
      index2Type = 1..WeeksPerYear;
      arrayType = array[index1Type, index2Type] of real;
```

A 7 by 52 array

```
var   MinTemps : arrayType;
```

These statements specify the ranges for two indexes: The first index can range from 1 to 7, while the second index can range from 1 to 52. Most people picture a two-dimensional array as a rectangular arrangement, or **matrix**, of elements that form rows and columns, as Figure 2-2 indicates. Each column in this matrix represents the seven daily minimum temperatures for a particular week.

To reference an element in a two-dimensional array, you must indicate both the row and the column that contain the element. You make these indications of row and column by writing two indexes. For example, *MinTemps[5, 12]* is the element in the 5th row and the 12th column. In the context of the temperature example, this element is the minimum temperature recorded for the 5th day of the 12th week. Turbo Pascal allows you to reference this element another way, by writing *MinTemps[5][12]*. Note that what was said about the indexes of one-dimensional arrays applies also to multidimensional arrays.

As an example of how to use a two-dimensional array in a program, consider the following procedure, which determines the smallest value in the previously described array *MinTemps*:

```
procedure LowestDailyTemp(MinTemps : arrayType;
            var LowestTemp : real;
            var DayOfWeek, WeekOfYear : integer);
{ -------------------------------------------------------
  Determines the lowest daily temperature during a 52-week
  period.
  Precondition: MinTemps is a 2-dimensional array of daily
  minimum temperatures for 52 weeks, where MinTemps[Day,
  Week] is the minimum temperature for day Day of week Week.
  Postcondition: LowestTemp is the smallest value in
  MinTemps, DayOfWeek and WeekOfYear are indexes such that
  LowestTemp = MinTemps[DayOfWeek, WeekOfYear], MinTemps is
  unchanged.
  ------------------------------------------------------- }
var Day, Week : integer;        { array indexes }
begin
    {initialize: assume lowest temperature is first in the
     array}
    LowestTemp := MinTemps[1,1];
    DayOfWeek := 1;
    WeekOfYear := 1;

    { search array for lowest temperature }
    for Week := 1 to WeeksPerYear do  { for all weeks }
       for Day := 1 to DaysPerWeek do { for all days in week }
```

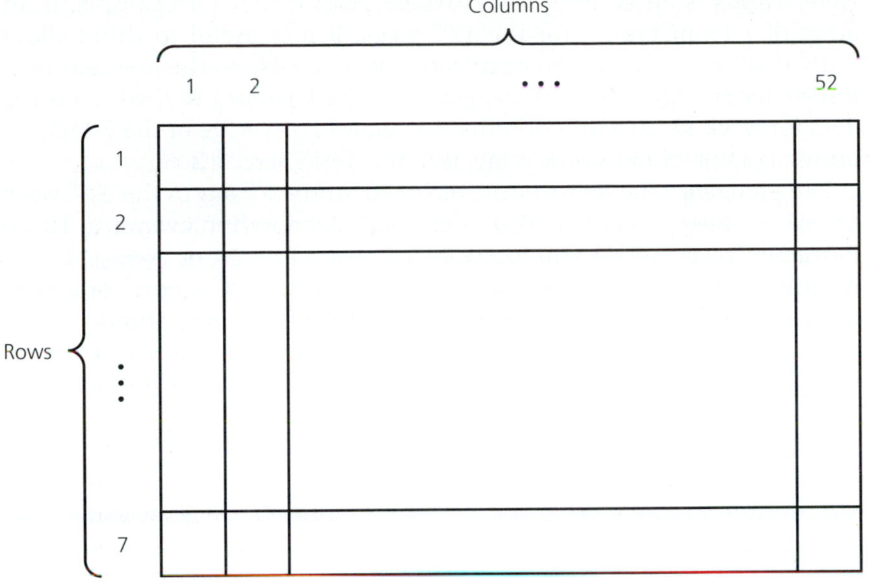

Figure 2-2

A two-dimensional array

```
begin
    if LowestTemp > MinTemps[Day,Week]
        then
        begin
            LowestTemp := MinTemps[Day,Week];
            DayOfWeek := Day;
            WeekOfYear := Week
        end  { if }
    end  { for }
end;  { LowestDailyTemp }
```

It is also entirely possible to declare *MinTemps* as a one-dimensional array of 364 (7 * 52) elements, in which case you might use *MinTemps[82]* instead of *MinTemps[5, 12]*. (Why? See Exercise 1 at the end of this chapter.) However, doing so will make your program harder to understand!

More than three dimensions is unusual

Although you can declare arrays with more than two dimensions, generally more than three dimensions is unusual. The techniques for working with such arrays are analogous to those for two-dimensional arrays.

Arrays of Arrays

Consider again the daily minimum temperatures for 52 weeks. Instead of declaring a two-dimensional array to represent these temperatures, as was done previously, you could declare a one-dimensional array of 52 one-dimensional, 7-element arrays, as follows:

```
type weekType = array[1..DaysPerWeek] of real;
     yearType = array[1..WeeksPerYear] of weekType;

var  Temps : yearType;
```

An array of 52 arrays

Here, *Temps* is an array of arrays where *Temps[12]*, for example, is an array of 7 temperatures for the 12th week. If it is useful to think about individual weeks, then this organization is preferable to the previous two-dimensional array. For example, you could pass *Temps[12]*, which is the data for week 12, to a function that calculates an average of the 7 temperatures in a one-dimensional array. (See Self-Test Exercise 2.)

You reference the temperature recorded for the 5th day of the 12th week by writing *Temps[12][5]*. You might find this notation awkward. Turbo Pascal, however, allows you to use either *Temp[12][5]* or *Temp[12, 5]* regardless of whether *Temp* is an array of arrays, as it is here, or a two-dimensional array. Even so, your choice of data structure should reflect your algorithm. Thus, if you will consider individual days rather than individual weeks, you may find that a two-dimensional array is preferable to an array of arrays.

STRINGS

Turbo Pascal includes the standard data type *string* that allows you to represent a string of characters. You can think of a string as a special array of characters. You can reference either individual characters in the string, just as you reference individual elements in an array, or the entire string.

String variables have a **current length**, which is the number of characters currently in the variable. The current length is dynamic; it changes as the contents of the string change. Like arrays, strings have a **maximum length**, which is established at compilation time. A string's current length ranges from a minimum of 0 characters (the empty or null string) to the maximum length defined for that string.

For example, consider the following statements:

```
const MaxLength = 30;
type  shortStringType = string[MaxLength];

var   Title : string;
      Name  : shortStringType;
```

Title is a string variable whose maximum length is 255 by default, whereas the maximum length of *Name* is 30. Note that *MaxLength* must be in the range 1 to 255. After the following statements execute, each variable has a current length of 17:

```
Title := 'Walls and Mirrors';
Name  := 'Dr. Jamie Perfect'
```

You use the Turbo Pascal function *length* to determine the current length of a string. Thus, *length(Title)* is 17.

You can reference the individual characters in a string by using the same index notation that you use for an array. Thus, *Title[5]* in the previous example is the letter *s*.

Strings are advantageous because you can reference the entire string simply by writing the string variable. For example, given the previous statement that assigns a string to *Title*, the statement

```
writeln(Title : 20)
```

writes *Walls and Mirrors* right-justified in a field of 20 spaces as

```
bbbWalls and Mirrors    (b indicates a blank space)
```

Similarly, you can read a string by using either *read* or *readln*. Blank spaces in the input line are treated like any other character and are read.

You can compare strings by using a relational operator between string variables to form a boolean expression, as the following examples indicate:

```
MyString = YourString    { are strings identical? }
MyString = 'quit'        { are strings identical? }
TheirString <> OurString { are strings different? }
```

You also can determine which of two strings comes before the other. The ordering of two strings is analogous to alphabetic ordering, but you use the ASCII table instead of the alphabet. Thus, the following boolean expressions are all true:

Examples of true expressions

```
'dig' < 'dog'     { 'i' < 'o' }
'Star' < 'star'   { 'S' < 's' }
'start' > 'star'
'd' > 'abc'
```

You can use boolean expressions that involve strings anywhere that you can use other boolean expressions, such as in *while*, *repeat*, and *if* statements.

You can concatenate two strings or a string and a character to form another string by using either the + operator or the Turbo Pascal function *concat*. The following expressions result in the same string:

Concatenation

```
'C' + 'omputer'
'Com' + 'puter'
concat('Compute', 'r')
```

If the resulting string exceeds its maximum declared length, it is truncated on the right.

The function *copy* allows you to extract a substring of a given string. The call

Extraction

```
copy(<string>, <first>, <length>)
```

where *<string>* is a string expression, returns the substring of *<string>* that begins at character number *<first>* and contains *<length>* characters, when available. If fewer than *<length>* characters are available for the substring, *copy* extracts the entire substring that begins at character number *<first>*.

Turbo Pascal includes other string functions and procedures; these are described in Appendixes F and G.

RECORDS

While an array is a collection of elements that are all of the same data type, a **record** is a group of related items that are not necessarily of the same data type. Each item in a record is called a **field**. For example, a record that describes you might contain three fields: your name, your age, and your grade point average. The following statements define a data type for such a record:

```
const StringLength = 25;  { length of string }
      MaxAge = 100;       { maximum age }

type  stringType = string[StringLength];
      ageType = 0..MaxAge;

      studentRecordType = record
          Name : stringType;
          Age  : ageType;
          GPA  : real
      end;  { record }
```

The identifiers *Name*, *Age*, and *GPA* are called **field identifiers**.

Now you can use the data type *studentRecordType* when declaring variables. To declare the record variable *Student1*, you would write

```
var   Student1 : studentRecordType;
```

Figure 2-3 depicts the record *Student1*. To reference the fields within a particular record, you **qualify** the field name by writing the record variable, a period, and the field identifier. For example, the second field in the record *Student1* is *Student1.Age*, as in the statement

```
Student1.Age := 21;
```

The third letter in the first field of *Student1* is

```
Student1.Name[3]
```

Notice that it is convenient to make a copy of an entire record. The following statement copies the record *Student1* into the record *Student2*:

Copying a record

```
Student2 := Student1
```

where *Student2* has a data type of *studentRecordType*.

Figure 2-3

The record *Student1*

Student1.Name	Student1.Age	Student1.GPA
Jamie Perfect	21	4.0

The *with* Statement

When you make several references to fields that are in a particular record, writing the record variable for each reference can get tedious. By using the *with* statement, you can reference the fields simply by writing the field identifiers. For example, to assign values to the three fields in the record *Student1*, which was defined previously, you could write

```
with Student1 do
begin
    Name := 'Jamie Perfect';
    Age := 21;
    GPA := 4.0
end;  { with }
```

Field identifiers that are within the *with* statement reference the fields that are within the record *Student1*. However, outside of the *with* statement, the record variable *Student1* is necessary, as in the following statement:

```
writeln(Student1.Name:15, ' has a GPA of ',
        Student1.GPA:4:2);
```

Although the *with* statement can save you a good deal of tedious typing, if overused it can detract from the readability of a program. The potential problem has to do with what some have called the **principle of locality**. This principle states that the effects of any statement should, as much as possible, be limited to other statements in its immediate locality. Adherence to this principle enhances readability, as it reduces the number of things that a reader must remember to understand the meaning of a statement.

A statement should affect only statements in its immediate locality

A *with* statement that has a scope of more than a few lines is likely to violate the principle of locality. You must remember that you are within the scope of a *with* statement to know that identifiers are field names of the same record rather than disjoint variables. You use a record to convey the message that its fields all contain information about the same entity; the use of a *with* statement tends to obscure this message.

Restrict the scope of a with statement to a few lines

There are a few situations in which a *with* statement is useful. Although no steadfast rules exist for when you should use *with*, here are three situations that come to mind.

Using the *with* Statement

KEY CONCEPTS

1. When reading values into the fields of a record, you can nest the *read* statement within a *with* statement.
2. When writing values out from the fields of a record, you can nest the *write* statement within a *with* statement.
3. When assigning values to the fields of a record, you can nest the block of assignment statements within a *with* statement.

Records Within Records

Fields can be records

Sometimes it is desirable for a field within a record to be itself a record. For example, suppose that you need to add an address field to the student's record that was defined earlier. It is convenient for the address to be a record with fields such as street, city, state, and zip code. The following definitions and declarations include these changes to the data type *studentRecordType*:

```
const StringLength = 25;  { length of string }
      MaxAge = 100;       { maximum age }

type  stringType = string[StringLength];
      ageType = 0..MaxAge;

      addressRecordType = record
          Street : stringType;
          City   : stringType;
          State  : string[2];
          Zip    : string[10]
      end;  { record }

      studentRecordType = record
          Name    : stringType;
          Age     : ageType;
          GPA     : real;
          Address : addressRecordType
      end;  { record }

var   Student1 : studentRecordType;
```

Note the order of the type definitions: The definition of *addressRecordType* must precede its use in *studentRecordType*. Now *Student1.Address.Zip* references the zip code field in the record *Student1*.

Arrays of Records

Now suppose that an instructor wants a record for each student in a class of no more than *MaxStudents* students, where *MaxStudents* is a named constant. You can add the data type

```
classType = array[1..MaxStudents] of studentRecordType;
```

to the previous type definitions and then declare, for example, the variable *CSC212* to be of the data type *classType*. The following are examples of references to this array:

CSC212[9].Name is the *Name* field in the ninth record.

CSC212[9].Name[1] is the first letter of the *Name* field in the ninth record.

CSC212[9].Address.State is the *State* field in the ninth record.

Variant Records

Sometimes, within a group of records there are fields that you use only for certain records. Rather than defining a record variable that contains all possible fields for all situations, you can use a **variant record** to save memory space. A variant record has a fixed part, which contains the fields that are common to all records, and a variant part, which contains fields that differ for certain records.

A variant record has a fixed part, which includes the tag field, and a variant part

For example, consider the following statements, which include a record definition for a student:

```
const StringLength = 25;  { length of string }
      MaxAge = 100;       { maximum age }

type  stringType = string[StringLength];
      ageType = 0..MaxAge;
      majorType = (CompSci, CompEgr, OtherEgr, Other);
      studentRecordType = record
          Name : stringType;
          Age  : ageType;
          GPA  : real;
          case Major : majorType of
               CompSci, CompEgr : ( CscGPA : real;
                                    CscCredits : integer );
               OtherEgr         : ( MajorGPA : real );
               Other            : ( )
      end;  {record }

var   Student2 : studentRecordType;
```

The fixed fields *Name*, *Age*, and *GPA* must appear first in the record definition. You define the variant part by using a construct similar to a *case* statement. The field *Major* is called the **tag field** and is analogous to the selector in a *case* statement. Notice, however, that you must declare the tag field's data type. For the possible values of the tag field, you describe the fields in the variant part of the record and enclose each description in parentheses. For example, when the value of the tag field *Major* is either *CompSci* or *CompEgr*, the variant part of the record contains two fields: *CscGPA* and *CscCredits*. Notice that the field identifiers must all be unique. Also notice that you can leave the variant part empty by writing ( ) and that there is no matching *end* for the reserved word *case*.

Figure 2-4 depicts some of the records that *Student2* can contain. Each version of the record uses the same amount of memory space, which is less than the space that would be required by a record containing all the different fields.

You must be careful to reference only those fields that exist for a particular value of the tag field. For example, within the record *Student2*, if the value of *Student2.Major* is *CompSci*, you can reference the field *Student2.CscGPA*, but not *Student2.MajorGPA*. You can reference the fixed fields within *Student2* for any value of *Student2.Major*.

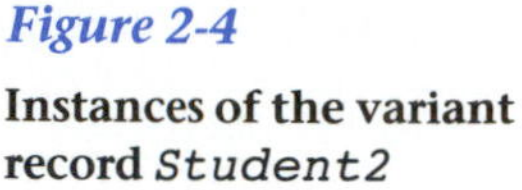

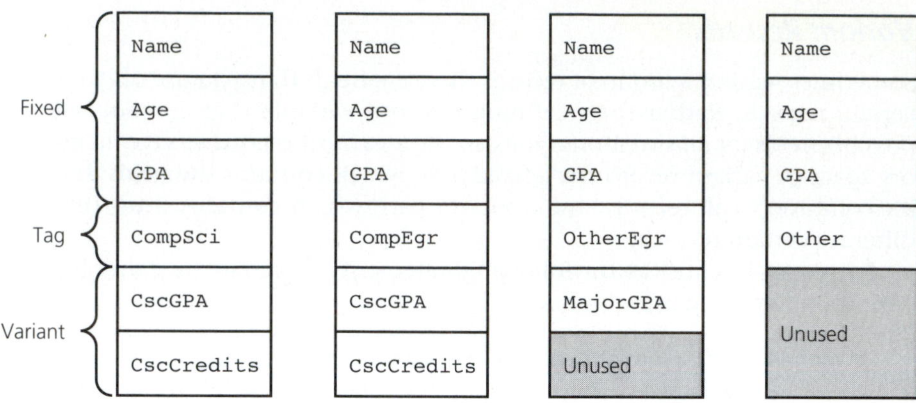

Figure 2-4

Instances of the variant record `Student2`

FILES

The components of a file must all be of the same data type

A **file** is a *sequence* of components of the same data type. The file is a structured data type; we will present and use it here in the same spirit as other data types. However, a file differs from the other data types in that a file can be permanent; it can live on after program execution terminates.

Variables that have data types other than a file data type represent memory that is accessible only within the program that creates them. When program execution terminates, the operating system reuses this memory and changes its contents. Files, on the other hand, reside in auxiliary storage, such as on a disk, and can exist and be accessible independently of any particular program. Files are thus more system dependent than the other data types because the mechanisms for creating and accessing them from outside a program depend on the particulars of a system. However, from within a Pascal program, files behave in a standard, system-independent manner.

You have used files ever since you wrote your first program. In fact, your Pascal source program is in a file. In addition, a typical program uses two files: one is called *`input`*, which is the **standard input file**, and the other is *`output`*, which is the **standard output file**. These particular files often represent your keyboard and monitor. That is, a program can take its input directly from the keyboard and display its output on the monitor. Note that you can specify that the standard input and output files be something other than your keyboard and monitor.

Standard Pascal provides both external and internal files. An **external file** exists after program execution. External files not only provide a permanent record for human users, they also allow communication between programs. Program *A* can write its output into a file that program *B* can later use for input. An **internal file** is temporary and exists only during program execution. Although an internal file resides in auxiliary storage, the system does not retain it after program execution ends. You use an internal file as a scratch pad when there is too much data to retain conveniently in memory. Although Turbo Pascal makes no provision for internal files, you can erase a file before program execution terminates, as you will see later in this chapter.

Files are classified further. A **textfile** is a file of characters that are organized into lines. The standard files *input* and *output* are textfiles, as are the files that you create—by using the Turbo Pascal integrated development environment—to contain your Pascal programs. A file that is not a textfile is called a **general file** or sometimes a **binary file** or a **nontext file**. The following statements declare textfiles and general files:

```
type intFileType   = file of integer;
     nameFileType = file of string;

     woodType      = (oak, pine, mahogany);
     woodFileType = file of woodType;

var  AgeFile     : intFileType;    { general file}
     GiftList    : nameFileType;   { general file}
     WoodFile    : woodFileType;   { general file}
     FileCabinet : text;           { textfile }
```

The type definition for a general file is of the form

```
file of <T>
```

where <*T*> is any predefined or user-defined data type other than *file*; you cannot have a file of files. The type definition for a textfile is the predefined data type *text*. A textfile is similar to a *file of char*; however, a textfile is divided into lines, but a *file of char* is not. Also, notice that even though *GiftList* contains characters, it is a general file—not a textfile—because each of its elements is a string, not a single character.

Declare all files except ***input*** *and* ***output*** *in the variable declaration section*

You reference a file by a **file variable**, which you declare in the variable declaration section of your program. A file variable can be any valid Pascal identifier. You do not declare the standard files *input* and *output*. You must associate each file variable with the name of an actual external file by using the *assign* statement. For example, the statement

Use ***assign*** *to associate a file variable with the name of a file*

```
assign(AgeFile, 'AGES.DAT')
```

associates the file variable *AgeFile* with the external file *AGES.DAT*.

It is useful to contrast files with their closest Pascal relatives, arrays. Files and arrays are similar in that they are both collections of components of the same type. For example, just as you can have an array of type *char*, so also can you have a file of type *char*. In both cases, the components are characters. However, in addition to the previous distinction between files and all other data types—including arrays—there are two other differences:

Differences between files and arrays

- **File size is dynamic; array size is static.** When you declare an array, you must specify its size. Thus, the Pascal compiler reserves a fixed amount of memory for the array. A well-written program always checks that an array can accommodate a new piece of data before attempting to insert it. If the array cannot accommodate the data, the program might have to terminate with a message of explanation. The only recourse is to increase the array size—hopefully by changing the value of a constant—and to compile and run the program again. On the other hand, if you declare the array's size to be larger than you need, you waste memory. In contrast, the size of a file is not fixed. When the system first creates a file, the file requires almost no storage space. As a program adds data to the file, the file's size increases dynamically. Thus, at any given time, the file occupies only as much space as it actually requires. This dynamic nature is a great advantage.

- **Textfiles provide sequential access; arrays provide direct access; general files provide both sequential access and direct access.** Before you get the impression that files are superior to arrays in all respects, consider that with arrays you can go directly to the element you want. If you want the 100th element in the array `A`, you can get at it by writing `A[100]`; you do not need to look at the elements `A[1]` through `A[99]` first. However, you can get to elements in a Pascal textfile only sequentially. If you want the 100th element in a textfile, you must read past the 99 elements that precede it. Textfile processing is therefore considerably slower and less flexible than array processing. The direct access nature of arrays is a great advantage. However, Turbo Pascal enables you to access the components of a general file either sequentially, much as you would a textfile, or directly, given their positions in the file. That is, you can access the ith component of a general file without first accessing its first $i - 1$ components, as you will see later in this chapter.

There is one last point to be made before we consider the details of textfiles and general files. Conceptually, you can think of a special **end-of-file (eof) symbol** that follows the last component in a file. Such a symbol may or may not actually exist in the file; however, allowing this slight abstraction permits a clear and concise explanation of the behavior of Pascal programs.

Textfiles

Textfiles are designed for easy communication with people. As such, textfiles are flexible and easy to use, but they are relatively inefficient with respect to computer time and storage. As you will see, some aspects of textfiles are true of all files, while other aspects are peculiar to textfiles.

Textfiles appear to contain lines

One special aspect of textfiles is that they *appear* to be divided into lines. This illusion is often the source of much confusion. In reality, a

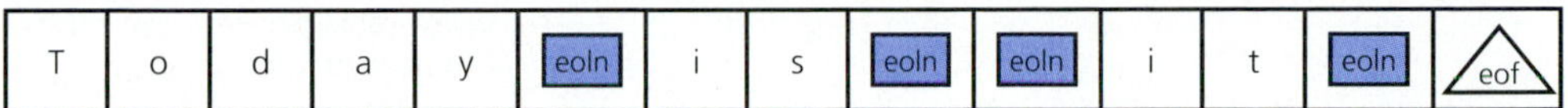

Figure 2-5

A textfile with end-of-line symbols

textfile—like any other file—is a sequence of components of the same type. That is, a textfile is a sequence of characters. A special **end-of-line (eoln) symbol** causes the illusion that a textfile contains lines by making the file *behave* as if it were divided into lines.

When you create a textfile by typing data at your keyboard, each time you press the Enter, or Return, key, you insert one end-of-line symbol into the file. Turbo Pascal's end-of-line symbol actually consists of two characters, a carriage return (ASCII 13) and a line feed (ASCII 10). Although you can read each of these characters separately into `char` variables, we will treat the two characters together as one end-of-line symbol to simplify our discussion. When an output device, such as a printer or monitor, encounters an end-of-line symbol in a textfile, the device moves to the beginning of the next line. In addition, Pascal treats all textfiles—including the empty file—as if they end with both an end-of-line symbol and an end-of-file symbol. Figure 2-5 depicts a textfile with these special symbols.

Associated with each file in a program is a **file window**, which marks the current position in the file. Because each component in a textfile is a character, a textfile's file window moves from character to character. The following sections describe the behavior of the file window.

You must use `reset` *before reading from a file for the first time*

Input. Before you can read anything from a file, you must prepare, or **open**, it for input by using the `reset` procedure. For the programmer, the important step in opening a file is the initialization of the file window's position. For example, for the file variable *F*,

```
reset(F)
```

moves the file window over the first component in the file, as Figure 2-6 illustrates. You can call the `reset` procedure at any time in your program, and you can reset the same file more than once. However, before you call `reset(F)` for the first time with a particular external file, you must call `assign` to associate *F* with the name of the file. If the named file does not exist, an error occurs. Note that you never use `reset` with the standard input file.

Never use `reset(input)`

When you use a file for input, the file window is over the component that you will read next. Thus, after you call `reset`, you are ready to read the first component. After reading several components, the file window

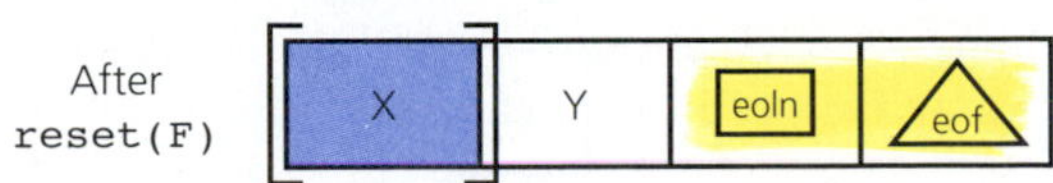

Figure 2-6

The effect of `reset` on a textfile

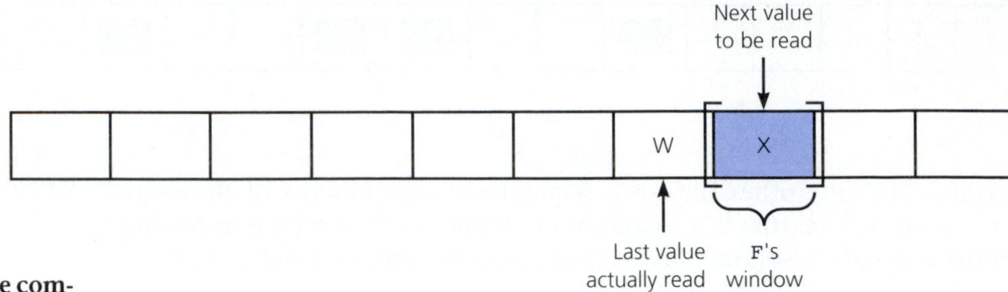

Figure 2-7

A file window over the component to be read next

will be as pictured in Figure 2-7. Although there is no way to move the file window to any particular component other than the first one, you can advance the window sequentially from one component to the next by using the Pascal procedure *read*, which you already know. When applied to files, *read* takes two arguments: The first is the file variable and the second is a variable to contain the result of the read operation. When this second variable is a character variable, the statement

```
read(F, x)
```

means

```
x := the value at the file window
Advance the file window to the next component
```

Figure 2-8 illustrates the effect of this *read* statement.

You can use the Pascal procedure *readln* only with textfiles. It reads a value from a file and then moves the window just past the next end-of-line symbol. Thus, as Figure 2-9 illustrates, the effect of

Use **readln** *only with textfiles*

```
readln(F, x)
```

Figure 2-8

The effect of *read(F, x)* **on a textfile**

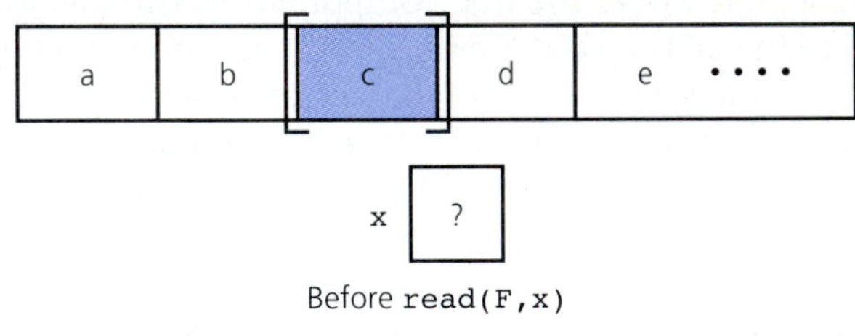

Before read(F,x)

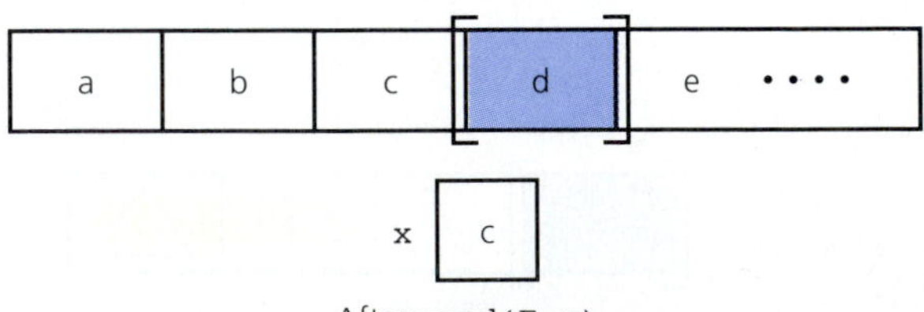

After read(F,x)

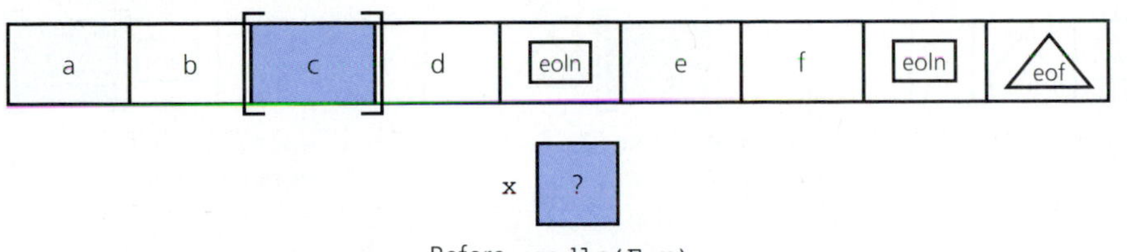

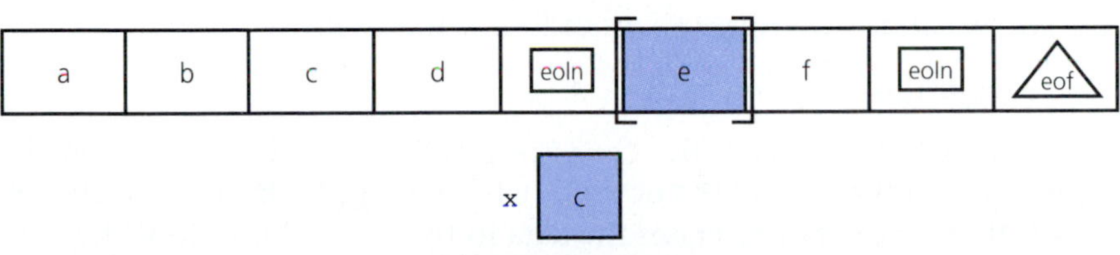

Figure 2-9

The effect of *readln(F, x)* on a textfile

means

```
x := the value at the file window
Advance the file window just beyond the next end-of-
  line symbol
```

***readln(F)* advances the file window just beyond the end-of-line symbol**

By omitting the assignment statement, you get the effect of *readln(F)* without the argument *x*. Thus, *readln(F)* advances the window just beyond the end-of-line symbol to what is usually the beginning of the next line.

You can detect when the file window has reached either the end of a line or the end of the file by using, respectively, the predefined boolean functions *eoln* and *eof*. The function *eoln(F)*, which is defined only when *F* is a textfile, returns *true* if *F*'s window is over the carriage return character of an end-of-line symbol or if *eof(F)* is *true*, and returns *false* otherwise. The function *eof(F)* returns *true* if *F*'s window is beyond the last end-of-line symbol or if the file is empty. Figure 2-10 illustrates the meaning of these functions.

To summarize, consider the textfile *F* that appears in Figure 2-9. If *Ch* is a character variable, the statements in the following sequence assign values to *Ch* as indicated:

```
reset(F);
read(F, Ch);      { Ch = 'a' }
readln(F, Ch);    { Ch = 'b' }
read(F, Ch);      { Ch = 'e' }
readln(F, Ch);    { Ch = 'f' }
reset(F);
read(F, Ch);      { Ch = 'a' }
readln(F, Ch);    { Ch = 'b' }
readln(F, Ch);    { Ch = 'e' }
read(F, Ch);      { attempted read past end of file }
```

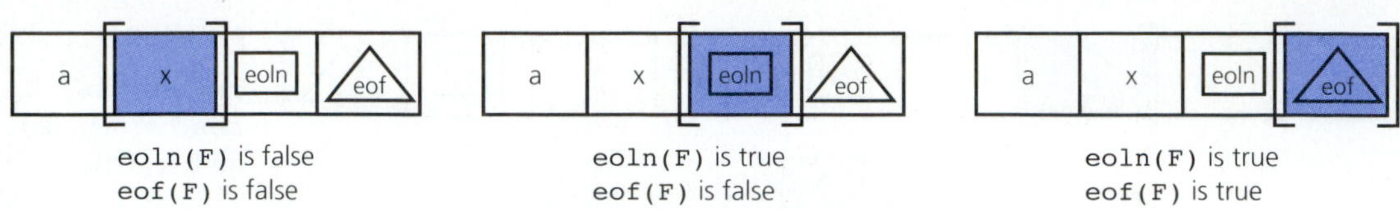

Figure 2-10
The end-of-line (*eoln*) and end-of-file (*eof*) functions

You must use `rewrite` before writing to a file for the first time

Output. Before you can write anything to a file *F*, you must open it for output by calling the *rewrite* procedure as follows:

```
rewrite(F)
```

`rewrite` creates a new file or erases the data in an existing file

Never use `rewrite(output)`

If you are creating a new file, *rewrite* positions the file window at the beginning (or the end) of the new file, which is empty. If the file *F* already exists, then *rewrite(F)* erases the data in the file and positions the window at the beginning (or the end) of the now empty file. You can call the *rewrite* procedure at any time in your program, and you can rewrite the same file more than once, although each time you do, you erase the file. However, before you call *rewrite(F)* for the first time with a particular external file, you must call *assign* to associate *F* with the name of the file. Note that you never use *rewrite* with the standard output file.

`write` appends a value to the file and advances the file window

The Pascal procedure *write*, which you already know, also applies to files. *Write* takes two arguments: The first is the file variable and the second is an expression whose value has the same data type as the components in the file. The statement

```
write(F, <expression>)
```

means

```
Write the value of <expression> at the position of the
  file window
Advance the file window
```

as Figure 2-11 illustrates.

Use `writeln` only with textfiles

You can use the Pascal procedure *writeln* only with textfiles. It appends a value to a file, writes an end-of-line symbol, and then moves the file window just past the end-of-line symbol. Thus, the effect of

```
writeln(F, <expression>)
```

is equivalent to

```
write(F, <expression>);
write(F, <end-of-line symbol>)
```

Figure 2-11
The effect of *write(F, 'X')* on a textfile

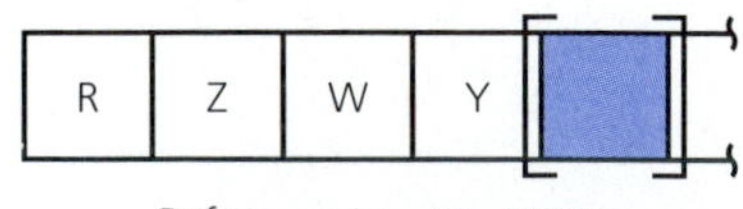

Before write(F,'X')

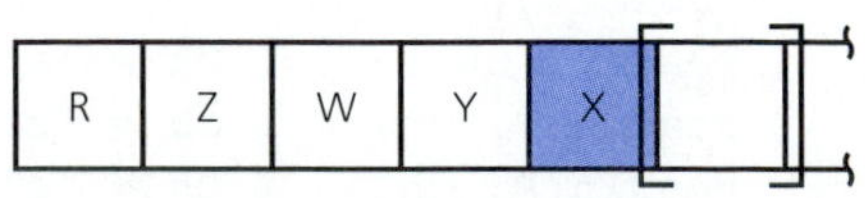

After write(F,'X')

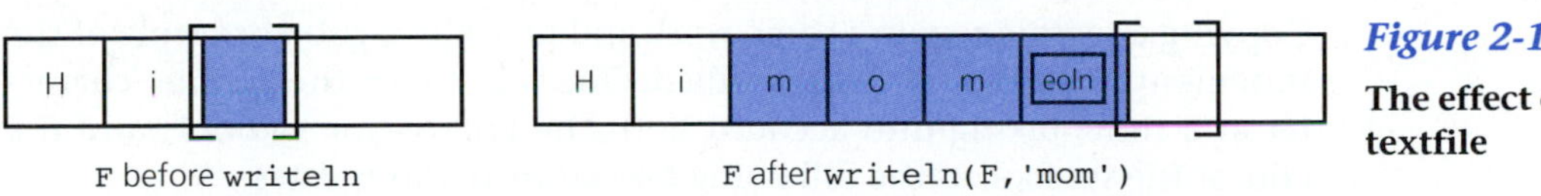

Figure 2-12

The effect of *writeln* on a textfile

Figure 2-12 illustrates the effect of such a *writeln* statement. Note that

```
writeln(F)
```

without the second (expression) argument appends just the end-of-line symbol to the file *F*.

Multiargument *read* and *write*. Pascal allows a single *read* or *readln* statement to read any number of values from a file, and a single *write* or *writeln* statement to write any number of values to a file. The statement

```
read(F, x1, x2, x3)
```

is exactly equivalent to

```
read(F, x1);
read(F, x2);
read(F, x3)
```

and the statement

```
readln(F, x1, x2, x3)
```

is exactly equivalent to

```
read(F, x1, x2, x3);
readln(F)
```

Similarly, the statement

```
write(F, <expression1>, <expression2>, <expression3>)
```

is exactly equivalent to

```
write(F, <expression1>);
write(F, <expression2>);
write(F, <expression3>)
```

and the statement

```
writeln(F, <expression1>, <expression2>, <expression3>)
```

is exactly equivalent to

```
write(F, <expression1>, <expression2>, <expression3>);
writeln(F)
```

Copying a textfile. Suppose that you have a textfile associated with the file variable *OriginalFile* and that you want to make a copy of it. Unfortunately, the following assignment statement is illegal:

```
CopyFile := OriginalFile { THIS STATEMENT IS ILLEGAL }
```

Copying a textfile requires some work and provides a good example of the statements that you have just studied. One way copies the file one character at a time, taking into account both the end-of-line symbols and the end-of-file symbol, as the following procedure demonstrates:

```
const NameLength = 12;

type  nameType = string[NameLength];

procedure CopyTextfile(OriginalFileName,
                       CopyFileName: nameType);
{ ---------------------------------------------------------
  Makes a duplicate copy of a textfile.
  Precondition: OriginalFileName is the name of an
  existing external textfile and CopyFileName is the name of
  the textfile to be created.
  Postcondition: The textfile named CopyFileName is a
  duplicate of the file named OriginalFileName. Both files
  are closed.
  --------------------------------------------------------- }
var OriginalFile, CopyFile : text;
    Ch : char;

begin
   writeln('Beginning file copy...');

   { associate file variables with external files }
   assign(OriginalFile, OriginalFileName);
   assign(CopyFile, CopyFileName);

   reset(OriginalFile);        { open given file for input }
   rewrite(CopyFile);          { open new file for output }

   while not eof(OriginalFile) do { read to end of file }
   begin
      { copy character from given file to new file }
      read(OriginalFile, Ch);
      write(CopyFile, Ch)
   end; { while }

   close(OriginalFile);        { close the files }
   close(CopyFile);

   writeln('File copy completed.')
end;   { CopyTextfile }
```

Notice that this procedure copies the carriage return and line feed characters that make up each Turbo Pascal end-of-line symbol just as it copies any other character. (*Caution:* This statement is not true for Standard Pascal, and therefore copying a textfile in Standard Pascal is not as simple as `CopyTextfile`.)

Another way to copy a textfile, if you know the length of the longest line in the file and this length does not exceed 255, is to replace the *read/write* pair in the previous procedure with

```
readln(OriginalFile, LineOfText);
writeln(CopyFile, LineOfText)
```

where *LineOfText* is a string of sufficient length.

In the previous procedure, notice the first and the last *writeln* statements that write messages to the standard output file. If they did not exist, you would receive no visible output when you ran the program. A program that produces no visible output is called a **silent program.** A silent program will probably bewilder its user, and for this reason, you should not write a program that produces no output to the standard output file.

Programs should not be silent

Adding to a textfile. You can use the same file for both input and output within a program. For example, consider the following sequence of *reset* and *rewrite* statements with the file *F*:

```
reset(F);      { You can now read the file F. }
  .
  .
  .
rewrite(F);    { You can now write to the file F,
                 but previous contents are lost. }
  .
  .
  .
reset(F);      { You can now read the file F. }
```

Observe that a textfile cannot be available simultaneously for both input and output. This rule makes it difficult to perform a task such as appending a new component to a file. For example, suppose that you first reset the file and then read to its end. Before you can write an additional component to the file, you must first call *rewrite*—but *rewrite* will destroy the file contents! Thus, to append a component to a file *F*, you must first call the Turbo Pascal procedure

append opens a file for output and positions the file window after the last component

```
append(F)
```

instead of *rewrite(F)*. *Append* opens the file for output and positions the file window after the file's last component. Thus, the old contents of the file are retained and you can write additional components. *Append* assumes that you have called *assign*.

Without *append*, you would need to make a copy of the file. Then, while the duplicate file was still open for output, you would write the new component to the file. You then have two files: the original file and an augmented copy. If desired, you could replace the original file with a copy of the augmented file. In this case, you could make the augmented file a temporary file, because once you have copied it into the original external file you have no need for it after program execution ends. To erase the temporary file, you call the *erase* procedure, as in

erase erases a temporary file

```
erase(TempFile)
```

Exercise 10 at the end of this chapter asks you to write a procedure that appends data to a textfile.

Numeric data within textfiles. As you know, you can read integer and real values from the standard input file into variables whose data types are *integer* or *real*, as appropriate. You also know that the standard input file is a textfile, and that a textfile is a sequence of characters. Although these facts may seem contradictory to you, integer and real values can be read from and written to a textfile. (You also can write, but not read, boolean values.) Although this presentation uses integers to illustrate the concepts, the other data types follow by analogy.

When your program reads from a textfile into an integer variable, the system expects a sequence of characters that it can convert into an integer. For example, if the textfile contains the character sequence '2', '3', '4' and if you read from the textfile into the integer variable *X*, the system will convert these three characters into the computer's internal representation for the integer 234 and assign this value to *X*. More precisely, the textfile contains the ASCII codes for the characters '2', '3', and '4'—which are, respectively, the decimal values 50, 51, and 52. However, these codes appear in the file in binary, as Figure 2-13a indicates. If you read those characters into the integer variable *X*, then *X* will contain the computer's internal representation for the integer 234, which appears in binary as shown in Figure 2-13b. The important point here is that the ASCII representation of digits in a textfile differs from the representation in memory of the number that those digits symbolize.

The representation of a numeric value in a textfile differs from its representation in an integer or real variable

To summarize, the statement

```
read(F, X)
```

where *F* is a textfile that contains valid integers and *X* is an integer variable, has the following effect:

```
Skip to the first nonblank character.
Convert into an integer the sequence of characters
  that begins at the current position of F's window
  and ends just before the next character c that is a
  blank or a control character.
Assign this integer value to X.
Advance the file window so that it is over the
  character c.
```

Figure 2-14 illustrates the effect of *read(F, X)*. Observe that if the sequence contains invalid characters or begins with a character other than +, −, or 0 through 9, an error will occur. For example, the system cannot

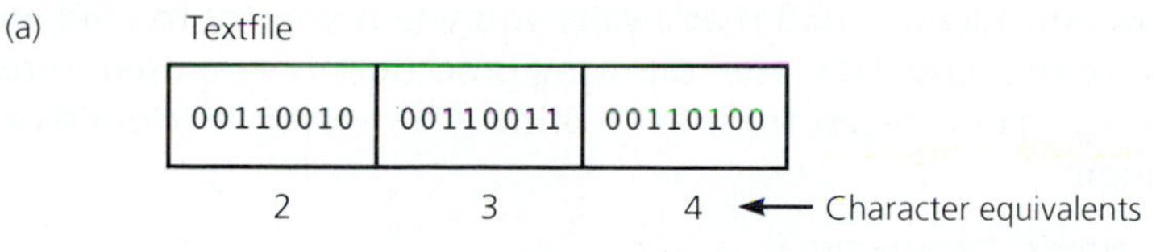

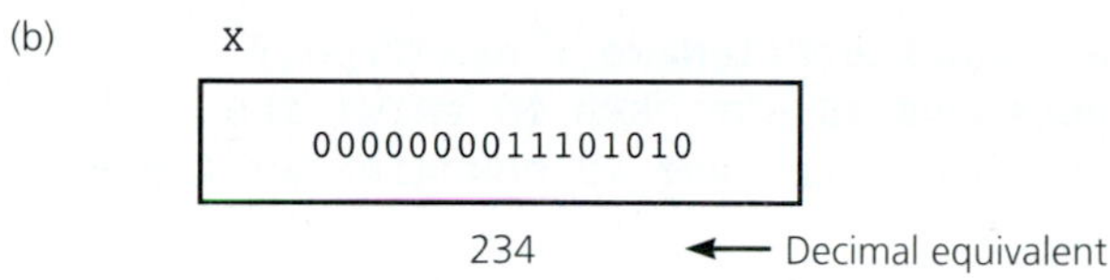

Figure 2-13

(a) The ASCII characters 2, 3, and 4 represented in binary in a textfile; (b) the internal binary representation of the integer 234

convert either the sequence *w123* or the sequence *123wrt45* into an integer.

When your program writes an integer value such as 234 to a textfile, the system first converts the integer from the computer's internal binary representation (0000000011101010) to the character sequence '2', '3', '4' and then writes these characters to the file. For the textfile `F` and the integer variable `X`, the statement

```
write(F,X)
```

has the following effect:

```
Convert the value of X into a sequence of characters.
Append this sequence of characters to the file F.
Position F's window just past the last character
  written.
```

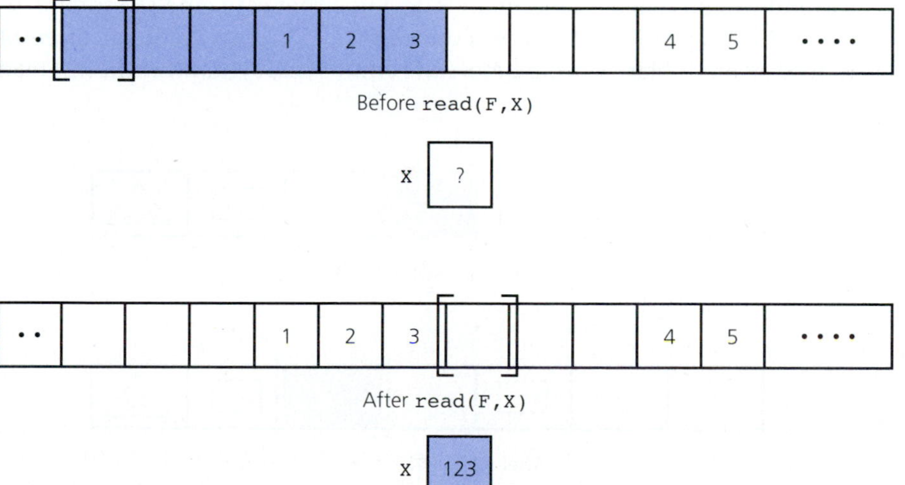

Figure 2-14

Reading an integer from a textfile

Now consider a pitfall that awaits you when you try to read an entire textfile of numeric data. The following procedure is supposed to read and print a series of integers from the textfile *F*. However, it contains an error in its logic.

```
const NameLength = 12;

type  nameType = string[NameLength];

procedure EchoFile(FileName : nameType);
{ THIS PROCEDURE IS SUPPOSED TO PRINT THE
  INTEGERS IN A FILE, BUT IT CONTAINS AN ERROR
  IN LOGIC. }
var  F : text;
     X : integer;
begin
   assign(F, FileName);
   reset(F);

   while not eof(F) do { read to end of file}
   begin
      read(F, X);
      writeln('Integer read is ', X)
   end;  { while }

   close(F)
end;  { EchoFile }
```

Given that each line in a textfile ends with an end-of-line symbol, this procedure either will print an extra, and incorrect, value or will read past the end-of-file symbol, producing an error. Why? After the procedure reads the last integer in the file, *F*'s window will be over either the end-of-line symbol or, if blanks exist at the end of the last line, a blank that is before the end-of-line symbol. (See Figure 2-15.) In either case, *eof(F)* is false, so the *while* loop will continue and the *read(F, X)* statement will attempt to read again. If blanks occur before the end-of-line symbol, *read* will read

Figure 2-15

Reading the last integer in a textfile

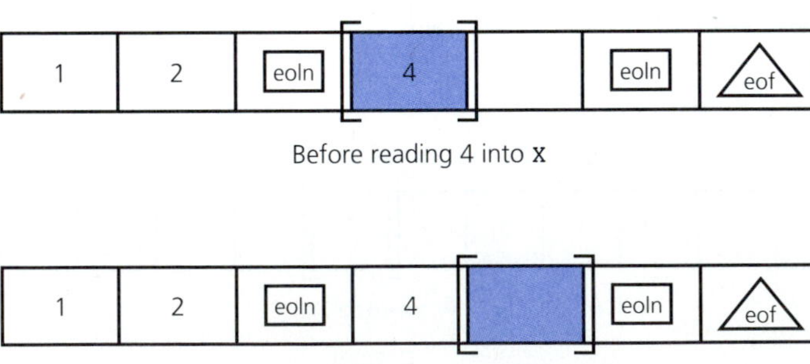

an incorrect value; otherwise *read* will attempt to advance *F*'s window beyond the end-of-file symbol, causing an error. However, this error will cause a run-time error message only if you specify the *$I+* compiler directive.

The simplest solution to this problem, if each line contains the same number of integers, is to use *readln* to read the entire line. For example, if the file contains three integers per line and if *X*, *Y*, and *Z* are integer variables, you could replace the previous *read* statement with

```
readln(F, X, Y, Z);
```

Another solution that works regardless of the number of integers per line is to use the *seekeoln* and the *seekeof* functions. The *seekeoln* function behaves like *eoln*, except that it skips over any blanks that might precede the end-of-line symbol. Similarly, the *seekeof* function behaves like *eof*, except that it skips over any blanks that might precede the end-of-file symbol. Thus, you can revise the previous procedure as follows:

```
procedure EchoFile(FileName : nameType);
{ Prints integers in a textfile. }
var  F : text;
     X : integer;
begin
   assign(F, FileName);
   reset(F);
   { read to end of file }
   while not seekeof(F) do
   begin
      { read to end of line }
      while not seekeoln(F) do
      begin
         read(F, X);
         writeln('Integer read is ', X)
      end  { while }
   end;   { while }

   close(F)
end; { EchoFile }
```

Default files. Several of the predefined functions and procedures that this section introduces use the standard input file or the standard output file as the default when you omit the file parameter. In particular,

- *read*, *readln*, *eof*, *eoln*, *seekeof*, and *seekeoln* all default to the standard input file *input* when you omit the file parameter.
- *write* and *writeln* default to the standard output file *output* when you omit the file parameter.

General Files

Files that are not textfiles are called **general** (or **binary** or **nontext**) **files.** Like a textfile, a general file is a sequence of components of the same data type, which is any type other than a file. Consider the following statements, which declare some general files:

```
const MaxSize = 10;
      NameLength = 12;

type  intFileType    = file of integer;
      realFileType   = file of real;

      intArrayType   = array[1..MaxSize] of integer;
      arrayFileType  = file of intArrayType;

      nameType       = string[NameLength];
      nameFileType   = file of nameType;

      personRecdType = record
          Name : nameType;
          <and other fields>
      end;  { record }

      peopleFileType = file of personRecdType;

var   I : intFileType;     { general file of integers }
      R : realFileType;    { general file of reals }
      A : arrayFileType;   { general file of arrays }
      S : nameFileType;    { general file of strings }
      P : peopleFileType;  { general file of records }
```

It is important to emphasize that each **file component** is an indivisible entity. For example, each component of the general file *I* is an integer in the computer's internal representation. If you write the integer value 234 to the integer file *I*, the system would write the computer's internal representation of 234, which is 0000000011101010 in binary, to the file, rather than the three ASCII characters '2', '3', '4', which are, respectively, 00110010, 00110011, and 00110100 in binary. If you could use a text editor to look at *I*, you would see gibberish. You create *I* not by using an editor—as you could for a textfile—but rather by running a program. Figure 2-16 illustrates the file *I*. Similar comments are true for the file *R* of real numbers.

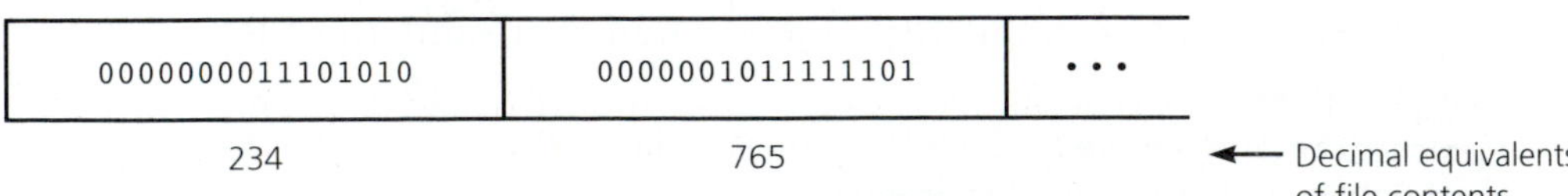

Figure 2-16

A general file of integers

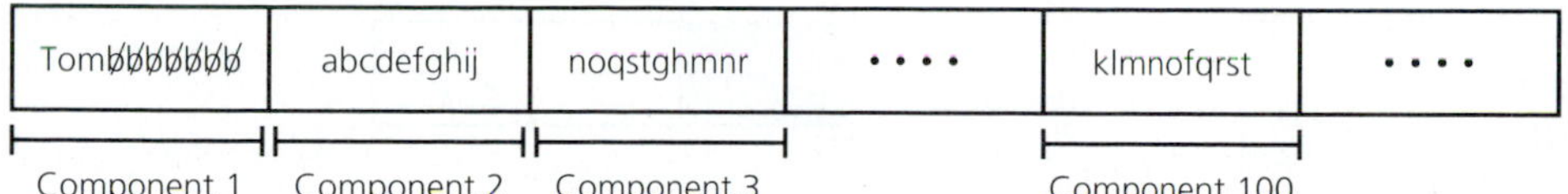

Figure 2-17

A file of strings

Similarly, consider the file *S*, where each component is a string of 10 characters, as Figure 2-17 illustrates in human-readable form. Input and output with the file *S* are at the string level, not the character level. Thus, if the variable *Name* has data type *nameType*, you could read an entire component, which is a string, from the file into *Name*. If the variable *Ch* has data type *char*, however, you could not read a single character from the file into either *Ch* or *Name[i]*. But once you have read a string into *Name*, you can access the individual characters as usual: *Name[i]* is the ith character in the string.

Finally, consider the file *P*, where each component is a record. Input and output with the file *P* are at the record level, not the field level. Thus, if the variable *Person* has data type *personRecdType*, you could read an entire record from the file into *Person*, but you could not read a field from the file. However, once you have read a record into *Person*, you can access the individual fields, such as *Person.Name*. General files of records are an important and useful data structure. Examples of such files appear later in this section. Note that textfiles cannot contain records.

A general file has an end-of-file symbol at its end, just as a textfile does. However, the notion of lines does not exist for a general file. Although a general file might contain data that coincidentally looks like an end-of-line symbol, you cannot detect it by using *eoln*. The Pascal procedures *assign*, *reset*, *rewrite*, *read*, *write*, and *erase*, as well as the function *eof* all apply to general files and are defined as they are for textfiles. For example, Figure 2-18 illustrates *reset*, *read*, and *eof* with a file of integers, which are indicated here in decimal rather than binary. Note that *readln*, *writeln*, *eoln*, *seekeoln*, *seekeof*, and *append* do not apply to general files.

Do not use eoln with general files

Recall that you can process components of a general file either sequentially or directly. The examples that follow demonstrate how to use general files. Given a general file of records, you will see how to search it sequentially and how to access a particular record directly.

You can process a general file either sequentially or directly

Searching a general file sequentially. Suppose that you have a general file of records of data type *personRecdType*, which was defined earlier in this section. Each record describes one of a company's employees, including the person's name. In this example, we assume that the records in the file appear alphabetically by the name field.

Given the name of an employee, you can search the file for the employee's record and thus determine other information about this person. A **sequential search** examines the records in the order that they appear in

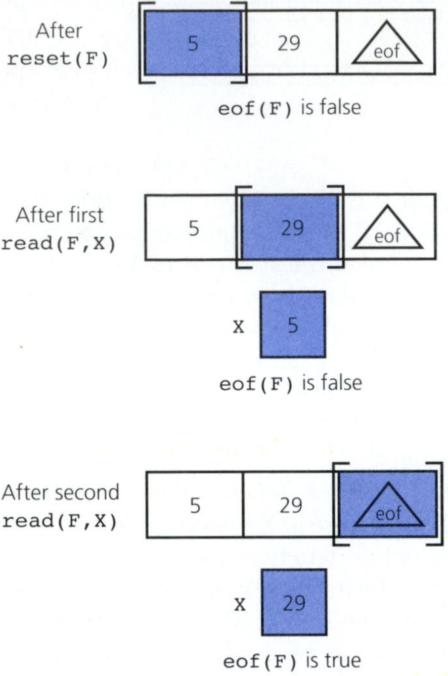

Figure 2-18

The effect of *reset*, *read*, and *eof* with a general file of integers

the file until the desired record is located. The following procedure performs such a sequential search:

```
procedure SearchFileSequentially(FileName, DesiredName : nameType;
             var DesiredRecord : personRecdType;
             var Found : boolean);
{ -------------------------------------------------------
  Searches a general file sequentially for a desired record.
  Precondition: FileName is the name of a general file of
  records about people. Each record contains a name field of
  data type nameType, as well as other fields. DesiredName
  is the name of the person whose record is sought.
  Postcondition: If DesiredName was found in a record in
  the file, DesiredRecord is that record and Found is true.
  Otherwise, Found is false and DesiredRecord is unchanged.
  The file is unchanged and closed.
  ------------------------------------------------------- }
var GF : peopleFileType;      { data types defined earlier }
    NextRecord : personRecdType;

begin
   assign(GF, FileName);
   reset(GF);

   Found := false;
```

```
   while (not Found) and (not eof(GF)) do
   begin
      read(GF, NextRecord);
      Found := (NextRecord.Name = DesiredName)
   end;  { while }

   if Found
      then DesiredRecord := NextRecord;

   close(GF)
end;  { SearchFileSequentially }
```

Accessing a general file directly. Although you can process a general file sequentially, you also can access directly the component stored at a given position without first accessing the preceding components.

The components of a general file are numbered sequentially, beginning with zero

The components in a Turbo Pascal general file are numbered sequentially in order of appearance in the file, beginning with zero. The *seek* procedure provides access to any component in the file, given the component's number. For example,

Use **seek** *to locate a record*

```
    seek(GF, 15)
```

advances the file window to the component numbered 15, which is actually the 16th component in the file because component numbers begin at zero. Immediately following the *seek*, you can use *read* to read the component.

The Turbo Pascal function *filesize* returns the number of components in a general file. If the components in the file *GF* are numbered 0 to 49, *filesize(GF)* returns 50.

Consider a general file of the employee records of data type *personRecdType*, as defined earlier. You can access any of these records by providing its component (record) number, as the following procedure demonstrates:

```
procedure SearchFileDirectly(FileName : nameType;
              DesiredRecordNumber : integer;
              var DesiredRecord : personRecdType;
              var Found : boolean);
{ ---------------------------------------------------------
  Searches a general file directly for a desired record.
  Precondition: FileName is the name of a general file of
  records about people. DesiredRecordNumber is the number of
  the desired record (0 is the first record).
  Postcondition: If the desired record was found,
  DesiredRecord is that record and Found is true. Otherwise,
  Found is false and DesiredRecord is unchanged. The file is
  unchanged and closed.
  --------------------------------------------------------- }
var GF : peopleFileType;
    LastRecordNumber : integer;
```

```
begin
   assign(GF, FileName);
   reset(GF);

   LastRecordNumber := filesize(GF) - 1;
   Found := (0 <= DesiredRecordNumber ) and
            (DesiredRecordNumber <= LastRecordNumber);
   if Found
      then
      begin
         seek(GF, DesiredRecordNumber);
         read(GF, DesiredRecord)
      end;

   close(GF)
end;  { SearchFileDirectly }
```

Admittedly, determining the number of the desired record usually is not a simple task, because typically the record numbers have no relationship to the contents of the records. In this example, you could maintain an array of employee names in the order that the employee records appear in the file. By searching the array for the desired name, you can determine the number of the corresponding record in the file (remembering that the first record in the file is record 0). Generally, searching this array will be faster than searching the file sequentially. Chapter 14 discusses the subject of searching files in more detail.

You can replace a particular record, thus updating its contents, by using the *seek* procedure. For example, if *GF* is the previously described file of employee records, the following steps locate, read, update, and replace the record whose number is *DesiredRecordNumber*:

Updating a record

```
{ update a record }
seek(GF, DesiredRecordNumber); { locate record }
read(GF, DesiredRecord);       { read record }

. . .                          { alter its fields }

seek(GF, DesiredRecordNumber); { locate record again }
write(GF, DesiredRecord);      { write updated record }
```

Finally, you can append a new record to a general file by using the function *filesize* and the procedure *seek*. The following statements append *NewRecord* to the file *GF*:

Appending a new record

```
seek(GF, filesize(GF));  { move file window just
                           after last record }
write(GF, NewRecord)     { write the new record }
```

Note that if the file contains 50 records, numbered 0 to 49, *filesize(GF)* returns 50, which is the number of the record to be added to the end of the file.

The case study in Chapter 3 further illustrates the use of files in the solution to a large, real-world problem.

SETS

In mathematics and in Pascal, a **set** is a collection of distinct elements. If you want your program to check a value against several possible values, you can use a set to make this determination. For example, suppose that the program reads a one-letter response to a yes-or-no question into the character variable `Response`. Acceptable values for `Response` would be *Y* or *y* for "yes" and *N* or *n* for "no." The boolean expression

```
Response in ['Y', 'y', 'N', 'n']
```

is true if the value of `Response` is valid—that is, if it is in the set `['Y', 'y', 'N', 'n']`. This section will review set declarations and set operations.

Declaring Sets and Assigning Them Values

You can declare a set data type by writing a statement of the following form within the type declaration section of your program:

```
set of <base_type>
```

Here, `<base_type>` represents any ordinal data type. For example, consider the following type and variable declarations:

```
const MaxAge = 100;
type  ageSetType     = set of 1..MaxAge;

      upperCaseType  = 'A'..'Z';
      letterSetType  = set of upperCaseType;

var   AgesPresent : ageSetType;
      LettersRead : letterSetType;
```

The variable `AgesPresent` is a set whose elements can be integers in the range 1 through 100. The variable `LettersRead` is a set whose elements can be uppercase letters. Note that the previous variable declarations *do not assign values to the variables*. A common mistake is to think that the value of `AgesPresent` is a set of 100 integers. However, the **base type** `ageSetType` simply specifies the permissible elements that the set `AgesPresent` can contain. Note that Turbo Pascal restricts the size of a set's base type to at most 256 possible values. The ordinal values of the bounds of the base type must be within the range 0 to 255.

Set variable declarations do not assign values to sets

Set constants. To assign values to a set, you use a set constant, which is a list of elements separated by commas and enclosed in square brackets. For example, you denote the set of the responses *Y* and *N* by using the set constant *['Y', 'N']*. Similarly, *[1, 4, 5]* is a set of the three integers 1, 4, and 5. In addition, *[18..21, 25]* has the same meaning as *[18, 19, 20, 21, 25]*. Note that *[]* is the empty set, which you can use to initialize a set variable. Thus, the following assignment statements are possible:

```
LettersRead := ['Y', 'N'];
AgesPresent := [18..21, 25];
AgesPresent := [];
```

Elements in a set are not ordered

You should also note that the elements within a set do not have an order, even though programmers often write the elements in order. Thus, the sets *['Y', 'N']* and *['N', 'Y']* are identical.

The following assignment statements are *illegal* for the reasons given:

Illegal assignments

```
AgesPresent := [5, 101]; { 101 is not in the set's base type }
LettersRead := 'A';      { 'A' is not a set; use ['A'] instead }
```

Now consider an enumerated data type as the base type for a set, as in the following statements:

```
type  errorType = (NegInput, ZeroInput, NonInteger, NoInput);
      errorSetType = set of errorType;

var   ErrorsOccurred : errorSetType;
```

A common mistake is to treat the data type *errorType* as a set. Here, the variable *ErrorsOccurred* is the set, and you could assign it a value such as *[ZeroInput, NoInput]*.

Note that in Turbo Pascal you can use set constants in the *const* statement. Thus, the following statement is legal:

```
const YesNo = ['Y', 'y', 'N', 'n']
```

Set-valued expressions. Set constants and set variables are two examples of set-valued expressions. A more general set-valued expression allows arbitrary expressions of the appropriate type to appear between the square brackets. For example, if *J* and *K* are integer variables, then *[J..K, J + K]* is a set-valued expression. You can form more complex set-valued expressions by combining set-valued expressions, parentheses, and set operators; set operators are considered next.

Set Operators

Eight set operators are available in Pascal: membership, equality, inequality, subset, superset, union, intersection, and difference. Each operator has two operands. The first five operators in this list are boolean valued: They return a value of *true* or *false*. The remaining three operators produce a set.

Membership in a set. Perhaps the most useful feature of sets is the test for membership in a set. Suppose that you want to determine whether or not the value of the integer variable *N* is in one of these ranges: *0..10*, *25..30*, or *50..100*. You could use either a lengthy boolean expression such as

```
((0 <= N) and (N <= 10)) or ((25 <= N) and (N <= 30))
or ((50 <= N) and (N <= 100))
```

or the simpler expression

```
N in [0..10, 25..30, 50..100]
```

Set membership simplifies range tests

Both expressions are true if *N* is within the desired range. The Pascal membership operator *in* has two operands. The first (*N*) is an expression of the same type as an individual element in the set that the second operand specifies; the second operand can be any set-valued expression.

The expression *not (N in [0..10])* is true when *N*'s value is not in the range 0 through 10. Notice that *N not in [0..10]* is syntactically incorrect.

Other set operators. The remaining seven set operators have set-valued expressions as operands. The first four operators return a boolean value, and the rest return a set. Here is a list of the operators and their definitions:

- **Equality (=).** If the sets *S* and *T* are identical, then they are **equal**. If *S* and *T* are equal, then the Pascal expression *S = T* is true; otherwise it is false.
- **Inequality (<>).** If the sets *S* and *T* are not identical, then they are **not equal**. If *S* and *T* are not equal, then the Pascal expression *S <> T* is true; otherwise it is false.
- **Subset (<=).** *S* is a **subset** of *T* if every element of *S* is also an element of *T*. If *S* is a subset of *T*, then *S <= T* is true.
- **Superset (>=).** *S* is a **superset** of *T* if *T* is a subset of *S*. If *S* is a superset of *T*, then *S >= T* is true.
- **Union (+).** The **union** of sets *S* and *T* (denoted in Pascal as *S + T*) is the set of all elements that are in either *S* or *T* (or both).
- **Intersection (*).** The **intersection** of sets *S* and *T* (*S * T*) is the set of all elements that are in both *S* and *T*.
- **Difference (–).** The **difference** of sets *S* and *T* (*S – T*) is the set of all elements that are in *S* but not in *T*.

Note that the following expressions are all true:

```
['Y', 'N'] = ['N', 'Y']
[2] <> [2, 3]
[2] <= [2, 3]
[2, 3] >= [2]
[2, 4, 6] + [8] = [2, 4, 6, 8]
[10..40] + [30..60] = [10..60]
```

Examples of true expressions

```
[10..60] * [50..70] = [50..60]
([10..40] + [30..60]) * [50..70] = [50..60]
[2, 4, 6, 8] - [4, 6, 9] = [2, 8]
```

Operator precedence

For expressions that involve the intersection (*), union (+), and difference (–) operators, intersection has a higher precedence than the union and difference operators. Thus, * has a higher precedence than + and –; this is the same precedence that the arithmetic operators *, +, and – have. In addition, if an expression involves both set-valued operators (*, +, –) and boolean-valued operators (=, <>, <=, >=, *in*), then the set-valued operators are always performed first. For example, the union operation is performed first in both the expression *S + T in R* and the expression *S + T >= R*. You should use parentheses in such expressions to clarify the order of the operations for readers of your program, even though such parentheses are technically unnecessary. Thus, you should write *(S + T) in R* and *(S + T) >= R*.

The operands of the set operators must be **type compatible**. Recall that the value of a set-valued expression is always a set, which contains a subrange or subranges of a single ordinal data type. This ordinal data type (*integer*, *char*, *boolean*, or user-defined enumerated) is called the **host type**. The operand sets must have the same host type to be type compatible. For example, the following sets are type compatible because their host types are the same—*integer*:

```
var S1 : set of 1..50;
    S2 : set of 1..100;
```

You cannot use sets directly in I/O statements

Finally, note that you cannot use sets directly in *read* and *write* statements. Instead, you can use the following statements to write the elements in the set *S1*, which was just declared:

```
writeln('The elements in the set S1 are: ');
for J := 1 to 50 do        { J is an integer variable }
    if J in S1
       then write(J:3);
```

Exercises 15 and 16 at the end of this chapter consider I/O with other sets, including those whose host type is an enumerated data type.

UNITS

Chapter 1 spoke of the virtues of modular programming. One of its advantages is that you can implement subprograms independently of other subprograms. You also may find it possible for several different programs to use a particular subprogram. As a result, you can build a library of subprograms that you can include in future programs.

How can you use previously written subprograms in a current program? Many modern operating systems support a **source-inclusion facility**, which allows the system to *include* the contents of a file automatically at a specified point in a program before the program is compiled. Thus, for example, you can store one or more subprograms in a file and have the system include it in any program that uses the subprograms. The assumption, of course, is that the subprograms are in **source** form—that is, they need to be compiled. Turbo Pascal provides the `$I` directive to indicate source inclusion. The system replaces the statement

```
{$I <filename>}
```

Including subprograms in source form

with the contents of the file `<filename>`.

It certainly would be more efficient to compile the subprograms once, independently of any particular program, and then later merge the results of the compilation with any program that you desire. Many programming languages allow you to do just that. Although Standard Pascal does not provide for this type of separate compilation, Turbo Pascal does. For example, you can compile a **unit**, which is a collection of subprograms, constant definitions, type definitions, and variable declarations, for later use in a program. That is, the unit is the result of previously compiled Pascal statements, which are no longer available to you. The unit may even be one that you did not write, just as you did not write the standard Pascal functions such as `sqrt`. Thus, you can use a unit in the same spirit that you use standard functions. Although standard functions are available to you automatically, you need to tell the compiler that you want to use a particular unit by writing a `uses` statement. If `Unit1` is the name of a unit, you can use it in your program by including the statement

Units are compiled separately from the program that uses them

```
uses Unit1
```

immediately after the program header.

The Sections of a Unit

A unit has a **public** portion that is available to its users, a **private** portion that is available only to itself, and an optional portion that provides for any desired initialization. An **interface section** provides the public portion; it is what you see when you want to use the unit. This section contains the variable declarations, constant definitions, data type definitions, and headers for procedures and functions that are available to the unit's users. This section can also contain a `uses` statement that references other units. The interface sections of such referenced units are available to both this unit and the programs that use this unit, but are not available to units that use this unit.

A unit's **implementation section** is its private portion. That is, you cannot see how the unit performs its task. Specifically, this section contains the complete definitions of the procedures and functions whose headers appear in the interface section. In addition, this section contains variable declarations and definitions for constants, data types, procedures, and functions that are available only within the unit itself. This section can also contain a *uses* statement that references other units. The interface sections of such units are available only to this unit, not to users of this unit.

Finally, a unit can optionally contain an **initialization section** that can, for example, initialize variables or open files. The statements in this section are executed before the statements in the main body of the program that uses the unit.

The general form of a unit is as follows:

The form of a unit

```
unit <unit name>;

interface

uses <list of units>; { optional }

{ declarations for public constants, data types,
  variables, procedures, and functions in any order }

implementation

uses <list of units>; { optional }

{ declarations for private constants, data
  types, and variables }

{ implementations of public procedures and functions}

{ implementations of private procedures and functions}

begin { optional initialization section }
    { optional initialization statements }
end.   { unit }
```

The name of the source file that contains a unit's Pascal statements must be the same as the first eight characters of the unit's name. Therefore, if <*unit name*> is *MyOwnUnit*, the source file name must be *MYOWNUNI.PAS*.

An example of a unit appears on pages 190–91 of Chapter 4.

Units and Information Hiding

Units enforce procedural abstraction

Units enforce procedural abstraction. Because the interface section indicates what is available to you, you must think of units in terms of what they can do for you and not how they are implemented. You should think of all your subprograms this way, even if you eventually implement them yourself.

Owned variables. Variables that are declared in the implementation section of a unit are called **owned variables.** (Other names include unit variables, static variables, and private variables.) Like a local variable, an owned variable is available only within its defining unit. However, like a global variable, not only is an owned variable available to all subprograms within its unit, but also it retains its value after any of these subprograms completes execution. This property allows you to use a unit's initialization section to assign to an owned variable a value that the unit's subprograms can use or modify. As you will see in Chapter 4, owned variables also allow you to hide the implementation of an abstract data type.

A FINAL COMMENT ON STANDARD PASCAL

Pascal is a very well-designed language, but it is not perfect. Perhaps its worst flaw is the behavior of its *and* and *or* operators. In particular, you know that when the boolean expression <*expression*$_1$> is false, then the expression

<*expression*$_1$> **and** <*expression*$_2$>

is false regardless of the value of <*expression*$_2$>. However, Standard Pascal evaluates <*expression*$_2$> anyway. Similarly, you know that when <*expression*$_1$> is true, then the expression

Standard Pascal always evaluates both operands of the operators **and** *and* **or**

<*expression*$_1$> **or** <*expression*$_2$>

is true regardless of the value of <*expression*$_2$>. Again, Standard Pascal evaluates <*expression*$_2$>. The problem in both of these examples is that if <*expression*$_2$> is ever undefined, then evaluating it will cause an error.

Happily, Turbo Pascal's *and* operator is defined so that it does not evaluate its second operand when the first operand is *false*. Such an operator is called a **conditional and**. Similarly, Turbo Pascal's *or* operator is a **conditional or** operator that does not evaluate its second operand if the first operand is *true*. This feature of Turbo Pascal is called **short-circuit boolean evaluation.**

For example, suppose that the array *A* is of the following data type:

```
type  arrayType = array[1..MaxSize] of integer;
```

Consider the following statements to determine whether or not the value of *Target*, which is an integer variable, occurs in the first *N* elements of *A*:

```
i := 1;
while (i <= N) and (A[i] <> Target) do
    i := succ(i);
if i <= N
    then writeln(Target, ' occurs at position ', i,
                 ' of the array.')
    else writeln(Target, ' does not occur in the array.')
```

In Standard Pascal a problem occurs when *N = MaxSize* and *Target* does not occur in *A*. Because Standard Pascal evaluates the expression *A[i]* <>

`Target` even though `i <= N` is false—that is, when `i = N + 1`—the reference to `A[N + 1]`, which does not exist, causes an error. However, in Turbo Pascal, when `N = MaxSize` and `i > N`, the expression `A[i] <> Target` is not evaluated.

Note that you can tell Turbo Pascal to evaluate boolean expressions in the same way as Standard Pascal by specifying the `$B+` compiler directive, which Appendix H describes.

We will use **`Cand`** *and* **`Cor`** *in pseudocode solutions*

The remainder of this book will use the notation **`Cand`** to mean *conditional and* and **`Cor`** to mean *conditional or* in pseudocode solutions to remind you of potential difficulties if either you use a compiler other than Turbo Pascal or you specify Turbo Pascal's `$B+` compiler directive. Thus, for example, we will write the pseudocode for the previous `while` loop as

```
i := 1
while (i <= N) Cand (A[i] <> Target) do
    increment i
```

SUMMARY

1. **An array is a collection of elements that have the same data type. You can refer to the elements of an array by using an index. A string is a special array of characters. You can reference either the entire string or its individual characters.**
2. **A record is a group of related items—called fields—which may be of different data types. You can use the `with` statement to simplify references to the fields within records.**
3. **Fields in a record can be records, arrays, sets, or any type of data except files.**
4. **A group of records is variant if the records contain both fixed fields, which are common to all records, and variant fields, which differ for certain records. A tag field references the fields in the variant part of the records.**
5. **A file is a sequence of components of the same data type. A file is the only Pascal data type that allows data to exist independently of a program. A program can write data to an external file, and this data will not disappear when the program terminates. An external file provides a way to keep a permanent record of a program's output as well as a way for one program to use another program's output as its input. An internal file exists only during program execution.**
6. **A textfile is a file of characters that contains end-of-line symbols that the function `eoln` can detect. In Turbo Pascal, an end-of-line**

symbol consists of two characters: a carriage return (ASCII 13) and a line feed (ASCII 10). If desired, you can read these characters just as you read any other character in the file.

7. In a textfile, when the file window reaches an end-of-line symbol, the function `eoln(F)` returns `true` and the function `eof(F)` returns `false`. If `F`'s window is beyond the last end-of-line symbol or if the file is empty, the functions `eof(F)` and `eoln(F)` each return `true`.

8. The standard input file `input` and the standard output file `output` are textfiles:

   a. Do not declare `input` or `output` in a variable declaration.
   b. Do not use the `reset` or `rewrite` procedures with these files; `input` is always open for reading and `output` is always open for writing.
   c. When you omit the file parameter from either a `read` or a `write` statement, the default files are `input` and `output`, respectively.

9. Although textfiles are files of characters, you can write integer, real, or boolean values to them. For example, if `x` contains the integer value 234, writing `x` to a textfile places the character sequence '2', '3', '4' in the file. The `write` procedure performs the conversion from the internal representation of the integer to the representation of the corresponding character sequence. Similarly, you can read characters, which represent either integer or real values, from a textfile into an appropriate integer or real variable.

10. A general file stores its components by using the computer's internal representation. Although you can only access the components of a textfile sequentially, you can access the components of a general file either sequentially or directly.

11. A set is a collection of distinct elements. Of the eight set operators, membership, equality, inequality, subset, and superset are boolean-valued operators, while union, intersection, and difference are set-valued operators.

12. Here are some situations where sets may be appropriate:

    a. There is no implied order for the objects.
    b. You need to keep track of which objects are present, but you do not need a count of how many of each object is present.
    c. You need to perform the standard set operations.

13. A unit is a collection of subprograms, constant definitions, type definitions, and variable declarations that you compile for later use in other programs. Units help you to enforce procedural abstraction.

COMMON PITFALLS / DEBUGGING

1. An array has a fixed size, which you choose before program execution. You must be careful that an index does not exceed this size. By default, Turbo Pascal does not check the range of array indexes. However, while debugging your program, you can use Turbo Pascal's ***$R+*** compiler directive to ensure that all array indexes are within their prescribed bounds. Similar comments apply to strings. (See Appendix H for more information about compiler directives.)

2. A string's current length, which can change during program execution, cannot exceed the string's maximum length, which you define at compilation time. Only string operations affect the current length. Thus, if you alter the individual characters within a string by using an index notation, you do not affect the string's current length. For example, the following statements write the empty string, because the current length of ***Title*** remains 0:

```
Title := '';              { the empty string, length 0 }
for Index := 1 to 5 do
   Title[Index] := '*';
writeln(Title);           { writes the empty string; }
                          { Title's length is still 0 }
```

   However, the previous statements will print five asterisks if you replace ***Title[Index] := '*'*** with

```
Title := concat(Title, '*')
```

   because the current length of ***Title*** will be 5.

3. Be careful when you reference the fields within a record. You must write both the record variable and the field identifier when you are outside the scope of a ***with*** statement. Be particularly careful when several record definitions have some of the same field identifiers.

4. The components in a file must all be of the same data type.

5. You must read a file's components into a variable of the corresponding type. For example, if the file is of type ***string***, you can read a component only into a variable of type ***string*** and not into a variable of type ***char***.

6. Do not forget to use ***reset(F)*** before you read from the file ***F*** and to use ***rewrite(F)*** before you write to ***F***. The standard input and output files are exceptions; do not use ***reset*** and ***rewrite*** with ***input*** and ***output***.

7. Remember that ***rewrite*** erases the data in an existing file.

8. Use ***readln***, ***writeln***, ***eoln***, ***seekeoln***, ***seekeof***, and ***append*** only with textfiles.

9. You must pass a file variable to a subprogram as a variable parameter. This restriction is a logical consequence of the more general restriction on files: You cannot use an assignment statement to copy one file to another file, even if the files are of the same type. Because a value parameter "copies" its value from the actual parameter, you cannot pass a file as a value parameter.

10. Be careful when reading integers (or reals) from a textfile. A common programming error can lead to an attempt to read past the end of the file while searching for the "last" integer. For example, the loop

```
{ F is a textfile, x is an integer variable }
while not eof(F) do
    read(F, x)
```

can cause such an error. If you specify the *$I+* compiler directive, this error results in program termination.

11. Generally, Pascal implementations impose a limit on the size of a set's base type. Turbo Pascal restricts the size of a set's base type to at most 256 possible values. The ordinal values of the bounds of the base type must be within the range 0 to 255.

12. By default, Turbo Pascal provides a "conditional and" operator and a "conditional or" operator, whereby the operator does not evaluate its second operand when the value of its first operand is sufficient to determine the result of the operation. However, if you either specify the *$B+* compiler directive or use Standard Pascal, an error can occur because both operands of the **and** and **or** operators are evaluated. Appendix B shows how to handle this situation.

SELF-TEST EXERCISES

1. Consider the array that the following statements define:

```
const DaysPerWeek = 7;
      WeeksPerYear = 52;

type  index1Type = 1..DaysPerWeek;
      index2Type = 1..WeeksPerYear;
      arrayType = array[index1Type, index2Type] of real;

var   MinTemps : arrayType;
```

Suppose, as you saw earlier in this chapter, that each column of the array represents the minimum temperatures for the seven days in a particular week. Write the Pascal statements that perform the following:

a. Write the minimum temperature for each day of the first week.

b. Write the minimum temperature for the first day of each of the first five weeks.

c. Write all of the minimum temperatures so that the temperatures for each week appear on a separate line.

2. Consider the array *Temps* that the following statements define:

```
const DaysPerWeek = 7;
      WeeksPerYear = 52;

type  weekType = array[1..DaysPerWeek] of real;
      yearType = array[1..WeeksPerYear] of weekType;

var   Temps : yearType;
```

Temps[12] is a one-dimensional array of seven real numbers. Suppose that you want to compute the average of these seven numbers by calling a function *Average*. Write the header statement for the function *Average* so that *Average(Temps[12])* returns the desired average.

3. Consider the definition of the record *Student1* within the section of this chapter entitled "Records Within Records." Write the Pascal references for the following items in this record:

a. The state
b. The first digit in the zip code
c. The GPA
d. The first letter in the name

4. Let *A*, *B*, and *C* be sets of integers. Assume that

A := [1..5, 9]; B := [2, 4, 6, 8]; and *C := [9..15, 20, 22]*

What is the value of each of the following expressions?

a. ***not*** *(8* ***in*** *A)*
b. *A - B*
c. *B - A*
d. *A + [9]*
e. *A * C*
f. *B <= A*
g. *A + B*
h. *A + C*

5. Consider the procedure *CopyTextfile*, which makes a copy of a textfile and was discussed in this chapter in the section "Textfiles." Trace the execution of this procedure when *OriginalFile* looks like

a b <eoln> c d <eoln> <eof>

where *<eoln>* represents the end-of-line symbol and *<eof>* represents the end-of-file symbol. Indicate the contents of *Ch* and *CopyFile*, the position of the file windows, and the values of the *eoln* and *eof* functions as you trace through the procedure.

EXERCISES

1. Assume the array *MinTemps* that Self-Test Exercise 1 describes. Consider the one-dimensional array *MT* of 364 (7 * 52) real numbers.
   a. Suppose that the first seven elements of *MT* represent the days in the first week, the second seven elements of *MT* represent the days in the second week, and so on. Which element of *MT* represents the 5th day in the 12th week? (That is, which element of *MT* corresponds to *MinTemps[5, 12]*?)
   b. Suppose that the first 52 elements of *MT* correspond to the first row of *MinTemps*, the second 52 elements of *MT* correspond to the second row of *MinTemps*, and so on. Which element of *MinTemps* corresponds to *MinTemps[5, 12]*?

2. Write the function *Average* that Self-Test Exercise 2 describes.

3. Consider the variable *CSC212* as defined in the section of this chapter entitled "Arrays of Records."
   a. Repeat Self-Test Exercise 3, but use the record *CSC212[3]* instead of *Student1*.
   b. Write statements that read names into the *Name* fields of *CSC212*. Do this both by using and by not using a *with* statement.

4. Change the definition of the *Name* field within the record type *studentRecordType*, which appears in the section "Records Within Records," so that *Name* is a record with three fields: *First*, *Middle*, *Last*.

5. Consider the variant record *Student2* that this chapter defines in the section "Variant Records." Write statements that display the fields in this record by using a *case* statement. Do this both by using and by not using a *with* statement.

6. Consider the following definitions:

```
const MaxSize = 80;

type  nameType = string[MaxSize];
      ageType = 0..maxint;

      personType = record
          Name : nameType;
          Age  : ageType
      end;  { record }

      nameFileType = file of nameType;
      personFileType = file of personType;
```

```
var   Ch : char;
      i : integer;
      AName : nameType;
      APerson : personType;
      F1 : nameFileType;
      F2 : personFileType;
```

What, if anything, is wrong with each of the following statements?

a. `read(AName);`

b. `for i := 1 to MaxSize do { syntactically correct }`
   `readln(AName[i]);`

c. `for i := 1 to MaxSize do`
   `read(F1, AName[i]);`

d. `if not eoln(F1)`
   `then read(F1, AName);`

e. `read(F2, APerson.Name)`

On the other hand, make sure that you understand that the following is legal and makes sense.

```
while not eof(F2) do
begin
    read(F2, APerson);
    writeln(APerson.Name, APerson.Age)
end
```

7. Consider two textfiles of integers. Suppose that each file is sorted into ascending order. You can **merge** the two files into a third file that is the sorted combination of the two original files. For example, if the first file contains the integers 1, 4, and 8, and the second file contains the integers 2 and 4, the third file will contain 1, 2, 4, 4, and 8.

Write a procedure that merges two sorted textfiles of integers, all of which are less than *maxint*, into a third sorted textfile of integers. Assume that each line of the files contains one integer.

Note that merging files becomes quite difficult in Turbo Pascal if you do not assume that all integers are less than *maxint*, because Turbo Pascal does not implement Standard Pascal's *get* procedure.

8. Write a procedure that merges two sorted general files of integers, all of which are less than *maxint*, into a third sorted general file of integers.

9. Write a procedure

```
AdvanceTo(var F : text; Target : char)
```

that will position the file window directly over the first occurrence in the file *F* of the character that *Target* specifies. If *Target* is a blank, the procedure should position the window over the first blank in the file and *not* over an end-of-line character. If *Target* does not appear in the file, the procedure should print a message to this effect.

10. a. Consider a textfile of integers. Write a procedure that appends to this file the 20 integers that you read from the standard input file. Use the *append* procedure.
    b. Consider a textfile of nonnumeric data. Write a procedure that appends to this file the 20 characters that you read from the standard input file. Use a temporary textfile instead of the *append* procedure.

11. Write a procedure that will append the contents of the textfile `F2` to the end of the general file `F1`. Assume that both files contain integer data. Recall that the call `rewrite(F1)` will destroy the contents of file `F1`. (*Hint:* Use a temporary file because you cannot use *append* with a general file.)

12. Repeat Exercise 11, but this time assume that `F2` is a general file instead of a textfile.

13. Let `F` be declared by

```
F : file of integer
```

Write a procedure that will write to the standard output file the *last five* integers in `F`. Your procedure may call `reset` only once. You must write the integers in the same order in which they appear in the file. If there are fewer than five integers in `F`, your program should print a message to that effect, and it should print as many integers as there are.

14. Let `A`, `B`, and `C` be sets of integers. Assume that

`A := [1..5, 9]; B := [2, 4, 6, 8];` and `C := [9..15, 20, 22]`

What is the value of each of the following expressions?

a. `(4 in A) and (4 in B)`
b. `(A * B) + [3]`
c. `A - C`
d. `C - [20]`
e. `A + [10]`
f. `B * C`
g. `A <= B`
h. `A >= (B - [6, 8])`
i. `C >= C`
j. `A + C`

15. Write some Pascal statements to read an integer into the set `S1` of `1..50`.

16. Assume the following declarations:

```
type   colorType = (red, blue, green, yellow);
var    ColorSet : set of colorType;
```

a. Write some Pascal statements to read color names into `ColorSet` by reading one-letter codes that correspond to the colors, and by adding the appropriate color name to the set by using a *case* statement.
b. Write some Pascal statements, including a *case* statement, to write the color names in the set `ColorSet`.

17. Write a Pascal procedure to determine which characters in a computer's character set appear at least once in a given textfile. Use a set of `char`. (Note that a reasonable alternative is to use a boolean array indexed by `char`.)

18. Write statements that keep track of which of several possible nonfatal errors occur in the course of a program's execution. Use a set of `errorType`, where `errorType` is an enumerated data type.

PROJECTS

19. Write a program that will read English prose and list in alphabetical order all the words that occur in the prose, along with a count of the number of times each word occurs.

The heart of this program will be a procedure that reads in a word. If you agree to treat any character other than the letters A through Z as a delimiter, then you can define a word to be any string of up to eight characters that is surrounded by delimiters. If a string between delimiters is more than eight characters, read the entire string, but truncate it to eight characters when you record it.

You can assume that there will be at most 100 distinct words in the text.

20. Write a program that simulates binary operations with n-bit quantities. Use a set of `1..n` to represent an n-bit quantity: The value i is in the set if and only if the ith bit of the n-bit quantity is 1. You can state the binary operations in terms of union, intersection, and difference.

CHAPTER 3

Linked Lists

PREVIEW This chapter introduces one more Pascal data type, the pointer, and discusses the linked list as a data structure. You can use pointers to implement a linked list in Pascal. We will develop algorithms for inserting items into and deleting items from a sorted linked list that is implemented with pointers. The techniques for performing these fundamental linked list operations are the basis of many of the data structures that appear throughout the remainder of this book. The material in this chapter is thus essential to much of the presentation in the following chapters.

The chapter concludes with a large case study of the development of a computerized system for managing the inventory of a videocassette store. The design and implementation of the solution will show you the principles and concepts of the previous two chapters in action. The size and complexity of this problem make it essential that the solution be developed in a top-down fashion and that the program be highly modular. The problem also provides a natural application for files and linked lists.

PRELIMINARIES

Why would you need another data structure, such as the linked list? We will answer this question by illustrating the deficiencies of an array. We then define Pascal pointers and use them to establish the structure of a linked list.

Maintaining Sorted Data in an Array

One of the most frequently performed computing tasks is the maintenance, in some specified order, of a collection of data. Many examples immediately come to mind: students placed in order by their names, baseball players listed in order by their batting averages, and corporations listed in order by their assets.

The problem of *maintaining* ordered data requires more than simply sorting the data. Often you need to insert some new data item into its proper, ordered place. Similarly, you often need to delete some data item. For example, suppose your university maintains an alphabetical list of the students who are currently enrolled. The registrar must insert names into and delete names from this list because students constantly enroll in and leave school.

Suppose that the array `Students` contains the list of students, as shown in Figure 3–1a. In Pascal, you could implement the array of students with the following definition:

```
const MaxStudents = 1000;
      NameLength = 20;
```

(a)

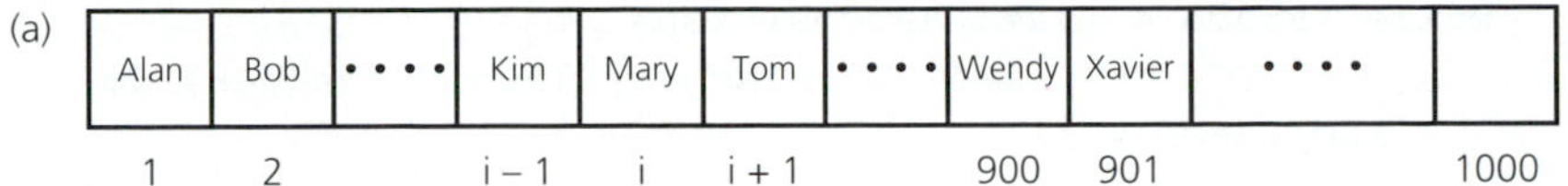

(b)

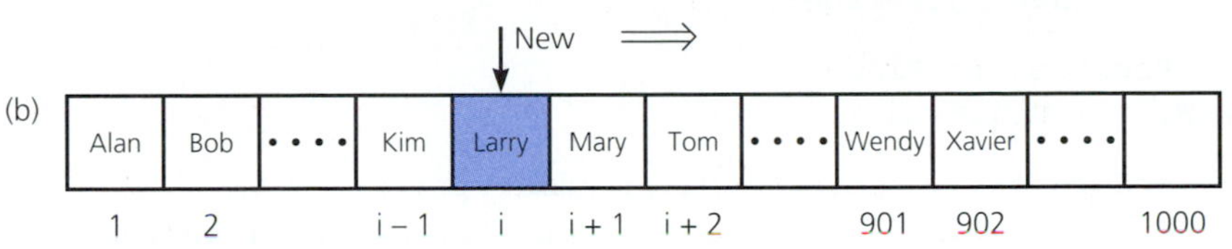

Figure 3-1

(a) An array of names;
(b) shifting for insertion

```
type   nameType = string[NameLength];
       nameListType = record
          LastPosition : 0..MaxStudents; { no. of students }
          Names : array[1..MaxStudents] of nameType
       end;    { record }

var    Students : nameListType;
```

Insertion into an array requires shifting elements to make room for the new item

To insert a new student name, you must find the position in the array where the name belongs, shift to the right the names from this position on, and insert the new name in the newly created opening. Figure 3–1b depicts this insertion, and the following Pascal procedures perform it.

```
function Position(Target: nameType;
                  List: nameListType): integer;
{ ---------------------------------------------------------
  Determines where a name belongs or exists in a sorted
  array of names.
  Precondition: The array List.Names contains
  List.LastPosition names in alphabetical order;
  List.LastPosition >= 0.
  Postcondition: Returns the position (in the range
  1..List.LastPosition) of the first element in the array
  List.Names that is greater than or equal to Target. If no
  such element exists, returns List.LastPosition + 1. If
  List.LastPosition = 0 (that is, List.Names is empty),
  returns 1. Target and List are unchanged.
  --------------------------------------------------------- }
var Place : integer;

begin
   Place := 1;

   { find the proper position in the array }
   { loop invariant:
     all elements in List.Names[1..Place-1] are < Target }
```

```
   while (Place < List.LastPosition)
                  and (List.Names[Place] < Target) do
       inc(Place);

   { check for insertion after the last name }
   if (List.LastPosition > 0) and (List.Names[Place] < Target)
       then inc(Place);

   Position := Place
end;   { Position }

procedure ArrayInsert(NewName: nameType;
            var List: nameListType; var Success: boolean);
{ -----------------------------------------------------------
  Inserts a name into a sorted array of names.
  Precondition: The array List.Names contains
  List.LastPosition names in alphabetical order.
  List.LastPosition >= 0.
  Postcondition: NewName is in its proper place in the
  array List.Names and Success is true, unless the array is
  full, in which case no insertion occurs and Success is
  false. If one or more elements already in the array are
  identical to NewName, NewName is in front of these
  elements. If insertion occurs, List.LastPosition is
  increased by 1.
  Calls: Position.
  ----------------------------------------------------------- }
var Index, Place : 1..MaxStudents;

begin
   if List.LastPosition >= MaxStudents
       then Success := false

       else
       begin
           {find insertion point}
           Place := Position(NewName, List);

           { make room for insertion by shifting elements }
           { Note: if Place = List.LastPosition+1, the loop
             is skipped; simply insert at end }
           for Index := List.LastPosition downto Place do
               List.Names[Index+1] := List.Names[Index];

           { insert element and count it }
           List.Names[Place] := NewName;
           inc(List.LastPosition);
           Success := true
       end   { if }
end; { ArrayInsert }
```

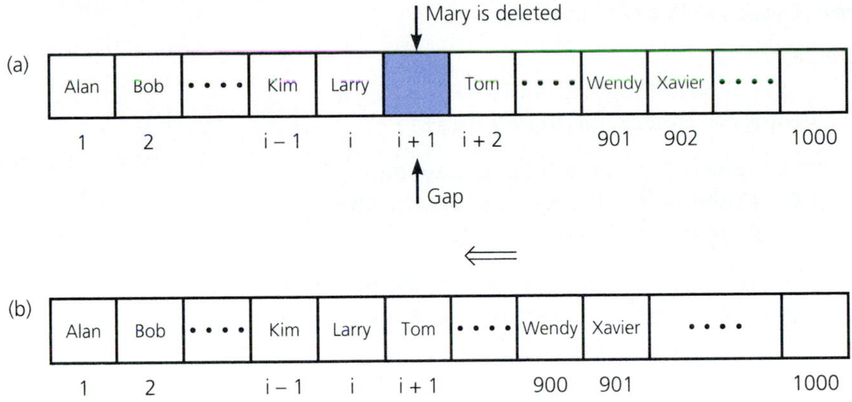

Figure 3-2

(a) Deletion causes a gap; (b) fill gap by shifting

Now consider how to delete a student's name from the list. You could blank it out after finding the name in the list. However, this strategy can lead to gaps in the array, as Figure 3-2a illustrates. An array that is full of gaps has two significant problems:

Problems with gaps in an array

- Variable `List.LastPosition` could have the value `MaxStudents` even though there are empty cells in the array. As a consequence, it could become impossible to insert new names into the array even when fewer than `MaxStudents` names are present.
- Because the names are spread out, the function `Position` might have to look at every cell of the array even when only a handful of names are present.

Thus, what you really need to do is shift the elements of the array to fill the gap left by the deleted name, as shown in Figure 3-2b

The following Pascal procedure performs the deletion by shifting. Both the type definitions and the function `Position` are the same as before.

```
procedure ArrayDelete(Name: nameType;
            var List: nameListType; var Success: boolean);
{ -------------------------------------------------------
  Deletes an element from a sorted array by shifting array
  elements.
  Precondition: The array List.Names contains
  List.LastPosition names in alphabetical order;
  List.LastPosition > 0.
  Postcondition: If deletion is successful, Name is
  deleted from the array List.Names, List.LastPosition is
  decreased by 1, and Success is true. However, if Name was
  not in the array, List is unchanged and Success is false.
  Calls: Position.
  ------------------------------------------------------- }
```

```
var Index, Place : integer;

begin
   { find position of Name in array }
   Place := Position(Name, List);

   { if position is after array end }
   if (Place > List.LastPosition) then
       Success := false

   { else if Name is not where expected }
   else if (Name <> List.Names[Place]) then
       Success := false

   else          { Name is present }
   begin         { shift to delete }
       dec(List.LastPosition);    { decrement count }
       for Index := Place to List.LastPosition do
           List.Names[Index] := List.Names[Index+1];
       Success := true
   end
end; { ArrayDelete }
```

Pointers and Linked Lists

Although the most intuitive means of imposing an order on data is to order it physically, this scheme has its disadvantages. In a physical ordering, the successor of an item *x* is the next data item in sequence after *x*, that is, the item "to the right" of *x*. An array orders its items physically, and as you have just seen, when you use an array to maintain the sorted list of student names, you must shift data both when you insert a new data item between a specified pair of data items and when you remove an item from a specified position. Other methods that do not require you to shift data for both insertions and deletions would be preferable. How can you avoid shifting data?

To get a conceptual notion of a scheme that would not involve shifting, consider Figure 3-3. This figure should help free you from the notion that the only way to maintain a given order of data is to store the data in that order. In these diagrams, each item of the list actually *points to* the next item. Thus, if you know where an item is, you can determine its successor, which can be anywhere physically. This flexibility not only allows you to insert and delete data items without shifting data, it also allows you to increase the size of the list easily. If you need to insert a new item, you simply find its place in the list and set two **pointers.** Similarly, to delete an item, you find the item and set a pointer to bypass the item.

An item on a linked list points to its successor

Because the items in this list are *linked* to one another, such a list is called a **linked list**. As you will see shortly, *a linked list is able to grow as needed, whereas an array can hold only a fixed number of data items.* In many applications, this flexibility gives a linked list a significant advantage.

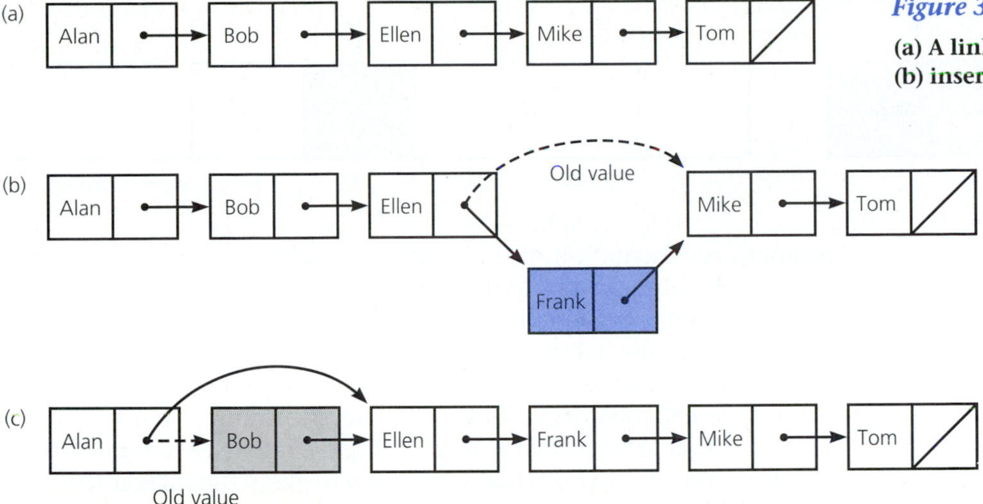

Figure 3-3

(a) A linked list of names; (b) insertion; (c) deletion

You can think of the linked list as an abstract data type (ADT). That is, you can describe operations on a linked list and design applications for a linked list without knowing—or caring—how to get one data item to point to another. Thus, if someone gave you Pascal subprograms that performed certain operations on a linked list, you could use them in a program to maintain a linked list without knowing the details of the subprograms' implementations. Chapter 4 will discuss abstract data types—including the linked list—in detail and demonstrate the importance of this concept. However, this chapter will focus on Pascal pointers and present the linked list as a data structure. That is, you will learn how to use pointers to implement a linked list. You should note, however, that you do not need pointers to implement linked lists; other implementations are possible.

Pascal pointers. When you declare an ordinary variable *X* to be `integer`, the Pascal compiler allocates a memory cell that can hold an integer. You use the identifier *X* to refer to this cell. To put the value 5 in the cell, you could write

```
X := 5
```

To print out the value that is in the cell, you could write

```
writeln('The value of X is ', X)
```

Now consider the following statements, which declare the variable *p* to be an integer **pointer variable**, or simply a **pointer:**

```
type ptrType = ^integer;
var  p : ptrType;
```

The variable *p* is said to be an *integer pointer variable* because it can *reference a memory cell* that contains an integer. (Similarly, you can declare pointers to any other type except files.) This reference to another memory cell is the

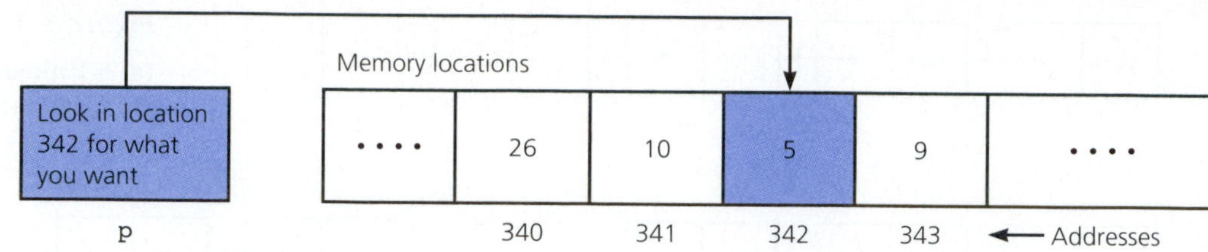

Figure 3-4

A pointer to an integer

computer's representation of the location, or **address** in memory, of the cell. Figure 3-4 illustrates a pointer that points to an integer.

The notion of one memory cell that references another memory cell is a bit tricky. In Figure 3-4, it is important to keep in mind that the content of *p* is not a typical value. The content of *p* is of interest only because it tells you where in memory to look for the integer value 5. That is, you can get to the integer value *indirectly* by following the reference that *p* contains.

Now consider how you actually can use *p* to get to the integer to which *p* points. In Pascal you may not look at the address that *p* contains. For example, you cannot say

```
writeln(p)
```

p^ is the memory cell pointed to by p

However, the notation *p^* refers to *the memory cell to which p points,* as shown in Figure 3-5. Thus, in this example, the value of *p^* is 5, and *writeln(p^)* writes 5. To summarize, *p* contains the address of a memory cell that contains the value 5, and the value of *p^* is 5.

You also use the *p^* notation to store a value in the memory cell to which *p* points. For example, you can put the value 7 into the memory cell that *p* points to by using the assignment statement

```
p^ := 7
```

After this assignment, the expression *p^* has the value 7, because 7 is now the value in the memory cell to which *p* points. Notice that the assignment statement

```
p := 7        { THIS STATEMENT IS ILLEGAL }
```

is illegal because there is a type clash: 7 is an integer, while *p* is a pointer, which can contain only a *reference* to (that is, an *address* of) a memory cell that contains an integer.

If you also had the declaration

```
var q : ptrType
```

you could assign to *q* the value in *p* by using the assignment statement

```
q := p
```

Pointer *q* now points to the same memory cell that *p* points to, as Figure 3-6 illustrates.

Figure 3-5

p* versus *p^

```
[•]-->[ 5 ]
 p     p^
```

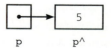

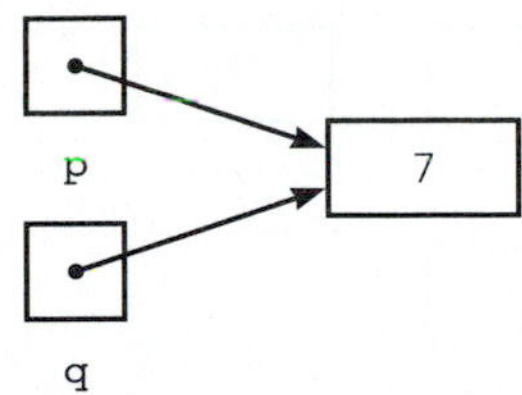

Figure 3-6

Two pointers that reference the same memory cell

Now for the big question: How do you get a pointer variable to point to a memory cell in the first place? To begin, memory is allocated either at compilation time or at execution time. Memory allocation at compilation time, that is, before the program executes, is called **static allocation**. A variable allocated then is called a **statically allocated variable**. Execution of the program does not affect the memory requirements of statically allocated variables.

For example, the statements

```
type ptrType = ^integer;

var  p, q : ptrType;
     X : integer;
```

cause the compiler to statically allocate memory for *p*, *q*, and *X*. Initially, the values of *p* and *q* are undetermined, as Figure 3-7a illustrates. However, you can place the address of *X* into *p* and therefore have *p* point to *X* by using Turbo Pascal's address-of (`@`) operator, as follows:

```
p := @X
```

Figure 3-7b illustrates the result of this assignment. (Notice that `p := X` is illegal.) Either of the assignment statements `X := 6` or `p^ := 6` assigns 6 to the memory statically allocated to *X*, as Figure 3-7c indicates.

Generally, static allocation of memory and the `@` operator will *not* be useful in an implementation of a linked list. Typically, you want pointer variables to point to memory cells that the system allocates at execution time instead of at compilation time. Memory allocation at execution time is called **dynamic allocation**. A variable allocated then is called a **dynamically allocated variable**. Pascal enables dynamic allocation of memory by providing the standard procedure *new*, which takes a pointer variable for its parameter, as in

***new* allocates memory dynamically**

```
new(p)
```

This procedure call allocates a new memory cell and initializes *p* so that *p* points to this new cell, as Figure 3-7d illustrates.

Observe that this newly created memory cell has no programmer-defined name. The only way to access its content or to put a value in it is indirectly via the pointer *p*. That is, *p^* references the newly created cell. As Figure 3-7e shows, the statement `p^ := 7` assigns 7 to the newly created memory cell.

Turbo Pascal also allows you to use *new* as a function with the same effect as that just described. Thus, you can write

```
q := new(ptrType)
```

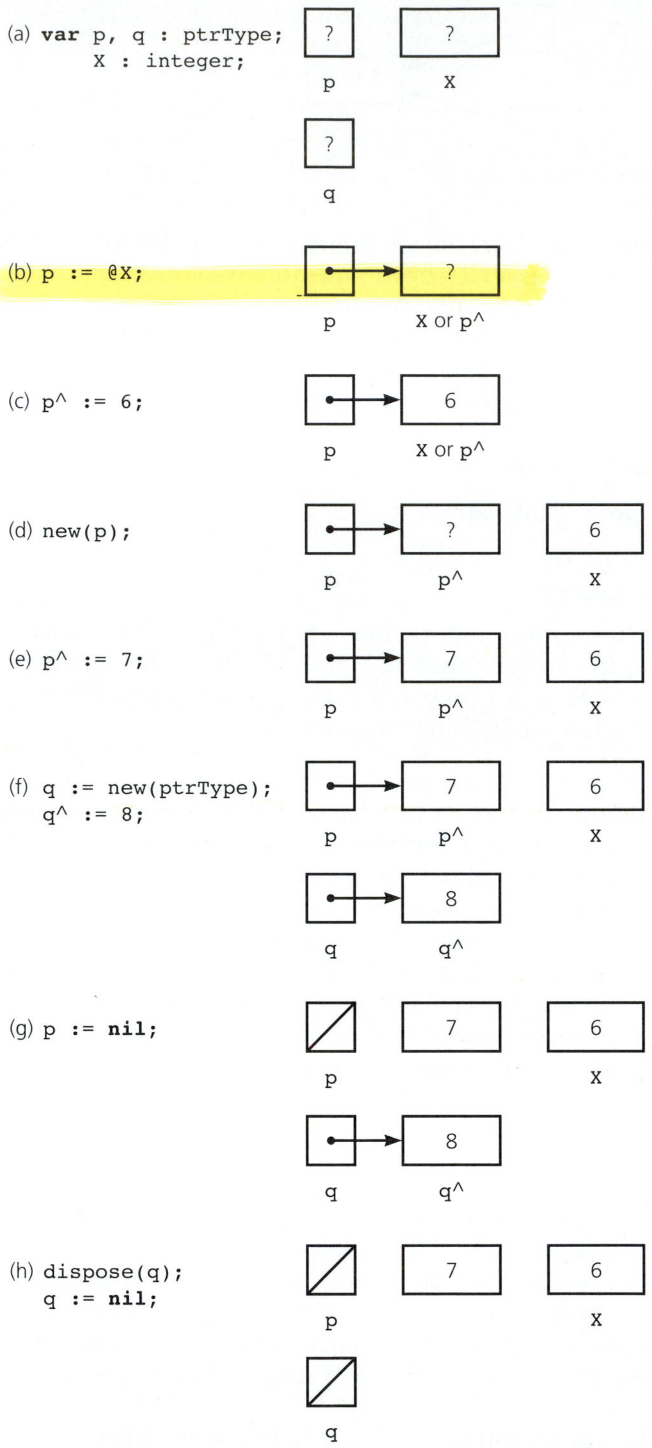

Figure 3-7

(a) Declaring pointer variables; (b) pointing to statically allocated memory; (c) assigning a value; (d) allocating memory dynamically; (e) assigning a value; (f) allocating memory dynamically and assigning a value; (g) assigning *nil* to a pointer variable; (h) deallocating memory

(a)
```
var p, q : ptrType;
    X : integer;
```


(b)
```
p := @X;
```


(c)
```
p^ := 6;
```


(d)
```
new(p);
```


(e)
```
p^ := 7;
```


(f)
```
q := new(ptrType);
q^ := 8;
```


(g)
```
p := nil;
```


(h)
```
dispose(q);
q := nil;
```

where the parameter is a pointer type; the function then returns a pointer to the newly allocated memory cell. In this example, *q* points to this new cell and *q*^ references the cell's content, as Figure 3-7f shows.

Suppose that you no longer need the value in a pointer variable. That is, you do not want the pointer to point to any particular memory cell. Pascal provides the constant `nil`, which you can assign to a pointer of any type. By convention, a `nil` pointer value means that the pointer does not point to anything. It is common to confuse a pointer variable whose value is `nil` with one whose value is not initialized. Until you explicitly assign a value to a pointer variable, its value—like that of any other variable—is undefined. You should not assume that its value is `nil`.

A pointer whose value is **`nil`** *does not point to anything*

Now suppose that you no longer need a dynamically allocated memory cell. Simply removing all references to the cell is wasteful, as the cell is no longer accessible, even though it remains allocated to the program. For example, Figure 3-7g shows the result of assigning `nil` to *p*. The cell containing 7, to which *p* originally pointed, is in limbo. To avoid this situation, Pascal provides the standard procedure *dispose* as a counterpart to *new*. Conceptually, the call

```
dispose(q)
```

dispose *returns memory to the system for reuse*

returns to the system the memory cell to which *q* points. That is, *dispose* in effect deallocates memory from a program, thus freeing the memory for future use by this program. Because in Turbo Pascal *dispose* does not affect *q* itself, a reference to *q*^ at this point can be disastrous. Thus, you should assign `nil` to *q* after the call to *dispose* as a precaution against following *q* to a deallocated memory cell. Figure 3-7h shows the results of these actions. The simple program in Figure 3-8 should serve to illustrate these concepts further.

Figure 3-8

Programming with pointer variables that reference dynamically allocated memory

```
program IllustratePointers;

type ptrType = ^integer;

var  p, q : ptrType;

begin

     new(p);            { Allocate a cell of type integer.     }

     p^ := 1;           { Assign a value to the new cell.      }
```

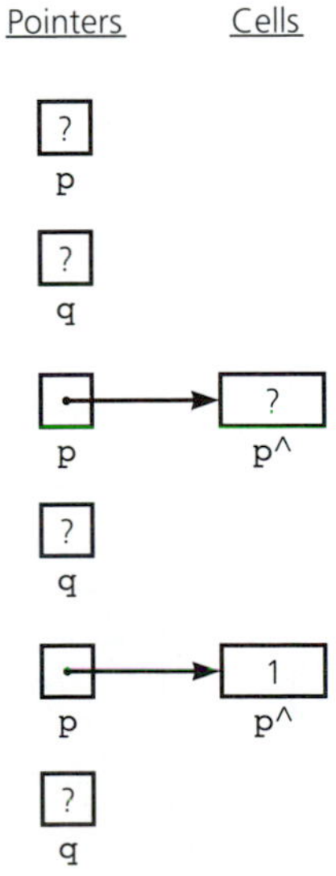

(continues)

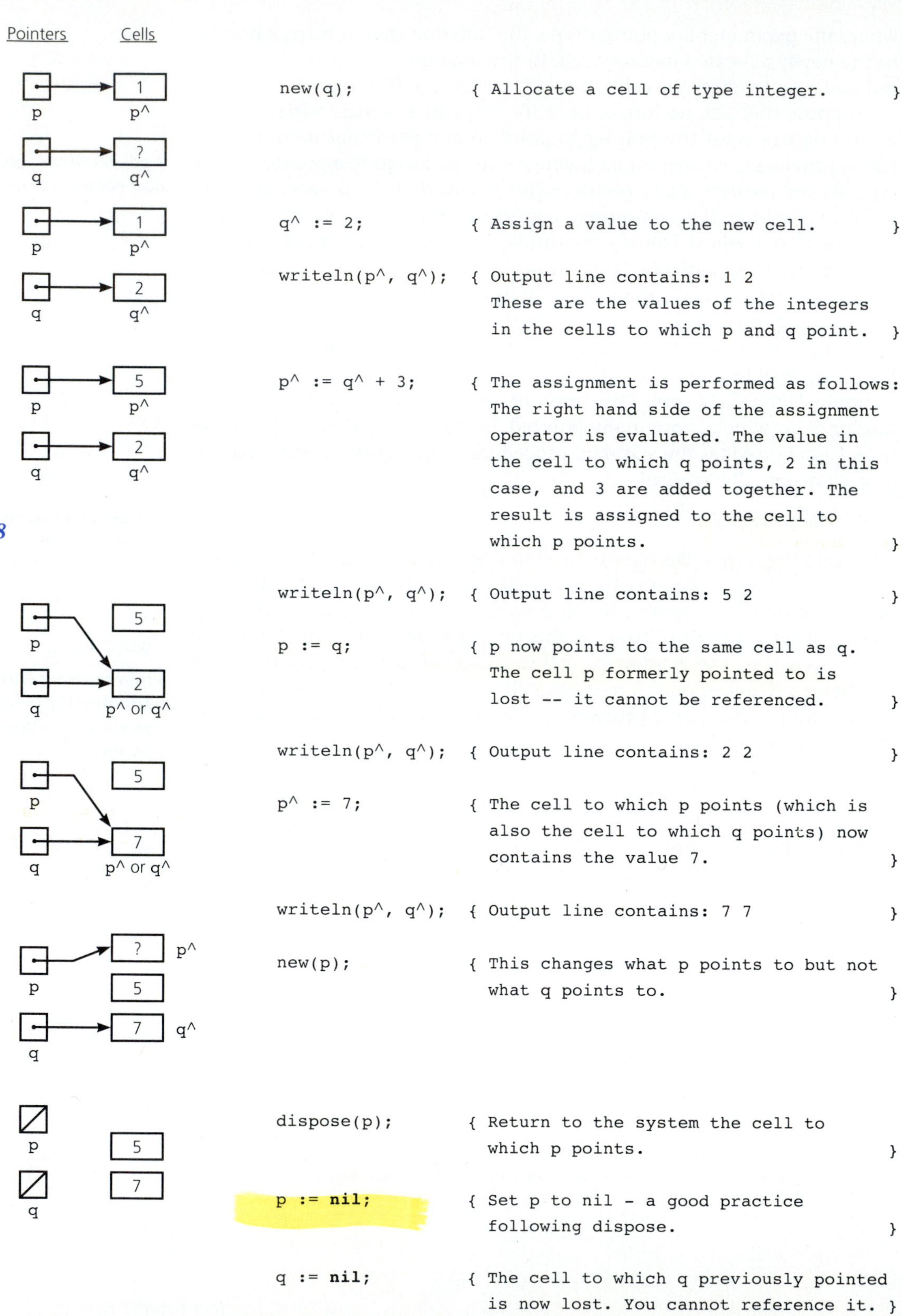

Pointers
Cells
new(q); { Allocate a cell of type integer. }
q^ := 2; { Assign a value to the new cell. }
writeln(p^, q^); { Output line contains: 1 2
These are the values of the integers
in the cells to which p and q point. }
p^ := q^ + 3; { The assignment is performed as follows:
The right hand side of the assignment
operator is evaluated. The value in
the cell to which q points, 2 in this
case, and 3 are added together. The
result is assigned to the cell to
which p points. }
writeln(p^, q^); { Output line contains: 5 2 }
p := q; { p now points to the same cell as q.
The cell p formerly pointed to is
lost -- it cannot be referenced. }
writeln(p^, q^); { Output line contains: 2 2 }
p^ := 7; { The cell to which p points (which is
also the cell to which q points) now
contains the value 7. }
writeln(p^, q^); { Output line contains: 7 7 }
new(p); { This changes what p points to but not
what q points to. }
dispose(p); { Return to the system the cell to
which p points. }
p := nil; { Set p to nil - a good practice
following dispose. }
q := nil; { The cell to which q previously pointed
is now lost. You cannot reference it. }
end.

Figure 3-8
continued

Because *p* is an integer pointer, the cell that *new(p)* allocates can contain only an integer. However, if you declare *p* as

```
type ptrType = ^char;
var  p : ^ptrType; { pointer to a character }
```

then *new(p)* would create a memory cell into which you could place a character.

Linked lists. Although we have illustrated most of the mechanics of pointers, using pointers to implement a linked list (like the one pictured in Figure 3-3) is not yet completely clear. After all, each item on a linked list contains both a data value—an integer, for example—and a pointer to the next item. Consider now how you can set up such a list, how you can print out the information on a linked list, and how you can insert into and delete from a linked list.

Since each item on the list must contain two pieces of information—the data value and a reference to the next item on the list—it is natural to conclude that each item on the list should be a record. One field of the record is the data and the other is a pointer. A record of this form is usually called a **node.**

Suppose that the data portion of each node contained an integer. What type of pointer should you use within a node, and to what will it point? You might guess that the pointer should point to an integer, but actually it must point to a record, because the nodes of the list are indeed records and not integers. Thus, a record of type *nodeType* will have as one of its fields a pointer to type *nodeType*. This idea is perhaps difficult to comprehend: Each record of type *nodeType* contains a pointer to another record of type *nodeType*.

The type definitions are thus

```
type  ptrType = ^nodeType; { nodeType is not yet defined }
      nodeType = record
          Data : integer;
          Next : ptrType
      end;
```

A node in a linked list is usually a record

Note that these statements define *ptrType* to be *^nodeType* before they define *nodeType*. In all other contexts, Pascal does not allow you to use a type in a *type* definition before you define it. However, for pointers, this syntax is legal. The compiler flags *nodeType* as an unknown type and comes back to that type when it eventually encounters its definition. Figure 3-9 illustrates a node described by the previous record definitions.

Now the declaration

```
var p : ptrType
```

declares a pointer variable *p* to be of type *ptrType*; that is, *p* can point to a node of type *^nodeType*.

There are two minor issues to consider. First, what is the value of the *Next* field in the last node on the list? By setting the *Next* field of the last

Figure 3-9

A list node

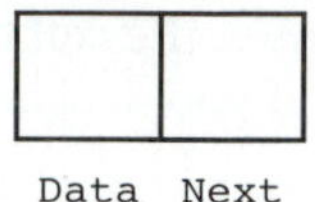

record of the list equal to *nil*, you can easily detect when you are at the end of the list.

Second, nothing points to the beginning of the list, and if you cannot get to the beginning of the list, you cannot get to the second node on the list, and if you cannot get to the second node on the list, you cannot get to the third node on the list, and so on. The solution is to have an additional pointer whose purpose is to point to the first node on the list. Such a node is called the **head pointer** or simply the **head** of the list. Figure 3-10 pictures a linked list with a head pointer.

The head pointer points to the first node on a linked list

Observe in Figure 3-10 that the pointer variable *Head* is different from the other pointers in the diagram in that it is not part of a record. Rather, it is a simple pointer variable that is external to the list, and it serves as a way of getting to the list's beginning. Thus, *Head* is an external pointer that is outside the list, whereas the *Next* fields are internal pointers within the nodes of the list. Also, note that the variable *Head* always exists, even at times when there are no nodes on the list. The declaration

```
var Head : ptrType
```

creates the variable *Head* whose value, like that of other uninitialized variables, is undefined. To what value should you initialize *Head* and to what value should you change it if a list ever becomes empty? In both cases, assigning *Head* the value *nil* is a logical choice, as this indicates that *Head* does not point to anything.

*If **Head** is **nil**, the list is empty*

It is a common mistake to think that before you can assign *Head* a value, you must make the call *new(Head)*. This misconception is rooted in the belief that the variable *Head* does not exist before the call. This is not at all true; *Head* is a declared pointer variable waiting to be assigned a value. Thus, for example, you can assign *nil* to *Head* without first calling *new(Head)*. In fact, the sequence

```
new(Head);        { An incorrect use of new }
Head := nil
```

causes the only reference—*Head*—to the newly created node to be lost, as Figure 3-11 illustrates. Thus, you needlessly have created a new node and made it inaccessible.

So far, you have seen that you can use pointer variables to implement a linked list. However, you have not seen how to perform operations that

Figure 3-10

A head pointer to a list

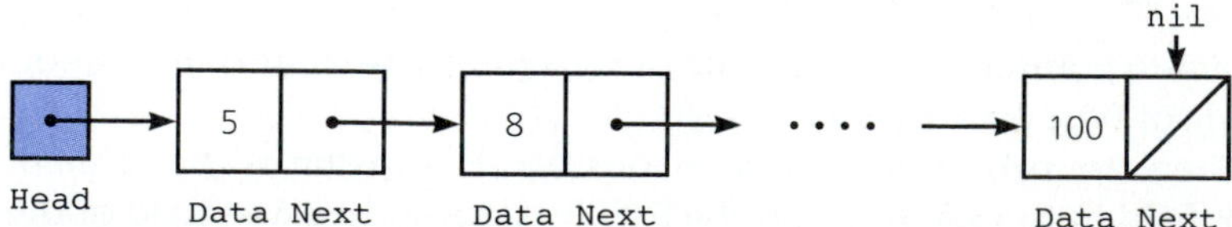

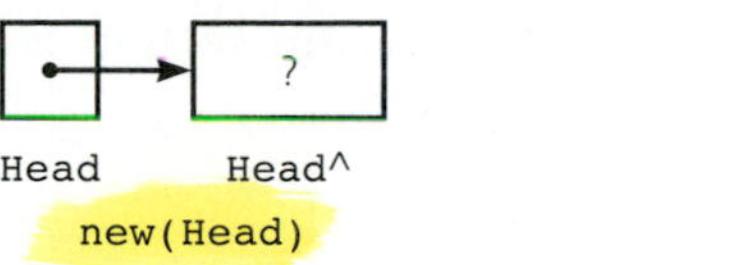

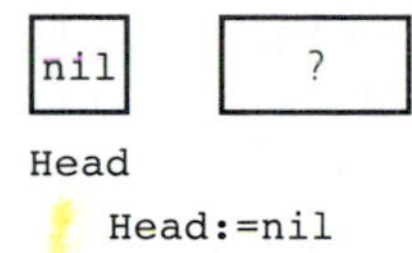

Figure 3-11

A lost cell

alter the structure of the list. The next section develops these operations. As you study the operations that alter the structure of a list, the potential advantages of a linked list over an array will become more apparent. One of these advantages was indicated already: You do not need to shift the data when you insert items into or delete items from a linked list. A second advantage of perhaps more importance is a result of the use of pointers to implement the linked list. It concerns the ability to use the Pascal procedure *new* to dynamically allocate memory cells for a program. Because you can use *new* to allocate memory cells as needed, you do not require an estimate of the amount of data that the program will have to handle. Contrast this with a static array. If you use an array to store a list of student names, you need an upper bound on the number of students that you must handle. *The ability of a linked list to grow as needed is a major advantage.*

Linked lists do not have a fixed size

However, linked lists can have disadvantages. For example, suppose that you wanted to access the nth node on the linked list in Figure 3-10. You would have to access the first node and get the pointer to the second node, access the second node and get the pointer to the third node, and so on until you finally accessed the nth node. Clearly, the time it takes you to access the first node is less than the time it takes to access the tenth node. That is, the **access time** depends on n. In contrast, you can access the nth item in the array `A` by using `A[n]`. Accessing either `A[1]` or `A[10]` takes the same amount of time. That is, the access time is constant for an array.

The time to access the nth node in a linked list depends on n

Beginning in the next sections and continuing through most of the book, we shall emphasize the importance of choosing between a **pointer-based solution** and an **array-based solution**. Although you have just seen the advantage of using a pointer-based linked list, it is not always the best choice. For many applications, an array-based solution is more appropriate. You will learn how to choose an appropriate structure to solve a particular problem as you progress through this book. For now, you should become comfortable with the mechanics of what was done in this section.

PROGRAMMING WITH LINKED LISTS

The previous section illustrated how you can use pointer variables to implement a linked list. This section develops algorithms for displaying the data portions of such a linked list and for inserting items into and deleting items from a sorted linked list. These linked list operations play a central role in the case study that appears later in this chapter, and they are the basis of many of the data structures that appear throughout the remainder of the book. Thus, the material in this section is essential to much of the discussion in the following chapters.

Displaying the Contents of a Linked List

Suppose now that you have a linked list, as was pictured in Figure 3-10, and that you want to write out the contents of its data fields. A high-level pseudocode solution is

```
Set a current pointer to point to the first node on the list
while the current pointer is not nil do
begin
   Write the data field of the current node
   Set the current pointer to the next field of the current
      node
end
```

This solution makes it clear that you need to keep track of the current position within the list. That is, you need a pointer variable to point to the node that you are working with. Thus, you must have the following additional declaration:

```
var Cur: ptrType; { pointer to current node }
```

To initialize *Cur* to point to the first node, simply let *Cur* point to the same node that *Head* points to by writing

```
Cur := Head
```

To write out the data field of the current node, you use the statement

```
writeln(Cur^.Data)
```

This statement makes sense because *Cur^* refers to a record, which you must qualify by supplying a field name. Finally, to advance the current position to the next node, you write

```
Cur := Cur^.Next
```

Figure 3-12 illustrates this action. If the previous assignment statement is not clear, consider

```
Temp := Cur^.Next;
Cur := Temp
```

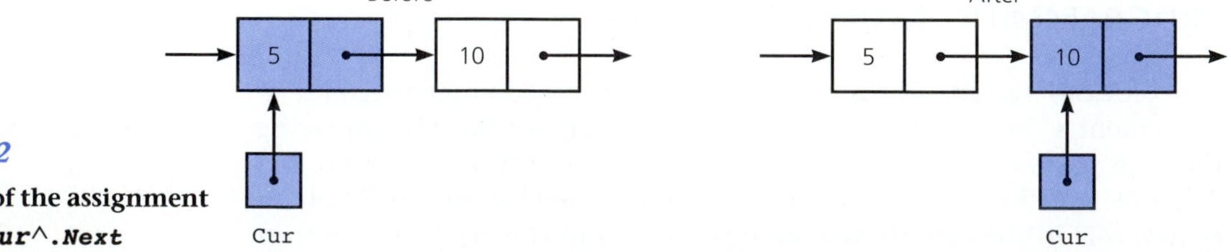

Figure 3-12
The effect of the assignment ***Cur := Cur^.Next***

and then convince yourself that the intermediate variable *Temp* is not necessary.

These ideas lead to the *PrintList* procedure.

```
procedure PrintList(Head : ptrType);
{ -------------------------------------------------------
  Prints the data in a linked list.
  Precondition: Head is a pointer variable that points to
  the linked list.
  Postcondition: Writes the data in the linked list to the
  standard output file. Both Head and the list are unchanged.
  ------------------------------------------------------- }
var Cur : ptrType;
begin
    Cur := Head;

    { Loop invariant: Cur points to the next node to be
      printed }
    while Cur <> nil do
    begin
       writeln(Cur^.Data);
       Cur := Cur^.Next
    end { while }
end; { PrintList }
```

Notice the condition in the *while* statement. As written, *Cur* points to each node in a nonempty list during the course of the *while* loop's execution, and so the data portion of each node is printed. After the last node is printed, *Cur* becomes *nil* and the *while* loop terminates. When the list is empty—that is, when *Head* is *nil*—the *while* loop is correctly skipped.

A common error is to use *Cur^.Next* instead of *Cur* in the *while* statement. When *Cur* points to the last node of a nonempty list, *Cur^.Next* is *nil*, and so the *while* loop would terminate before printing the data in the last node. In addition, when the list is empty—that is, when *Cur* is *nil*—*Cur^.Next* is undefined. You should be aware that Turbo Pascal does not produce a run-time error message if you reference *Cur^.Next* when *Cur* is *nil*. However, such a reference is wrong and causes unpredictable results.

The procedure *PrintList* uses **list traversal**, which is a common operation. A traversal sequentially **visits** each node on the list until it reaches the end of the list. *PrintList* prints the data field of each node when it visits the node. Later in this book, you will see that there are other useful things that you can do to a node during a visit.

A traverse operation visits each node on the list

To write the contents of a linked list, you had to assume that somehow the linked list was set up in advance. We will now show you operations that actually alter the structure of a linked list. These operations allow you to delete nodes from and insert nodes into an existing linked list. Ultimately, you will see how to build a linked list from scratch.

Deleting a Specified Node from a Linked List

So that you can address the problem of deleting a specified node from a linked list, assume that the list shown in Figure 3-13 already exists. Notice that, in addition to *Head*, the diagram includes two external pointer variables, *Cur* and *Prev*, which the following statements declare:

```
var    Cur  : ptrType;   { pointer to current node }
       Prev : ptrType;   { pointer to previous node }
```

The task is to delete the node to which *Cur* points. The role of the pointer variable *Prev* will become apparent in a moment.

As Figure 3-13 indicates, you can delete node *N*, to which *Cur* points, by altering the value of the pointer field *Next* in the node that precedes *N*. You need to set this pointer so that it points to the node that follows *N*, thus bypassing *N* on the chain. Notice that this pointer change does not directly affect the node *N*. Node *N* remains in existence, and it points to the same node that it pointed to before the deletion. However, the node has effectively been deleted from the list. For example, notice that the procedure *PrintList* from the previous section would not print the contents of the node *N*.

To accomplish this pointer change in Pascal, notice first that if you had only the pointer *Cur* that points to *N*, there would be no direct way of getting to the node that precedes *N*. After all, you cannot follow the links on the list backward. However, notice the pointer variable *Prev* in Figure 3-13. *If you are to delete the node N from a linked list, you need a pointer to the node that precedes N.*

If you do have a pointer variable *Prev* that points to the node preceding *N*, the pointer change suggested by Figure 3-13 is easy to implement in Pascal. The following assignment statement is all that you require to delete the node that *Cur* points to:

Deleting an interior node

```
Prev^.Next := Cur^.Next
```

There are two questions to answer about the deletion of a node from a linked list.

- How did the variables *Cur* and *Prev* come to point to the appropriate nodes?
- Does the previous method work for any node *N*, regardless of where in the linked list it appears?

To answer the first question, consider the context in which you might expect to delete a node. In one common situation, you need to delete a node that contains a particular data value. In other words, you do not pass the values of *Cur* and *Prev* to the deletion procedure, but instead the procedure establishes these values as its first step by searching the list for the node *N* that contains the data value to be deleted. Once the procedure finds the node *N*—and the node that precedes *N*—the deletion of *N* pro-

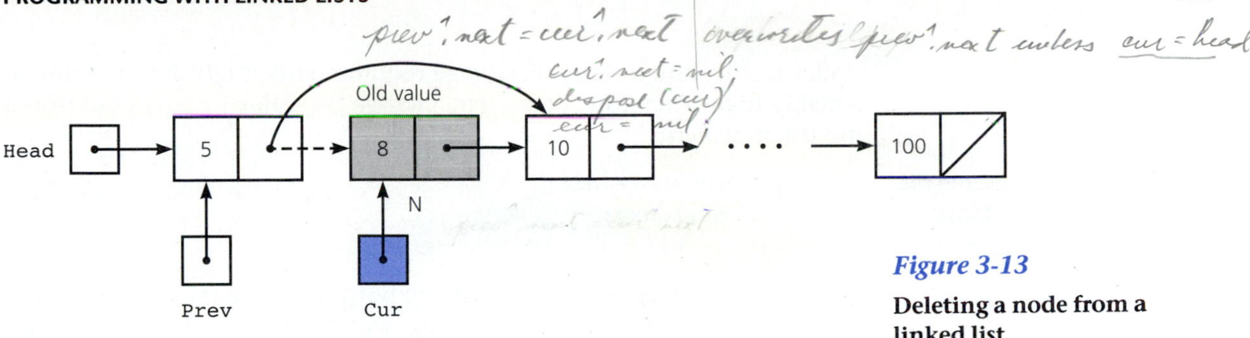

Figure 3-13

Deleting a node from a linked list

ceeds as described previously. The details of such a deletion procedure appear later in this section.

In answer to the second question, the method described does not work if the node to be deleted is the *first* node on the list. If the node to be deleted is the first node on the list, it certainly does not make sense to assert that `Prev` points to the node that precedes this node! Thus, *deletion of the first node on a linked list is a special case,* as Figure 3-14 depicts.

When you delete the first node of the list, you must change the value of `Head` to reflect the fact that, after the deletion, there is a new first node on the list. That is, the node that was second prior to the deletion is now first. You make this change to `Head` by using the assignment statement

Deleting the first node

```
Head := Cur^.Next
```

As was the case for the deletion of an interior node, the pointers bypass the old first node, although it still exists. Notice also that if the node to be deleted is the *only* node on the list—and thus it is both the first node and the last node—the previous assignment statement assigns the value `nil` to the variable `Head`. Recall that the value `nil` in `Head` indicates an empty list, and so this assignment statement handles the deletion of the only node on a list correctly.

It is really a bit wasteful that node *N* still exists after its deletion from the list. Once you change the value of `Cur` so that it no longer points to *N*, *N* will be in a state of limbo—it still requires storage space, even though the program can no longer access it. If a program were to accumulate many

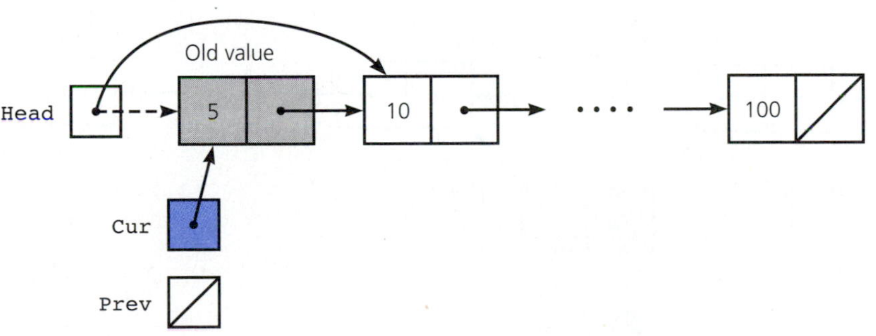

Figure 3-14

Deleting the first node

nodes in this limbo state, its storage requirements might become unreasonably high. Therefore, before you change the value of *Cur*, you should use the statements

Return deleted nodes to the system by using ***dispose***

```
Cur^.Next := nil;
dispose(Cur);
Cur := nil
```

to return node *N* to the system. Setting both *Cur^.Next* and *Cur* to *nil* are examples of defensive programming, which can avoid devastating, subtle errors later in the program.

You have seen the mechanics of deleting a specified node from a linked list. Shortly, we shall incorporate these techniques into a Pascal procedure for deleting a node that contains a specified data value.

Inserting a Node into a Specified Position

Figure 3-15 illustrates the technique of inserting a new node into a specified position of a linked list. You insert the new node, to which the pointer variable *NewPtr* points, between the two nodes that *Prev* and *Cur* point to. As the diagram suggests, you can accomplish the insertion by using the pair of assignment statements

Inserting a node between nodes

```
NewPtr^.Next := Cur;
Prev^.Next := NewPtr
```

The following two questions are analogous to those previously asked about the deletion of a node:

- How did the variables *NewPtr*, *Cur*, and *Prev* come to point to the appropriate nodes?
- Does the method work for inserting a node into any position of a list?

The answer to the first question, like the answer to the corresponding question for deletion, is found by considering the context in which you will use the insertion operation. The case study given later in this chapter, for example, maintains a sorted linked list of cassette titles. That problem

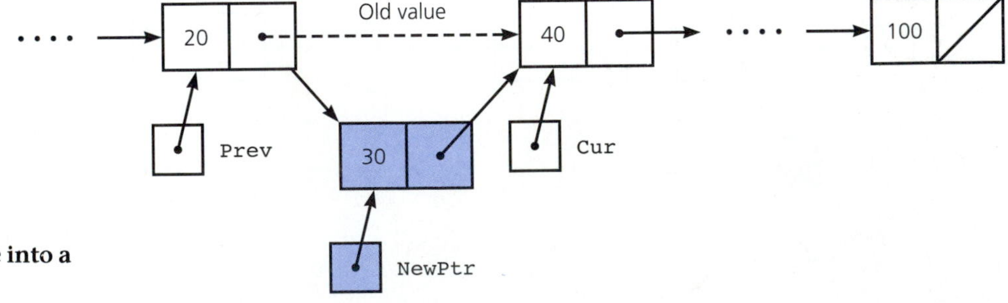

Figure 3-15

Inserting a new node into a linked list

requires a procedure to insert a new title into its proper sorted position in the list. The first step of such a procedure is to establish the values of *Cur* and *Prev* by traversing the list until you find the proper sorted position for the new title. You then create a new node, to which *NewPtr* points, by calling Pascal's *new* procedure:

```
new(NewPtr)
```

After you establish the data portion of this new node, you insert it into the list, as was just described. The details of the insertion procedure appear in the next section.

The answer to the second question is that *insertion, like deletion, must account for special cases.* First, consider the insertion of a node at the beginning of the list, as shown in Figure 3-16. You must make *Head* point to the new node and the new node point to the node that had been at the beginning of the list. You accomplish this by using these statements:

Inserting a node at the beginning of a list

```
NewPtr^.Next := Head;
Head := NewPtr
```

Observe that if the list is empty before the insertion, *Head* is *nil*, so the *Next* field of the new item is set to *nil*. This step is correct because the new item is the last item—as well as the first item—on the list.

Inserting a new node at the end of a list, as shown in Figure 3-17, is potentially a special case because the intention of the pair of assignment statements

If ***Cur*** *is* ***nil****, inserting at the end of a list is not a special case*

```
NewPtr^.Next := Cur;
Prev^.Next := NewPtr
```

is to insert the new node *between* the node that *Cur* points to and the node that *Prev* points to. If you are to insert the new node at the end of the list, to what node should *Cur* point? In this situation it makes sense to view the value of *Cur* as *nil* because as you traverse the list, *Cur* becomes *nil* as it moves past the end of the list. Observe that if *Cur* has the value *nil* and *Prev* points to the last node on the list, then the previous pair of assignment statements will indeed insert the new node at the end of the list.

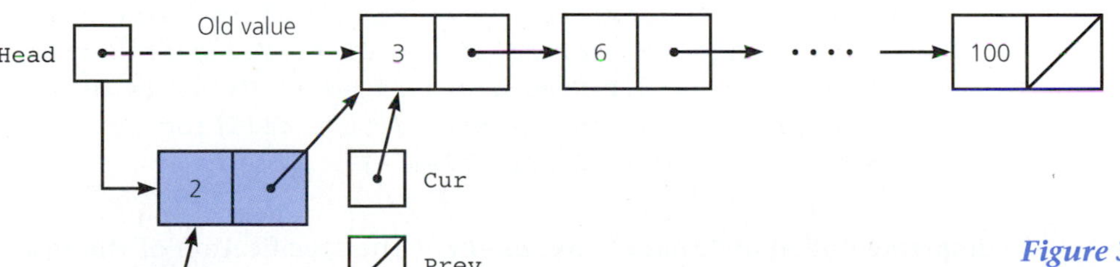

Figure 3-16

Inserting at the beginning of a linked list

Figure 3-17

Inserting at the end of a linked list

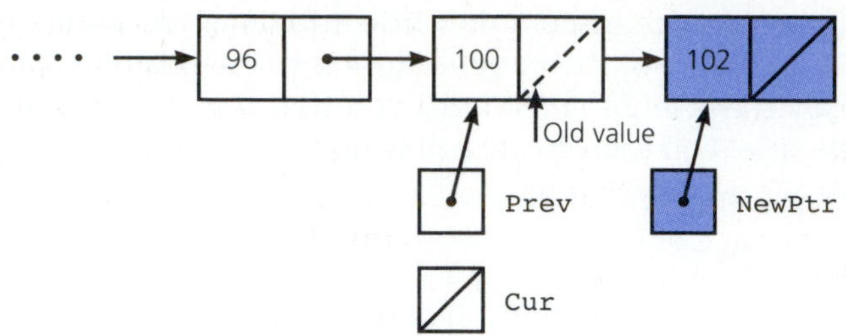

Insertion and Deletion Procedures for a Sorted Linked List

You will often have a linked list that is sorted by its data values. The case study at the end of this chapter presents an application that uses such a linked list. There are also many problems that require you to order a linked list in ways other than by its data values. Examples of such problems and their solutions appear throughout Part III of this book. This section constructs procedures to insert into and delete from a sorted linked list by using the previously developed techniques.

To be more precise, this section implements the following two procedures:

```
LinkedListInsert(Head, NewValue, Success)

{ Inserts a new node into a sorted linked list.
  Precondition: Head points to a sorted linked list of
  distinct items. NewValue is the value to be inserted.
  Postcondition: Inserts NewValue into its proper sorted
  position in the sorted linked list unless the list already
  contains an item with that value, in which case no insertion
  occurs. NewValue is unchanged; the list and possibly Head are
  changed if NewValue is inserted. The boolean flag Success is
  true if the insertion is successful, otherwise it is false. }

LinkedListDelete(Head, Value, Success)

{ Deletes a specified node from a sorted linked list.
  Precondition: Head points to a sorted linked list of
  distinct items. Value is the value to be deleted.
  Postcondition: Deletes the data item equal to Value, if it
  is present, from the sorted linked list. Value is unchanged;
  the list and possibly Head are changed if Value is deleted.
  The boolean flag Success is true if the deletion is
  successful, otherwise it is false. }
```

Implementation of *`LinkedListInsert`*. The specification of the insertion procedure does not allow the list to contain two items with the same value. This restriction is arbitrary, and, in fact, you might very well wish to allow duplicate values in some applications, in which case you would modify the procedure accordingly. In the case study to follow, duplicates are not allowed, so this implementation of `LinkedListInsert` does not allow duplicates. However, the treatment of duplicates is a final refinement to the solution. Initially, the assumption is that the list does not already contain the new data that you want to insert.

There are three high-level steps in the insertion process:

Three steps to insert a new node

```
1. Determine the point of insertion.
2. Create a new node and store the new data in it.
3. Connect the new node to the list by changing pointers.
```

As was observed previously, to determine the point at which the value `NewValue` should be inserted into a sorted list, you must traverse the list from its beginning until you find the appropriate place for `NewValue`. This appropriate place is just before the node that contains the first data item greater than `NewValue`. You know that you will need a pointer `Cur` to the node that is to follow the new node; that is, `Cur` points to the node that contains the first data item greater than `NewValue`. You also need a pointer `Prev` to the node that is to precede the new node; that is, `Prev` points to the node that contains the last data item smaller than `NewValue`. Thus, as you traverse the list, you keep a *trailing* pointer. When you reach the node that contains the first value larger than `NewValue`, the trailing pointer points to the previous node. At this time, you can insert the new node between the two nodes that `Prev` and `Cur` point to, as was described earlier.

A first attempt at some pseudocode that refines the three steps in the algorithm follows:

A first attempt at a solution

```
{ STEP 1: Determine the point of insertion }
{ initialize Prev and Cur to start the traversal from the
  beginning of the list }
Prev := nil
Cur := Head

{ advance Prev and Cur as long as NewValue > the current
  data item }
{ Loop invariant: NewValue > all data portions in node 1
  through node that Prev points to }
while NewValue > Cur^.Data do
begin
    Prev := Cur
    Cur := Cur^.Next
end

{ STEP 2: Create a new node—with NewPtr pointing to it—and
          store the new data in it }
new(NewPtr)
NewPtr^.Data := NewValue
```

```
{ STEP 3 : Connect the new node, to which NewPtr points, to
           the list by changing pointers so that insertion
           is between the two nodes that Prev and Cur point to }
NewPtr^.Next := Cur
Prev^.Next := NewPtr
```

The earlier discussion should have alerted you to the fact that there are two special cases to watch for:

Special cases

- The insertion of a node at the beginning of the list
- The insertion of a node at the end of the list

You have already seen how to handle these special cases, but in the context of this insertion procedure, the detection of the special cases is somewhat tricky.

First consider the insertion of a node at the beginning of the list. This situation arises when the value to be inserted is *smaller* than all the values currently on the list. In this case, the `while` loop in Step 1 of the previous pseudocode is never entered, so `Prev` and `Cur` maintain their original values. In particular, `Prev` maintains its original value of `nil`. Since this is the only situation in which the value of `Prev` is equal to `nil` after the `while` loop, you can detect an insertion at the beginning of the list by comparing `Prev` to `nil`. Thus, you can refine the insertion pseudocode by replacing Step 3 with the following:

When `Prev = nil`, insertion is at the beginning of the list

Correct version of Step 3

```
{ STEP 3 : Connect the new node }
{ test for insertion at the beginning of the list }
if (Prev = nil)
    then          { insert new node at beginning of the list }
    begin
       NewPtr^.Next := Head
       Head := NewPtr
    end

    else          { insert new node between the two nodes that }
    begin         { Prev and Cur point to }
       NewPtr^.Next := Cur
       Prev^.Next := NewPtr
    end
```

The second special case, insertion at the end of the list, arises when the value to be inserted is *greater* than all the values currently on the list. As was noted earlier, you can handle insertion at the end of the list by using the standard pair of assignment statements

```
NewPtr^.Next := Cur
Prev^.Next := NewPtr
```

provided that `Prev` points to the last node on the list and that the value of `Cur` is `nil`. However, the `while` loop

The loop in Step 1 causes a problem

```
while NewValue > Cur^.Data do    { this loop is wrong }
begin
   Prev := Cur
   Cur := Cur^.Next
end
```

in Step 1 of the pseudocode causes a difficulty because the new value is greater than all the values on the list. Eventually, the *while* statement compares *NewValue* to the value in the last node. During that execution of the loop, *Cur* is assigned the value *nil*. After this iteration, *NewValue* is again compared to *Cur^.Data*. This value, when *Cur* is *nil*, is unpredictable.

To solve this problem, you need another test in the termination condition of the *while* loop so that the loop exits when *Cur* becomes *nil*. Thus, in Step 1 of the pseudocode, you replace the *while* statement with

The correct **while** *statement for Step 1*

```
while (Cur <> nil) Cand (NewValue > Cur^.Data) do
```

Recall that the *Cand* (conditional and) operator does not evaluate its second operand if its first operand is false. (Also recall that the *and* operator in Turbo Pascal behaves like the *Cand* operator by default, unless you use the *$B+* compiler directive.) Thus, the pseudocode for Step 1 is

Pseudocode for Step 1

```
Prev := nil
Cur := Head

{ advance Prev and Cur as long as NewValue > the
  current data item }
{ Loop invariant: NewValue > all data portions in
  node 1 through node that Prev points to }
while (Cur <> nil) Cand (NewValue > Cur^.Data) do
begin
    Prev := Cur
    Cur := Cur^.Next
end
```

Notice how the *while* statement solves the problem of inserting a node at the end of the list. In the case where *NewValue* is greater than all the values on the list, *Prev* points to the last node on the list and *Cur* becomes *nil*, thus terminating the *while* loop. Therefore, you can insert the new node at the end of the list by using the standard pair of assignment statements

Insertion at the end of the list is not a special case

```
NewPtr^.Next := Cur
Prev^.Next := NewPtr
```

Observe that the solution correctly handles insertion into an empty list as a special case of insertion at the beginning of the list. When the list is empty, the statement *Cur := Head* assigns *Cur* an initial value of *nil*, and thus the *while* loop is never entered. Therefore, *Prev* maintains its original value of *nil*, indicating an insertion at the beginning of the list. In the revised Step 3, the statement *NewPtr^.Next := Head* executes next and assigns *nil* to the new node's *Next* field. Thus, the new node is set up correctly as both the first and the last node on the list.

You now have a satisfactory solution at the pseudocode level for inserting a value into a linked list that does not already contain that value. Notice that if *NewValue* did exist in the list and if you allowed duplicates, then the solution would insert *NewValue* before the first node that contained *NewValue*.

Now suppose that you want to prevent the insertion of a value that is already present in the list. You can accomplish this task by checking, upon termination of the *while* loop in Step 1, whether *NewValue* is equal to the value in the node that *Cur* points to. If it is, then a duplicate of *NewValue* is in the list, so the insertion is disallowed. Notice that you must be careful to avoid this check when the value of *Cur* is *nil*. You can write this check most naturally in pseudocode by using the *Cor* (conditional or) operator as follows:

Disallow duplicates

```
{ STEP 1a: Check for duplicates }
if (Cur = nil) Cor (NewValue <> Cur^.Data)
   then NewValue is not a duplicate value
   else NewValue is a duplicate value
```

Recall that the *or* operator in Turbo Pascal behaves like the *Cor* operator by default, unless you use the *$B+* compiler directive.

There is only one small Pascal issue that is left to discuss: how to pass the list's head pointer variable to the procedure *LinkedListInsert*. Should the head pointer be a value parameter or a variable (*var*) parameter? It must be a variable parameter, but the reasoning is complex. If your first instinct is that *Head* must be a variable parameter because the procedure will alter the nodes on the list to which *Head* points, you have reached the right conclusion, but for the wrong reason.

Consider what would happen if you passed the head pointer as a value parameter. Figure 3-18 illustrates that although the procedure copies the actual parameter *MyListPtr* into the formal parameter *Head*, the list nodes themselves are *not* copied. Thus, if the procedure makes any changes to the nodes on the list, the changes are made to the actual nodes, not to local copies of the nodes; that is, *any changes the procedure makes to the list are not localized to the procedure.*

Thus, passing the head of a list to a procedure as a value parameter allows the procedure to modify the nodes on the list and even to insert and delete nodes. Therefore, it now would seem that *Head* could be a value parameter in the procedure. This assumption would be correct if not for the possibility that the procedure will change the value of *Head* itself. If the procedure inserts the new node at the beginning of the list, it changes the value of *Head*, and this change must be reflected in the actual parameter (*MyListPtr* in Figure 3-18) that corresponds to *Head*. This required

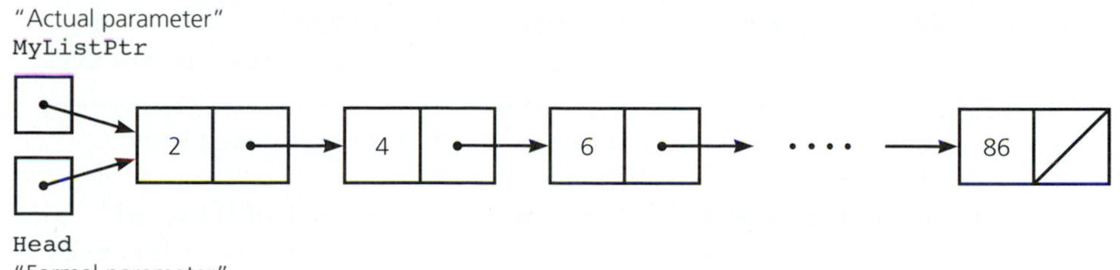

Figure 3-18

A head pointer as a value parameter

change in *MyListPtr* is the only reason that *Head* needs to be a variable parameter!

The Pascal version of the insertion procedure follows. Notice that Step 1 of the pseudocode is implemented as the procedure *FindPosition*, which *LinkedListInsert* calls.

Step 1 implemented as ***FindPosition***

```
procedure FindPosition(Value : integer; Head : ptrType;
                       var Prev, Cur : ptrType);
{ ---------------------------------------------------------
  Determines where an item belongs or exists in a sorted
  linked list.
  Precondition: Value is the value of the data portion of
  the node to be located; Head points to a sorted linked
  list of distinct integers; $B- is in effect.
  Postcondition: If Value is not on the list, Prev and
  Cur point to two adjacent nodes between which Value
  belongs. If Value is on the list, Cur points to the node
  that contains Value. If this node is not first on the
  list, Prev points to the preceding node, otherwise
  Prev = nil.
  --------------------------------------------------------- }
begin
   { initialize Prev and Cur to start the traversal from }
   { the beginning of the list }
   Prev := nil;
   Cur := Head;

   { advance Prev and Cur while Value > current data item }

   { Loop invariant: Value > all data portions in node 1
     through node to which Prev points }
   while (Cur <> nil) and (Value > Cur^.Data) do
   begin
      Prev := Cur;
      Cur := Cur^.Next
   end   { while }
end;   { FindPosition }
```

The final code for ***LinkedListInsert***

```
procedure LinkedListInsert(var Head: ptrType;
                NewValue: integer; var Success: boolean);
{ ---------------------------------------------------------
  Inserts a node into a sorted linked list; disallows
  duplicates.
  Precondition: Head points to a sorted linked list of
  distinct integers. NewValue is the value to be inserted.
  $B- is in effect.
  Postcondition: Inserts NewValue into its proper sorted
  position in the sorted linked list unless the list already
  contains an item with that value, in which case no
  insertion occurs. NewValue is unchanged; the list and
  possibly Head are changed if NewValue is inserted. The
  boolean flag Success is true if the insertion is
  successful, otherwise it is false.
  --------------------------------------------------------- }
var Cur, Prev, NewPtr : ptrType;
begin
   { STEP 1: Determine the point of insertion }
   FindPosition(NewValue, Head, Prev, Cur);

   { STEP 1a: Check for duplicates:
              is NewValue in list already? }
   if (Cur = nil) or (NewValue <> Cur^.Data)
       then           { NewValue is not a duplicate value }
       begin
          { STEP 2: create a new node, which NewPtr points
            to, and store the new data in it }
          new(NewPtr);
          NewPtr^.Data := NewValue;

          { STEP 3: Connect the new node to the list }
          if (Prev = nil) {is insertion at beginning of list?}
              then  { insert new node at beginning of list }
              begin
                  NewPtr^.Next := Head;
                  Head := NewPtr
              end

              else  { insert new node between the two nodes }
              begin {   that Prev and Cur point to }
                  NewPtr^.Next := Cur;
                  Prev^.Next := NewPtr
              end;
              Success := true { insertion is successful }
       end  { NewValue is not a duplicate }
       else Success := false   { disallow insertion
                                  - NewValue in list already }
end;  { LinkedListInsert }
```

Implementation of *LinkedListDelete*. Now turn your attention to implementing the deletion procedure for a sorted linked list. Much of the reasoning for *LinkedListDelete* is analogous to that for *LinkedList-Insert*, so we present only one level of pseudocode and leave the Pascal procedure as an exercise. You may wish to review the earlier discussion of the mechanics of deleting a specified node.

There are three high-level steps in the deletion process.

Three steps to delete a node

```
1. Locate the node in the list that you want to delete.
2. Disconnect this node from the list by changing
   pointers.
3. Return the node to the system.
```

These steps refine into the following pseudocode for the deletion procedure. Note the use of the previous *FindPosition* procedure.

```
LinkedListDelete(Head, Value, Success)

{ Deletes a specified node from a sorted linked list.
  Precondition: Head points to a sorted linked list of
  distinct integers. Value is the value to be deleted.
  Postcondition: Deletes the data item equal to Value, if
  it is present, from the sorted linked list. Value is
  unchanged; the list and possibly Head are changed if
  Value is deleted. The boolean flag Success is true if
  the deletion is successful, otherwise it is false.
  Calls: FindPosition. }
begin
   { STEP 1: Locate node that you want to delete }
   FindPosition(Value, Head, Prev, Cur)

   { STEP 2: If Value is present, disconnect its
     node from the list by changing pointers. }
   if (Cur <> nil) Cand (Value = Cur^.Data)
      then     { Value is present; disconnect its node }
      begin
         if (Prev = nil) { first or interior node? }
            then Head := Cur^.Next          { first }
            else Prev^.Next := Cur^.Next    { interior }

         { STEP 3: Return node to the system }
         Cur^.Next := nil
         dispose(Cur)
         Cur := nil

         Success := true
      end

      else Success := false { Value not in list,
                              deletion impossible }
end   { LinkedListDelete }
```

The implementation of *LinkedListDelete* is left as an exercise.

There is one more issue to raise: What is the fate of any pointer variable that points to a disposed node? The procedure call *dispose(p)* does not affect *p* in Turbo Pascal. Thus, it is possible for a program to follow *p* to a node that is no longer active, which is why you should assign *nil* to *p* immediately after calling *dispose*. However, consider the situation

The pointer q points to a disposed node

```
q := p;
dispose(p);
p := nil
```

as illustrated in Figure 3-19. Even though *p* is *nil*, *q* still points to the disposed node. Later the system might reallocate this node—via the *new* procedure—and *q* may still point to it. You can imagine some of the errors that might ensue if a program mistakenly followed the pointer *q* and reached a node within an entirely unexpected data structure! It would be useful if the *dispose* procedure could eliminate the potential for this type of program error by setting to *nil* all pointers to a disposed node. Unfortunately, this task is very difficult. Because the procedure *dispose* cannot determine which variables—in addition to *p*—point to the node to be freed, it will have to remain the programmer's responsibility not to follow a pointer to a freed node.

Saving and Restoring a Linked List by Using a File

As a final problem, we discuss how you can save and restore a linked list by using an external file, so that you can preserve the list between runs of a program. The case study in this chapter utilizes this technique in a business application. The program maintains a linked list of information about a retail store's inventory. Since the program is not running continually, you need a way to save the list so that the program can restore it each time you run the program.

The technique is demonstrated here by saving and restoring a linked list of integers like the lists that were used earlier in this chapter. Recall the following definitions and declaration:

```
type   ptrType = ^nodeType;
       nodeType = record
           Data : integer;
           Next : ptrType;
       end;

var    Head : ptrType;
```

To begin, suppose that your program needs to write a linked list of integers to a file in a way that will allow you to restore the list later. What should you write to the file? You might be tempted to write each node in its entirety—that is, to write each entire record, which contains an integer field and a pointer field, to a file of type *nodeType*. However, writing the pointer fields serves no useful purpose, because once the program has ter-

Do not write the pointer fields to the file

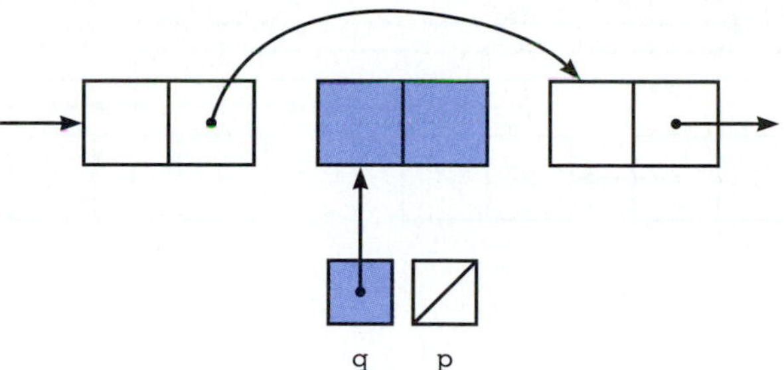

Figure 3-19

An incorrect reference to a deleted and disposed node

minated, the saved pointer values from the records are meaningless. Although the address in a pointer field, which referenced a memory location, was valid before you wrote the list out to the file, the interpretation of the address is not well defined after program execution terminates. For example, when you execute the program again, the saved address may reference a memory location of some completely different structure within the program or even within another program altogether. Thus, the solution of writing out the entire node to a file is not a good one.

It turns out that all you need to do is to write the data portion—in this case an integer—of each node to the file, because it is easy to restore the list structure from only this information. The following procedure, *SaveList*, performs this task by writing the integers to a general file of integers, although you just as easily could write them to a textfile. Figure 3-20 illustrates the action of *SaveList*.

Save a linked list by writing only its data to a file

```
const NameLength = 12;

type  nameType = string[NameLength];

procedure SaveList(Head: ptrType; SaveFileName: nameType);
{ ----------------------------------------------------------
  Saves a linked list's data in a general file of integers.
  Precondition: Head points to the linked list.
  SaveFileName is the name of an external general file to
  be created.
  Postcondition: The general file SaveFileName of
  integers contains the linked list's data. The file is
  closed; Head and the linked list are unchanged.
  ---------------------------------------------------------- }
var  Cur : ptrType;
     F : file of integer;

begin
{ initialize }
    assign(F, SaveFileName);
    rewrite(F);
    Cur := Head;
```

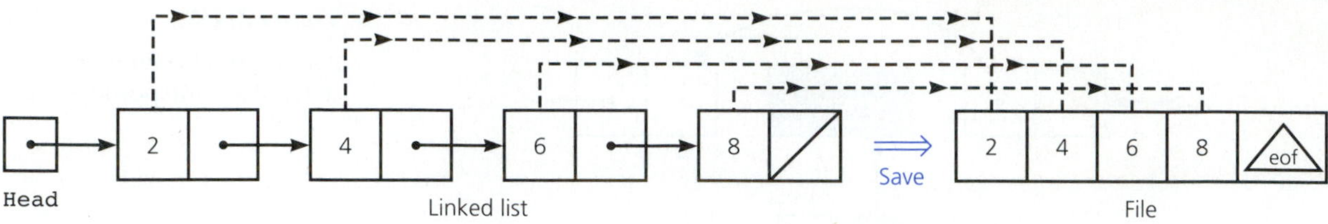

Figure 3-20

Saving a linked list in a file

```
{ traverse the list to the end, writing out each item }
   while (Cur <> nil) do
   begin
      write(F, Cur^.Data);
      Cur := Cur^.Next
   end;  { while }
   close(F)
end;  { SaveList }
```

Once you have saved the linked list's data in the file, you can re-create the list anytime you wish. After the program that originally created the list has terminated, the data endures in the file. Thus, when the program (or another program) is active again, it can restore the list by reading the data from the file.

To develop a procedure to restore a linked list, you should first notice that the procedure *SaveList* writes the integers to the file in the order that they appear on the list. The *RestoreList* procedure thus must build the list by reading the file and placing each newly read integer at the end of the list, as Figure 3-21 illustrates.

A pseudocode solution for *RestoreList* is

```
while not end of file do
begin
    Read in the next integer
    Append the integer to the end of the list
end
```

To add a new integer to the end of the list, you must perform these four steps:

Four steps to add a node to the end of a linked list

1. Use `new` to allocate a new node for the list.
2. Set the pointer field in the last node on the list to point to the new node.
3. Put the new integer in the new node.
4. Set the pointer field in the new node to `nil`.

Use a tail pointer to facilitate adding nodes to the end of a linked list

Each time you read a new integer, you must get to the last node on the list. One way to accomplish this is to traverse the list each time you read a new integer. A much more efficient method uses a pointer variable *Tail* to remember where the end of the list is—just as *Head* remembers where the

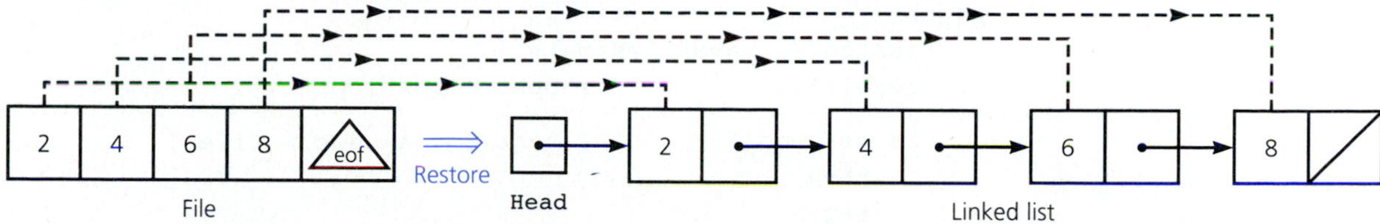

Figure 3-21

Restoring a linked list from a file

beginning of the list is. Like *Head*, *Tail* is external to the list. Figure 3-22 illustrates a linked list that has both head and tail pointers.

With *Tail* pointing to the end of the list, you can perform both Step 1 and Step 2 by using the single statement

```
new(Tail^.Next)
```

This call to *new* allocates a new node and sets the *Next* field of the last node on the list to point to this new node. Notice that you could have accomplished the same task by using a temporary pointer variable as follows:

```
new(Temp);
Tail^.Next := Temp
```

You thus have an easy method for adding a new integer to the end of the list. Initially, however, when you insert the first integer into an empty list, *Tail* does not point to anything. One way to handle this fact is to treat the first insertion as a special case before the *while* loop. This approach leads to the Pascal procedure *RestoreList*:

Treat the first insertion as a special case

Creating a linked list from data in a file

```
procedure RestoreList(var Head : ptrType;
                      SaveFileName : nameType);
{ ---------------------------------------------------------
  Creates a linked list from the data in a general file.
  Precondition: SaveFileName is the name of an existing
  external general file of integers.
  Postcondition: Head points to the created linked list;
  if the file is empty, Head is nil. The file is unchanged
  and closed.
  --------------------------------------------------------- }
var  Tail : ptrType;
     F : file of integer;
```

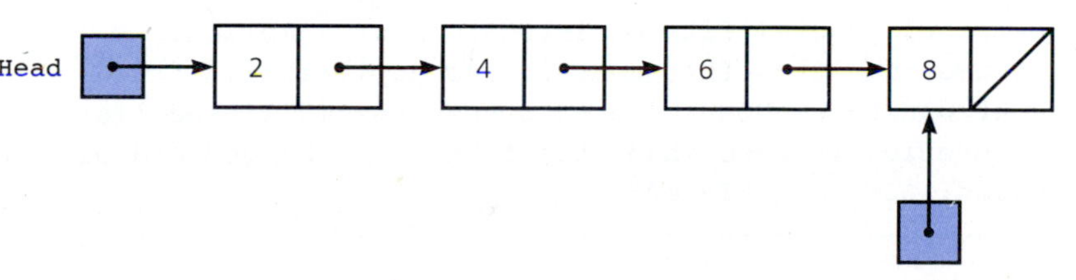

Figure 3-22

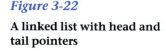

A linked list with head and tail pointers

```
begin
   assign(F, SaveFileName);
   reset(F);               { open F for input }

   if not eof(F)           { test for an empty file }
      then
      begin
         { add the first integer to the list }
         new(Head);
         read(F, Head^.Data);
         Head^.Next := nil;
         Tail := Head;

         { add the remaining integers to the list }
         while not eof(F) do
         begin
            new(Tail^.Next);
            Tail := Tail^.Next;
            read(F, Tail^.Data);
            Tail^.Next := nil
         end { while }
      end   { then }

      else Head := nil;   { the file is empty - return the
                            empty list }
   close(F)
end; { RestoreList }
```

Now suppose that a file contains integers that are not in the order you want. For example, suppose that you want the integers to appear in ascending order on your linked list, but in the file they are in no particular order at all. You can solve this problem easily by using the previous *LinkedListInsert* procedure. Because *LinkedListInsert* inserts new items into their proper sorted order, the following Pascal procedure will create an ordered linked list from an unordered file:

Creating a sorted linked list from arbitrary data in a file

```
procedure BuildSortedList(var Head : ptrType;
                              DataFileName : nameType);
{ ---------------------------------------------------------
  Constructs a linked list that contains in sorted order the
  integers from a general unordered file of integers.
  Precondition: DataFileName is the name of an existing
  external general file of integers. For simplicity,
  assume that this file contains no duplicates.
  Postcondition: Head points to the created linked list,
  as previously described; the file is unchanged and closed.
  Calls: LinkedListInsert.
  --------------------------------------------------------- }
```

```
var  Value : integer;
     F : file of integer;
     Success : boolean; { Success is provided for
            LinkedListInsert, which always returns Success =
            true because the file contains no duplicates.
            Thus, Success is ignored here.}
begin
   assign(F, DataFileName);
   reset(F);
   Head := nil;
   while (not eof(F)) do
   begin
      read(F, Value);
      LinkedListInsert(Head, Value, Success)
   end; { while }

   close(F)
end;    {BuildSortedList}
```

This type of sorting algorithm is known as an **insertion sort** and is among the sorting algorithms that Chapter 7 will consider.

Using Structured Types in Data Fields

Although for simplicity the previous linked lists used integer data fields, you need not restrict yourself to simple data types. In fact, the advantages of a linked list are more dramatic when you use data fields of a structured data type such as an array or a record. For example, suppose that you want a linked list of customer names, where each name is a string of characters. The following statements describe such a list:

```
const MaxString = 20;
type  dataType = string[MaxString];
      ptrType = ^nodeType;
      nodeType = record
          Data : dataType;
          Next : ptrType
      end; { record }

var   Head : ptrType;
```

In fact, you could redefine *dataType* so that it is a record with several fields that include additional details about each customer. (Notice how easy such a change would be. The use of *dataType* is one way to make a program simple to modify.)

VARIATIONS OF THE LINKED LIST

This section briefly introduces several variations of the linked list that you have just seen. These variations often are useful, and you will encounter them later in this text. Many of the implementation details are left as exercises. Note that in addition to the data structures discussed in this section, it is possible to have structures such as arrays of pointers to linked lists and linked lists of linked lists. These structures are also left as exercises.

Circular Linked Lists

When you access a computer by using a remote terminal, you are sharing the computer with many other users. The **time-sharing system** must organize the users so that only one user at a time has access to CPU time. By ordering the users, the system can give each user a turn. Because users regularly enter and exit the system (by logging on or logging off), a linked list of user names allows the system to maintain order without shifting names when it makes insertions to and deletions from the list. Thus, the system can traverse the linked list from the beginning and give each user on the list a turn at CPU time. What must the system do when it reaches the end of the list? It must return to the beginning of the list. However, the fact that the last node of a linked list does not point to another node can be an inconvenience.

If you want to access the first node of a linked list after accessing the last node, you must resort to the head pointer. Suppose that you change the `Next` field of the list's last node so that, instead of containing `nil`, it points to the first node. The result is a **circular linked list**, as illustrated in Figure 3-23. In contrast, the linked list you saw earlier is said to be **linear**.

Every node on a circular linked list has a successor

Every node on a circular linked list points to a successor, so you can start at any node and traverse the entire list. Although you could think of a circular list as not having either a beginning or an end, you still would have an external pointer to one of the nodes on the list. Thus, it remains natural to think of both a first and a last node on a circular list. If the external pointer points to the "first" node, you still would have to traverse the list to get to the last node. However, if the external pointer—call it `List`—points to the "last" node, as it does in Figure 3-24, you can access both the first and last nodes without a traversal, because `List^.Next`

Figure 3-23
A circular linked list

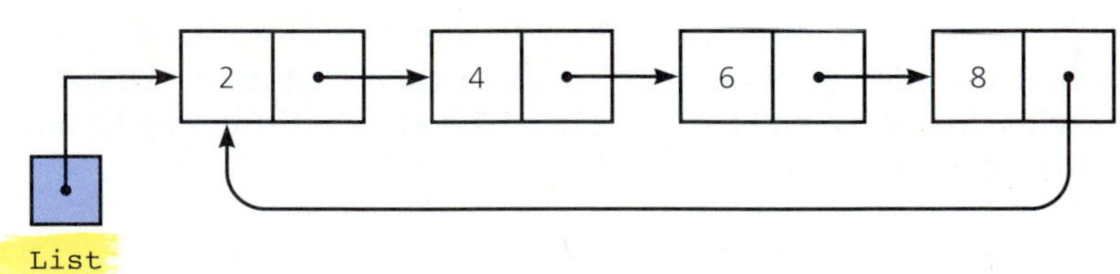

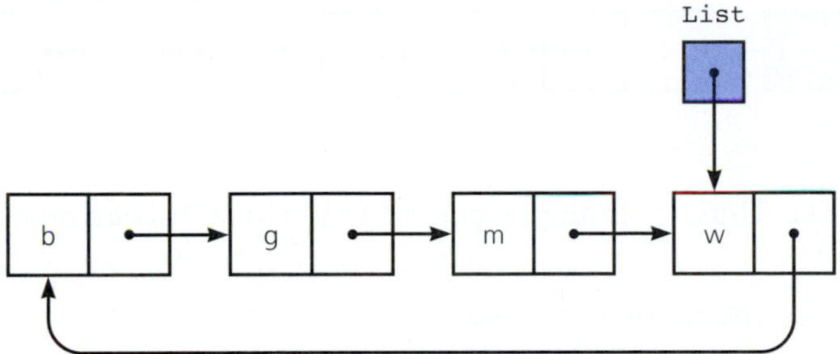

Figure 3-24

A circular linked list with an external pointer to the last node

points to the first node. In fact, the somewhat strange notation *List^.Next^.Data* is the data field of the first node.

A *nil* value in the external pointer indicates an empty list, as it did for a linear list. However, no node on a circular list contains *nil* in its *Next* field. Thus, you must alter the algorithm for detecting when you have traversed an entire list. By simply comparing the current pointer *Cur* to the external pointer *List*, you can determine when you have traversed the entire circular list. For example, the following Pascal statements write the data fields of every node on a circular list, assuming that *List* points to the "last" node and *Print* is a procedure to write a data field in an appropriate format:

No node on a circular linked list contains **nil**

Write the data that is on a circular linked list

```
if List <> nil
    then                          { if list is not empty }
    begin
       Cur := List;               { initialize Cur }
       repeat
          Cur := Cur^.Next;       { point to next node }
          Print(Cur^.Data)        { write data portion }
       until Cur = List           { quit at end of list }
    end
```

Operations such as insertion into and deletion from a circular linked list are left as exercises.

Dummy Head Nodes

Both the *LinkedListInsert* and *LinkedListDelete* procedures presented earlier for linear lists require a special case to handle action at the first position of a list. Although these procedures correctly handle this case, many people prefer a method that eliminates the need for the special case. One such method is to add a **dummy head node**—as Figure 3-25 depicts—that is always present, even when the list is empty. In this way, the item at the first position of the list is actually in the second node.

When you use a dummy head node, there is no special case in the *LinkedListInsert* and *LinkedListDelete* procedures, because these procedures will initialize *Prev* to point to the dummy head node rather

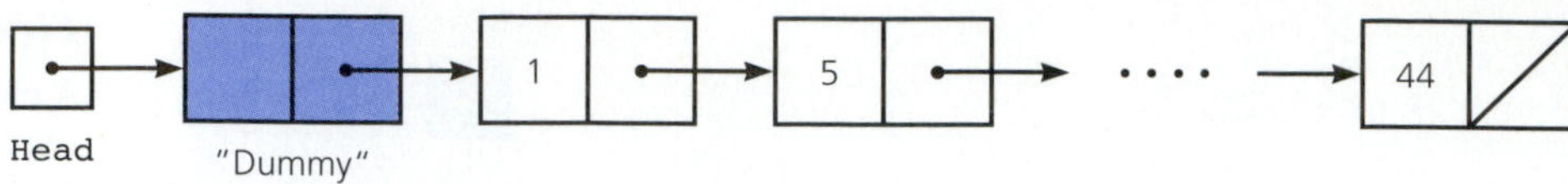

Figure 3-25

A dummy head node

than to *nil*. Thus, for example, in the *LinkedListDelete* procedure the statement

```
Prev^.Next := Cur^.Next
```

deletes from the list the node to which *Cur* points, regardless of whether or not this node is the first element on the list.

Despite the fact that a dummy head node eliminates the need for a special case, we do not, in general, advocate its use with a linked list. We feel that handling the first list position separately is less distracting than is altering the list's structure by adding a dummy head node. However, dummy head nodes are useful with doubly linked lists, as you will see in the next section.

Some people like to put global information about the list—such as its length and the smallest and largest value on the list—in a dummy head node, as Figure 3-26a shows. Unless the dummy head node is exactly the same type of record as the other nodes on the list, the list operations will still require a special case for the first position. This situation occurs because one Pascal pointer variable can point to only one type of record. Thus, if the data type of the dummy head node differs from the other nodes, you cannot use the same pointer variable to point both to the dummy head node and to another list node. For example, you cannot initialize *Prev* to point to the dummy head node and then advance it to traverse down the list. One way to program around this problem is to use a variant record.

Our own preference for handling global information is to put the information **in a head record** that contains the external pointer to the first node on the list, as shown in Figure 3-26b. The following Pascal statements

Figure 3-26

(a) A dummy head node with global information; (b) a head record with global information

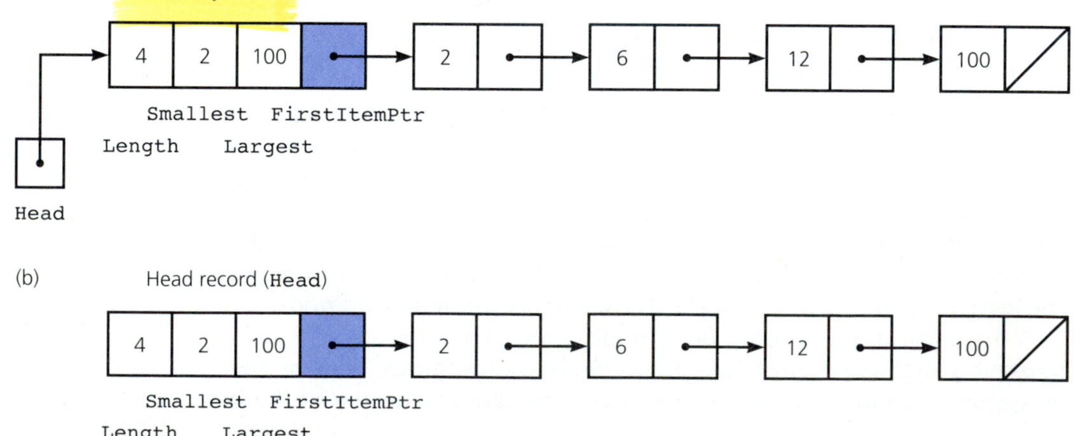

establish the head record *Head*:

```
type headRecordType = record
        Length, Smallest, Largest : integer;
        FirstItemPtr : ptrType    { ptrType = ^nodeType
                                    as before }
     end;    { record }

var  Head : headRecordType;
```

You can use a head record for global information instead of a dummy head node

Whether or not you use a dummy head node or a head record is, however, a matter of personal taste.

Doubly Linked Lists

Suppose that you have a method for directly accessing the node that you wish to delete from a linked list. If you have been able to locate the node without a traversal, you will not have established a trailing pointer to the node that precedes it on the list. Without a trailing pointer, you will be unable to delete the node. You could overcome this problem if you had a way to back up from the node that you wish to delete to the node that precedes it. A **doubly linked list** will solve this problem because each of its nodes has pointers to both the next node and the previous node.

Each node on a doubly linked list points to both its predecessor and its successor

Consider a sorted list of customer names such that each node contains, in addition to its data fields, two pointer fields, *Precede* and *Next*. As usual, the *Next* field of node *N* points to the node that follows *N* on the list. The *Precede* field points to the node that precedes *N* on the list. Thus, the form of the sorted linked list of customers is as shown in Figure 3-27.

Notice that if *Cur* points to a node *N*, you can get a pointer to the node that precedes *N* on the list by using the assignment statement

```
Prev := Cur^.Precede
```

A doubly linked list thus allows you to delete a node without traversing the list to establish a trailing pointer.

Because there are more pointers to set, the mechanics of inserting into and deleting from a doubly linked list are a bit more involved than for a singly linked list. In addition, the special cases at the beginning or the end of the list are more complicated. It is common to eliminate the special cases by structuring a doubly linked list to contain a dummy head node. Although dummy head nodes may not be worthwhile for singly linked

Figure 3-27

A doubly linked list

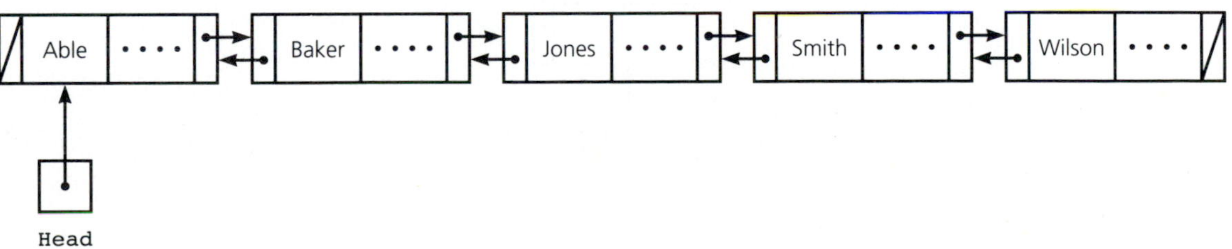

Dummy head nodes are useful in doubly linked lists

lists, the more complicated special cases for doubly linked lists make them very attractive.

As is shown in Figure 3-28a, the external pointer `ListHead` always points to the dummy head node. Notice that the head node is of the same type as the other nodes on the list; thus it also contains `Precede` and `Next` pointer fields. You can link the list so that it becomes a **circular doubly linked list.** The `Next` field of the head node then points to the first "real node"—for example, the first customer name—on the list, and the `Precede` field of the first real node points back to the head node. Similarly, the `Precede` field of the head node then points to the last node on the list, and the `Next` field of the last node points to the head node. Note that the dummy head node is present even when the list is empty. In this case, both pointer fields of the dummy head node point to the head node itself, as Figure 3-28b illustrates.

A circular doubly linked list eliminates special cases for insertion and deletion

By using a circular doubly linked list, you can perform insertions and deletions without special cases: Inserting into and deleting from the first or last position is the same as for any other position. First consider how to delete the node *N* that `P` points to. As Figure 3-29 illustrates, you need to

1. Change the `Next` field of the node that precedes *N* so that it points to the node that follows *N*.
2. Change the `Precede` field of the node that follows *N* so that it points to the node that precedes *N*.

The following assignment statements accomplish these two steps:

Deleting a node

```
{ delete the node that P points to }
P^.Precede^.Next := P^.Next;
P^.Next^.Precede := P^.Precede
```

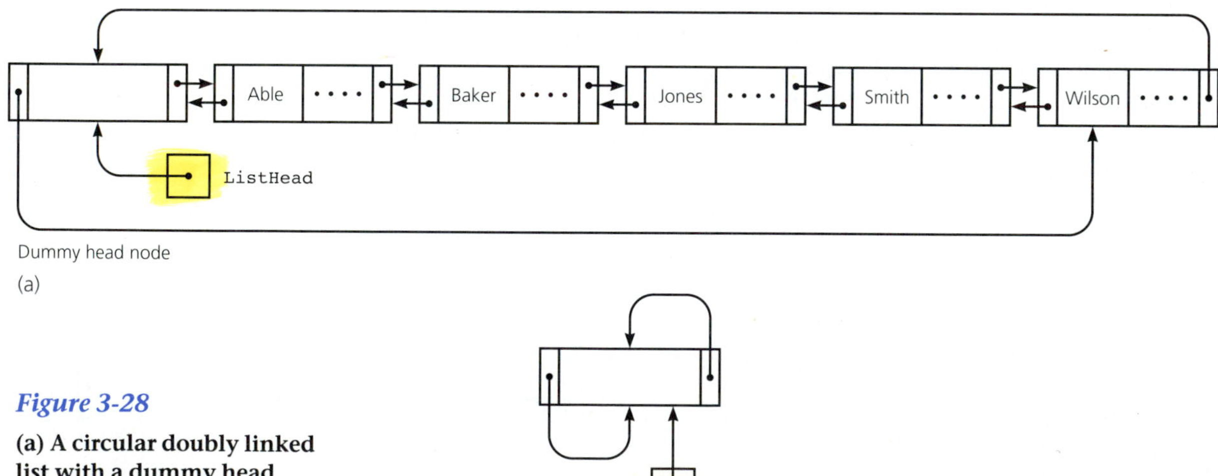

Figure 3-28

(a) A circular doubly linked list with a dummy head node; (b) an empty list with a head node

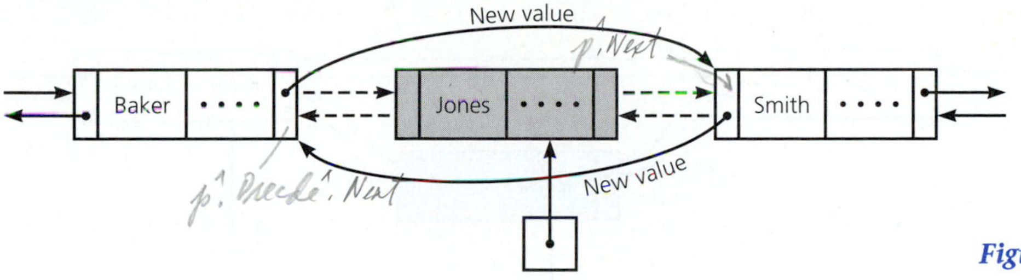

Figure 3-29
Pointer changes for deletion

You should convince yourself that these statements work even when the node to be deleted is the first, last, or only data (nonhead) node on the list.

Now consider how to insert a node into a circular doubly linked list. In general, the fact that the list is doubly linked does not save you from having to traverse the list to find the proper place for the new item. For example, if you insert a new customer name, you must find the proper place within the sorted linked list for the new record. The following traversal sets *Cur* to point to the node that should follow the new node on the list:

Traverse the list to locate the insertion point

```
Cur := ListHead^.Next
while (Cur <> ListHead) Cand (NewName > Cur^.Name) do
    Cur := Cur^.Next
```

Notice that if you want to insert the new record either at the end of the list or into an empty list, the loop will set *Cur* to point to the dummy head node.

As Figure 3-30 illustrates, once *Cur* points to the node that is to follow the new node, you need to

1. Set the *Next* field of the new node to point to the node that is to follow it.
2. Set the *Precede* field of the new node to point to the node that is to precede it.
3. Set the *Precede* field of the node that is to follow the new node so that it points to the new node.
4. Set the *Next* field of the node that is to precede the new node so that it points to the new node.

The following assignment statements accomplish these four steps, assuming that *P* points to the new node:

Inserting a node

```
{ insert the new node pointed to by P before the node
  pointed to by Cur }
P^.Next := Cur;
P^.Precede := Cur^.Precede;
P^.Next^.Precede := P;
P^.Precede^.Next := P
```

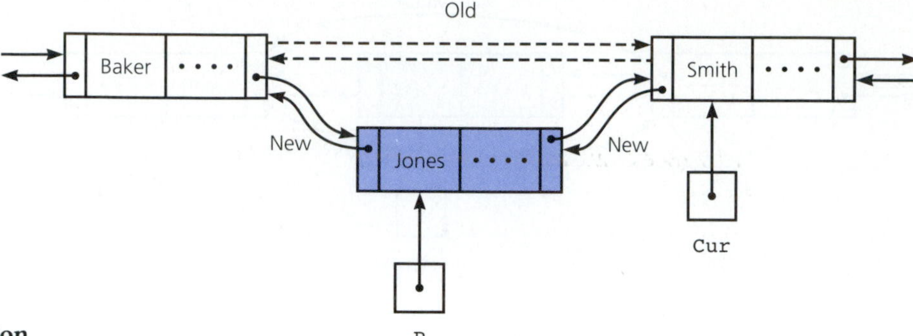

Figure 3-30

Pointer changes for insertion

You should convince yourself that these statements work even when you insert the node into the beginning of a list, at the end of a list—in which case `Cur` points to the head node—or into an empty list, in which case `Cur` also points to the head node.

A CASE STUDY: MAINTAINING AN INVENTORY

The case study in this section illustrates the issues of program design and development that the previous chapters discuss. The solution to this particular problem, maintaining an inventory, demonstrates how you can solve a complex problem effectively by using the principles of top-down design and modularity. The solution also illustrates Pascal list processing and file handling.

Statement of the Inventory Problem

The object is to write an interactive program that will maintain an inventory for a videocassette dealer. The inventory consists of a list of movie titles and the following inventory information associated with each title:

- **Have value:** number of cassettes currently in stock.
- **Want value:** number of cassettes that should be in stock. (When the have value is less than the want value, more cassettes are ordered.)
- **Wait list:** list of names of people waiting for the title if it is sold out.

Because the inventory program will not be running at all times, there should be a mechanism for saving the inventory in a file and for restoring the inventory when the program is run again.

Input and output are as follows:

INPUT

- A file that contains a previously saved inventory.
- A file that contains information on an incoming shipment of cassettes. (See command D under "Action Commands.")
- Single-letter commands—with arguments where necessary—that inquire about or modify the inventory and that the user will enter interactively.

OUTPUT

- A file that contains the updated inventory. (Note that any inventory items with have value = 0, want value = 0, and an empty wait list are removed from the inventory and do not appear in the file.)
- Output as specified by the individual commands.

The program should be able to execute the following commands:

Information Commands

H	(help)	Print a summary of the available commands.
I <*title*>	(inquire)	Print the inventory information for a specified title.
L	(list)	List the entire inventory (in alphabetical order by title).

Action Commands

A <*title*>	(add)	Add a new title to the inventory. Prompt for initial want value.
M <*title*>	(modify)	Modify the want value for a specified title.
D	(delivery)	Take delivery of a shipment of cassettes, assuming that the clerk has entered the shipment information (titles and counts) into a file. Read in the file, mail out cassettes to the people on the wait list, and update the have values in the inventory accordingly. Note that the program must add an item to the inventory if a delivered title is not present in the current inventory.
O	(order)	Write a purchase order for additional cassettes based on a comparison of the have and want values in

		the inventory, so that the have value is brought up to the want value.
R	(return)	Write a return order based on a comparison of the have and want values in the inventory and decrease the have values accordingly (make the return). The object is to reduce the have value to the want value.
S <*title*>	(sell)	Decrease the count for the specified title by 1. If the title is sold out, put a name on the wait list for the title.
Q	(quit)	

You can use this problem statement as a high-level specification for a computer program. The sections that follow describe the process of going from a statement of the problem to a program that effectively solves the problem—that is, meets its specification. You can view this problem-solving process as having three main stages:

1. The top-down design of a solution
2. The bottom-up implementation of the solution
3. The final set of refinements to the program

Although these stages appear as isolated topics in the following discussion, you must always keep a global perspective. You cannot complete a stage in total isolation from the others.

Top-Down Design of a Solution

This section describes the highlights of a methodical, top-down approach to the inventory problem. At many steps in the development of the solution, you must make choices. Although the following discussion may give the illusion that the choices are clear-cut, such is not always the case. In reality there are more trade-offs between the choices and more false starts (wrong choices considered) than we possibly can describe in a reasonable amount of space. However, the presentation tries to convey, as much as possible, the spirit of the problem-solving process.

The discussion may also give the illusion that we solved all subproblems in complete isolation from other subproblems. In reality, as we have said, many are best solved in tandem with other subproblems and with a perspective of the overall picture in mind. The methodology that we describe gives a framework for the systematic solution of large problems. We deal with some of the more subtle aspects of weighing trade-offs and keeping the big picture in proper perspective in Parts III and IV of this book.

Consider now the top-down design of a solution to the inventory problem. From the statement of the inventory problem, it is clear that at the highest level you can break the inventory problem into the following subtasks, as Figure 3-31 illustrates:

I. Restore the current inventory from an external file.

II. Execute user commands to ask about or modify the inventory.

III. Save the current inventory in an external file.

Before proceeding with the refinement of the three subproblems, consider the choice of a data structure. Both Chapter 4 and Part III of this book demonstrate that you should base the choice of an abstract data type on the operations that you expect to perform on the data. Because the ADT is an integral part of all phases of the solution process, you should refine it in a top-down fashion along with the algorithm. At this time, however, the emphasis is on using data structures rather than on developing and choosing among ADT's.

The problem description suggests some common operations that you will perform on the inventory:

- List the inventory in alphabetical order by title (L command).
- Find the inventory item associated with a title (I, M, D, and S commands).
- Insert new inventory items (A and D commands).

Recall that associated with each title there might be a list of people who are waiting for that title. You must be able to add new people to the end of this list when they want a cassette that is sold out and to delete people from the beginning of the list when new cassettes are delivered.

Part III of this book discusses various ADT's that support these kinds of operations in an efficient way. For now, we settle for a data structure that is both reasonable with respect to more advanced analysis and is consistent

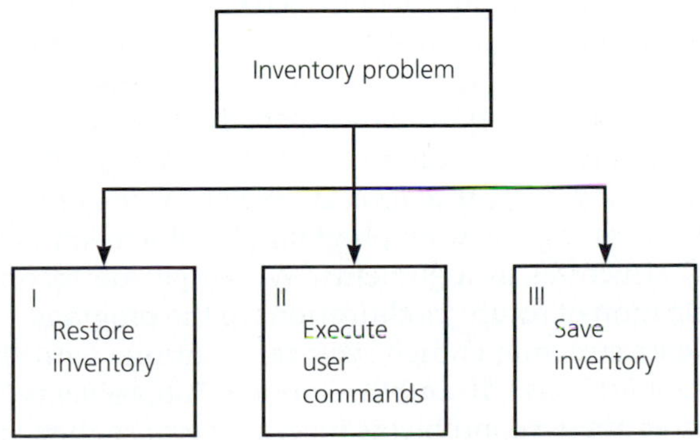

Figure 3-31

Division of the problem into subproblems

with the level of material presented so far. Chapter 12 revises this solution so that it utilizes ADT's and more sophisticated data structures.

You can represent the inventory as follows:

- The inventory will be a linked list of data items, sorted by the title that each item represents.
- Each item will contain a title, the number in stock (a have value), the number desired (a want value), and a pointer to the beginning of a linked list of people's names (the wait list).
- Because you must be able to add new names to the end of an item's wait list, each item will also contain a pointer to the last name on its list. (Recall the insertion and deletion operations for a linked list that were illustrated earlier in the chapter.)

Figure 3-32 and the following Pascal type definitions summarize these choices:

```
const MaxString = 15;
type  nameType = string[MaxString];
      { wait list - people waiting for certain cassettes }
      waitPtrType = ^waitNodeType;
      waitNodeType = record
          Who  : nameType;
          Next : waitPtrType
      end;   { record }

      { inventory list - list of stock items }
      stockPtrType = ^stockNodeType;
      stockNodeType = record
          Title : nameType;
          Have, Want : integer;
          Wait, Last : waitPtrType;
          Next : stockPtrType
      end;   { record }
```

Now consider how the data structures will interact with the rest of the program. In Chapter 1 you saw reasons for avoiding global structures in general, but it might be appropriate to make a structure global if it is an integral part of all (or almost all) aspects of the program. If you design the inventory program to operate on a single, fixed inventory, then it is reasonable to treat the inventory structure globally. However, if you design—or might later modify—the program to manipulate more than one inventory (for example, if you want to look at saved histories of the inventory), then you want to have general subprograms, to which you can pass different inventory structures as arguments. We chose the second approach here, in anticipation of future modifications to the program.

With the data structure chosen, you can continue with the design of solutions to Subproblems I, II, and III. Consider Subproblems I and III first. You can consider these subproblems together because they are so closely

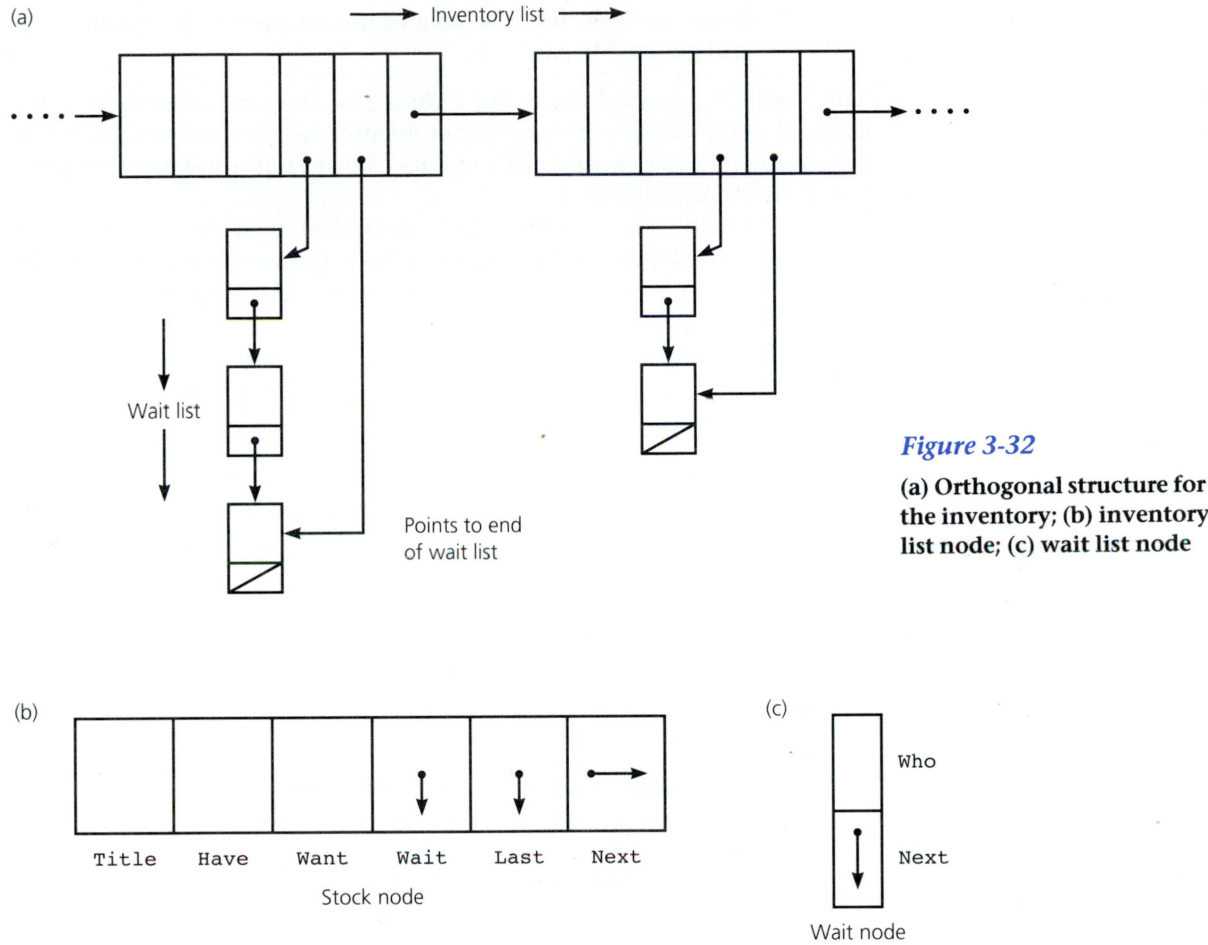

Figure 3-32

(a) Orthogonal structure for the inventory; (b) inventory list node; (c) wait list node

associated: They both deal with communication between the internal data structure for processing the inventory and an external file for saving the inventory.

At the highest level, Subproblem I requires you to read the inventory from a file into the data structure. Thus, for each inventory item you must be able to read the title, the have and want values, and the wait list. Similarly, Subproblem III requires you to write the inventory to a file.

Before you can proceed, you must consider how you will save the inventory in a file. Recall that you save a linked list in a file by saving only the data portion of the list items. However, there is one slight complication here: Each inventory item has an associated sublist—the wait list. Thus,

- You need a second file for the names on the wait lists because the items in a file must all be of the same type.
- To restore the wait lists, you must know their lengths. In particular, if you store the names on all the wait lists together in a

single file, you must be able to determine where one list ends and the next begins.

The need for a second file is not a difficulty, but you must modify the original statement of the inventory problem to accommodate this change because it specifies "a file." This change is not at all unreasonable given the spirit of the problem.

To address the second observation, recall that the have value of a stock item is the number of items currently in stock. It is reasonable to adopt the convention that a negative have value is the number of cassettes that you are short—the size of the wait list!

The following statements summarize this discussion. They contain a slight modification to the previous type definitions and new definitions for the two files.

```
const MaxString = 15;
type  nameType = string[MaxString];
      { wait list - people waiting for certain
        cassettes }
      waitPtrType = ^waitNodeType;
      waitNodeType = record
          Who  : nameType;
          Next : waitPtrType
      end;    { record }

      { data fields for a single stock item }
      stockInfoType = record
          Title : nameType;
          Have, Want : integer
      end;    { record }

      { node on inventory list }
      stockPtrType = ^stockNodeType;
      stockNodeType = record
          Item : stockInfoType ;
          Wait, Last : waitPtrType;
          Next : stockPtrType
      end;    { record }

      { file of stock items for the inventory list }
      stockFileType = file of stockInfoType;

      { file of names for the wait lists }
      nameFileType = file of nameType;
```

If you redefine the inventory record, as Figure 3-33 shows, so that it contains a subrecord that consists of the title, its have value, and its want value, you can keep these items together in the file. Thus, the previous concern of saving and restoring a linked list is addressed.

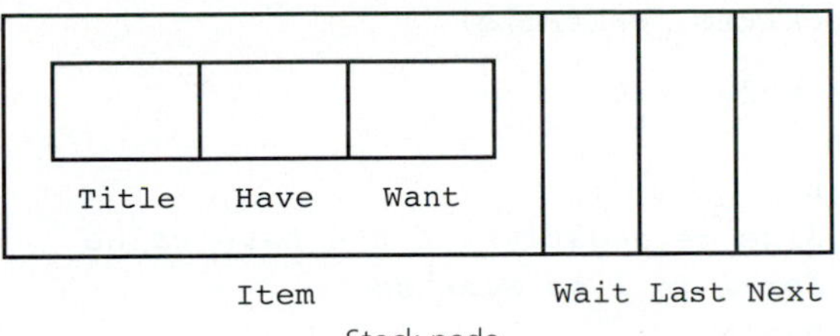

Figure 3-33

Modified node structure

With this data structure, you can attempt the first version of a solution to Subproblem I.

Subproblem I: Restore the current inventory from external files. At a very high level, the following procedure, `GetInv`, solves this subproblem:

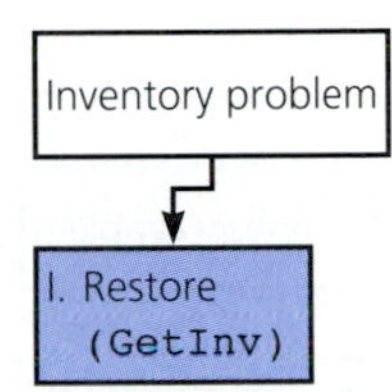

Figure 3-34

```
GetInv(InvList, InvFile, WaitFile)

    while not eof(InvFile) do
    begin
       Read a stock item from the inventory file
       Add the item to the end of the inventory list
       Read in the wait list associated with the stock item
    end
```

As was described earlier, the addition of the first node to a linked list is a special case. Therefore, you can refine the first attempt as follows:

```
GetInv(InvList, InvFile, WaitFile)

    if not eof(InvFile)
       then
       begin
          { get the first item for the inventory list }
          Read the first item from the inventory file
          Add it as the first item on the inventory list
          GetWait(StockItem, WaitFile) { Subproblem I.1 }

          { get the rest of the list }
          while not eof(InvFile) do
          begin
             Read the next item from the inventory file
             Add it to the end of the inventory list
             GetWait(StockItem, WaitFile)
          end
       end
```

Figure 3-35

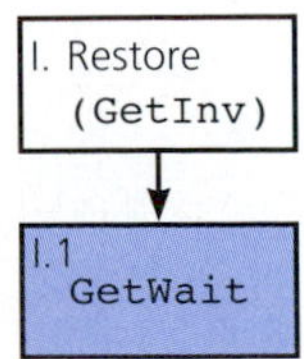

Subproblem I.1: Read in the wait list for a stock item. This procedure uses the fact that you can determine the size of the wait list from the have value of the stock item.

```
GetWait(StockItem, WaitFile)

    if have value < 0
       then
       begin
           Size := negative of the have value
           for i := 1 to Size do
           begin
               Read a name from the wait file
               Add the name to the end of the wait list
           end
       end
```

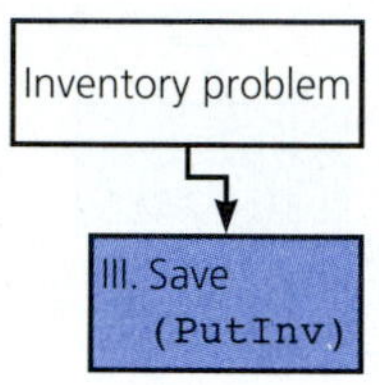

Figure 3-36

Subproblem III: Save the current inventory in external files.

FIRST PASS

```
PutInv(InvList, InvFile, WaitFile)

    for each item in the inventory do
    begin
       if the item is still part of the inventory
           then save the item (and its wait list)
    end
```

SECOND PASS

Recall that you remove an item from the inventory—by not saving it in the file—if both its want value and have value are zero and its wait list is empty. The following refinement implements this convention:

```
PutInv(InvList, InvFile, WaitFile)

    for each item in the inventory do
    begin
       if (the have value is not zero) or
              (the want value is not zero) or
              (the wait list is not empty)
          then
          begin
              { write the wait list to WaitFile }
              PutWait(StockItem, WaitFile) { Subproblem III.1 }

              Write out the stock item to the inventory file
          end
    end
```

Subproblem III.1: Save the wait list for a stock item in an external file.

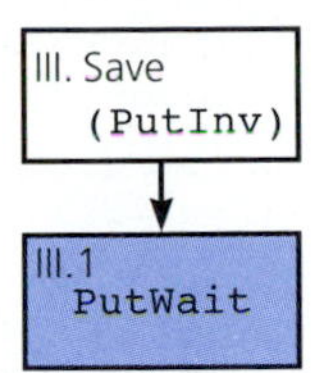

Figure 3-37

```
PutWait(StockItem, WaitFile)

    Trav = StockItem.Wait
    while Trav <> nil do
    begin
       Write out the wait name to WaitFile
       Trav := Trav^.Next
    end
```

Note that the preceding assumes, for both saving and restoring the inventory, that the have value is a true indicator of the size of the wait list, which will be the case if the entire program is working correctly. But what if something goes wrong? For example, if a later modification to the program causes a violation of this indicator, the inventory structure could become invalid or the program could abort in a very inelegant way—a way that would be very unsatisfactory to a user. For example, when restoring the inventory, the program could attempt to read past the end of the file if it expected some wait list to be longer than it was.

As a fail-safe measure, you should check that the have counts truly reflect the sizes of the wait lists whenever you save or restore the inventory. However, you can postpone this important detail now and view it as one refinement to the program that you will make during the third and final stage of the problem-solving process.

With this portion of the problem out of the way, we can turn to the core of the inventory problem, Subproblem II. Many of the subproblems that we solve are very simple and have high-level solutions that are self-explanatory. We explain the solution only where it is necessary to support or clarify the refinements.

Subproblem II: Execute user commands to ask about or modify the inventory. You process user commands until the quit command occurs. At a very high level, you can state Subproblem II as follows:

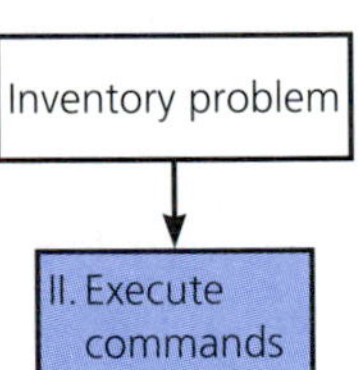

Figure 3-38

FIRST PASS

```
main program

    Read the first command
    while command is not Q (quit) do
    begin
       Execute the appropriate command
       Read the next command
    end
```

SECOND PASS

```
main program

   GetCmnd(Command)                    { Subproblem II.1 }
   while Command <> 'Q' do
   begin
      case Command of
          'H' : ProcH                  { Subproblem II.2 }
          'I' : ProcI(inventory)       { Subproblem II.3 }
          'L' : ProcL(inventory)       { Subproblem II.4 }
          'A' : ProcA(inventory)       { Subproblem II.5 }
          'M' : ProcM(inventory)       { Subproblem II.6 }
          'D' : ProcD(inventory)       { Subproblem II.7 }
          'O' : ProcO(inventory)       { Subproblem II.8 }
          'R' : ProcR(inventory)       { Subproblem II.9 }
          'S' : ProcS(inventory)       { Subproblem II.10 }
      end
      GetCmnd(Command)
   end
```

As part of the final refinement of the user interface, you should test for undefined commands.

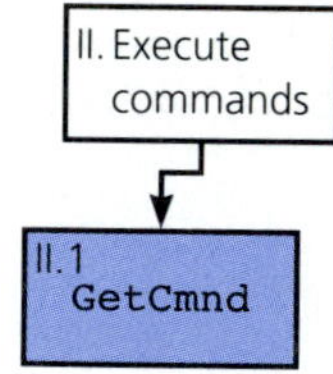

Figure 3-39

Subproblem II.1: Read the next command. You should provide a flexible input format. At first, however, you can assume that *the command will be a single uppercase letter* and leave the addition of flexibility for the final refinement of the program. Because as a procedure *GetCmnd* is an isolated module, the later refinements should cause no difficulties. Of course, the choice is really arbitrary as to how simple the original input procedure should be and how much refinement you should postpone for later.

FIRST PASS

```
GetCmnd(Command)

   Skip blanks in the input file
   Read the command
```

As a safeguard against an unexpected end of file, *GetCmnd* equates end of file with the quit command, as follows:

SECOND PASS

```
GetCmnd(Command)

   { skip blanks, get first nonblank in the input file }
   SkipBlanks(input, Ch)                 { Subproblem II.1.1 }

   { assign command - test for end of file }
   if eof(input)
      then Command := 'Q'
      else Command := Ch
```

Subproblem II.1.1: Skip blanks in a file.

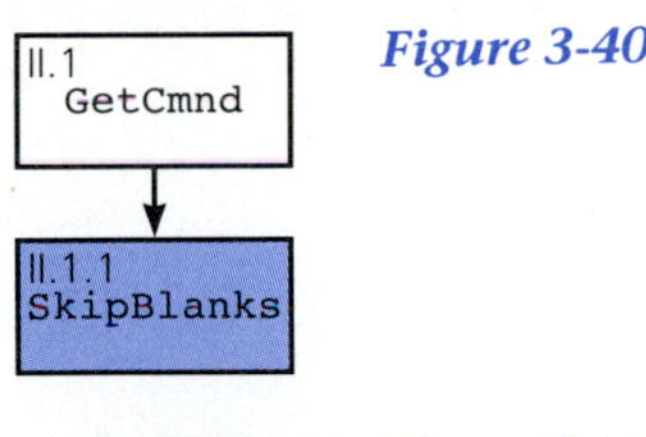

Figure 3-40

```
SkipBlanks(InFile, Ch)

    Ch := ' '
    while (not eof(InFile)) and (Ch = ' ') do
        read(InFile,Ch)
```

Subproblem II.2: Process command H (summarize the available commands).

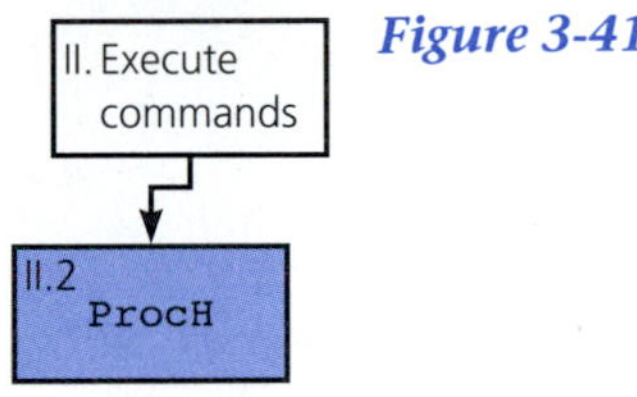

Figure 3-41

```
ProcH

    Write out a summary of each command
```

Subproblem II.3: Process command I (print information for a specified title).

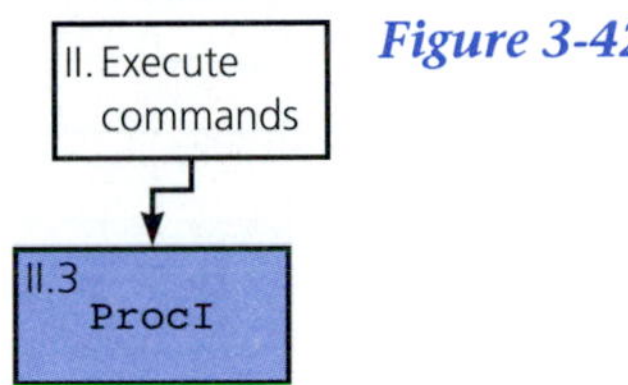

Figure 3-42

FIRST PASS

```
ProcI(InvList)

    Read in a title argument
    Find the title in the inventory
    Write out the title, have value, and want value
    Write out the associated wait list
```

SECOND PASS

```
ProcI(InvList)

    { get the title argument }
    GetTitle(ATitle)                    { Subproblem II.3.1 }

    { find the title in the inventory }
    Loc := Find(InvList, ATitle)        { Subproblem II.3.2 }

    { write out the information }
    if Loc <> nil
       then
       begin
           with Loc^.Item do
               writeln(Title, Have, Want)
           Waitnames(Loc^.Wait)        { Subproblem II.3.3 }
       end
```

Subproblem II.3.1: Read in a title.

FIRST PASS

```
GetTitle(ATitle)

    Initialize the title to all blanks
    Skip blanks in the input file
    Read characters until ATitle is full or
     end of line is reached
```

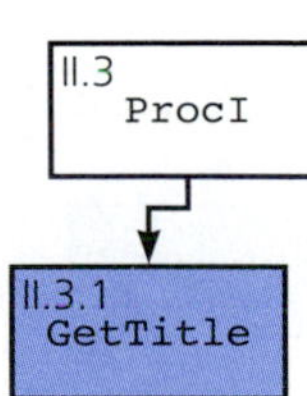

Figure 3-43

SECOND PASS

```
GetTitle(ATitle)

    { read in the string }
    SkipBlanks(input, Ch)
    if not eof(input)
       then
       begin
          readln(CharString)
          ATitle := concat(Ch, CharString)
       end

       else ATitle := ''
```

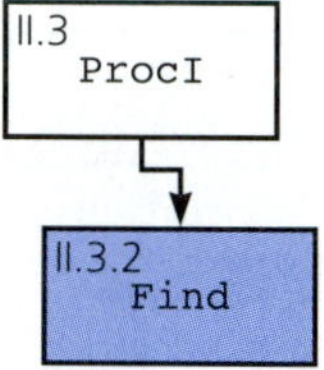

Figure 3-44

Subproblem II.3.2: Find a title in the inventory. Return *nil* if the title is not found. Observe that this task is very similar to the *FindPosition* procedure discussed earlier in this chapter.

```
function Find(InvList, ATitle): returns pointer to stock item

    { locate the title }
    Cur := InvList
    while (Cur <> nil) Cand (Cur^.Item.Title < ATitle) do
       Cur := Cur^.Next

    { set the function value }
    if (Cur <> nil) Cand (Cur^.Item.Title = ATitle)
       then Find := Cur
       else Find := nil
```

Again, note the use of the *Cand* operator.

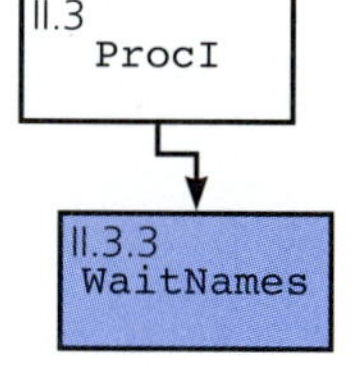

Figure 3-45

Subproblem II.3.3: Write out the names on the specified wait list.

```
WaitNames(NamePtr)

    while NamePtr <> nil do
    begin
       Write out the name that NamePtr points to
       NamePtr := NamePtr^.Next
    end
```

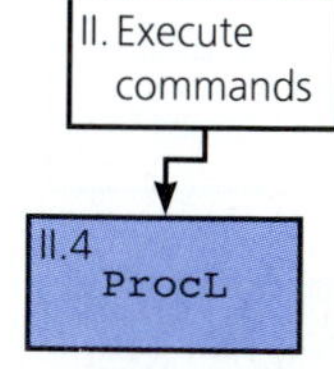

Figure 3-46

Subproblem II.4: Process command L (list the current inventory).

FIRST PASS

```
ProcL(InvList)

    for each item in the inventory do
    begin
       Write out the title, have value, and want value
       Write out the associated wait list
    end
```

SECOND PASS

```
ProcL(InvList)

    Trav := InvList
    while Trav <> nil do
    begin
       with Trav^.Item do
           writeln(Title, Have, Want)
       WaitNames(Trav^.Wait)
       Trav := Trav^.Next
    end
```

Subproblem II.5: Process command A (add a new title to the inventory). You can define the A command to mean that it will add a new title if the title does not already exist. If the title does exist, you can prompt the user to modify the existing want value.

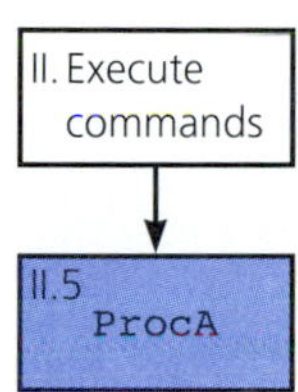

Figure 3-47

FIRST PASS

```
ProcA(InvList)

    Read in a title argument
    Insert the new title in the inventory (if it is
       not there already)
    Read the want value
```

SECOND PASS

```
ProcA(InvList)

    { get the title argument }
    GetTitle(ATitle)

    { insert a new stock item if necessary
      -- return Loc pointing to the item }
    InvInsert(InvList, ATitle, Loc)  { Subproblem II.5.1 }

    { update the want value for the stock item }
    read the want value
```

Subproblem II.5.1: Insert a new item in the inventory, if it is not present already. Return a pointer to the item.

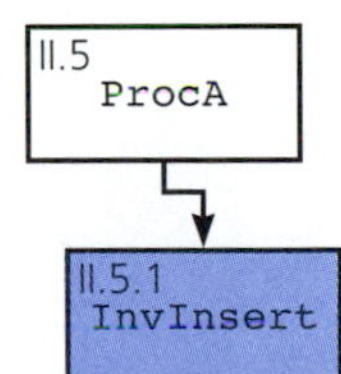

Figure 3-48

FIRST PASS

```
InvInsert(InvList, ATitle, Loc)

    Locate where the title should go
    Insert it if it is not there already
    Return a pointer to the item
```

SECOND PASS

```
InvInsert(InvList, ATitle, Loc)

    { locate where the title should go }
    Prev := nil
    Cur := InvList
    while (Cur <> nil) Cand (Cur^.Item.Title < ATitle) do
    begin
       Prev := Cur
       Cur := Cur^.Next
    end

    { insert title if necessary }
    if (Cur = nil) Cor (Cur^.Item.Title <> ATitle)
       then insert new node between Prev and Cur

    Loc is a pointer to the item
```

Note the use of the *Cand* and *Cor* operators.

Figure 3-49

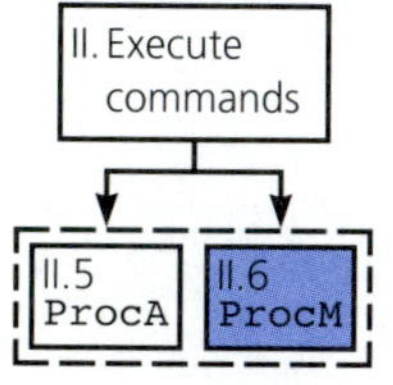

Subproblem II.6: Process command M (modify the want value for a specified title). The M command is supposed to modify the want value of an existing title. You can define it to include the addition of a new title, if it does not exist already. Note that *ProcA* and *ProcM* are identical, so you can combine them into one routine, *ProcAM*.

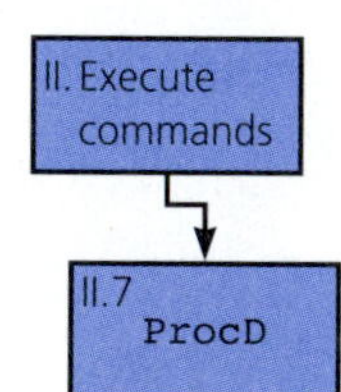

Figure 3-50

Subproblem II.7: Process command D (take delivery of a shipment). The D command specifies that the shipment information for a delivery will be in an external file, so add the following variable declaration to the existing declarations:

```
var ShipFile : text
```

In the following, the shipment file name is passed to the procedure *ProcD* as a parameter.

FIRST PASS

```
ProcD(InvList, ShipFile)

    while not eof(ShipFile) do
    begin
       Read the delivery information (titles and counts)
       Locate the title (insert it if it is not there already)
       Update the have value for the title
       Hold cassettes for people on the wait lists
    end
```

SECOND PASS

```
ProcD(InvList, ShipFile)

    while not eof(ShipFile) do
    begin
       { read the count and title }
       read(ShipFile, Count)
       GetTitle(ATitle)

       { update the have value in the inventory
         -- create a new item if necessary }
       InvInsert(InvList, ATitle, Loc)
       Update the have value

       { process back orders if necessary }
       while (wait list is not empty) and (Count > 0) do
       begin
           Hold one cassette for the first person on the
               wait list
           Delete the first person from the wait list
           Count := Count - 1
       end
    end
```

Note that procedure `GetTitle` reads title arguments from the input file (for commands I, A, M, and S) and reads titles from the delivery file (for command D). You can accommodate these tasks by having procedure `GetTitle` take a file name as an argument *(procedure `GetTitle(ATitle, InFile)`).*

Subproblem II.8: Process command O (write a purchase order).

```
ProcO(InvList)

    for each item in the inventory do
    begin
       if have value < want value
           then write a purchase order
    end
```

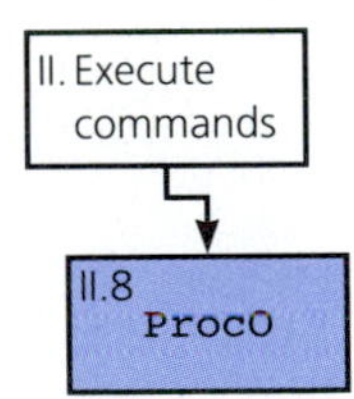

Figure 3-51

Figure 3-52

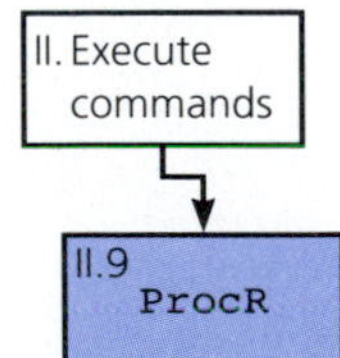

Subproblem II.9: Process command R (write a return order).

```
ProcR(InvList)

    for each item in the inventory do
    begin
       if have value < want value
           then
```

```
          begin
              Write a return order
              Decrease the have value accordingly
          end
    end
```

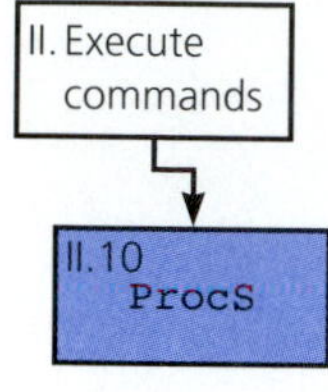

Figure 3-53

Subproblem II.10: Process command S (sell a cassette).

FIRST PASS

```
ProcS(InvList)

     Read in a title argument
     Find the title in the inventory
     if the title is not in the inventory then
        Print a message
     else if the have value = 0 then
        Decrease the have value by 1
     else read in a name for the wait list
```

SECOND PASS

```
ProcS(InvList)

     { get the title argument }
     GetTitle(ATitle, InFile)

     { find the title in the inventory }
     Loc := Find(InvList, ATitle)

     { decrease the have value by 1 if possible }
     if Loc = nil then
        Print message
     else if have value > 0 then
        have value := have value - 1
     else
     begin   { get a name for the wait list }
        GetName(Name, InFile)
        Add the name to the end of the wait list
     end
```

Observe that procedure `GetName` is really identical to procedure `GetTitle`, which was defined earlier. Therefore, rename `GetTitle` and `GetName` with the more general name `GetString`. (`GetString(AString, InFile)`).

A top-down design of a solution to the inventory problem is now complete. Figure 3-54 summarizes this design. The place at which the design of a solution ends and its implementation with a program begins is not at all clear. You easily could justify refining the solution further before turning to the coding. However, the intention of this discussion is not to walk

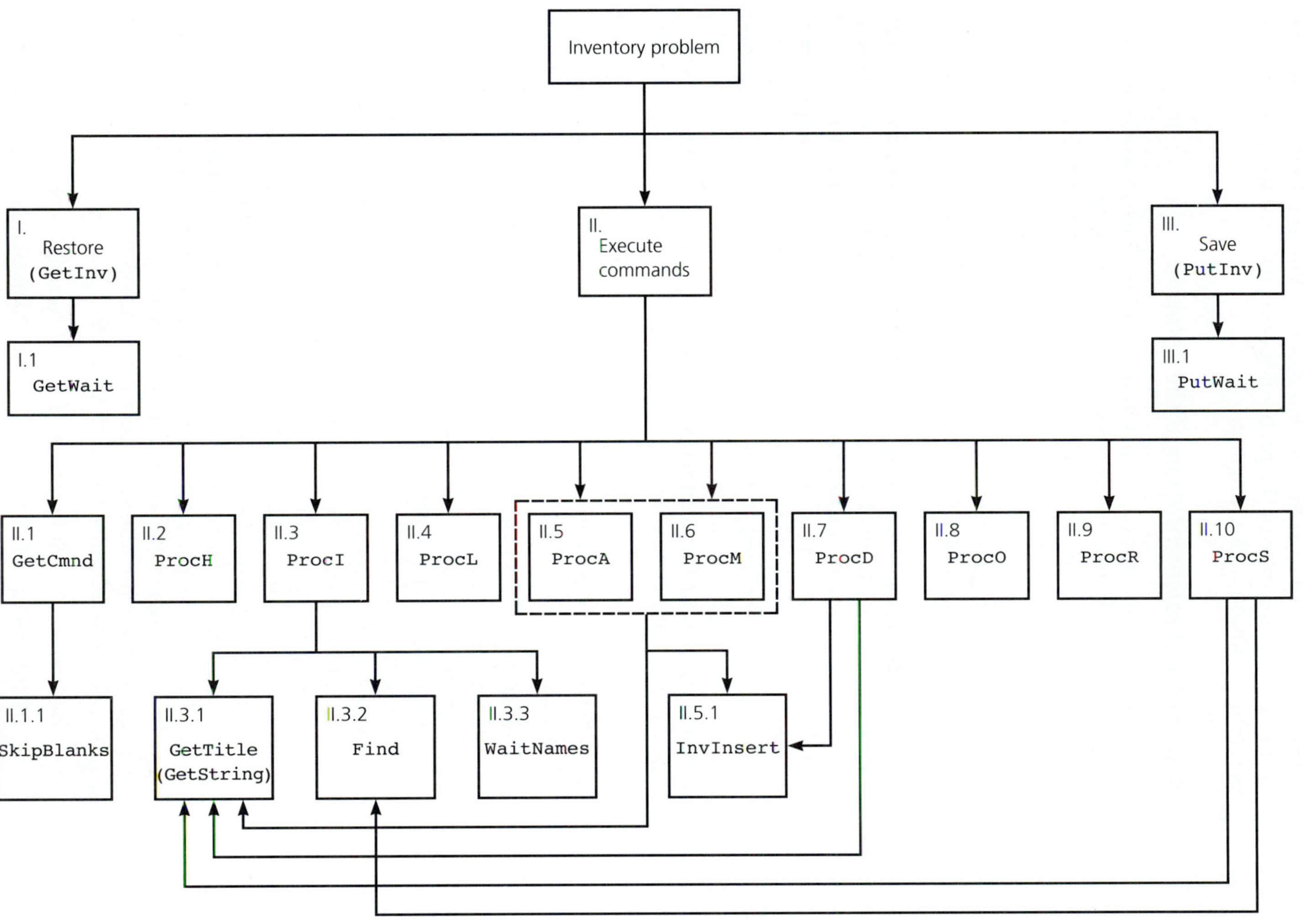

Figure 3-54
Complete design hierarchy

you through every detail of this particular problem, but rather to give you a good feel for the spirit of the solution process. With this in mind, we now turn to the second stage of the problem-solving process: the implementation of the solution with a program.

Bottom-Up Implementation of the Solution

This stage of the process takes the solution and produces a working Pascal program. Although there is much coding detail at this stage, we emphasize the organization of the implementation and the order of doing things rather than programming details. That is, we demonstrate how to build a program systematically from the bottom up, adding a few new routines at a time until the program is complete. We shall summarize here the major steps that we took to get from the pseudocode solution to a complete working program.

The development of this program occurred in two main phases. In the first phase, we essentially chose to ignore the wait lists by treating calls to the wait list operations (procedures *`GetWait`*, *`PutWait`*, and *`WaitNames`*) as stubs. Recall that stubs are placeholder procedures, which simply report that they have been called. We chose this approach because the wait list operations are peripheral to the main focus of the problem. The second phase of the implementation consisted of replacing the stubs with the implementations of the corresponding modules. Within each phase, we added a few routines at a time, got them to work, and then added more routines.

Phase 1: Omit the wait list operations. This discussion is broken into the following five steps:

1. One of the most useful and important procedures that you can write is often not part of the solution at all. During the development of a large program, it is useful to have a special debugging procedure that writes out the status of the primary data structures and program variables. Having this as a separate procedure allows you easily to either add diagnostics to or remove them from any place in the code during the remainder of the program development.

   In this particular program, the debugging routine also happens to be one of the routines for the program: Procedure *`ProcL`* lists the current inventory. Therefore, procedure *`ProcL`* should be one of the first routines written. Note, however, that you cannot test *`ProcL`* unless there is some data in the data structure. Thus, the first coding task is to define and implement some minimal subset of the solution that would put something into the data structure and allow you to test *`ProcL`*. The following procedures accomplish this task:

`GetCmnd`	{ Subproblem II.1 }	Read in a command.
`SkipBlanks`	{ II.1.1 }	Skip blanks in an input file (needed for *`GetCmnd`*).

`ProcAM`	{ II.5 and II.6 }	Insert new items into the inventory.
`InvInsert`	{ II.5.1 }	Insert a new node into the data structure (needed for `ProcAM`).

We then implemented

`ProcL`	{ II.4 }	List the current inventory.

2. After the procedures in the previous step were working satisfactorily, we turned our attention to adding a new set of routines to expand the scope of the program. We chose from among many possibilities and decided to write the routines for saving and restoring the inventory:

`GetInv`	{ I }	Restore the inventory from a file.
`PutInv`	{ III }	Save the inventory in a file.

   One reason for this decision was that it allowed us to continue the development of the program over a series of runs without having to create a new inventory from scratch each time. We did not code the procedures `PutWait` and `GetWait` (for saving and restoring the wait lists) until Phase 2 of the program development.

   Notice that the program never actually deletes nodes from the linked list of inventory items. It removes items from the inventory simply by not writing them out to the file when it executes the Q command (that is, when it executes `PutInv`). Because this removal occurs just before the program terminates—and all memory is returned to the system—nothing is gained by explicitly disposing of these particular nodes.

3. At this point, the program was starting to look like a solution to the original problem. We chose to add the following routines next, primarily because they were easy to write:

`ProcH`	{ II.2 }	Write out a summary of the commands.
`ProcO`	{ II.8 }	Write a purchase order.
`ProcR`	{ II.9 }	Write a return order.

4. The choices here were fairly arbitrary. We focused on the addition of procedure `ProcI`.

`ProcI`	{ II.3 }	Write information about a specified title.
`GetString`	{ II.3.1 }	Read a title argument (needed for `ProcI`).
`Find`	{ II.3.2 }	Locate a title in the inventory (needed for `ProcI`).

5. Finally, we added the last two procedures:

`ProcD`	{ II.7 }	Process a delivery.
`ProcS`	{ II.10 }	Sell a cassette.

Phase 2: Implement the wait list operations. At this point we had a working program that supported all the inventory commands but did not account for the wait lists. It was fairly easy to add the remaining subprograms:

`GetWait`	{ I.1 }	Read in (from a file) the wait list for a stock item.
`PutWait`	{ III.1 }	Write out (to a file) the wait list for a stock item.
`WaitNames`	{ II.3.3 }	Write out the wait list for a stock item.

Final Set of Refinements to the Program

After completing the bottom-up implementation of the solution, we had a complete working program for the original problem. During this last stage of the problem-solving process, we refined the program to make it more sophisticated. This stage included the following kinds of refinements:

1. During the top-down design of the solution, we made temporary simplifying assumptions about the input data. In this final stage we removed these assumptions.

   For example, in the pseudocode given earlier for Subproblem II.1 (the procedure `GetCmnd`) we made the assumption that commands would consist of single uppercase letters. In the final set of refinements, we removed this assumption by allowing both lowercase commands and uppercase commands and by adding code to recognize commands that appear as the first character of a word. The advantage of this second feature is that it allows a user to type, for example, the word "order" instead of the single character "O". The first version of the program would not have recognized "order" and would have ignored it.

2. A second type of refinement was to make the user interface more "intelligent." For example, you might want a program that is easy to use for both sophisticated and unsophisticated users. An example of a modification that can enhance the appeal of the program is as follows: If a command requires an argument such as the title of a cassette, then the user should be able to type either the full command with arguments (if the user is familiar with the command) or only the command name and get prompted for the arguments (if the user is not familiar with the command). That is, the program prompts for arguments only if the user omits them. We added this feature by modifying the `Get-`

String procedure and by adding a procedure *Prompt* to prompt the user to give the appropriate input.

3. A third kind of refinement concerned adding internal checks to the program to test for program errors. Given the nature of the program, it is reasonable to assume that other people might modify it in the future. These modifications might violate some of the assumptions about the data and data structures, and the program should help you to avoid any serious consequences as a result of modification. This is in keeping with the discussion of fail-safe programming in Chapter 1.

   For example, consider the operations that restore and save the inventory. The correctness of the inventory program depends heavily on the integrity of these operations, and these operations in turn depend on the validity of the have value of each inventory item as a true indicator of the size of the associated wait list. If a modification to a program caused a violation of the relationship between the have value and the size of the wait list, the results could be severe: The entire inventory structure could lose its validity. One type of enhancement to this program was to include checks of this relationship in the places where the inventory structure was vulnerable to ruin. We chose to build this extra testing into the procedures *GetWait* and *PutWait*. Note that *GetInv* and *PutInv*—the procedures that restore and save the inventory structure—call *GetWait* and *PutWait*.

One of the reasons that we like this inventory problem is because there is so much room for growth. The exercises at the end of this chapter suggest modifications and enhancements. We hope that the ease of changing and adding to the program will help to convince you of the value and effectiveness of top-down design and modularity.

SUMMARY

1. **Pointer variables are an extremely useful data type. You can use them to implement the data structure known as a linked list by using statements such as the following:**

```
type    ptrType = ^nodeType;
        nodeType = record
             Data : <any data type except file>;
             Next : ptrType
        end;
var     Head : ptrType
```

   If *P* is a variable of type *ptrType* that points to a node in this linked list, then

   - ***P^* is the node.**
   - ***P^.Data* is the data portion of the node.**
   - ***P^.Next* points to the next node.**

2. The linked list is highly versatile and you will encounter it throughout the book. Algorithms for inserting data into and deleting data from a sorted linked list consist of two steps: Traverse the list from the beginning until you reach the appropriate position; perform pointer changes to alter the structure of the list.
3. An important advantage of a pointer-based linked list over an array is that you can increase the size of a linked list simply by using the ***new*** command to dynamically allocate additional nodes when needed. You can also insert items into and delete items from a linked list without shifting data.
4. While you can access any element of an array directly, you must traverse a linked list to access a particular node. Therefore, the access time for an array is constant, whereas the access time for a linked list depends upon the location of the node within the list.
5. Pascal's ***dispose*** procedure allows a program to recycle its nodes by returning them to the system for reallocation by the ***new*** procedure.
6. You can store a linked list in a file by writing the data portion of the nodes in the order in which they appear on the list. As a result, it is easy to restore the linked list directly from the file at a later time.
7. In a circular linked list, the last node points to the first node, so that every node has a successor. If the list's external pointer points to the last node instead of the first node, you can access both the last node and the first node without traversing the list.
8. Dummy head nodes provide a method for eliminating the special cases for insertion into and deletion from the beginning of a linked list. The use of dummy head nodes is a matter of personal taste for singly linked lists, but it is helpful for a doubly linked list.
9. A head record contains global information about a linked list—such as its length—in addition to a pointer to the first node on the list.
10. A doubly linked list allows you to traverse the list in either direction. Each node points to its successor as well as its predecessor. Because insertions and deletions with a doubly linked list are more involved than with a singly linked list, it is convenient to use both a dummy head node and a circular structure to eliminate complicated special cases for the beginning and end of the list.
11. The case study demonstrated how you can use a methodical top-down approach to solve a large problem. The case study illustrated several problem-solving principles, including the following:

a. You should split the problem into modules that you successively refine. For the most part, you should perform the refinements in isolation, although you should keep the overall picture in mind.
b. After you have completed the design of the initial solution, you have a hierarchy of modules. As you begin implementing the modules with Pascal subprograms, you must decide which modules to code first. If the development of a module *M* depends on the actions of its submodules, then a reasonable approach is to start at the bottom of the hierarchy and work up. On the other hand, if the modules that *M* uses are peripheral, you can implement them initially by using dummy procedures—called stubs—that simply report that they have been called. By using stubs you can focus on the more central aspects of the problem.
c. Before you consider the programming task complete, you should carefully perform a final set of refinements that include making the input modules as flexible as possible, adding fail-safe features, and polishing the documentation.

COMMON PITFALLS / DEBUGGING

1. You cannot look at the value of a pointer variable `P`. For example, `write(P)` is illegal.
2. An uninitialized pointer variable has an undefined value, not the value `nil`.
3. If `P` is an uninitialized pointer variable, you must call `new(P)` before assigning a value to `P^`. Failure to do so can cause catastrophic results.
4. An attempt to reference a pointer variable that has the value `nil` is wrong, but not illegal, in Turbo Pascal. For example, if `P` has the value `nil`, you should avoid statements such as `write(P^.Data)` and `P := P^.Next`, even though Turbo Pascal will not object. Failure to do so can cause a program to run incorrectly the first time that you run it, even though it runs correctly the second time.
5. Insertions into and deletions from the beginning of a linked list are special cases unless you use dummy head nodes. Failure to recognize this fact can result in a reference to a pointer whose value is `nil`; such a reference is incorrect.
6. When traversing a linked list by using the pointer variable `Cur`, you must be careful not to reference `Cur` after it has "passed" the last node on the list, because it will have the value `nil` at that point. For example, the loop

```
while (Value > Cur^.Data) do
    Cur := Cur^.Next
```

is incorrect if ***Value*** is greater than all the data values in the linked list, because ***Cur*** becomes ***nil***. At the pseudocode level, the ***Cand*** operator solves this problem:

```
while (Cur <> nil) Cand (Value > Cur^.Data) do
    Cur := Cur^.Next
```

7. After you have returned a node to the system by using ***dispose(P)***, you should not reference any pointer variable that still points to the node, including ***P***. To help you avoid this kind of error, you should assign ***nil*** to ***P*** after executing ***dispose(P)***. However, if variables other than ***P*** point to the freed node, the possibility of error still exists.

8. A doubly linked list is a construct that programmers tend to overuse. However, a doubly linked list is appropriate when you can access a node directly, without performing a traversal from the beginning of the list. Because doubly linking the list provides an easy way to get to the node's predecessor as well as its successor, you can, for example, delete the node readily.

SELF-TEST EXERCISES

1. Eliminate the statements that are syntactically incorrect in this program, and then trace the execution by hand.

```
program TestPointers;

type    intPtrType = ^integer;
        intPtrPtrType = ^intPtrType;

var     p, q : intPtrType;
        pp : intPtrPtrType;

begin
    new(p);
    new(q);
    writeln(p, q);

    p^ := 7;
    q^ := 11;
    writeln(p^, q^);

    new(pp);
    pp^  := 20;
    pp^ := p;
    writeln(p^, pp^);

    pp^^ := pp^^ + q^;
    writeln(p^, pp^^);
```

```
        new(pp^);
        pp^^ := -3;
        pp^^ := q^ + p^ + pp^^;
        writeln(p^, q^, pp^^)
    end.
```

2. Consider a sorted linked list of nodes that each contain a single character in the data portion. Initially, the list contains three nodes, as Figure 3-55 depicts. In addition, *Prev* points to the first node in this list and *Cur* points to the second node. Do not use any of the subprograms that were presented in this chapter when writing the solutions to this exercise.
   a. Write Pascal statements that delete the second node and return it to the system. (*Hint:* First modify Figure 3-55.)
   b. Now assume that *Cur* points to the first node of the remaining two nodes of the original list. Write Pascal statements that delete the first node and return it to the system.
   c. Now *Head* points to the only node that is left on the list. Write Pascal statements that insert a new node that contains "A" into the list so that the list remains sorted.
   d. Revise Figure 3-55 so that your new diagram reflects the results of the previous deletions and insertion.

3. Write a procedure that will print only the Nth node in a linked list of integers. You can assume that the linked list contains at least N nodes.

4. How many assignment operations does the procedure that you wrote for Self-Test Exercise 3 require?

5. Consider the array *Lists* of pointers that the following statements define:

```
const MaxList = 10;
type  ptrType = ^nodeType;
      nodeType = record
          Data : integer;
          Next : ptrType
      end;    { record }

      ptrArrayType = array[1..MaxList] of ptrType;
var   Lists : ptrArrayType;
```

You can think of *Lists* as an array of linked lists. Suppose that each linked list is ordered. How can you use the *LinkedListInsert* and *LinkedListDelete* procedures, as developed in this chapter, on the ith linked list in *Lists*?

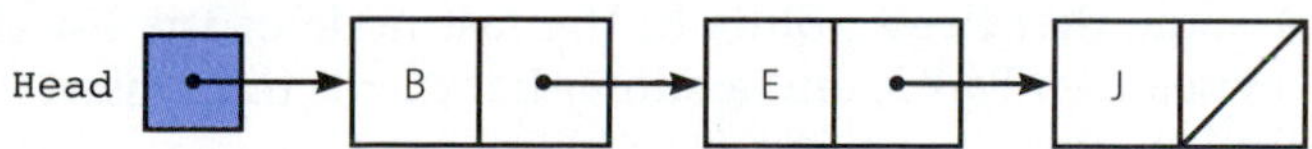

Figure 3-55

Linked list for Self-Test Exercise 2

EXERCISES

1. Trace the execution of the following program by hand, and show its output.

```
program TestPointers;
const   MaxName = 8;
        MaxFamily = 100;

type    personType = record
             Name : string[MaxName];
             Age : 0..maxint
        end;  { record }

        familyType = array[1..MaxFamily] of personType;

        personPtrType = ^personType;
        familyPtrType = ^familyType;

var     PPtr : personPtrType;
        FPtr : familyPtrType;

begin
     new(PPtr);
     PPtr^.Age := 25;
     PPtr^.Name := 'Fred';
     write(PPtr^.Name);
     writeln(' is ', PPtr^.Age:1,' years old.');

     new(FPtr);
     FPtr^[10] := PPtr^;
     write(FPtr^[10].Name);
     writeln(' is ', FPtr^[10].Age:1,' years old.')
end.
```

2. This exercise assumes that you have completed Self-Test Exercise 2 and know the final status of the linked list. For each of the following, write the Pascal statements that perform the requested operation on the list. Also draw a picture of the status of the list after each operation is complete. When you delete a node from the list, return it to the system. All insertions into the list should maintain the list's sorted order. Do not use any of the subprograms that were presented in this chapter.

   a. Assume that `Prev` points to the first node and `Cur` points to the second node. Insert "F" into the list.
   b. Assume that `Prev` points to the second node and that `Cur` points to the third node of the list after you revised it in Part *a*. Delete the last node on the list.
   c. Assume that `Prev` points to the last node of the list after you revised it in Part *b*, and assume that `Cur` is `nil`. Insert "G" into the list.

3. a. Complete the Pascal implementation of the procedure *LinkedListDelete* described in the section "Insertion and Deletion Procedures for a Sorted Linked List."
   b. Write a unit for a sorted linked list that contains the operations *LinkedListInsert*, *LinkedListDelete*, *SaveList*, and *RestoreList*. The procedure *FindPosition* that *LinkedListInsert* and *LinkedListDelete* call should be private.

4. Consider an unordered linked list.
   a. Write a procedure that inserts a node at the beginning of the linked list and a procedure that deletes the first node of the linked list.
   b. Repeat Part *a*, but this time perform the insertion and deletion at the end of the list instead of at the beginning.

5. Compare the number of operations that the *PrintList* procedure—described in the section "Displaying the Contents of a Linked List"—requires to print each node on a linked list of integers with the number of operations that a procedure requires to print each item in an array of integers.

Exercises 6 through 27 all refer to the following definitions:

```
type    nodePtrType = ^nodeType;
        nodeType = record
            Data : integer;
            Next : nodePtrType
        end
```

6. Write a function

   ```
   function Count(Head : nodePtrType) : integer;
   ```

   to count the number of records on the linked list pointed to by *Head*.

7. Write a procedure that will return to the system all the nodes on a linked list. Use the procedure *dispose*.

8. Write a procedure that will copy a linked list to a new linked list.

9. Given a linked list, write a procedure that creates a second linked list whose nodes are the nodes of the first list in reversed order. That is, the first node on the first list is the last node of the second list.

10. Given a linked list, write a procedure that reverses its links. Thus, the last node becomes first and the first node becomes last. This exercise differs from Exercise 9 in that there is only one list.

11. Consider an unordered linked list of integers. Write a procedure that creates two additional unordered linked lists: One list contains the even integers that are on the original list, and the other contains the odd integers. Do not destroy the original list.

12. Repeat Exercise 11, but this time do not use the *new* procedure. Instead, move each node from the original list into one of the new

lists as appropriate. When you are done, the original list will be empty.

13. Repeat Exercise 12, but this time move only the odd integers from the original list into a new list. When you are done, the original list will contain the even integers and the new list will contain the odd integers.

14. Repeat Exercises 11, 12, and 13, but this time assume that all of the lists are sorted.

15. Write a procedure that will delete the ith node from a linked list.

16. Write a function

```
function Position(Head : nodePtrType;
     Target : integer) : nodePtrType;
```

to return a pointer to the first record on an unordered linked list that contains the value in `Target`. If there is no such record on the list, `Position` should return `nil`. Assume that `Head` points to the linked list.

17. Write a procedure that will delete from a linked list the node that contains the largest data value. Can you do this with a single traversal of the list?

18. Write a procedure that will merge two linked lists that are sorted by data value. The result should be a linked list that is the sorted combination of the original lists.

19. Repeat Exercises 7, 8, and 15 through 18 for a circular linked list.

20. Assume that the pointer `List` points to the first node of a circular linked list. Write a loop that will print the data portion of every node on the list.

21. Write a procedure that will determine whether two circular lists are identical. Do this in two different ways as follows:

   a. In the first version, you may assume that a data item will occur at most once on any list.

   b. In the second version, you must account for possible duplicates on a list.

22. Write a procedure `MakeLinear(var P : nodePtrType)` that converts a circular list to a linear list that starts at the node that contains the smallest integer on the list. The parameter `P` points to some arbitrary node on the circular linked list. Upon return from the procedure, `P` points to the head of the new linear list.

23. Write a procedure that will reverse the links of a circular linked list, as Figure 3-56 depicts.

24. Write a program that will read a file of integers, insert each into a linked list so that the list is sorted by data value, and write out the final list.

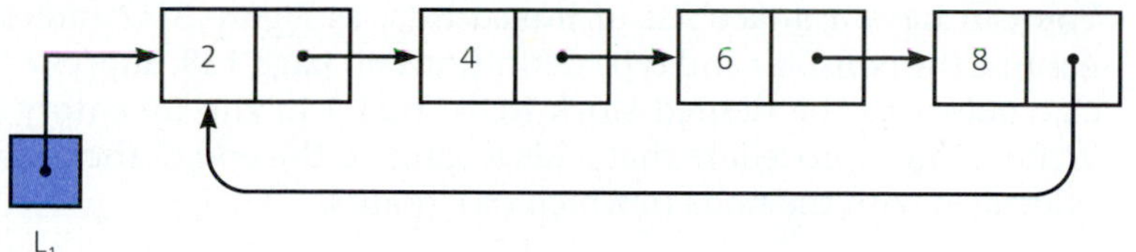

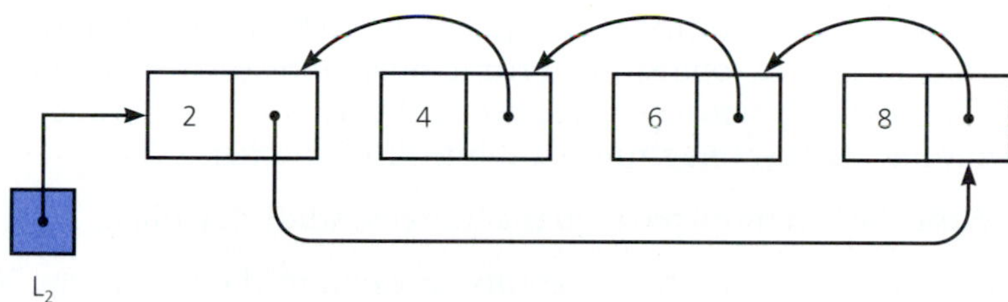

Figure 3-56

Two circular lists, one the reverse of the other

25. Write the type definitions for the dummy head node that Figure 3-26a pictures. Also declare the pointer variable `Head`.

26. Write procedures for insertion into and deletion from a sorted linked list that has a dummy head node.

27. Write a type definition for a variant record that will allow you to keep global information about a list in a dummy head node.

28. You can implement a character string as a linked list of characters. Write subprograms for some typical string operations such as concatenation (append one string to another) and length computation. How can you implement the string so that you can obtain its length without traversing the linked list and counting?

29. Consider the ordered doubly linked list shown in Figure 3-28. This list is circular and has a dummy head node. Suppose that `NewName` contains a name that you want to add to the list in its proper order. Write a loop that traverses the list backward from the last node and sets `Cur` to point to the node that should precede the new node in the list.

30. Write insertion and deletion procedures for the ordered doubly linked list shown in Figure 3-28. The list is circular and has a dummy head node. Each procedure has a pointer parameter `P`. The insertion procedure should insert the new node pointed to by `P` in its proper order in the list. The deletion procedure should delete the node to which `P` points.

31. Repeat Exercise 30 for the ordered doubly linked list shown in Figure 3-27. This list is not circular and does not have a dummy head node. Watch out for the special cases at the beginning and end of the list.

32. You can have a linked list of linked lists, as Figure 3-32 indicates. Assume the constant and type definitions on page 138. Suppose that `Cur` points to the desired stock item (node) in the inventory list. Write a Pascal procedure that adds a name to the end of the wait list associated with the node to which `Cur` points.

PROJECTS

33. Write a complete string manipulation package (see Exercise 28), including more sophisticated string operations such as finding the index of the leftmost occurrence of a character in a string and determining whether one string is a substring of another.

34. Write the inventory program that the case study describes.

35. Modify and expand the inventory program in the case study. Here are a few suggestions:

a. Add the ability to manipulate more than one inventory with the single program.

b. Add the ability to keep various statistics about each of the inventory items (such as the average number sold per week for the last 10 weeks).

c. Add the ability to modify the have value for an inventory item (for example, when a cassette is damaged or returned from a customer). Consider the implications for maintaining the relationship between a have value and the size of the corresponding wait list.

d. Make the wait lists more sophisticated. For example, keep names and addresses and mail letters automatically when a cassette comes in.

e. Make the ordering mechanism more sophisticated. For instance, do not order cassettes that have been ordered already but have not been delivered.

II

Problem-Solving Tools

CHAPTER 4

Data Abstraction: The Walls

PREVIEW The first three chapters of this book reinforced principles of program design and implementation. Our primary concern now is to develop a repertoire of problem-solving tools. This chapter elaborates on data abstraction, which was introduced in Chapter 1, as a tool for increasing the modularity of a program—for building "walls" between a program and its data structures. During the design of a solution, you will discover that you need to support several operations on the data and therefore need to define abstract data types. Only after you have clearly defined the operations of an abstract data type should you consider data structures for implementing it. This chapter will introduce some simple abstract data types and use them to demonstrate the advantages of abstract data types in general. In Part III of this book, which involves the management of data, you will see several other important ADT's.

This chapter also introduces the fundamental principles of object-oriented programming, a technique that enforces data abstraction. Examples of objects will demonstrate these principles and show you how to apply this new problem-solving tool. Although several programming languages support object-oriented programming, this chapter restricts its discussion to the features that are available in Turbo Pascal.

ABSTRACTION

By now the advantages of top-down design should be quite clear. Throughout the previous chapters of this book, we have espoused its virtues via argument and illustration. You can develop programs by piecing together functions and procedures that have yet to be written. The trick is to decide what *you would like* the subprograms to do and to proceed under the assumption that they exist and work. In this way you can write the subprograms in relative isolation from one another, knowing *what* each one will do but not necessarily *how* each will eventually do it. The underlying principle, which is called **procedural abstraction**, yields **modular** programs, whose advantages you saw in Chapter 1. To summarize those advantages, modularity is a method that keeps the complexity of a large program manageable by systematically controlling the interaction of its components. Thus, a modular program is easier to write because you can focus on one task at a time without other distractions.

Recall from Chapter 1 that procedural abstraction involves writing module specifications and in addition identifying details that you can hide within the module from other modules. The principle of **information hiding** involves not only hiding these details, but also making them *inaccessible* from outside a module. A graphic way to understand procedural abstraction and information hiding is to imagine **walls** around the various tasks a program performs. These walls prevent the tasks from becoming entangled. The wall around each task *T* prevents the other tasks from "see-

Isolate the implementation details of a module from other modules

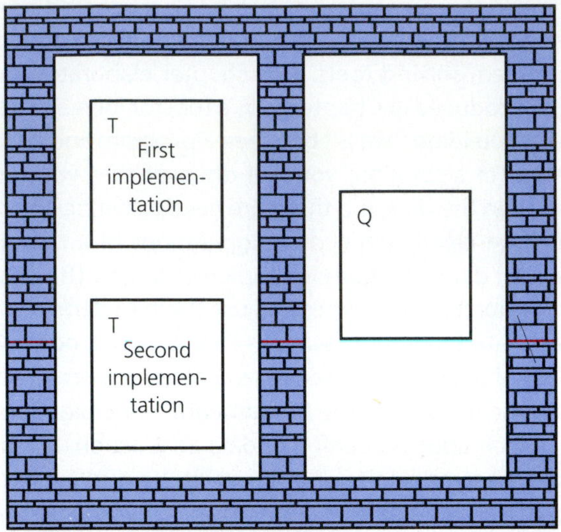

Figure 4-1

Isolated tasks: the implementation of task *T* does not affect task *Q*

ing" how *T* is performed. As Figure 4-1 illustrates, one benefit of this isolation is that if the method for performing task *T* should change, task *Q* will not be affected, because the wall prevents task *Q*'s method of solution from depending on task *T*'s method of solution.

The isolation of the modules cannot be total, however. Although task *Q* is oblivious to *how* task *T* is performed, it may well have to know *what* task *T* is and how to initiate it. For example, suppose that a program needs to operate on a sorted array of names. The program may, for instance, need to search the array for a given name or print out the names in alphabetical order. The program thus needs a module *S* that sorts an array of names. Although the rest of the program knows that module *S* will sort an array, it should not care how *S* accomplishes its task.

When you as program designer realize that there is a need to sort the names, you write the specifications for the sort routine. For example,

Write specifications for each module before implementing it

> The routine will receive an array of no more than `MaxNames` names. The length of each name is no more then `NameLength` characters. The routine will return the array with the names in ascending alphabetical order.

You can view these specifications as the terms of a **contract** that states that the program can rely on *S* to sort the array. If you alone write the entire program, this contract helps systematically decompose the problem into smaller tasks. If the program is a team project, the contract helps to delineate responsibilities. Whoever writes the sort routine has this contract to live up to. After the sort routine has been written and tested, the rest of the program will rely on it. The contract tells the other modules how to use the routine and the result of doing so. For example, the contract will specify how to call the sort routine properly and will state that upon return, the array is sorted in ascending order.

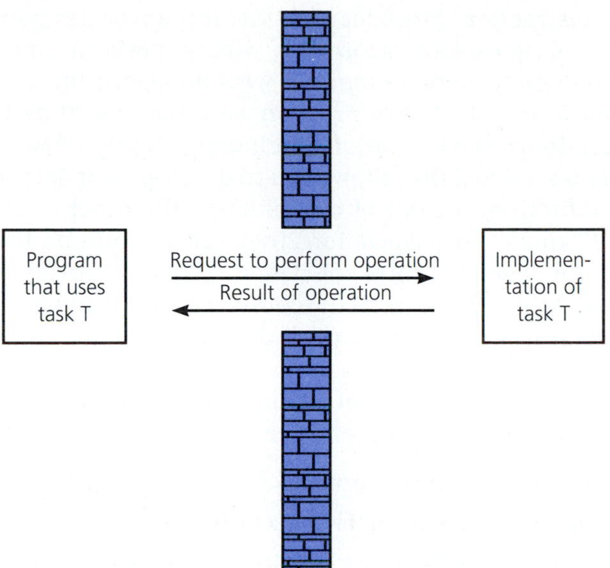

Figure 4-2
A slit in the wall

Thus, imagine a tiny slit in each wall, as Figure 4–2 illustrates. Things can pass through the slit into and out of the module. For example, you can pass the array into the sort routine, and the routine can pass the sorted array out to you. What goes in and comes out is governed by the terms of the module's contract: *If you use me in this way, this is exactly what I'll do for you.* It is very important to notice, however, that a module's contract does not commit the module to a particular method of performing its task. If another part of the program assumes anything about the method, it does so at its own risk. Thus, for example, if at some later date you use a different sort routine, you should not need to change the rest of the program at all. The slit in the wall is not large enough to allow the outside world to see the inner workings of the module. As long as the new module honors the terms of the original contract, the rest of the program should be oblivious to the change.

Specifications do not indicate how to implement a module

This discussion should not be news to you. Although we have not explicitly used the terms "wall" and "contract" before, the concepts certainly permeate the previous chapters of this book. For example, we have used the standard function `sqrt` as an example of a module that you know how to use. You know that if you pass `sqrt` either a real or an integer expression, it will return the real square root of the value of that expression. You can use `sqrt` even though you do not know its implementation. In fact, the `sqrt` function is precompiled and is an example of a **unit**, which was introduced in Chapter 2. You do not have access to `sqrt`'s source statements. Furthermore, it may be that `sqrt` was written in a language other than Pascal! There is so much about `sqrt` that you do not know, yet you can use it in your program without concern.

We have given you this synopsis of procedural abstraction now because we are about to expand on the other half of modular program develop-

Both procedural and data abstraction ask you to think what, *not* how

ment: **data abstraction**. Procedural abstraction advocates partitioning a program into independent algorithms, which perform small, isolated tasks, and asks you to think in terms of *what* an algorithm does independently of *how* it does it. Data abstraction asks that you think in terms of *what* you can do to a collection of data independently of *how* you do it. Data abstraction is a tool that allows you to develop each data structure in relative isolation from the rest of the solution. The other modules of the solution will "know" what operations they can perform on the data, but they should not depend on how the data is stored or how the operations are performed. Again, the terms of the contract are *what* and not *how*. Thus, data abstraction is a natural extension of procedural abstraction to data structures.

Often the solution to a problem requires the performance of operations that are broadly described in one of three ways:

- **Add** data to a data collection.
- **Remove** data from a data collection.
- **Ask questions** about the data in a data collection.

The details of the operations, of course, vary from application to application, but the overall theme is the management of data. Realize, however, that not all problems, and certainly not all ADT's, use or require these operations.

ABSTRACT DATA TYPES

A collection of data values together with a set of operations on that data are called an **abstract data type**, or ADT. The definition of the operations must be rigorous enough to specify completely the effect that they have on the data, yet the definition must not specify how to store the data nor how to carry out the operations. For example, the ADT operations cannot specify whether to store the data in consecutive memory locations or in disjoint memory locations that are linked with pointers. You choose a particular **data structure** when you implement an ADT. Recall that a data structure is a construct that you can define within a programming language to store a collection of data. For example, a Pascal array is a data structure.

The specifications of ADT operations indicate what they do, but not how to implement them

Data structures implement ADT's

Data structures and structured data types are related. All structured data types—arrays, records, files, and sets—are data structures. There are, however, other data structures, which could be either user-defined data types in Pascal or data types in another language, that you could invent. For example, suppose that you wanted a data structure to store both the names and salaries of a group of employees. You could use the following definitions:

```
const MaxNumber = 500;
      NameLength = 20;
```

```
type   nameType = string[NameLength];
       nameArrayType = array[1..MaxNumber] of nameType;
       salaryArrayType = array[1..MaxNumber] of real;
var    Names : nameArrayType;
       Salaries : salaryArrayType;
```

Here the employee *Names[I]* has a salary of *Salaries[I]*. The two arrays *Names* and *Salaries* together form a data structure, yet there is no single Pascal data type that describes it.

ADT's and data structures are not the same

An abstract data type is not another name for a data structure. To give you a better idea of the conceptual difference between an ADT and a data structure, consider the machine in Figure 4-3. This machine accepts ice cubes as input and produces as output either crushed ice or cold water according to which one of two buttons you push. The machine is analogous to an abstract data type. The ice cubes are analogous to a data collection; the operations are *Crush* and *Liquefy*. At this level of design, the machine is a black box. You are not concerned with how it will perform its operations, only that it performs them. If you want crushed ice, do you really care how the machine accomplishes its task as long as it does so correctly? Thus, after you have specified the machine's functions, you can design many uses for crushed ice and cold water without knowing how the machine accomplishes its tasks and without the distraction of engineering details.

Eventually someone must build the machine. Exactly how will this machine produce crushed ice, for example, from ice cubes? It might crush

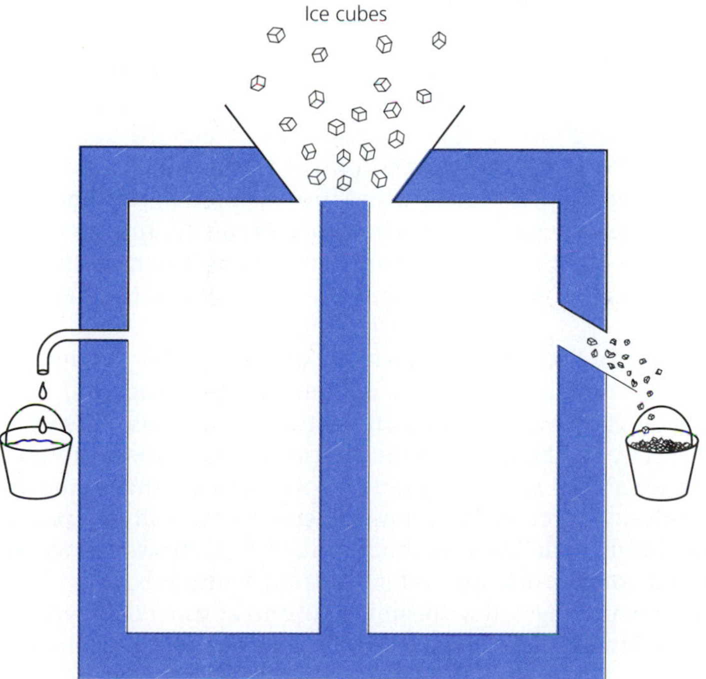

Figure 4-3

A machine that transforms ice cubes into either crushed ice or water

the cubes between two steel rollers, or it might use hammers to smash the cubes into small pieces. The internal structure of the machine corresponds to the implementation of the ADT in Pascal, that is, to a data structure. Although the user of the machine does not care about its inner workings, certainly the machine's manufacturer cares. Which design is easiest and cheapest to build? Which design is the most efficient in its operation? These are the same concerns that you should have when you choose a data structure to implement an ADT in Pascal.

Notice that the interior mechanisms for each operation are surrounded by steel walls. The only breaks in the walls accommodate the input (ice cubes) to the machine and its output (crushed ice or cold water). Thus, the machine's mechanisms are not only hidden from the user but also are inaccessible. In addition, the mechanism of one operation is hidden from and inaccessible to the other operation. There are other benefits of the machine's design as a result of its modularity. You can improve the operation *Crush* by modifying its module without affecting the *Liquefy* module. You could also add an operation by adding another module to the machine without affecting the original two operations. Thus, both abstraction and information hiding are at work here.

Carefully specify an ADT's operations before you implement them

When a program must perform data operations that are not directly supported by the language, you must construct the data structures. You should first design an abstract data type and then carefully specify what the ADT operations are to do (the contract). Then—*and only then*—should you implement the operations with a data structure. If you implement the operations properly, the rest of the program will be able to assume that the operations perform as specified—that is, that the terms of the contract are honored. However, the program must not depend on a particular method for supporting the operations.

A program should not depend on the details of an ADT's implementation

To summarize, data abstraction results in walls between a program and its data structures. A slit in each wall allows you to pass requests to perform operations through to the data structure and allows the data structure to pass back the results of these operations, as Figure 4-4 illustrates. The data structure's specifications govern what those operations are and what they do: *This is the exact result of each of my operations.* This approach allows the program to be oblivious to any change in the implementations of its data structures. Much of the remainder of the book uses this data-abstraction approach.

Providing for the requirements of an ADT sounds like a formidable task, and indeed it is. An ADT is both a mathematical concept and a problem-solving tool. The formal mathematical study of ADT's uses systems of **axioms** to specify the behavior of the operations. Our goal is to give you a sense of the value of ADT's as a problem-solving tool rather than to develop mathematically rigorous definitions. Therefore, we will rely primarily on informal, intuitive definitions. From time to time, however, we shall present a few axiomatic definitions for illustrative purposes.

The following pages describe how to use an abstract data type to realize data abstraction's goal of separating the operations on data from the imple-

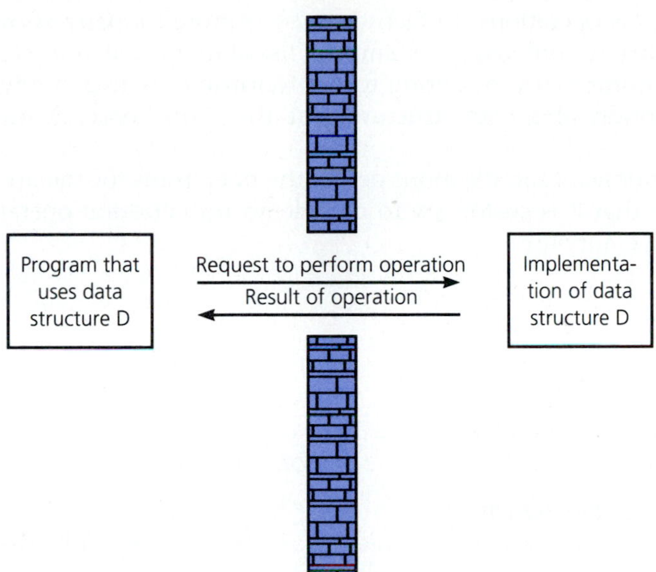

Figure 4-4

A wall that isolates data structures

mentation of these operations. In doing so, several examples of ADT's will be presented.

The ADT Ordered List

To elaborate on the notion of an abstract data type, consider the familiar grocery list pictured in Figure 4-5. Although the six items on the list are in sequential order, they are not necessarily sorted by name. Perhaps the list items appear in the order in which they occur on the grocer's shelves, but more likely they appear in the order in which they occurred to you.

What can you do to such a list? You might count the items to determine the length of the list, insert an item at position *i* on the list, delete the item at position *i,* or look at the item at position *i.* Thus, you could define the ADT "grocery list" as a collection of grocery items together with

Figure 4-5

A grocery list

the previous operations. In fact, this ADT is more formally known as an **ordered list**. An ordered list is simply a list of items that you reference by position number. Do not bring to the following discussion any preconceived notion of a data structure that the term "ordered list" might suggest.

The following specifications define the operations for the ADT ordered list. Note that it is customary to include an initialization operation that creates an empty list.

KEY CONCEPTS

ADT Ordered List Operations

```
CreateOrderedList(OL)
{ Creates an empty ordered list OL. }

OrderedListLength(OL)
{ Returns the number of items that are in the ordered list
  OL. }

OrderedListInsert(OL, Position, NewItem)
{ Inserts NewItem at position Position of ordered list OL,
  where 1 <= Position <= OrderedListLength(OL)+1.
  If Position <= OrderedListLength(OL), items are shifted as
  follows: The item at Position becomes the item at
  Position+1, the item at Position+1 becomes the item at
  Position+2, and so on.}

OrderedListDelete(OL, Position)
{ Deletes the item at position Position of the ordered list
  OL, where 1 <= Position <= OrderedListLength(OL).
  If Position < OrderedListLength(OL), items are shifted as
  follows: The item at Position+1 becomes the item at
  Position, the item at Position+2 becomes the item at
  Position+1, and so on.}

OrderedListRetrieve(OL, Position, DataItem)
{ Sets DataItem to the item at position Position of the
  ordered list OL, where 1 <= Position <=
  OrderedListLength(OL). The list is left unchanged by this
  operation.}
```

An ADT definition should not include implementation issues

The specifications of these five operations are the terms of the contract for the ADT ordered list. Notice that the specifications of the operations contain no mention of how to store the ordered list or how to perform the operations. The ADT definition tells you only what you can do to an ordered list. It is of fundamental importance that the definition of an ADT *not* include implementation issues. This restriction on the definition of an ordered list is what allows you to build a wall between an implementation of an ordered list and the program that uses it. The ADT operations are the sole terms of the contract between an implementation and a program: *If you request that these operations be performed, this is what will happen.* The behavior of the operations is the only thing on which a program should depend.

A program should depend only on the behavior of the ADT

What does the definition of the ADT ordered list tell you about its behavior? It is apparent that the ordered list operations fall into the three broad categories presented earlier in this chapter.

- The operation `OrderedListInsert` **adds** data to a data collection.
- The operation `OrderedListDelete` **removes** data from a data collection.
- The operations `OrderedListRetrieve` and `OrderedListLength` **ask questions** about the data in a data collection.

These descriptions of the operations are only general, but the definition of an ordered list does specify exactly what the operations do. To get a more precise idea of how the operations work, apply them to this grocery list:

L = <milk, eggs, butter, apples, bread, chicken>

The notation implies that milk is the first item on the list and chicken is the last item.

To begin, consider how you can construct this list by using the ordered list operations. One way is first to create an empty list and then to use a series of insertion operations to successively append the items to the list as follows:

```
CreateOrderedList(L)
OrderedListInsert(L, 1, milk)
OrderedListInsert(L, 2, eggs)
OrderedListInsert(L, 3, butter)
OrderedListInsert(L, 4, apples)
OrderedListInsert(L, 5, bread)
OrderedListInsert(L, 6, chicken)
```

Notice that the ordered list's insertion operation can insert new items into any position of the list, not just its end. The definition of `OrderedListInsert` specifies that if a new item is inserted into position *i*, then the position of each item that was at a position of *i* or greater is increased by 1. Thus, for example, if you start with the previous grocery list and you perform the operation

```
OrderedListInsert(L, 4, nuts)
```

then the list becomes

L = <milk, eggs, butter, nuts, apples, bread, chicken>

All items that were at position numbers greater than or equal to 4 before the insertion are moved and are now each at the next higher position number after the insertion.

Similarly, the deletion operation specifies that if an item is deleted from position *i*, then the position of each item that was at a position greater than *i* is decremented by 1. Thus, for example, if *L* is the list

L = <milk, eggs, butter, nuts, apples, bread, chicken>

and you perform the operation

```
OrderedListDelete(L, 5)
```

then the list becomes

L = <milk, eggs, butter, nuts, bread, chicken>

All items that were at position numbers greater than 5 before the deletion are moved and are now each at the next lower position number after the deletion.

These examples illustrate that the definition of an ADT can specify the effects of its operations without having to indicate how to store the data. However, we have stated the terms of an ordered list's contract—that is, the specifications of its operations—rather informally. For instance, we are relying on your intuition to know what we mean when we say that an item is "at position *i*" in the ordered list. This notion is simple, and most people will understand its intentions. However, some abstract data types are much more complex and less intuitive than an ordered list. For such ADT's it is necessary to use a more rigorous method of defining the behavior of their operations: You must supply a set of **axioms**. For example, the axiom

```
OrderedListRetrieve(OrderedListInsert(OL, I, X), I) = X
```

specifies that `OrderedListRetrieve` retrieves from position `I` the item that `OrderedListInsert` has put there.[1]

Once you have satisfactorily specified the behavior of an ADT, you can design applications that access and manipulate the ADT's data solely in terms of its operations and without regard for its implementation. As a very simple example, suppose that you want to design a procedure that prints out the items in an ordered list. Even though the wall between the implementation of the ADT ordered list and the rest of the program prevents you from knowing how the ordered list is stored, you can write a

[1]This axiom contains inconsistencies in the way we have used the operations. For the above axiom to be syntactically correct, both `OrderedListInsert` and `OrderedListRetrieve` must be Pascal-like functions instead of procedures, as we defined them earlier in this section. In particular, `OrderedListInsert(OL, I, X)` must return as its value the ordered list that results after the insertion, and `OrderedListRetrieve(OL, I)` must return the value in position `I` of `OL`. These inconsistencies result from our desire to define the operations on an intuitive level. As long as you are aware of the issue, it should not cause any difficulties.

procedure `PrintList` in terms of the operations that define the ADT ordered list. The pseudocode for such a procedure follows:

An implementation-independent application of the ADT ordered list

```
PrintList(OL)
{ Prints the items on the ordered list OL (in order) }

    for Position := 1 to OrderedListLength(OL) do
    begin
        OrderedListRetrieve(OL, Position, DataItem)
        Print DataItem
    end
```

Notice that as long as the ADT ordered list is implemented correctly, the `PrintList` procedure will perform its task; the procedure does not depend on *how* you implement the ordered list. Figure 4-6 illustrates the wall between `PrintList` and the implementation of the ADT ordered list.

As another application of the ADT operations, suppose that you want a procedure `Swap` that interchanges the items currently in positions *I* and *J* of the ordered list. The following pseudocode for such a procedure assumes that there actually are items in positions *I* and *J* of the ordered list:

```
Swap(OL, I, J)
{ Swaps the I^th and J^th items in the ordered list OL. }

    OrderedListRetrieve(OL, I, IthItem)  { copy I^th item }
    OrderedListRetrieve(OL, J, JthItem)  { copy J^th item }

    replace I^th item with J^th }
    OrderedListDelete(OL, I)
    OrderedListInsert(OL, I, JthItem)

    { replace J^th item with I^th }
    OrderedListDelete(OL, J)
    OrderedListInsert(OL, J, IthItem)
```

Notice that the order of operations is important because when you delete an item, `OrderedListDelete` renumbers the remaining items. Like `PrintList`, the `Swap` procedure does not depend on how you implement the ordered list.

You can use ADT operations in an application without the distraction of implementation details

In both of the preceding examples, notice how you can focus on the task at hand without the distraction of implementation details such as arrays or pointers. With less to worry about, you are less likely to make an error in your logic when you use the ADT operations in applications such as `PrintList` and `Swap`. Likewise, when you finally implement the ADT operations in Pascal, you will not be distracted by these applications. In addition, you will not have to change `PrintList` and `Swap`, because they do not depend on any implementation decisions that you make. These assertions assume that you do not change the specifications of the ADT operations during their implementation. However, as Chapter 1 pointed out, developing software is not a linear process. You may realize during implementation that you need to refine your specifications. Clearly, changes to

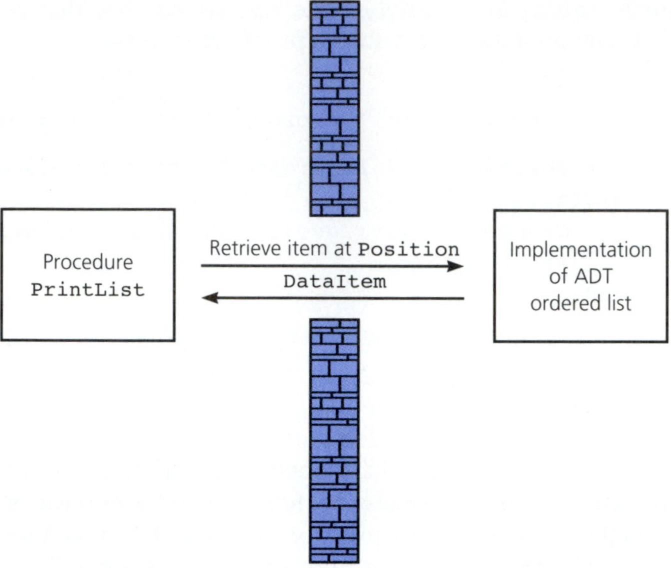

Figure 4-6

The wall between *PrintList* and the implementation of the ADT ordered list

the specification of any module affect any already-designed uses of that module.

To summarize, you can specify the behavior of an ADT independently of its implementation, either with informal definitions or with more formal axioms. Given such a specification, and without any knowledge of how the ADT will be implemented, you can design applications that utilize the ADT's operations to access its data.

Designing an ADT

You will see two implementations of the ADT ordered list later in this chapter. However, you probably have some ideas for implementations because the ADT ordered list shares some behaviors with both arrays and linked lists. Consider now some ADT's whose implementations will be less obvious to you. In doing so, you will learn more about the nature of an ADT and see that you should design ADT's as part of your solution to a problem.

The design of an abstract data type should evolve naturally during the problem-solving process. As an example of how this process might occur, suppose that you want to determine the dates of all the holidays in a given year. One way to do this is to examine a calendar. That is, you could consider each day in the year and ascertain whether that day is a holiday. The following pseudocode is thus a possible solution to this problem:

```
ListHolidays(Year)
{ Prints the dates of all holidays in the given year. }

   Date := date of first day of Year
```

```
while Date is before the first day of succ(Year) do
begin
   if Date is a holiday
        then write(Date, ' is a holiday')
   Date := date of next day
end  { while }
```

What data is involved here? Clearly, this problem operates on dates, where a date consists of a month, day, and year. Pascal does not have a standard data type *dateType*, so you will have to define your own. However, a Pascal user-defined (enumerated) data type does not suffice here. Even if you could specify all the dates that you require by using a user-defined data type, the data type would not specify and restrict the legal operations on the dates. For example, the standard data type *integer* implies arithmetic operations such as addition and multiplication as well as boolean operations such as comparison. An abstract data type differs from a user-defined data type in that an ADT specifies certain operations on the data values.

An ADT differs from a Pascal user-defined data type

What operations will you need to solve the holiday problem? You can see from the previous pseudocode that you must

- Determine the date of the first day of a given year.
- Determine whether a date is before another date.
- Determine whether a date is a holiday.
- Determine the date of the day that follows a given date.

Thus, you could define the following operations for your ADT:

```
FirstDay(Year)
{ Returns the date of the first day of the year specified. }

IsBefore(Date1, Date2)
{ Returns true if Date1 is before Date2, otherwise returns false. }

IsHoliday(Date)
{ Returns true if Date is a holiday, otherwise returns false. }

NextDay(Date)
{ Returns the date of the day after the specified date. }
```

All of these operations happen to be specified as functions.

The *ListHolidays* pseudocode now appears as follows:

```
ListHolidays(Year)
{ Prints the dates of all holidays in the year Year. }

   Date := FirstDay(Year)
   while IsBefore(Date, FirstDay(succ(Year))) do
   begin
      if IsHoliday(Date)
           then write(Date, ' is a holiday ')
      Date := NextDay(Date)
   end  { while }
```

Thus, you can design an ADT by choosing operations that are suitable to your problem. After specifying the operations, you use them to solve your problem independently of the implementation details of the ADT.

An appointment book. As another example of an ADT design, imagine that you want to create a computerized appointment book that spans a one-year period. Suppose that you make appointments only on the hour and half hour between 8 a.m. and 5 p.m. You want your system to store a brief notation about the nature of each appointment along with the date and time.

Thus, you can define an ADT appointment book. The data items in this ADT are the appointments, where an appointment consists of a date, time, and purpose. What are the operations? Two obvious operations are

- Make an appointment for a certain date, time, and purpose.
- Cancel the appointment for a certain date and time.

You will want to be careful that you do not make an appointment at an already occupied time. In addition to these operations, it is likely that you will want to

- Ask whether you have an appointment at a given time.
- Determine the nature of your appointment at a given time.

These two operations are related and can be combined. After all, you cannot determine the nature of an appointment unless you have one, and if you have an appointment, you probably will want to know its purpose. Finally, ADT's typically have an initialization operation.

Thus, the ADT appointment book can have the following operations:

```
CreateAppointmentBook(AppointmentBook)
{ Creates an empty appointment book. }

MakeAppointment(AppointmentBook, Date, Time, Purpose)
{ Inserts an appointment for the Date, Time, and Purpose
  specified. Assumes that there is not already an
  appointment at that time. }

CancelAppointment(AppointmentBook, Date, Time)
{ Deletes the appointment for the Date and Time specified. }

CheckAppointment(AppointmentBook, Date, Time,
                                   IsAppointment, Purpose)
{ Determines whether there is an appointment for the Date
  and Time specified. If there is, sets IsAppointment to
  true and returns the purpose of the appointment in
  Purpose; otherwise sets IsAppointment to false. }
```

You can use these ADT operations to design other operations on the appointments. For example, suppose that you want to change the day or time of a particular appointment. The following pseudocode indicates how to accomplish this task by using the previous ADT operations:

```
{ change the date or time of an appointment }
read (OldDate, OldTime, NewDate, NewTime)
CheckAppointment(AppointmentBook, OldDate, OldTime,
                                  IsAppointment, Purpose)
if IsAppointment { if old date/time is booked }
    then
    begin          { then see if new date/time is available }
       CheckAppointment(AppointmentBook, NewDate, NewTime,
                                  IsAppointment, Purpose)
       if IsAppointment { if new date/time is booked }
           then write('You already have an appointment at ',
                           NewTime, ' on ', NewDate)
           else    { new date/time is available }
           begin
               MakeAppointment(AppointmentBook, NewDate,
                                          NewTime, Purpose)
               CancelAppointment(AppointmentBook, OldDate,
                                                   OldTime)
           end
    end

    else write('You do not have an appointment at ', OldTime,
                  ' on ', OldDate)
```

Again notice that you can design applications for ADT operations without knowing how the ADT is implemented. The exercises at the end of this chapter provide examples of other tasks you can perform with this ADT.

ADT's that suggest other ADT's. This final example shows that the design of one ADT can suggest other ADT's. In fact, you can use one ADT to implement another ADT.

Suppose that you want to design a data base of recipes. You could think of this data base as an ADT: The recipes are the data items, and some typical operations on the recipes could include the following:

```
CreateRecipeBook(RecipeBook)
{ Creates an empty data base. }

InsertRecipe(RecipeBook, Recipe)
{ Inserts a recipe into the data base RecipeBook. }

DeleteRecipe(RecipeBook, Recipe)
{ Deletes a recipe from the data base RecipeBook. }

RetrieveRecipe(RecipeBook, Name, Recipe)
{ Retrieves the named recipe from the data base RecipeBook. }
```

This level of the design does not indicate such details as where `InsertRecipe` will place a recipe into the data base.

Now imagine that you want to write a procedure that scales a recipe retrieved from the data base. If the recipe is for *n* people, you want to revise it so that it will serve *m* people. Suppose that the recipe contains measurements such as 2½ cups, 1 tablespoon, and ¼ teaspoon. That is, the quantities are given as mixed numbers—integers and fractions—in units of cups, tablespoons, and teaspoons.

This problem suggests another ADT—measurement—with the following operations:

```
ReadMeasure(Measure)
{ Reads a Measure. }

WriteMeasure(Measure)
{ Writes a Measure. }

ScaleMeasure(Measure, NewMeasure, ScaleFactor)
{ Multiplies a Measure by a fractional ScaleFactor, which
  has no units, to obtain NewMeasure. }

ConvertMeasure(Measure, OldUnits, NewMeasure, NewUnits)
{ Converts Measure from its old units to a NewMeasure in new
  units. }
```

The ADT measurement requires that you perform fractional arithmetic. As there is no Pascal data type `fraction`, another ADT called fraction is in order. Its operations could include addition, subtraction, multiplication, and division of fractions. For example, you could specify addition as

```
AddFractions(First, Second, Sum)
{ Adds two fractions and reduces the sum to lowest terms }
```

Moreover, you could include operations to convert a mixed number to a fraction and to convert a fraction to a mixed number when feasible.

When you finally implement the ADT measurement, you can use the ADT fraction. That is, you can use one ADT to implement another ADT. The exercises at the end of this chapter ask you to implement these ADT's.

The Linked List As an ADT

Although Chapter 3 presented the linked list as a data structure that involved pointers, you could design an ADT linked list, which you could implement in ways other than by using Pascal pointers. For example, you could define the ADT linked list of sorted integers that has the following operations:

```
CreateLinkedList(LL)
{ Creates an empty linked list LL. }
```

```
LinkedListInsert(LL, NewValue)
{ Inserts NewValue into its proper sorted position in a
  sorted linked list LL unless the list already contains a
  node with that value, in which case no insertion occurs. }

LinkedListDelete(LL, Value)
{ Deletes the data item equal to Value, if it is present,
  from the sorted linked list LL. }

LinkedListRetrieve(LL, NodeNumber, RetrievedValue)
{ Sets RetrievedValue to the data item in node NodeNumber
  of the linked list LL. }

LinkedListPosition(LL, Value)
{ Returns the position number in the linked list LL of the
  node that contains Value. }
```

As you did in Chapter 3, you can implement this ADT by using pointers. However, you also can implement it by using arrays, as Exercise 10c at the end of this chapter considers. Similarly, you can define other Pascal data structures such as files and sets as ADT's, but we leave these to you as exercises.

IMPLEMENTING ADT'S

Data structures implement ADT's

The question of how to **implement** an ADT—that is, how to store the data and carry out the operations—is in the realm of **data structures**. In other words, data structures implement ADT's. What does it mean to implement an ADT once its operations are clearly defined? Your first reaction to this question might be that an implementation is a set of Pascal type definitions, functions, and procedures. Although this point of view is not incorrect, hopefully you have learned not to jump right into code. Just as you use successive refinement in the top-down design of algorithms, so should you refine an ADT through successive levels of abstraction. You can view each of the successively more concrete descriptions of the ADT as implementing its more abstract predecessors. As you will see, there are decisions that you should make carefully at each level of the implementation. In a formal course on data structures, you will learn how to weigh quantitatively the trade-offs involved. For now, however, our analyses are at the intuitive level.

The refinement process stops when you reach an implementation at a level of abstraction that the programming language supports—that is, when the ADT is transformed gradually from a set of operations into a form that can be realized in a programming language. If the implementation uses constructs such as records and pointers, you can stop if your language is Pascal, because Pascal supports records and pointers. On the other hand, if your language is FORTRAN, you must devise a way to implement records and pointers by using the constructs that FORTRAN supplies. The more primitive your language, the more levels of implementation you will require.

Implementations of the ADT Ordered List

The implementation of the ADT ordered list will illustrate ADT implementation in general. Recall that the ADT ordered list operations are

```
CreateOrderedList(OL)
OrderedListLength(OL)
OrderedListInsert(OL, Position, NewItem)
OrderedListDelete(OL, Position)
OrderedListRetrieve(OL, Position, DataItem)
```

An array-based implementation. Your first thought about implementing an ordered list is probably to store the list's items in an array. In fact, you might believe that the ordered list is simply a fancy name for an array. If you do, we hope that by the time you finish reading this chapter, you will see the error in this point of view.

In any case, the array-based implementation appears to be a natural choice because both an array `Items` and an ordered list reference their items by position number. Thus, you can store the ordered list's K^{th} item in `Items[K]`. How much of the array will the ordered list occupy? Possibly all of the array, but probably not. That is, you need to keep track of the array elements that you have assigned to the ordered list and those that are available for use in the future. The length of the array is a known, fixed value such as `MaxLength`. Thus, a simple solution is to keep track of the number of items on the list, that is, the list's length. An obvious benefit is that implementing the operation `OrderedListLength(OL)` will be easy.

You should implement each ADT operation as either a procedure or a function. Each operation will require both the array `Items` and the current number of items on the ordered list. One way to facilitate the passing of both `Items` and `Size` to each subprogram is to define the ordered list `OL` as a record with two fields:

An ordered list as a record with two fields

`Size`: an integer that is the current number of items on the list

`Items`: an array that contains the items on the list

as Figure 4-7 illustrates. Thus, the following statements declare `OL` to be an ordered list:

```
const  MaxLength = <maximum length of list>;
type   itemType = <desired type of list item>;
       ordListType = record
            Size : integer;
            Items : array[1..MaxLength] of itemType
       end;
var    OL : ordListType;
```

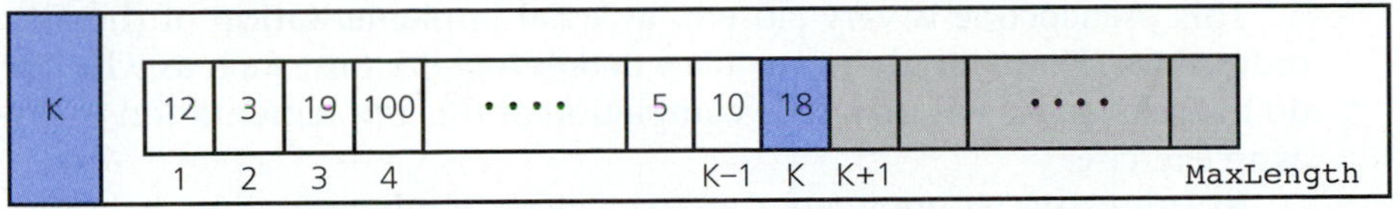

Figure 4-7

An array-based implementation of an ordered list

The pseudocode for the five ordered list operations follows:

```
CreateOrderedList(OL)

    OL.Size := 0

OrderedListLength(OL)

    OrderedListLength := OL.Size

OrderedListInsert(OL, Position, NewItem)

    OLLength := OrderedListLength(OL)
    if (Position < 1) or (Position > succ(OLLength))
                                   or (OLLength = MaxLength)
        then indicate an error

        else
        begin
           { shift all items at positions >= Position
              ( no shift if Position = succ(OLLength) ) }
           for J := OLLength downto Position do
               OL.Items[J + 1] := OL.Items[J]
           { insert new item }
           OL.Items[Position] := NewItem
           OL.Size := succ(OL.Size)
        end

OrderedListDelete(OL, Position)

    OLLength := OrderedListLength(OL)
    if (Position < 1) or (Position > OLLength)
        then indicate an error

        else
        begin
           { shift all items at positions > Position
              ( no shift if Position = OLLength ) }
           for J := succ(Position) to OLLength do
               OL.Items[J - 1] := OL.Items[J]
           OL.Size := pred(OL.Size)
        end

OrderedListRetrieve(OL, Position, DataItem)

    if (Position < 1) or (Position > OrderedListLength(OL))
        then indicate an error
        else return the item OL.Items[Position]
```

This pseudocode is very close to a Pascal implementation of the ADT ordered list. However, there are a few details to work out, such as what to do in the event of an error. The completion of this implementation is left as an exercise.

In summary, to implement an ADT, given implementation-independent specifications of the ADT operations, you first must choose a data structure. Next, you must write constant and type definitions not only for the data structure, but also for the parameters that the ADT operations require. You should realize that the calling module, as well as the ADT operations, must have access to these constant and type definitions. However, the calling module must access data only by using the ADT operations.

A pointer-based implementation. A close examination of the array-based implementation uncovers a difficulty. An array has a fixed size—at least in most commonly used programming languages—but the ADT ordered list can have an arbitrary length. Thus, in the strict sense, you cannot use an array to implement an ordered list, because it is certainly possible for the number of items on the list to exceed the fixed size of the array. When developing implementations for ADT's, you are often confronted with this **fixed-size** problem. In many contexts, you must reject an implementation that has a fixed size in favor of an implementation that can grow dynamically.

Thus, this section considers how you can develop a dynamic implementation. Pascal supports the dynamic allocation of storage through its predefined procedure *new*. Recall that the procedure call *new(p)* returns *p* pointing to a newly allocated node of storage. You can use the techniques developed in Chapter 3 to link these nodes together, thereby creating a linked list that represents the ADT ordered list. As the length of the ordered list increases, you need only use the procedure *new* to allocate nodes for the additional items. Unlike the array-based implementation, a pointer-based implementation does not impose a fixed maximum length on the list—except, of course, as imposed by the storage limits of the system.

Figure 4-8 indicates one possible way to design a linked list to implement an ordered list. You can use a head record *OL* that has two fields as follows:

A head record that points to an ordered list

Size: an integer that is the current number of items on the list

Head: a pointer to the item in the first position on the list

Thus, the following statements declare *OL* to be an ordered list:

```
type  itemType = <desired type of list item>;
      ptrType = ^nodeType;
      nodeType = record
            Item : itemType;
            Next : ptrType
      end;  { record }
```

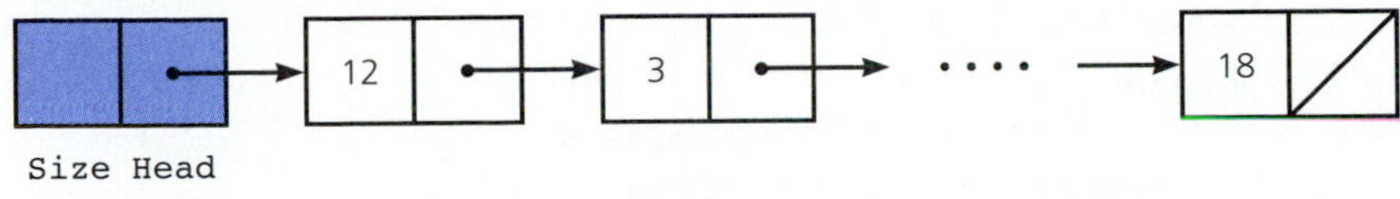

Figure 4-8

A pointer-based implementation of an ordered list

```
        ordListType = record
              Size : integer;
              Head : ptrType
        end;  { record }
  var   OL : ordListType;
```

Of the five ordered list operations, *CreateOrderedList* and *OrderedListLength* are straightforward:

```
CreateOrderedList(OL)

    OL.Size := 0
    OL.Head := nil

OrderedListLength(OL)

    OrderedListLength := OL.Size
```

For the implementation of the remaining operations, it is convenient to define a function *PtrTo*, which returns a pointer to the node at a specified position on the list. Because a linked list does not provide direct access to a specified position, *PtrTo* must traverse the list from its beginning until the specified point is reached. As you will see, this task is common to the implementation of the retrieval, insertion, and deletion operations. The pseudocode for *PtrTo* is as follows:

```
PtrTo(OL, Position)
{ Returns a pointer to the node at position Position in
  ordered list OL. If Position < 1 or Position > the length
  of OL, PtrTo returns nil. }

   if (Position < 1) or (Position > OrderedListLength(OL))
       then PtrTo := nil

       else { count from the beginning of the list }
       begin
          Trav := OL.Head
          for Skip := 1 to pred(Position) do
              Trav := Trav^.Next
          PtrTo := Trav
       end
```

Now the retrieval operation appears in pseudocode as follows:

```
OrderedListRetrieve(OL, Position, DataItem)

   if (Position < 1) or (Position > OrderedListLength(OL))
       then indicate an error
```

```
    else
    begin
       P := PtrTo(OL, Position)
       Return the item P^.Item
    end
```

Notice that this implementation of `OrderedListRetrieve` is substantially less efficient than the array-based implementation. The array-based implementation accesses the ith item directly because it is stored in `Items[i]`. The pointer-based implementation, on the other hand, traverses the linked list until the ith item is encountered.

The pointer-based implementations of `OrderedListInsert` and `OrderedListDelete` use the general linked list processing techniques developed in Chapter 3. To insert an item after the first item of an ordered list, you must first obtain a pointer to the preceding item. Insertion into the first position of an ordered list is a special case.

```
OrderedListInsert(OL, Position, NewItem)

   if (Position < 1) or (Position > succ(OrderedListLength(OL)))
       then indicate an error

       else
       begin
          OL.Size := succ(OL.Size)
          if Position = 1
             then insert NewItem at beginning of list

             else
             begin
                Prev := PtrTo(OL, pred(Position))
                Insert NewItem after node to which
                  Prev points
             end
       end
```

The deletion operation is analogous to insertion. To delete an item that occurs after the first item of an ordered list, you must first obtain a pointer to the preceding item. Deletion from the first position of an ordered list is a special case.

```
OrderedListDelete(OL, Position)

   if (Position < 1 ) or (Position > OrderedListLength(OL))
       then indicate an error

       else
       begin
          OL.Size := pred(OL.Size)
          if Position = 1
             then delete the first node from the list
```

```
            else
            begin
               Prev := PtrTo(OL, pred(Position))
               Delete the node after the node to
                 which Prev points
            end
      end
```

The completion of this pointer-based implementation is left as an exercise.

Because *PtrTo* returns a pointer, you would not want any module outside of the ADT to call it. To do so would violate the walls of the ADT. That is, the walls should hide the pointer-based implementation of the ADT from the modules outside of the ADT. Such modules should be able to use the ADT without knowledge of the pointers that the implementation uses. Thus, only the ADT ordered list operations should call *PtrTo*. It is perfectly reasonable for the implementation of an ADT to define private variables, procedures, and functions that are not accessible by the rest of the program. Although Standard Pascal does not provide a way to prevent this access, Turbo Pascal does if you define the ADT within a unit. We outline a unit for the ADT ordered list later in this chapter.

***PtrTo* is hidden from the user within the walls of the ADT**

Violating the walls. Recall the *PrintList* procedure that printed the items on an ordered list *OL*.

```
PrintList(OL)
{ Prints the items on the ordered list OL (in order) }

   for Position := 1 to OrderedListLength(OL) do
   begin
      OrderedListRetrieval(OL, Position, DataItem)
      Print DataItem
   end
```

Again note that this procedure invokes the ADT operations *OrderedListLength* and *OrderedListRetrieve*, and therefore is independent of the particular implementation of the ADT ordered list that you happen to choose. That is, *PrintList* will work regardless of whether you use an array-based implementation, a pointer-based implementation, or some other implementation. This feature is a definite advantage of abstract data types. In addition, by thinking in terms of the available ADT operations, you will not be distracted by implementation details such as pointers. For example, the following is an implementation of *PrintList* that assumes the pointer-based implementation that was just described:

```
PrintList2(OL)
{ Prints the items on the ordered list OL (in order).
  Assumes a pointer-based implementation. }

   Cur := Head
```

```
while Cur <> nil do
begin
   Print Cur^.Item
   Cur := Cur^.Next
end
```

`PrintList2` certainly takes more effort to write than `PrintList`. (Note that `PrintList2` is like the `PrintList` procedure in Chapter 3.)

Suppose that after writing `PrintList2`, you decide to change from the pointer-based implementation that `PrintList2` assumes to an array-based implementation of the ADT ordered list. You would need a completely new implementation of `PrintList2` because it depends on the data structure—the linked list—that you chose for the implementation of the ordered list. Violating the walls of the ADT is a definite disadvantage here.

Sometimes people use the ADT operations but violate the walls of the ADT inadvertently. For example, under the array-based ordered list implementation that we described earlier in this chapter, you might accidentally reference the first item in the ordered list by writing `OL.Items[1]` instead of `OrderedListRetrieve(OL,1,FirstItem)`. If you changed to another implementation, your program would be incorrect. To correct your program, you must locate and change all references to `OL.Items[1]`—but first you must realize that `OL.Items[1]` is in error! Unfortunately, Pascal does not help you to avoid this violation, unless you define the ADT within a unit.

Implementing an ADT Within a Unit

You have seen the advantages of information hiding, abstract data types, and honoring the walls of an ADT. However, if you simply include an ADT's type, procedure, and function definitions within your program, violating the ADT's walls not only is easy, it is legal. Whereas Standard Pascal relies on the honor system to protect an ADT from its users, Turbo Pascal provides a way for you to enforce an ADT's walls by implementing the ADT within a unit.

Recall from Chapter 2 that the user of a unit has access to all constants, data types, variables, procedures, and functions that the unit's interface section declares. Likewise, you can hide from a unit's user all constants, data types, variables, procedures, and functions that appear in the unit's implementation section. For example, consider the pointer-based implementation of the ADT ordered list discussed earlier in this chapter. By including `PtrTo` within the implementation section but not the interface section of a unit, you make `PtrTo` unavailable to any program that uses the unit. However, `PtrTo` is still available to the ADT operations, as the following unit demonstrates:

This unit hides `PtrTo` from the unit's user, but does not hide the ordered list

```
unit OrdList1;    { unit of ADT ordered list operations }
interface
```

```
type   itemType = <desired type of list item>;
       ptrType = ^nodeType;
       nodeType = record
           Item : itemType;
           Next : ptrType
       end;    { record }

       ordListType = record
           Size : integer;
           Head : ptrType
       end;    { record }

procedure CreateOrderedList(var OL : ordListType);
function OrderedListLength(OL : ordListType): integer;
procedure OrderedListInsert(var OL : ordListType;
                Position : integer; NewItem : itemType;
                var Success : boolean);
procedure OrderedListDelete(var OL : ordListType;
                Position : integer; var Success : boolean);
procedure OrderedListRetrieve(var OL : ordListType;
                Position : integer; var DataItem : itemType;
                var Success : boolean);

implementation

function PtrTo(OL : ordListType; Position : integer) : ptrType;

{ Implementations of PtrTo and the five ADT operations
  appear here. }

end.    { unit }
```

Because the type definitions for the ADT appear in the interface section of the unit, any user of the unit can violate the walls of the ADT. However, this unit has a distinct advantage: Because the data type *ordListType* is public and the ordered list is a parameter of the ADT operations, the user can have several different ordered lists in simultaneous existence by using only this unit, as the following program segment demonstrates:

```
program DemonstrateOrderedListUnitOne;

uses OrdList1;             { ADT ordered list operations }

var OList1, OList2 : ordListType;
    Name, Title : itemType;

begin    { Main Program }
    CreateOrderedList(OList1);       { create first list }
    CreateOrderedList(OList2);       { create second list }

    readln(Name, Title);
    OrderedListInsert(OList1, 1, Name, Success);
    OrderedListInsert(OList2, 1, Title, Success);
    . . .
```

Another approach that completely hides the ADT's implementation, but allows only one ordered list, is possible. You must hide the type definitions, but you cannot simply move them to the unit's implementation section, because the subprogram headers in the interface section use the data type *ordListType* in their parameter lists. You can avoid this dilemma by removing the ordered list *OL* from the parameter lists and declaring *OL* as an owned variable in the implementation section. Thus, the ADT operations can access *OL* globally, yet this access is denied to all users of the unit. The following unit demonstrates these ideas for a pointer-based implementation of the ADT ordered list:

*This unit hides both **PtrTo** and the ordered list from the unit's user*

```
unit OrdList2;  { unit of ADT ordered list operations }

interface

type itemType = <desired type of list item>;

procedure CreateOrderedList;
function OrderedListLength : integer;
procedure OrderedListInsert(Position : integer;
                  NewItem : itemType; var Success : boolean);
procedure OrderedListDelete(Position : integer;
                  var Success : boolean);
procedure OrderedListRetrieve(Position : integer;
                  var DataItem: itemType;
                  var Success : boolean);

implementation

type ptrType = ^nodeType;
     nodeType = record
         Item : itemType;
         Next : ptrType
     end;   { record }

     ordListType = record
         Size : integer;
         Head : ptrType
     end;   { record }

var  OL : ordListType;

function PtrTo(Position : integer) : ptrType;

{ Implementations of PtrTo and the five ADT operations
   appear here. }

end. { unit }
```

If you want to have more than one ordered list in existence simultaneously, you need a unit like the previous one for each list. If, for example, you had two units named *UnitOne* and *UnitTwo*, you could qualify calls to the ADT operations as follows:

```
UnitOne.CreateOrderedList;
UnitTwo.CreateOrderedList;
```

You can avoid qualifying such calls by using different names for the corresponding ADT operations within each unit. For example, you could replace *CreateOrderedList* with *CreateNameList* in one unit and *CreateTitleList* in the other unit.

Comparing Array-Based and Pointer-Based Implementations

Typically, the various implementations that a programmer contemplates for a particular ADT have advantages and disadvantages. When you must select an implementation, you should weigh these advantages and disadvantages before you make your choice. As you will see, the decision between possible implementations of an ADT is one that you must make time and time again. This section compares the two implementations of the ADT ordered list that you just saw as an example of how you should proceed in general.

Arrays are easy to use, but they have a fixed size

The array-based implementation appears to be a reasonable approach. An array behaves like an ordered list, and arrays are easy to use. However, as was already mentioned, an array has a fixed size; it is possible for the number of items in the ordered list to exceed this fixed size. In practice, when choosing among implementations of an ADT, you must ask the question, does the fixed-size restriction of an array-based implementation present a problem in the context of a particular application? The answer to this question depends on two factors. The obvious factor is whether or not, for a given application, you can predict in advance the maximum number of items in the ADT at any one time. If you cannot, then the array-based solution is not adequate; it is quite possible that an operation—and hence the entire program—will fail because the ADT in the context of a particular application requires more storage than the array can provide.

Can you predict the maximum number of items in the ADT?

On the other hand, if you can predict in advance the maximum number of items in the ADT at any one time for a given application, you must explore a more subtle factor: Would you waste storage by declaring an array to be large enough to accommodate this maximum number of items? Consider a case in which the maximum number of items is large, but you suspect that this number will rarely be achieved. For example, suppose that there could be as many as 10,000 items in an ordered list, but the actual number of items in the ordered list rarely exceeds 10. Although you must declare at least 10,000 array locations, at least 9,990 array locations will be wasted for the majority of the program's execution.

Will an array waste storage?

In both of the previous cases, the pointer-based implementation of an ordered list is preferable to the array-based implementation. Because a pointer-based implementation uses the *new* procedure to provide dynamic storage allocation, it will provide as much storage as the ordered list needs (within the bounds of the particular computer, of course).[2] Thus, you need not be able to predict the maximum size of the ordered list. Also, the ordered list will be allocated only as much storage as it needs, so you will not waste storage. In addition, the pointer-based implementation recycles storage for use elsewhere by using the *dispose* procedure.

Thus, there are many types of applications for which the fixed-size restriction of an array-based implementation of an ADT is unacceptable. The need for dynamic storage is one factor that would lead you to choose a pointer-based implementation. There are also other, more subtle factors that would push you in this direction. Some of these factors will come to light in Chapter 7, which examines the efficiency of algorithms, and in Chapter 10, which compares implementations of the ADT **table**.

It is important to point out, however, that there are many contexts in which the fixed-size limitation of an array-based implementation is not a problem. For example, it would not be a problem if, from the context of the application, you knew that the length of an ordered list would never be greater than 25. You could allocate enough storage in the array for the ordered list and know that you would waste little storage when the ordered list contained only a few items.

The item after the Ith item in an array is implied; in a linked list, it is pointed to explicitly

There are other contrasts in the natures of the array-based and pointer-based implementations. Any time you store a collection of data in a structure such as an array or a linked list, the data items become ordered; that is, there is a first item, a second item, and so on. This order implies that given any item in the structure there is a notion of the next item after it. In an array *A*, the location of the next item after the item in *A[I]* is *implicit*—it is in *A[I + 1]*. In a linked list, however, the location of the next item after the item in node *N* must be determined *explicitly* by using the pointer in the node *N*. This notion of an implicit versus explicit next item is one of the primary differences between an array and a linked list.

Thus, the most obvious advantage of an array-based implementation is that it saves space because it does not have to store explicit information about where to find the next data item. Another, more subtle advantage is that it can provide **direct access** to a specified item. For example, if you use the array *Items* to implement an ordered list, you know that the item associated with list position *I* is stored in *Items[I]*. On the other hand, if you use a linked list to implement the ordered list, you have no way of knowing the location of the node that contains this item. To get to the appropriate node, you would have to use the *Next* pointers to traverse the linked list from its beginning until you reached the Ith node. The advantages provided by direct access will be considered often as we select implementations for many of the ADT's in the remainder of this book.

---

[2]Turbo Pascal allows you to detect when a call to *new* is unsuccessful due to insufficient memory by using the *HeapError* variable. For simplicity, we will assume throughout this book that sufficient memory always exists.

Changing from One Implementation to Another

Suppose that your program originally employs the array-based ordered list implementation, but you soon realize that the limitations of a fixed-sized ordered list are not acceptable for your particular application. Because the wall created by the data-abstraction approach isolates a program from changes in the implementations of its ADT's, changing from one implementation to another requires only a minimal amount of surgery. Indeed, if you define each ADT within a unit, you must change only a program's `uses` statement. Regardless of the organization of the ADT, however, certain changes to it are necessary.

In theory, you must replace only the body of each of the five ordered list operations. In practice, however, you must make a few other small changes. As an example, the following summarizes the necessary program modifications for changing from an array-based to a pointer-based implementation of the ADT ordered list:

1. **Change the subprograms.** As you would expect, you must remove the five subprograms that the array-based implementation uses to perform the ordered list operations and replace them with the subprograms for the pointer-based implementation.
2. **Change global type definitions.** The need for this modification is really a result of Pascal's requirement that the type definitions for the ordered list be global: Because variables that are not local to the routines—for example, actual parameters in the procedure calls—must use the type definitions, the definitions must be global. If the type definitions could be local to the subprograms that implement the ordered list operations, then the definitions would be replaced as a result of replacing the subprograms. As this is not the case, you have to replace the type definitions that you saw earlier in this chapter as well as the subprograms.
3. **Change the calling sequence.** Although this change does not apply to our implementations of the ADT ordered list, we note it here anyway. Sometimes there will be slight differences between the parameters of a subprogram in one implementation and those of the corresponding subprogram in another implementation. If this is the case, you could change the calling sequences when you change implementations. However, this change does violate the spirit of the ADT contract. Instead you could revise the specifications of the ADT operations to remove any implementation dependencies; that is, you could change the definitions of the subprograms so that their parameter lists correspond to an implementation-independent calling sequence.

These modifications are like the ones that you generally must make when you change from one implementation of an ADT to another. Notice that none of the modifications require any sort of substantial revisions to the program. For all practical purposes, the wall allows the rest of the program to be oblivious to a change in the implementation of an ADT.

OBJECT-ORIENTED PROGRAMMING (*OPTIONAL*[3])

By now, you have seen the advantage of the walls that hide an ADT's implementation from its users. You also realize that the users of the ADT have a responsibility to honor these walls. However, if you define an ADT within a Turbo Pascal unit, you can enforce the walls somewhat by omitting private subprograms from the unit's interface section.

Object-oriented programming, or OOP, is a software engineering technique that provides more structure, modularity, and abstraction than the techniques you have learned so far. Instead of viewing a program as a sequence of actions, OOP views it as a collection of components called **objects** that interact. You can use an object to implement an ADT.

OOP embodies three fundamental principles:

KEY CONCEPTS ***Three Principles of Object-Oriented Programming***

1. Encapsulation: Objects combine data and operations.
2. Inheritance: Objects can inherit properties from other objects.
3. Polymorphism: Objects can determine appropriate operations at execution time.

The following discussion describes these three principles in detail.

Encapsulation

Typically, in an non-object-oriented environment, you apply data abstraction to design an abstract data type. During the implementation of the ADT, you choose a data structure and write subprograms that operate on its data. The resulting ADT operations form a wall between the user and the data structure. That is, the user agrees to access the data structure by using only the ADT operations, as Figure 4-9 illustrates. You have seen, however, that the user can violate this wall by accessing the data structure directly.

Both the data structure and the ADT operations are distinct pieces, as Figure 4-9 indicates. Object-oriented programming combines an ADT's data with its operations—now called **methods**—to form an **object**, which is a new data type. Combining data and methods to form an object, as Figure 4-10 illustrates, is called **encapsulation**. To *encapsulate* means to encase or enclose; thus, encapsulation is an information hiding technique. Whereas procedures and functions encapsulate actions, objects encapsulate data as

---

[3]You can cover this section now, cover it later, or skip it entirely.

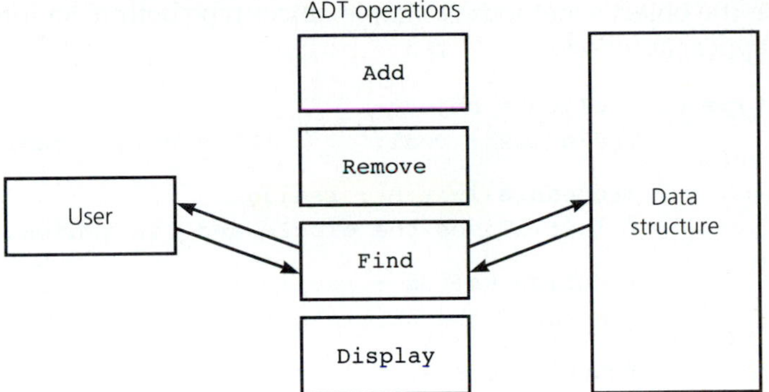

Figure 4-9

ADT operations provide access to a data structure

well as actions. Rather than thinking of the many components of the ADT in Figure 4-9, you can think at a higher level of abstraction when you consider the object in Figure 4-10 because it is a single entity. Whereas an ADT's operations act on a data structure, an object operates on itself. Thus, the inner detail of the object is hidden from the user of the object.

Although you may have been unaware of them, you have seen objects before. The alarm clock that awoke you this morning encapsulates time and operations such as "set the alarm." Even though you request the clock to perform certain functions, you do not see the details of these operations. A circle could be another example of an object. When you imagine a circle of a given radius, you probably also think of its diameter and area. You could think of a circle as embodying methods that return these values.

How do you actually construct an object? In Turbo Pascal,[4] a type definition for an object resembles a type definition for a record, but you replace the reserved word `record` with `object`. An object type definition can contain data fields, but unlike a record type definition, an object type definition includes procedure and function headers—in any order—that

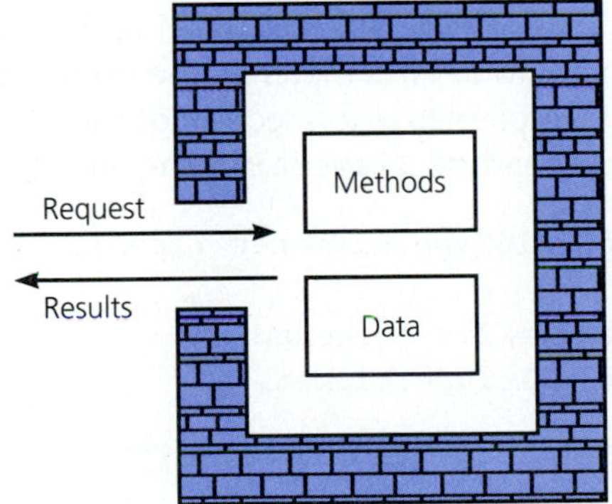

Figure 4-10

An object's data and methods are encapsulated

[4]Versions 5.5 and later

describe the object's methods. A simple object type definition for a circle would appear as follows:

```
type circleType = object
        TheRadius : real;     { the circle's radius }

        procedure Init(R : real);
        { Initializes the circle and its radius. }

        function Radius : real;
        { Returns the circle's radius. }

        function Diameter : real;
        { Returns the circle's diameter. }

        function Area : real;
        { Returns the circle's area. }

        function Circumference : real;
        { Returns the circle's circumference. }

        procedure DisplayStatistics;
        { Displays statistics of the circle. }
    end;    { object }
```

The identifiers that you use for a method's name and formal parameters must differ from those that you use for the object's fields.

The object variable *MyCircle*, which is of data type *circleType* and is declared as

```
var  MyCircle : circleType;
```

is called an **instance** of type *circleType*. Note that *MyCircle* contains one data field, *TheRadius*, and that upon request it can initialize itself; return its radius; compute its diameter, area, and circumference; and display these statistics. By the way, requests to an object are called **messages** and are simply calls to procedures or functions. Thus, an object responds to a message by acting on its data.

You still must implement the procedures and functions that are the object's methods; you do so either later in the program or, if the object is part of a unit, in the implementation section of the unit. For example, you could implement the method *Diameter* of the object *circleType* as

```
function circleType.Diameter : real;
begin
   Diameter := 2.0 * TheRadius
end;   { circleType.Diameter }
```

When you implement a method, qualify its name with the object's data type

Note that the name of this function is *circleType.Diameter*, not simply *Diameter*. When you implement a method, you must qualify the method's name with the object type to distinguish it from methods with the same name in other objects.

Within the body of the subprogram that defines an object's method, you can reference the object's data fields and other methods without such qualification. However, when you invoke a method from outside the object definition, that is, from other parts of the program, you must qualify the method name with an object variable, much as you do for records. For example, you could write

When you invoke a method, qualify its name with an object variable

```
MyCircle.Init(5.1);
writeln(MyCircle.Diameter)
```

to initialize a circle object of radius 5.1 and display its diameter. You can also use the *with* statement, as in

```
with MyCircle do
begin
   Init(5.1);
   writeln(Diameter)
end;    { with }
```

Note that you can reference an object's data fields directly from outside the method definitions. For example, you can write *MyCircle.TheRadius*. However, accessing the data fields directly from outside the method definitions is a practice that you should avoid. Instead, you should treat the data fields as hidden from the user of the object and provide methods within the object that access these fields for the user. Such is the purpose of the function *circleType.Radius*; it simply returns the value of *TheRadius*, which is the circle's radius.

Private fields and methods. You can restrict access to any of an object's data fields and methods by defining a **private section**[5] as follows:

```
type DooDad = object
      { public section }
         Doo : boolean;                { public field }

         procedure Init;               { public method }
         procedure DisplayValue;       { public method }

      { private section }
      private
         Dad : real;                   { private field }

         function Value : real;        { private method }
      end;    { object }
```

Note that the private section must follow the public section in the object type definition.

Private fields and methods are accessible only within the unit or program that contains the object type definition. Thus, private sections are

[5]Available beginning with version 6.0 of Turbo Pascal

effective only when you organize your objects into one or more units, as described next. Generally, private fields are desirable.

Defining an object as a unit. Defining your objects within one or more units frequently provides a convenient way for you to use objects in other programs. More importantly, however, when you define an object within a unit, the object's private section is hidden from the program that uses the unit.

The following unit contains a complete, but slightly modified, definition of *circleType*, which we just discussed. Here, the data field *TheRadius* is private.

```
unit UCircle;

interface

type circleType = object
        procedure Init(R : real);
        { -------------------------------------------
          Initializes the circle and its radius.
          Precondition: R is the desired radius.
          Postcondition: TheRadius = R.
          ------------------------------------------- }
        function Radius : real;
        { -------------------------------------------
          Determines the circle's radius by accessing
          the private field TheRadius.
          Precondition: Init has been called.
          Postcondition: Returns the radius.
          ------------------------------------------- }
        function Diameter : real;
        { -------------------------------------------
          Computes the circle's diameter.
          Precondition: Init has been called.
          Postcondition: Returns the diameter.
          ------------------------------------------- }
        function Area : real;
        { -------------------------------------------
          Computes the circle's area.
          Precondition: Init has been called.
          Postcondition: Returns the area.
          ------------------------------------------- }
        function Circumference : real;
        { -------------------------------------------
          Computes the circle's circumference.
          Precondition: Init has been called.
          Postcondition: Returns the circumference.
          ------------------------------------------- }
```

```
            procedure DisplayStatistics;
            { -------------------------------------------
              Displays statistics of the circle.
              Precondition: Init has been called.
              Postcondition: Displays the radius,
              diameter, circumference, and area.
              ------------------------------------------- }

         private
            TheRadius : real;
         end;   { object }

   implementation

   procedure circleType.Init(R : real);
   begin
      TheRadius := R
   end;  { circleType.Init }

   function circleType.Radius : real;
   begin
      Radius := TheRadius
   end;  { circleType.Radius }

   function circleType.Diameter : real;
   begin
      Diameter := 2.0 * TheRadius
   end;  { circleType.Diameter }

   function circleType.Area : real;
   begin
      Area := Pi * sqr(TheRadius)
   end;  { circleType.Area }

   function circleType.Circumference : real;
   begin
      Circumference := Pi * Diameter
   end;  { circleType.Circumference }

   procedure circleType.DisplayStatistics;
   begin
      writeln;
      writeln('Radius = ', Radius:6:1);
      writeln('Diameter = ', Diameter:6:1);
      writeln('Circumference = ', Circumference:10:1);
      writeln('Area = ', Area:10:1)
   end;  { circleType.DisplayStatistics }

   end.  { unit }
```

From within `DisplayStatistics`, you can invoke the method `Radius`, or access the private field `TheRadius`

Note that within the method *DisplayStatistics*, you can invoke the method *Radius*, as we did here, or access the field *TheRadius* directly.

The following program demonstrates how to use this unit:

```
program DemonstrateCircleObjectUnit;

uses UCircle;

var MyCircle : circleType;

begin  { Main Program }
{ set radius }
    MyCircle.Init(5.1);

{ display radius, diameter, circumference, area }
    MyCircle.DisplayStatistics;
end.   { Program }
```

*A reference to the private field **TheRadius** would be illegal within this program*

Because the object type definition is within the unit that this program uses, you can invoke any of the object's methods from within the program, but you cannot access the object's private data field *TheRadius*.

Inheritance

When you think of inheritance, you might imagine the one million dollars that you hope some long-lost wealthy relative will bequeath to you. In OOP, however, **inheritance** describes the ability of a data type to inherit properties from a previously defined data type. These properties are like the genetic characteristics that you received from your parents: Some traits are the same, some are similar but different, and some are new.

Consider the object type *circleType* that the previous section defined. An instance of *circleType* has one field and six methods. Imagine that you want an object type *sphereType*, which is like *circleType*, but adds a method *Volume* and changes some other methods. For example, you might write

```
type sphereType = object(circleType)
     { substitute methods: }
        function Area : real; { surface area }
        procedure DisplayStatistics;

     { new method }
        function Volume : real;
     end;   { object }
```

Adding *(circleType)* after *object* indicates that *circleType* is an **ancestor** type of *sphereType*, which in turn is a **descendent** type of *circleType*. Any descendents of *sphereType* would be descendents of *circleType* and, if there were ancestors of *circleType*, they also would be ancestors of *sphereType*. However, *circleType* is an **immediate ancestor** of *sphereType* and *sphereType* is an **immediate descendent** of *circleType*. Although an object type can have many immediate descendents, it can have only one immediate ancestor.

A descendent object type inherits all data fields and methods from its ancestor type. Thus, objects of type *sphereType* have all the data fields and methods that *circleType* defines as well as a new method *Volume* and substitute methods *Area* and *DisplayStatistics*. Suppose that you have

```
var  MyCircle : circleType;
     MySphere : sphereType;
```

MySphere.Diameter, for example, returns *MySphere*'s diameter by using the method *Diameter* that *sphereType* inherits from *circleType*.

Inheritance reduces the effort necessary to add features to an existing object

You can add as many new fields and methods to the definition of a descendent type as you like. New fields can be objects, but not of the type currently being defined (*sphereType*, in the previous example). In addition, new fields must have different identifiers than those defined in the ancestor type. Thus, you cannot change an ancestor's fields. You can, however, add methods that have any names. If a new method has the same name as an ancestor method—*Area*, for example—instances of the new object will use the new method, while instances of the ancestor object will use the original method.[6] Thus, *MyCircle.Area* invokes the method *circleType.Area*, whereas *MySphere.Area* invokes the method *sphereType.Area*. The method *circleType.Area* is hidden from objects of type *sphereType*.

This example exhibits a simple kind of **polymorphism**, which literally means *many forms*. The method *Area* has two forms. Because the compiler can determine which form to use at compilation time—as opposed to execution time—this situation is called **early binding**. We will elaborate on polymorphism shortly.

The following unit defines *sphereType* and uses the previously defined unit *UCircle*.

```
unit USphere;

interface

uses UCircle;

type sphereType = object(circleType)
       function Area : real;   { surface area }
       { ------------------------------------------
         Computes the sphere's surface area.
         Precondition: Init has been called.
         Postcondition: Returns the surface area.
         ------------------------------------------ }
```

[6]You can avoid confusion about which method *Area* represents by using *SurfaceArea* rather than *Area* to name *sphereType*'s area method. Although this approach is desirable stylistically, we do not take it here so that we can illustrate polymorphism later.

```
      function Volume : real;
      { ------------------------------------------
        Computes the sphere's volume.
        Precondition: Init has been called.
        Postcondition: Returns the volume.
        ------------------------------------------ }
      procedure DisplayStatistics;
      { ------------------------------------------
        Displays statistics of the sphere.
        Precondition: Init has been called.
        Postcondition: Displays the radius,
        diameter, equator length, surface area, and
        volume.
        ------------------------------------------ }
    end;  { object }

implementation

function sphereType.Area : real;
begin
   { you cannot reference TheRadius directly }
   { because it is private in circleType }
   Area := 4.0 * Pi * sqr(Radius)   { surface area }
end;  { sphereType.Area }

function sphereType.Volume : real;
var R : real;
begin
   R := Radius;
   Volume := 4.0 * Pi * R * sqr(R)/3.0
end;  { sphereType.Volume }

procedure sphereType.DisplayStatistics;
begin
   writeln;
   writeln('Radius = ', Radius:6:1);
   writeln('Diameter = ', Diameter:6:1);
   writeln('Equator length = ', Circumference:10:1);
   writeln('Surface area = ', Area:10:1);
   writeln('Volume = ', Volume:10:1)
end;  { sphereType.DisplayStatistics }

end.  { unit }
```

*Users of the unit that defines **`circleType`** cannot access **`circleType`**'s private field **`TheRadius`***

Notice that you may not directly reference *`circleType`*'s private field *`TheRadius`* from within the unit *`USphere`*. You can reference *`TheRadius`* only within the unit *`UCircle`* that contains *`circleType`*. Also, objects of type *`sphereType`* cannot reference *`TheRadius`* directly. However, you can—and should—use the method *`Radius`* to access the value of *`TheRadius`*. Note that if you compile the object types *`circleType`* and *`sphereType`* into one unit, they both have access to *`TheRadius`* directly.

Even so, using the method *Radius* to access *TheRadius* is preferable stylistically.

The following program demonstrates how to use the preceding unit:

```
program DemonstrateSphereObjectUnit;

uses UCircle, USphere;

var  MyCircle : circleType;
     MySphere : sphereType;

begin  { Main Program }
   MyCircle.Init(2.0);
   writeln('Display statistics of my circle:');
   MyCircle.DisplayStatistics;

   MySphere.Init(5.1);
   writeln('Display statistics of my sphere:');
   MySphere.DisplayStatistics;
end.  { Program }
```

Because the main program directly references an object of type *circleType*, the unit *UCircle* must appear in the *uses* statement even though it appears in *USphere*'s *uses* statement.

Object type compatibility. A descendent object type is type-compatible with all of its ancestor object types. Thus, you can use an instance of a descendent type instead of an instance of an ancestor type, but not the other way around. To remember this fact, realize that a descendent begins with its ancestor's features and probably augments them. Thus, whereas an assignment such as

```
AncestorInstance := DescendentInstance
```

completely defines *AncestorInstance*,

```
DescendentInstance := AncestorInstance;    { ILLEGAL }
```

does not completely define *DescendentInstance* and is illegal.

In addition, the object type of an actual parameter in a call to a subprogram can be a descendent of the corresponding formal parameter's object type. For example, consider the following ordinary procedure—that is, one that is not a method—in the previous program *DemonstrateSphereObjectUnit*:

```
procedure DisplayDiameter(Thing: circleType);
begin
   writeln('The diameter is ', Thing.Diameter:6:1)
end;  { DisplayDiameter }
```

The following calls to this procedure are legal:

```
DisplayDiameter(MyCircle);{ display MyCircle's diameter}
DisplayDiameter(MySphere);{ display MySphere's diameter}
```

The data type of the actual parameter *MySphere* is *sphereType*, which is a descendent of the data type of the formal parameter *Thing*. Moreover, if you define *planetType* as a descendent of *sphereType* and let *Saturn* be an instance of *planetType*, then

```
DisplayDiameter(Saturn)
```

is also legal. Note that object type compatibility applies to both value and variable parameters.

Abstract object types. Object type compatibility allows you to define an object type that is the basis of a family of other object types. For example, the previous object types *circleType* and *sphereType* describe points that are equidistant from the origin of a coordinate system: a two-dimensional coordinate system for *circleType* and a three-dimensional coordinate system for *sphereType*. The object type *equidistantPointsType* that defines one field *TheRadius* and one method *Init* could be the ancestor of *circleType*. Although instances of *equidistantPointsType* would not exist, this new type could be the common ground for *circleType* and *sphereType*, and thus would serve an important organizational purpose. *EquidistantPointsType* is an **abstract object type**; it defines characteristics for its descendents to inherit, but it does not have instances. You will see another example of an abstract object type later in this chapter.

Abstract object types have descendents, not instances

Polymorphism

Recall our previous object types *circleType* and *sphereType*:

```
type circleType = object
        procedure Init(R : real);
        function Radius : real;
        function Diameter : real;
        function Area : real;
        function Circumference : real;
        procedure DisplayStatistics;

     private
        TheRadius : real;
     end;   { object }

     sphereType = object(circleType)
        function Area : real; { surface area }
        function Volume : real;
        procedure DisplayStatistics;
     end;   { object }
```

In the previous section, you saw that the procedures *circleType.DisplayStatistics* and *sphereType.DisplayStatistics* each contain a call to the function *Area*. Which version of *Area* is called?

The compiler will choose *circleType*'s version of *Area* for *circleType.DisplayStatistics* and *sphereType*'s version of *Area* for *sphereType.DisplayStatistics*. As was mentioned earlier, because these choices are made at compilation time as opposed to execution time, they are examples of early binding. The methods are called **static methods** because the choices the compiler makes cannot be altered during execution.

Imagine that you omit the procedure *sphereType.DisplayStatistics* from the definition of *sphereType*, letting *sphereType* inherit *circleType*'s *DisplayStatistics*. If *MySphere* is an instance of *sphereType*, the statement *MySphere.DisplayStatistics* will display correct values for *MySphere*'s radius, diameter, and circumference (equator length), but it will display an incorrect value for *MySphere*'s surface area. Because *sphereType* inherits *circleType*'s methods *Radius*, *Diameter*, and *Circumference*, calls to these methods by *MySphere.DisplayStatistics* provide the correct values for *MySphere*. However, as we just noted, the compiler chooses *circleType*'s version of *Area*, not *sphereType*'s version of *Area*, when it compiles *circleType.DisplayStatistics*. Thus, you get the area of a circle instead of *MySphere*'s surface area.

Polymorphism allows an object's method to have the same name as an ancestor method. Whereas early binding means that the compiler determines the appropriate version of a method, **late binding** means that this choice is postponed until execution time. In fact, under late binding you write only one version of a method, which you can use with various objects with dramatically different results.

To enable one version of *DisplayStatistics* to select the appropriate version of *Area* at execution time, you must make *Area* a **virtual method** instead of a static method. With *Area* defined as a virtual method, when an instance of *sphereType* calls *DisplayStatistics*, *DisplayStatistics* will call *sphereType.Area*, yet when an instance of *circleType* calls *DisplayStatistics*, *DisplayStatistics* will call *circleType.Area*. Thus, objects can process data types that are unknown at compilation time. Figure 4-11 illustrates the general effect of a virtual method.

To indicate that a method such as *Area* is virtual, you simply write the reserved word *virtual* after the subprogram's header in the object type definition. *Virtual* simply indicates that late binding rather than early binding is in effect for the particular method. Any method in a descendent object type that has the same name as an ancestor's virtual method must also be virtual and must have the same parameters. In fact, the headers for all implementations of a virtual method must be identical. This stipulation is not necessary for static methods.

Object types that contain virtual methods must define a constructor

Virtual methods have another requirement: The object type that contains a virtual method must have a **constructor**, which is an initialization method that you must call before you call a virtual method. You denote a constructor by using the reserved word *constructor* instead of *proce-*

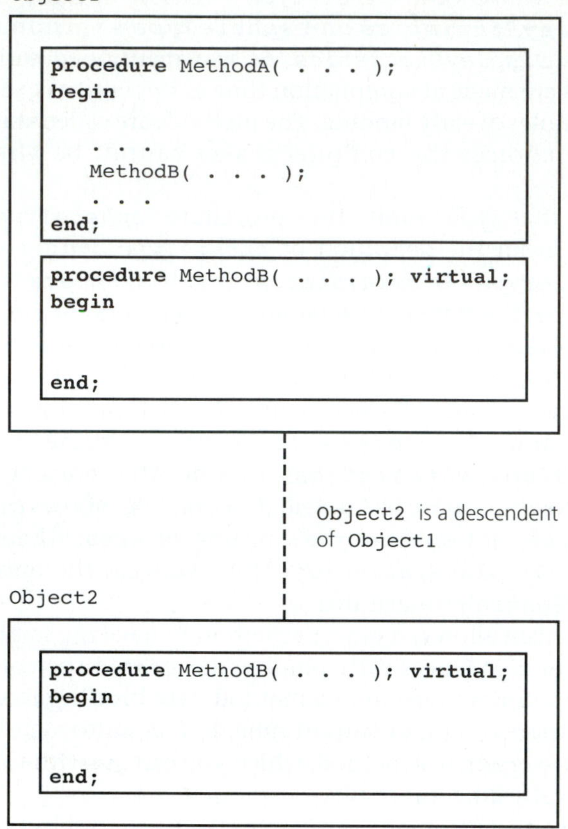
Object1
procedure MethodA(. . .);
begin
. . .
MethodB(. . .);
. . .
end;
procedure MethodB(. . .); virtual;
begin
end;
Object2 is a descendent of Object1
Object2
procedure MethodB(. . .); virtual;
begin
end;

Figure 4-11

Calls to virtual methods: *Object1.MethodA* calls *Object1*'s *MethodB*; *Object2.MethodA* calls *Object2*'s *MethodB*

dure, and typically you name it *Init*. Thus, the previous object definitions become

```
type circleType = object
         constructor Init(R : real);
         function Radius : real;
         function Diameter : real;
         function Area : real; virtual;
         function Circumference : real;
         procedure DisplayStatistics;

      private
         TheRadius : real;
      end;   { object }

      sphereType = object(circleType)
         { the constructor is inherited }
         function Area : real; virtual;
         function Volume : real;
      end;   { object }
```

Note that an object can inherit a constructor instead of defining its own. Note also that constructors themselves cannot be virtual.

You must call the constructor for every instance of an object. Thus, if *MyCircle* and *YourCircle* are instances of *circleType*, you must include the statements

```
MyCircle.Init;
YourCircle.Init
```

in your program. Note that the following is incorrect:

```
MyCircle.Init;
YourCircle := MyCircle    { ILLEGAL }
```

Also note that an object's methods should not call the constructor. Finally, an object that has only static methods can have a constructor, and any object can have several constructors.

Constructors are less mysterious when you consider some of Turbo Pascal's implementation details. Every object type that defines a virtual method has a **virtual method table**, or VMT. For every virtual method in the object, the VMT contains a pointer to the actual instructions that implement the method. A call to the constructor establishes this pointer. Thus, when an instance of an object calls its constructor, the constructor establishes within the VMT pointers to the versions of the virtual methods that are appropriate for the object's instance. Realize that each instance of an object type does not have its own VMT; each object type has only one VMT.

Use $R+ to check the initialization status of virtual methods

You should use Turbo Pascal's *$R+* directive to check the initialization status of the virtual methods. When this directive is in effect, a call to an uninitialized virtual method causes a range check error during execution. If you fail to use *$R+*, a call to an uninitialized virtual method can cause Turbo Pascal to behave unpredictably.

When to use virtual methods. Although static methods use less memory and execution time than virtual methods, unless space and time efficiency is essential, your objects should use virtual methods instead of static methods. Why? Object types that define virtual methods are **extensible**. That is, you can add capabilities to a descendent object type without access to the ancestor's source statements.

For example, imagine a unit that defines the previous object type *circleType*. *CircleType* contains the method *DisplayStatistics*, which calls the virtual method *Area*. Now consider a program that uses this unit and defines the previous object type *sphereType*, which inherits *DisplayStatistics* and contains its own virtual method *Area*. An instance of *sphereType* can use the inherited method *DisplayStatistics*, which, because *Area* is virtual, calls *sphereType*'s version of *Area*. Thus, you can change the behavior of *DisplayStatistics* even though it may have been written and compiled long ago. If *Area* were not a virtual method within *circleType*, you would need to define an entirely new *DisplayStatistics* method within *sphereType*.

Dynamic Object Types

In Chapter 3, you saw the advantages that dynamic memory allocation has over static allocation. These same advantages also make dynamic allocation desirable for objects. You can allocate an object's fields dynamically; in fact, you can allocate entire objects dynamically.

Allocation. An instance *MyCircle* of *circleType*, which we defined in the previous section, is an example of a **statically allocated object**. Memory for *MyCircle* is allocated at compilation time and remains allocated for the duration of the program's execution. In contrast, the memory for a **dynamically allocated object** is allocated during program execution and remains allocated only as long as you want.

To allow dynamically allocated instances of *circleType*, you add the statements

```
type circlePtrType = ^circleType;

var  MyCirclePtr : circlePtrType;
```

You then create an instance of the dynamic object by using either the *new* procedure

Use new to allocate an object dynamically

```
new(MyCirclePtr)
```

or the *new* function

```
MyCirclePtr := new(circlePtrType)
```

If the object type contains virtual methods, as *circleType* does, you must call its constructor next:

```
MyCirclePtr^.Init(5.1)
```

Note that the pointer variable and the caret replace the object variable that you use for a statically allocated object.

Turbo Pascal extends *new* to incorporate these two steps into one. You can write either

```
new(MyCirclePtr, Init(5.1))
```

or

```
MyCirclePtr := new(circlePtrType, Init(5.1))
```

Notice that you do not qualify *Init* with *MyCirclePtr^* —*MyCirclePtr* is, as yet, undefined. *New* determines the correct constructor from the type of its first parameter.

Deallocation and destructors. When you are finished with a dynamically allocated object, you can deallocate its memory by a call to the *dispose* procedure, such as

```
dispose(MyCirclePtr)
```

If you dynamically allocate either an object or its fields, and the object contains virtual methods, you must define a special method—called a **destructor**—within the object. The destructor, which by convention you name *Done*, performs all tasks necessary to deallocate the object. Exactly what you do within a destructor depends upon the intricacy of the object. Sometimes you do nothing special and the destructor is empty:

Dynamically allocated objects that contain virtual methods must define a destructor

```
destructor circleType.Done;
begin
end;    { circleType.Done }
```

However, even empty destructors perform a necessary service because the compiler generates instructions that access the object type's VMT in response to the reserved word *destructor*.

To deallocate a dynamic object that has virtual methods, you use an extended form of the *dispose* procedure:

```
dispose(MyCirclePtr, Done);
```

If the object contains dynamically allocated fields, the object's destructor must also call *dispose*. The examples that follow demonstrate possible destructors.

An object can inherit its destructor from an ancestor object. An object even can have several destructors to treat various situations, but you call only one destructor per instance of the object. Destructors can be either static or virtual, but virtual destructors are recommended to ensure that future descendents of the object can deallocate themselves correctly. Finally, note that even if a statically allocated object with static fields contains virtual methods, you do not need a destructor. Destructors are necessary only for dynamically allocated objects or objects with dynamically allocated fields. However, including a destructor in all objects permits dynamic allocation in the future even if you presently use only static allocation.

Virtual destructors are recommended for all objects

An Example of Dynamic Objects

In this example, we have revised the previous object types *circleType* and *sphereType* not only to make them dynamic, but also to incorporate some other ideas discussed in this chapter. Notice the ancestor object types *genericObjectType* and *equidistantPointsType*, which serve as abstract object types. *GenericObjectType* is organized as a separate unit because later examples will also use it. Within *equidistantPointsType*, notice the new field *Identifier*, which is simply a string that names each object. The fields within *equidistantPointsType* are private and can be accessed through the use of methods. We have omitted any implementations of methods that are the same as those you have seen already. To save space, we also have omitted pre- and postconditions, which are similar to those presented earlier.

```
unit UGeneric; { Dynamic abstract object }

interface

type genericObjectPtrType = ^genericObjectType;
     genericObjectType = object
        constructor Init;
        destructor Done; virtual;
        procedure Display; virtual;
     end;   { object }

implementation

constructor genericObjectType.Init;
begin
end;   { genericObjectType.Init }

destructor genericObjectType.Done;
begin
end;   { genericObjectType.Done }

procedure genericObjectType.Display;
begin
end;   { genericObjectType.Display }

end.   { unit }

unit UEquidistantPoints;
{ Dynamic circle and sphere objects }

interface

uses  UGeneric;         { Dynamic abstract object }

const NameLength = 20;

type  nameType = string[NameLength];

      equidistantPointsPtrType = ^equidistantPointsType;
      equidistantPointsType = object(genericObjectType)
         constructor Init(R : real);
            { sets radius to R and name to 'generic' }
         destructor Done; virtual;
         function Radius : real;          { Returns radius }
         function Name : nameType;        { Returns name }
         procedure Display; virtual;
            { Displays name, radius }

      private
         TheRadius : real;
         Identifier : nameType; { object's name }
      end;  { object }

      circlePtrType = ^circleType;
      circleType = object(equidistantPointsType)
```

```
      constructor Init(R : real);
         { sets radius to R and name to 'circle' }
      { the destructor is inherited }
      function Diameter : real;
      function Circumference : real;
      function Area : real; virtual;
   end;  { object }

   spherePtrType = ^sphereType;
   sphereType = object(circleType)
      constructor Init(R : real);
         { sets radius to R and name to 'sphere' }
      { the destructor is inherited }
      function Area : real; virtual;{surface area}
      function Volume : real;
   end;   { object }

implementation

constructor equidistantPointsType.Init(R : real);
begin
   TheRadius := R;
   Identifier := 'generic'
end;   { equidistantPointsType.Init }

destructor equidistantPointsType.Done;
begin
end;   { equidistantPointsType.Done }

function equidistantPointsType.Radius : real;
begin
   Radius := TheRadius
end;   { equidistantPointsType.Radius }

function equidistantPointsType.Name : nameType;
begin
   Name := Identifier
end;   { equidistantPointsType.Name }

procedure equidistantPointsType.Display;
begin
   writeln('a ', Name, ' of radius ', Radius:6:1)
end;   { equidistantPointsType.Display }

constructor circleType.Init(R : real);
begin
   TheRadius := R;
   Identifier := 'circle'
end;   { circleType.Init }

{ circleType.Diameter, circleType.Circumference, and
  circleType.Area are the same as on page 201. }
```

```
constructor sphereType.Init(R : real);
begin
   TheRadius := R;
   Identifier := 'sphere'
end;    { sphereType.Init }

{ sphereType.Area and sphereType.Volume are the same
  as on page 204. }

end.    { unit }
```

We included *circleType.Init* and *sphereType.Init* simply to set the identifier field appropriately. Otherwise, *circleType* and *sphereType* could inherit *Init* from *equidistantPointsType*, just as they inherit the destructor *Done*.

If *MySpherePtr* is an instance of *spherePtrType*, the following statements demonstrate the dynamic allocation, use, and subsequent deallocation of a *sphereType* object:

```
{ allocate sphere of radius 5.1 }
   new(MySpherePtr, Init(5.1));

{ display name and radius }
   MySpherePtr^.Display;            { Display inherited }

{ display diameter, surface area, and volume }
   writeln(MySpherePtr^.Diameter);  { Diameter inherited }
   writeln(MySpherePtr^.Area);      { sphere surface area }
   writeln(MySpherePtr^.Volume);    { sphere volume }

{ deallocate sphere }
   dispose(MySpherePtr, Done);
```

The *sphereType* object inherits *Display* from *equidistantPointsType* and *Diameter* from *circleType*. Notice that you allocate and deallocate a dynamic object within the program that uses the object.

A Family of List Objects

Consider a list that you might encounter, such as a list of chores, a list of important dates, or a list of addresses. You might choose to place the items on your list arbitrarily, chronologically, or perhaps alphabetically. As you saw earlier in this chapter, the ADT ordered list specifies none of these orders. The ADT ordered list is simply a list of items that you reference by position number. However, suppose that the items on your list occur alphabetically. That is, your list is a sorted list. You can define operations on your list in terms of the ADT ordered list operations. For example, to insert an item into a sorted list, you first need to determine the position in the list where the new item belongs. You then can use *OrderedListInsert* to insert the item into that position on the list.

Thus, your list can be a descendent of the ADT ordered list. Furthermore, the ADT ordered list can descend from a generic list, whose characteristics are common to all the lists mentioned here. For example, you can count the items on any of these lists.

The following example defines a family of list objects. An abstract object type is the ancestor of an ordered list object, which is the ancestor of a sorted list object. A pointer-based implementation is used.

```
unit ULists; { a family of list objects }

interface

type itemType = <desired type of list item>;

     ptrType = ^nodeType;
     nodeType = record
        Item : itemType;
        Next : ptrType
     end;  { record }

     listType = object              { abstract object type }
        constructor Init;
        { ----------------------------------------------
          Initializes the list.
          Precondition: None.
          Postcondition: The list's length is 0.
          ---------------------------------------------- }
        destructor Done; virtual;
        { ----------------------------------------------
          Deallocates the list.
          Precondition: Init has been called.
          Postcondition: All storage associated with
          the items on the list is deallocated; the
          list's length is 0.
          ---------------------------------------------- }
        function ListLength : integer; virtual;
        { ----------------------------------------------
          Determines the length of the list.
          Precondition: Init has been called.
          Postcondition: Returns the number of items
          that are currently on the list.
          ---------------------------------------------- }
        procedure DisplayList;
        { ----------------------------------------------
          Displays the items on the list.
          Precondition: Init has been called.
          Postcondition: Each item that is currently on
          the list is displayed.
          ---------------------------------------------- }
```

```
private
   { private fields }
   TheHead : ptrType; { pointer to the linked list }
   Size : integer;    { number of items on list }

   { private methods }
   function Head : ptrType;
   { ----------------------------------------------
     Precondition: Init has been called.
     Postcondition: Returns list's head pointer.
     ---------------------------------------------- }

   procedure SetHead(NewHead : ptrType);
   { ----------------------------------------------
     Precondition: Init has been called. NewHead
     is a pointer.
     Postcondition: Sets the list's head pointer
     to NewHead.
     ---------------------------------------------- }
   procedure SetSize(NewSize : integer);
   { ----------------------------------------------
     Precondition: Init has been called.
     Postcondition: Sets the list's Size field to
     NewSize.
     ---------------------------------------------- }
end;  { object }

ordListType = object(listType)
   { the constructor and destructor are inherited }
   procedure OrderedListInsert(Position : integer;
          NewItem: itemType; var Success : boolean);
   { ----------------------------------------------
     Inserts an item into an ordered list.
     Precondition: Init has been called. Position
     indicates where the insertion should occur,
     NewItem is the item to be inserted.
     Postcondition: If 1 <= Position <=
     ListLength+1, NewItem is at position Position
     in the list, other items are renumbered
     accordingly, and Success is true; else Success
     is false.
     ---------------------------------------------- }
   procedure OrderedListDelete(Position : integer;
                              var Success : boolean);
   { ----------------------------------------------
     Deletes an item from an ordered list.
     Precondition: Init has been called. Position
     indicates where the deletion should occur.
```

```
      Postcondition: If 1 <= Position <= ListLength,
      the item at position Position in the list is
      deleted, other items are renumbered accordingly,
      and Success is true; else Success is false.
      --------------------------------------------- }
   procedure OrderedListRetrieve(Position: integer;
                         var DataItem : itemType;
                         var Success : boolean);
   { ---------------------------------------------
      Retrieves a list item by position number.
      Precondition: Init has been called. Position
      is the number of the item to be retrieved.
      Postcondition: If 1 <= Position <= ListLength,
      DataItem is the value of the desired item and
      Success is true; else Success is false.
      --------------------------------------------- }

private
   function PtrTo(Position : integer) : ptrType;
   { ---------------------------------------------
      Determines a pointer to an item in an ordered
      list.
      Precondition: Init has been called. Position
      is the position of the desired item in the
      list.
      Postcondition: If 1 <= Position <= ListLength,
      returns a pointer to the indicated item. If
      Position < 1, returns a pointer to the first
      item; if Position > ListLength, returns a
      pointer to the last item.
      --------------------------------------------- }
end;  { object }

sortedListType = object(ordListType)
   { the constructor and destructor are inherited }
   procedure LocatePosition(DataItem : itemType;
      var Position: integer; var Success : boolean);
   { ---------------------------------------------
      Determines the position of an item in a sorted
      list.
      Precondition: Init has been called. The items
      in the list are sorted into ascending order.
      DataItem is the desired item.
      Postcondition: If DataItem is in the list,
      Position is its position number and Success is
      true; otherwise Position is the location where
      DataItem should occur if inserted and Success
      is false.
      --------------------------------------------- }
```

```
      procedure SortedListInsert(NewItem : itemType;
                                 var Success : boolean);
      { ---------------------------------------------
        Inserts an item into a sorted list.
        Precondition: Init has been called. The items
        in the list are sorted into ascending order.
        NewItem is the item to be inserted.
        Postcondition: NewItem is in its proper
        sorted location within the list and Success is
        true. Duplicate items are allowed.
        --------------------------------------------- }
      procedure SortedListDelete(AnItem : itemType;
                                 var Success : boolean);
      { ---------------------------------------------
        Deletes an item from a sorted list.
        Precondition: Init has been called. The items
        in the list are sorted into ascending order.
        AnItem is the item to be deleted.
        Postcondition: The first occurrence of AnItem
        is deleted from the list and Success is true.
        If AnItem does not occur on the list, Success is
        false.
        --------------------------------------------- }
   end;  { object }

implementation

constructor listType.Init;
begin
   Size := 0;
   TheHead := nil
end;  { listType.Init }

destructor listType.Done;
var Cur, Temp : ptrType;
begin
   Cur := TheHead;
   while Cur <> nil do
   begin
      Temp := Cur;
      Cur := Cur^.Next;
      dispose(Temp)
   end;   { while }

   TheHead := nil;
   Size := 0
end;  { listType.Done }
```

```
function listType.ListLength;
begin
   ListLength := Size
end;  { listType.ListLength }

procedure listType.DisplayList;
var Cur : ptrType;
    Position : integer;
begin
   writeln('List length is ', Size);

   Position := 1;
   Cur := TheHead;

   { Loop invariant: Cur points to the next node to be
     printed }
   while Cur <> nil do
   begin
      writeln(Position,' : ', Cur^.Item);
      Cur := Cur^.Next;
      Position := succ(Position)
   end { while }
end;  { listType.DisplayList }

function listType.Head : ptrType;
begin
   Head := TheHead
end;  { listType.Head }

procedure listType.SetHead(NewHead : ptrType);
begin
   TheHead := NewHead
end;  { listType.SetHead }

procedure listType.SetSize(NewSize : integer);
begin
   Size := NewSize
end;  { listType.SetSize }

function ordListType.PtrTo(Position : integer) : ptrType;
var Trav : ptrType;
    Skip : integer;
begin
   { if Position is out of range, assume default value }
   if Position < 1 then
      Position := 1
   else if Position > ListLength then
      Position := ListLength;
```

```
   { traverse to desired item }
   Trav := Head;
   for Skip := 1 to pred(Position) do
      Trav := Trav^.Next;
   PtrTo := Trav   { return pointer to desired item }
end;  { ordListType.PtrTo }

procedure ordListType.OrderedListInsert(Position : integer;
               NewItem : itemType; var Success : boolean);
var Prev, Cur : ptrType;
begin
   if (Position < 1) or (Position > succ(ListLength))
      then Success := false

      else
      begin
         Success := true;
         SetSize(succ(ListLength));

         new(Cur);
         Cur^.Item := NewItem;

         if Position = 1
            then
            begin  { insert at list's beginning }
               Cur^.Next := Head;
               SetHead(Cur)
            end

            else  { insert into list's interior }
            begin
               Prev := PtrTo(pred(Position));
               Cur^.Next := Prev^.Next;
               Prev^.Next := Cur
            end
      end
end;   { ordListType.OrderedListInsert }

procedure ordListType.OrderedListDelete(Position : integer;
                                   var Success : boolean);
var Prev, Cur : ptrType;
begin
   if (Position < 1) or (Position > ListLength)
       then Success := false

       else
       begin
          Success := true;
          SetSize(pred(ListLength));
```

```
          if Position = 1
              then { delete first item }
              begin
                 Cur := Head;
                 SetHead(Head^.Next);
              end

              else { delete interior item }
              begin
                 Prev := PtrTo(pred(Position));
                 Cur := Prev^.Next;
                 Prev^.Next := Cur^.Next;
              end;

          dispose(Cur)
       end
end;   { ordListType.OrderedListDelete }

procedure ordListType.OrderedListRetrieve(Position : integer;
             var DataItem : itemType; var Success : boolean);
var Cur : ptrType;

begin
   if (Position < 1) or (Position > ListLength)
       then Success := false

       else
       begin
          Cur := PtrTo(Position);
          DataItem := Cur^.Item;
          Success := true
       end
end;  { ordListType.OrderedListRetrieve }

procedure sortedListType.LocatePosition(DataItem : itemType;
              var Position : integer; var Success : boolean);
var Trav : ptrType;
begin
   Position := 1;
   Trav := Head;
   { Loop invariant: all data items before the one to
     which Trav points are < DataItem }
   while (Position < ListLength) and
                                 (Trav^.Item < DataItem) do
   begin
      Position := succ(Position);
      Trav := Trav^.Next
   end;  { while }
```

```
   { check whether proper position is after end of list }
   if (ListLength > 0) and (Trav^.Item < DataItem)
       then Position := succ(Position);

   if Position > ListLength then
       Success := false
   else if DataItem <> Trav^.Item then
       Success := false
   else Success := true
end;  { SortedListType.LocatePosition }

procedure sortedListType.SortedListInsert(NewItem : itemType;
                                      var Success : boolean);
var InsertionPosition : integer;
begin
   LocatePosition(NewItem, InsertionPosition, Success);
   OrderedListInsert(InsertionPosition, NewItem, Success)
end;  { sortedListType.SortedListInsert }

procedure sortedListType.SortedListDelete(AnItem : itemType;
                                     var Success : boolean);
var DeletionPosition : integer;
begin
   LocatePosition(AnItem, DeletionPosition, Success);
   if Success then
       OrderedListDelete(DeletionPosition, Success)
end;  { sortedListType.SortedListDelete }

end.  { unit }
```

The following program demonstrates how to use this unit, with the assumption that *itemType = integer*.

```
program DemonstrateListObjectsUnit;

uses ULists;

var OL : ordListType;
    SL : sortedListType;
    Item : itemType;
    Success : boolean;

begin  { Main program }
    OL.Init;

    OL.OrderedListInsert(1, 21, Success);
    OL.OrderedListInsert(2, 14, Success);

    writeln('The list contains ', OL.ListLength, ' items');
    OL.DisplayList;

    OL.Done;
```

```
    SL.Init;

    SL.SortedListInsert(52, Success);
    writeln('The list contains ', SL.ListLength, ' items');

    SL.DisplayList;

    SL.OrderedListRetrieve(1, Item, Success);
    writeln('The item in position 1 is ', Item);

    SL.Done
end.  { Program }
```

Notice that both `OL` and `SL` inherit the methods `Init`, `ListLength`, `DisplayList`, and `Done` from the abstract object type `listType`. Also notice that `SL` inherits the retrieval method from `ordListType`.

Although the items on a list are dynamically allocated, the list objects themselves are statically allocated. Thus, after `OL.Done` executes, for example, you are left with an empty ordered list object. That is, the instance `OL` of the object remains. Although statically allocated objects do not require a destructor, including one permits dynamic allocation in the future. You can implement dynamic allocation by defining the following pointers to the list objects:

```
type listPtrType = ^listType;
     ordListPtrType = ^ordListType;
     sortedListPtrType = ^sortedListType;
```

Exercise 13 at the end of this chapter asks you to make these changes.

The Advantages of OOP

The time that you expend on program design can increase when you use object-oriented programming. In addition, the solution that OOP techniques produce typically will be more general than is absolutely necessary to solve the problem at hand. This excess, however, usually is worth the extra effort that OOP requires.

To design a solution to a problem, you need to identify objects that fit the problem. More likely, you will want a family of related objects. This stage of the design process is time-consuming, particularly if you have no existing objects upon which to build. Once you implement an ancestor object, however, the implementation of each descendent proceeds more rapidly than if it did not inherit its ancestor's methods. Looking ahead, you can reuse previously implemented objects in future programs, either as is or with modifications that can include new objects that descend from your existing ones. This reuse of objects can actually reduce the time requirements of an object-oriented design.

OOP also has a positive effect on program maintenance. You can make one modification to an ancestor object and affect all of its descendents.

Without inheritance, you would make the same change to many modules. In addition, you can add new features to a program by adding descendent objects that do not affect their ancestors and, therefore, do not introduce errors into the rest of the program. You can also add a descendent object that modifies its ancestor's original behavior, even though that ancestor was written and compiled long ago.

SUMMARY

1. **Data abstraction is a technique for controlling the interaction between a program and its data structures. It builds walls around a program's data structures, just as other aspects of modularity build walls around a program's algorithms. Such walls make programs easier to design, implement, read, and modify.**
2. **The specification of a set of data-management operations together with the data values upon which they operate define an abstract data type (ADT).**
3. **Only after you have fully defined an ADT should you think about how to implement it with a data structure. The proper choice of a data structure to implement an ADT depends both on the details of the ADT operations and on the context in which you will use the operations.**
4. **Even after you have selected an implementation for an ADT, the remainder of the program should not depend on your particular choice. That is, you should access the data structure by using only the ADT operations. Thus, you hide the data structure behind a wall of ADT operations.**
5. **An array-based implementation uses an implicit ordering scheme—for example, the item that follows `A[I]` is stored in `A[I + 1]`. A pointer-based implementation uses an explicit ordering scheme—for example, the item that follows the one in node *N* is found by following node *N*'s pointer.**
6. **You often must choose between an array-based and a pointer-based implementation. One important criterion on which to base this choice is whether or not, in the context of a particular problem, the fixed-size limitations of an array are acceptable. If not, the dynamic storage allocation provided by a pointer-based implementation is required. On the other hand, an array provides direct access to its elements, whereas a linked list does not. In the chapters that follow, you will encounter applications with a wide range of data-management requirements. The process of selecting data structures for these applications will illustrate some of the other important criteria on which to base the choice of a data structure.**

7. Organizing the implementation of an ADT as a unit increases the modularity of the program that uses the ADT. A unit also enables you to hide from the ADT's user the subprograms that the ADT implementation requires.
8. Object-oriented programming, or OOP, extends data abstraction by hiding both data and operations, called methods, within an object. Thus, an object encapsulates both data and methods. OOP views a program as a collection of objects that interact.
9. An object type definition can have private data fields and private methods, which are accessible only within the unit or program that contains the object type definition.
10. Object types can have ancestor and descendent relationships. Descendent object types inherit data fields and methods from previously defined ancestor object types. In addition, descendent object types are type-compatible with their ancestor object types.
11. Inheritance enables you to define a family of object types that descend from an abstract object type, which typically has descendents but not instances.
12. Polymorphism allows you to write one version of a method that behaves differently for each object that inherits the method. Such a method calls other methods that are virtual. Object types that contain virtual methods must include an initialization method `Init`, called a constructor.
13. Dynamic objects, which are allocated at execution time, use pointer variables that are analogous to the ordinary pointer variables with which you are familiar. Dynamic object types that contain virtual methods must include a destructor, which is a cleanup method that deallocates the storage assigned to the object.
14. Because certain object types have applications in many programs, you should take steps to facilitate their use. First, you can define particular object types within units. Secondly, you can make your object type a descendent of an abstract object type that has only the essential data fields and methods necessary for its descendents. When you use such a unit in your program, you can define another descendent object type that tailors the data fields and methods to suit the present application.

COMMON PITFALLS / DEBUGGING

1. A program should not depend upon the particular implementations of its ADT's.
2. If you choose an array-based implementation for an ADT, there will

be a maximum number of items that you can store. Thus, the implementation will have to check whether there is room in the data structure before inserting a new item, and the calling program will have to take appropriate action if there is no room.

3. **Both Turbo and Standard Pascal do not allow functions to return complex structures such as arrays and records. Therefore, you generally should write an ADT's retrieval operations as procedures that use a variable parameter to return the item. This approach allows you to define the ADT's items to be of any type.**

4. **The syntax of Pascal requires you to place the type definitions of ADT's globally, outside of the ADT subprograms. As a consequence, when switching from one implementation to another, you must replace the type definitions as well as the subprograms.**

5. **When implementing an object's method, be sure to qualify the method's name with the object type identifier. Compiler messages such as `Unknown identifier` or `Undefined forward reference` indicate failure to qualify the method's name.**

6. **You must call the constructor for every instance of an object type that has virtual methods. Calling an uninitialized virtual method will cause program execution to hang. To guard against this error, use Turbo Pascal's `$R+` directive at least during the debugging stages of program development.**

7. **If you use `procedure` instead of `constructor` for an object type that contains a virtual method, you will not receive a syntax error message, but execution will probably hang.**

8. **All occurrences of the header of a particular virtual method—within the definition of the object type as well as the implementation of the method—must be identical. This requirement applies both to the original object type and its descendents. Note, however, that you write `virtual` only after a header that is in the definition of an object type, not after the header of a method's implementation.**

SELF-TEST EXERCISES

1. What is the significance of "wall" and "contract"? Why do these notions help you to become a better problem solver?

2. Write a procedure that replaces the Ith item in an ordered list *OL*. Define the procedure in terms of the ADT ordered list operations. Thus, your procedure should be independent of any particular implementation of the ordered list.

3. You can think of a Pascal textfile abstractly. Define a set of operations that are a part of the ADT textfile.

4. Write preconditions and postconditions for each of the ADT ordered list operations.

5. Define an object type `cylinderType` that is a descendent of `circleType`, as defined in the section "Encapsulation."

6. Define a dynamic object type `squareType` that is a descendent of `genericObjectType`, as defined in the unit `UGeneric` that appears in the section "An Example of Dynamic Objects."

EXERCISES

1. Develop a unit that contains an array-based implementation of the ADT ordered list. Be sure to consider the issue of error checking and handling.

2. Develop a unit that contains a pointer-based implementation of the ADT ordered list.

3. Compare the array-based and pointer-based implementations of the `OrderedListDelete(OL, Position)` operation for an ordered list. Describe the work required for various values of `Position` under each implementation. What are the implications for efficiency if the cost of shifting data is large compared to the cost of following a pointer? When would this situation occur? What if the costs are approximately the same?

4. Implement the procedure `Swap(OL, I, J)` that interchanges the Ith and J^{th} items of the ordered list `OL`, as described in the section "The ADT Ordered List." Add a parameter `Success` that indicates whether the swap was successful.

5. Use the procedure `Swap` that you wrote in Exercise 4 to write the following procedures:
   a. Write a procedure that reverses the order of the items in an ordered list `OL`.
   b. Write a procedure that sorts the items in an ordered list `OL` into ascending order.

6. If Pascal did not contain sets, you could define your own abstract data type set. Define operations that are a part of the ADT set. (Exercise 10b asks you to implement this ADT.)

7. Define operations that are a part of the ADT character string.

8. Write a pseudocode procedure in terms of the ADT appointment book, described in the section "Designing an ADT," for each of the following tasks:
   a. Change the purpose of the appointment at a given date and time.
   b. Print all the appointments for a given date.

   Do you need to add operations to the ADT to perform these tasks?

9. Consider the ADT polynomial—polynomials in a single variable x—that the following operations define:

```
CreatePolynomial(P)
{ Initializes P to be the zero polynomial. }

Degree(P)
{ Returns the degree of the polynomial P. The degree is
  the highest power of a term with a nonzero
  coefficient. }

SetCoefficient(P, i, Value)
{ Sets the coefficient of the degree i (x^i) term to
  Value. }

RetrieveCoefficient(P, i)
{ Returns the coefficient of the degree i (x^i) term. }
```

For this problem, consider only polynomials—such as the following polynomial—whose exponents are nonnegative integers:

$P = 4x^5 + 7x^3 - x^2 + 9$

The following examples demonstrate the ADT operations on this polynomial:

`Degree(P)` = 5 (the highest power of a term with a nonzero coefficient)

`RetrieveCoefficient(P, 3)` = 7 (the coefficient of the degree 3 (x^3) term)

`RetrieveCoefficient(P, 2)` = −1 (the coefficient of the degree 2 (x^2) term)

`RetrieveCoefficient(P, 4)` = 0 (the coefficient of a missing term is implicitly 0)

`RetrieveCoefficient(P, 6)` = 0 (the coefficient of a missing term is implicitly 0)

`SetCoefficient(P, 7, -3)` produces the polynomial:

$$P = -3x^7 + 4x^5 + 7x^3 - x^2 + 9$$

By using these ADT operations, write statements to perform the following tasks:

a. Print the coefficient of the term that has the highest degree.
b. Increase the coefficient of the x^3 term by 8.

10. Some programming languages—for example, FORTRAN—do not directly support the data types *record*, *set*, and *pointer*. In these languages, you have to implement structures such as records, sets, and linked lists by using the structures that are available.

a. Define an ADT record and implement it by using only arrays and simple variables. How can you implement an array of records?

b. Define an ADT set and implement it by using only arrays and simple variables. (See Exercise 6.)

c. Implement the ADT linked list of sorted integers as described in the section "The Linked List As an ADT" by using two integer arrays—`Data` and `Next`—and a single integer-valued variable `Head`. When appropriate, use a boolean parameter, `Success`, to indicate whether an operation is successful.

On the surface, it may seem to you that this implementation sacrifices the primary motivation for having linked structures: dynamic allocation. In Chapter 10, however, you will see that dynamic allocation is not the only motivation for having linked structures; a fixed-sized array-based implementation of a linked structure can in fact be useful. Furthermore, in a more advanced course on data structures, you will be exposed to techniques for using large arrays that will be "shared" by several data structures. In this context you will see that a linked list that has been implemented with arrays can indeed be viewed as a dynamic structure.

Exercises 11 through 15 involve object-oriented programming.

11. Define an object type `ovalType` and then define an object type `circleType` as a descendent of `ovalType`. `CircleType` should be similar to the object defined within the unit `UCircle` that appears in the section "Encapsulation."

12. The object type `ordListType`, which is defined in the section "A Family of List Objects," does not contain a method `Position` that returns the number of a particular item, given the item's value. Such a method allows you to pass the node's number to `OrderedListDelete`, for example, to delete the item.

Define a descendent of `ordListType` that has a `Position` method and includes methods that insert, delete, and retrieve items by their values instead of their positions. Thus, insertions into the list are made at an arbitrary position in the list. Although the items on this list are not sorted, the new object type is analogous to `sortedListType`, which contains the method `LocatePosition`.

13. Revise the object type `ordListType`, as defined in the section "A Family of List Objects," so that it is dynamically allocated. Write a small program that demonstrates how to allocate, use, and deallocate your new dynamic object type.

14. Revise the object type `ordListType`, as defined in the section "A Family of List Objects," so that the items on the list are dynamically allocated objects that descend from `genericObjectType`, as defined in the section "An Example of Dynamic Objects." Write a small program that demonstrates how to allocate, use, and deallocate your new object. Include a procedure that allocates objects that descend from `genericObjectType`.

15. a. Implement the ADT linked list of sorted integers as an object within a unit. Then implement the ADT circular linked list as a descendent object of the linked list.
    b. Revise the object types that you defined in Part *a* so that they are dynamic.

PROJECTS

16. Consider the ADT character string that you defined in Exercise 7. Develop an implementation for your operations. (Note that Exercises 28 and 33 of Chapter 3 asked you to write a pointer-based implementation of character strings.)

17. Consider the ADT polynomial that Exercise 9 defined.
    a. Define the ADT polynomial operations in terms of the ADT ordered list operations.
    b. Write a procedure ***Add*** that will add two polynomials. Write ***Add*** in terms of the ADT polynomial operations.
    c. Consider a sparse implementation of the ADT polynomial. That is, suppose you would like to implement the ADT in such a way that only the terms with nonzero coefficients are explicitly stored. For example, you can represent the polynomial *P* in Exercise 9 with the linked list in Figure 4-12. Complete the sparse implementation.
    d. Define a traverse operation for the ADT polynomial that will allow you to add two sparse polynomials without having to consider terms with zero coefficients explicitly.

18. Implement the ADT appointment book, described in the section "Designing an ADT." Add operations as necessary. For example, you should add operations to read and write appointments.

19. a. Pascal does not have a data type ***fraction*** for the rational numbers. Define an ADT fraction that addresses this deficiency. Provide operations that read, write, add, subtract, multiply, and divide fractions. The results of all arithmetic operations should be in lowest terms, so include a private procedure ***ReduceToLowestTerms***. Exercise 19 in Chapter 5 will help you with the details of this method. (Should your read and write operations call ***ReduceToLowestTerms***?) To simplify the determination of a fraction's sign, you can assume that its denominator is positive.

Figure 4-12

A sparse polynomial

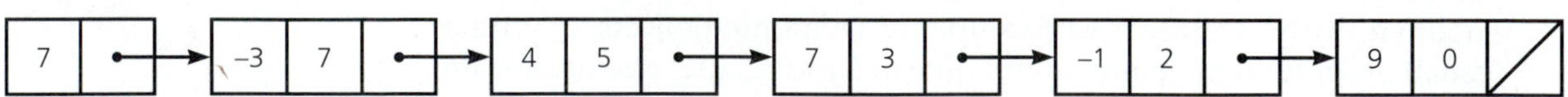

Define the ADT within a unit and write a program that demonstrates its operations.

b. Pascal does not have a data type for mixed numbers, each of which consists of an integer portion and a fractional portion in lowest terms. Define such an ADT that assumes the existence of the ADT fraction. Provide operations that read, write, add, subtract, multiply, and divide mixed numbers. The results of all arithmetic operations should have fractional portions that are in lowest terms. Also include an operation that converts a fraction to a mixed number.

Define the ADT within a unit that uses the unit of Part *a*, and write a program that demonstrates its operations.

c. Implement the ADT recipe book as described in the section "Designing an ADT" and, in doing so, implement the ADT measurement. Add operations as necessary. For example, you should add operations to recipe book to read, write, and scale recipes.

20. Repeat Projects 16 through 19, but this time implement the ADT's as objects within units. Use private fields where appropriate.

CHAPTER 5

Recursion: The Mirrors

PREVIEW The goal of this chapter is to help you to develop a basic understanding of recursion, which is one of the most powerful methods of solution available to the computer scientist. Several relatively simple problems demonstrate the thought processes that lead to recursive solutions. These problems are diverse and include examples of computing, counting, and searching. In addition to presenting recursion from a conceptual viewpoint, this chapter discusses methods that will help you to understand the mechanics of recursion. These methods are particularly useful for tracing and debugging recursive subprograms.

RECURSIVE SOLUTIONS

Typically, solutions to problems use either **iteration**—that is, they involve loops—or **recursion**. You should know at the outset that not all recursive solutions are better than iterative solutions. In fact, some recursive solutions are impractical. However, recursive algorithms often provide elegantly simple solutions to problems of great complexity. Such solutions are, in general, very well structured and modular. In fact, the manner in which the modules of a recursive solution interact is precisely what makes recursion such a powerful and unique problem-solving tool.

Recursion will play a major role in many of the solutions that appear throughout the remainder of this book. This chapter and the next present several important applications of recursion, including recursive search algorithms and recursive grammars for defining the syntax of languages. Chapter 7 examines recursive sorting algorithms as part of its discussion of algorithm efficiency. Recursion will also be an integral part of many of the data structures studied in Parts III and IV.

What exactly is recursion? It is a technique for performing a task T by performing another task T'. So far, this sounds like top-down design, in which you solve a large problem by breaking it up into smaller problems. The difference is that, with recursion, the task T' has *exactly the same nature* as the original task T. Thus, a recursive solution of task T might be described as follows:

```
Solution to T:
    Solve task T', which is identical in nature to
      task T
```

It may seem strange to solve a task by solving another task just like it. What have you gained? The crucial point is that, although T' is identical in nature to T, it is in some sense *smaller* than T.

As an illustration of the elements in a recursive solution, consider the problem of looking up a word in a dictionary. Suppose you wanted to look up the word "vademecum." Imagine starting at the beginning of the dictionary and looking at every word in order until you found "vademecum."

That is precisely what a **sequential search** does, and, for obvious reasons, you want a faster way to perform the search. One such method is the **binary search**, which in spirit is similar to the way in which you use a dictionary. Although you can write an iterative binary search algorithm, consider the following recursive binary search of the dictionary:

```
{ Search the dictionary for a word }

   if the dictionary contains only one page
     then scan the page for the word

     else
     begin
        Open the dictionary to a point near the middle
        Determine which half of the dictionary contains the
          word

        if the word is in the first half of the dictionary
          then search the first half of the dictionary for
                 the word
          else search the second half of the dictionary for
                 the word
     end
```

Parts of this solution are intentionally vague: How do you scan a single page? How do you find the middle of the dictionary? Once the middle is found, how do you determine which half contains the word? The answers to these questions are not difficult, but we will not obscure the solution strategy with these details at present.

The previous search strategy reduces the problem of searching the dictionary for a word to a problem of searching half of the dictionary for the word, as Figure 5-1 illustrates. Notice two important points. First, once you have divided the dictionary in half, you already know how to search the appropriate half: You can use exactly the same strategy that you employed to search the original dictionary. Second, note that there is a special case that is different from all the other cases: After you have divided the dictionary so many times that you are left with only a single page, the halving ceases. At this point, the problem is sufficiently small that you can solve it directly by scanning the single page that remains for the word. This special case is called the **degenerate case**, or the **base case**.

A degenerate case is a special case whose solution you know

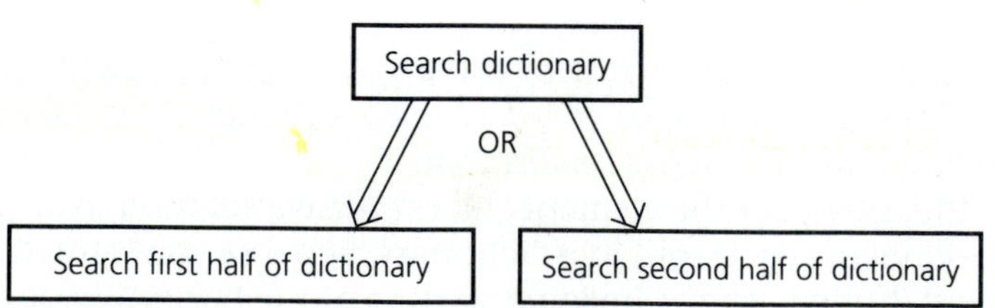

Figure 5-1

A recursive solution

This strategy is one of **divide and conquer**. You solve the dictionary search problem by first *dividing* the dictionary into two halves and then *conquering* the appropriate half. You solve the smaller problem by using the same divide-and-conquer strategy. The dividing continues until you reach the degenerate case. As you will see, this strategy is inherent in many recursive solutions.

A binary search uses a divide-and-conquer strategy

To further explore the nature of the solution to the dictionary problem, consider a slightly more rigorous formulation.

```
Search(Dictionary, Word)

   if Dictionary is one page in size
      then scan the page for Word

      else
      begin
          Open Dictionary to a point near the middle
          Determine which half of Dictionary contains Word

          if Word is in the first half of Dictionary
              then Search(first half of Dictionary, Word)
              else Search(second half of Dictionary, Word)
      end
```

Writing the solution as a procedure allows several important observations:

Four observations about a recursive solution

1. One of the actions of the procedure is to call itself; that is, the procedure `Search` calls the procedure `Search`. This action is what makes the solution recursive. The solution strategy is to split `Dictionary` in half, determine which half contains `Word`, and apply the same strategy to the appropriate half.
2. Each call to the procedure `Search` made from within the procedure `Search` passes a dictionary that is one-half the size of the previous dictionary. That is, at each successive call to `Search(Dictionary, Word)`, the size of `Dictionary` is cut in half. The procedure solves the search problem by solving another search problem that is identical in nature *but smaller in size*.
3. There is one search problem that you handle differently from all of the others. When `Dictionary` contains only a single page, you use another method: You scan the page directly. Searching a one-page dictionary is the degenerate case of the search problem. When you reach the degenerate case, the recursive calls stop and you solve the problem directly.
4. The manner in which the size of the problem diminishes ensures that you will eventually reach the degenerate case.

These facts describe the general form of a recursive solution. Though not all recursive solutions fit these criteria as nicely as this solution does, the similarities are far greater than the differences. As you attempt to construct a new recursive solution, you should keep in mind the following four questions:

KEY CONCEPTS

Four Questions for Constructing Recursive Solutions

1. How can you define the problem in terms of a smaller problem of the same type?
2. How does each recursive call diminish the size of the problem?
3. What instance of the problem can serve as the degenerate case?
4. As the problem size diminishes, will you reach this degenerate case?

Now consider two relatively simple problems: computing the factorial of a number and writing a string backward. Their recursive solutions further illustrate the points raised by the solution to the dictionary search problem. These examples also illustrate the difference between a recursive function and a recursive procedure.

A Recursive Function: The Factorial of n

Consider a recursive solution to the problem of computing the factorial of an integer n. We chose to start with this problem because its recursive solution is easy to understand and neatly fits the mold we described earlier. However, because there is a simple and efficient nonrecursive solution to the problem, you probably would not use the recursive solution in practice.

To begin, consider the familiar iterative definition of *Factorial*(n) (more commonly written $n!$):

An iterative definition of Factorial

$$Factorial(n) = n * (n-1) * (n-2) * \cdots * 1 \text{ for any integer } n > 0$$
$$Factorial(0) = 1$$

The factorial of a negative integer is undefined. You should have no trouble writing an iterative factorial function based on this definition.

To define *Factorial*(n) recursively, you first need to define *Factorial*(n) in terms of the factorial of a smaller number. To do so, simply observe that the factorial of n is equal to the factorial of $(n - 1)$ multiplied by n; that is,

A recurrence relation

$$Factorial(n) = n * Factorial(n-1)$$

The definition of *Factorial*(n) in terms of *Factorial*($n - 1$), which is an example of a **recurrence relation**, implies that you can also define *Factorial*($n - 1$) in terms of *Factorial*($n - 2$), and so on. This process is analogous to the dictionary search solution, in which you search a dictionary by searching a smaller dictionary in exactly the same way.

The definition of *Factorial(n)* lacks one key element: the degenerate case. As was done in the dictionary search solution, here you must define one case differently from all the others, or else the recursion will never stop. The degenerate case for the factorial function is *Factorial*(0), which you know is 1. Because *n* originally is greater than or equal to zero and each call to *Factorial* decrements *n* by 1, you will always reach the degenerate case. With the addition of the degenerate case, the complete recursive definition of the factorial function is

$$Factorial(n) = \begin{cases} 1 & \text{if } n = 0 \\ n * Factorial(n - 1) & \text{if } n > 0 \end{cases}$$

***A recursive definition of* Factorial**

To be sure that you understand this recursive definition, apply it to the computation of *Factorial*(4). Since $4 > 0$, the recursive definition states that

$$Factorial(4) = 4 * Factorial(3)$$

Similarly,

$$Factorial(3) = 3 * Factorial(2)$$
$$Factorial(2) = 2 * Factorial(1)$$
$$Factorial(1) = 1 * Factorial(0)$$

You have reached the degenerate case, and the definition directly states that

$$Factorial(0) = 1$$

At this point, the application of the recursive definition stops and you still do not know the answer to the original question: What is *Factorial*(4)? However, the information to answer this question is now available:

Since *Factorial*(0) = 1, then *Factorial*(1) = 1 * 1 = 1
Since *Factorial*(1) = 1, then *Factorial*(2) = 2 * 1 = 2
Since *Factorial*(2) = 2, then *Factorial*(3) = 3 * 2 = 6
Since *Factorial*(3) = 6, then *Factorial*(4) = 4 * 6 = 24

Notice that the recursive definition of *Factorial*(4) yields the same result as the iterative definition, which gives $4 * 3 * 2 * 1 = 24$. To prove that the two definitions of *Factorial* are equivalent for all nonnegative integers, you would use **mathematical induction**. (See Appendix A.) Chapter 6 discusses the close tie between recursion and mathematical induction.

The recursive definition of the factorial function has illustrated two points: (1) *Intuitively*, you can define *Factorial(n)* in terms of *Factorial(n* – 1), and (2) *mechanically*, you can apply the definition to determine the value of a given factorial. Even in this simple example, applying the recursive definition required quite a bit of work. That, of course, is where the computer comes in.

Once you have a recursive definition of *Factorial(n)*, it is easy to construct a Pascal function that implements the definition:

```
type nonnegType = 0..maxint;

function Fact(n : nonnegType) : nonnegType;
{ -----------------------------------------------------
  Computes the factorial of the nonnegative integer n.
  Precondition: n must be greater than or equal to 0.
  Postcondition: Returns the factorial of n; n is
  unchanged.
  ----------------------------------------------------- }
begin
   if n = 0
      then Fact := 1
      else Fact := n * Fact(n - 1)
end;  { Fact }
```

Suppose that the statement *writeln(Fact(3))* calls the function from the main program. Figure 5-2 depicts the sequence of computations that this call would require.

This function fits the model of a recursive solution given earlier in this chapter as follows:

***Fact* satisfies the four criteria of a recursive solution**

1. One action of *Fact* is to *call itself.*
2. At each recursive call to *Fact*, the integer whose factorial you need to compute is *diminished by 1.*
3. The function handles the factorial of 0 differently from all the other factorials: It does not generate a recursive call. Rather, you know that *Fact(0)* is 1. Thus, $n = 0$ is the *degenerate case.*
4. Given that n is nonnegative, point 2 of this list assures you that you will always *reach the degenerate case.*

Figure 5-2

Fact(3)

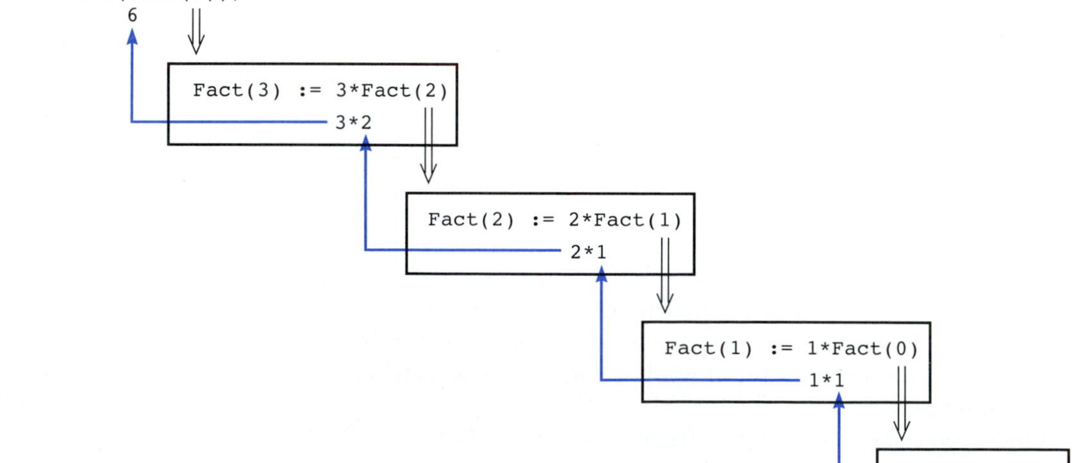

At an intuitive level, it should be clear that the function *Fact* implements the recursive definition of *Factorial*. Now consider the mechanics of executing this recursive function. *Fact* is straightforward except perhaps for the assignment statement in the *else* clause (*Fact := n * Fact(n - 1)*). This assignment statement has the following effect:

1. To evaluate the expression to the right of the assignment operator, each operand of the product is evaluated.
2. The second operand—*Fact(n - 1)*—is a call to the function *Fact*. Although this is a recursive call (the function *Fact* calls the function *Fact*), there really is nothing special about it. Imagine substituting a call to another function—Pascal's function *abs*, for example—for the recursive call to *Fact*. The principle is the same: Simply evaluate the function.

In principle, evaluating a recursive function is no more difficult than evaluating a nonrecursive function. In practice, however, the bookkeeping can quickly get out of hand.

Thus, we shall introduce the **box method**, which is a systematic way to trace the actions of a recursive function or procedure. You can use the box method both to help you to understand recursion and to debug recursive subprograms. However, such a mechanical device is no substitute for an intuitive understanding of recursion. The box method is illustrative of how compilers frequently implement recursion. As you read the following description of the method, realize that each box roughly corresponds to an **activation record**, which a compiler typically uses in its implementation of a subprogram call. Chapter 8 will discuss this implementation further.

An activation record is created for each subprogram call

The box method. The box method is illustrated here for the recursive function *Fact*. As you will see in the next section, this method is somewhat simpler for a recursive procedure, as no value needs to be returned.

1. Label each recursive call in the body of the recursive subprogram. There may be several recursive calls, and it will be important to distinguish among them. These labels help you to keep track of the correct place to which you must return after a function call completes. For example, mark the expression *Fact(n - 1)* within the body of the function with the letter A:

```
function Fact(n : nonnegType) : nonnegType;
begin
    if n = 0
       then Fact := 1
       else Fact := n * Fact(n - 1)
end;  { Fact }                   (A)
```

Label each recursive call in the subprogram

You return to point A after each recursive call, substitute the computed value for *Fact(n - 1)*, and continue execution by evaluating the expression *n * Fact(n - 1)*.

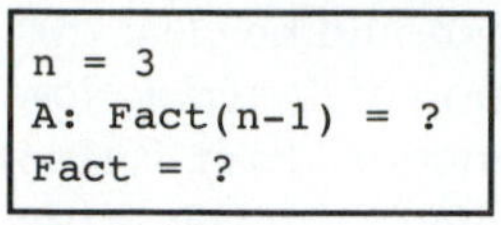

Figure 5-3

A box

```
n = 3
A: Fact(n-1) = ?
Fact = ?
```

Each time a subprogram is called, a new box represents its local environment

2. Represent each call to the subprogram during the course of execution by a new box in which you note the subprogram's **local environment**. More specifically, each box will contain
   a. The value parameters of the formal parameter list.
   b. The subprogram's local variables.
   c. A placeholder for the value returned by each recursive call from the current box. Label this placeholder to correspond to the labeling in Step 1.
   d. The value of the function itself.

   When you first create a box, you will know only the values of the parameters. You fill in the values of the other items as you determine them from the subprogram's execution. For example, you would create the box in Figure 5-3 for the call *`Fact(3)`*. (You will see in later examples that you must handle both variable parameters and global variables somewhat differently from value parameters and local variables.)
3. Draw an arrow from the statement that initiates the recursive process to the first box. Then, when you create a new box after a recursive call, as described in Step 2, you draw an arrow from the box that makes the call to the newly created box. Label each arrow to correspond to the label (from Step 1) of the recursive call; this label indicates exactly where to return after the call completes. For example, Figure 5-4 shows the first two boxes generated by the statement *`writeln(Fact(3))`* in the main program.
4. After you create the new box and arrow as described in Steps 2 and 3, start executing the body of the subprogram. Each reference to an item in the subprogram's local environment references the corresponding value in the current box, regardless of how you generated the current box.
5. On exiting the subprogram, cross off the current box and follow its arrow back to the box that called the subprogram. This box now becomes the current box, and the label on the arrow specifies the exact location at which execution of the subprogram should continue. Sub-

Figure 5-4

The beginning of the box method

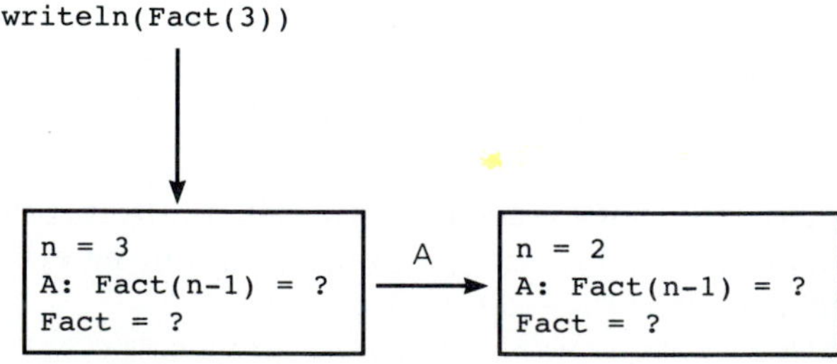

stitute the value returned by the just-terminated function call into the appropriate item in the current box.

Figure 5-5 is a complete box trace for the call `Fact(3)`, which is in the main program. In the sequence of diagrams in this figure, it is always clear which box is the current box: It is the deepest along the path of arrows and appears in color.

Figure 5-5

Box trace of `Fact(3)`

The initial call is made, and function `Fact` begins execution:

```
n            =3
A: Fact(n-1)=?
Fact         =?
```

At point A, a recursive call is made and the new invocation of the function `Fact` begins execution:

```
n            =3    A   n            =2
A: Fact(n-1)=?    -->  A: Fact(n-1)=?
Fact         =?        Fact         =?
```

At point A, a recursive call is made and the new invocation of the function `Fact` begins execution:

```
n            =3    A   n            =2    A   n            =1
A: Fact(n-1)=?    -->  A: Fact(n-1)=?    -->  A: Fact(n-1)=?
Fact         =?        Fact         =?        Fact         =?
```

At point A, a recursive call is made and the new invocation of the function `Fact` begins execution:

```
n            =3    A   n            =2    A   n            =1    A   n            =0
A: Fact(n-1)=?    -->  A: Fact(n-1)=?    -->  A: Fact(n-1)=?    -->  A: Fact(n-1)=?
Fact         =?        Fact         =?        Fact         =?        Fact         =?
```

This is the degenerate case, so this invocation of `Fact` completes.

```
n            =3    A   n            =2    A   n            =1    A   n            =0
A: Fact(n-1)=?    -->  A: Fact(n-1)=?    -->  A: Fact(n-1)=?    -->  A: Fact(n-1)=?
Fact         =?        Fact         =?        Fact         =?        Fact         =1
```

The function value is returned to the calling box, which continues execution.

```
n            =3    A   n            =2    A   n            =1        n            =0
A: Fact(n-1)=?    -->  A: Fact(n-1)=?    -->  A: Fact(n-1)=1        A: Fact(n-1)=?
Fact         =?        Fact         =?        Fact         =?        Fact         =1
```

The current invocation of `Fact` completes.

```
n            =3    A   n            =2    A   n            =1        n            =0
A: Fact(n-1)=?    -->  A: Fact(n-1)=?    -->  A: Fact(n-1)=1        A: Fact(n-1)=?
Fact         =?        Fact         =?        Fact         =1        Fact         =1
```

(continues)

Figure 5-5
continued

The function value is returned to the calling box, which continues execution.

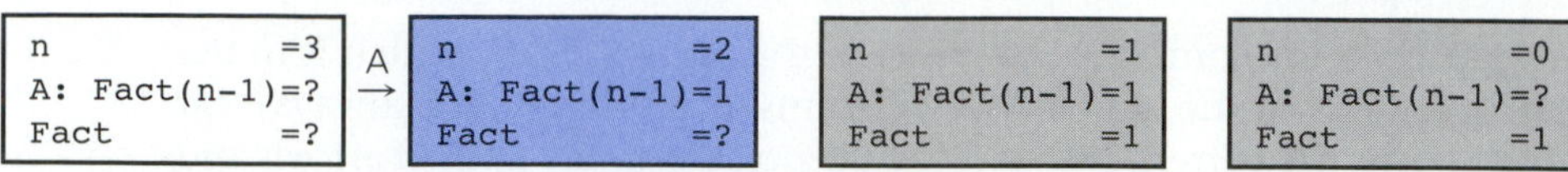

The current invocation of `Fact` completes.

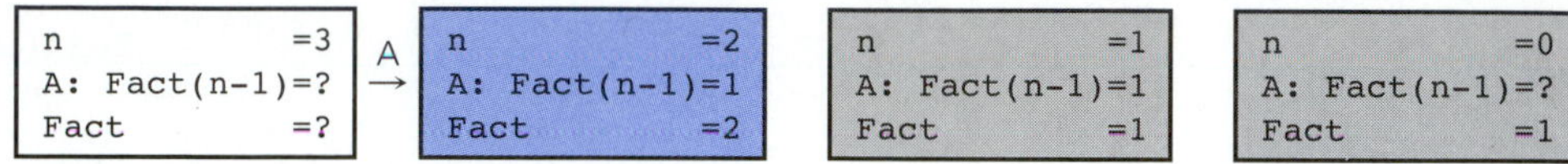

The function value is returned to the calling box, which continues execution.

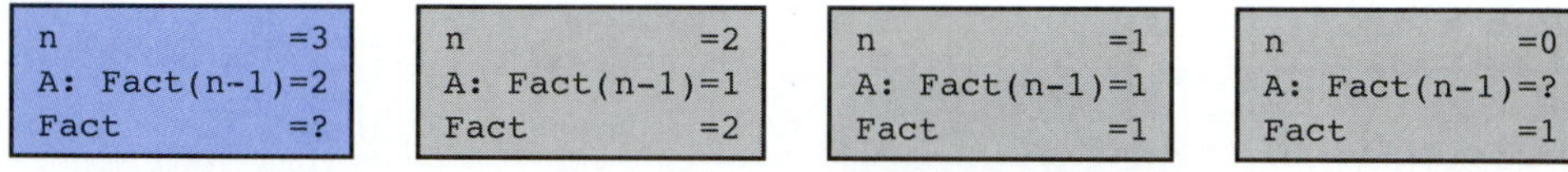

The current invocation of `Fact` completes.

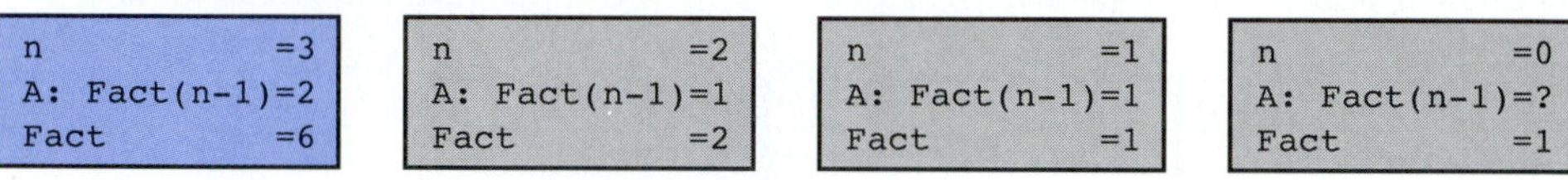

The value 6 is returned to main call.

Well-placed `write` statements can help you to debug a recursive subprogram

The box method should give you a good indication of the special techniques you need to employ to debug a recursive subprogram. You should include *`write`* statements to report the values of all parameters and local variables at both entry to and exit from the subprogram. *`Write`* statements also should report the point in the program where each recursive call occurred. You will see this technique used in the next example.

We end this section with a brief discussion of error checking within *`Fact`*. By declaring the function's parameter *n* to be of type *`nonnegType`* rather than simply *`integer`* and by specifying the *`$R+`* directive, you can guard against errors in the logic of the calling program. If the calling program ever passed a negative value to the function *`Fact`*, the program would abort immediately because of a type clash. On the other hand, if you had declared *n* as an integer, passing a negative value to *`Fact`* would result in an infinite sequence of recursive calls, terminated only by a system-defined limit, because the function would never reach the degenerate case. For example, *`Fact(-4)`* would call *`Fact(-5)`*, which would call *`Fact(-6)`*, and so on.

We admit that using Pascal's type checking to guard against logic errors does not result in a user-friendly function. However, Chapter 1 indicated that such error checking should be your last line of defense. In addition to declaring n to be of type `nonnegType`, the function should test n and, if $n < 0$, the function should either issue an error message or set a flag. Chapter 1 discussed these ideas in the two sections "Fail-Safe Programming" and "Style"; you might want to review that discussion at this time.

A Recursive Procedure: Writing a String Backward

Now consider a problem that is slightly more difficult: Given a string of characters, print it out in reverse order. For example, write the string 'cat' as 'tac'. To construct a recursive solution, you should ask the four questions in the "Key Concepts" box on page 236.

You can construct a solution to the problem of writing a string of length n backward in terms of the problem of writing a string of length $n - 1$ backward. That is, each recursive step of the solution diminishes by 1 the length of the string to be written backward. The fact that the strings get shorter and shorter suggests that the problem of writing some "very short" string backward can serve as the degenerate case. One very short string is the empty string, the string of length zero. Thus, you can choose for the degenerate case the problem

The degenerate case

```
Write the empty string backward
```

The solution to this problem is to do nothing at all—a very straightforward solution indeed! (Alternatively, you could use the string of length 1 as the degenerate case.)

How can you write an n-character string backward, if you can write an (n − 1)-character string backward?

Exactly how can you use the solution to the problem of writing a string of length $n - 1$ backward to solve the problem of writing a string of length n backward? This approach is analogous to the construction of the solution to the factorial problem, where you specified how to use *Factorial*($n - 1$) in the computation of *Factorial*(n). Unlike the factorial problem, however, with the string problem it is not immediately clear how to proceed. Obviously, not any string of length $n - 1$ will do. For example, there is no relation between writing 'apple' (a string of length 5) backward and writing 'pear' (a string of length 4) backward. You must choose the smaller problem carefully so that you can use its solution in the solution to the original problem.

The string of length $n - 1$ that you choose must be a substring (part) of the original string. Suppose that you strip away one character from the original string, leaving a substring of length $n - 1$. For the recursive solution to be valid, the ability to write the substring backward, combined with the ability to perform some minor task, must result in the ability to write the original string backward. Compare this approach with the way you computed *Factorial* recursively: The ability to compute *Factorial*($n - 1$), combined with the ability to multiply this value by n, resulted in the ability to compute *Factorial*(n).

You need to decide which character to strip away and which minor task to perform. Consider the minor task first. Since you are printing characters,

Figure 5-6

A recursive solution

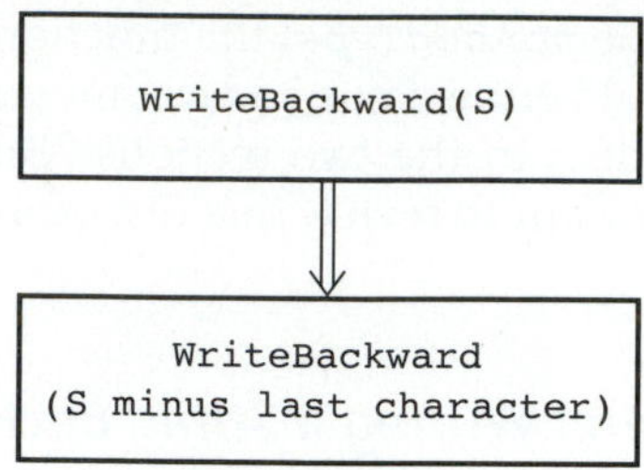

a likely candidate for the minor task is printing a single character. As for the character that you should strip away from the string, there are several possible alternatives. Two of the more intuitive alternatives are

Strip away the last character

or

Strip away the first character

Consider the first of these alternatives, stripping away the last character, as Figure 5-6 illustrates.

For the solution to be valid, you must print the last character in the string first. Therefore, you must print the last character before you write the remainder of the string backward. A high-level recursive solution, given the string *S*, is

***WriteBackward** writes a string backward*

```
WriteBackward(S)

    if the string is empty
       then do not do anything--this is the degenerate case

       else
       begin
           Print the last character of S
           WriteBackward(S minus its last character)
       end
```

This solution to the problem is conceptual. To obtain a Pascal procedure, you must resolve a few implementation issues. Suppose that the procedure will receive two parameters: a string *S* to be written backward and an integer *Size* that specifies the length of the string. To simplify matters, you can assume that the string begins at position 1 and ends at position *Size*. That is, all characters, including blanks, in that range are part of the string. The Pascal procedure *WriteBackward* appears as follows:[1]

```
procedure WriteBackward(S : string; Size : integer);
{ ---------------------------------------------------------
  Writes a character string backward.
  Precondition: The string is S[1..Size], where Size >= 0.
```

[1]You can use Turbo Pascal's *Length* and *Copy* functions in this procedure instead of the parameter *Size*, but we think that this version is easier to understand.

```
  Postcondition: Writes the string backward; does not change
  either parameter.
  ---------------------------------------------------------- }
begin
   if Size > 0
      then
      begin
         { write the last character }
         write(S[Size]);

         { write the rest of the string backward }
         WriteBackward(S, Size - 1)           {A}
      end

      { Size = 0 is the degenerate case - do nothing }
end;  { WriteBackward }
```

Notice that the recursive calls to *WriteBackward* use successively smaller values of *Size*. This decrease in *Size* has the effect of stripping away the last character of the string and ensures that the degenerate case will be reached.

You can trace the execution of *WriteBackward* by using the box method. As was true for the function *Fact*, each box contains the local environment of the recursive call—in this case, the value parameters *S* and *Size*. Because *WriteBackward* is a procedure rather than a function, it returns no computed value. Figure 5-7 illustrates the box method for the procedure *WriteBackward* with the string 'cat'.

*The procedure **WriteBackward** does not return a computed value*

Now consider a slightly different approach to the problem. Recall that we mentioned two alternatives for the character that you could strip away from the string: the last character or the first character. The solution just given strips away the last character of the string. It will now be interesting to construct a solution based on the second alternative:

Strip away the first character

To begin, consider a simple modification of the previous pseudocode solution that replaces each occurrence of "last" with "first." Thus, the procedure prints the first character rather than the last and then recursively writes the remainder of the string backward.

__WriteBackward1__ does not write a string backward

```
WriteBackward1(S)

   if the string is empty
      then do not do anything--this is the degenerate case

      else
      begin
         Print the first character of S
         WriteBackward1(S minus its first character)
      end
```

Does this solution do what you want it to? If you think about this procedure, you will realize that it prints the string in its normal left-to-

Figure 5-7

Box trace of `WriteBackward('cat', 3)`

The initial call is made, and the procedure begins execution:

S = 'cat'
Size = 3

Point A (`WriteBackward(S, Size-1)`) is reached, and the recursive call is made.

Output line just before call: **t**

The new invocation begins execution.

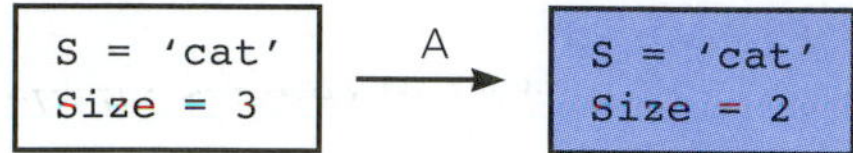

Point A is reached, and the recursive call is made.

Output line just before call: **ta**

The new invocation begins execution.

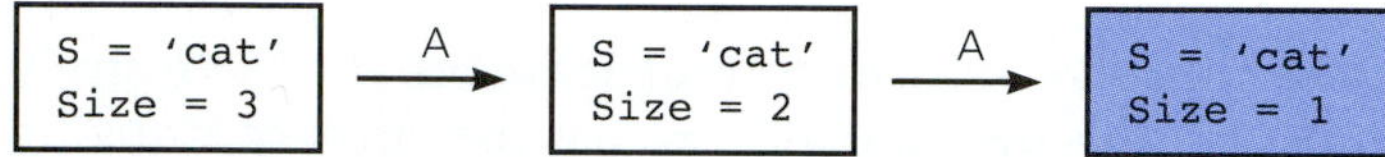

Point A is reached, and the recursive call is made.

Output line just before call: **tac**

The new invocation begins execution.

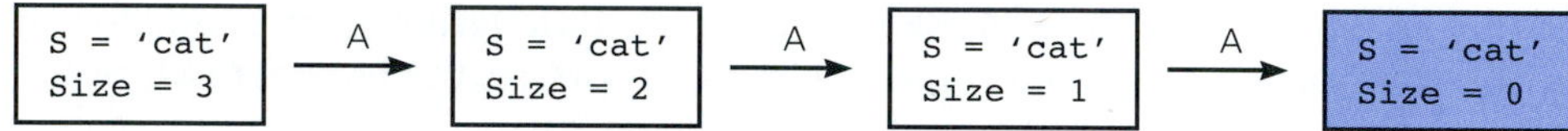

This is the degenerate case, so this invocation completes.
Control returns to the calling box, which continues execution.

S = 'cat'
Size = 3
A
S = 'cat'
Size = 2
A
S = 'cat'
Size = 1
S = 'cat'
Size = 0

Output line just after return from last call: **tac**

This invocation completes. Control returns to the calling box, which continues execution.

S = 'cat'
Size = 3
A
S = 'cat'
Size = 2
S = 'cat'
Size = 1
S = 'cat'
Size = 0

Output line just after return from last call: **tac**

This invocation completes. Control returns to the calling box, which continues execution.

S = 'cat'
Size = 3
S = 'cat'
Size = 2
S = 'cat'
Size = 1
S = 'cat'
Size = 0

Output line just after return from last call: **tac**

This invocation completes. Control returns to the statement following the main call.

right direction instead of backward. After all, the steps in the pseudocode are

```
Print the first character of S
Write the rest of S
```

These steps simply print the string `S`. Naming the procedure `WriteBackward` does not guarantee that it will actually write the string backward—recursion really is not magic!

You can write `S` backward correctly by using the following recursive formulation:

```
Write S minus its first character backward
Print the first character of S
```

In other words, you write the first character of `S` only *after* you write the rest of `S` backward. This approach leads to the following pseudocode procedure:

`WriteBackward2` writes a string backward

```
WriteBackward2(S)

   if the string is empty
      then do not do anything--this is the degenerate case

      else
      begin
         WriteBackward2(S minus its first character)
         Print the first character of S
      end
```

The translation of `WriteBackward2` into Pascal is similar to that of the original `WriteBackward` procedure and is left as an exercise.

It is instructive to carefully trace the actions of the two pseudocode procedures `WriteBackward` and `WriteBackward2`. First, add `writeln` statements to each procedure, to provide output that is useful to the trace, as follows:

```
WriteBackward(S)

   writeln('Enter WriteBackward with string: ', S)
   if the string is empty
      then do not do anything--this is the degenerate case

      else
      begin
         writeln('About to print last character of string: ',S)

         Print the last character of S
         WriteBackward(S minus its last character)        {A}
      end
   writeln('Leave WriteBackward with string: ', S)
```

```
WriteBackward2(S)

    writeln('Enter WriteBackward2 with string: ', S)
    if the string is empty
      then do not do anything--this is the degenerate case

      else
      begin
        WriteBackward2(S minus its first character)      {A}
        writeln('About to print first character of string: ',S)
        Print the first character of S
      end
    writeln('Leave WriteBackward2 with string: ', S)
```

Figures 5-8 and 5-9 show the output of the revised procedures *WriteBackward* and *WriteBackward2*, when initially given the string 'cat'.

You need to be comfortable with the differences between these two procedures. The recursive calls that the two procedures make generate a different sequence of values for the parameter *S*. Despite this fact, both procedures correctly write the string argument backward. They compensate for the difference in the sequence of values for *S* by printing different characters in the string at different times relative to the recursive calls. In terms of the box traces in Figures 5-8 and 5-9, procedure *WriteBackward* prints a character just before generating a new box (just before a new recursive call), whereas procedure *WriteBackward2* prints a character just after crossing off a box (just after returning from a recursive call). When these differences are put together, the result is two procedures that employ different strategies to accomplish the same task.

This example also illustrates the value of the box method, combined with well-placed *write* statements, in debugging recursive subprograms. The *write* statements at the beginning, interior, and end of the recursive procedures report the value of the parameter *S*. In general, when debugging a recursive subprogram, you should also report both the values of local variables and the point in the subprogram where each call occurs, as shown in the example that follows on page 253.

Figure 5-8

Box trace of *`WriteBackward('cat')`* in pseudocode

The output file is initially empty.

The initial call is made and the procedure begins execution.

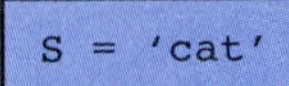

Point A is reached, and the recursive call is made.

Output file just before call:

```
Enter WriteBackward with string: cat
About to print last character of string: cat
t
```

The new invocation begins execution.

Point A is reached, and the recursive call is made.

Output file just before call:

```
Enter WriteBackward with string: cat
About to print last character of string: cat
t
Enter WriteBackward with string: ca
About to print last character of string: ca
a
```

The new invocation begins execution.

S = 'cat' —A→ S = 'ca' —A→ S = 'c'

Point A is reached, and the recursive call is made.

Output file just before call:

```
Enter WriteBackward with string: cat
About to print last character of string: cat
t
Enter WriteBackward with string: ca
About to print last character of string: ca
a
Enter WriteBackward with string: c
About to print last character of string: c
c
```

The new invocation begins execution.

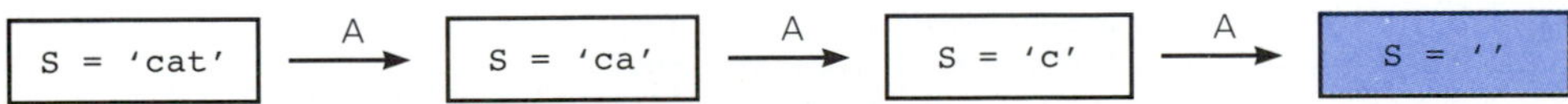

This invocation completes execution and a return is made.

(continues)

Figure 5-8
continued

Output file just after return:

```
Enter WriteBackward with string: cat
About to print last character of string: cat
t
Enter WriteBackward with string: ca
About to print last character of string: ca
a
Enter WriteBackward with string: c
About to print last character of string: c
c
Enter WriteBackward with string:
Leave WriteBackward with string:
```

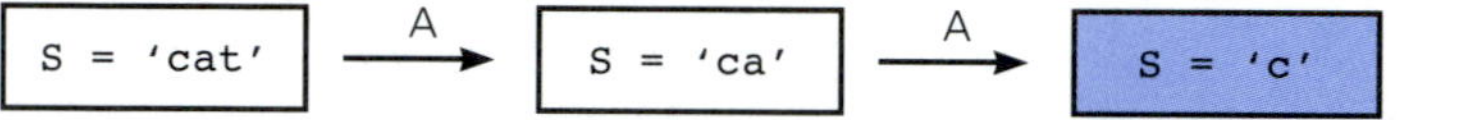

This invocation completes execution and a return is made.

Output file just after return:

```
Enter WriteBackward with string: cat
About to print last character of string: cat
t
Enter WriteBackward with string: ca
About to print last character of string: ca
a
Enter WriteBackward with string: c
About to print last character of string: c
c
Enter WriteBackward with string:
Leave WriteBackward with string:
Leave WriteBackward with string: c
```

This invocation completes execution and a return is made.

Output file just after return:

```
Enter WriteBackward with string: cat
About to print last character of string: cat
t
Enter WriteBackward with string: ca
About to print last character of string: ca
a
Enter WriteBackward with string: c
About to print last character of string: c
c
Enter WriteBackward with string:
Leave WriteBackward with string:
Leave WriteBackward with string: c
Leave WriteBackward with string: ca
```

S = 'cat'　S = 'ca'　S = 'c'　S = ''

This invocation completes execution and a return is made.

Output file just after return:

```
Enter WriteBackward with string: cat
About to print last character of string: cat
t
Enter WriteBackward with string: ca
About to print last character of string: ca
a
Enter WriteBackward with string: c
About to print last character of string: c
c
Enter WriteBackward with string:
Leave WriteBackward with string:
Leave WriteBackward with string: c
Leave WriteBackward with string: ca
Leave WriteBackward with string: cat
```

Figure 5-9

Box trace of *Write-Backward2('cat')* in pseudocode

The output file is initially empty.

The initial call is made, and the procedure begins execution.

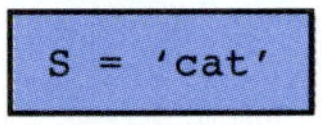

```
S = 'cat'
```

Point A is reached, and the recursive call is made.

Output file just before call:

```
Enter WriteBackward2 with string: cat
```

The new invocation begins execution.

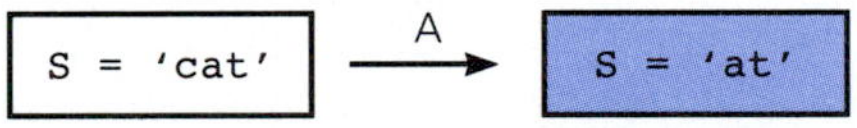

```
S = 'cat'  --A-->  S = 'at'
```

Point A is reached, and the recursive call is made.

Output file just before call:

```
Enter WriteBackward2 with string: cat
Enter WriteBackward2 with string: at
```

The new invocation begins execution.

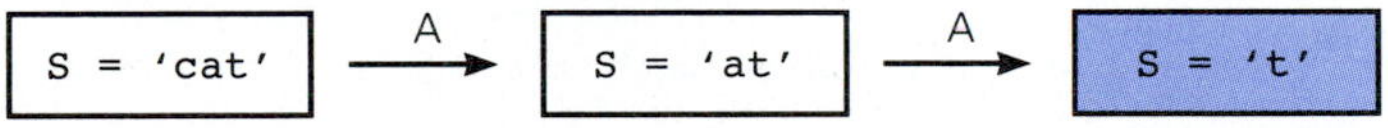

```
S = 'cat'  --A-->  S = 'at'  --A-->  S = 't'
```

Point A is reached, and the recursive call is made.

Output file just before call:

```
Enter WriteBackward2 with string: cat
Enter WriteBackward2 with string: at
Enter WriteBackward2 with string: t
```

(continues)

Figure 5-9
continued

The new invocation begins execution.

This invocation completes execution and a return is made.

Output file just after return

```
Enter WriteBackward2 with string: cat
Enter WriteBackward2 with string: at
Enter WriteBackward2 with string: t
Enter WriteBackward2 with string:
Leave WriteBackward2 with string:
```

s = 'cat' —A→ s = 'at' —A→ s = 't'   s = ''

This invocation completes execution and a return is made.

Output file just after return:

```
Enter WriteBackward2 with string: cat
Enter WriteBackward2 with string: at
Enter WriteBackward2 with string: t
Enter WriteBackward2 with string:
Leave WriteBackward2 with string:
About to print first character of string: t
t
Leave WriteBackward2 with string: t
```

s = 'cat' —A→ s = 'at'   s = 't'   s = ''

This invocation completes execution and a return is made.

Output file just after return:

```
Enter WriteBackward2 with string: cat
Enter WriteBackward2 with string: at
Enter WriteBackward2 with string: t
Enter WriteBackward2 with string:
Leave WriteBackward2 with string:
About to print first character of string: t
t
Leave WriteBackward2 with string: t
About to print first character of string: at
a
Leave WriteBackward2 with string: at
```

s = 'cat'   s = 'at'   s = 't'   s = ''

Output file just after return:

```
Enter WriteBackward2 with string: cat
Enter WriteBackward2 with string: at
Enter WriteBackward2 with string: t
Enter WriteBackward2 with string:
Leave WriteBackward2 with string:
About to print first character of string: t
t
Leave WriteBackward2 with string: t
About to print first character of string: at
a
Leave WriteBackward2 with string: at
About to print first character of string: cat
c
Leave WriteBackward2 with string: cat
```

Example: Using *write* statements to debug a recursive subprogram. The following pseudocode indicates where to place *write* statements within a recursive subprogram during debugging:

Sample write statements that help to debug a recursive subprogram

```
procedure R(... )

    writeln('Calling procedure R from point A.',...)
    R(... ) { this is point A }
    writeln('Calling procedure R from point B.',...)
    R(... ) { this is point B }
```

In addition to reporting each recursive call, the *write* statements should display the values of all parameters and local variables.

Before leaving the *WriteBackward* problem, suppose that *S* is in a linked list rather than a string. Given the nature of linked lists, the strategy of *WriteBackward* is very difficult to implement; however, the strategy of *WriteBackward2* is simple to implement. You will see why in the next chapter when you learn to process linked lists recursively.

COMPUTING THINGS

You should now be able to solve some more-challenging problems recursively. The next two problems require you to compute some specified value.

Raising an Integer to a Power

Pascal has no exponentiation operator. That is, if you want to know the value of x^n, you have to write a function to compute it. This section presents three functions for performing exponentiation. To simplify matters, consider only integers raised to nonnegative integer powers.

Assuming the type definition

```
type nonnegType = 0..maxint
```

the following *iterative* Pascal function performs the exponentiation:

***Pow1* computes x^n iteratively**

```
function Pow1(x : integer; n : nonnegType) : longint;
{ ---------------------------------------------------------
  Exponentiation function--ITERATIVE SOLUTION.
  Precondition: x is an integer; n is a nonnegative integer.
  Postcondition: Returns x raised to the nth power.
  --------------------------------------------------------- }
var   Temp : longint;
      Exponent : integer;

begin
    Temp := 1;
    for Exponent := 1 to n do
       Temp := x * Temp;
    Pow1 := Temp
end;  { Pow1 }
```

Now consider a recursive solution. How can you define raising x to the nth power in terms of raising x to a smaller power? The answer is found in the "rule of exponents":

$$x^n = x * x^{n-1}$$

That is, you can compute x^n by computing x^{n-1} and multiplying the result by x. This recursive solution lacks only a degenerate case. Recall that, by definition,

$$x^0 = 1$$

You thus have the following recursive formulation:

Computing x^n recursively

$$x^0 = 1$$
$$x^n = x * x^{n-1} \quad \text{if } n > 0$$

Since n is nonnegative, you will always reach the degenerate case, $n = 0$.

The following Pascal function implements this solution directly:

***Pow2* computes x^n recursively**

```
function Pow2(x : integer; n : nonnegType) : longint;
{ ---------------------------------------------------------
  Exponentiation function--RECURSIVE SOLUTION.
  Precondition: x is an integer; n is a nonnegative integer.
  Postcondition: Returns x raised to the nth power.
  --------------------------------------------------------- }
begin
    if n = 0
       then Pow2 := 1
       else Pow2 := x * Pow2(x, n-1)
end;  { Pow2 }
```

To compute x^n, the function *Pow2* is called $n + 1$ times: once from the main program and n times recursively. You can reduce this number of calls greatly by exploiting another rule of exponents:

$$x^n = (x^{n/m})^m$$

In particular, for $m = 2$

$$x^n = (x^{n/2})^2$$

You can use this rule to construct a more efficient recursive power function. The strategy of the following function is to halve the value of n at each recursive call rather than simply to decrement it by 1. The result is that the function reaches the degenerate case with far fewer recursive calls than *Pow2*.

Pow3* computes x^n recursively and more efficiently than *Pow2

```
function Pow3(x : integer; n : nonnegType) : longint;
{ -------------------------------------------------------
  Exponentiation function--MORE EFFICIENT RECURSIVE SOLUTION.
  Precondition: x is an integer; n is a nonnegative integer.
  Postcondition: Returns x raised to the nth power.
  ------------------------------------------------------- }
begin
   if n = 0 then
      Pow3 := 1
   else if odd(n) then
      Pow3 := x * sqr(Pow3(x, n div 2))
   else Pow3 := sqr(Pow3(x, n div 2))
end;  { Pow3 }
```

Observe that the function *Pow3* has a case for even n (when *odd(n)* is false) and a different case for odd n (when *odd(n)* is true). Consider first the case for even n. Here the function computes the value x^n as

```
sqr(Pow3(x, n div 2))
```

(*sqr* is a predefined Pascal function for raising integers to the power of 2). This computation is valid because, when n is even,

$$(x^{n \text{ div } 2})^2 = (x^{n/2})^2 = x^n$$

Now consider the case when n is odd. Notice that the value of *n div 2* is not the same as *n/2* when n is odd. For example, the value of *13 div 2* is 6 rather than 6.5, and consequently $(x^{13 \text{ div } 2})^2$ is equal to x^{12} rather than x^{13}. In general, when n is odd,

$$(x^{n \text{ div } 2})^2 = x^{n-1}$$

To compensate for this fact, when n is odd the function *Pow3* computes

```
x * sqr(Pow3(x, n div 2))
```

Figure 5-10 illustrates the dramatic reduction in the number of required calls to the power function that you can achieve by halving n rather than

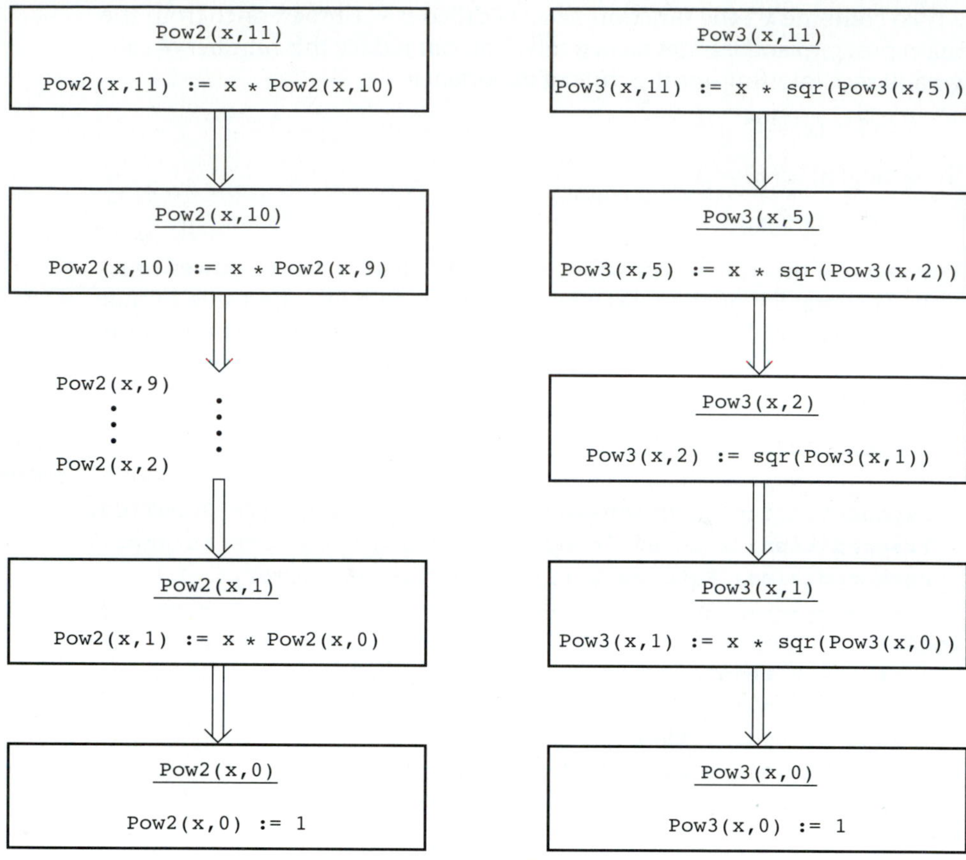

Figure 5-10

Pow2(x, 11) versus ***Pow3(x, 11)***

decrementing n by 1. Exercise 15 further discusses the efficiency of the power functions.

Multiplying Rabbits (The Fibonacci Sequence)

Rabbits are very prolific breeders. If rabbits did not die, their population would quickly get out of hand. Suppose we assume the following "facts," which we obtained in a recent survey of randomly selected rabbits:

- Rabbits never die.
- A rabbit reaches sexual maturity exactly two months after birth, that is, at the beginning of its third month of life.
- Rabbits are always born in male-female pairs. At the beginning of every month, each sexually mature male-female pair gives birth to exactly one male-female pair.

Suppose you started with a single newborn male-female pair. How many pairs would there be in month 6, counting the births that took place at the beginning of month 6? Since 6 is a relatively small number, you can figure out the solution easily:

Month 1:	1 pair, the original.
Month 2:	1 pair still, since it is not yet sexually mature.
Month 3:	2 pairs; the original pair has reached sexual maturity and has given birth to a second pair.
Month 4:	3 pairs; the original pair has given birth again, but the pair born at the beginning of month 3 is not yet sexually mature.
Month 5:	5 pairs; all rabbits alive in month 3 (2 pairs) are now sexually mature. Add their offspring to those pairs alive in month 4 (3 pairs) to yield 5 pairs.
Month 6:	8 pairs; 3 newborn pairs from the pairs alive in month 4 plus 5 pairs alive in month 5.

You can now construct a recursive solution for computing *Rabbit(n)*, the number of pairs alive in month *n*. You must determine how you can use *Rabbit(n* − 1) to compute *Rabbit(n)*. Observe that *Rabbit(n)* is the sum of the number of pairs alive just prior to the start of month *n* and the number of pairs born at the start of month *n*. Just prior to the start of month *n*, there are *Rabbit(n* − 1) pairs of rabbits. Not all of these rabbits are sexually mature at the start of month *n*. Only those who were alive in month *n* − 2 are ready to reproduce at the start of month *n*. That is, the number of pairs born at the start of month *n* is *Rabbit(n* − 2). Therefore, you have the relationship

$$Rabbit(n) = Rabbit(n-1) + Rabbit(n-2)$$

The number of pairs in month **n**

Figure 5-11 illustrates this relationship.

This recursive relationship introduces a new point. In some cases, you solve a problem by solving more than one smaller problem of the same type. This change does not add much conceptual difficulty, but you must be very careful when selecting the degenerate case. The temptation is simply to say that *Rabbit*(1) should be the degenerate case because its value is 1 according to the problem's statement. But what about *Rabbit*(2)? Applying the recursive definition to *Rabbit*(2) would yield

$$Rabbit(2) = Rabbit(1) + Rabbit(0)$$

Thus, the recursive definition would need to specify the number of pairs alive in month 0—an undefined quantity.

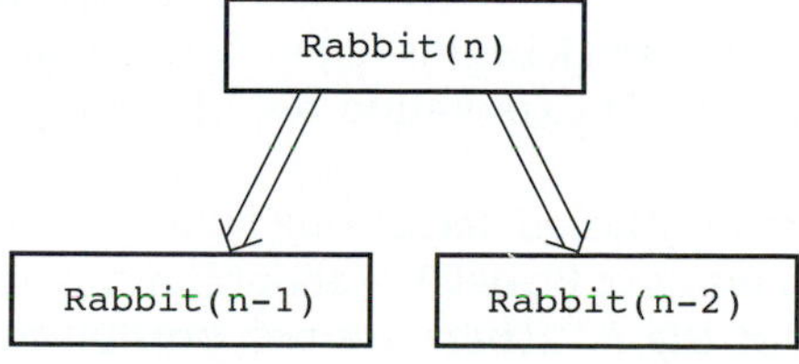

Figure 5-11

Recursive solution to the rabbit problem

Two degenerate cases are necessary because there are two smaller problems

One possible solution is to define *Rabbit*(0) to be 0, but this approach seems artificial. A slightly more attractive alternative is to treat *Rabbit*(2) itself as a special case with the value of 1. Thus, the recursive definition has two degenerate cases, *Rabbit*(2) and *Rabbit*(1). The recursive definition becomes

$$Rabbit(n) = \begin{cases} 1 & \text{if } n \leq 2 \\ Rabbit(n-1) + Rabbit(n-2) & \text{if } n > 2 \end{cases}$$

Incidentally, the series of numbers *Rabbit*(1), *Rabbit*(2), *Rabbit*(3), and so on is known as the **Fibonacci sequence**, which models many naturally occurring phenomena.

A pseudocode function to compute *Rabbit*(*n*) is easy to write from the previous definition:

`Rabbit` computes the Fibonacci sequence, but does so inefficiently

```
function Rabbit(n) : returns a positive integer
{ Assumption: n is a positive integer. }

   if n <= 2
      then Rabbit := 1
      else Rabbit := Rabbit(n - 1) + Rabbit(n - 2)
```

Should you implement this function in Pascal and run it? Figure 5-12 illustrates the recursive calls that `Rabbit(7)` generates. (To save space, the figure uses `Rab` instead of `Rabbit`.) Think about the number of recursive calls that `Rabbit(10)` generates. At best, the function `Rabbit` is inefficient; for large values of *n*, it is infeasible to use. We shall discuss this problem in more detail at the end of this chapter, at which time we shall give some techniques for generating a more efficient solution from this same recursive relationship.

COUNTING THINGS

The next two problems require you to count certain combinations of events or things.

Mr. Spock's Dilemma (Choosing k *out of* n *Things)*

The five-year mission of the *U.S.S. Enterprise* is to explore new worlds. The five years are almost up, but the *Enterprise* has just entered an unexplored solar system that contains *n* planets. Unfortunately, time will allow for only *k* explorations. Mr. Spock begins to ponder how many different ways he can choose *k* planets for exploration out of the *n* planets in the solar system.

Mr. Spock is especially fascinated by one particular planet, Planet *X*. He begins to think—in terms of Planet *X*—about how many ways there are to pick *k* planets out of the *n*. "There are two possibilities: Either we visit

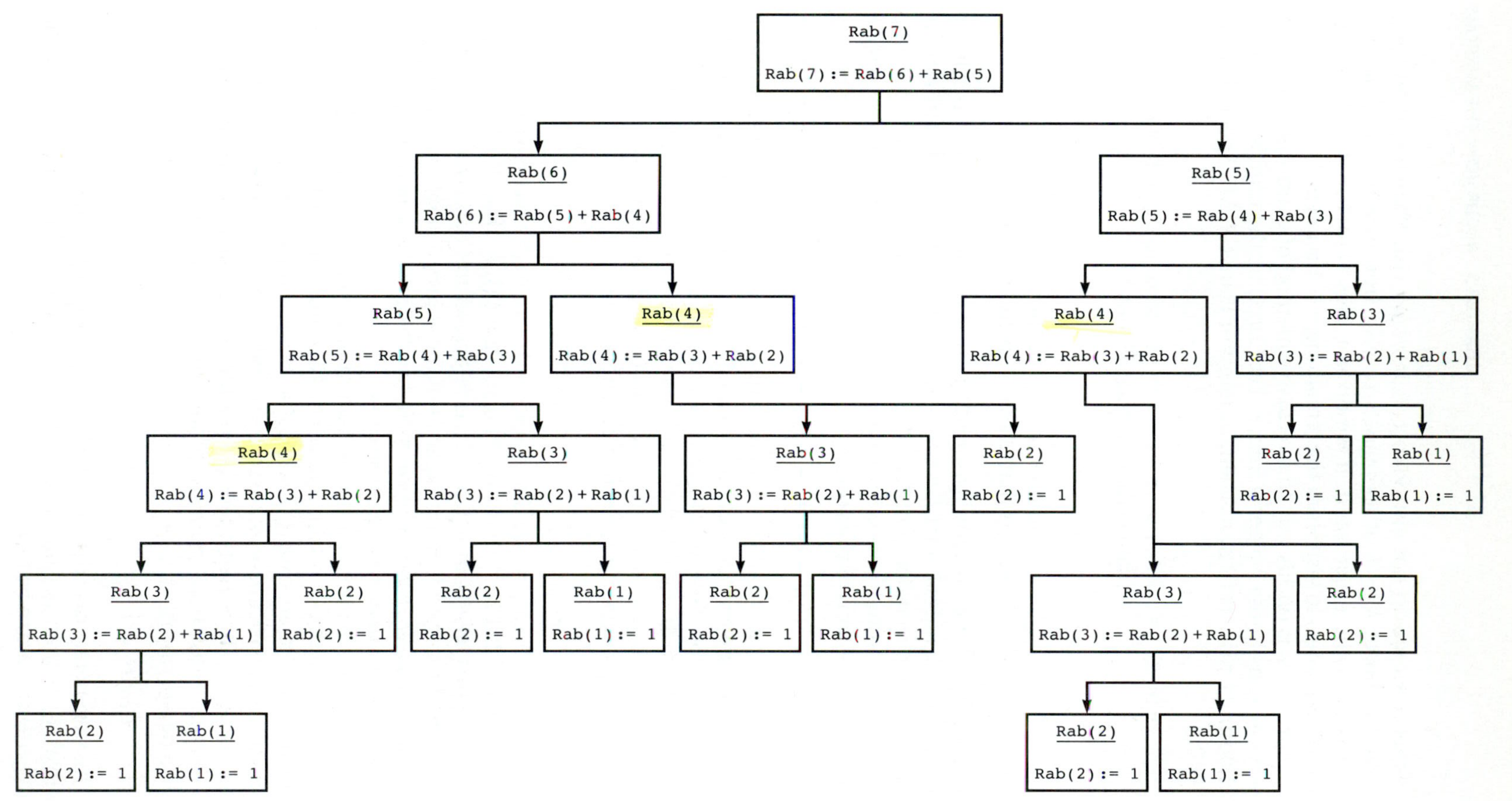

Figure 5-12

The recursive calls that ***Rabbit(7)*** generates

Planet X, or we do not visit Planet X. If we *do* visit Planet X, then I will have to choose $k - 1$ other planets to visit from the $n - 1$ remaining planets. On the other hand, if we do not visit Planet X, I will have to choose k planets to visit from the remaining $n - 1$ planets."

Mr. Spock is on his way to a recursive method of counting how many ways he can choose k planets from n. Let $C(n, k)$ be the number of ways of choosing k planets from n. Then, in terms of Planet X, Mr. Spock deduces that

$C(n, k)$ = (the number of ways of choosing a group of k planets that includes Planet X)

+

(the number of ways of choosing a group of k planets that does not include Planet X)

But Mr. Spock has already reasoned that the number of ways to select a group that includes Planet X is $C(n - 1, k - 1)$, and the number of ways to select a group that does not include Planet X is $C(n - 1, k)$. Mr. Spock has figured out a way to solve his counting problem in terms of two smaller counting problems of the same type:

The number of ways to choose k out of n things is the sum of the number of ways to choose k − 1 out of n − 1 things and the number of ways to choose k out of n − 1 things

$$C(n, k) = C(n - 1, k - 1) + C(n - 1, k)$$

Mr. Spock now has to worry about the degenerate case(s). He also needs to demonstrate that each of the two smaller problems eventually reaches a degenerate case. First, what selection problem does he immediately know the answer to? If the *Enterprise* had time to visit all the planets (that is, if $k = n$), there would be no need for a decision; there is only one way to select all the planets. Thus, the first degenerate case is

Degenerate case: There is one way to choose everything

$$C(k, k) = 1$$

If $k < n$, it is easy to see that the second term in the recursive definition $C(n - 1, k)$ is "closer" to the degenerate case $C(k, k)$ than is $C(n, k)$. However, the first term, $C(n - 1, k - 1)$, is not closer to $C(k, k)$ than is $C(n, k)$—they are the same "distance" apart. *When you solve a problem by solving two (or more) smaller problems, each of the smaller problems must be closer to a degenerate case than the original problem.*

Mr. Spock realizes that there is another trivial selection problem that the first term does, in fact, approach. This problem is the counterpart of his first degenerate case, $C(k, k)$. Just as there is only one way to select all the planets to visit ($k = n$), there is also only one way to select zero planets to visit ($k = 0$). When there is no time to visit any of the planets, the *Enterprise* must head home without any exploration. Thus the second degenerate case is

Degenerate case: There is one way to choose nothing

$$C(n, 0) = 1$$

This degenerate case does indeed have the property that $C(n - 1, k - 1)$ is closer to it than is $C(n, k)$. (Alternatively, you could define the second degenerate case to be $C(n, 1) = n$.)

Mr. Spock adds one final part to his solution:

$$C(n, k) = 0 \qquad \text{if } k > n$$

Although k could not be greater than n in the context of this problem, the addition of this case makes the recursive solution more generally applicable.

To summarize, the following recursive solution solves the problem of choosing k out of n things:

$$C(n, k) = \begin{cases} 1 & \text{if } k = 0 \\ 1 & \text{if } k = n \\ C(n-1, k-1) + C(n-1, k) & \text{if } 0 < k < n \\ 0 & \text{if } k > n \end{cases}$$

The number of ways to choose k *out of* n *things recursively*

You can easily derive the following pseudocode function from this recursive definition:

```
function C(n, k) : returns a nonnegative integer
{ Assumption: n and k are nonnegative integers. }

   if k > n then
      C := 0
   else if k = n then
      C := 1
   else if k = 0 then
      C := 1
   else C := C(n-1, k-1) + C(n-1, k)
```

The comments about efficiency that we made following the rabbit problem apply here also. Figure 5-13 shows the number of recursive calls that the computation of `C(4, 2)` requires.

The Mad Scientist Problem

The mad scientist wishes to make a chain out of plutonium and lead pieces. There is a problem, however. If the scientist places two pieces of plutonium next to each other, BOOM! The question is, in how many ways can the scientist safely construct a chain of length n?

Assume that pieces of the same element are indistinguishable and that the scientist has at least n pieces of plutonium and n pieces of lead. Also note that the question asks for the number of ways to construct a chain. The chains *lead-plutonium* and *plutonium-lead*, for example, are different chains and count as two ways.

The scientist realizes that there are two classes of safe chains: safe chains that end with a lead piece and safe chains that end with a plutonium piece. The answer to the question is simply the sum of the number of chains of each type. That is, let

$C(n)$ be the number of safe chains of length n

$L(n)$ be the number of safe chains of length n that end with a piece of lead

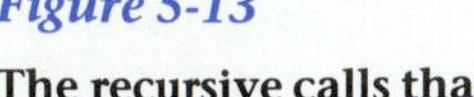

Figure 5-13

The recursive calls that `C(4, 2)` generates

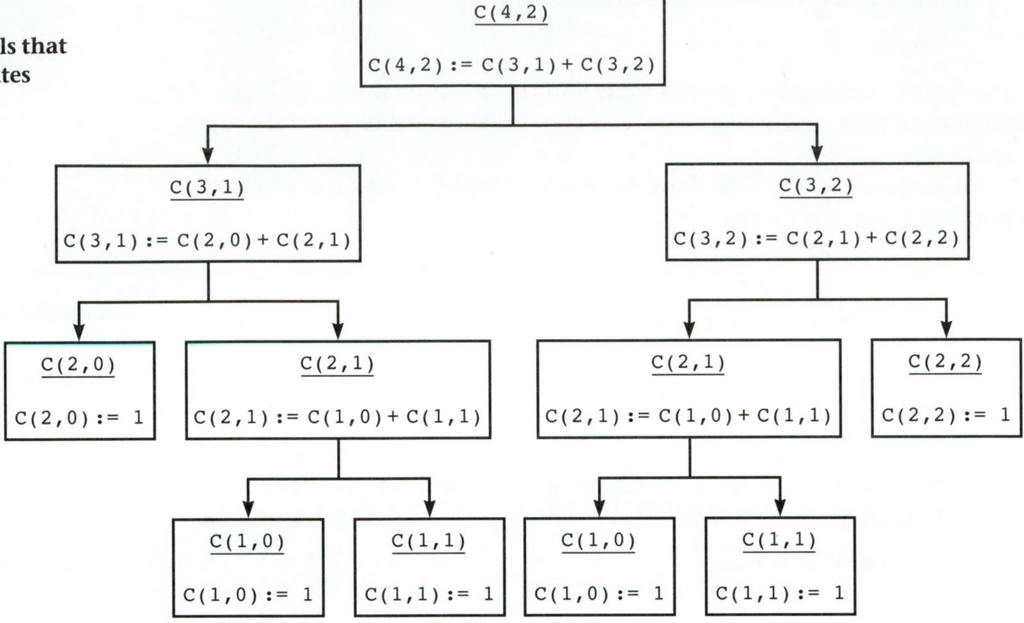

$P(n)$ be the number of safe chains of length n that end with a piece of plutonium

Then

$$C(n) = L(n) + P(n)$$

First, consider $L(n)$. The scientist can create a safe chain of length n that ends with a lead piece simply by tacking a lead piece onto the end of *any* safe chain of length $n - 1$. Hence, the number of safe chains of length n that end with a lead piece is precisely equal to the total number of safe chains of length $n - 1$; that is,

The number of safe chains of length n *that end in lead*

$$L(n) = C(n - 1)$$

Next, consider $P(n)$. The only way a safe chain can end with a plutonium piece is if the piece just before the end is lead. (If it is plutonium, the scientist cannot add another plutonium piece.) Thus, the only way to make a safe chain of length n that ends in plutonium is first to make a safe chain of length $n - 1$ that ends in lead and then add a piece of plutonium to the end. Therefore, the number of safe chains of length n that end with a plutonium piece is precisely equal to the number of safe chains of length $n - 1$ that end with a lead piece:

$$P(n) = L(n - 1)$$

The scientist then uses the earlier fact that $L(n) = C(n - 1)$ to obtain

The number of safe chains of length n *that end in plutonium*

$$P(n) = C(n - 2)$$

Thus, the scientist has solved $L(n)$ and $P(n)$ in terms of the smaller problems $C(n-1)$ and $C(n-2)$, respectively. The scientist then uses

$$C(n) = L(n) + P(n)$$

to obtain

$$C(n) = C(n-1) + C(n-2)$$

The number of safe chains of length **n**

The form of this recurrence relation is identical to the solution for the multiplying rabbits problem.

As you saw in the rabbit problem, two degenerate cases are necessary because the recurrence relation defines a problem in terms of two smaller problems. As you did for the rabbit problem, you can choose $n = 1$ and $n = 2$ for the degenerate cases. Although both problems use the same n's for their degenerate cases, there is no reason to expect that they use the same values for these degenerate cases. That is, there is no reason to expect that *Rabbit*(1) is equal to $C(1)$ and that *Rabbit*(2) is equal to $C(2)$.

A little thought reveals that for the chain problem,

Two degenerate cases are necessary because there are two smaller problems

$C(1) = 2$ (Chains that consist of either a single piece of plutonium or a single piece of lead.)

$C(2) = 3$ (The safe chains of length 2 are *lead-lead, plutonium-lead*, and *lead-plutonium*.)

In summary, the solution to this problem is

A recursive solution

$$C(1) = 2$$
$$C(2) = 3$$
$$C(n) = C(n-1) + C(n-2) \qquad \text{for } n > 2$$

Moral of the story: Sometimes you can solve a problem by breaking it up into cases—for example, chains that end in plutonium and chains that end in lead.

Another moral of the story: The values that you use for the degenerate cases are extremely important. Although the recurrence relations for C and *Rabbit* are the same, the different values for their degenerate cases ($n = 1$ or 2) cause different values for larger n. For example, *Rabbit*(20) = 6,765, while $C(20) = 17{,}711$. The larger the value of n, the larger the discrepancy. You should think about why this is so.

SEARCHING FOR THINGS

Searching is an important task that occurs frequently. This chapter began with an intuitive approach to a binary search algorithm. In this section we will develop the binary search and examine other searching problems that have recursive solutions. Our goal is to develop further your notion of recursion.

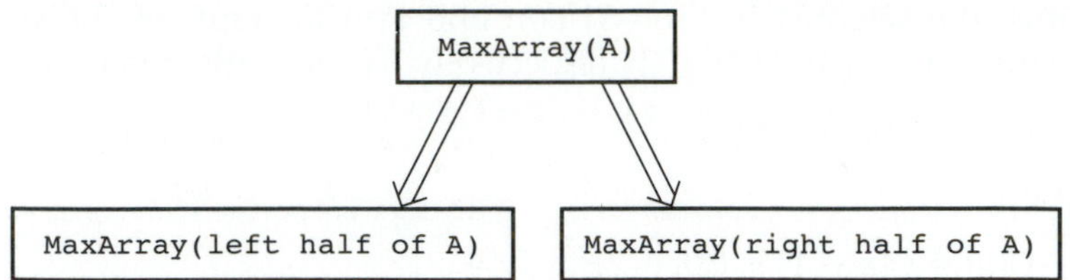

Figure 5-14

Recursive solution to the largest-element problem

Finding the Largest Element of an Array

This section begins by outlining a solution to a simple problem. You should complete the solution before continuing.

Suppose you have an array `A` of integers and you want to find its maximum element. You could construct an iterative solution without too much difficulty, but instead consider a recursive formulation:

```
if A has only one element then
    MaxArray(A) is the element in A

else if A has more than one element then
    MaxArray(A) is the maximum of
      MaxArray(left half of A) and MaxArray(right half of A)
```

Notice that this strategy fits the divide-and-conquer model we discussed at the beginning of this chapter when we introduced the binary search algorithm. That is, the algorithm proceeds by dividing the problem and conquering the subproblems, as Figure 5-14 illustrates. However, there is a difference between this algorithm and the binary search algorithm. While the binary search algorithm conquers only one of its subproblems at each step, *MaxArray* conquers both. In addition, after *MaxArray* conquers the subproblems, it must reconcile the two solutions—that is, it must find the maximum of the two maximums. Figure 5-15 illustrates the computations that are necessary to find the largest element in the array that contains 1, 6, 8, and 3 (denoted here by <1, 6, 8, 3>).

`MaxArray` conquers both of its subproblems at each step

We leave it to you to develop a recursive solution based on this strategy. In so doing, you may stumble on several subtle programming issues. We discuss virtually all of these issues in the binary search problem that follows, but this is a good opportunity for you to get some practice implementing a recursive solution.

Binary Search

At the beginning of this chapter, we presented—at a high level—a recursive binary search algorithm for finding a word in a dictionary. We will now fully develop this algorithm, illustrating some important programming issues.

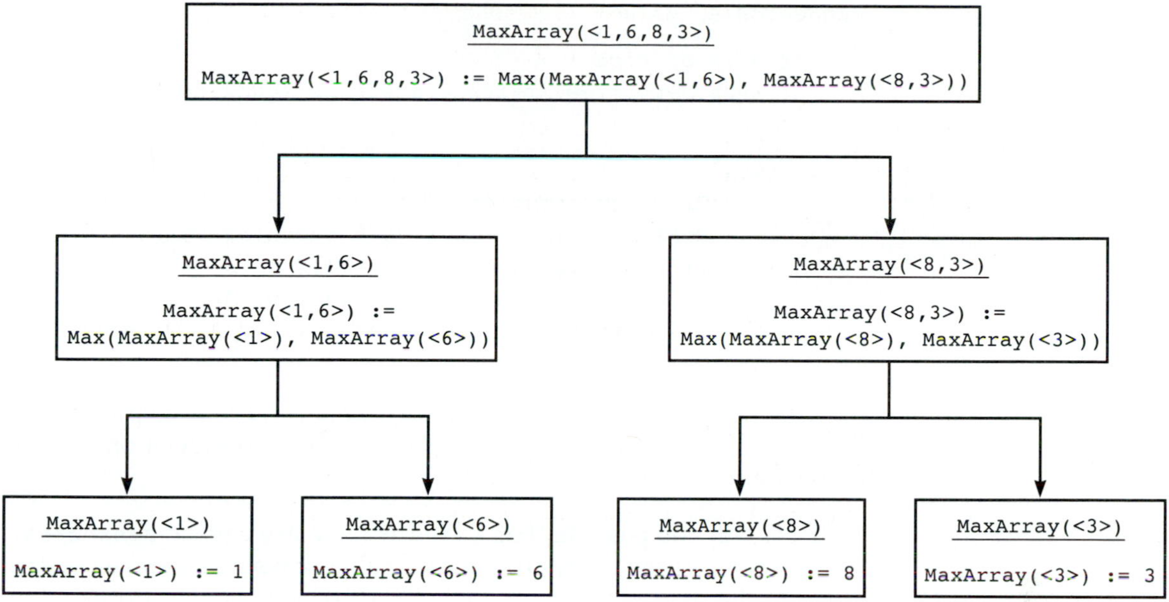

Figure 5-15

The recursive calls that `MaxArray(<1,6,8,3>)` generates

Recall the earlier solution to the dictionary problem:

A binary search conquers one of its subproblems at each step

```
Search(Dictionary, Word)

   if Dictionary is one page in size
      then scan the page for Word

      else
      begin
         Open Dictionary to a point near the middle
         Determine which half of Dictionary contains Word

         if Word is in the first half of Dictionary
            then Search(first half of Dictionary, Word)
            else Search(second half of Dictionary, Word)
      end
```

Now alter the problem slightly by searching an array `A` of integers for a given value. The array, like the dictionary, must be sorted, or else a binary search is not applicable. Hence, assume that

An array must be sorted before you can apply a binary search to it

$$A[1] \leq A[2] \leq A[3] \leq \cdots \leq A[Size]$$

where `Size` is the size of the array. A high-level binary search for the array problem is

```
BinSearch(A, Value)

    if A is of size 1
       then determine if its element is equal to Value

       else
       begin
           Find the midpoint of A
           Determine which half of A contains Value
           if Value is in the first half of A
               then BinSearch(first half of A, Value)
               else BinSearch(second half of A, Value)
       end
```

Although the solution is conceptually sound, various considerations demand changes in its organization. Three of these considerations are the following:

1. **How will you pass "half of *A*" to the recursive calls to `BinSearch`?** You can pass the entire array at each call, but have `BinSearch` search only the portion `A[First..Last]`. Thus, you would also pass the integers `First` and `Last` to `BinSearch`:

   ```
   BinSearch(A, First, Last, Value)
   ```

   With this convention, the new midpoint is given by

   ```
   Mid := (First + Last ) div 2
   ```

   The array halves are `A[First..Mid-1]` and `A[Mid+1..Last]`; neither "half" contains `A[Mid]`

   Then `BinSearch(first half of A, Value)` becomes

   ```
   BinSearch(A, First, Mid - 1, Value)
   ```

   and `BinSearch(second half of A, Value)` becomes

   ```
   BinSearch(A, Mid + 1, Last, Value)
   ```

2. **How do you determine which half of the array contains `Value`?** One possible implementation of

   ```
   if Value is in the first half of A
   ```

   is

   ```
   if Value < A[Mid]
   ```

   Determine whether `A[Mid]` is the value you seek

   However, there is no test for equality between `Value` and `A[Mid]`. This omission can cause the algorithm to miss `Value`: After the previous halving algorithm splits `A` into halves, `A[Mid]` is not in either half of the array. (In this case, two halves do not make a whole!) Therefore, you must determine whether `A[Mid]` is the value you seek *now* because later it will not be in the remaining half of the array. The interaction between the halving criterion and the termination condition (the degenerate case) is subtle and is often a source of error. We need to rethink the degenerate case.

3. **What should the degenerate case(s) be?** As written, *BinSearch* terminates only when an array of size 1 occurs; this is the only degenerate case. By changing the halving procedure so that *A[Mid] remains in one of the halves,* it is possible to implement the binary search correctly so that it has only this single degenerate case. However, we believe that it is clearer to have two distinct degenerate cases as follows:

   Two degenerate cases

   a. *First > Last*. You will reach this degenerate case when *Value* is not in the original array.
   b. *Value = A[Mid]*. You will reach this degenerate case when *Value* is in the original array.

   These degenerate cases are a bit different from any you have encountered previously. In a sense, the algorithm determines the answer to the problem from the degenerate case it reaches. Many search problems have this flavor.

The Pascal function *BinSearch*, which follows, returns the index of the array element that is equal to *Value*. Because we plan to show you a box trace of this function, we have labeled—as *X* and *Y*—the two recursive calls to *BinSearch*.

```
{ Size is a constant equal to the size of the array }
type arrayType = array[1..Size] of integer;

function BinSearch(A: arrayType; First, Last: integer;
                                  Value: integer): integer;
{ ---------------------------------------------------------
  Searches the array A[First..Last] for Value by using a
  binary search.
  Precondition: 1 <= First, Last <= Size, and
  A[First] <= A[First+1] <= ... <= A[Last].
  Postcondition: If Value is in the array, returns
  BinSearch > 0 such that A[BinSearch] = Value; otherwise
  returns BinSearch = 0.
  --------------------------------------------------------- }
var Mid : integer;

begin
    if First > Last

        then BinSearch := 0 { Value not in original array }

        else
        { Invariant:
            If Value is in A, A[First] <= Value <= A[Last] }
        begin
            Mid := (First + Last) div 2;
            if Value = A[Mid] then
                BinSearch := Mid    { Value found at A[Mid] }
```

```
            else if Value < A[Mid] then
               BinSearch :=
                  BinSearch(A, First, Mid-1, Value) { X }
            else
               BinSearch :=
                  BinSearch(A, Mid+1, Last, Value) { Y }
         end
end;   { BinSearch }
```

Notice that *BinSearch* has the following invariant: If *Value* occurs in the array, then *A[First]* ≤ *Value* ≤ *A[Last]*.

Figure 5-16 shows a box trace of *BinSearch* when it searches the array containing 1, 5, 9, 12, 15, 21, 29, and 31. Notice how the labels *X* and *Y* of the two recursive calls to *BinSearch* appear in the diagram. Exercise 6 at the end of this chapter asks you to perform other box traces with this function.

There is another implementation issue, which deals specifically with Pascal, to consider. In the function *BinSearch*, *A* is a value parameter. This fact implies that at each call to *BinSearch*, the function makes a copy of *A* and places it in its local environment. If *A* is large, many calls to *BinSearch* may be necessary, with each call requiring a copy of a large array.

There are two obvious ways to avoid this problem, but neither is satisfactory. Either you could declare the array *A* as a global variable or you

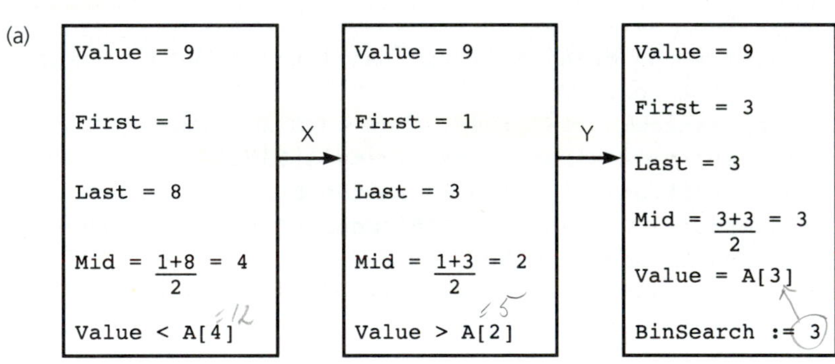

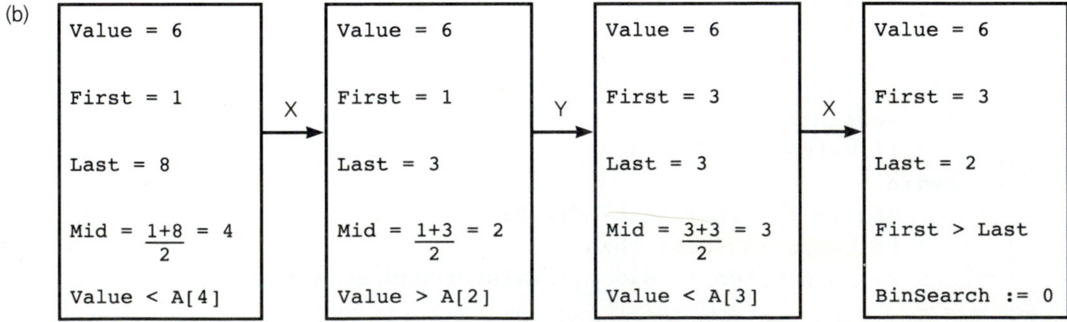

Figure 5-16

Box traces of *Binsearch* with *A* = <1,5,9,12,15,21,29,31>: (a) a successful search; (b) an unsuccessful search

could pass *A* to *BinSearch* as a variable parameter. Both of these solutions undermine modularity, however. First, you usually should avoid global variables, as they destroy the clean interface between a subprogram and the remainder of the program. Global variables also make the subprogram less general. In the case of *BinSearch*, a global declaration of the array *A* would allow the function to search only this specific array. Second, passing *A* as a variable parameter suggests that the function *BinSearch* makes a change to *A*. However, *BinSearch* does not change *A*, so passing *A* as a variable parameter conveys misinformation about *BinSearch*'s interface with the rest of the program.

Passing A either globally or as a variable parameter is not satisfactory

A third possibility is to embed the recursive search function within a nonrecursive function, which is called a **nonrecursive shell**. In the following, the function *ValueIndex* performs the recursive binary search—as *BinSearch* did earlier—and *BinSearch* is the nonrecursive shell:

BinSearch is a nonrecursive shell

A is global to ValueIndex

```
{ Size is a constant equal to the size of the array }
type arrayType = array[1..Size] of integer;

function BinSearch(A: arrayType; N : integer;
                                  Value: integer): integer;
{ -------------------------------------------------------
  Searches the array A for Value by using a binary search.
  Precondition: A[1..N] is sorted in ascending order.
  Postcondition: If Value is in the array, returns
  BinSearch > 0 such that A[BinSearch] = Value; otherwise
  returns BinSearch = 0.
  ------------------------------------------------------- }

    function ValueIndex(First, Last : integer;
                        Value: integer): integer;
    { ---------------------------------------------------
      Precondition: A is global to this function.
      1 <= First, Last <= Size.
      Postcondition: If Value is in A[First..Last],
      returns ValueIndex > 0 such that A[ValueIndex] =
      Value; otherwise returns ValueIndex = 0.
      --------------------------------------------------- }
    var Mid : integer;
    begin
        if First > Last
            then ValueIndex := 0

            else
            { Invariant:
                If Value is in A,
                  A[First] <= Value <= A[Last] }
            begin
                Mid := (First + Last) div 2;
                if Value = A[Mid] then
                    ValueIndex := Mid
```

```
                else if Value < A[Mid] then
                    ValueIndex :=
                        ValueIndex(First, Mid-1, Value)
                else
                    ValueIndex :=
                        ValueIndex(Mid+1, Last, Value)
            end
    end;   { ValueIndex }

begin   { BinSearch }
    BinSearch := ValueIndex(1, N, Value)
end;   { BinSearch }
```

The only action of the function `BinSearch` is to call the function `ValueIndex`, which is local to `BinSearch` and performs the actual binary search. You pass the array `A` to `BinSearch` as a value parameter, and `ValueIndex` accesses it as a nonlocal variable; that is, `A` is global to `ValueIndex`. Because you call `BinSearch` only once (for each search problem), only one copy of `A` is made. The fact that `ValueIndex` is local to `BinSearch` minimizes the objection that `ValueIndex` accesses a nonlocal variable `A`: Only `BinSearch` invokes `ValueIndex`. The function `ValueIndex` can make no changes to `A` that will propagate outside `BinSearch`. `BinSearch` is general because you can pass it any array of the appropriate type. The solution is a good compromise between the concerns of programming style and efficiency.

A nonrecursive shell allows a compromise between efficiency and style

However, there are some situations where even one copy of `A` is too many, and in these situations it is necessary to pass the array `A` as a variable parameter. You will need some mathematical techniques for analyzing algorithms to identify such a situation. Chapter 7 introduces some of these techniques briefly, but not until you take a formal course on the analysis of algorithms will you be exposed to them in earnest. Until then, we recommend that you use the nonrecursive shell approach as a reasonable compromise between efficiency and style.

Represent global variables and variable parameters outside of the boxes in a box trace

A box trace of the recursive function `ValueIndex` reveals a new consideration. Because the array `A` is neither a value parameter nor a local variable, it is not a part of `ValueIndex`'s local environment, and so `A` should not appear within each box. Therefore, as Figure 5-17 shows, you represent the array `A` outside the boxes, and all references to `A` affect this single representation. Note that you represent a variable parameter in the box method in the same way as you represent a global variable.

`BinSearch` is inappropriate for a linked list

As a final comment, notice that the binary search algorithm is inappropriate for a linked list: How would you locate its midpoint? Chapter 10 examines a linked structure that permits a binary search.

Finding the kth Smallest Element of an Array

The previous two examples presented recursive methods for finding the largest element in an arbitrary array and for finding an arbitrary element in a sorted array. We conclude this discussion of searching with a high-

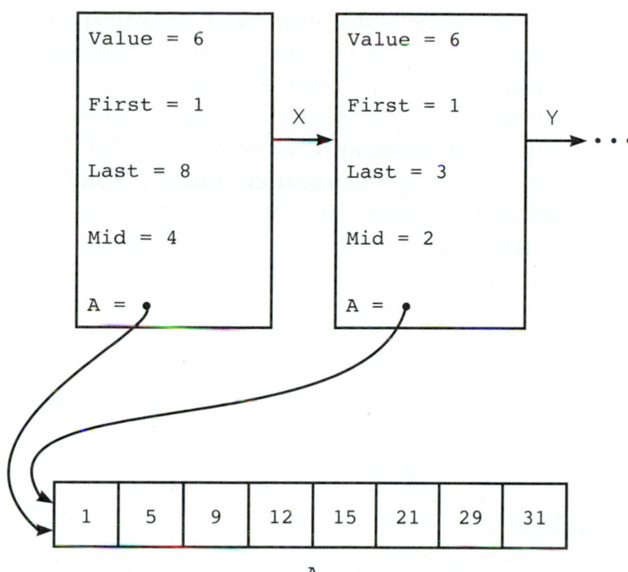

Figure 5-17

Box method with either a global variable or a variable parameter

level description of a recursive solution for finding the kth smallest element in an arbitrary array `A`. Would you ever be interested in such an element? Statisticians often want the median value in a collection of data. The median value in an ordered collection of data occurs in the middle of the collection. In an unordered collection of data, there are about the same number of values smaller than the median value as there are larger values. Thus, if you have 49 elements, the 25th smallest element is the median value.

Obviously, you could solve this problem by sorting the array. Then the kth smallest element would be `A[k]`. Although this approach is a legitimate solution, it does more than the problem requires; a more efficient solution is possible. The solution that we outline here finds the kth smallest element without completely sorting the array.

By now, you know that you solve a problem recursively by writing its solution in terms of one or more smaller problems of the same type in such a way that this notion of *smaller* ensures that you will always reach a degenerate instance of the problem. For all of the earlier recursive solutions, the amount of the reduction in problem size between recursive calls is *predictable*. For example, in the factorial problem, you always decrease the problem size by 1; in the exponentiation problem, you always halve the problem size. In addition, the degenerate cases for all the previous problems except the binary search have a static, predefined size. Thus, by knowing only the size of the original problem, you can determine the number of recursive calls that are necessary before you reach the degenerate case.

For all previous examples, you know the amount of reduction made in the problem size by each recursive call

The solution that we are about to present for finding the kth smallest element departs from these traditions. Although you solve the problem in terms of a smaller problem, just how much smaller this problem is depends on the elements in the array and cannot be predicted in advance. Also, the

You cannot predict in advance the size of either the smaller problems or the degenerate case in the recursive solution to the kth-smallest-element problem

size of the degenerate case depends on the elements in the array, as it did for the binary search. (Recall that you reach a degenerate case for a binary search when the middle element is the one sought.)

This "unpredictable" type of solution is caused by the nature of the problem: The relationship between the rankings of the elements in any predetermined parts of the array and the ranking of the elements in the entire array is not strong enough to determine the kth smallest element. For example, suppose that `A` contains the elements shown in Figure 5-18. Notice that `A[4]` = 6 is the third-smallest element in the first half of `A` and that `A[5]` = 8 is the third-smallest element in the second half of `A`. Can you conclude from this anything about the location of the third-smallest element in all of `A`? The answer is no; this relationship is not strong enough to allow you to draw any useful conclusions. You should experiment with other fixed splitting schemes as well.

The recursive solution proceeds by

1. Selecting a **pivot element** in the array
2. Cleverly arranging, or **partitioning**, the elements in the array about this pivot element
3. Recursively applying the strategy to *one* of the partitions

Now consider the details of the recursive solution. Suppose that you want to find the kth smallest element in the array segment `A[F..L]`. Let the pivot p be any element of the array segment. (For now, ignore how to choose p.) You can partition the elements of `A[F..L]` into three regions: S_1, which contains the elements less than p; the pivot p itself; and S_2, which contains the elements greater than or equal to p. Notice that this partition implies that all the elements in S_1 are smaller than all the elements in S_2. Figure 5-19 illustrates this partition.

Partition `A` into three parts: elements < p, p, and elements ≥ p

In terms of array subscripts, all elements in `A[F..PivotIndex-1]` are less than p and all elements in `A[PivotIndex+1..L]` are greater than or equal to p. Notice that the sizes of the regions S_1 and S_2 depend on both p and the other elements of `A[F..L]`.

This partition induces three "smaller problems," such that the solution to one of the problems will solve the original problem:

1. If there are k or more elements in S_1 = `A[F..PivotIndex-1]` (that is, if $k <$ `PivotIndex` $- $ `F` $+ 1$), then S_1 contains the k smallest elements of the array segment `A[F..L]`. In this case, the kth smallest element must be in S_1.

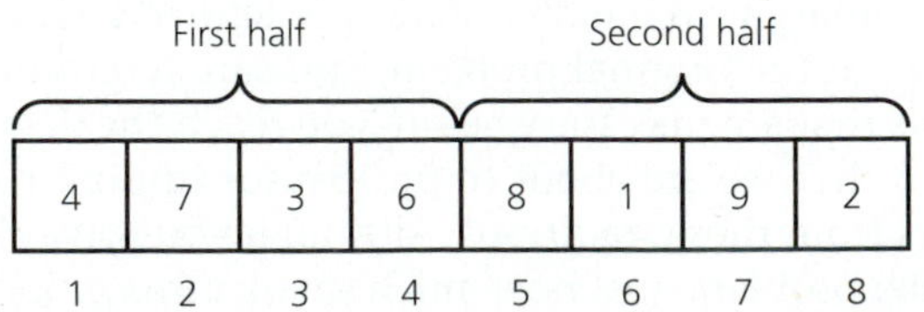

Figure 5-18
A sample array

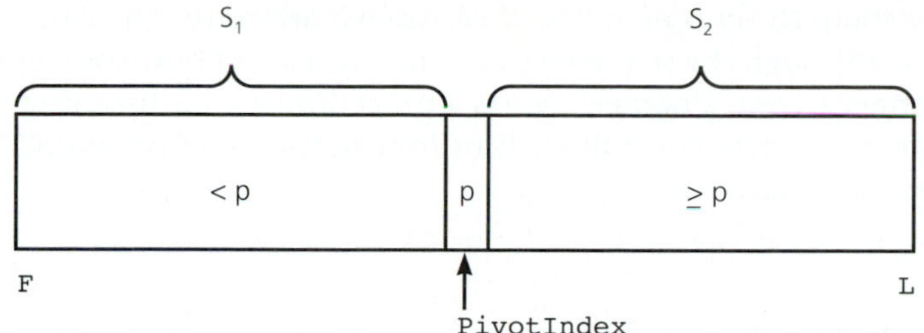

Figure 5-19

A partition about a pivot

2. If there are $k - 1$ elements in S_1 (that is, if k = `PivotIndex` − `F` + 1), then the kth smallest element must be the pivot p; this is the degenerate case.
3. If there are fewer than $k - 1$ elements in S_1 (that is, if k > `PivotIndex` − `F` + 1), then the kth smallest element in `A[F..L]` must be in S_2 = `A[PivotIndex+1..L]`. Because there are `PivotIndex - F` elements in S_1, the kth smallest element in `A[F..L]` is the (k − (`PivotIndex` − `F` + 1))st smallest element in S_2.

A recursive definition can summarize this discussion. Let

`KSmall(k, A, F, L)` = k^{th} smallest element in `A[F..L]`

After you select the pivot element p and partition `A[F..L]` into S_1 and S_2, you have that

The k*th* *smallest element in* `A[F..L]`

```
KSmall(k, A, F, L)

    ⎧ KSmall(k, A, F, PivotIndex-1) if k < PivotIndex-F+1
  = ⎨ p                             if k = PivotIndex-F+1
    ⎩ KSmall(k - (PivotIndex-F+1), A, PivotIndex+1, L)
                                    if k > PivotIndex-F+1
```

There is always a pivot, and since it is not part of either S_1 or S_2, the size of the array segment to be searched decreases by at least 1 at each step. Thus, you will eventually reach the degenerate case: The desired element is a pivot. A high-level pseudocode solution is as follows:

```
function KSmall(k, A, F, L) : returns a value from the array

    Choose a pivot element p from A[F..L]
    Partition the elements of A[F..L] about p

    if k < PivotIndex - F + 1 then
       KSmall := KSmall(k, A, F, PivotIndex-1)
    else if k = PivotIndex - F + 1 then
       KSmall := p
    else KSmall :=
              KSmall(k-(PivotIndex-F+1), A, PivotIndex+1, L)
```

This pseudocode is not far from a Pascal function. The only questions that remain are how to choose the pivot element p and how to partition the array about the chosen p. The choice of p is arbitrary. Any p in the array will work, although the sequence of choices will affect how soon you reach the degenerate case. Chapter 7 gives a procedure for partitioning the elements about p. There you will see how to turn the function `KSmall` into a sorting algorithm.

RECURSION AND EFFICIENCY

Recursion is a powerful problem-solving tool that often produces very clean solutions to even the most complex problems. Recursive solutions can be easier to understand and to describe than iterative solutions. By using recursion, you can often write simple, short implementations of your solution.

The overriding concern in this chapter has been to give you a solid understanding of recursion so that you will be able to construct recursive solutions on your own. However, there are some drawbacks to recursion, which we briefly point out in this section.

These drawbacks have to do with the issue of efficiency. It is often the case that a nonrecursive, iterative subprogram is more efficient than a recursive one. Two factors contribute to the inefficiency of some recursive solutions:

Factors that contribute to the inefficiency of some recursive solutions

- The overhead associated with subprogram calls
- The inherent inefficiency of some recursive algorithms

The first of these factors does not pertain specifically to recursive subprograms but is true of subprograms in general. In most implementations of Pascal and other high-level programming languages, a subprogram call incurs a bookkeeping overhead. As we mentioned earlier, each subprogram call produces an activation record, which is analogous to a box in the box method. Recursive subprograms magnify this overhead because a single initial call to the subprogram can generate a large number of recursive calls. For example, the call *Factorial*(n) generates n recursive calls. On the other hand, the use of recursion, as is true with modularity in general, can greatly clarify complex programs. This clarification frequently more than compensates for the additional overhead. Thus, the use of recursion is often consistent with the view of the cost of a computer program.

Recursion can clarify complex solutions

However, you should not use recursion just for the sake of using recursion. For example, you probably should not use the recursive *Factorial* function in practice. You can easily write an iterative *Factorial* function given the iterative definition that we stated earlier in this chapter. The iterative function is almost as clear as the recursive one and is more efficient. There is no reason to incur the overhead of recursion when its use does not gain anything. *The true value of recursion is as a tool for solving problems for which there is no simple nonrecursive solution.*

Recursion is not always appropriate, particularly when a clear, efficient iterative solution exists

The second point about recursion and efficiency is that some recursive algorithms are inherently inefficient. This inefficiency is a very different issue than that of overhead. It has nothing to do with how a compiler happens to implement a recursive subprogram but rather is related to the method of solution that the algorithm employs.

As an example, recall the recursive solution for the multiplying rabbits problem that you saw earlier in this chapter:

$$Rabbit(n) = \begin{cases} 1 & \text{if } n \leq 2 \\ Rabbit(n-1) + Rabbit(n-2) & \text{if } n > 2 \end{cases}$$

The recursive version of **Rabbit** *is inherently inefficient*

The diagram in Figure 5-12 illustrated the computation of *Rabbit*(7); we asked you to think about what the diagram would look like for *Rabbit*(10). If you thought about this question, you may have come to the conclusion that such a diagram would fill up most of this chapter. The diagram for *Rabbit*(100) would fill up most of this universe!

The fundamental problem with *Rabbit* is that it computes the same values over and over again. For example, in the diagram for *Rabbit*(7), you can see that *Rabbit*(3) is computed five times. When *n* is moderately large, many of the values are recomputed literally trillions of times. Even if the computation of each of these values required only a trivial amount of work (for example, if you could perform a million of these computations per second), the enormous number of times that the values are recomputed still would make the solution infeasible.

You can use **Rabbit's** *recurrence relation to construct an efficient iterative solution*

However, do not conclude that the recurrence relation is of no use. One way to solve the rabbit problem is to construct an iterative solution based on this same recurrence relation. The iterative solution goes forward instead of backward and computes each value only once. You can use the following iterative function to compute *Rabbit*(*n*) even for very large values of *n*.

```
function IterativeRabbit(n : integer): longint;
{ ---------------------------------------------------------
  Iterative solution to the rabbit problem.
  --------------------------------------------------------- }
var Next, Current, Previous : longint;
    i : integer;

begin
   { initialize degenerate cases: }
   Previous := 1;        { Rabbit(1) }
   Current := 1;         { Rabbit(2) }
   Next := 1;            { Rabbit(i) when i <= 2 }

   { compute next Rabbit values when n >= 3 }
   for i := 3 to n do
   begin
```

```
      { Current = Rabbit(i-1), Previous = Rabbit(i-2) }
      Next := Current + Previous;     { Rabbit(i) }

      Previous := Current;            { get ready for }
      Current := Next                 { next iteration }
   end;  { for }

   IterativeRabbit := Next
end;    { IterativeRabbit }
```

Convert from recursion to iteration if it is easier to discover a recursive solution but more efficient to use an iterative solution

There are thus times when an iterative solution is more efficient than a recursive solution. In certain cases, however, it may be easier to discover a recursive solution than an iterative solution. Therefore, you may need to convert a recursive solution to an iterative solution. This conversion process is easier if your recursive subprogram calls itself once, instead of several times. Be careful when deciding whether your subprogram calls itself more than once. Although the function *Rabbit* calls itself twice, the function *BinSearch* calls itself once, even though you see two calls in the Pascal code. Those two calls appear within an *if* statement; only one of them will be executed.

Conversion from a recursive solution to an iterative solution is even easier when the solitary recursive call is the last *action* that the subprogram takes. This situation is called **tail recursion.** For example, the procedure *WriteBackward* exhibits tail recursion because its recursive call is the last action that the procedure takes. Before you conclude that this observation is obvious, consider the function *Fact*. Although its recursive call appears last in the function definition, *Fact*'s last action is the multiplication. Thus, *Fact* is not tail recursive.

Although the original recursive formulation of the *Rabbit* algorithm was inherently inefficient, there are recursive algorithms that are extremely efficient. For example, the recursive binary search algorithm is quite efficient. You will develop the ability to determine whether a recursive algorithm is adequately efficient in more advanced courses concerned with the analysis of algorithms. For now, we shall continue to present recursive algorithms without worrying too much about this issue.

SUMMARY

1. **Recursion is a technique that solves a problem by solving a smaller problem of the same type.**
2. **When constructing a recursive solution, keep the following four questions in mind:**
   - **a. How can you define the problem in terms of a smaller problem of the same type?**
   - **b. How does each recursive call diminish the size of the problem?**
   - **c. What instance of the problem can serve as the degenerate case?**
   - **d. As the problem size diminishes, will you reach this degenerate case?**

3. You can use the box method to trace the actions of a recursive subprogram. These boxes resemble activation records, which many compilers use to implement recursion. (Chapter 8 discusses implementing recursion further.) Although the box method is useful, it cannot replace an intuitive understanding of recursion.

4. Recursion often produces straightforward solutions to even the most complex problems. Recursive solutions can be easier to understand, describe, and implement than iterative solutions. However, some recursive solutions can be less efficient than a corresponding iterative solution due to their inherently inefficient algorithms and the overhead of subprogram calls.

COMMON PITFALLS / DEBUGGING

1. A recursive algorithm must have a degenerate case, whose solution you know directly without making any recursive calls. Without a degenerate case, a recursive subprogram will generate an infinite sequence of calls.

2. A recursive solution must be stated in terms of one or more problems that are each closer to a degenerate case than is the original problem. When a recursive subprogram contains more than one recursive call, there often must be more than one degenerate case.

3. The box method, in conjunction with well-placed ***write*** statements, can be a good aid in debugging recursive subprograms. ***Write*** statements should report the values of parameters and local variables at both entry to and exit from the subprogram. ***Write*** statements should also report the point in the program from which each recursive call occurs.

4. A recursive solution that recomputes certain values frequently can be inefficient. In such cases, iteration may be preferable to recursion.

SELF-TEST EXERCISES

1. The following function computes the product of the $n \geq 1$ real numbers in an array. Show how this function satisfies the properties of a recursive function.

```
const Size = 50;
type  arrayType = array[1..Size] of real;
function Product(A : arrayType; n : integer) : real;
{ Precondition: 1 <= n <= Size.
  Postcondition: Returns the product of n elements in A;
  A is unchanged. }
```

```
begin
   if n = 1
      then Product := A[1]
      else Product := A[n] * Product(A, n-1)
end
```

2. Rewrite the function in Self-Test Exercise 1 as a procedure.
3. Write a recursive function that computes the product of the elements in the array *A[First..Last]*.
4. Given an integer $N > 0$, write a recursive procedure *PrintIntegers* that prints the integers $N, N-1, \cdots, 1$.
5. What is the purpose of a nonrecursive shell?
6. Of the following recursive procedures and functions that you saw in this chapter, identify those that exhibit tail recursion: *Fact*, *WriteBackward*, *WriteBackward2*, *Pow2*, *Rabbit*, *C* in the Spock problem, *C* in the mad scientist problem, *MaxArray*, *BinSearch*, and *KSmall*.

EXERCISES

1. Given an integer $N > 0$, write a recursive Pascal procedure that prints the integers $1, 2, \cdots, N$.
2. Write a recursive Pascal procedure that prints the digits of a positive decimal integer in reverse order.
3. The following recursive function *NumberEqual* counts the number of integers in the array *A* that are equal to the integer *X*. For example, if *A* contains the 10 integers 1, 2, 4, 4, 5, 6, 7, 8, 9, and 12, then *NumberEqual(A, 10, 4)* returns the value 2 because 4 occurs twice in *A*.

```
const Size = 50;
type  arrayType = array[1..Size] of integer;
function NumberEqual(A: arrayType;
                     N, X: integer): integer;
var Count : integer;
begin
   if N <= 0
      then NumberEqual := 0

      else
      begin
         if A[N] = X
            then Count := 1
            else Count := 0;
         NumberEqual := NumberEqual(A, N-1, X) + Count
      end
end;  { NumberEqual }
```

Demonstrate that this function is recursive by listing the criteria of a recursive solution and stating how the function meets each criterion.

4. Embed the function *NumberEqual* that Exercise 3 defines in a nonrecursive shell.

5. Perform a box trace of the following calls to recursive subprograms that appear in this chapter. Clearly indicate each subsequent recursive call.

   a. *Rabbit(5)*
   b. *Pow3(2, 5)*
   c. *PrintIntegers(5)* (You wrote *PrintIntegers* in Self-Test Exercise 4.)

6. Perform a box trace of the recursive function *BinSearch*, which appears in the section "Binary Search," with the array 1, 5, 9, 12, 15, 21, 29, 31 for each of the following search values: **a.** 5; **b.** 13; **c.** 16.

7. What output does the following program produce?

```
program Mystery;

function TheValue(A, B, N : integer) : integer;
var C : integer;
begin
    writeln('Enter: A = ', A:2, ' B = ', B:2);

    C := (A + B) div 2;
    if (sqr(C) <= N)
       then TheValue := C
       else TheValue := TheValue(A, C-1, N);

    writeln('Leave: A = ', A:2, ' B = ', B:2);
end; { TheValue }

begin { Main Program }
   writeln(TheValue(1, 7, 7))
end.  { Program }
```

8. What output does the following program produce?

```
program Mystery;

function FSqrt(N : integer) : integer;

    function Search(First, Last : integer) : integer;
    var Mid : integer;
    begin
       writeln('Enter: First = ', First:2,' Last = ',
                                                 Last:2);

       Mid := (First + Last) div 2;
       if (sqr(Mid) <= N) and (N < sqr(Mid+1)) then
           Search := Mid
```

```
          else if sqr(Mid) > N then
             Search := Search(First, Mid-1)
          else Search := Search(Mid + 1, Last);
          writeln('Leave: First = ',First:2,' Last = ',
                                                    Last:2)
       end;  { Search }
begin
   FSqrt := Search(1, N)
end;  { FSqrt }

begin { Main Program }
   writeln(FSqrt(30))
end.  { Program }
```

9. Consider the following procedure, which converts a positive decimal number to base 8 and displays the result.

```
type posIntType = 1..maxint;

procedure PrintOctal(N : posIntType);
begin
    if N > 0
       then
       begin
          if N div 8 > 0
               then PrintOctal(N div 8);
          write(N mod 8 : 1)
       end
end; { PrintOctal}
```

Describe how the algorithm works. Hand-execute the procedure with $N = 100$.

10. Consider the following program:

```
program Demonstration;

var Temp : integer;

function F(N : integer) : integer;
{ Precondition: N >= 0. }
begin
    writeln('function entered with N = ', N:2);

    case N of
       0..2: F := succ(N)
    else F := F(N-2) * F(N-4)
    end { case }
end; { F }

begin { Main Program }
    Temp := F(8);
    writeln('The value of F(8) is ', Temp:4)
end.  { Program }
```

Show the exact output of the program. Are there any parameter values that you could pass to the function *F* that would cause the program to run forever? If so, describe all such values.

11. Consider the following procedure:

```
procedure R(X, Y : integer);
begin
    if Y > 0
       then
       begin
          X := X + 1;
          Y := Y - 1;
          writeln(X, Y);
          R(X, Y);
          writeln(X, Y)
       end
end
```

Execute the procedure with *X* = 5 and *Y* = 3. How is the output affected if *X* is a variable (*var*) parameter instead of a value parameter?

12. Implement *WriteBackward2*, discussed in the section "A Recursive Procedure: Writing a String Backward," as a Pascal procedure.

13. Implement *MaxArray*, discussed in the section "Finding the Largest Element of an Array," as a Pascal function. What other recursive definitions of *MaxArray* can you describe?

14. Write a recursive function that will sum the elements in an array.

15. Consider the functions *Pow1*, *Pow2*, and *Pow3* discussed in the section "Raising an Integer to a Power." How many multiplications will each function perform (counting calls to function *sqr* as one multiplication) to compute 3^{32}? 3^{19}? How many recursive calls will *Pow2* and *Pow3* make to compute 3^{32}? 3^{19}?

16. Modify the recursive *Rabbit* function so that it is visually easy to follow the flow of execution. Instead of just adding "Enter" and "Leave" messages, indent the trace messages according to how "deep" the current recursive call is. For example, the call *Rabbit(4)* should produce the output

```
Enter Rabbit:   n = 4
    Enter Rabbit:   n = 3
        Enter Rabbit:   n = 2
        Leave Rabbit:   n = 2   value = 1
        Enter Rabbit:   n = 1
        Leave Rabbit:   n = 1   value = 1
    Leave Rabbit:   n = 3   value = 2
    Enter Rabbit:   n = 2
    Leave Rabbit:   n = 2   value = 1
Leave Rabbit:   n = 4   value = 3
```

Note how this output corresponds to figures such as Figure 5-12.

17. Consider the following recurrence relation:

$f(1) = 1; f(2) = 1; f(3) = 1; f(4) = 3; f(5) = 5;$
$f(n) = f(n-1) + 3 * f(n-5)$ for all $n > 5$.

a. Compute $f(n)$ for the following values of n: 6, 7, 12, 15.

b. If you were careful, rather than computing $f(15)$ from scratch (the way a recursive Pascal subprogram would compute it), you would have computed $f(6)$, then $f(7)$, then $f(8)$, and so on up to $f(15)$, recording the values as you computed them. This ordering would have saved you the effort of ever computing the same value more than once. (Recall the nonrecursive version of the `Rabbit` program discussed at the end of this chapter.)

Note that during the computation, you never need to remember all the previously computed values—only the last five. By taking advantage of these observations, write a Pascal function that uses a variation of the ADT ordered list to compute $f(n)$ for arbitrary values of n.

18. Write iterative versions of the following recursive subprograms: `Fact`, `WriteBackward`, `BinSearch`, `KSmall`.

***19.** Consider the problem of finding the **greatest common divisor (GCD)** of two positive integers a and b. The algorithm we present is a variation of Euclid's algorithm, which is based on the following theorem:

THEOREM. If a and b are positive integers with $a > b$ such that b is not a divisor of a, then GCD(a, b) = GCD(b, a mod b).

This relationship between GCD(a, b) and GCD(b, a mod b) is the heart of the recursive solution. It specifies how you can solve the problem of computing GCD(a, b) in terms of another problem of the same type. Also, if b does divide a, then b = GCD(a, b), so an appropriate choice for the degenerate case is (a mod b) = 0.

This theorem leads to the following recursive definition:

$$\text{GCD}(a, b) = \begin{cases} b & \text{if } (a \bmod b) = 0 \\ \text{GCD}(b, a \bmod b) & \text{otherwise} \end{cases}$$

The following Pascal function implements this recursive algorithm:

```
type posIntType = 1..maxint;
     nonnegType = 0..maxint;

function GCD(a, b : posIntType) : nonnegType;
{ Returns the greatest common divisor of a and b. }
begin
   if (a mod b) = 0          { degenerate case }
      then GCD := b
      else GCD := GCD(b, a mod b)

end;   { GCD }
```

a. Prove the theorem.

b. What happens if $b > a$?

c. What is the notion of smaller? (That is, do you always approach a degenerate case?) Why is the degenerate case appropriate?

***20.** Let $C(n)$ be the number of different ways to select integers from the integers 1 through $n - 1$ so that they add up to n (for example, $4 = 1 + 1 + 1 + 1 = 1 + 1 + 2 = 2 + 2 \cdots$). Write recursive definitions for $C(n)$ under the following variations:

a. Permutations are distinct versus permutations are not distinct (for example, $4 = 1 + 2 + 1$ and $4 = 1 + 1 + 2$).

b. You count n itself in the sum versus you do not count n (for example, $C(1) = 0$ versus $C(1) = 1$).

21. Consider the following recursive definition:

$$Acker(m, n) = \begin{cases} n + 1 & \text{if } m = 0 \\ Acker(m - 1, 1) & \text{if } n = 0 \\ Acker(m - 1, Acker(m, n - 1)) & \text{otherwise} \end{cases}$$

This function, called **Ackermann's function,** is of interest because it grows rapidly with respect to the sizes of m and n. What is *Acker(1, 2)*? Implement the function in Pascal and do a box trace of *Acker(1, 2)*. (*Caution:* Even for modest values of m and n, Ackermann's function requires many recursive calls.)

CHAPTER 6

Recursion as a Problem-Solving Tool

PREVIEW Most of the problems in this chapter are both difficult and important. For many of these problems, the recursive solutions are far more elegant and concise than the best of their nonrecursive counterparts. For example, the classic Towers of Hanoi problem appears to be quite difficult, yet it has an extremely simple recursive solution.

Although this chapter considers linked lists again—recursion simplifies the operations that you saw in Chapter 3—for the most part, it introduces new concepts such as backtracking and formal grammars. Backtracking is a technique that involves guesses at a solution. Formal grammars enable you to define, for example, syntactically correct algebraic expressions. The chapter concludes with a discussion of the close relationship between recursion and mathematical induction; you will learn how to use mathematical induction to study properties of algorithms.

More applications of recursion appear in the next chapter, where you will study some recursive sorting algorithms.

Now that we have presented the basic concepts of recursion, we are ready to move on to some extremely useful and somewhat complex applications. The examples in this chapter include two puzzles, recursive processing of linked lists, and grammars for defining languages.

DOING THINGS

This section uses recursion to "do things." Specifically, given some data organized in one way, the problem is to recursively organize the data in another way. Because you actually must effect some change and not, for example, simply search the data, you must use procedures rather than functions to accomplish such a task. The first problem of this section is called the Towers of Hanoi. Although this problem probably has no direct real-world application, we nevertheless begin with it because its solution so well illustrates the use of recursion.

The Towers of Hanoi

Many, many years ago, in a distant part of the Orient—in the Vietnamese city of Hanoi—the Emperor's wiseperson passed on to meet his ancestors. The Emperor needed a replacement wiseperson. Being a rather wise person himself, the Emperor devised a puzzle, declaring that its solver could have the job of wiseperson.

The Emperor's puzzle consisted of N disks (he didn't say exactly how many) and three poles: A (the source), B (the destination), and C (the spare). The disks were of different sizes and had holes in the middle so that they could fit on the poles. Because of their great weight, the disks could be placed only on top of disks larger than themselves. Initially, all the disks were on pole *A*, as shown in Figure 6-1a. The puzzle was to move the disks, one by one, from pole *A* to pole *B*. A person could also use pole *C* in the course of the transfer, but again a disk could be placed only on top of a disk larger than itself.

As the position of wiseperson was generally known to be a soft job, there were many applicants. Scholars and peasants alike brought the Emperor their solutions. Many solutions were thousands of steps long, and many contained `goto`'s. "I can't understand these solutions," bellowed the Emperor. "There must be an easy way to solve this puzzle."

And indeed there was. A great Buddhist monk came out of the mountains to see the Emperor. "My son," he said, "the puzzle is so easy, it almost solves itself." The Emperor's security chief wanted to throw this strange person out, but the Emperor let him continue.

"If there is only one disk (that is, $N = 1$), move it from pole *A* to pole *B*." So far, so good, but even the village idiot got that part right. "If there is more than one disk (that is, $N > 1$), simply

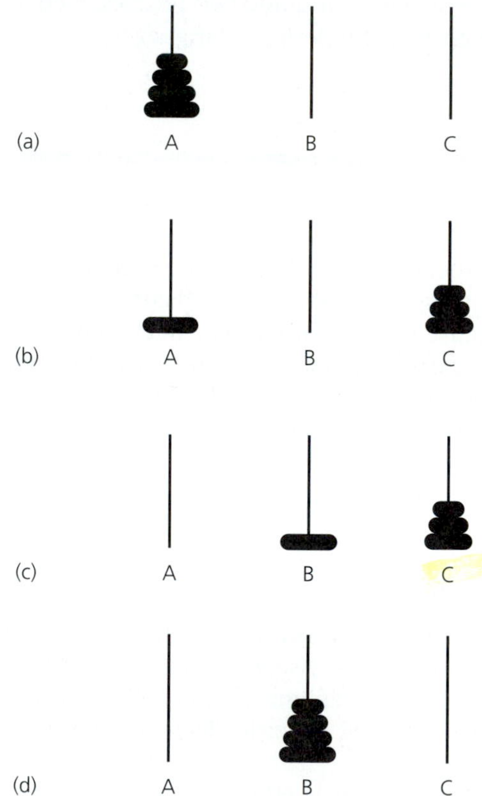

Figure 6-1

(a) The initial state; (b) move *N* – 1 disks from *A* to *C*; (c) move one disk from *A* to *B*; (d) move *N* – 1 disks from *C* to *B*

1. Ignore the bottom disk and solve the problem for $N - 1$ disks, with the small modification that pole C is the destination and pole B is the spare. (See Figure 6-1b.)
2. After you have done this, $N - 1$ disks will be on pole C, and the largest disk will remain on pole A. So solve the problem for $N = 1$ (recall that even the village idiot could do this) by moving the large disk from A to B. (See Figure 6-1c.)
3. Now all you have to do is move the $N - 1$ disks from pole C to pole B; that is, solve the problem with pole C as the source, pole B as the destination, and pole A as the spare." (See Figure 6-1d.)

There was silence for a few moments, and finally the Emperor said impatiently, "Well, are you going to tell us your solution or not?" The monk simply gave an all-knowing smile and vanished.

The Emperor obviously was not a recursive thinker, but you should realize that the monk's solution is perfectly correct. The key to the solution is the observation that you can solve the Towers problem of N disks by solving three smaller—in the sense of number of disks—Towers problems. Let `Towers(Count, Source, Dest, Spare)` denote the problem of moving `Count` disks from pole `Source` to pole `Dest`, using pole `Spare` as a spare. Notice that this definition makes sense even if there are more than `Count` disks on pole `Source`; in this case, you concern yourself with only the top `Count` disks and ignore the others. Similarly, the poles `Dest` and `Spare` might have disks on them before you begin; you ignore these, too, except that you may place only smaller disks on top of them.

The problem statement

You can restate the Emperor's problem as follows: Beginning with N disks on pole A and 0 disks on poles B and C, solve `Towers(N, A, B, C)`. You can state the monk's solution as follows:

The solution

Step 1. Starting in the initial state—with all the disks on pole A—solve

```
Towers(N-1, A, C, B)
```

That is, ignore the bottom (largest) disk and move the top $N - 1$ disks from pole A to pole C, using pole B as a spare. When you are finished, the largest disk will remain on pole A, and all the other disks will be on pole C.

Step 2. Now, with the largest disk on pole A and all others on pole C, solve

```
Towers(1, A, B, C)
```

That is, move the largest disk from pole A to pole B. Because this disk is larger than the disks already on the spare pole C, you really could not use the spare. However, fortunately—and obviously—you do not need to use the spare in this degenerate case. When you are done, the largest disk will be on pole B and all other disks will remain on pole C.

Step 3. Finally, with the largest disk on pole *B* and all the other disks on pole *C*, solve

```
Towers(N-1, C, B, A)
```

That is, move the $N - 1$ disks from pole *C* to pole *B*, using *A* as a spare. Notice that the destination pole *B* already has the largest disk, which you ignore. When you are done, you will have solved the original problem: All the disks will be on pole *B*.

A pseudocode description of the solution is

```
Towers(Count, Source, Dest, Spare)

   if Count = 1
      then move the disk directly from Source to Dest

      else
      begin
          Solve Towers(Count-1, Source, Spare, Dest)
          Solve Towers(1, Source, Dest, Spare)
          Solve Towers(Count-1, Spare, Dest, Source)
      end
```

This recursive solution follows the same basic pattern as the recursive solutions you saw in the previous chapter:

The solution to the Towers problem satisfies the four criteria of a recursive solution

1. You solve a Towers problem by solving other Towers problems.
2. These other Towers problems are smaller than the original problem; there are fewer disks to move. In particular, the number of disks decreases by 1 at each recursive call.
3. When there is only one disk—the degenerate case—the solution is easy to solve directly.
4. The way that the problems become smaller ensures that you will reach a degenerate case.

Notice that this recursive solution will call itself many, many times. Figure 6-2 illustrates the calls for three disks.

Now consider a Pascal version of the Towers solution. Notice that since most computers do not have arms (at the time of this writing), the procedure moves a disk by printing directions to a human. Thus, the formal parameters that represent the poles are of type `char`, and the corresponding actual parameters are `'A'`, `'B'`, and `'C'`. The call `Towers(3, 'A', 'B', 'C')` produces this output:

The solution for three disks

```
Move disk from pole A to pole B
Move disk from pole A to pole C
```

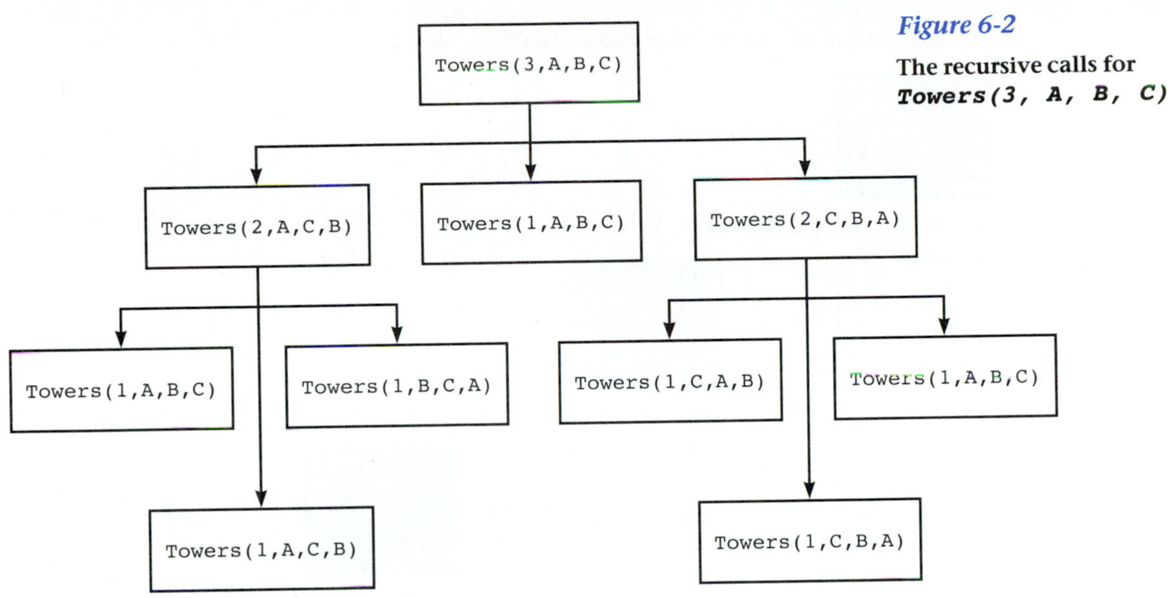

Figure 6-2

The recursive calls for *Towers(3, A, B, C)*

```
Move disk from pole B to pole C
Move disk from pole A to pole B
Move disk from pole C to pole A
Move disk from pole C to pole B
Move disk from pole A to pole B
```

The Pascal procedure follows:

```
procedure Towers(Count : integer; Source, Dest, Spare : char);
begin
    if Count = 1
       then writeln('Move disk from pole ', Source:1,
                    ' to pole ', Dest:1)
       else
       begin
           Towers(Count-1, Source, Spare, Dest);    { X }
           Towers(1, Source, Dest, Spare);          { Y }
           Towers(Count-1, Spare, Dest, Source)     { Z }
       end
end;  { Towers }
```

The three recursive calls in the procedure are labeled *X*, *Y*, and *Z*. These labels appear in the box trace of *Towers(3, 'A', 'B', 'C')*. (See Figure 6-3.)

The initial call is made, and procedure `Towers` begins execution:

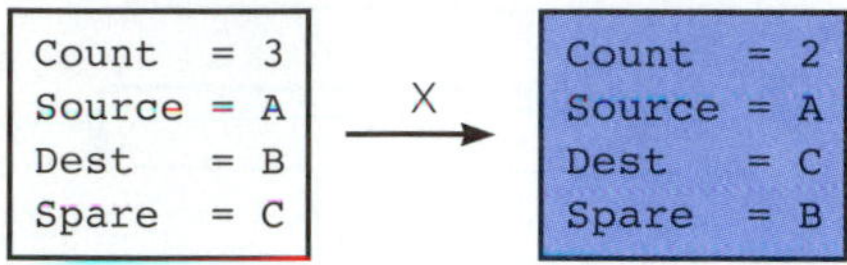

At point X, a recursive call is made, and the new invocation of the procedure begins execution:

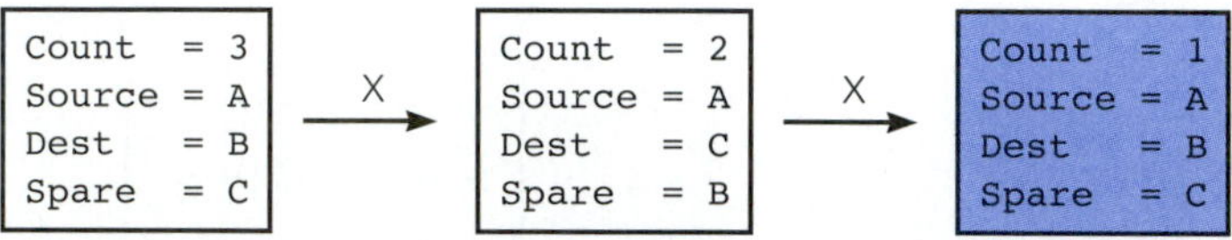

At point X, a recursive call is made, and the new invocation of the procedure begins execution:

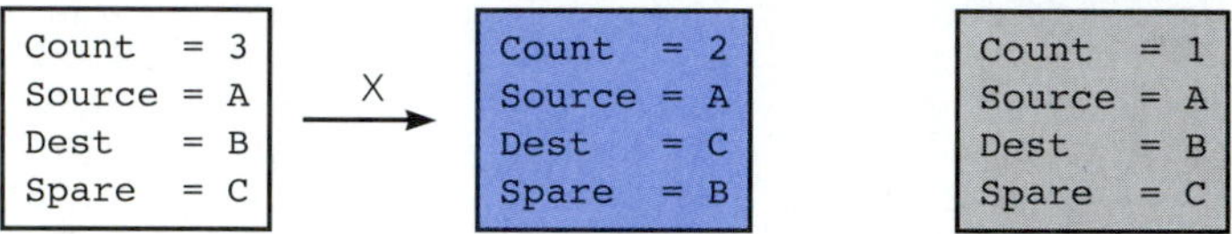

This is the degenerate case, so a disk is moved, the return is made, and the procedure continues execution.

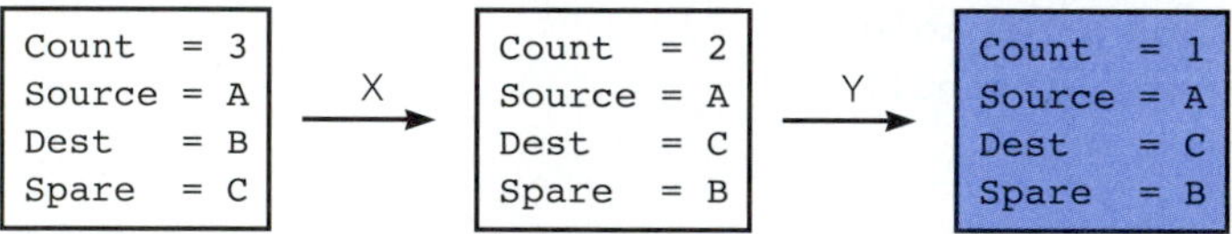

At point Y, a recursive call is made, and the new invocation of the procedure begins execution:

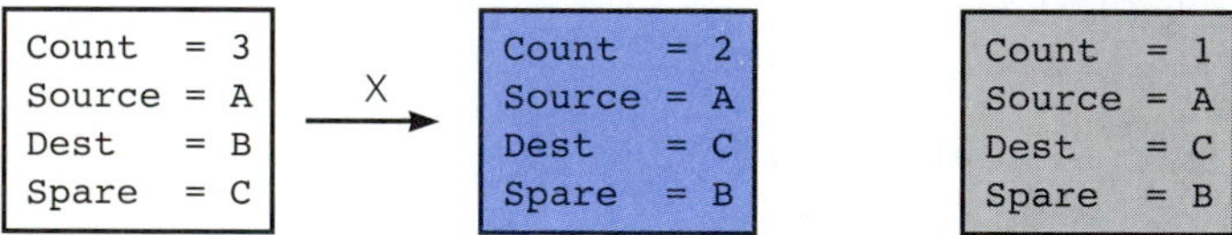

This is the degenerate case, so a disk is moved, the return is made, and the procedure continues execution.

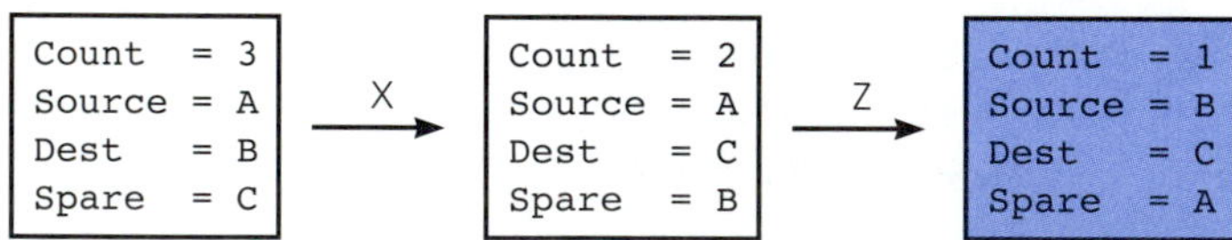

At point Z, a recursive call is made, and the new invocation of the procedure begins execution:

Count = 3 Source = A Dest = B Spare = C	X →	Count = 2 Source = A Dest = C Spare = B	Z →	Count = 1 Source = B Dest = C Spare = A

Figure 6-3

Box trace of *`Towers(3, 'A', 'B', 'C')`*

This is the degenerate case, so a disk is moved, the return is made, and the procedure continues execution.

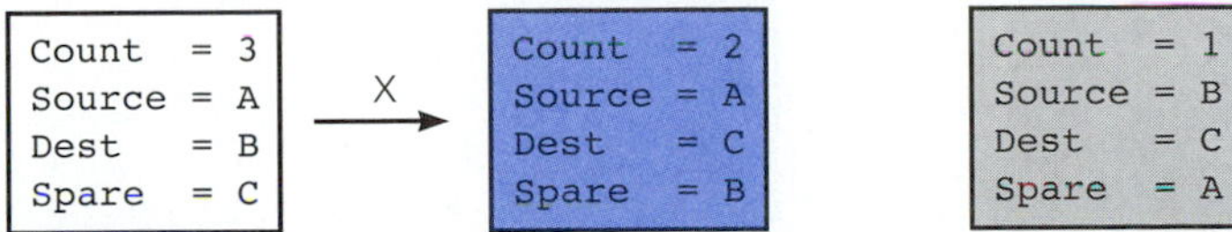

This invocation completes, the return is made, and the procedure continues execution.

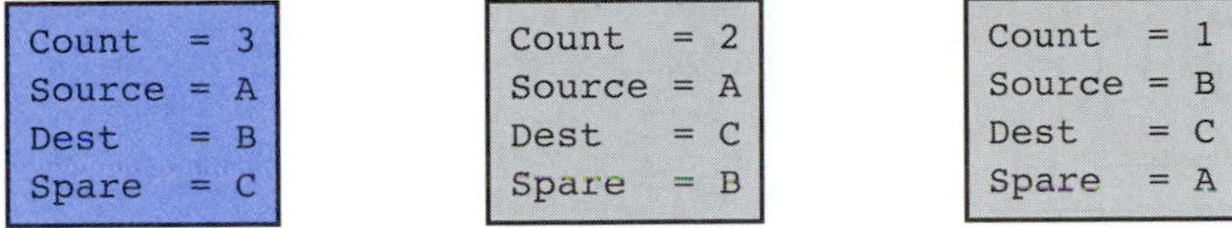

At point Y, a recursive call is made, and the new invocation of the procedure begins execution:

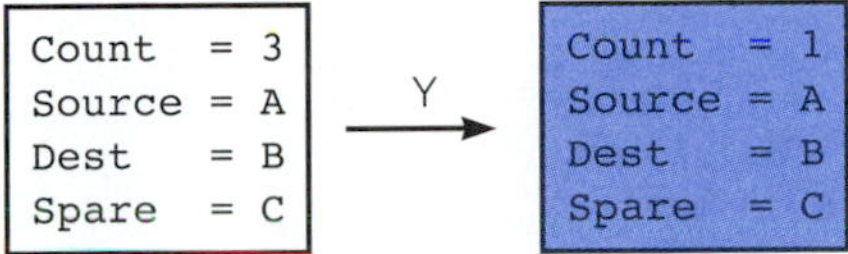

This is the degenerate case, so a disk is moved, the return is made, and the procedure continues execution.

At point Z, a recursive call is made, and the new invocation of the procedure begins execution:

```
Count  = 3        Count  = 2
Source = A   Z    Source = C
Dest   = B  --->  Dest   = B
Spare  = C        Spare  = A
```

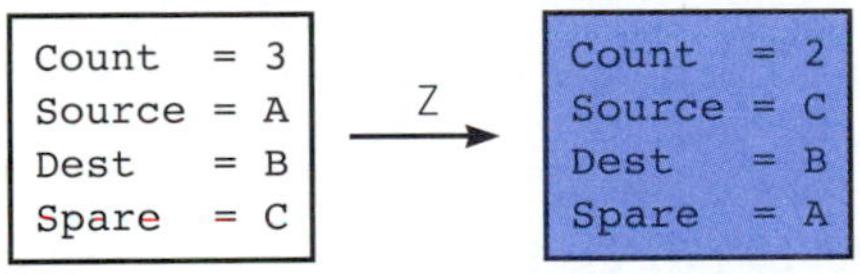

At point X, a recursive call is made, and the new invocation of the procedure begins execution:

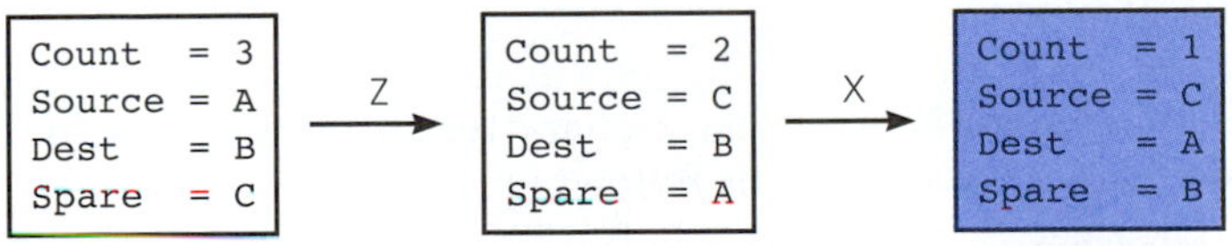

```
Count  = 3        Count  = 2        Count  = 1
Source = A   Z    Source = C   X    Source = C
Dest   = B  --->  Dest   = B  --->  Dest   = A
Spare  = C        Spare  = A        Spare  = B
```

This is the degenerate case, so a disk is moved, the return is made, and the procedure continues execution.

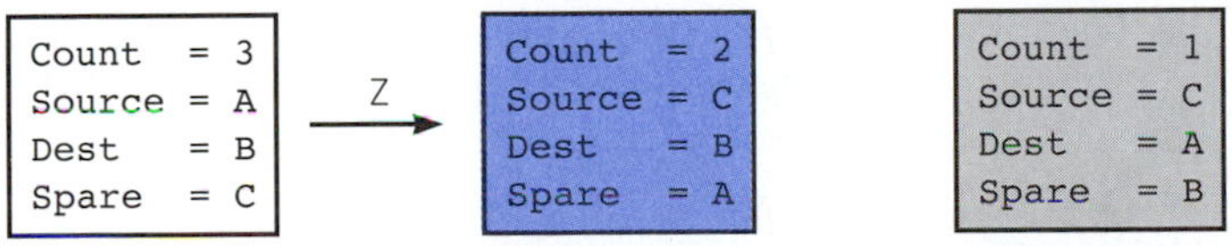

```
Count  = 3        Count  = 2        Count  = 1
Source = A   Z    Source = C        Source = C
Dest   = B  --->  Dest   = B        Dest   = A
Spare  = C        Spare  = A        Spare  = B
```

At point Y, a recursive call is made, and the new invocation of the procedure begins execution:

```
Count  = 3        Count  = 2        Count  = 1
Source = A   Z    Source = C   Y    Source = C
Dest   = B  --->  Dest   = B  --->  Dest   = B
Spare  = C        Spare  = A        Spare  = A
```

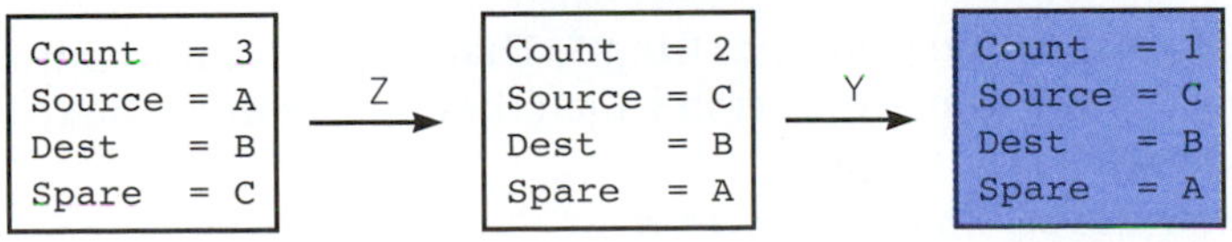

(continues)

Figure 6-3
continued

This is the degenerate case, so a disk is moved, the return is made, and the procedure continues execution.

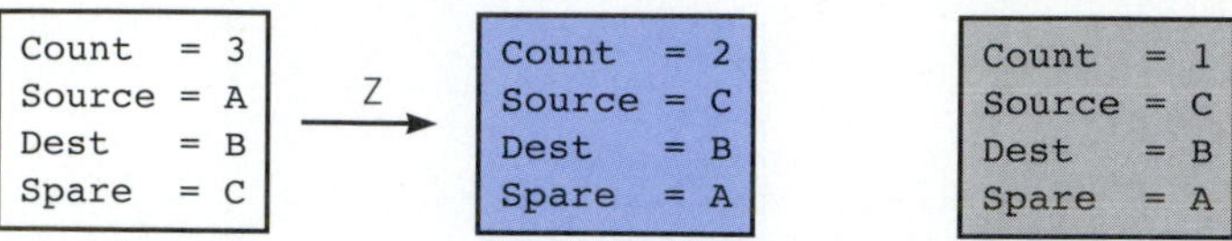

At point Z, a recursive call is made, and the new invocation of the procedure begins execution:

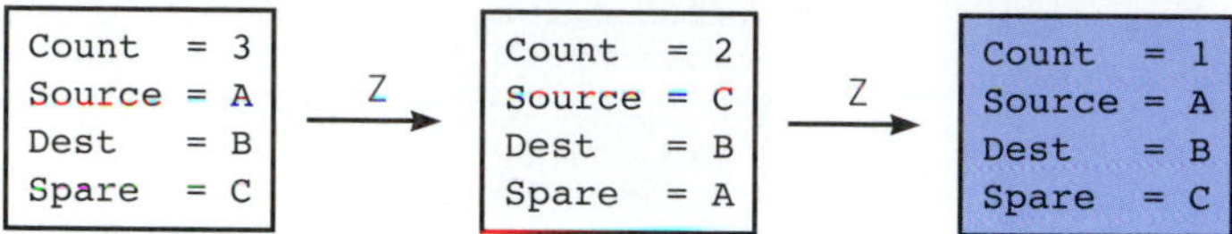

This is the degenerate case, so a disk is moved, the return is made, and the procedure continues execution.

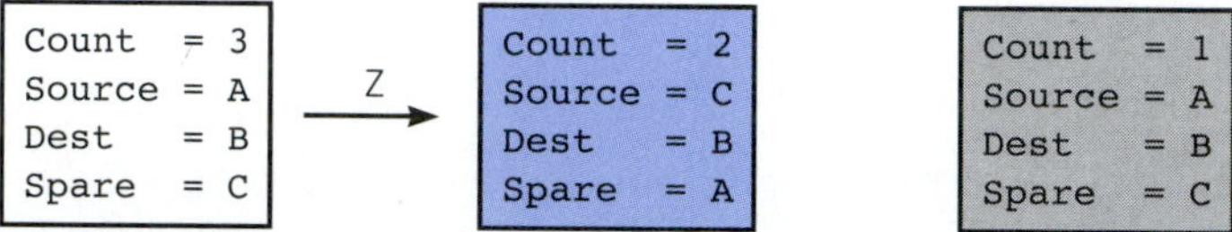

This invocation completes, the return is made, and the procedure continues execution.

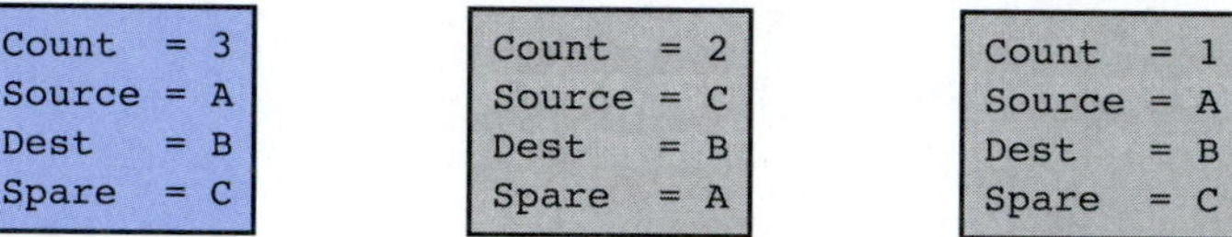

Processing Linked Lists Recursively

It is possible, and sometimes desirable, to process linked lists recursively. This section examines the examples of recursive traversal and insertion operations on a linked list.

Traversal. As a first example, consider a character string *S* that is in a linked list. That is, assume you have the following:

Definitions for a linked list that contains a character string

```
type    ptrType = ^nodeType;
        nodeType = record
            Letter : char;
            Next   : ptrType
        end;
var     StringPtr : ptrType;
```

The pointer variable `StringPtr` points to the head of the list that contains the string.

Suppose that you want to print the string *S*. That is, you want to print the characters in the string in the order in which they appear in the linked list. The recursive strategy is simply

```
Print the first character of S
Write S minus its first character
```

The following Pascal procedure implements this strategy:

```
procedure WriteForward(StringPtr : ptrType);
{ ---------------------------------------------------------
  Writes a string.
  Precondition: The string is in a linked list to which
  the pointer StringPtr points.
  Postcondition: The string is printed. The linked list
  and StringPtr are unchanged.
  --------------------------------------------------------- }
begin
   if StringPtr <> nil
      then
      begin
         { print first character }
         write(StringPtr^.Letter);

         { print string minus its first character }
         WriteForward(StringPtr^.Next)
      end
end;  { WriteForward }
```

This procedure is uncomplicated. It requires that you have direct access only to the first character of the string. The linked list provides this direct access because the list's first node, to which the list's head *StringPtr* points, contains the string's first character. Furthermore, you easily can pass the string minus its first character to *WriteForward*: If *StringPtr* points to the beginning of the string, then *StringPtr^.Next* points to the string minus its first character. You should compare *WriteForward* to the iterative procedure *PrintList* that appears in Chapter 3.

*Compare the recursive **WriteForward** to Chapter 3's **PrintList**, which is iterative*

Now suppose that you want to print the string backward. The previous chapter already developed two recursive strategies for writing a string *S* backward. Recall that the strategy of the procedure *WriteBackward* is

Print the last character of S
Write S minus its last character backward

The strategy of the procedure *WriteBackward2* is

Write S minus its first character backward
Print the first character of S

You saw that these two strategies work equally well when *S* is a Turbo Pascal string. However, when *S* is in a linked list, the first strategy is very difficult to implement: If *StringPtr* points to the node that contains the first character of the string, how do you get to the last character? Even if you had some way to get to the last node on the list quickly—such as by having a tail pointer, as described in Chapter 3—it would be very difficult for you to move toward the front of the string at each recursive call. That is, it would be difficult for you to access the ends of the successively shorter strings that the recursive calls generate. (However, a doubly linked list would solve this problem. Why?)

This discussion illustrates one of the primary disadvantages of linked lists: whereas a Turbo Pascal string provides direct access to any character in the string, a linked list does not. Fortunately, however, the strategy of procedure *WriteBackward2* requires that you have direct access only to the first character of the string. This access is the same that *WriteForward* requires: The list's head *StringPtr* points to the first character of the string *S*, and *StringPtr^.Next* points to *S* minus its first character.

When the string is in a linked list, **WriteBackward2** *is much easier to implement recursively than* **WriteBackward**

The following is a Pascal procedure for implementing *WriteBackward2* when *S* is stored in a linked list:

```
procedure WriteBackward2(StringPtr : ptrType);
{ ---------------------------------------------------------
  Writes a string backward.
  Precondition: The string is in a linked list to which
  the pointer StringPtr points.
  Postcondition: The string is printed backward. The
  linked list and StringPtr are unchanged.
  --------------------------------------------------------- }
begin
   if StringPtr <> nil
      then
      begin
      { print backward string minus its first character }
         WriteBackward2(StringPtr^.Next);

      { print first character }
         write(StringPtr^.Letter)
      end
end; { WriteBackward2 }
```

Insertion. Now view the insertion of a node into a sorted linked list from a new perspective, that is, recursively. Later in this book you will need a recursive algorithm to perform this insertion. Interestingly, recursive insertion eliminates the need for both a trailing pointer and a special case for inserting into the beginning of the list.

Consider the following recursive view of a sorted linked list: A linked list is sorted if its first data item is less than its second data item and the list that begins with the second data item is sorted. More formally, you can state this definition as follows:

A recursive definition of a sorted linked list

The linked list to which *L* points is a sorted list if

L is *nil* (the empty list is a sorted linked list)

or

L^.Next is *nil* (a list with a single node is a sorted linked list)

or

L^.Data < *L^.Next^.Data*, and *L^.Next* points to a sorted linked list

You can base a recursive insertion procedure on this definition. Notice that the following algorithm inserts the node at one of the degenerate cases—either when the list is empty or when the new data item is smaller than all the data items on the list. In both cases, you need to insert the new data item at the beginning of the list.

```
LinkedListInsert(L, NewValue)
{ Inserts NewValue into its proper sorted position in a
  sorted linked list. L points to the list. NewValue does
  not exist already in the list. }

    if (L = nil) Cor (NewValue < L^.Data) { Cor was described in
                                             Chapter 2 }
       then { degenerate case }
       begin
          { Insert the new node at the beginning of the
            list to which L points }
          new(p)
          p^.Data := NewValue
          p^.Next := L
          L := p
       end

       else LinkedListInsert(L^.Next, NewValue)
```

Insertion occurs at the degenerate case

Although *LinkedListInsert* does not maintain a trailing pointer, the insertion of the new node is accomplished easily when the degenerate case is reached. The conceptually difficult part of this algorithm is the statement

```
L := p
```

This assignment is all that is necessary to make the pointer field of the appropriate node point to the new node. Note that *L* points to the beginning of a sorted list. Recall that to insert the node to which *p* points at the beginning of this list, you need to make *L* point to that node. But does this action really change the appropriate pointer field in the actual argument list (the original list that the external pointer *ListHead* points to)? Yes it does, assuming that *L* is passed as a *variable parameter.*

***L* must be a variable parameter**

To understand the previous remarks, first consider the case in which the new item is to be inserted at the beginning of the original list to which the external pointer *ListHead* points. In this case, no recursive calls are made, and thus when the degenerate case is reached (*NewValue < L^.Data*), *ListHead* is the actual parameter that corresponds to *L*, as Figure 6-4a illustrates. Hence, assuming that *L* is a variable parameter, the assignment *L := p* sets the value of *ListHead* to *p*—that is, *ListHead* now points to the new node, as Figure 6-4b shows.

The general case in which the new item is inserted into the interior of the list to which *ListHead* points is very similar. When the degenerate case is reached, what is the actual parameter that corresponds to *L*? It is the *Next* field of the node that should precede the new node; that is, it is the

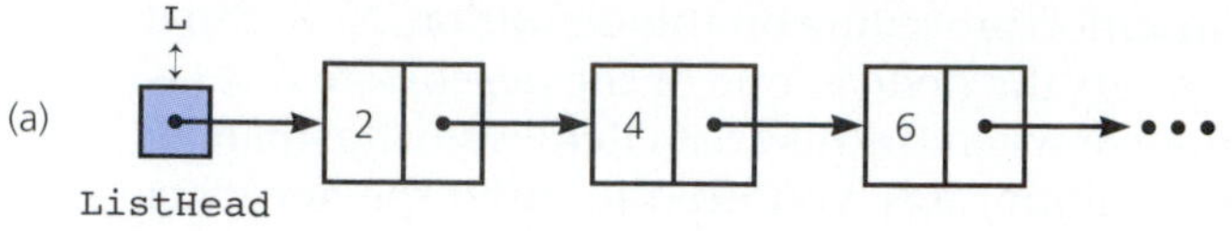

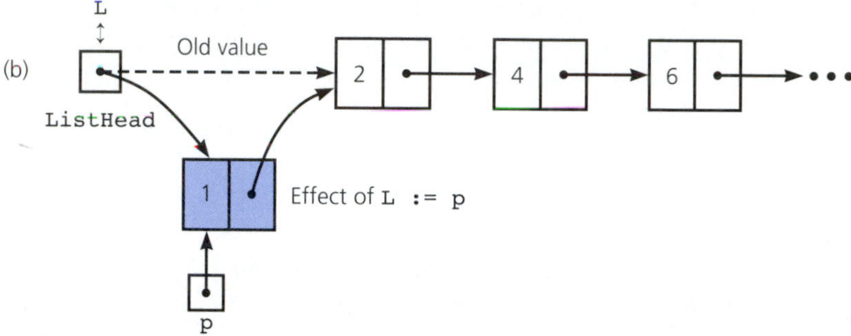

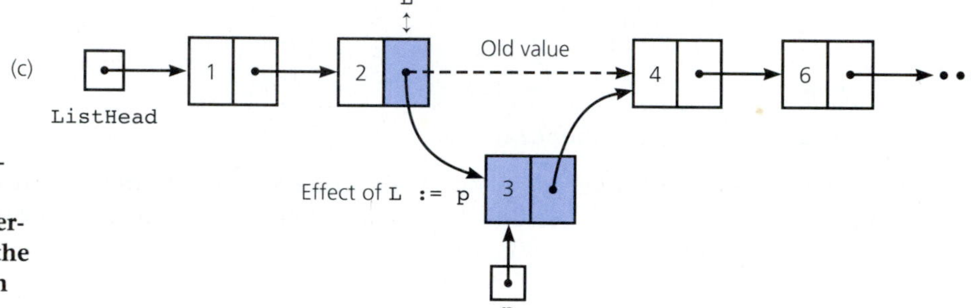

Figure 6-4

(a) The degenerate case—first node of list; (b) the assignment made for insertion at the beginning of the list; (c) the search stops in the middle of the list

Next field of the last node whose data item is less than *NewValue*. Therefore, since *L* is a variable parameter, the assignment *L := p* sets the *Next* field of the appropriate node to point to the new node.

Though we could argue that you should perform the operations on a sorted linked list recursively (after all, recursion does eliminate special cases and the need for a trailing pointer), the primary purpose in presenting the recursive *LinkedListInsert* is to prepare you for the binary search tree algorithms that we will present in Chapter 10.

BACKTRACKING

Backtracking is a strategy for guessing at a solution and backing up when an impasse is reached

This section considers an organized way to make successive guesses at a solution. If a particular guess leads to a dead end, you back up to that guess and replace it with a different guess. This strategy of backing up when you reach an impasse is known as **backtracking**. You can combine recursion and backtracking to solve the following problem.

The Eight Queens Problem

A chessboard contains 64 squares that form 8 rows and 8 columns. One of the most powerful pieces in the game of chess is the queen because it can attack any other piece within its row, within its column, or along its diagonal. The Eight Queens problem asks you to place eight queens on the chessboard so that no queen can attack any other queen.

Place eight queens on the chessboard so that no queen can attack any other queen

One strategy is to guess at a solution. However, there are 4,426,165,368 ways to arrange 8 queens on a chessboard of 64 squares—so many ways that it would be exhausting to check all of them for a solution to this problem. (Remember Mr. Spock's problem in Chapter 5!) Nevertheless, a simple observation eliminates many arrangements from consideration: No queen can reside in a row or a column that contains another queen. Alternatively, each row and column can contain exactly one queen. Thus, attacks along rows or columns are eliminated, leaving only 8! = 40,320 arrangements of queens to check for attacks along diagonals. A solution appears more feasible.

Suppose that you provide some organization for the guessing strategy by placing one queen per column, beginning with the first square of column 1. When you consider column 2, you eliminate its first square because row 1 contains a queen, you eliminate its second square because of a diagonal attack, and you finally place a queen in the third square of column 2. Figure 6-5 shows the placement of five queens as a result of this procedure. The dots in the figure indicate squares that are rejected because a queen in that square is subject to attack by another queen in an earlier column.

Place queens one column at a time

Notice that the five queens in Figure 6-5 can attack any square in column 6. Therefore, you cannot place a queen in column 6, so you must back up to column 5 and move its queen. As Figure 6-6 indicates, the next possible square in column 5 is in the last row. When you consider column 6 once again, there are still no choices for a queen in that column. As you have exhausted the possibilities in column 5, you must back up to column 4. The next possible square in column 4 is in row 7, as Figure 6-7 indicates. You then consider column 5 again and place a queen in row 2.

If you reach an impasse, backtrack to the previous column

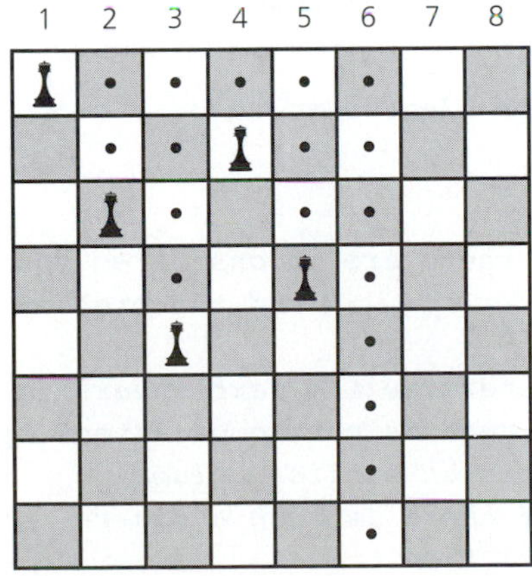

Figure 6-5

Five queens that cannot attack each other, but that can attack all of column 6

Figure 6-6

Backtracking to column 5 to try another square for the queen

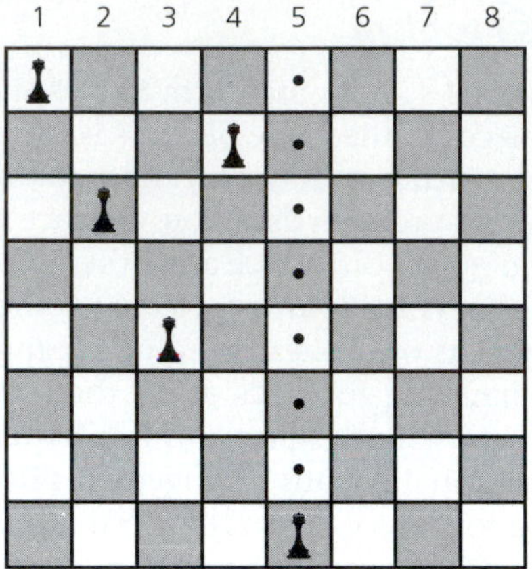

How can you use recursion in the solution that was just described? Consider a procedure that places a queen in a column, given that you have placed queens correctly in the preceding columns. First, if there are no more columns to consider, you are finished; this is the degenerate case. Otherwise, after you successfully place a queen in the current column, you need to consider the next column. That is, you need to solve the same problem with one fewer column; this is the recursive step. Thus, you begin with eight columns, consider smaller problems that decrease in size by one column at each recursive step, and reach the degenerate case when you have a problem with no columns.

This solution appears to satisfy the criteria for a recursive solution. However, you do not know that you can *successfully place a queen in the current column.* If you can, then the procedure calls itself recursively for the next column. If you cannot place a queen in the current column, then you need to backtrack, as has already been described. The following pseudocode describes the algorithm for placing queens in columns, given that the previous columns contain queens that cannot attack each other:

The solution combines recursion with backtracking

```
PlaceNextQueen(Column)
{ Places queens in columns Column through 8. }

  if Column > 8
     then the problem is solved

     else
     begin
        while there are unconsidered squares in the column
                       and the problem is unsolved do
        begin
           Determine the next square in the column
             that is not under attack by a queen
             in an earlier column
           if there is such a square
              then
```

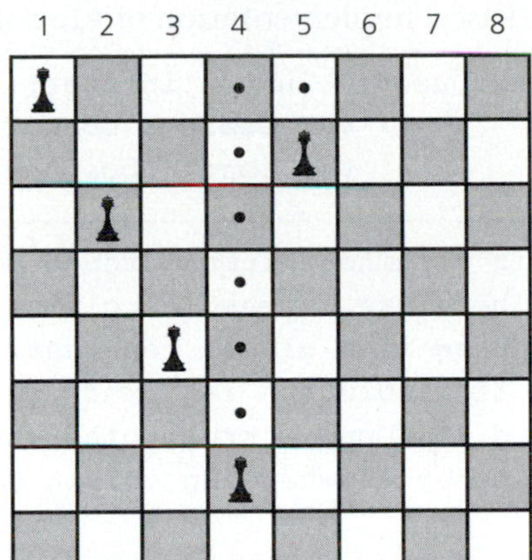

Figure 6-7

Backtracking to column 4 to try another square for the queen and then considering column 5 again

```
            begin
               Place a queen in the square
               { try next column}
               PlaceNextQueen(Column+1)
               if no queen possible in column Column+1
                  then remove queen from column
                     Column and consider next
                     square in the column
            end { if }
      end { while }
   end { if }
```

Before you implement *PlaceNextQueen* in Pascal, you need to consider a few details. For simplicity, you can use a two-dimensional array to represent the board. (The exercises at the end of this chapter consider other possibilities.) You can use an enumerated data type to represent the two states of each square on the board: A square either contains a queen or is empty. Thus,

The chessboard can be a two-dimensional array

```
const BoardSize = 8;
type  squareType = (Queen, Empty);
      boardType = array[1..BoardSize, 1..BoardSize] of squareType;
var   Board : boardType
```

The procedure *PlaceNextQueen* needs to determine whether the squares in the given column can be attacked by the queens in previous columns. Here the function `Attack`, which returns *true* if a given square can be attacked by queens that are in previous columns, makes this determination.

Finally, the procedure *PlaceNextQueen* is used in the following context:

Using **PlaceNextQueen**

```
ClearBoard              { set all squares to Empty }
PlaceNextQueen(1)       { begin with the first column }
if there is a solution
   then PrintBoard      { print solution }
   else print message   { no solution found }
```

The following is the Pascal implementation of *PlaceNextQueen*:

```
procedure PlaceNextQueen(Column : integer;
                         var Board : boardType;
                         var Done : boolean);
{ ---------------------------------------------------------
  Places queens in columns Column through BoardSize of Board.
  Precondition: There are queens in columns 1 through
  Column-1. BoardSize is a global constant.
  Postcondition: If a solution is found, queens are in all
  columns of Board and Done = true; otherwise, there is no
  solution for a queen anywhere in column Column and Done =
  false.
  Calls: Attack.
  --------------------------------------------------------- }
var Row : integer;          { square number in column }
begin
    if Column > BoardSize
        then Done := true   { degenerate case }

        else
        begin
            Done := false;
            Row := 1;
            while (Row <= BoardSize) and (not Done) do
            begin
               { if square can be attacked, }
               if Attack(Board, Row, Column)
                   then Row := succ(Row) { then consider next
                                           square in column }

                   else                  { otherwise }
                   begin
                       { place queen and consider next column }
                       Board[Row, Column] := Queen;
                       PlaceNextQueen(Column+1, Board, Done);

                       { if no queen possible in next column, }
                       if not Done
                          then               { then backtrack }
                          begin
                             { remove queen placed earlier and
                               try next square in column }
                             Board[Row, Column] := Empty;
                             Row := succ(Row)
                          end  { then }
                   end  { else }
            end  { while }
        end  { if }
end;  { PlaceNextQueen }
```

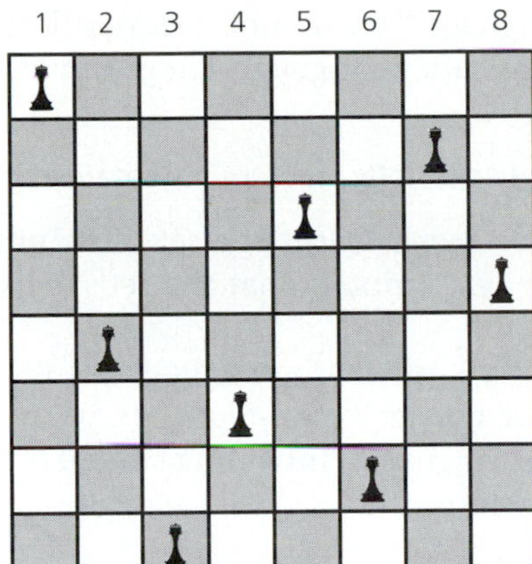

Figure 6-8

A solution to the Eight Queens problem

Figure 6-8 indicates the solution that the previous algorithm finds.

By modifying the use of `PlaceNextQueen`, you can discover other solutions to the Eight Queens problem. You can also improve this algorithm. Although we used an 8 by 8 array to represent the board because it simplified the implementation, such an array is inefficient; after all, only 8 squares out of 64 are used. The exercises at the end of this chapter consider modifications and improvements to this algorithm.

DEFINING THINGS

This section demonstrates how to define languages by using recursion. A **language** is nothing more than a set of strings of symbols. For example, consider the language that comprises all syntactically correct Pascal programs. If you view a program as one long string of characters, you can define the set

A language is a set of strings of symbols

Pascal-Programs = {strings *w* : *w* is a syntactically correct Pascal program}

Notice that whereas all programs are strings, not all strings are programs. A Pascal compiler is a program that, among other things, determines whether a given string is a member of the set *Pascal-Programs;* that is, the compiler determines whether the string is a syntactically correct Pascal program. Of course, this definition of *Pascal-Programs* is not descriptive enough to allow the construction of a compiler. The definition specifies a characteristic of the strings in the set *Pascal-Programs*: The strings are syntactically correct Pascal programs. However, the definition does not give the rules for determining whether a string is in the set or not; that is, the definition does not specify what is meant by a syntactically correct Pascal program.

When we say "language," we do not necessarily mean a programming language or a communication language. For example, consider the following language:

Algebraic-Expressions = {*w* : *w* is an algebraic expression}

The language *Algebraic-Expressions* is the set of strings that meets certain rules of syntax. Once again, notice that the set's definition does not give these rules.

A grammar states the rules for forming the strings in a language

A **grammar** states the rules of a language. As it is a complex task to present a grammar for the set *Pascal-Programs*, we instead present grammars for some simpler languages, including several different common languages of algebraic expressions.

The Basics of Grammars

A grammar is a device for defining a language. One of the great benefits of using a grammar to define a language is that you can often write a straightforward recursive algorithm, based on the grammar, that determines whether a given string is a member of the language. Such an algorithm is called a **recognition algorithm** for the language.

A grammar uses several special symbols:

Symbols that grammars use

- $x \mid y$ means x or y.
- $x\ y$ means x followed by y. (When the context requires clarification, we will write $x \cdot y$.)
- <*word*> means any instance of *word* that the definition defines.

As an example of a grammar, consider the language

Pascal-Ids = {*w* : *w* is a legal Pascal identifier}

As you know, a legal Pascal identifier must begin with a letter and be followed by zero or more letters and digits. For simplicity, do not use the underscore (_) and assume that there is no restriction on the maximum length of an identifier. One way to represent this definition of an identifier is with a syntax diagram, as shown in Figure 6-9.

A syntax diagram is convenient for people to use, but a grammar is a better starting point if you want to write a program that will recognize an identifier. A grammar for the language *Pascal-Ids* is

A grammar for the language of Pascal identifiers

<*identifier*> = <*letter*> | <*identifier*> <*letter*> | <*identifier*> <*digit*>

<*letter*> = A | B | ··· | Z

<*digit*> = 0 | 1 | ··· | 9

The definition reads as follows:

An identifier is a letter, or an identifier followed by a letter, or an identifier followed by a digit.

The most striking aspect of this definition is that *identifier* appears in its own definition: This grammar is recursive, as are many grammars.

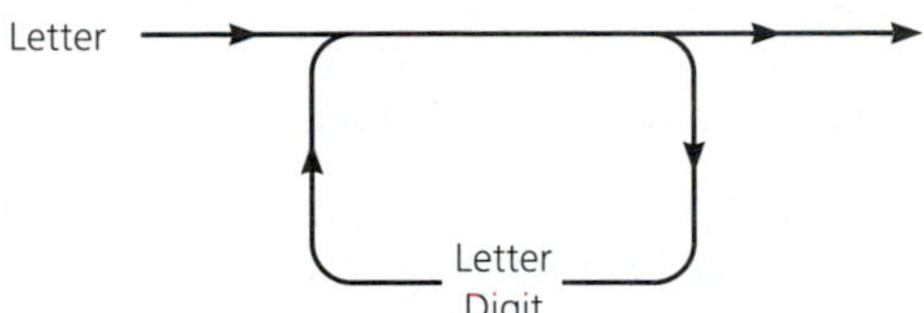

Figure 6-9

A syntax diagram for Pascal identifiers

Given a string *w*, you can determine whether the string is in the language *Pascal-Ids* by using the grammar to construct the following recognition algorithm: If *w* is of length 1, then it is in the language if the character is a letter. (This statement is the degenerate case, so to speak.) If *w* is of length greater than 1, then it is in the language if the last character of *w* is either a letter or a digit, and *w* minus its last character is an identifier.

The pseudocode for a recursive function that determines whether a string is in *Pascal-Ids* follows:

A recognition algorithm for Pascal identifiers

```
function IsId(w) : returns a boolean value
{ Determines whether w is a legal Pascal identifier. }

   if w is of length 1 then        { degenerate case }
      if w is a letter
         then IsId := true
         else IsId := false

   else if the last character of w is a letter then
      IsId := IsId(w minus its last character)
   else if the last character of w is a digit then
      IsId := IsId(w minus its last character)
   else IsId := false
```

Two Simple Languages

Now consider two more simple examples of languages, their grammars, and resulting recognition algorithms.

Palindromes. A palindrome is a string that reads the same from left to right as it does from right to left. For example, "radar" and "deed" are both palindromes. You can define the language of palindromes as follows:

Palindromes = {*w* : *w* reads the same left to right as right to left}

How can you use a grammar to define the language *Palindromes*? You need to devise a rule that allows you to determine whether or not a given string *w* is a palindrome. In the spirit of recursive definitions, you should state this rule in terms of determining whether a *smaller string* is a palindrome. Your first instinct might be to choose *w* minus its last (or first) character for the smaller string. However, this does not work because there is no relationship between the statements

w is a palindrome

and

w minus its last character is a palindrome

That is, *w* might be a palindrome, although *w* minus its last character is not, as is the case for "deed." Similarly, *w* minus its last character might be a palindrome, although *w* is not, as is the case for "deeds."

A little thought reveals that you must consider characters in pairs: There *is* a relationship between the statements

w is a palindrome

and

w minus its first and last characters is a palindrome

Specifically, *w* is a palindrome if and only if

A recursive description of a palindrome

- The first and last characters of *w* are the same

and

- *w* minus its first and last characters is a palindrome

You need a degenerate case that you will reach after stripping away enough pairs of characters. If *w* is of even length, you will eventually be left with two characters, and then, after you strip away another pair, you will be left with zero characters. A string of length zero is called the **empty string** and is a palindrome. If *w* is of odd length, you will eventually be left with one character, after which you cannot strip away another pair. Hence, you must have a second degenerate case: A string of length 1 is a palindrome.

Strings of length 0 or 1 are the degenerate case

This discussion leads to the following grammar for the language *Palindromes*:

A grammar for the language of palindromes

<*pal*> = empty string | <*ch*> | a <*pal*> a | b <*pal*> b | ··· | Z <*pal*> Z
<*ch*> = a | b | ··· | z | A | B | ··· | Z

Based on this grammar, you can construct a recursive function for recognizing palindromes. The pseudocode for such a function follows:

A recognition algorithm for palindromes

```
function IsPal(w) : returns a boolean value
{ Determines whether the string w of letters is a palindrome. }

  if (w is the empty string) or (w is of length 1) then
     IsPal := true

  else if the first and last characters of w are
             the same letter then
     IsPal := IsPal(w minus its first and last characters)

  else IsPal := false
```

Strings of the form A^nB^n. The symbol A^nB^n is standard notation for the string that consists of *n* consecutive A's followed by *n* consecutive B's.

Another simple language consists of such strings:

$$L = \{w : w \text{ is of the form } A^nB^n \text{ for some } n \geqslant 0\}$$

The grammar for this language is actually very similar to the grammar for palindromes. You must strip away both the first and last characters and check to see that the first character is an "A" and the last character is a "B". Thus, the grammar is

<*legalword*> = empty string | A <*legalword*> B

A grammar for the language of strings A^nB^n

The pseudocode for a recognition function for this language follows:

A recognition algorithm for strings A^nB^n

```
function IsAnBn(w) : returns a boolean value
{ Determines whether w is of the form AⁿBⁿ. }

  if the length of w is zero then
    IsAnBn := true

  else if (the first character of w is A) and
               (the last character of w is B) then
    IsAnBn := IsAnBn(w minus its first and last characters)

  else IsAnBn := false
```

Algebraic Expressions

One of the tasks a compiler must perform is to recognize and evaluate algebraic expressions. For example, consider the Pascal assignment statement

```
y := x + z * (w/k + z * (7 * 6))
```

A Pascal compiler must determine whether the right side is a syntactically legal algebraic expression; if so, the compiler then must indicate how to compute the expression's value.

There are several common definitions for a "syntactically legal" algebraic expression. Some definitions force an expression to be fully parenthesized, whereas others are more lenient. In general, the stricter a definition, the easier it is to recognize a syntactically legal expression. On the other hand, it is an inconvenience for the programmer to have to conform to overly strict rules of syntax. For example, if the syntax rule requires full parenthesization, you would have to write `((x * y) * z)` rather than `x * y * z`.

This section presents three different languages for algebraic expressions. The expressions in these languages are easy to recognize and evaluate but are generally inconvenient to use. However, these languages provide us with good, nontrivial applications of grammars. We will mention other languages of algebraic expressions whose members are difficult to recognize and evaluate but are convenient to use. To avoid unnecessary complications, assume you have only the binary operators +, −, *, and / (no unary operators or exponentiation). Also assume that all operands in the expression are single-letter identifiers.

Infix, prefix, and postfix expressions. The type of algebraic expressions you learned about in grade school are called **infix expressions.** The term "infix" indicates that every binary operator appears between its operands. For example, in the expression

$a + b$

the operand + is between its operands a and b. This convention necessitates associativity rules, precedence rules, and the use of parentheses to avoid ambiguity. For example, the expression

$a + b * c$

is ambiguous. What is the second operand of the +? Is it b or is it $(b * c)$? Similarly, the first operand of the * could be either b or $(a + b)$. The rule that * has higher precedence than + removes the ambiguity by specifying that b is the first operand of the * and that $(b * c)$ is the second operand of the +. If you want another interpretation, you must use parentheses:

$(a + b) * c$

Even with precedence rules, there is ambiguity in an expression like

$a / b * c$

Typically, / and * have equal precedence, so you could interpret the expression either as $(a / b) * c$ or as $a / (b * c)$. The common practice is to *associate from left to right*, thus yielding the first interpretation.

Two alternatives to the traditional infix convention are **prefix** and **postfix**. Under these conventions, an operator appears before its operands and after its operands, respectively. Thus, the infix expression

$a + b$

is written in prefix form as

In a prefix expression, an operator precedes its operands

$+ a b$

and in postfix form as

In a postfix expression, an operator follows its operands

$a b +$

To further illustrate the conventions, consider the two interpretations of the infix expression $a + b * c$ just considered. You write the expression

$a + (b * c)$

in prefix form as

$+ a * b c$

The + appears before its operands a and $(* b c)$, and the * appears before its operands b and c. The same expression is written in postfix form as

$a b c * +$

The * appears after its operands b and c, and the + appears after its operands a and $(b c *)$.

Similarly, you write the expression

$(a + b) * c$

in prefix form as

$* + a\, b\, c$

The * appears before its operands (+ *a b*) and *c*, and the + appears before its operands *a* and *b*. The same expression is written in postfix form as

$a\, b + c\, *$

The + appears after its operands *a* and *b*, and the * appears after its operands (*a b* +) and *c*.

The advantage of prefix and postfix expressions is that they never need precedence rules, association rules, and parentheses. Therefore, the grammars for prefix and postfix expressions are quite simple. In addition, the algorithms that recognize and evaluate these expressions are relatively straightforward.

Prefix and postfix expressions never need precedence rules, association rules, and parentheses

Prefix expressions. A grammar that defines the language of all prefix expressions is

<pre-exp> = *<letter>* | *<operator>* *<pre-exp>* *<pre-exp>*
<operator> = + | − | * | /
<letter> = A | B | ··· | Z

From this grammar you can construct a recursive algorithm that recognizes prefix expressions. Suppose that you treat the expression in question as a substring `S[First..Last]`. If the expression is of length 1, then it is a prefix expression if and only if `S[First]` is a single uppercase letter. Expressions of length 1 can be the degenerate case. If the length of the expression is greater than 1, then for it to be a legal prefix expression, it must be of the form

<operator> *<pre-exp>* *<pre-exp>*

Thus, the algorithm must check to see that

- The first character `S[First]` is an operator

and

- `S[First+1..Last]` consists of two consecutive prefix expressions

The first task is trivial, but the second is a bit tricky. How can you determine whether you are looking at two consecutive prefix expressions? A key observation is that if you add *any* string of characters to the end of a prefix expression, you will no longer have a prefix expression. That is, if *E* is a prefix expression and *Y* is any nonempty string, then *E Y* cannot be a prefix expression. This is a subtle point; Exercise 18 at the end of this chapter asks you to prove it.

If* E *is a prefix expression,* E Y *cannot be

Given this observation, you can begin to determine whether the string `S[First+1..Last]` consists of two consecutive prefix expressions by identifying a first prefix expression. If you cannot find one, then the original string itself is not a prefix expression. If you do find one, you need to know where it ends. Notice that the previous observation implies that there is only one possible endpoint for this first expression: Given that `S[First+1..End1]` is a prefix expression, there can be no other prefix expression that begins at `S[First+1]`. That is, it is not possible that `S[First+1..End2]` is a prefix expression for any `End2` ≠ `End1`.

If you find that the first prefix expression ends at position `End1`, you then attempt to find a second prefix expression beginning at position `End1 + 1` and ending at or before position `Last`. If you find the second expression, you must check that you are at the end of the string in question. That is, you must make sure that there are no nonblank characters in `S` between the end of the second expression and position `Last`.

You can construct a function `EndPre(S, First, Last)` that returns either the position of the end of the prefix expression that begins at `S[First]` or the value 0, which signals that there is no prefix expression that begins at `S[First]`. The function appears in pseudocode as follows:

If there is a prefix expression beginning at `S[First]`, `EndPre` *determines its end*

```
function EndPre(S, First, Last) : returns an index into
                                  the substring S[First..Last]
{ Returns the index of the end of the prefix expression that
begins at S[First], if there is one. Otherwise, returns 0. }

   if (First < 1) or (First > Last) then
      EndPre := 0

   else if S[First] is an identifier then
      EndPre := First

   else if S[First] is an operator then
      begin
          { find the end of the first prefix expression }
          FirstEnd := EndPre(S, First + 1, Last)

          { find the end of the second prefix expression
              if the end of the first one was found }
          if (FirstEnd > 0)
              then EndPre := EndPre(S, FirstEnd + 1, Last)
              else EndPre := 0
      end

   else EndPre := 0
```

Now you can use the function `EndPre` to determine whether `S[1..Size]` is a prefix expression as follows:

A recognition algorithm for prefix expressions

```
function IsPre(S, Size) : returns a boolean value
{ Determines if S[1..Size] is a legal prefix expression. }
   LastChar := EndPre(S, 1, Size)
```

```
    if (LastChar <> 0) and there are no nonblank characters
            in S[LastChar+1..Size]
        then IsPre := true
        else IsPre := false
```

The following Pascal program demonstrates how you can use the previous functions to determine whether or not an expression is in prefix form. The recursive function *EndPre* is nested within the function *IsPre* so that *EndPre* can access the expression globally.

```
program RecognizePrefix;
{ *********************************************************
  RECOGNIZES A PREFIX EXPRESSION.
  Input: An expression (string of 80 or fewer characters).
  An operand is a single uppercase letter; an operator is
  one of +, -, *, and /.
  Output: Prints a message that indicates whether the
  string is a prefix expression. Note that valid prefix
  expressions do not contain embedded blanks.
  Subprograms: Calls IsBlank, IsPre, and ReadWriteExpr.
  ********************************************************* }
const MaxStringLength = 80;
type  expressionType = string[MaxStringLength];

function IsBlank(SubString : expressionType;
                 First, Last : integer) : boolean;
{ ---------------------------------------------------------
  Determines if a substring is all blank.
  Precondition: SubString[First..Last] is a substring.
  Postcondition: Returns true if the substring is all
  blanks; else returns false.
  Assumption: The substring is small, so it is searched in
  its entirety.
  --------------------------------------------------------- }
var Index : integer;
begin
   IsBlank := true;
   for Index := First to Last do
      if SubString[Index] <> ' '
         then IsBlank := false
end;  { IsBlank }

function IsPre(Expression : expressionType) : boolean;
{ ---------------------------------------------------------
  Determines if an expression is a valid prefix expression.
  Note that valid prefix expressions do not contain
  embedded blanks.
```

```
  Precondition: Expression is a character string.
  Postcondition: Returns true if Expression is in prefix
  form, else returns false. Expression is unchanged.
  Calls: IsBlank and the local recursive function EndPre.
  -------------------------------------------------------- }
   function EndPre(First, Last : integer) : integer;
   { ------------------------------------------------------
     Finds the end of the legal prefix expression that
     begins at a given character. Uses the grammar <pre> =
     <letter> | <operator><pre><pre> where <letter> is a
     single uppercase letter.
     Precondition: Expression[First..Last] is global to
     this function and contains a character string.
     Postcondition: Returns the index of the last
     character in the prefix expression that begins at
     First, or returns 0 if there is no such prefix
     expression.
     ---------------------------------------------------- }
   var FirstEnd : integer;
   begin
      { test the bounds }
      if (First < 1) or (First > Last) then
         EndPre := 0    { assume empty string }

      { degenerate case - a single letter }
      else if Expression[First] in ['A'..'Z'] then
         EndPre := First

      { general case - apply the recursive definition }
      else if Expression[First] in ['+','-','*','/']
         then
         begin
            { find end of the first prefix expression }
            FirstEnd := EndPre(First+1, Last);

            { find end of the second prefix expression }
            if FirstEnd > 0
               then EndPre := EndPre(FirstEnd+1, Last)
               else EndPre := 0
         end
      else EndPre := 0
   end;   { EndPre }

var LastChar: integer;{ index to last char of prefix expr}
    Size: integer;  { length of input string }

begin   { body of IsPre }
{ the end of the legal expression that begins at index 1
  must be the last nonblank character of the input string }
```

```
    Size := length(Expression);
    LastChar := EndPre(1, Size);
    IsPre := (LastChar > 0) and
                 IsBlank(Expression, LastChar+1, Size)
end; { IsPre }

procedure ReadWriteExpr(var Expression : expressionType);
{ ----------------------------------------------------------
  Reads and echo prints an expression.
  Precondition: MaxStringLength is a global constant.
  Postcondition: Expression contains input expression,
  which is printed, but is not followed by a carriage
  return.
  ---------------------------------------------------------- }
begin
   write('Enter expression of no more than ');
   writeln(MaxStringLength, ' characters. ');
   readln(Expression);

   writeln;
   write(Expression)
end;  { ReadWriteExpr }

var Expression: expressionType;
begin   { Main Program - demonstrate function IsPre }
    ReadWriteExpr(Expression); { read and print expression }
    if IsPre(Expression)       { test expression }
        then writeln(' is a legal prefix expression.')
        else writeln(' is NOT a legal prefix expression.')
end.   { Program }
```

The following provides samples of the program's output:

```
A                  is a legal prefix expression.
+AB                is a legal prefix expression.
+/AB-CD            is a legal prefix expression.
A+B                is NOT a legal prefix expression.
                   is NOT a legal prefix expression.
+A                 is NOT a legal prefix expression.
+ABC               is NOT a legal prefix expression.
AB                 is NOT a legal prefix expression.
A B                is NOT a legal prefix expression.
```

Postfix expressions. A grammar that defines the language of all postfix expressions is

$$<post\text{-}exp> = <letter> \mid <post\text{-}exp> <post\text{-}exp> <operator>$$
$$<operator> = + \mid - \mid * \mid /$$
$$<letter> = A \mid B \mid \cdots \mid Z$$

Chapter 8 presents a nonrecursive algorithm for *evaluating* postfix expressions. Here we shall develop an algorithm for converting a prefix expression to a postfix expression. These two algorithms, combined with the prefix recognition algorithm, give you a method for evaluating a prefix expression *E*, as Figure 6-10 illustrates. To simplify the conversion algorithm, assume that by using the prefix recognition algorithm, you have a syntactically correct prefix expression.

If you think recursively, the conversion from prefix form to postfix form is straightforward. If the prefix expression *E* is a single letter, then

Postfix(E) = E

Otherwise *E* must be of the form

<operator> <pre-exp1> <pre-exp2>

The corresponding postfix expression is then

<post-exp1> <post-exp2> <operator>

where *<pre-exp1>* converts to *<post-exp1>* and *<pre-exp2>* converts to *<post-exp2>*. Therefore,

Postfix(E) = Postfix(pre-exp1) · Postfix(pre-exp2) · <operator>

The conversion algorithm is

An algorithm that converts a prefix expression to postfix form

```
if E is a single letter
   then Postfix(E) := E
   else Postfix(E) := Postfix(pre-exp1) · Postfix(pre-exp2)
                                             · <operator>
```

The following Pascal procedure accomplishes this conversion process. The string `Pre` contains the prefix expression, and the string `Post` will contain the postfix expression that the procedure constructs. The recursive procedure `Convert` is nested within the nonrecursive `ConvertPreTo-Post` procedure so that `Convert` can access the strings `Pre` and `Post` globally. Notice that each recursive call to `Convert` returns the index `PreIndex`, which points to the location within the string `Pre` that follows the end of the prefix expression that `Convert` just converted. This index

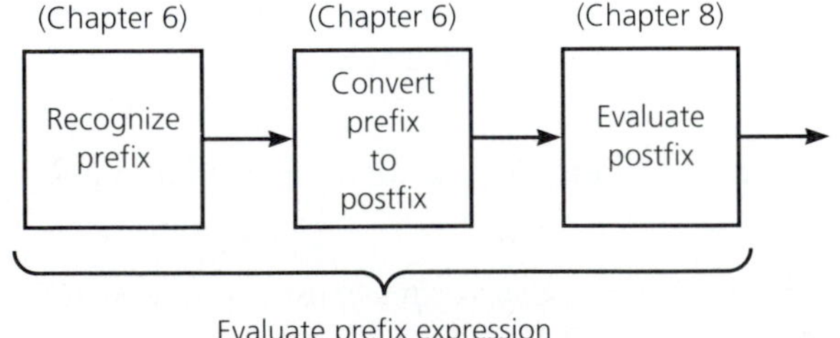

Figure 6-10

Combining algorithms to evaluate a prefix expression

is the starting point of the prefix expression that the next recursive call to *Convert* will convert.

```
const MaxStringLength = 80;   { maximum string length }

type  expressionType = string[MaxStringLength];

procedure ConvertPreToPost(Pre: expressionType;
                           var Post: expressionType);
{ ---------------------------------------------------------
  Converts a prefix expression to postfix form.
  Precondition: Pre is an algebraic expression in
  syntactically correct prefix form. An operand is a single
  uppercase letter; an operator is one of +, -, *, and /.
  Postcondition: Post is the equivalent postfix
  expression; Pre is unchanged.
  Calls: The local recursive procedure Convert.
  --------------------------------------------------------- }

    procedure Convert(var PreIndex : integer);
    { ---------------------------------------------------
      Recursively converts a prefix expression to postfix
      form.
      Precondition: The prefix expression in Pre begins
      at the index PreIndex. Pre and Post are global to
      this procedure.
      Postcondition: The prefix expression is converted
      into postfix form and concatenated to the end of
      Post. Sets PreIndex to 1 past the end of the given
      prefix expression.
      --------------------------------------------------- }
    var Ch : char;

    begin
        { check the first character of the prefix string }
        Ch := Pre[PreIndex];   { get first character }
        inc(PreIndex);         { advance pointer }

        if Ch in ['A'.. 'Z']   { check character }
            then    { degenerate case - single identifier }
                Post := concat(Post, Ch)

            else
            begin  { do the conversion recursively }
                Convert(PreIndex);         { first operand }
                Convert(PreIndex);         { second operand }
                Post := concat(Post, Ch)  { operator }
            end
    end;   { Convert }
```

```
var PreIndex : integer;

begin   { body of ConvertPreToPost }
    { initialize }
    PreIndex := 1;
    Post := ''; { empty string }

    { do the conversion }
    Convert(PreIndex)
end;    { ConvertPreToPost }
```

Fully parenthesized expressions. Most programmers would object to using prefix or postfix notation for their algebraic expressions, so most programming languages use infix notation. However, infix notation requires parenthesization, precedence rules, and rules for association to avoid ambiguity within the expressions.

The simplest scheme for recognizing and evaluating infix expressions requires all expressions to be *fully parenthesized*. A grammar for the language of all fully parenthesized expressions is

A grammar for the language of fully parenthesized algebraic expressions

<*expression*> = <*letter*> | (<*expression*> <*operator*> <*expression*>)
<operator> = + | − | * | /
<letter> = A | B | ··· | Z

This definition requires that you place parentheses around each pair of operands together with their operator so that there is no possibility for ambiguity. Thus, precedence and association rules are unnecessary. However, the scheme is rather inconvenient for programmers.

Therefore, most programming languages support a definition of algebraic expressions that includes both precedence rules for the operators and rules of association so that fully parenthesized expressions are not required. However, the grammars for defining such languages are more involved and the algorithms for recognizing and evaluating their expressions are more difficult than those you have seen in this section. Project 20 at the end of this chapter involves algebraic expressions with precedence rules. Chapter 8 presents a nonrecursive algorithm for evaluating algebraic expressions that allow both precedence and left-to-right association rules.

THE RELATIONSHIP BETWEEN RECURSION AND MATHEMATICAL INDUCTION

A very strong relationship exists between recursion and mathematical induction. Recursion solves a problem by specifying a solution to one or more degenerate cases and then demonstrating how to derive the solution to a problem of an arbitrary size from the solutions to smaller problems of the same type. Similarly, mathematical induction proves a property about the natural numbers by proving the property about a base case—usually 0 or 1—and then proving that the property must be true for an arbitrary natural number N if it is true for the natural numbers smaller than N.

Given the similarities between recursion and mathematical induction, it should not be surprising that induction is often employed to prove properties about recursive algorithms. What types of properties? You can, for example, prove that an algorithm actually performs the task that you intended. As an illustration, we will prove that the recursive *Factorial* algorithm of Chapter 5 does indeed compute the factorial of its argument. Another use of mathematical induction is to prove that a recursive algorithm performs a certain amount of work. For example, we will prove that the solution to the Towers of Hanoi problem makes exactly $2^N - 1$ moves when it starts with N disks.

You can use induction to prove that a recursive algorithm is either correct or performs a certain amount of work

The Correctness of the Recursive Factorial Function

The following pseudocode describes a recursive function that computes the factorial of a nonnegative integer *n:*

```
Factorial(n)

    if n = 0
       then Factorial := 1
       else Factorial := n * Factorial(n - 1)
```

You can prove that the function `Factorial` returns the values

`Factorial(0)` $= 0! = 1$
`Factorial(n)` $= n! = n * (n-1) * (n-2) * \cdots * 1$ if $n > 0$

The proof is by induction on n.

Basis. *Show that the property is true for* $n = 0$. That is, you must show that `Factorial(0)` returns 1. But this result is simply the degenerate case of the function: `Factorial(0)` returns 1 by its definition.

You now must establish that

property is true for an arbitrary k $\Rightarrow$ *property is true for k* $+ 1$

Inductive hypothesis. *Assume that the property is true for* $n = k$. That is, assume that

`Factorial(k)` $= k * (k-1) * (k-2) * \cdots * 2 * 1$

Inductive conclusion. *Show that the property is true for* $n = k + 1$. That is, you must show that `Factorial(k + 1)` returns the value

$(k+1) * k * (k-1) * (k-2) * \cdots * 2 * 1$

By definition of the function `Factorial`, `Factorial(k + 1)` returns the value

$(k+1) *$ `Factorial(k)`

But by the inductive hypothesis, `Factorial(k)` returns the value

$$k * (k - 1) * (k - 2) * \cdots * 2 * 1$$

Thus, `Factorial(k + 1)` returns the value

$$(k + 1) * k * (k - 1) * (k - 2) * \cdots * 2 * 1$$

which is what you needed to show to establish that

property is true for an arbitrary k $\Rightarrow$ *property is true for k + 1*

The inductive proof is thus complete.

The Cost of Towers of Hanoi

At the beginning of this chapter, we presented the following solution to the Towers of Hanoi problem:

```
Towers(Count, Source, Dest, Spare)

   if Count = 1
      then move the disk directly from Source to Dest

      else
      begin
         Solve Towers(Count-1, Source, Spare, Dest)
         Solve Towers(1, Source, Dest, Spare)
         Solve Towers(Count-1, Spare, Dest, Source)
      end
```

We now pose the following question: If you begin with N disks, how many moves does `Towers` make to solve the problem?

Let $Moves(N)$ be the number of moves made starting with N disks. When $N = 1$, the answer is easy:

$$Moves(1) = 1$$

When $N > 1$, the value of $Moves(N)$ is not so apparent. An inspection of the `Towers` procedure, however, reveals three recursive calls. Therefore, if you knew how many moves the procedure made starting with $N - 1$ disks, you could figure out how many moves it made starting with N disks; that is,

$$Moves(N) = Moves(N - 1) + Moves(1) + Moves(N - 1)$$

Thus, you have a recurrence relation for the number of moves required for N disks:

A recurrence relation for the number of moves that `Towers` *requires for* N *disks*

$$Moves(1) = 1$$
$$Moves(N) = 2 * Moves(N - 1) + 1 \text{ if } N > 1$$

For example, you can determine $Moves(3)$ as follows:

$$\begin{aligned} Moves(3) &= 2 * Moves(2) + 1 \\ &= 2 * (2 * Moves(1) + 1) + 1 \\ &= 2 * (2 * 1 + 1) + 1 \\ &= 7 \end{aligned}$$

Although the recurrence relation gives you a way to compute *Moves(N)*, a **closed-form formula**—such as an algebraic expression—would be more satisfactory because you could substitute any given value for *N* and obtain the number of moves made. However, the recurrence relation is useful because there are techniques for obtaining a closed-form formula from it. Unfortunately, these techniques are beyond the scope of this book. Therefore, we simply pull the formula out of the blue and use mathematical induction to prove that it is correct.

The solution to the previous recurrence relation is

A closed-form formula for the number of moves that `Towers` *requires for* N *disks*

$$Moves(N) = 2^N - 1, \text{ for all } N \geq 1$$

Notice that $2^3 - 1$ agrees with the value 7 that was just computed for *Moves*(3).

The proof that $Moves(N) = 2^N - 1$ is by induction on *N*.

Basis. *Show that the property is true for N = 1.* Here, $2^1 - 1 = 1$, which is consistent with the recurrence relation's specification that *Moves*(1) = 1.

You now must establish that

property is true for an arbitrary k ⇒ *property is true for k + 1*

Inductive hypothesis. *Assume that the property is true for N = k.* That is, assume

$$Moves(k) = 2^k - 1$$

Inductive conclusion. *Show that the property is true for N = k + 1.* That is, you must show that $Moves(k + 1) = 2^{k+1} - 1$. Now

$$\begin{aligned} Moves(k + 1) &= 2 * Moves(k) + 1 && \text{from the recurrence relation} \\ &= 2 * (2^k - 1) + 1 && \text{by the inductive hypothesis} \\ &= 2^{k+1} - 1 \end{aligned}$$

which is what you needed to show to establish that

property is true for an arbitrary k ⇒ *property is true for k + 1*

The inductive proof is thus complete.

We do not wish to leave you with the false impression that proving properties of programs is an easy matter. These two proofs are about as easy as any will be. We do, however, wish to reiterate that well-structured programs are far more amenable to these techniques than are poorly structured programs.

Appendix A provides more information about mathematical induction.

SUMMARY

1. **Recursion allows you to solve problems whose iterative solutions are difficult to conceptualize. The Towers of Hanoi is such a problem.**

2. You can use recursion to perform operations on linked lists. Such use will eliminate special cases and the need for a trailing pointer.
3. Backtracking is a solution strategy that involves both recursion and a sequence of guesses that ultimately lead to a solution. If a particular guess leads to an impasse, you back up, replace that guess, and try to complete the solution again.
4. A grammar is a device for defining a language, which is a set of strings of symbols. A benefit of using a grammar to define a language is that you often can construct a recognition algorithm that is directly based on the grammar. Grammars are frequently recursive, which allows you to describe vast languages concisely.
5. We illustrated the use of grammars by defining several different languages of algebraic expressions. These different languages have their relative advantages and disadvantages. Prefix and postfix expressions, while difficult for the programmer to use, eliminate problems of ambiguity. Infix expressions, on the other hand, require parentheses, precedence rules, and rules of association to eliminate ambiguity.
6. There is a very close relationship between mathematical induction and recursion. Induction is often used to establish the correctness of a recursive algorithm and to prove properties about it. For example, you can prove that an algorithm is correct and derive the amount of work an algorithm requires.

COMMON PITFALLS / DEBUGGING

1. When developing a recursive solution, you must be sure that the solutions to the smaller problems really do give you a solution to the original problem. For example, the recursive insertion algorithm for a sorted linked list works because each smaller linked list is also sorted. When the algorithm makes an insertion at the beginning of one of these lists, the inserted node will be in the proper position in the original list.
2. You must be sure that the subproblems that a recursive solution generates eventually reach a degenerate case. Failure to do so could result in an algorithm that does not terminate. For example, the recursive insertion algorithm for a sorted linked list is guaranteed to terminate because each smaller list contains one fewer node than the preceding list and because the empty list is a degenerate case.
3. Grammars, like recursive algorithms, must have carefully chosen degenerate cases. You must ensure that when a string is decomposed far enough, it will always reach the form of one of the grammar's degenerate cases.

4. The subtleties of some of the algorithms you encountered in this chapter indicate the need for mathematical techniques to prove their correctness. The application of these techniques during the design of the various components of a solution can help to eliminate errors in logic before they appear in the program. One such technique is mathematical induction; another is the use of loop invariants, which we discussed in Chapter 1 and will discuss again in the next chapter.

SELF-TEST EXERCISES

1. Trace the execution of the procedure `Towers` to solve the Towers of Hanoi problem for two disks.
2. Write a recursive Pascal procedure that retrieves the contents of the ith integer in a linked list of integers. Assume that $i \geq 1$ and that the linked list contains at least i nodes. (*Hint:* If $i = 1$, return the first integer in the list; otherwise retrieve the $(i - 1)^{st}$ integer from the rest of the list.)
3. Consider a Four Queens problem, which has the same rules as the Eight Queens problem but uses a 4 by 4 board. Find all solutions to this new problem by applying backtracking by hand.
4. Write the prefix expression that represents the following infix expression:

   $(A / B) * C - (D + E) * F$
5. Write the postfix expression that represents the following infix expression:

   $(A * B - C) / D + (E - F)$
6. Write the infix expression that represents the following prefix expression:

   $--A/B+C*DEF$
7. Consider the language of these strings: $, cc$d, cccc$dd, cccccc$ddd, and so on. Write a recursive grammar for this language.

EXERCISES

1. Consider the following recursive function:

```
function p(x : integer) : integer;
begin
    if x < 3
       then p := x
       else p := p(x-1) * p(x-3)
end;
```

Let $A(n)$ be the number of multiplication operations that the execution of `p(n)` performs. Write a recursive definition of $A(n)$.

2. Consider palindromes that consist only of lowercase letters such as "level" and "deed," but not "RadaR," "ADA," or "101." Let $C(n)$ be the number of palindromes of length n. Give a recursive definition of $C(n)$.

3. Let L be the language

$L = \{S : S \text{ is of the form } A^nB^{2n}, \text{ for some } n >= 0\}$

Thus, a string is in L if and only if it starts with a sequence of A's and is followed by a sequence of twice as many B's. For example, AABBBB is in L, but ABBB and ABBABB are not in L.

a. Give a grammar for the language L.
b. Write a recursive function that determines whether the character string `Str[First..Last]` is in L.

4. Consider the language that the following grammar defines:

<*S*> = $ | <*W*> | $<*S*>
<*W*> = abb | a<*W*>bb

Write all strings that are in this language and that contain seven or fewer characters.

5. Is *+∗A−B/C++DE−FG* a prefix expression? Explain in terms of the grammar for prefix expressions.

6. Is *AB/C∗EFG∗H/+D−+* a postfix expression? Explain in terms of the grammar for postfix expressions.

7. Consider the language that the following grammar defines:

<*S*> = <*L*> | <*D*> <*S*> <*S*>
<*L*> = A | B
<*D*> = 1 | 2

a. Write all three-character strings that are in this language.
b. Write one string in this language that contains more than three characters.

8. Consider a language of the following character strings: The letter A; the letter B; the letter C followed by a string that is in the language; the letter D followed by a string in the language. For example, these strings are in this language: A, CA, CCA, DCA, B, CB, CCB, DB, and DCCB.

a. Write the grammar for this language.
b. Is CAB in this language? Explain.

9. Trace the following recursive subprograms:

a. `EndPre` with the expression *−∗/ABCD*
b. `IsPal` with the string abcdeba
c. `Towers` with two disks

10. Consider the language that the following grammar defines:

<*word*> = \$ | a<*word*>a | b<*word*>b | ··· | y<*word*>y | z<*word*>z

Equivalently,

$L = \{w\$\text{reverse}(w) : w \text{ is a string of letters of length} \geq 0\}$

Note that this language is very similar to the language of palindromes, but there is a special middle character here.

The algorithm that we gave for recognizing palindromes can be adapted easily to this language. The algorithm, which is recursive and processes the string `Str[First..Last]` from both ends toward the middle, is based on the following facts:

- A string with no characters (`Last < First`) is not in the language.
- A string with exactly one character (`First = Last`) is in the language if the character is a \$.
- A longer string (`First < Last`) is in the language if the ends are identical letters and the inner string (`First+1` to `Last-1`) is in the language.

Describe a recursive recognition algorithm that processes the string from left to right, reading one character at a time and not explicitly saving the string for future reference. Write a Pascal function that implements your algorithm.

11. Write recursive procedures that will perform insertion and deletion operations on a sorted linked list.

12. Write a recursive procedure that will reverse a linked list. (See Exercise 10 in Chapter 3.)

13. Write a recursive procedure that will merge two sorted linked lists into a single sorted linked list. You need not preserve the original lists. (See Exercise 18 in Chapter 3.)

14. Write a nonrecursive solution to the Towers of Hanoi problem. By studying the recursive solution that was presented in this chapter, you can gain some insight into how to proceed.

15. Complete the program that solves the Eight Queens problem.

16. Revise the program that you just wrote for the Eight Queens problem so that it answers the following questions:

a. How many backtracks occur? That is, how many times does the program remove a queen from the board?
b. How many calls to `Attack` are there?
c. How many recursive calls to `PlaceNextQueen` are there?
d. Can you make `Attack` more efficient? For example, as soon as you detect that a queen can attack a given square, do you still look for another queen?

***17.** You can begin the Eight Queens problem by placing a queen in the second square of the first column instead of the first square. You can then call `PlaceNextQueen` to begin with the second column. This revision should lead you to a new solution. Write a program that finds all solutions to the Eight Queens problem.

***18.** Prove the following for single-letter operands: If E is a prefix expression and Y is a nonempty string of characters, then $E\ Y$ cannot be a legal prefix expression. (*Hint*: Use a proof by induction on the length of E.)

19. Chapter 5 gave the following definition for $C(n, k)$, where n and k are assumed to be nonnegative integers:

$$C(n, k) = \begin{cases} 1 & \text{if } k = 0 \\ 1 & \text{if } k = n \\ C(n-1, k-1) + C(n-1, k) & \text{if } 0 < k < n \\ 0 & \text{if } k > n \end{cases}$$

Prove by induction on n that the following is a closed form for $C(n, k)$:

$$C(n, k) = \frac{n!}{(n-k)!k!}$$

PROJECTS

20. The following is a grammar that allows you to omit parentheses in infix algebraic expressions when the precedence rules remove ambiguity. For example, $a + b * c$ means $a + (b * c)$. However, the grammar requires parentheses when ambiguity would otherwise result. That is, the grammar does not permit left-to-right association when several operators have the same precedence. For example, $a / b * c$ is illegal. Notice that the definitions introduce **factors** and **terms.**

<expression> = *<term>* | *<term>* + *<term>* | *<term>* − *<term>*
<term> = *<factor>* | *<factor>* * *<factor>* | *<factor>* / *<factor>*
<factor> = *<letter>* | (*<expression>*)
<letter> = A | B | ··· | Z

With this grammar, you can apply the operators * and / only to a factor—that is, to an operand that is either a single letter or enclosed in parentheses. You can apply the operators + and − to any term—that is, to an operand that is either a factor or the (possibly unparenthesized) product or quotient of a pair of factors.

The recognition algorithm is based on a recursive chain of subtasks: *find an expression* → *find a term* → *find a factor*. What makes this a recursive chain is that *find an expression* uses *find a term*, which in turn uses *find a factor*. *Find a factor* either detects a degenerate case or uses *find an expression*, thus forming the recursive chain.

The pseudocode for the recognition algorithm follows:

```
FIND AN EXPRESSION
{ The grammar specifies that an expression is either a
  single term or a term followed by a + or a -, which
  then must be followed by a second term. }

     Find a term
     if the next symbol is a + or a -
         then find a term

FIND A TERM
{ The grammar specifies that a term is either a single
  factor or a factor followed by a * or a /, which must
  then be followed by a second factor. }

     Find a factor
     if the next symbol is a * or a /
         then find a factor

FIND A FACTOR
{ The grammar specifies that a factor is either a
  single letter (the degenerate case) or an expression
  enclosed in parentheses. }

     if the next symbol is a letter then
         done
     else if the next symbol is a '(' then
         begin
             Find an expression
             Check for ')'
         end
     else there is no factor
```

Implement this recognition algorithm. Use conventions similar to those in this chapter. The following sample output indicates the results that your program should produce:

```
A+(B-C) is a legal expression.
((A)(B) is NOT a legal expression.
A+B-C   is NOT a legal expression.
  A     is NOT a legal expression.
```

(The last expression is not legal because it contains leading blanks.)

21. Instead of using an 8 by 8 array to represent the board in the Eight Queens program, you can use a one-dimensional array to represent only the squares that contain a queen. Let `Col[1..8]` be an array of integers such that

`Col[k]` = *row number of the queen in column k*

For example, if `Col[2] = 4`, then there is a queen in the fourth row (square) of the second column; that is, in `Board[4, 2]`. Thus, you use `Col[k]` to represent a queen instead of `Board[Col[k], k]`.

This scheme requires that you also store information about whether each queen is subject to attack. Because only one queen per column is permitted, you do not have to check columns. To check for a row attack, define a boolean array `RowAttack` such that

`RowAttack[k]` *is true if the queen in column k can be attacked by a queen in its row*

To check for diagonal attacks, observe that diagonals have either a positive slope or a negative slope. Those with a positive slope are parallel to the diagonal that runs from the lower left corner of the board to the upper right corner. Diagonals with a negative slope are parallel to the diagonal that runs from the upper left corner to the lower right corner. Convince yourself that if `Board[i, j]` represents a square, then `i + j` is constant for squares that are in a diagonal with a positive slope, and `i - j` is constant for squares that are in a diagonal with a negative slope. You will find that `i + j` ranges from 2 to 16 and that `i - j` ranges from −7 to +7. Thus, define boolean arrays `PosDiagonal` and `NegDiagonal` such that

`PosDiagonal[k]` *is true if the queen in column* `k` *can be attacked by a queen in its positive-sloped diagonal, and*

`NegDiagonal` *is true if the queen in column* `k` *can be attacked by a queen in its negative-sloped diagonal*

Use these ideas to write a program that solves the Eight Queens problem.

22. You can use backtracking to find your way through a maze. Consider a rectangular maze that you divide into squares. Imagine that you color certain squares to indicate the walls of the maze. By representing the maze with a two-dimensional array and by using backtracking, write a program that finds a path through your maze.

CHAPTER 7

Algorithm Efficiency and Sorting

PREVIEW This chapter will show you how to analyze the efficiency of algorithms. The basic mathematical techniques for analyzing algorithms are central to more advanced topics in computer science and give you a way to formalize the notion that one algorithm is significantly more efficient than another. As examples, you will see analyses of some algorithms that you have studied before, including those that search data. In addition, this chapter examines the important topic of sorting data. You will study some simple algorithms, which you may have seen before, and some more sophisticated recursive algorithms. Sorting algorithms provide varied and relatively easy examples of the analysis of efficiency.

MEASURING EFFICIENCY OF ALGORITHMS

The comparison or **analysis of algorithms** is a topic that is central to computer science. Measuring an algorithm's efficiency is quite important because your choice of algorithm for a given application often makes a great deal of difference. Previous chapters have informally compared different methods for performing a task. For example, we compared a sequential search of an array with a binary search and concluded that the binary search is significantly faster. Before formalizing this comparison, we need to give a more rigorous meaning to the term "significantly faster." This section introduces **order-of-magnitude analysis** and illustrates how you can use it to formalize the intuitive notion that one algorithm is significantly faster than another.

Suppose you have two algorithms that perform the same task, such as searching. What does it mean to compare the algorithms and conclude that one is better than the other? Chapter 1 discussed the cost of a computer program and the several components that constitute this cost. Some of these components involve the cost of human time—the time of the people who develop, maintain, and use the program. The other components involve the cost of program execution—that is, the program's efficiency—measured by the amount of computer time and space that the program requires to execute.

We have, up to this point, emphasized the human cost components. The early chapters of this book stressed style and readability. They pointed out that well-structured algorithms reduce the human costs of implementing the algorithm with a program, of maintaining the program, and of modifying the program. Our primary concern has been that you develop good problem-solving skills and programming style. We have and shall continue to concentrate our efforts in that direction; we have not changed our minds about what is important. However, we are also interested in the efficiency of algorithms. Efficiency is a criterion that you should use when selecting an algorithm and its implementation. The solutions in this book, in addition to illustrating what we feel to be a good programming style, are frequently based on algorithms that are relatively efficient.

Consider efficiency when selecting an algorithm

The analysis of algorithms is the area of computer science that provides tools for contrasting the differing efficiency of methods of solution. Notice that we said methods of solution rather than programs because we want to emphasize that the analysis concerns itself primarily with *significant* differences in efficiency—differences that you usually can obtain only through superior methods of solution and rarely through clever tricks in coding. Reductions in computing costs due to clever coding tricks are often more than offset by reduced program readability, which increases human costs. An analysis should focus on gross differences in the efficiency of algorithms that are likely to dominate the overall cost of a solution. To do otherwise could very well result in the selection of an algorithm that runs a small fraction of a second faster than another algorithm yet requires many more hours of human time to implement and maintain.

A comparison of algorithms should focus on significant differences in efficiency

How do you compare the time efficiency of two algorithms that solve the same problem? One possible approach is to implement the two algorithms in Pascal and run the programs. There are at least three fundamental difficulties with this approach:

Three difficulties with comparing programs instead of algorithms

1. **How are the algorithms coded?** If algorithm A_1 runs faster than A_2, it could be the result of better programming. Thus, if you compare the running times of the programs, you are really comparing implementations of the algorithms rather than the algorithms themselves. You should not compare implementations, because they are sensitive to factors such as programming style that tend to cloud the issue of which algorithm is inherently more efficient.
2. **What computer should you use?** The particular computer on which the programs are run also obscures the issue of which algorithm is inherently more efficient. It may be that because of the particular operations that the algorithms require, A_1 runs faster than A_2 on one computer, while the opposite is true on another computer. You should compare the efficiency of the algorithms independently of a particular computer.
3. **What data should the programs use?** Perhaps the most important difficulty in this list is the selection of the data for the programs to use. There is always the danger that you will select instances of the problem for which one of the algorithms runs uncharacteristically fast. For example, when comparing a sequential and a binary search, you might happen to search for the smallest item in a sorted array. In such a case, the sequential search will find the item more quickly than the binary search because the item is first in the array and so is the first item that the sequential search will examine. Any analysis of efficiency must be independent of specific data.

Order-of-Magnitude Analysis

Algorithm analysis should be independent of specific implementations, computers, and data

To overcome the previous problems, computer scientists employ mathematical techniques that analyze algorithms independently of specific implementations, computers, or data. The mathematical approach considers an algorithm's time requirement as a function of the problem size. The way to measure a problem's size depends on the application—typical examples are the size of an array, the number of nodes on a linked list, the number of records in a file, or the number of items on an ordered list.

Measure an algorithm's time requirement as a function of the problem size

What specifically do you want to know about the time requirement of an algorithm? The most important thing to learn is how quickly the algorithm's time requirement grows as a function of the problem size. Typically, this growth rate is stated as a proportion of the problem size. For example, if N is the size of the problem, you might conclude that an algorithm requires time proportional to N, N^2, 2^N, or $\log N$. (When speaking of proportional growth rates, you need not specify the base of the log. Exercise 10 at the end of this chapter asks you to show why you can omit the base.)

Consider the statement

Algorithm A requires time proportional to N^2

What can you conclude from this statement? One thing that you cannot conclude is the exact amount of time that *A* will require to solve a problem of size N: The statement is equally valid if *A* required N^2 seconds, $5 * N^2$ seconds, or $N^2/10$ seconds to solve a problem of size N.

Such characterizations of an algorithm's efficiency might thus appear to be of little use. However, what would it mean if you said that

Algorithm A requires $5 * N^2$ *seconds to solve a problem of size N*

The previous discussion indicated the difficulties with such a statement: On what computer does the algorithm require $5 * N^2$ seconds? What implementation of the algorithm requires $5 * N^2$ seconds? Is there another implementation of the algorithm that requires only $3 * N^2$ seconds, but is perhaps less readable? On the other hand, an assertion like "*A* requires time proportional to N^2" is exactly the kind of statement that characterizes the inherent efficiency of an algorithm independently of such factors as particular computers and implementations.

The significance of an algorithm's proportional time requirement will become apparent if you compare two algorithms for which the requirement differs. For example, suppose that you have a second algorithm *B* such that

Algorithm B requires time proportional to N

Compare algorithm efficiencies for large problems

Although you cannot determine the exact amount of time that either algorithm *A* or algorithm *B* requires, you can determine that for large problems, *B* will require significantly less time than *A*. That is, the amount of time—as a function of the problem size N—that *B* requires increases at a slower rate than the amount of time that *A* requires, because N increases at a slower rate than N^2. Even if *B* actually requires $5 * N$ seconds and *A* actually requires $N^2/10$ seconds, as N increases, the amount of time that *B* requires will become significantly less than the time that *A* requires.

To further dramatize the significance of an algorithm's proportional growth rate, consider the table and graph in Figure 7-1. The table (Figure

(a)

Function	N					
	10	100	1,000	10,000	100,000	1,000,000
$\log_2 N$	3	6	9	13	16	19
N	10	100	1,000	10,000	100,000	1,000,000
$N * \log_2 N$	30	664	9,965	10^5	10^6	10^7
N^2	10^2	10^4	10^6	10^8	10^{10}	10^{12}
N^3	10^3	10^6	10^9	10^{12}	10^{15}	10^{18}
2^N	10^3	10^{30}	10^{301}	$10^{3,010}$	$10^{30,103}$	$10^{301,030}$

(using the fact that $2^{10} \cong 10^{3.0103}$)

(b)

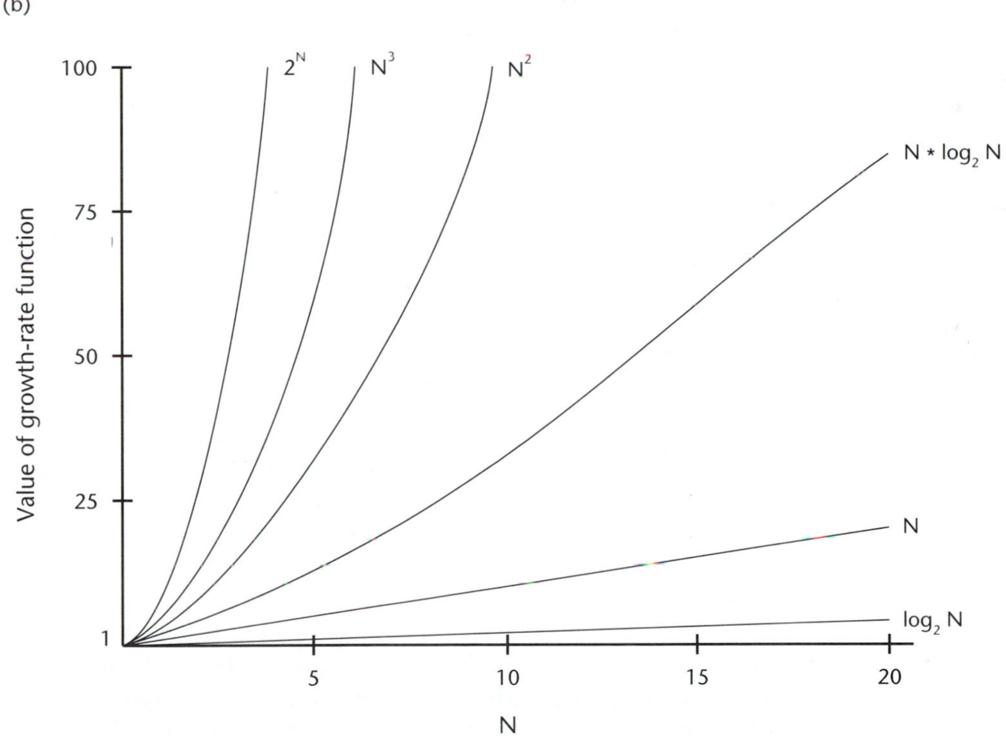

Figure 7-1

A comparison of growth-rate functions: (a) in tabular form; (b) in graphical form

7-1a) gives for various values of *N* the approximate values of six common growth-rate functions, which are listed in order of growth. The table demonstrates how much more quickly the value of a function grows than does that of the functions that precede it in the table. (Figure 7-1b represents the growth-rate functions graphically.) If algorithm *A* requires time that is proportional to function *f* and algorithm *B* requires time that is proportional to a slower-growing function *g*, then it is apparent that *B* will always be significantly more efficient than *A* for large enough problems. For large problems, the proportional growth rate dominates all other factors in determining an algorithm's efficiency.

Big O Notation

We now formalize the concept of an algorithm's proportional growth rate. The statement

Algorithm A requires time proportional to f(N)

means that given any (reasonable) implementation of the algorithm and any (reasonable) computer, there is some **constant of proportionality** *c* such that *A* requires no more than

*c * f(N) time units (such as seconds)*

to solve a problem of size *N*. Algorithm *A* is said to be **order *f*(*N*)**, which is denoted as **O(*f*(*N*))**; *f*(*N*) is called the algorithm's **growth-rate function.** Because the notation uses the capital letter O to denote *order*, it is called the **Big O notation.**

KEY CONCEPTS

Definition of the Order of an Algorithm

Algorithm *A* is order *f*(*N*) (denoted O(*f*(*N*))) if for any (reasonable) implementation of the algorithm and any (reasonable) computer, there is some constant *c* such that for all but a finite number of values of *N*, *A* requires no more than *c* * *f*(*N*) time units to solve a problem of size *N*.

If a problem requires a constant time that is independent of the problem's size *N*, the problem is O(1). If a problem of size *N* requires time that is directly proportional to *N*, then the problem is O(*N*). If the time requirement is directly proportional to N^2, then the problem is O(N^2), and so on.

Notice that the definition of O(*f*(*N*)) does allow *A* to require more than *c* * *f*(*N*) time units for a finite number of problem sizes. This characteristic simply allows you to discount finitely many values of *N*, that is, to consider only sufficiently large values of *N*. For example, the function log *N* takes on the value 0 when $N = 1$. Thus, the fact $c * \log 1 = 0$ for all constants *c* implies an unrealistic time requirement; presumably, all algorithms require more than 0 time units even to solve a problem of size 1. Thus, you can discount problems of size $N = 1$ in this case.

There are many important mathematical properties of Big O notation that you will see in later courses. However, some of these properties are simple enough to cover now:

Some properties of growth-rate functions

1. **You can ignore low-order terms in an algorithm's growth-rate function.** For example, if an algorithm is O($N^3 + 4 * N^2 + 3 * N$), then it is also O(N^3). By examining the table in Figure 7-1a, you can see that

the N^3 term is significantly larger than either $(4 * N^2)$ or $(3 * N)$, particularly for large values of N. For large N, the growth rate of $N^3 + 4 * N^2 + 3 * N$ is the same as the growth rate of N^3. Realize that the growth rate of $f(N)$, not the value of $f(N)$, is what is important here. Thus, even if an algorithm is $O(N^3 + 4 * N^2 + 3 * N)$, we say that it is simply $O(N^3)$. In general, you are usually able to conclude that an algorithm is $O(f(N))$, where f is a function similar to the ones listed in Figure 7-1.

2. **You can ignore a multiplicative constant in the high-order term of an algorithm's growth-rate function.** For example, if an algorithm is $O(5 * N^3)$, then it is also $O(N^3)$. This observation follows from the definition of $O(f(N))$, if you let $c = 5$.
3. $\mathbf{O(f(N)) + O(g(N)) = O(f(N) + g(N))}$. You can combine growth-rate functions. For example, if an algorithm is $O(N) + O(N)$, then it is also $O(2 * N)$, which you write simply as $O(N)$ by applying property 2.

An algorithm can require different times to solve different problems of the same size

There is one final point to make about the definition of the order of an algorithm: Algorithm A might require different times to solve different problems of the same size. For example, the time that an algorithm requires to search N items might depend on the nature of the items. Usually you consider the maximum amount of time that an algorithm can require to solve a problem of size N—that is, the worst case. **Worst-case analysis** concludes that A is $O(f(N))$ if, in the worst case, A requires no more than $c * f(N)$ time units to solve a problem of size N for all but a finite number of values of N.

An **average-case analysis** attempts to determine the average amount of time that an algorithm requires to solve problems of size N. In an average-case analysis, A is $O(f(N))$ if the average amount of time that A requires to solve a problem of size N is no more than $c * f(N)$ time units for all but a finite number of values of N. Average-case analysis is, in general, far more difficult to perform than worst-case analysis. One difficulty is determining the relative probabilities of encountering various problems of a given size; another is determining the distributions of various data values. Worst-case analysis is more practical to calculate and is thus more common.

An Example: The Efficiency of List Traversal

As an example of how to analyze the efficiency of a particular algorithm, consider a traversal of a linked list. Recall from Chapter 3 that you can print the contents of a linked list by using the `PrintList` procedure, which appears in pseudocode as

An example of list traversal

```
PrintList(Head)
{ Prints the data in a linked list. }
    Cur := Head
    while Cur <> nil do
    begin
        writeln(Cur^.Data)
        Cur := Cur^.Next
    end
```

If there are N nodes in the list, then the number of operations that the procedure requires is proportional to N. For example, there are $N + 1$ assignments and N print operations, which together are $2 * N + 1$ operations. According to the previous discussion, you ignore both the coefficient 2 and the constant 1. Therefore, `PrintList` is $O(N)$; that is, the time that `PrintList` requires to print N nodes is proportional to N. This conclusion makes sense intuitively: It takes longer to print, or traverse, a list of 100 items than it does a list of 10 items.

`PrintList` is O(N)

The Effect of Different ADT Implementations on Efficiency

You can use order-of-magnitude analysis to help you choose an implementation for an abstract data type. Recall that Chapter 4 introduced the ADT ordered list and presented two implementations. One implementation stored the list's items in an array, the other stored the items in a linked list. There is a potentially significant difference in the efficiency with which the two implementations support the ADT operations.

For example, the operation `OrderedListRetrieve(OL, N)` retrieves the value of the item at the Nth position in an ordered list. The array-based implementation can access the Nth item directly because it is stored in `OL.Items[N]`. This access is independent of `N`; `OrderedListRetrieve` takes the same time to access either the 100th item or the first item on the list. Thus, the array-based implementation of the retrieval operation is $O(1)$. However, the pointer-based implementation must traverse the list from its beginning until the Nth node is reached. Like the previous `PrintList` algorithm, the pointer-based implementation of `OrderedListRetrieve` is $O(N)$.

An array-based `OrderedListRetrieve` is O(1)

A pointer-based `OrderedListRetrieve` is O(N)

Throughout the course of an analysis, you should always keep in mind that you are interested only in *significant* differences in efficiency. Is the difference in efficiency for the two implementations of `OrderedListRetrieve` significant? Notice that as the size of the list grows, the pointer-based implementation might require more time to retrieve the desired node, because the node can be farther away from the beginning of the list. In contrast, regardless of how large the list is, the array-based implementation always requires the same constant amount of time to retrieve any particular item. Thus, no matter what your notion of a significant difference in time is, you will reach this time difference if the list is large enough.

In this example, observe that the difference in efficiency for the two implementations is worth considering only when the problem is large enough. If the ordered list never has more than 10 elements, for example, the difference in the implementation is not significant at all.

Keeping Your Perspective

Before continuing with additional order-of-magnitude analyses of specific algorithms, it is appropriate to present a few words about perspective. Frequently when evaluating an algorithm's efficiency, you have to weigh carefully the trade-offs between a solution's execution time requirements and its memory requirements. You rarely are able to make a statement as strong as "Method *A* is the best method of performing the task." A solution that requires a relatively small amount of computer time often also requires a relatively large amount of memory. It may not even be possible to say that one solution requires less time than another. Solution *A* may perform some components of the task faster than solution *B,* while solution *B* performs other components of the task faster than solution *A*. Often you must analyze the solutions in the light of a particular application.

For example, consider an ADT ordered list of *N* items. Suppose that an application *X* frequently retrieves items from the ordered list, but rarely inserts or deletes an item. We recently observed that the retrieval operation for an array-based implementation of an ordered list is faster than for a pointer-based implementation. Thus, you should choose an array-based implementation of the ordered list for application *X*. On the other hand, if application *Y* requires frequent insertions and deletions, but rarely retrieves an item, you should choose a pointer-based implementation of the ordered list. The most appropriate implementation of an ADT for a given application strongly depends on how frequently the application is to perform the operations.

When choosing an ADT's implementation, consider how frequently particular ADT operations occur in a given application

Soon we will compare a searching algorithm that is O(*N*) with one that is $O(\log_2 N)$. While it is true that an $O(\log_2 N)$ searching algorithm requires significantly less time on large arrays than an O(*N*) algorithm, on small arrays—say $N < 25$—the time requirements might not be significantly different at all. In fact, it is entirely possible that, because of factors such as the size of the constant of proportionality—that is, the *c* in the definition of Big O—the O(*N*) algorithm will run faster on small problems. It is only on large problems that the slower growth rate of an algorithm necessarily gives it a significant advantage. Thus, in general, if the maximum size of a given problem is small, the time requirements of any two solutions for that problem likely will not differ significantly. If you know that your problem size will always be small, do not overanalyze: Simply choose the algorithm that is easiest to code and understand.

If the problem size is always small, you can probably ignore an algorithm's efficiency

In summary, it is important to examine an algorithm for both style and efficiency. The analysis should focus only on gross differences in efficiency and not reward coding tricks that save milliseconds. Any finer differences in efficiency are likely to interact with coding issues, which we feel should not interfere with the development of your programming style. If you find a method of solution that is significantly more efficient than others, you should select it, unless you know that the maximum problem size is quite small. If you will solve only small problems, it is possible that a less efficient algorithm is more appropriate. That is, other factors, such as the simplicity of the algorithm, would become more significant than minor differences in efficiency. In fact, performing an order-of-magnitude analysis implicitly assumes that an algorithm will be used to solve large problems. This assumption allows you to focus on growth rates because, regardless of other factors, an algorithm with a slow growth rate will require less time

Compare algorithms for both style and efficiency

Order-of-magnitude analysis focuses on large problems

than an algorithm with a fast growth rate, provided that the problems to be solved are sufficiently large.

The Efficiency of Searching Algorithms

As another example of order-of-magnitude analysis, consider the efficiency of two search algorithms: the sequential search and the binary search of an array.

Sequential search. In a sequential search of N array elements, you look at each element in turn, beginning with the first one, until either you find the desired element or you reach the end of the data collection. In the best case, the desired element is the first one that you examine, so only one comparison is necessary. Thus, in the best case, a sequential search is O(1). In the worst case, the desired element is the last one you examine, so N comparisons are necessary. Thus, in the worst case, the algorithm is O(N). In the average case, you would find the desired element in the middle of the collection, making $N/2$ comparisons; thus, the algorithm is O(N) in the average case.

Sequential search. Worst-case: O(N); average case: O(N); best case: O(1)

What is the algorithm's order when you do not find the desired element? Does the algorithm's order depend on whether or not the initial data is sorted? We leave these questions for you in Self-Test Exercise 10 at the end of this chapter.

Binary search. Is a binary search of an array more efficient than a sequential search? The binary search algorithm, which was presented in Chapter 5, searches a sorted array for a particular item by repeatedly dividing the array in half. The algorithm determines which half the item must be in—if it is indeed present—and discards the other half. Thus, the binary search algorithm searches arrays of successively smaller sizes: The size of an array is approximately one-half the size of the array previously searched.

At each division, the algorithm makes a comparison. How many comparisons does the algorithm make when it searches an array of N elements? The exact answer depends, of course, on where the sought-for item resides in the array. However, you can compute the maximum number of comparisons that a binary search requires—that is, the worst case. The number of comparisons is equal to the number of times that the algorithm divides the array in half. Suppose that $N = 2^k$ for some k. The search requires the following steps:

1. Inspect the middle item of an array of size N.
2. Inspect the middle item of an array of size $N/2$.
3. Inspect the middle item of an array of size $N/2^2$, and so on.

To inspect the middle item of an array, you first must divide the array in half. If you divide an array of N elements in half, then divide one of those halves in half, and continue dividing halves until only one element remains, you will have performed k divisions. This fact is true because $N/2^k = 1$. (Remember, we assumed that $N = 2^k$.) In the worst case, the algorithm performs k divisions and, therefore, k comparisons. Because $N = 2^k$,

$$k = \log_2 N$$

Thus, the algorithm is $O(\log_2 N)$ in the worst case when $N = 2^k$.

What if N is not a power of 2? You can easily find the smallest k such that

$$2^{k-1} < N < 2^k$$

(For example, if N is 30, then $k = 5$, because $2^4 = 16 < 30 < 32 = 2^5$.) The algorithm still requires at most k divisions to obtain a subarray with one element. Now it follows that

$$k - 1 < \log_2 N < k$$
$$k < 1 + \log_2 N < k + 1$$
$$k = 1 + \log_2 N \text{ rounded down}$$

Thus, the algorithm is still $O(\log_2 N)$ in the worst case when $N \neq 2^k$. In general, the algorithm is $O(\log_2 N)$ in the worst case for any N.

Binary search is O(log$_2$N) in the worst case

Is a binary search better than a sequential search? Much better! For example $\log_2 1{,}000{,}000 = 19$, so a sequential search of one million sorted items can require one million comparisons, but a binary search of the same items will require at most 20 comparisons. For large arrays, the binary search has an enormous advantage over a sequential search.

Realize, however, that maintaining the array in sorted order requires an overhead cost, which can be substantial. The next section examines the cost of sorting an array.

SORTING ALGORITHMS AND THEIR EFFICIENCY

Sorting is a process that organizes a collection of data into either ascending[1] or descending order. The need for sorting arises in many situations. You may simply want to sort a collection of data before displaying it for human consumption. Often, however, you must perform a sort as an initialization step for certain algorithms. For example, searching for data is one of the most common tasks performed by computers. When the collection of data to be searched is large, an efficient method for searching—such as the binary search algorithm—is desirable. However, the binary search algorithm requires that the data be sorted. Thus, sorting the data is a step that must precede a binary search on a collection of data that is not already sorted. Good sorting algorithms, therefore, are quite valuable.

[1]To allow for duplicate data items, we use *ascending* to mean nondecreasing and *descending* to mean nonincreasing.

The sorts in this chapter are internal sorts

There are two categories of sorting algorithms. An **internal sort** requires that the collection of data fit entirely in the computer's main memory. The algorithms that are presented in this chapter are internal sorting algorithms. An **external sort** is used when the collection of data will not fit in the computer's main memory all at once, but must reside in secondary storage, such as on a disk. Chapter 14 examines external sorts.

The data elements to be sorted might be integers, character strings, or even records. It is easy to imagine the results of sorting a collection of integers or character strings, but consider a collection of records. If there is one field in each record, sorting the records is really no different than sorting a collection of integers. However, when each record contains several fields, you must know which field determines the order of the entire record within the collection of data. This field is called the **sort key**. For example, if the records contain information about people, you might want to sort on their names, their ages, or their zip codes. Regardless of your choice of sort key, the sorting algorithm orders entire records based on only one field, the sort key.

For simplicity, this chapter assumes that the data elements are quantities such as numbers or character strings. Data elements that are records with several fields are considered in the exercises. All algorithms in this chapter sort the data into ascending order. Modifying these algorithms to sort data into descending order is simple. Finally, each example assumes that the data resides in an array and that the indexes to that array are integers.

Selection Sort

Imagine some data that you can examine all at once. To sort it, you could select the largest item and put it in its place, select the next largest and put it in its place, and so on. For a card player, this process is analogous to looking at an entire hand of cards and ordering it by selecting cards one at a time in their proper order. The **selection sort** formalizes these intuitive notions. To sort an array into ascending order, you first search it for the largest element. Because you want the largest element to be in the last position of the array, you swap the last element with the largest element, even if these elements happen to be identical. Now, ignoring the last—and largest—element of the array, you search the rest of the array for its largest element and swap it with its last element, which is the next-to-last element in the original array. You continue until you have selected and swapped $N - 1$ of the N elements in the array. The remaining element, which is now in the first position of the array, is in its proper order, so it is not considered further.

Select the largest element

Figure 7-2 provides an example of a selection sort. Beginning with five integers, you select the largest—37—and swap it with the last integer—13. (As the elements in this figure are ordered, they appear in boldface. We will use this convention throughout this chapter.) Next you select the larg-

Underlined elements are selected;
boldface elements are in order.

Initial array:	29	10	14	<u>37</u>	13
After 1st swap:	<u>29</u>	10	14	13	**37**
After 2nd swap:	13	10	<u>14</u>	**29**	**37**
After 3rd swap:	<u>13</u>	10	**14**	**29**	**37**
After 4th swap:	**10**	**13**	**14**	**29**	**37**

Figure 7-2

A selection sort of an array of five integers

est integer—29—from among the first four integers in the array and swap it with the next-to-last integer in the array—13. Notice that the next selection—14—is already in its proper position, but the algorithm ignores this fact and performs a swap of 14 with itself. It is more efficient in general to occasionally perform an unnecessary swap than to continually ask whether the swap is necessary. Finally, you select the 13 and swap it with the element in the second position of the array—10. The array is now sorted into ascending order.

A Pascal procedure that performs a selection sort on an array `A` of `N` elements follows:

```
const  MaxSize = <maximum number of elements in array>;
type   dataType = <type of array element>;
       arrayType = array[1..MaxSize] of dataType;

procedure SelectionSort(var A : arrayType; N : integer);
{ ---------------------------------------------------------
  Sorts the elements of an array into ascending order.
  Precondition:  A[1..N] is an array of N elements.
  Postcondition: The array A is sorted into ascending order;
  N is unchanged.
  Calls: IndexOfLargest, Swap.
  --------------------------------------------------------- }
var L : integer;          { index of largest element found }
    Last : integer;       { index of last element in subarray }
begin
    for Last := N downto 2 do
    { Invariant: A[Last+1..N] is sorted and > A[1..Last] }
    begin
       { select largest element in A[1..Last] }
       L := IndexOfLargest(A, Last);

       { swap largest element A[L] with A[Last] }
       Swap(A[L], A[Last])
    end  { for }
end;  { SelectionSort }
```

The procedure uses two simple subprograms as follows:

```
function IndexOfLargest(var A : arrayType;
                        Size : integer) : integer;
{ --------------------------------------------------------
  Finds the largest element in an array.
  Precondition: A[1..Size] is an array, Size >= 1.
  Postcondition: Returns the index of the largest element in
  the array. The parameters are unchanged.
  -------------------------------------------------------- }
var LargestElement,       { largest element found so far }
    Current : integer;    { index of current element }
begin
    LargestElement := A[1];
    IndexOfLargest := 1;

    for Current := 2 to Size do
    { Invariant: LargestElement >= A[1..Current-1] }
        if A[Current] > LargestElement
            then
            begin
                LargestElement := A[Current];
                IndexOfLargest := Current
            end  { if, for }
end; { IndexOfLargest }

procedure Swap(var X, Y : dataType);
{ --------------------------------------------------------
  Swaps X and Y.
  Precondition: None.
  Postcondition: Contents of actual locations that X and Y
  represent are swapped.
  -------------------------------------------------------- }
var Temp : dataType;
begin
    Temp := X;
    X := Y;
    Y := Temp
end;  { Swap }
```

Analysis. As you can see from the previous sorting algorithm, sorting in general requires both comparisons and exchanges of elements. As a first step in analyzing algorithms, you should count the number of comparisons and exchanges that sorting N elements requires. It is easy to see that the *for* loop in the procedure *SelectionSort* executes $N - 1$ times. Thus, there are $N - 1$ calls to each of the subprograms *IndexOfLargest* and *Swap*. Each call to *IndexOfLargest* causes its loop to execute *Last* $- 1$ times. Thus, the $N - 1$ calls to *IndexOfLargest*, for values of *Last* that range from N down to 2, cause its loop to execute in total the following number of times:

$$(N - 1) + (N - 2) + \cdots + 1 = \frac{N * (N - 1)}{2}$$

Each execution of `IndexOfLargest`'s loop performs one comparison. Therefore, a selection sort of N elements requires

$$\frac{N * (N - 1)}{2}$$

comparisons.

The $N - 1$ calls to `Swap` result in $N - 1$ exchanges. Each exchange requires three assignments, or data moves. Thus, a selection sort of N elements requires

$$3 * (N - 1)$$

moves.

Together, there are

$$\begin{aligned} &N * (N - 1)/2 + 3 * (N - 1) \\ &= N^2/2 + 5 * N/2 - 3 \end{aligned}$$

major operations.

Thus, selection sort is $O(N^2)$. Note that the algorithm does not depend on the initial arrangement of the data, which is an advantage of a selection sort. However, $O(N^2)$ grows rapidly.

Selection sort is $O(N^2)$

Also, notice that while there are $O(N^2)$ comparisons, there are only $O(N)$ data moves. A selection sort could be a good choice over other methods when data moves are costly but comparisons are not. Such might be the case if each data item is lengthy but the sort key is short. Of course, storing the data in a linked list allows inexpensive data moves for any algorithm.

Bubble (Exchange) Sort

The next sorting algorithm is one that you may have seen already. That is precisely why we want to include it for analysis later, because it is not a particularly good algorithm. The **bubble sort**, or **exchange sort**, compares adjacent elements and exchanges them if they are out of order. This sort usually requires several passes over the data. During the first pass, you compare the first two elements in the array. If they are out of order, you exchange them. You then compare the elements in the next pair—that is, in positions 2 and 3 of the array. If they are out of order, you exchange them. You proceed, comparing and exchanging elements two at a time until you reach the end of the array.

Figure 7-3a illustrates the first pass of a bubble sort of an array of five integers. You compare the elements in the first pair—29 and 10—and exchange them because they are out of order. Next you consider the sec-

Figure 7-3

The first two passes of a bubble sort of an array of five integers: (a) pass 1; (b) pass 2

	(a) Pass 1					(b) Pass 2				
Initial array:	29	10	14	37	13	10	14	29	13	**37**
	10	29	14	37	13	10	14	29	13	**37**
	10	14	29	37	13	10	14	29	13	**37**
	10	14	29	37	13	10	14	13	**29**	**37**
	10	14	29	13	**37**					

ond pair—29 and 14—and exchange these elements because they are out of order. The elements in the third pair—29 and 37—are in order, and so you do not exchange them. Finally, you exchange the elements in the last pair—37 and 13.

When you order successive pairs of elements, the largest element bubbles to the top (end) of the array

Although the array is not sorted after the first pass, the largest element has "bubbled" to its proper position at the end of the array. During the second pass of the bubble sort, you return to the beginning of the array and consider pairs of elements in exactly the same manner as the first pass. You do not, however, include the last—and largest—element of the array. That is, the second pass considers the first $N - 1$ elements of the array. After the second pass, the second largest element in the array will be in its proper place in the next-to-last position of the array, as Figure 7-3b illustrates. Now, ignoring the last two elements, which are in order, you continue with subsequent passes until the array is sorted.

Bubble sort usually requires several passes through the array

Notice that although a bubble sort requires at most $N - 1$ passes to sort the array, it is possible that fewer passes will be necessary to sort a particular array. Thus, you could terminate the process if no exchanges occur during any pass. The following Pascal procedure `BubbleSort` uses a boolean variable to signal when an exchange occurs during a particular pass. The procedure uses the previous `Swap` procedure.

```
procedure BubbleSort(var A : arrayType; N : integer);
{ ---------------------------------------------------------
  Sorts the elements of an array into ascending order.
  Precondition:  A[1..N] is an array of N elements.
  Postcondition: The array A is sorted into ascending order;
  N is unchanged.
  Calls: Swap.
  --------------------------------------------------------- }
var Index, NextIndex, Pass : integer;
    Sorted: boolean;     { false when exchanges occur }
begin
   Pass := 1;
   Sorted := false;

   while (Pass < N) and (not Sorted) do
   { Invariant: A[N+2-Pass..N] is sorted
                      and > A[1..N+1-Pass] }
```

```
    begin
       Sorted := true;                    { assume sorted }
       for Index := 1 to N-Pass do
       begin
          { Invariant: A[1..Index-1] <= A[Index] }
          NextIndex := succ(Index);
          if A[Index] > A[NextIndex]
              then
              begin   { exchange elements }
                 Swap(A[Index], A[NextIndex]);
                 Sorted := false    { signal exchange }
              end   { if }
       end;    { for }

       { Assertion: A[1..N-Pass] < A[N-Pass+1] }
       Pass := succ(Pass)
    end   { while }
end;   { BubbleSort }
```

Analysis. As was noted earlier, the bubble sort requires at most $N - 1$ passes through the array. During pass 1, there are $N - 1$ comparisons and at most $N - 1$ exchanges; during pass 2, there are $N - 2$ comparisons and at most $N - 2$ exchanges. In general, during pass i, there are $N - i$ comparisons and at most $N - i$ exchanges. Therefore, in the worst case, there will be a total of

$$(N-1) + (N-2) + \cdots + 1 = \frac{N * (N-1)}{2}$$

comparisons and the same number of exchanges. Recall that each exchange requires three data moves. Thus, altogether there are

$$2 * N * (N-1) = 2 * N^2 - 2 * N$$

major operations in the worst case. Therefore, the bubble sort algorithm is $O(N^2)$ in the worst case.

Bubble sort. Worst case: ***O(N²)****; best case:* ***O(N)***

The best case occurs when the original data is already sorted: *BubbleSort* uses one pass, during which there are $N - 1$ comparisons and no exchanges. Thus, the bubble sort is $O(N)$ in the best case.

Insertion Sort

Imagine once again arranging a hand of cards, but now you pick up one card at a time and insert it into its proper position; in this case you are performing an **insertion sort**. Chapter 3 introduced the insertion sort algorithm in the context of a linked list; the procedure *BuildSortedList* created a sorted linked list from a file of unsorted integers. You can use the insertion sort strategy to sort items that reside in an array. This version of the insertion sort partitions the array into two regions: sorted and

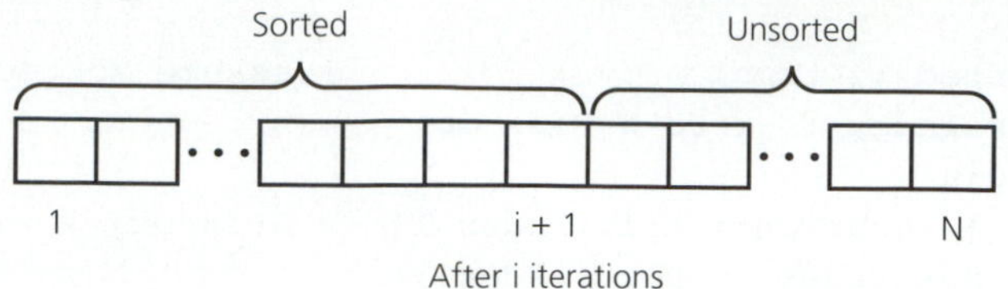

Figure 7-4
An insertion sort partitions the array into two regions

Take each element from the unsorted region and insert it into its correct order in the sorted region

unsorted, as Figure 7-4 depicts. Initially, the entire array is the unsorted region. At each step, the insertion sort takes the first item of the unsorted region and places it into its correct position in the sorted region. However, the first step is trivial: Moving `A[1]` from the unsorted region to the sorted region really does not require moving data. Therefore, you can omit this first step by considering the initial sorted region to be `A[1]` and the initial unsorted region to be `A[2..N]`. Note that an invariant of the algorithm is that the items in the sorted region are sorted among themselves. Because at each step the size of the sorted region grows by 1 and the size of the unsorted region shrinks by 1, the entire array will be sorted when the algorithm terminates.

Figure 7-5 illustrates an insertion sort of an array of five integers. Initially, the sorted region is `A[1]`, which is 29, and the unsorted region is the rest of the array. You take the first element in the unsorted region—the 10—and insert it into its proper position in the sorted region. Notice that insertion into the sorted region requires that you shift array elements to make room for the insertion. You then take the first element in the new unsorted region—the 14—and insert it into its proper position in the sorted region, and so on.

A Pascal procedure that performs an insertion sort on an array of *N* elements follows:

```
procedure InsertionSort(var A : arrayType; N : integer);
{ ---------------------------------------------------------
  Sorts the elements of an array into ascending order.
  Precondition: A[1..N] is an array of N elements. $B- is
  in effect to enable conditional and.
  Postcondition: The array A is sorted into ascending order,
  N is unchanged.
  --------------------------------------------------------- }
var    Unsorted : integer;  { first index of unsorted region }
       Loc : integer;       { index of insertion in sorted
                              region }
       NextItem : dataType; { next item in unsorted region }

{ Initially, sorted region = A[1] and unsorted region =
  A[2..N]. In general, sorted region = A[1..Unsorted-1] and
  unsorted region = A[Unsorted..N] }
begin
    for Unsorted := 2 to N do
    { Invariant: A[1..Unsorted-1] is sorted }
```

Initial array:	**29**	10	14	37	13	copy 10
	29	29	14	37	13	shift 29
	10	**29**	14	37	13	insert 10; copy 14
	10	29	29	37	13	shift 29
	10	**14**	**29**	37	13	insert 14; copy 37, insert 37 on top of itself
	10	**14**	**29**	**37**	13	copy 13
	10	14	14	29	37	shift 14, 29, 37
Sorted array:	**10**	**13**	**14**	**29**	**37**	insert 13

Figure 7-5

An insertion sort of an array of five elements

```
    begin
       { find the proper position (Loc) in A[1..Unsorted]
         for A[Unsorted], which is the first element in the
         unsorted region--shift, if necessary, to make room }
       NextItem := A[Unsorted];
       Loc := Unsorted;
       while (Loc > 1) and (A[Loc-1] > NextItem) do { Cand }
       begin                   { shift A[Loc-1] to the right }
          A[Loc] := A[Loc -1];
          Loc := pred(Loc)
       end;  { while }
       { Assertion: A[Loc] is where NextItem belongs }

       { insert NextItem into sorted region }
       A[Loc] := NextItem
    end  { for }
end;  { InsertionSort }
```

Analysis. The *for* loop in the procedure *InsertionSort* executes $N - 1$ times. Within this loop there is a *while* loop that executes at most *Unsorted* − 1 times for values of *Unsorted* that range from 2 to N. Thus, in the worst case, the algorithm's comparison occurs the following number of times:

$$1 + 2 + \cdots + (N - 1) = \frac{N * (N - 1)}{2}$$

In addition, the algorithm moves data items at most the same number of times. Together, there are

$$N * (N - 1) = N^2 - N$$

major operations in the worst case.

Therefore, the insertion sort algorithm is $O(N^2)$ in the worst case. For small arrays—say, fewer than 50 items—the simplicity of the insertion sort makes it an appropriate choice. For large arrays, however, an insertion sort can be prohibitively inefficient.

Insertion sort is O(N²) in the worst case

Mergesort

Divide and conquer

Two important divide-and-conquer sorting algorithms, mergesort and quicksort, have elegant recursive formulations and are highly efficient. The presentations here are in the context of sorting arrays, but—as you shall see in Chapter 14—mergesort generalizes to external files. It will be convenient to express the algorithms in terms of the array `A[F..L]`.

Halve the array, recursively sort its halves, and then merge the halves

Mergesort is a recursive sorting algorithm that always gives the same performance, regardless of the initial order of the array elements. Suppose that you divide the array into halves, sort each half, and then **merge** the sorted halves into one sorted array, as Figure 7-6 illustrates. In this figure, the halves *1, 4, 8* and *2, 3* are merged to form the array *1, 2, 3, 4,* 8. This merge step compares an element in one half of the array with an element in the other half and moves the smaller element to a temporary array. This process continues until there are no more elements to consider in one half. At that time, you simply move the remaining elements to the temporary array. Finally, you copy the temporary array back into the original array.

Although the merge step of mergesort produces a sorted array, how do you sort the array halves prior to the merge step? Mergesort sorts the array halves by using mergesort—that is, by calling itself recursively. Thus, the pseudocode for mergesort is

```
Mergesort(A, F, L)
{ Sorts A[F..L]. }

   if F < L
      then
      begin
         Mid := (F + L) div 2       { get midpoint }
         Mergesort(A, F, Mid)       { sort A[F..Mid] }
         Mergesort(A, Mid+1, L)     { sort A[Mid+1..L] }
```

Figure 7-6

A mergesort with an auxiliary temporary array

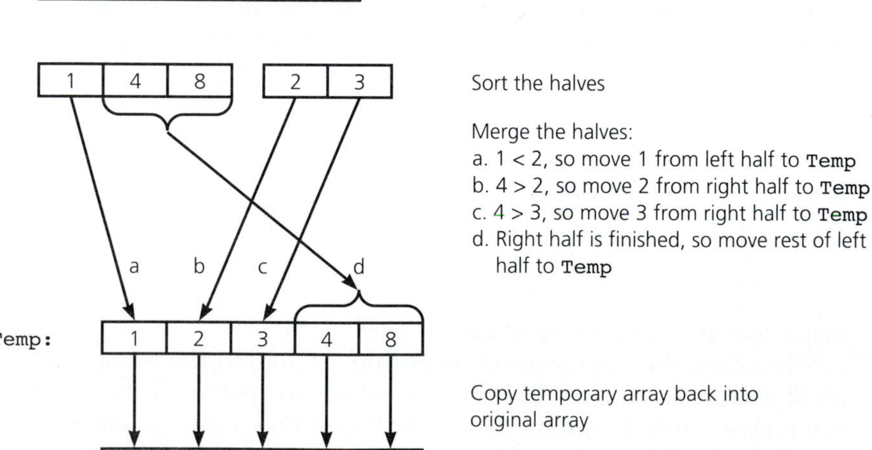
A:
8 1 4 3 2
Divide the array in half
1 4 8 2 3
Sort the halves
Merge the halves:
a. 1 < 2, so move 1 from left half to Temp
b. 4 > 2, so move 2 from right half to Temp
c. 4 > 3, so move 3 from right half to Temp
d. Right half is finished, so move rest of left half to Temp
a b c d
Temp:
1 2 3 4 8
Copy temporary array back into original array
A:
1 2 3 4 8

```
              { merge sorted halves A[F..Mid] and A[Mid+1..L] }
              Merge(A, F, Mid, L)
          end

          else quit
```

Clearly, most of the effort in the mergesort algorithm is in the merge step, but does this algorithm actually sort? The recursive calls continue dividing the array into pieces until each piece contains only one element; obviously an array of one element is sorted. The algorithm then merges these small pieces into larger sorted pieces until one sorted array results. Figure 7-7 illustrates both the recursive calls and the merge steps in a mergesort of an array of six integers.

The following Pascal procedures implement the *Mergesort* algorithm. Note that to sort an array *A[1..N]*, you would invoke *Mergesort* by writing *Mergesort(A, 1, N)*.

```
const  MaxSize = <maximum number of elements in array>;
type   dataType = <type of array element>;
       arrayType = array[1..MaxSize] of dataType;

procedure Merge(var A : arrayType; F, Mid, L : integer);
{ ---------------------------------------------------------
  Merges two sorted array segments A[F..Mid] and A[Mid+1..L]
  into one sorted array.
  Precondition: F <= Mid <= L. The subarrays A[F..Mid] and
  A[Mid+1..L] are each sorted in increasing order.
  Postcondition: A[F..L] is sorted.
  Implementation note: This procedure merges the two
  subarrays into a temporary array, and copies the result
  into the original array A.
  --------------------------------------------------------- }
var    TempArray : arrayType;  { temporary array }
       First1, Last1, First2, Last2, Index : integer;
begin
    { initialize the local indexes to the subarrays }
    First1 := F;            { beginning of first subarray }
    Last1 := Mid;           { end of first subarray }
    First2 := succ(Mid);    { beginning of second subarray }
    Last2 := L;             { end of second subarray }

    { next available location in TempArray }
    Index := First1;

    { while both subarrays are not empty, copy the smaller
      element into the temporary array }
    while ( (First1 <= Last1) and (First2 <= Last2) ) do
    { Invariant: TempArray[First1..Index-1] is in order }
    begin
       if A[First1] < A[First2]
       then
```

Figure 7-7

A mergesort of an array of six integers

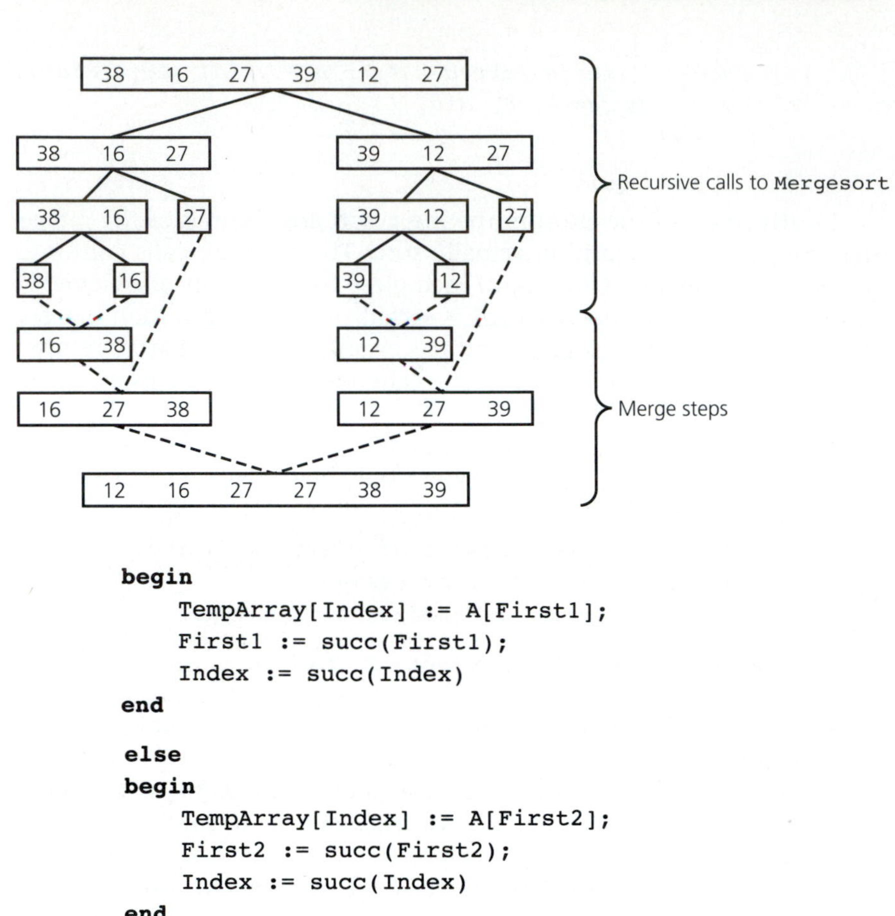


```
      begin
         TempArray[Index] := A[First1];
         First1 := succ(First1);
         Index := succ(Index)
      end

      else
      begin
         TempArray[Index] := A[First2];
         First2 := succ(First2);
         Index := succ(Index)
      end
   end;  { while }

   { finish off the nonempty subarray }

   { finish off the first subarray if necessary }
   while (First1 <= Last1) do
   { Invariant: TempArray[First1..Index-1] is in order }
   begin
      TempArray[Index] := A[First1];
      First1 := succ(First1);
      Index := succ(Index)
   end;  { while }

   { finish off the second subarray if necessary }
   while (First2 <= Last2) do
   { Invariant: TempArray[First1..Index-1] is in order }
   begin
      TempArray[Index] := A[First2];
      First2 := succ(First2);
      Index := succ(Index)
   end;  { while }
```

```
    { copy the result back into the original array }
    for Index := F to L do
       A[Index] := TempArray[Index]
end;  { Merge }

procedure Mergesort(var A : arrayType; F, L : integer);
{ ----------------------------------------------------------
  Sorts an array by using mergesort.
  Mergesort is a recursive algorithm that sorts by:
    1. sorting the first half of the array
    2. sorting the second half of the array
    3. merging the two sorted halves
  Precondition: A[F..L] is an array.
  Postcondition: A[F..L] is sorted in ascending order.
  Calls: Merge.
  ---------------------------------------------------------- }
var Mid : integer;
begin
    if F < L
       then
       begin
          { sort each half }
          Mid := (F + L) div 2;
          Mergesort(A, F, Mid);    { sort left half A[F..Mid]}
          Mergesort(A, Mid+1, L); { sort right half A[Mid+1..L]}

          { merge the two halves }
          Merge(A, F, Mid, L)
       end
end;  { Mergesort }
```

Notice that because each call to the procedure *Mergesort* must alter the array *A*, *A* is passed as a variable parameter. Recall from Chapter 5 that when you use the box method to trace the execution of a recursive procedure, you must represent variable parameters differently than value parameters. You view a variable parameter as external to the boxes instead of as part of the local environment of each recursive call. Within each box that corresponds to a call's local environment, you associate the name of the formal parameter with the actual parameter, as Figure 5-17 of Chapter 5 illustrates. References to the formal parameter from within different recursive calls to the subprogram lead to the same actual parameter.

*Pass the array **A** as a variable parameter*

Analysis. Because the merge step of the algorithm requires the most effort, we begin the analysis there. Each merge step merges *A[F..Mid]* and *A[Mid+1..L]*. Figure 7-8 provides an example of a merge step that requires the maximum number of comparisons. If the total number of elements in the two array segments to be merged is *N*, then merging the

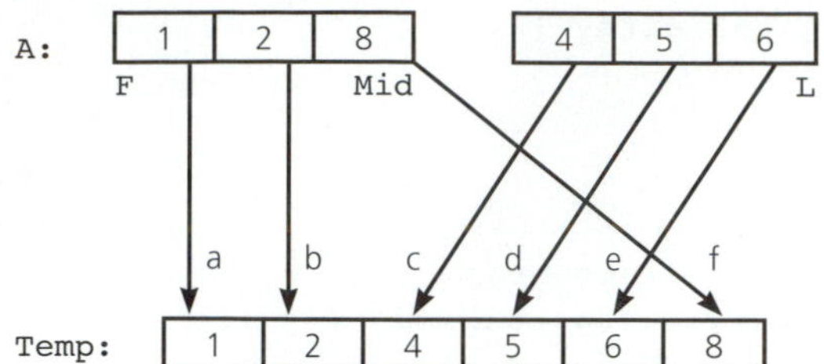

Merge the halves:

a. 1 < 4, so move 1 from `A[F..Mid]` to `Temp`
b. 2 < 4, so move 2 from `A[F..Mid]` to `Temp`
c. 8 > 4, so move 4 from `A[Mid+1..L]` to `Temp`
d. 8 > 5, so move 5 from `A[Mid+1..L]` to `Temp`
e. 8 > 6, so move 6 from `A[Mid+1..L]` to `Temp`
f. `A[Mid+1..L]` is finished, so move 8 to `Temp`

Figure 7-8

A worst-case instance of the merge step in *Mergesort*

segments requires at most $N - 1$ comparisons. (For example, in Figure 7-8 there are six elements in the segments and five comparisons.) In addition, there are N moves from the original array to the temporary array, and N moves from the temporary array back to the original array. Thus, there are $3 * N - 1$ major operations in each merge step.

Each call to *Mergesort* recursively calls itself twice. As Figure 7-9 illustrates, if the original call to *Mergesort* is at level 0, then there are two calls to *Mergesort* at level 1 of the recursion. Each of these calls then calls *Mergesort* twice, so there are four calls to *Mergesort* at level 2 of the recursion, and so on. How many levels of recursion are there?

Each call to *Mergesort* halves the array. After halving the array the first time, there are two pieces. The next recursive calls to *Mergesort* halve each of these two pieces to produce four pieces of the original array; the next recursive calls halve each of these four pieces to produce eight pieces, and so on. The recursive calls continue until the array pieces each contain one element—that is, until there are N pieces, where N is the number of elements in the original array. If N is a power of 2 ($N = 2^k$), then the recursion goes $k = \log_2 N$ levels deep. For example, in Figure 7-9 there are eight elements in the original array. Because $8 = 2^3$, there are three levels of recursive calls to *Mergesort*. If N is not a power of 2, then there are $1 + \log_2 N$ (rounded down) calls to *Mergesort*.

The original call to *Mergesort* (at level 0) calls *Merge* once. *Merge* merges all N elements and requires $3 * N - 1$ operations, as was shown earlier. At level 1 of the recursion, there are two calls to *Mergesort*, and hence to *Merge*. Each of these two calls to *Merge* merges $N/2$ elements and requires $3 * (N/2) - 1$ operations. Together these two calls to *Merge* require $2 * (3 * (N/2) - 1)$, or $3 * N - 2$ operations. At level m of the recursion there are 2^m calls to *Merge*; each of these calls merges $N/2^m$ elements and so requires $3 * (N/2^m) - 1$ operations. Together the 2^m calls to *Merge* require $3 * N - 2^m$ operations. Thus, there are $O(N)$ operations at each level of the recursion. Because there are either $\log_2 N$ or $1 + \log_2 N$ levels, *Mergesort* is $O(N * \log_2 N)$ in both the worst and average cases. You should look at Figure 7-1 again to convince yourself that $O(N * \log_2 N)$ is significantly faster than $O(N^2)$.

***Mergesort* is $O(N * \log_2 N)$**

Although *Mergesort* is an extremely efficient algorithm with respect to time, it does have one drawback: To perform the step

```
Merge sorted halves A[F..Mid] and A[Mid+1..L]
```

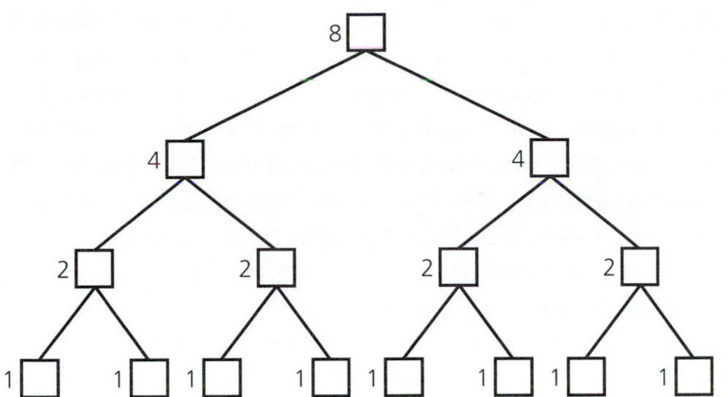

Figure 7-9

Levels of recursive calls to `Mergesort`, given an array of eight elements

the algorithm requires an auxiliary array whose size equals the size of the original array. In situations where storage is limited, this requirement might not be acceptable.

Quicksort

Another divide-and-conquer algorithm

Consider the first two steps of the solution to the problem of finding the kth smallest element of the array `A[F..L]` that was discussed in Chapter 5:

```
Choose a pivot element p from A[F..L]
Partition the elements of A[F..L] about p
```

Quicksort partitions an array into elements that are < the pivot and those that are ≥ the pivot

Recall that this partition, which is pictured again in Figure 7-10, has the property that all elements in S_1 = `A[F..PivotIndex-1]` are less than the pivot `p`, and all elements in S_2 = `A[PivotIndex+1..L]` are greater than or equal to `p`. Though this property does not imply that the array is sorted, it does imply an extremely useful fact: The elements in positions `F` through `PivotIndex - 1` remain in positions `F` through `PivotIndex - 1` when the array is properly sorted, although their positions relative to one another may change. Similarly, the elements in positions `PivotIndex + 1` through `L` will remain in positions `PivotIndex + 1` through `L` when the array is sorted, although their relative positions may change. Finally, the pivot element remains in its position in the final, sorted array.

Partitioning places the pivot in its correct position within the array

The partition induces relationships between the array elements that are the ingredients of a recursive solution. Arranging the array elements

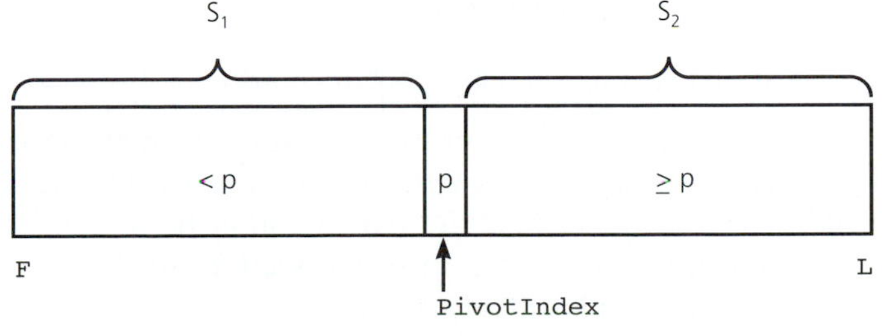

Figure 7-10

A partition about a pivot

around the pivot *p* generates two smaller sorting problems—sort the left section of the array (S_1), and sort the right section of the array (S_2). The relationships between the array elements imply that once you solve the left and right sorting problems, you will have solved the original sorting problem. That is, partitioning the array before the recursive calls places the pivot in its correct position and ensures that when the smaller array segments are sorted, their elements will be in the proper relation to the rest of the array. Notice that you are assured that the left and right sorting problems are indeed smaller problems and are each closer than the original sorting problem to the degenerate case—which is an array containing one element—because the pivot is not part of either S_1 or S_2. Thus, the quicksort algorithm will eventually terminate.

The pseudocode for quicksort follows:

```
Quicksort(A, F, L)
{ Sorts A[F..L]. }

   if F < L
      then
      begin
          Choose a pivot element p from A[F..L]
          Partition the elements of A[F..L] about p
          { the partition is A[F..PivotIndex..L] }

          Quicksort(A, F, PivotIndex-1)       { sort S1 }
          Quicksort(A, PivotIndex+1, L)       { sort S2 }
      end
   { if F >= L, there is nothing to do }
```

It is worth contrasting `Quicksort` with the pseudocode function given for the kth smallest integer problem in Chapter 5:

```
function KSmall(k, A, F, L) : returns a value from the array

   Choose a pivot element p from A[F..L]
   Partition the elements of A[F..L] about p

   if k < PivotIndex - F + 1 then
      KSmall := KSmall(k, A, F, PivotIndex-1)
   else if k = PivotIndex - F + 1 then
      KSmall := p
   else KSmall :=
             KSmall(k-(PivotIndex-F+1), A, PivotIndex+1, L)
```

There are two fundamental differences between `KSmall` and `Quicksort`:

Differences between `KSmall` and `Quicksort`

- `KSmall` is called recursively only on the section of the array that contains the desired element, and it is not called at all if the desired element is the pivot. On the other hand, `Quicksort` is called recursively on both unsorted sections of the array. Figure 7-11 illustrates this difference.

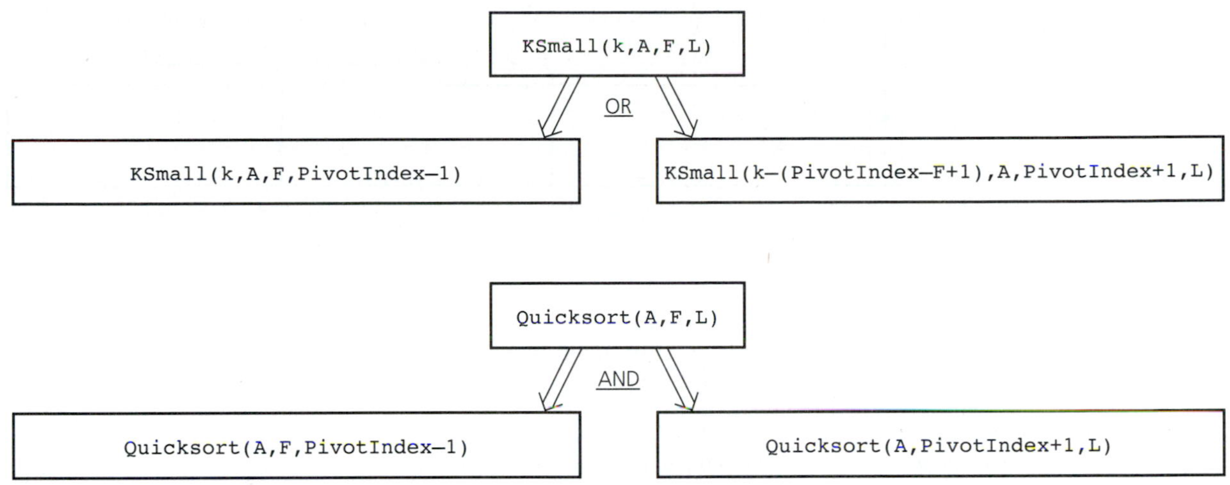

Figure 7-11

`KSmall` versus **`Quicksort`**

- `KSmall` is a function that does not alter the array it is passed—it simply returns a value—whereas `Quicksort` is a procedure that does alter the array it is passed.

Using an invariant to develop a partition procedure. Now consider the partition procedure that both `KSmall` and `Quicksort` require. Partitioning an array section about a pivot element is actually the most difficult part of these two problems.

The partition procedure will receive an array segment `A[F..L]` as a parameter. The procedure must arrange the elements of the array segment into two regions: S_1, the set of elements less than the pivot, and S_2, the set of elements greater than or equal to the pivot. The procedure arranges the array so that S_1 is `A[F..PivotIndex–1]` and S_2 is `A[PivotIndex+1..L]`, as you saw in Figure 7-10.

What pivot should you use? If the elements in the array are arranged randomly, you can choose a pivot randomly. For example, you can choose `A[F]` as the pivot. (We will say more about the choice of pivot later.) While you are developing the partition, it is convenient to retain the pivot in the `A[F]` position.

It is also useful to impose another region, called the unknown region, on the array. Thus, you should view the array as shown in Figure 7-12. The array indexes `F`, `LastS1`, `FirstUnknown`, and `L` divide the array as was just described. Throughout the entire partitioning process, the following is true:

Invariant

> *The elements in the region S_1 are all less than the pivot, and those in S_2 are all greater than or equal to the pivot.*

This statement is the invariant for the partitioning algorithm. The relationship between the elements in the unknown region—which is `A[FirstUnknown..L]`—and the pivot is, simply, unknown!

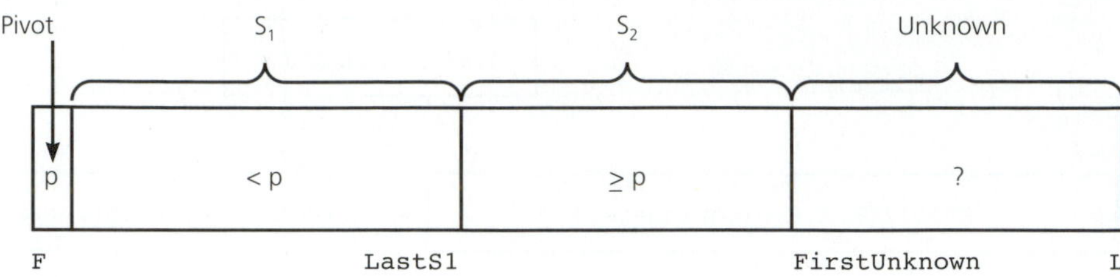

Figure 7-12

Invariant for the partition algorithm

For the invariant to be true at the start of the procedure, the array's indexes must be initialized as follows so that the unknown region spans all of the array segment to be partitioned except the pivot:

Initially, all elements except the pivot `A[F]` constitute the unknown region

```
LastS1 := F
FirstUnknown := succ(F)
```

Figure 7-13 shows the initial status of the array.

At each step of the partition procedure, you examine one element of the unknown region, determine in which of the two regions S_1 or S_2 it belongs, and place it there. Thus, the size of the unknown region decreases by 1 at each step. The procedure terminates when the size of the unknown region reaches 0—that is, when `FirstUnknown > L`.

The following pseudocode describes the partitioning algorithm:

The partitioning algorithm

```
Partition(A, F, L, PivotIndex)
{ Partition A[F..L] }

   { choose the pivot, p, initialize S1 and S2
     to empty and unknown to A[F+1..L] }
   p := A[F]
   LastS1 := F
   FirstUnknown := succ(F)

   while (FirstUnknown <= L) do
   begin
      { consider the placement of the "leftmost"
          element in the unknown region }
      if A[FirstUnknown] < p
        then Move A[FirstUnknown] into S1
        else Move A[FirstUnknown] into S2
   end

   { place pivot in proper position between S1 and S2 and
       mark its new location }
   Swap A[F] with A[LastS1]
   PivotIndex := LastS1
```

The algorithm is straightforward enough, but its move operations need clarification. Consider the two possible actions that you need to take at each iteration of the `while` loop:

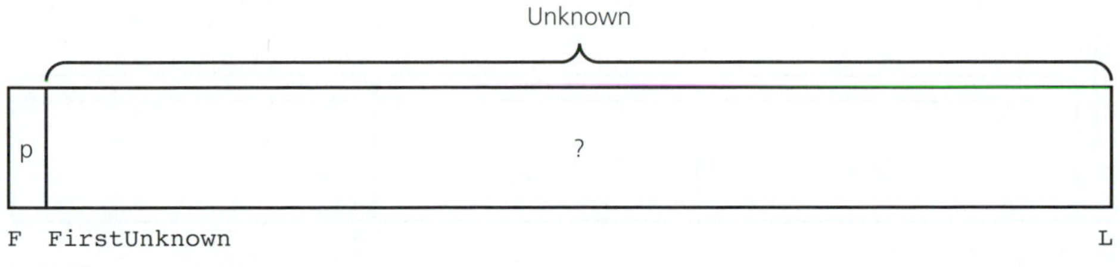

Figure 7-13

Initial state of the array

Move `A[FirstUnknown]` into S_1. S_1 and the unknown region are, in general, not adjacent: S_2 is between the two regions. However, if you swap `A[FirstUnknown]` with the first element of S_2—which is `A[LastS1 + 1]`, as Figure 7-14 illustrates—and then increment `LastS1` by 1, the element that was in `A[FirstUnknown]` will be at the rightmost position of S_1. Now, what about the element of S_2 that was moved to `A[FirstUnknown]`? If you increment `FirstUnknown` by 1, then that element becomes the rightmost member of S_2. Thus, you should execute the following statements to move `A[FirstUnknown]` into S_1:

```
Swap A[FirstUnknown] with A[LastS1+1]
LastS1 := succ(LastS1)
FirstUnknown := succ(FirstUnknown)
```

This strategy works even when S_2 is empty. In this case, after `LastS1` is incremented, it will equal `FirstUnknown`, and thus the swap simply exchanges an element with itself. *Note that this move preserves the invariant.*

Figure 7-14

Moving `A[FirstUnknown]` into S_1 by swapping it with `A[LastS1+1]` and by incrementing both `LastS1` and `FirstUnknown`

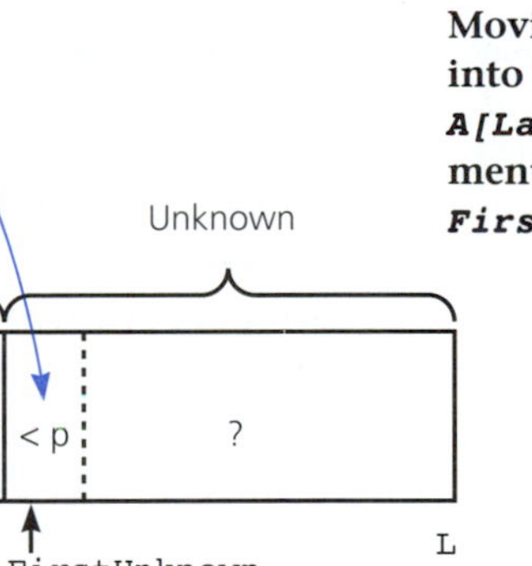

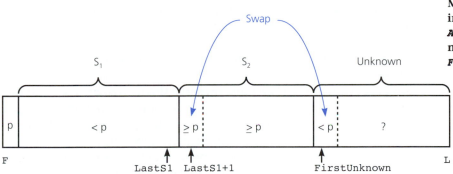

Move `A[FirstUnknown]` into S_2. This move is simple. Recall that the rightmost boundary of the region S_2 is at position `FirstUnknown - 1`; that is, regions S_2 and the unknown region are adjacent, as Figure 7-15 illustrates. Thus, to move `A[FirstUnknown]` into S_2, simply increment `FirstUnknown` by 1: S_2 expands to the right. *Note that this move preserves the invariant.*

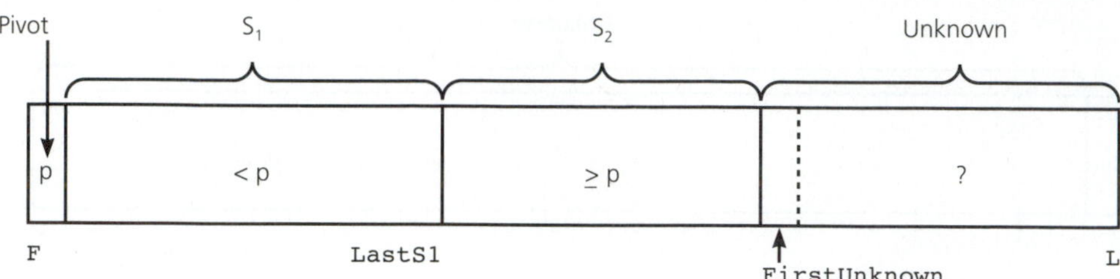

Figure 7-15

Moving `A[FirstUnknown]` into S_2 by incrementing `FirstUnknown`

After all elements have been moved from the unknown region into S_1 and S_2, there is one final task to perform. You must place the pivot between the segments S_1 and S_2. Observe that `A[LastS1]` is the rightmost element in S_1. If you interchange this element with the pivot, which is `A[F]`, you will place the pivot in its correct location. Then the statement

```
PivotIndex := LastS1
```

allows the procedure to return the location of the pivot. Note that you can use this index to determine the boundaries of S_1 and S_2. Figure 7-16 shows a partition of an array of six integers when the pivot is the first element.

Before continuing the implementation of `Quicksort`, note that you can establish the correctness of the partition algorithm by using invariants. Again, the loop invariant for the partition procedure is

> *All elements in S_1 (`A[F+1..LastS1]`) are less than the pivot, and all elements in S_2 (`A[LastS1+1..L]`) are greater than or equal to the pivot.*

Recall that when you use invariants to establish the correctness of an iterative algorithm, a four-step process is required:

The proof that the partitioning algorithm is correct uses an invariant and requires four steps

1. **The invariant must be true initially**, before the loop begins execution. In the partition algorithm, before the loop that swaps array elements is entered, the pivot is `A[F]`, the unknown region is `A[F+1..L]`, and S_1 and S_2 are empty. The invariant is clearly true initially.
2. **An execution of the loop must preserve the invariant.** That is, if the invariant is true before any given iteration of the loop, then you must show that it is true after the iteration. In the partition algorithm, at each iteration of the loop a single element moves from the unknown region into either S_1 or S_2, depending on whether or not the element is less than the pivot. Thus, if the invariant was true before the move, it will remain true after the move.
3. **The invariant must capture the correctness of the algorithm.** That is, you must show that if the invariant is true when the loop terminates, the algorithm is correct. In the partition algorithm, the termination condition is that the unknown region is empty. But if the unknown region is empty, each element of `A[F+1..L]` must be in either S_1 or S_2—in which case the invariant implies that the partition algorithm has done what it was supposed to do.
4. **The loop must terminate.** That is, you must show that the loop will

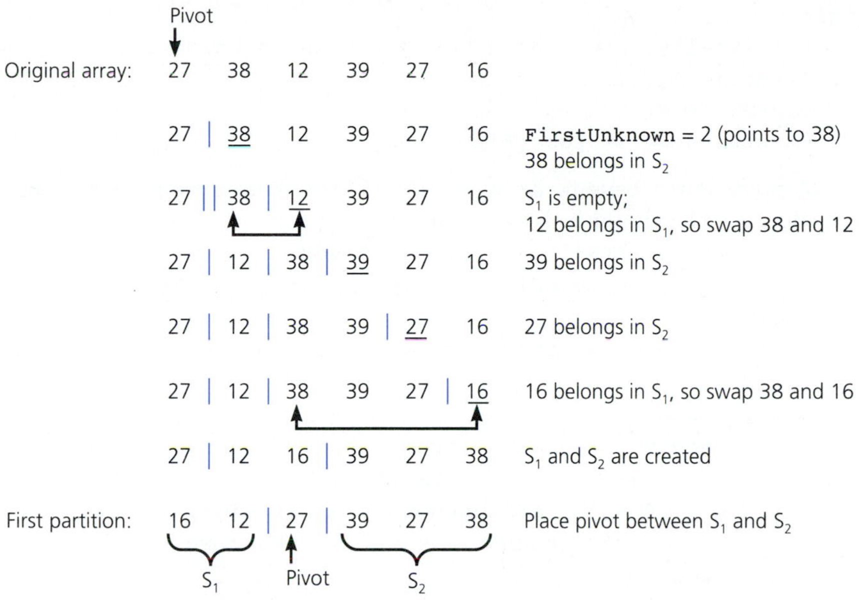

	Pivot						
Original array:	27	38	12	39	27	16	
	27 |	<u>38</u>	12	39	27	16	FirstUnknown = 2 (points to 38) 38 belongs in S_2
	27 ||	38 |	<u>12</u>	39	27	16	S_1 is empty; 12 belongs in S_1, so swap 38 and 12
	27 |	12 |	38 |	<u>39</u>	27	16	39 belongs in S_2
	27 |	12 |	38	39 |	<u>27</u>	16	27 belongs in S_2
	27 |	12 |	38	39	27 |	<u>16</u>	16 belongs in S_1, so swap 38 and 16
	27 |	12	16 |	39	27	38	S_1 and S_2 are created
First partition:	16	12 |	27 |	39	27	38	Place pivot between S_1 and S_2
	S_1		Pivot		S_2		

Figure 7-16

The first partition of an array when the pivot is the first element

terminate after a finite number of iterations. In the partition algorithm, the size of the unknown region decreases by 1 at each iteration. Therefore, the unknown region becomes empty after a finite number of iterations, and thus the termination condition for the loop will be met.

The following Pascal procedures implement the quicksort algorithm. Note that the required procedure *Swap* is the same one that *SelectionSort* uses. To sort an array *A[1..N]*, you invoke *Quicksort* by writing *Quicksort(A, 1, N)*.

```
const  MaxSize = <maximum number of elements in array>;
type   dataType = <type of array element>;
       arrayType = array[1..MaxSize] of dataType;

procedure Partition(var A : arrayType ; F, L : integer;
                    var PivotIndex : integer);
{ ---------------------------------------------------------
  Partitions A[F..L] for quicksort.
  Precondition: F <= L; assumes pivot is A[F].
  Postcondition: Partitions A[F..L] such that:
     S1 = A[F..PivotIndex-1] <  Pivot
          A[PivotIndex]       =  Pivot
     S2 = A[PivotIndex+1..L] >= Pivot
  Calls: Swap.
  --------------------------------------------------------- }
var    FirstUnknown : integer;
       LastS1 : integer;
       Pivot : dataType;
```

```
begin
    { initially, everything but pivot is in unknown }
    Pivot := A[F];
    LastS1 := F;
    FirstUnknown := succ(F);

    { move one element at a time until unknown region is empty }
    while (FirstUnknown <= L) do
    { Invariant: A[F+1..LastS1] <  Pivot
                 A[LastS1+1..FirstUnknown-1] >= Pivot }
    begin
       { move element from unknown to proper region }
       if A[FirstUnknown] < Pivot
           then
           begin   { element from unknown belongs in S1 }
               LastS1 := succ(LastS1);
               Swap(A[FirstUnknown], A[LastS1]);
               FirstUnknown := succ(FirstUnknown)
           end

           { else element from unknown belongs in S2 }
           else FirstUnknown := succ(FirstUnknown)
    end; { while }

    { place pivot in proper position and mark its location }
    Swap(A[F], A[LastS1]);
    PivotIndex := LastS1
end;  { Partition }

procedure Quicksort(var A : arrayType; F, L : integer);
{ ----------------------------------------------------------
  Sorts an array by using quicksort.
  Precondition: A[F..L] is an array.
  Postcondition: A[F..L] is sorted.
  Calls: Partition.
  ---------------------------------------------------------- }
var PivotIndex : integer;
begin
   if F < L
     then
     begin
       { create the partition: S1, Pivot, S2 }
       Partition(A, F, L, PivotIndex);

       { sort regions S1 and S2 }
       Quicksort(A, F, PivotIndex-1);
       Quicksort(A, PivotIndex+1, L)
     end
end;  { Quicksort }
```

As was true with *Mergesort*, each call to the procedure *Quicksort* must alter the array *A*, so *A* is passed as a variable parameter.

Pass the array A as a variable parameter

You can use an element other than *A[F]* as the pivot: Simply interchange your pivot with *A[F]* and then use the previously described partition algorithm. In the analysis to follow, you will learn that it is desirable to avoid a pivot that makes either S_1 or S_2 empty. A good choice of pivot is one that is near the median of the array elements. Exercise 12 at the end of this chapter considers this choice of pivot.

Place your choice of pivot in A[F] before partitioning

Quicksort and *Mergesort* are similar in spirit, but whereas *Quicksort* does work before its recursive calls, *Mergesort* does work after its recursive calls. That is, while *Quicksort* has the form

```
Quicksort(A, F, L)

   if F < L
     then
     begin
       Prepare array for recursive calls
       Quicksort(S1 region of A)
       Quicksort(S2 region of A)
     end

     else quit
```

Mergesort has the general form

```
Mergesort(A, F, L)

   if F < L
     then
     begin
       Mergesort( Left half of A )
       Mergesort( Right half of A )
       Tidy up array after the recursive calls
     end

     else quit
```

The preparation in *Quicksort* is to partition the array into regions S_1 and S_2. The algorithm then sorts S_1 and S_2 independently, because every element in S_1 belongs to the left of every element in S_2. In *Mergesort*, on the other hand, no work is done before the recursive calls: The algorithm sorts each half of the array with respect to itself. However, the algorithm still must deal with the interaction between the elements of the two halves. That is, the algorithm merges the two halves of the array after the recursive calls.

Analysis. The major effort in the *Quicksort* procedure occurs during the partitioning step. As you consider each element in the unknown region, you compare *A[FirstUnknown]* with the pivot and move *A[FirstUnknown]* into either S_1 or S_2. It is possible for one of S_1 or S_2 to remain empty. For example, if the pivot is the smallest element in the array segment, then S_1 will remain empty. This occurrence is the worst case because S_2 decreases in size by only 1 at each recursive call to `Quicksort`. Thus, the maximum number of recursive calls to `Quicksort` will occur.

`Quicksort` is slow when the array is already sorted

Notice what happens when the array is already sorted into ascending order. Figure 7-17 shows the results of the first call to `Partition` for a sorted array. The pivot is the smallest element in the array, and S_1 remains empty. `Partition` requires $N - 1$ comparisons to partition the N elements in this array. On the next recursive call to `Quicksort`, `Partition` is passed $N - 1$ elements, so it will require $N - 2$ comparisons to partition them. Again S_1 will remain empty. Because the array segment that `Quicksort` considers at each level of recursion decreases in size by only 1, $N - 1$ levels of recursion are required. Therefore, `Quicksort` requires

$$1 + 2 + \cdots + (N - 1) = \frac{N * (N - 1)}{2}$$

comparisons. However, recall that a move into S_2 does not require an exchange of array elements; it requires only a change in the index `FirstUnknown`.

Similarly if S_2 remains empty at each recursive call, $N * (N - 1) / 2$ comparisons are required. In addition, however, an exchange is necessary to move each unknown element to S_1. Thus, $N * (N - 1) / 2$ exchanges are necessary. (Again, each exchange requires three data moves.) Thus, you can conclude that `Quicksort` is $O(N^2)$ in the worst case.

In contrast, Figure 7-18 shows an example in which S_1 and S_2 contain the same—or in general, nearly the same—number of elements. In this average case, assuming random arrangements of array items, fewer recursive calls to `Quicksort` occur. As you did in the previous analysis of `Mergesort`, you can conclude that there are either $\log_2 N$ or $1 + \log_2 N$ calls to `Quicksort`. Each call to `Quicksort` involves m comparisons and at most m exchanges, where m is the number of elements in the subarray to be sorted. Clearly $m \leq N - 1$.

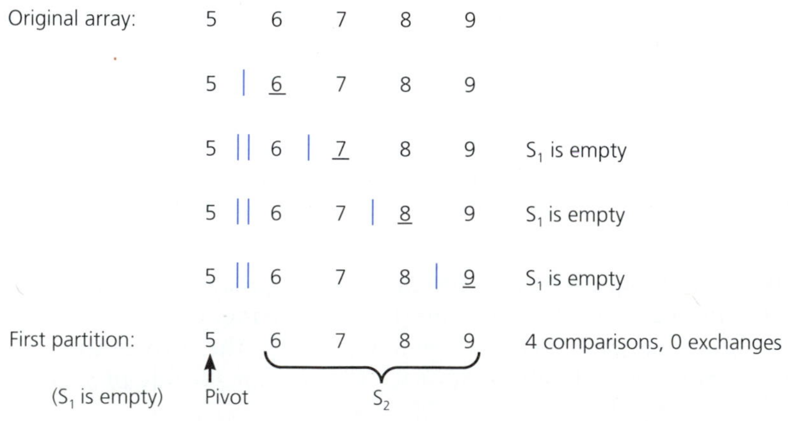

Figure 7-17

A worst-case partitioning with `Quicksort`

Original array:	5 6 7 8 9	
	5 | 6 7 8 9	
	5 || 6 | 7 8 9	S_1 is empty
	5 || 6 7 | 8 9	S_1 is empty
	5 || 6 7 8 | 9	S_1 is empty
First partition:	5 6 7 8 9	4 comparisons, 0 exchanges
(S_1 is empty)	Pivot (5); S_2 (6 7 8 9)	

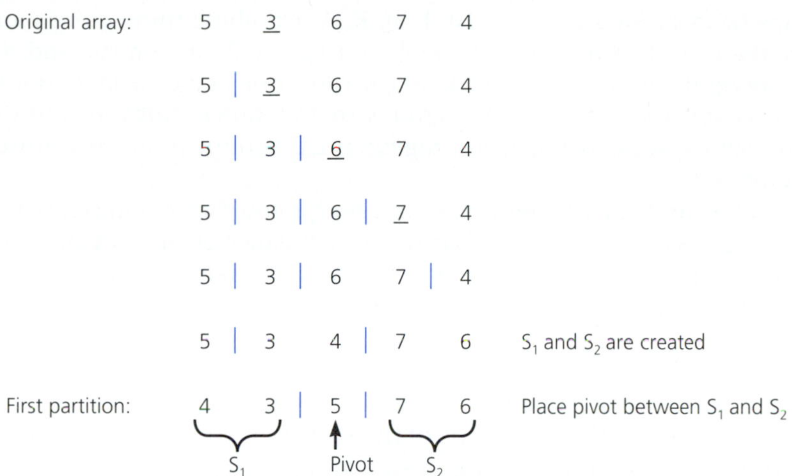

Figure 7-18

An average-case partitioning with `Quicksort`

`Quicksort`. Worst case: $O(N^2)$; average case: $O(N * \log_2 N)$

A formal analysis of `Quicksort`'s average-case behavior would show that it is $O(N * \log_2 N)$. Thus, on large arrays you can expect `Quicksort` to run significantly faster than `InsertionSort`, although in its worst case `Quicksort` will require roughly the same amount of time as an insertion sort.

It might then seem surprising that `Quicksort` is often used to sort large arrays. The reason for `Quicksort`'s popularity is that it is usually extremely fast in practice, despite its unimpressive theoretical worst-case behavior. Although a worst-case situation is not typical, even if the worst case occurs, `Quicksort`'s performance is acceptable for moderately large arrays.

The fact that `Quicksort`'s average-case behavior is far better than its worst-case behavior distinguishes it from the other sorting algorithms considered in this chapter. If the original arrangement of data in the array is "random," `Quicksort` performs at least as well as any known sorting algorithm that involves comparisons. Unless the array is already ordered, `Quicksort` is best.

`Mergesort`'s efficiency is somewhere between the possibilities for `Quicksort`: Sometimes `Quicksort` is faster, and sometimes `Mergesort` is faster. While the worst-case behavior of `Mergesort` is of the same order of magnitude as `Quicksort`'s average-case behavior, in most situations `Quicksort` will run somewhat faster than `Mergesort`. However, in its worst case `Quicksort` will be significantly slower than `Mergesort`.

Radix Sort

The final sorting algorithm in this chapter is quite different from the others. It is for this reason that we include it here.

Imagine one last time you are sorting a hand of cards. This time you pick up the cards one at a time and arrange them by rank into 13 possible groups in this order: 2, 3, ··· , 10, J, Q, K, A. Combine these groups and place the cards face down on the table so that the 2's are on top and the aces are on the bottom. Now pick up the cards one at a time and arrange them by suit into four possible groups in this order: clubs, diamonds, hearts, and spades. When taken together, the groups result in a sorted hand of cards.

A **radix sort** uses this idea of forming groups and then combining them to sort a collection of data. The sort treats each data element as a character string. As a first simple example of a radix sort, consider this collection of three-letter strings:

```
ABC, XYZ, BWZ, AAC, RLT, JBX, RDT, KLT, AEO, TLJ
```

The sort begins by organizing the data according to their rightmost (least significant) letters. Although none of the strings end in A or B, two strings end in C. Place those two strings into a group. Continuing through the alphabet, you will form the following groups:

Group strings by rightmost letter

```
(ABC, AAC) (TLJ) (AEO) (RLT, RDT, KLT) (JBX) (XYZ, BWZ)
```

The strings in each group end with the same letter, and the groups are ordered by that letter. The strings within each group retain their relative order from the original list of strings.

Now combine the groups into one as follows. Take the elements in the first group in their present order, follow them with the elements in the second group in their present order, and so on. The following group results:

Combine groups

```
ABC, AAC, TLJ, AEO, RLT, RDT, KLT, JBX, XYZ, BWZ
```

Next, form new groups as you did before, but this time use the middle letter of each string instead of the last letter:

Group strings by middle letter

```
(AAC) (ABC, JBX) (RDT) (AEO) (TLJ, RLT, KLT) (BWZ) (XYZ)
```

Now the strings in each group have the same middle letter, and the groups are ordered by that letter. As before, the strings within each group retain their relative order from the previous group of all strings.

Combine these groups into one group, again preserving the relative order of the elements within each group:

Combine groups

```
AAC, ABC, JBX, RDT, AEO, TLJ, RLT, KLT, BWZ, XYZ
```

Now form new groups according to the first letter of each string:

Group strings by first letter

```
(AAC, ABC, AEO) (BWZ) (JBX) (KLT) (RDT, RLT) (TLJ) (XYZ)
```

Finally, combine the groups into the final sorted collection of data, again maintaining the relative order within each group:

Sorted strings

```
AAC, ABC, AEO, BWZ, JBX, KLT, RDT, RLT, TLJ, XYZ
```

The strings are now in sorted order.

In the previous example, all character strings had the same length. If the character strings have varying lengths, you can treat them as if they were the same length by padding them on the right with blanks as necessary.

To sort numeric data, the radix sort treats a number as a character string. You can treat numbers as if they were padded on the left with zeros, making them all appear to be the same length. You then form groups according to the rightmost digits, combine the groups, form groups according to the next-to-last digits, combine them, and so on, just as you did in the previous example. Figure 7-19 shows a radix sort of eight integers.

The following pseudocode describes the algorithm for a radix sort of *N* decimal integers of *d* digits each:

```
RadixSort(A, N, d)
{ Sorts N d-digit integers in the array A. }

   for j := d downto 1 do
   begin
      Initialize 10 groups to empty
      Initialize a counter for each group to 0

      for i := 1 to N do
      begin
         k := jth digit of A[i]
         Place A[i] at the end of group k
         Increase kth counter by 1
      end  { end for i }

      Replace the elements in A with all the elements in
         group 1, followed by all the elements in group 2,
         and so on.
   end { for j }
```

Analysis. From the pseudocode for the radix sort, you can see that this algorithm requires *N* moves each time it forms groups and *N* moves to

0123, 2154, 0222, 0004, 0283, 1560, 1061, 2150	Original array
(156**0**, 215**0**) (106**1**) (022**2**) (012**3**, 028**3**) (215**4**, 000**4**)	Grouped by fourth digit
1560, 2150, 1061, 0222, 0123, 0283, 2154, 0004	Combined
(00**0**4) (02**2**2, 01**2**3) (21**5**0, 21**5**4) (15**6**0, 10**6**1) (02**8**3)	Grouped by third digit
0004, 0222, 0123, 2150, 2154, 1560, 1061, 0283	Combined
(0**0**04, 1**0**61) (0**1**23, 2**1**50, 2**1**54) (0**2**22, 0**2**83) (1**5**60)	Grouped by second digit
0004, 1061, 0123, 2150, 2154, 0222, 0283, 1560	Combined
(**0**004, **0**123, **0**222, **0**283) (**1**061, **1**560) (**2**150, **2**154)	Grouped by first digit
0004, 0123, 0222, 0283, 1061, 1560, 2150, 2154	Combined (sorted)

Figure 7-19

A radix sort of eight integers

combine them again into one group. The algorithm performs these $2 * N$ moves d times. Therefore, the radix sort requires $2 * N * d$ moves to sort N strings of d characters each. However, notice that no comparisons are necessary. Thus, radix sort is $O(N)$.

Even though radix sort is O(N), it is not appropriate as a general-purpose sorting algorithm

Despite its efficiency, radix sort has some difficulties that make it inappropriate as a general-purpose sorting algorithm. For example, to perform a radix sort of strings of uppercase letters, you need to accommodate 27 groups—one group for blanks and one for each letter. If there are N strings in the original data collection, each group must be able to contain N strings. For large N this requirement demands substantial memory, if you use arrays for both the original data and the resulting groups. However, you can save memory by using a linked list for each of the 27 groups. Thus, a radix sort is more appropriate for a linked list than for an array.

A Comparison of Sorting Algorithms

Figure 7-20 summarizes the worst-case and average-case orders of magnitude for the sorting algorithms that appear in this chapter. For reference purposes, we have included another algorithm—**heapsort**—here, even though you will not see it until Chapter 12.

SUMMARY

1. **Order-of-magnitude analysis and Big O notation enable you to analyze the efficiency of an algorithm without regard for such factors as computer speed and programming skill that are beyond your control. When you compare the inherent efficiencies of algorithms, you typically concentrate only on significant differences in their growth-rate functions.**
2. **Worst-case analysis considers the maximum amount of work an algorithm will require on a problem of a given size, while average-case analysis considers the expected amount of work that it will require.**
3. **Quicksort and mergesort are two very efficient recursive sorting algorithms. In the "average" case, quicksort is among the fastest**

Figure 7-20

Approximate growth rates with respect to time of seven sorting algorithms

	Worst Case	Average Case
Selection sort	N^2	N^2
Bubble sort	N^2	N^2
Insertion sort	N^2	N^2
Mergesort	$N * \log N$	$N * \log N$
Quicksort	N^2	$N * \log N$
Radix sort	N	N
Heapsort	$N * \log N$	$N * \log N$

known sorting algorithms. However, for certain cases quicksort can be significantly slower than other sorting algorithms. For example, quicksort's worst-case behavior is not nearly as good as mergesort. Fortunately, these cases rarely occur in practice. Mergesort is not quite as fast as quicksort in the average case, but its performance is consistently good in all cases. Mergesort has the disadvantage of requiring extra storage equal to the size of the array to be sorted.

COMMON PITFALLS / DEBUGGING

1. In general, you should avoid analyzing an algorithm solely by studying the running times of a specific implementation. Running times are influenced by such factors as programming style, the particular computer, and the data on which the program is run.
2. When comparing the efficiencies of various solutions, look only at significant differences. This rule is consistent with the multidimensional view of the cost of a computer program.
3. If a problem is small, do not overanalyze it. In such a situation, the primary concern should be simplicity. For example, if you are sorting an array that contains only a small number of elements—say, fewer than 50—a simple $O(N^2)$ algorithm such as an insertion sort is appropriate.
4. If you are sorting a very large array, an $O(N^2)$ algorithm could well be too inefficient. Although quicksort's worst-case behavior is $O(N^2)$, the worst case rarely occurs in practice. Quicksort is appropriate when you are confident that the data in the array to be sorted is arranged randomly.

SELF-TEST EXERCISES

1. Trace the selection sort as it sorts the following array into ascending order: `20 80 40 25 60 30`
2. Repeat Self-Test Exercise 1, but instead sort the array into descending order.
3. Trace the bubble sort as it sorts the following array into ascending order: `25 30 20 80 40 60`
4. Trace the insertion sort as it sorts the array in Self-Test Exercise 3 into ascending order.
5. Show that the mergesort algorithm satisfies the four criteria of recursion that Chapter 5 describes.

6. Trace *Quicksort*'s partitioning algorithm as it partitions the following array. Use the first element as the pivot.

   `38 16 40 39 12 27`

7. How many comparisons of array elements do the following loops contain?

```
for J := 1 to N-1 do
begin
    I := succ(J);
    repeat
       if A[I] < A[J]
           then Swap(A[I], A[J]);
       I := succ(I)
    until I > N
end;  {for}
```

8. Repeat Self-Test Exercise 7, but first replace the statement `I := succ(J)` with `I := J`.

9. What order is an algorithm that has as a growth-rate function

   a. $8 * N^3 - 9 * N$ b. $7 * \log_2 N + 20$ c. $7 * \log_2 N + N$

10. Consider a sequential search of N data elements.

    a. If the data is sorted into ascending order, how can you determine that your desired element is not in the data collection without always making N comparisons?
    b. What is the order of the sequential search algorithm when the desired element is not in the data collection? Do this for both sorted and unsorted data, and consider the best, average, and worst cases.
    c. Show that if the sequential search algorithm finds the desired element in the data collection, then the algorithm's order does not depend upon whether or not the data is sorted.

EXERCISES

1. Trace the insertion sort as it sorts the following array into ascending order: `20 80 40 25 60`

2. Apply selection sort, bubble sort, and insertion sort to

   a. an inverted array: `8 6 4 2`
   b. an ordered array: `2 4 6 8`

3. Find an array that makes *BubbleSort* exhibit its worst behavior.

4. Revise the procedure *SelectionSort* so that it sorts records according to one field, which is the search key.

5. Write the procedure *SelectionSort* so that it uses recursion.

6. Trace the mergesort as it sorts the following array into ascending order: 20 80 40 25 60 30

7. Trace the quicksort as it sorts the following array into ascending order: 20 80 40 25 60 10 15

8. Suppose you remove the call to *Merge* from the *Mergesort* algorithm to obtain

```
Mystery(A, N)
{ Mystery algorithm for A[1..N]. }

    if N > 1
      then
      begin
          Mergesort( Lefthalf(A) )
          Mergesort( Righthalf(A) )
      end

      else quit
```

What does this new algorithm do?

9. Show that any polynomial $f(x) = c_k x^k + c_{k-1} x^{k-1} + \cdots + c_1 x + c_0$ is $O(x^k)$.

10. Show that for all constants $a, b > 1$, $f(N)$ is $O(\log_a N)$ if and only if $f(N)$ is $O(\log_b N)$. Thus, you can omit the base when you write $O(\log N)$. (*Hint*: Use the identity $\log_a N = \log_b N / \log_b a$ for all constants $a, b > 1$.)

11. Recall that the partition procedure that *Quicksort* uses moves one item at a time from the unknown region into the appropriate region S_1 or S_2. Note that if the item to be moved belongs in region S_1, and if S_2 is empty, then the procedure will swap an array element with itself. Modify the partition procedure to eliminate this unnecessary swapping.

12. You can choose any element of the array as pivot in *Quicksort*. Simply interchange elements so that your pivot is in *A[F]*. One way to choose a pivot is to take the middle value of the three values *A[1]*, *A[L]*, and *A[(F + L) div 2]*. How many recursive calls are necessary to sort an array of size N if you always choose the pivot in this way?

13. Use invariants to show that the procedure *SelectionSort* is correct.

14. Add a counter to the procedures *InsertionSort* and *Mergesort* that counts the number of comparisons that are made. Run the two procedures on problems of various sizes. On what size does the difference in the number of comparisons become significant? How does this size compare with the size that the Big O's for these algorithms predict?

***15.** Describe an iterative version of `Mergesort`. Define an appropriate invariant and show the correctness of your algorithm.

16. One criterion used to evaluate sorting algorithms is stability. A sorting algorithm is **stable** if it does not exchange records with the same sort key. That is, records with the same sort key (possibly differing in other fields) will maintain their positions relative to one another. For example, you might want to take an array of student records that is sorted by name and produce an array that is sorted by class. Sorting the array (by class) with a stable sorting algorithm will ensure that within each class the students will remain sorted by name. Some applications mandate a stable sorting algorithm. Others do not. Which of the sorting algorithms described in this chapter are stable?

17. When we introduced the radix sort, we sorted a hand of cards by first ordering the cards by rank and then by suit. To implement a radix sort for this example, you could use two characters to represent a card, if you used T to represent a 10. For example, S2 is the 2 of spades and HT is the 10 of hearts.

a. Trace the radix sort for this example.

b. Suppose that you did not use T to represent a 10—that is, suppose that H10 is the 10 of hearts—and that you padded the two-character strings on the right with a blank to form three-character strings. How would a radix sort order the entire deck of cards in this case?

18. You can sort a large array of integers that are in the range `1..100` by using an array `Count[1..100]` to count the number of occurrences of each integer in the range `1..100`. Fill in the details of this sorting algorithm, which is called a **bucket sort**, and write a Pascal procedure that implements it. What is the order of the bucket sort? Why is the bucket sort not useful as a general sorting algorithm?

19. Implement the radix sort for both a linked list and an array.

20. **a.** Implement the mergesort algorithm for a linked list.

b. Implement any other sorting algorithms that are appropriate for a linked list.

PROJECT

21. **a.** Modify the partition procedure for `Quicksort` so that S_1 and S_2 will never be empty.

b. Another partitioning strategy for `Quicksort` is possible. Let an index `Low` traverse the array segment `A[F..L]` from `F` to `L` and stop when it encounters the first element that is greater than the pivot element. Similarly, let a second index `High` traverse the array segment from `L` to `F` and stop when it encounters the first element that is smaller than the pivot element. Then swap these two elements, increment `Low`, decrement `High`, and continue until `High` and `Low` meet somewhere in the middle. Implement this version of `Quicksort` in Pascal. How can you ensure that the regions S_1 and S_2 are not empty?

c. There are several variations of this partitioning strategy. What other strategies can you think of? How do they compare to the two that have been given?

Problem Solving with Abstract Data Types

CHAPTER 8

Stacks

PREVIEW This chapter introduces a well-known ADT called a stack and presents both array-based and pointer-based implementations. You will see how the operations on a stack give it a last-in, first-out behavior. Two of the several important applications of a stack that the chapter considers are evaluating algebraic expressions and searching for a path between two points. Finally, the chapter discusses the important relationship between stacks and recursion.

INTRODUCTION

Parts I and II of this book reviewed aspects of problem solving that are closely related to programming issues; developed the linked list, which is an important data structure that you will see throughout this book; discussed procedural abstraction and data abstraction as important ways to increase a solution's modularity; introduced recursion, a problem-solving tool useful in the construction of algorithms; studied the efficiency of algorithms; and compared sorting algorithms. The primary concerns of Parts III and IV are the aspects of problem solving that involve the *management of data*—that is, the identification and implementation of some of the more common data-management operations.

Part III deals both with data organized by *position* and with data organized by *value*. In general, these organizations are appropriate for applications of rather different natures. For example, if an application needs to ask a question about the first person in a line, the data should be organized by position. On the other hand, if an application needs to ask a question about the employee named Smith, the data should be organized by value. Part IV considers a few advanced techniques for organizing data by value, including techniques for organizing data stored in an external file.

Our study of data management has three aspects. The first is the identification of useful sets of operations—that is, the identification of abstract data types. The second aspect is the presentation of applications that use these abstract data types. The third aspect is the development of implementations for the abstract data types—that is, the development of data structures. As you will discover, the nature of the operations of an abstract data type, along with the application in which you will use it, greatly influence the choice of its implementation.

The next section defines an important ADT known as a stack and, in doing so, illustrates how to use an ADT approach in program development.

THE STACK AS AN EXAMPLE OF AN ADT IN PROGRAM DEVELOPMENT

Suppose that you want to read a single line of text and then print it in reversed order. Assume that your keyboard has no backspace key; thus, if you make a data-entry error, you must use the # character to correct your mistake as follows: Each # erases the previous character entered, but consecutive # characters do not cancel out; instead they are applied in sequence and so erase several characters. For instance, if the input line is

```
abc defgh#2klmnopqr##wxyz
```

the corrected input would be

```
abc defg2klmnopwxyz
```

Given that this line is the corrected input, the reversed output is

```
zyxwponmlk2gfed cba
```

Consider now the process of constructing a solution to this problem. One design decision that you must make eventually is how to store the input line. In accordance with the ADT approach, you should postpone this decision until you have a better idea of what operations you will need to perform on the data. You can begin by breaking the problem into two tasks:

Two tasks solve the problem

```
Read the line, correcting "errors" along the way
Print the line in reversed order
```

You can refine the first of these tasks as

Initial refinement of the first task

```
{ Read the line, correcting "errors" along the way }
while (not end of line) do
begin
    Read a new character Ch
    if Ch is not a '#'
       then add Ch to the data structure
       else remove from the data structure the
            item that was added most recently
end
```

This refinement calls to attention two of the operations that the ADT will have to include:

Two ADT operations that are required

- *Insert a new item into the data structure.*
- *Remove from the data structure the item that was added most recently.*

Notice that there is a potential for trouble if you type a # when the data structure is empty, that is, when there are no characters in the data structure. If this situation should occur, you have two options: (1) have the program terminate and print an error message, or (2) have the program ignore the # and continue. Either option is reasonable: Suppose that you decide to ignore the # and continue. Therefore, the algorithm becomes

The "read and correct" algorithm

```
{ Read the line, correcting "errors" along the way }
while (not end of line) do
```

```
begin
    Read a new character Ch
    if Ch is not a '#' then
       Add Ch to the data structure
    else if the data structure is not empty then
       Remove from the data structure the
           item that was added most recently
    else ignore the #
end
```

From this pseudocode you can identify a third operation required by the ADT:

- *Determine whether the data structure is empty.*

Another ADT operation that is required

By reading the line, you have performed the first task, so now move on to the second task, printing the line in reversed order. At first, it appears that you can accomplish this task by using the three ADT operations already identified, as follows:

A false start at printing the line in reverse order

```
{ Print the line in reversed order }
while the data structure is not empty do
begin
    Remove from the data structure the item
       that was added most recently
    Print .....Uh-oh!
end
```

Because the *Remove* operation deletes the item from the data structure, the item is gone, so you cannot print it. What you should have done was to *retrieve* from the data structure the item that was added most recently. Recall that the retrieval operation in Chapter 4 meant to *look at, but leave unchanged.* Only after retrieving and printing the item should you remove it from the data structure. The print-backward algorithm therefore becomes

The "print-backward" algorithm

```
{ Print the line in reversed order }
while the data structure is not empty do
begin
    Retrieve from the data structure the item
       that was added most recently and put it in Ch
    Print Ch
    Remove from the data structure the item
       that was added most recently
end
```

Thus, a fourth operation is required by the ADT:

- *Retrieve from the data structure the item that was added most recently.*

Another ADT operation that is required

You now have a high-level solution to the problem. Although you have yet to think about what the data structure is, you know that you must be able to perform the following four operations:

Four operations that the solution requires

- *Determine whether the data structure is empty.*
- *Insert a new item into the data structure.*
- *Remove from the data structure the item that was added most recently.*
- *Retrieve from the data structure the item that was added most recently.*

These operations define the ADT you need. It turns out that this is a very well-known ADT, which is usually called a **stack.**

There is a fifth operation, which seems so obvious that there might be a tendency to neglect it. This operation creates a new stack. In terms of a Pascal implementation, *CreateStack* corresponds roughly to declaring a variable of the appropriate type and initializing the variable so that it represents an empty stack. The *CreateStack* operation is also important from a more theoretical point of view, as it allows you to state precisely the results of performing a sequence of one or more operations beginning with an empty stack.

Thus, the following operations define the ADT stack. The operation names given here conform to convention:

KEY CONCEPTS

ADT Stack Operations

```
CreateStack(S)
{ Creates an empty stack S. }

StackIsEmpty(S)
{ Determines whether stack S is empty. }

Push(S, NewItem)
{ Adds NewItem to stack S. }

Pop(S)
{ Removes from stack S the item that was added most
  recently. }

StackTop(S)
{ Retrieves from stack S the item that was added
  most recently, leaving S unchanged. }
```

As was mentioned in Chapter 4, intuitive definitions such as these are not really sufficient to define an ADT formally. For example, to capture formally the intuitive notion that the last item inserted into the stack is the first item to be removed, you could write an axiom such as

```
Pop(Push(S, NewItem)) = S
```

An example of an axiom

In addition, before you implement any ADT operations, you should specify both their preconditions and their postconditions. Realize, however, that during program design, the first attempt at specification is often informal and is only later made precise by the writing of preconditions and postconditions. The preconditions and postconditions for the ADT stack operations appear later in this chapter as comments in their Pascal implementations.

You can now put together the solution to the line-reversal problem. You can write a nearly complete pseudocode solution by using the previous stack operations. Notice that not only are these operations as yet unwritten, but also that you do not know what a stack looks like. Because the ADT approach builds a wall around the implementation of the stack, you can write the rest of the program independently of the stack's implementation. So long as the rest of the program correctly uses the ADT operations—that is, so long as it honors the contract—it will work regardless of how you implement the ADT.

The pseudocode solution follows:

```
program LineReverse

{ The following subprograms are the specified stack
operations. }

CreateStack(S)       { Creates an empty stack }

StackIsEmpty(S)      { Determines whether stack is empty }

Push(S, NewItem)     { Adds NewItem to stack }

Pop(S)               { Removes most recently added item from
                       stack }

StackTop(S)          { Retrieves most recently added item
                       from stack }

ReadAndCorrect(S)
{ Reads the input line. For each character read, either
  enters it into stack S or, if it is #, corrects the
  contents of S. }

begin
    while (not end of line) do
    begin
       read(NewChar)

       if NewChar <> '#' then
           Push(S, NewChar)
       else if not StackIsEmpty(S) then
           Pop(S)
    end  { while }
end  { ReadAndCorrect }
```

```
PrintBackward(S)
{ Prints the reversed line by printing contents of stack S. }
begin
    while ( not StackIsEmpty(S) ) do
    begin
       NewChar := StackTop(S)
       write(NewChar)
       Pop(S)
    end
end  { PrintBackward }

begin  { Main Program }
    CreateStack(S)
    ReadAndCorrect(S)
    PrintBackward(S)
end  { Program }
```

MORE ON THE NATURE OF THE ABSTRACT DATA TYPE STACK

The term "stack" is intended to conjure up visions of things encountered in daily life, such as a stack of dishes in the school cafeteria, a stack of books on your desk, or a stack of assignments waiting for you to work on them. In common English usage, "stack of" and "pile of" are synonymous. To computer scientists, however, a stack is not just any old pile. A stack has the property that the last item placed on the stack will be the first item removed. This property is commonly referred to as **last in, first out**, or simply LIFO.

Last in, first out

A stack of dishes in a cafeteria makes a very good analogy of the abstract data type stack, as Figure 8-1 illustrates. As new dishes are added, the old dishes drop farther into the well beneath the surface. At any particular time, only the dish last placed on the stack is above the surface and visible. This dish is the one that must be removed next. In general, the dishes are removed in exactly the opposite order from that in which they were added.

The LIFO property of stacks seems inherently unfair. Think of the poor person who finally gets the last dish on the cafeteria's stack, a dish that

Figure 8-1

Stack of cafeteria dishes

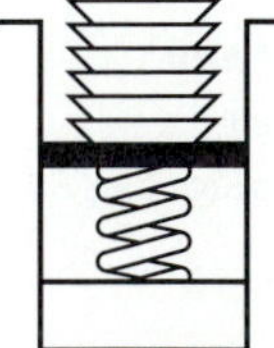

may have been placed there six years ago. Or how would you like to be the first person to arrive on the stack for a movie—as opposed to the line for a movie. You would be the last person allowed in! These examples demonstrate the reason that stacks are not especially prevalent in everyday life. The property that we usually desire in our daily lives is **first in, first out**, or FIFO. A **queue**, which we present in the next chapter, is the abstract data type with the FIFO property. Most people would much prefer to wait in a movie *queue*—as a line is commonly called in Britain—than in a movie *stack*. However, while the LIFO property of stacks is not appropriate for very many day-to-day situations, it is precisely what is needed for a large number of problems that arise in computer science.

Notice how well the analogy holds between the abstract data type stack and the stack of cafeteria dishes. The five operations that define the ADT stack are the *only* operations of the ADT stack, and they correspond to the only things that you can do to a stack of dishes. You can determine whether the stack of dishes is empty but not how many dishes are on the stack; you can inspect the top dish but no other dish; you can place a dish on top of the stack but at no other position; and you can remove a dish from the top of the stack but from no other position. If you were permitted to perform any other operations, or if you were not permitted to perform any of the five operations, the data type would not be a stack.

An alternate definition of **Pop**

We should point out, however, that there are some common variations of our definition of a stack. For example, you could define `Pop(S, Item)`, which removes the top item and returns its value in `Item`, and omit the operation `StackTop(S)`. If you were to adopt this definition of a stack, how could you inspect the top item of a stack without removing it? If this inspection were necessary, you could write an auxiliary function `AuxStackTop` that utilizes both `Pop` and `Push` as follows:

```
function AuxStackTop(S)

    Pop(S, Item)
    Push(S, Item)
    AuxStackTop := Item
```

This function is a bit awkward, but on the other hand it is very common to have to inspect and remove the top item of a stack simultaneously. Whereas the original definition of a stack requires the sequence

```
Item := StackTop(S)
Pop(S)
```

to make a copy of the top item and then remove it, this task is accomplished by the single operation

```
Pop(S, Item)
```

under the alternative definition. Both definitions of a stack are reasonable, each having its relative advantage. For the remainder of this book, we shall use the original definition presented.

Although the stack of cafeteria dishes suggests that, as you add or remove dishes, the other dishes move, do not have this expectation of the ADT stack. The stack operations involve only the top item and say nothing about the other items in the stack. Implementations of the ADT stack operations might or might not move the stack's items. The implementations in the next section do not move data items.

IMPLEMENTATIONS OF THE ADT STACK

Fixed size versus dynamic size

This section develops two Pascal implementations of the ADT stack: array based and pointer based. The array-based implementation uses an array to represent the stack, while the pointer-based implementation uses a linked list. Figure 8-2 illustrates these two implementations. Once again the issue of fixed versus dynamic size is the primary consideration for making the choice between implementations. If you were to choose an array-based implementation, you would have to place a restriction on the `Push` operation so that it would not attempt to add an item to the stack if the stack's size limit, which is the size of the array, has been reached. If this restriction is not acceptable, you must use a pointer-based implementation. For the line-reversal problem, for example, it is conceivable that the fixed-size restriction may not present a problem: If the system allows a line length of only 80 characters, you could use the array-based implementation, which is described in the next section.

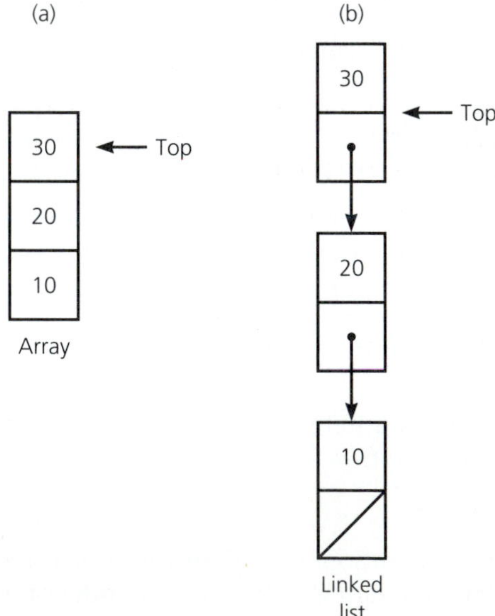

Figure 8-2

Implementations of the ADT stack: (a) array based; (b) pointer based

An Array-Based Implementation of the ADT Stack

Consider the array-based implementation of the ADT stack in Figure 8-3. This figure suggests that you represent a stack with a record that contains both the array *Items* and an index *Top* to a position in *Items*. Assuming such a representation, the following unit contains an array-based implementation of the ADT stack:

```
unit StackOps;
{ *******************************************************
  BASIC STACK OPERATIONS - Array-Based Implementation

    CreateStack, StackIsEmpty, Push, Pop, and GetStackTop

  ******************************************************* }
interface

const  MaxStack = <maximum size of stack>;

type   itemType = <desired type of stack item>;

       stackType = record
          Top      : 0..MaxStack;
          Items    : array[1..MaxStack] of itemType
       end; { record }

procedure CreateStack(var S : stackType);
{ -------------------------------------------------------
  Creates an empty stack.
  Precondition: None.
  Postcondition: The stack S is empty.
  ------------------------------------------------------- }
function StackIsEmpty(S : stackType) : boolean;
{ -------------------------------------------------------
  Determines whether a stack is empty.
  Precondition: CreateStack(S) has been called.
  Postcondition: Returns true if S was empty, else returns
  false.
  ------------------------------------------------------- }
procedure Push(var S : stackType; NewItem : itemType;
               var Success : boolean);
{ -------------------------------------------------------
  Adds an item to the top of a stack.
  Precondition: CreateStack(S) has been called.
  Postcondition: If S was not full, NewItem is on the top
  of the stack S and Success is true; otherwise Success is
  false.
  Note: S is full if it has MaxStack items.
  ------------------------------------------------------- }
```

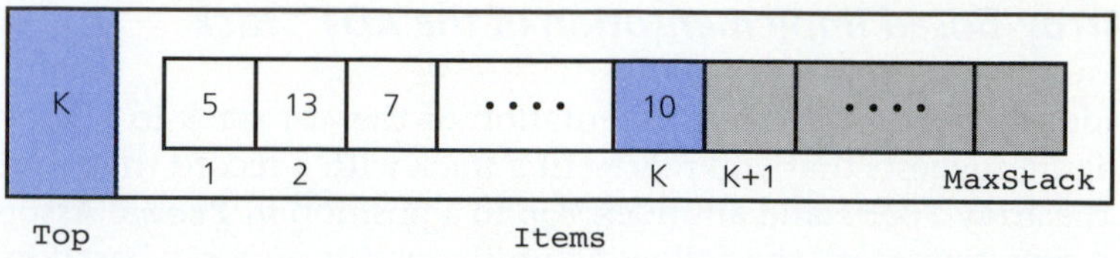

Figure 8-3

An array-based implementation


```
procedure Pop(var S : stackType; var Success : boolean);
{ ---------------------------------------------------------
  Removes the top of a stack.
  Precondition: CreateStack(S) has been called.
  Postcondition: If S was not empty, the item that was
  added most recently to S is removed and Success is true.
  However, if S was empty, deletion is impossible and
  Success is false.
  ------------------------------------------------------- }
procedure GetStackTop(S : stackType;
             var StackTop: itemType; var Success : boolean);
{ ---------------------------------------------------------
  Retrieves the top of a stack.
  Precondition: CreateStack(S) has been called.
  Postcondition: If S was not empty, StackTop contains the
  item that was added most recently to S and Success is
  true. However, if S was empty, the operation fails and
  Success is false. S is unchanged.
  ------------------------------------------------------- }

implementation

procedure CreateStack(var S : stackType);
begin
   S.Top := 0
end; { CreateStack }

function StackIsEmpty(S : stackType) : boolean;
begin
   StackIsEmpty := (S.Top < 1)
end; { StackIsEmpty }

procedure Push(var S : stackType; NewItem : itemType;
               var Success : boolean);
begin
   Success := (S.Top < MaxStack);

   if Success
      then { stack is not full }
      begin
         S.Top := succ(S.Top);
         S.Items[S.Top] := NewItem;
      end
end; { Push }
```

```
procedure Pop(var S : stackType; var Success : boolean);
begin
   Success := not StackIsEmpty(S);

   if Success
      then S.Top := pred(S.Top)
end; { Pop }

procedure GetStackTop(S : stackType;
                  var StackTop: itemType; var Success : boolean);
begin
   Success := not StackIsEmpty(S);
   if Success
      then StackTop := S.Items[S.Top]
end; { GetStackTop }

end. { unit }
```

A program that uses this unit could begin as follows:

```
program DemonstrateStack;
uses StackOps;     { array-based stack operations }

var S : stackType;
    Entry : itemType;
    Success : boolean;

begin
    CreateStack(S);
    readln(Entry);
    Push(S, Entry, Success);
    . . .
```

There are several things to notice about this implementation. Consider the point when the programmer and the program designer draw up a contract for the implementation of the ADT stack in Pascal. Suppose that you are the programmer. The program designer tells you that the following five operations are needed:

```
CreateStack(S)        { Creates an empty stack. }

StackIsEmpty(S)       { Determines whether stack is empty. }

Push(S, NewItem)      { Adds NewItem to stack. }

Pop(S)                { Removes most recently added item from
                        stack. }

StackTop(S)           { Retrieves most recently added item
                        from stack, leaving stack unchanged. }
```

In the course of developing these Pascal routines, you and the program designer would have to work out a few details of the contract. For example, consider the implementation of the *Push* operation. Presumably, you and the designer determined at the outset that the fixed-size restriction of the

The designer and the programmer must agree on some details in their contract

array-based implementation was acceptable. Even so, both of you still must agree on the details of how the `Push` operation should handle an attempt to add an item to a full stack. The decision made in the previous implementation is that the procedure `Push` will return a flag—that is, a boolean-valued variable parameter—with the value `false` if `Push` attempts to add an item to a full stack. This flag, `Success`, allows the calling routine to take appropriate action.

Furthermore, you and the designer need to decide whether `StackTop` is a procedure or a function. In the previous implementation, `StackTop` is a procedure (`GetStackTop`). The primary reason for this choice is to allow full generality of what `itemType` can be—that is, what type of items the stack can contain. Because Pascal allows functions to return only simple values, you could not use a function `StackTop` if `itemType` were, for instance, a record or an array.

Finally, you and the designer would have to decide how to handle two other eventualities: What to do if either `GetStackTop` or `Pop` is called when the stack is empty. The previous implementation handles these situations in a manner analogous to the way it handles the stack-full situation. If either `GetStackTop` or `Pop` is called with an empty stack, it will return the flag `Success` with the value `false`, thereby allowing the calling routine to take appropriate action.

This decision to return a boolean flag `Success` that indicates whether a retrieval is successful is another reason for implementing the operation `StackTop` as a procedure. Recall that functions should not have side effects, such as an output parameter. You could, of course, write `StackTop` as a function with the precondition that the stack is not empty. This restriction allows you to omit `Success` as a parameter.

These choices regarding the boolean `Success` parameters and the proper calling sequences for the operations all should be summarized in the final version of the contract between the designer and the programmer.

A Pointer-Based Implementation of the ADT Stack

Many applications require a pointer-based implementation of a stack so that it can grow and shrink dynamically. Figure 8-4 illustrates a pointer-based implementation of a stack where `S` is a pointer to the head of a linked list of items.

The following unit contains a pointer-based implementation of the ADT stack:

```
unit StackOps;
{ *********************************************************
  BASIC STACK OPERATIONS - Pointer-Based Implementation

    CreateStack, StackIsEmpty, Push, Pop, and GetStackTop

  ********************************************************* }
```

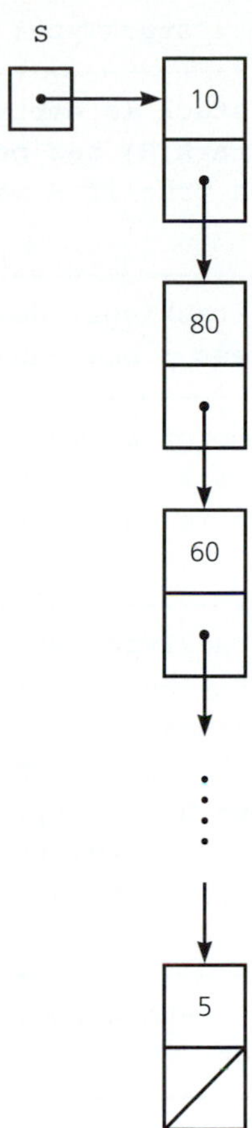

Figure 8-4

A pointer-based implementation

```
interface

type  itemType = <desired type of stack item>;

      ptrType = ^nodeType;
      nodeType = record
          Item : itemType;
          Next : ptrType
      end; { record }

      stackType = ptrType;

procedure CreateStack(var S : stackType);
{ -------------------------------------------------------
  Creates an empty stack.
  Precondition: None.
  Postcondition: The stack S is empty.
  ------------------------------------------------------- }
```

```
function StackIsEmpty(S : stackType) : boolean;
{ ---------------------------------------------------------
  Determines whether a stack is empty.
  Precondition: CreateStack(S) has been called.
  Postcondition: Returns true if S was empty, else returns
  false.
  --------------------------------------------------------- }
procedure Push(var S : stackType; NewItem : itemType;
               var Success : boolean);
{ ---------------------------------------------------------
  Adds an item to the top of a stack.
  Precondition: CreateStack(S) has been called.
  Postcondition: NewItem is on the top of the stack S and
  Success is true.
  --------------------------------------------------------- }
procedure Pop(var S : stackType; var Success : boolean);
{ ---------------------------------------------------------
  Removes the top of a stack.
  Precondition: CreateStack(S) has been called.
  Postcondition: If S was not empty, the item that was
  added most recently to S is removed and Success is true.
  However, if S was empty, deletion is impossible and
  Success is false.
  --------------------------------------------------------- }
procedure GetStackTop(S : stackType;
             var StackTop: itemType; var Success : boolean);
{ ---------------------------------------------------------
  Retrieves the top of a stack.
  Precondition: CreateStack(S) has been called.
  Postcondition: If S was not empty, StackTop contains the
  item that was added most recently to S and Success is
  true. However, if S was empty, the operation fails and
  Success is false. S is unchanged.
  --------------------------------------------------------- }

implementation

procedure CreateStack(var S : stackType);
begin
    S := nil
end; { CreateStack }

function StackIsEmpty(S : stackType) : boolean;
begin
    StackIsEmpty := (S = nil)
end; { StackIsEmpty }

procedure Push(var S : stackType; NewItem : itemType;
               var Success : boolean);
```

```
var NewTopPtr : ptrType;
begin
    { create a new node }
    new(NewTopPtr);
    NewTopPtr^.Item := NewItem;

    { insert the new node }
    NewTopPtr^.Next := S;
    S := NewTopPtr;
    Success := true
end; { Push }

procedure Pop(var S : stackType; var Success : boolean);
var TopPtr : ptrType;
begin
    Success := not StackIsEmpty(S);

    if Success
       then        { stack is not empty }
       begin
          TopPtr := S;
          S := S^.Next;
          dispose(TopPtr)
       end
end; { Pop }

procedure GetStackTop(S : stackType;
             var StackTop: itemType; var Success : boolean);
begin
    Success := not StackIsEmpty(S);

    if Success
       then StackTop := S^.Item
end;  { GetStackTop }

end. { unit }
```

As you did with the array-based implementation, here you and the program designer must work out some points in the contract. If you assume that your computer has sufficient memory, as you did in Chapter 4, you have no concern about the stack-full condition for the *Push* operation, as you had in the array-based implementation. However, the comments made about boolean flags with respect to the array-based implementation's *Pop* and *GetStackTop* procedures apply here as well. As it did for the array-based implementation, the final version of the contract for the pointer-based implementation should include all this information.

The Stack As an Object (Optional)

You can implement the ADT stack as an object. This section presents two possible approaches. The first approach closely models the pointer-based implementation of the ADT stack just discussed. The second approach defines the stack as a descendent of the object *ordListType*, which Chapter 4 defined on page 216.

A pointer-based stack. The following pointer-based implementation of a stack object has many similarities with the pointer-based implementation of the ADT stack that you just saw:

```
unit StackObj;
interface

type itemType = <desired type of stack item>;
     ptrType = ^nodeType;

     nodeType = record
        Item : itemType;
        Next : ptrType
     end; { record }

     stackType = object
        constructor Init;
        { ------------------------------------------------
          Creates an empty stack
          Precondition: None.
          Postcondition: The stack is empty.
          ------------------------------------------------ }
        destructor Done; virtual;
        { ------------------------------------------------
          Deallocates a stack.
          Precondition: Init has been called.
          Postcondition: All storage associated with
          the stack is deallocated. The stack is empty.
          ------------------------------------------------ }
        function StackIsEmpty : boolean;
        { ------------------------------------------------
          Determines whether a stack is empty.
          Precondition: Init has been called.
          Postcondition: Returns true if the stack was
          empty, else returns false.
          ------------------------------------------------ }
        procedure Push(NewItem : itemType;
                       var Success : boolean);
        { ------------------------------------------------
          Adds an item to the top of a stack.
          Precondition: Init has been called.
          Postcondition: NewItem is on the top
          of the stack and Success is true.
          ------------------------------------------------ }
```

```
      procedure Pop(var Success : boolean);
      { ------------------------------------------------
        Removes the top of a stack.
        Precondition: Init has been called.
        Postcondition: If the stack was not empty,
        the item that was added most recently is
        removed and Success is true. However, if the
        stack was empty, deletion is impossible and
        Success is false.
        ------------------------------------------------ }
      procedure GetStackTop(var StackTop : itemType;
                            var Success : boolean);
      { ------------------------------------------------
        Retrieves the top of a stack.
        Precondition: Init has been called.
        Postcondition: If the stack was not empty,
        StackTop contains the item that was added most
        recently and Success is true. However, if the
        stack was empty, the operation fails and Success
        is false. The stack is unchanged.
        ------------------------------------------------ }
    private
      Top : ptrType;
    end;  { object }

implementation

constructor stackType.Init;
begin
  Top := nil
end; { stackType.Init }

destructor stackType.Done;
var Cur, Temp : ptrType;
begin
  Cur := Top;
  Top := nil;
  while Cur <> nil do
  begin
    Temp := Cur;
    Cur := Cur^.Next;
    dispose(Temp)
  end  { while }
end; { stackType.Done }

function stackType.StackIsEmpty : boolean;
begin
  StackIsEmpty := (Top = nil)
end; { stackType.StackIsEmpty }
```

```
procedure stackType.Push(NewItem : itemType;
                         var Success : boolean);
var NewTopPtr : ptrType;
begin
   { create a new node and set its value }
   new(NewTopPtr);
   NewTopPtr^.Item := NewItem;

   { insert the new node }
   NewTopPtr^.Next := Top;
   Top := NewTopPtr;
   Success := true
end; { stackType.Push }

procedure stackType.Pop(var Success : boolean);
var TopPtr : ptrType;
begin
   Success := not StackIsEmpty;
   if Success
      then { stack not empty }
      begin
         TopPtr := Top;
         Top := Top^.Next;
         dispose(TopPtr)
      end
end; { stackType.Pop }

procedure stackType.GetStackTop(var StackTop : itemType;
                                var Success : boolean);
begin
   Success := not StackIsEmpty;
   if Success
      then StackTop := Top^.Item
end; { stackType.GetStackTop }

end. { unit }
```

Compare the implementation of this object with the previous pointer-based implementation of the ADT stack. The differences are as follows: *stackType* qualifies each method name (for example, *stackType.Push*), *StackIsEmpty* replaces each occurence of *StackIsEmpty(S)*, and *Top* replaces each instance of *S*.

The following statements demonstrate how to use this object:

```
var AnItem : itemType;
    S : stackType;
    Success : boolean;

begin  { Main Program }
    S.Init;
```

```
      readln(AnItem);
      S.Push(AnItem, Success);
```

A stack that descends from *ordListType*. You can implement a stack as an ordered list. If the item in position 1 of an ordered list represents the top of the stack, you can implement the stack operation *Push(NewItem)* as *OrderedListInsert(1, NewItem)*. Similarly, you can implement the stack operation *Pop* as *OrderedListDelete(1)* and the stack operation *GetStackTop(StackTop)* as *OrderedListRetrieve(1, StackTop)*.

Recall that Chapter 4 presented the ordered list as the object *ordListType*. Object inheritance allows you to conveniently define a stack as an object that descends from *ordListType*. The stack object uses its ancestor's methods to implement its own methods, as the following unit demonstrates. Pre- and postconditions are omitted to save space but are the same as those just given in the previous object definition.

```
unit StackObj;
interface

uses ULists;   { contains definition of ordListType }

type itemType = <desired type of stack item>;
     ptrType = ^nodeType;

     nodeType = record
        Item : itemType;
        Next : ptrType
     end;  { record }

     stackType = object(ordListType)
        { constructor and destructor are inherited }
        function StackIsEmpty : boolean;
        procedure Push(NewItem : itemType;
                       var Success : boolean);
        procedure Pop(var Success : boolean);
        procedure GetStackTop(var StackTop : itemType;
                              var Success : boolean);
     end;  { object }

implementation

function stackType.StackIsEmpty : boolean;
begin
   StackIsEmpty := (ListLength = 0);
end;  { stackType.StackIsEmpty }
```

```
procedure stackType.Push(NewItem : itemType;
                         var Success : boolean);
begin
   OrderedListInsert(1, NewItem, Success)
end;  { stackType.Push }

procedure stackType.Pop(var Success : boolean);
begin
   if StackIsEmpty
      then Success := false
      else OrderedListDelete(1, Success)
end;  { stackType.Pop }

procedure stackType.GetStackTop(var StackTop : itemType;
                                var Success : boolean);
begin
   if StackIsEmpty
      then Success := false
      else OrderedListRetrieve(1, StackTop, Success)
end;  { stackType.GetStackTop }

end.  { unit }
```

Notice how simple it is to implement a stack object, once you have implemented the ordered list.

Exercise 14 of Chapter 4 asked you to revise *ordListType* so that each item on the ordered list is a dynamically allocated object. Notice that once you make that change, enabling *stackType* to stack dynamically allocated objects is straightforward. Exercise 19 at the end of this chapter asks you to make this revision.

TWO SIMPLE APPLICATIONS OF THE ADT STACK

This section and the next present several applications for which the LIFO property of stacks is appropriate. The first two examples are rather simple; the others are more substantial. Keep in mind throughout that you are using the ADT stack to solve the problems. You can use the five stack operations, but you may not assume any particular implementation. You choose a specific implementation only as a last step.

Checking for Balanced Parentheses

One application of a stack is to verify that a given input string contains balanced parentheses. For example, the parentheses in the string

```
abc(defg(ijk)(l(mn))op)qr
```

are balanced, while the parentheses in the string

```
abc(def))(ghij(kl)m
```

are not balanced. You can check whether a string contains balanced parentheses by traversing it from left to right. As you move from left to right, you match each successive close parenthesis ")" with the most recently encountered unmatched open parenthesis "("; that is, the "(" must be to the left of the current ")". The parentheses are balanced if

Requirements for balanced parentheses

1. Each time you encounter a ")", it matches an already encountered "("
2. When you reach the end of the string, you have matched each "("

The solution requires that you keep track of each unmatched "(" and discard one each time you encounter a ")". One way to perform this task is to push each "(" encountered onto a stack and pop one off each time you encounter a ")". Thus, a first-draft pseudocode solution is

Initial draft of a solution

```
while not at the end of the string do
begin
    if the next character is a '(' then
       Push(S, '(')
    else if the character is a ')' then
       Pop(S)
end
```

Although this solution correctly keeps track of parentheses, missing from it are the checks that conditions 1 and 2 are met—that is, that the parentheses are indeed balanced. To verify condition 1 when a ")" is encountered, you must check to see whether the stack is empty before popping from it. If it is empty, you terminate the loop and report that the string is not balanced. To verify condition 2, you check that the stack is empty when the end of the string is reached.

The pseudocode solution for the string `Str` thus becomes

A detailed pseudocode solution

```
CreateStack(S)
Continue := true
I := 1

while (I <= length(Str)) and Continue do
begin
   { ignore all characters other than parentheses }
   if (Str[I] <> ')') and (Str[I] <> '(') then
      I := succ(I)

   { push an open parenthesis }
   else if Str[I] = '(' then
      begin
         Push(S, '(', Success)
         I := succ(I)
      end
```

```
      { close parenthesis: pop a matching open parenthesis }
      else if not StackIsEmpty(S) then
         begin
            Pop(S, Success)
            I := succ(I)
         end

      { close parenthesis, but no matching open parenthesis }
      else Continue := false
end  { while }

{ note that if Continue is false, I <= length(Str),
  so no test of Continue is necessary }
if (I > length(Str)) and StackIsEmpty(S)
      then is balanced
      else not balanced
```

Figure 8-5 shows the stacks that result when this algorithm is applied to several simple examples.

It may have occurred to you that a simpler solution to this problem is possible. You need only keep a count of the current number of unmatched left parentheses. Each time you encounter a left parenthesis, you increment the count; each time you encounter a right parenthesis, you decrement the count. If this count ever falls below zero or if it is greater than zero when the end of the string is reached, then the string is unbalanced. You need not actually store the left parentheses on a stack. However, the stack-based solution is conceptually useful as it previews more legitimate uses of stacks, such as those in the next example.

Exercise 2 at the end of this chapter asks you to extend the algorithm given here to check for balanced square brackets and braces in addition to parentheses.

Figure 8-5

Traces of the algorithm that checks for balanced parentheses

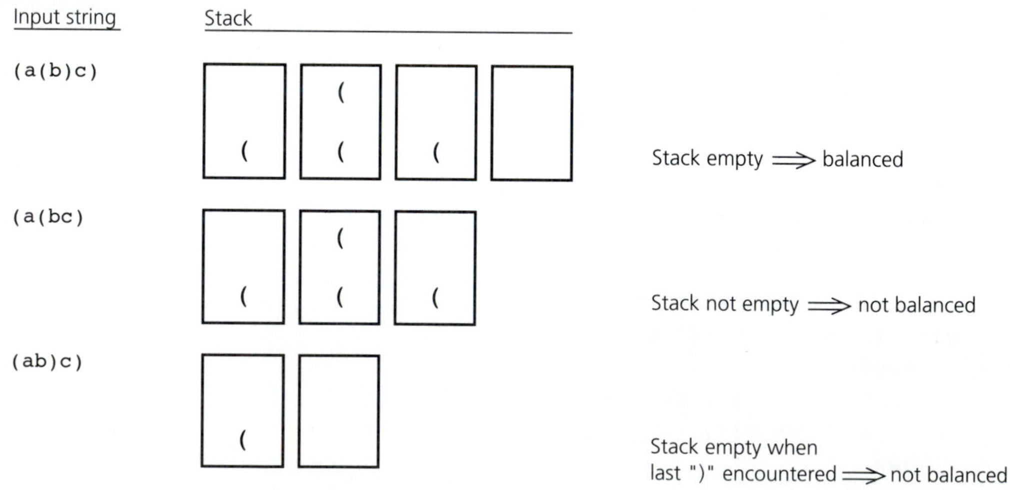

Recognizing Strings in a Language

Consider the problem of recognizing whether or not a particular string is in the language

$$L = \{w\$w' : w \text{ is string of characters other than } \$, w' = \text{reverse}(w)\}$$

For example, the string *ABC$CBA* is in the language. (Exercise 10 in Chapter 6 introduced a similar language.) A stack is very useful in determining whether a given string is in *L*. If you traverse the first half of the string and push each character onto a stack, when you reach the $ you can undo the process: For each character in the second half of the string, you pop a character off the stack. However, you must match the popped character with the current character in the string to ensure that the second half of the string is the reverse of the first half. The stack must be empty when—and only when—you reach the end of the string; otherwise, one "half" of the string is longer than the other, and so the string is not in *L*.

The following algorithm implements this strategy. To avoid unnecessary complications, assume that the string `Str` contains exactly one $.

***A pseudocode recognition algorithm for the language* L**

```
CreateStack(S)

{ push characters in w (the characters before $) onto stack }
I := 1
while (Str[I] <> '$') do
begin
    Push(S, Str[I])
    I := succ(I)
end

{ skip the $ }
I := succ(I)

{ match the reverse of w }
Continue := true
while (I <= length(Str)) and Continue do
begin
    { first half is shorter than second half }
    if StackIsEmpty(S) then
       Continue := false

    { characters do not match }
    else if (StackTop(S) <> Str[I]) then
       Continue := false

    { characters match }
    else
    begin
       Pop(S)
       I := succ(I)
    end
end  { while }
```

```
{ note that if Continue is false, I <= length(Str)
  so no test of Continue is needed }
if (I > length(Str))and StackIsEmpty(S)
    then in language
    else not in language
```

Notice that the two algorithms presented in this section depend only on the fact that the stack operations are supported and not on how the stack is implemented. The primary consideration in choosing between an array-based and a pointer-based implementation for the stack in the previous examples is whether there is a reasonable limit on the size of the string to be analyzed. For example, if the string is a Pascal string, an array-based stack implementation can use a maximum stack size that corresponds to the maximum string length (255 in Turbo Pascal). On the other hand, if the string is stored in a linked list or in a file, a pointer-based stack implementation might be required.

MORE COMPLEX APPLICATIONS OF STACKS

This section contains several problems that you can solve neatly by using the ADT stack. The first problems involve algebraic expressions, which were discussed in Chapter 6.

Algebraic Expressions

Chapter 6 presented recursive grammars that specified the syntax of algebraic expressions. Recall that prefix and postfix expressions avoid the ambiguity inherent in the evaluation of infix expressions. We now present stack-based solutions to the problems of evaluating infix and postfix expressions. To avoid distracting programming issues, we will allow only the binary operators *, /, +, and −, and disallow unary operators and exponentiation.

To evaluate an infix expression, first convert it to postfix form and then evaluate the postfix expression

The strategy we shall adopt here is first to develop an algorithm for evaluating postfix expressions and then to develop an algorithm for transforming an infix expression into an equivalent postfix expression. This strategy eliminates the need for an algorithm that directly evaluates infix expressions, a more difficult problem.

Evaluating postfix expressions. Consider an example that illustrates how you can evaluate a postfix expression. Some hand-held calculators use a postfix convention. For example, to compute the value of

2 * (3 + 4)

you would enter the sequence 2, 3, 4, +, *, which corresponds to the postfix expression

2 3 4 + *

Key entered	Calculator action	Stack S
2	Push(S, 2)	2
3	Push(S, 3)	2 3
4	Push(S, 4)	2 3 4
+	Oprnd2 ← StackTop(S)	2 3 4
	Pop(S)	2 3
	Oprnd1 ← StackTop(S)	2 3
	Pop(S)	2
	Result ← Oprnd1 + Oprnd2	2
	Push(S, Result)	2 7
*	Oprnd2 ← StackTop(S)	2 7
	Pop(S)	2
	Oprnd1 ← StackTop(S)	2
	Pop(S)	
	Result ← Oprnd1 * Oprnd2	
	Push(S, Result)	14

Figure 8-6

The action of a postfix calculator when evaluting the expression 2 * (3 + 4)

Each time you enter an operand, the calculator pushes it onto a stack. When you enter an operator, the calculator applies it to the top two operands on the stack, pops the operands from the stack, and pushes the result of the operation onto the stack. Thus, the action of the calculator for the previous sequence is as shown in Figure 8-6. The final result, 14, is on the top of the stack. Thus, the ADT stack provides the required operations for this problem.

You can formalize the action of the calculator to obtain an algorithm that evaluates a postfix expression, which is entered as a string of characters. To avoid issues that cloud the algorithm with programming details, assume that

Simplifying assumptions

- The string is a syntactically correct postfix expression.
- There are no unary operators.
- There is no exponentiation operator.
- Operands are single uppercase letters that represent integer values.

A pseudocode algorithm that evaluates postfix expressions

```
for each character Ch in the string do
begin
   if Ch is an operator named Op
      then
      begin
         { evaluate and push the result }
         Oprnd2 := StackTop(S)
         Pop(S)
         Oprnd1 := StackTop(S)
         Pop(S)
         Result := Oprnd1 Op Oprnd2
         Push(S, Result)
      end  { then }
      else Push(S, Ch) { Ch is an operand }
end
```

Upon termination of the algorithm, the value of the expression will be on the top of the stack. Exercise 11 at the end of this chapter asks you to implement this algorithm.

Converting infix expressions to postfix form. The next problem is to convert an infix expression into a postfix expression. Taken together, the solution to the previous problem of evaluating a postfix expression and the solution to this new problem provide a way to evaluate infix expressions.

The infix expressions here are the familiar ones. They allow parentheses, operator precedence, and left-to-right association. If you manually convert a few infix expressions to postfix form, you will discover three important facts:

Facts about converting from infix to postfix

- The operands always stay in the same order with respect to one another.
- An operator will move only "to the right" with respect to the operands; that is, if, in the infix expression, the operand *X* precedes the operator *Op,* it is also true that in the postfix expression the operand *X* precedes the operator *Op*.
- All parentheses are removed.

As a consequence of these three facts, the primary task of the conversion algorithm is determining where to place each operator.

The following high-level pseudocode solution converts an infix expression to a postfix expression, which is the string *PE*:

A high-level algorithm that converts an infix expression to postfix form

```
Initialize PE to the null string
for each character Ch in the infix expression do
    case Ch of
       Ch is an operand  : Append Ch to the end of PE
       Ch is an operator : Store Ch until it can be
                             determined where to place it
       Ch is '(' or ')'  : Discard Ch
    end  { case }
```

You may have guessed that you really do not want simply to discard the parentheses, as they play an important role in determining the placement of the operators. Because in any infix expression a set of matching parentheses defines an isolated subexpression that consists of an operator and its two operands, the algorithm must evaluate the subexpression independently of the rest of the expression. Regardless of what the rest of the expression looks like, the operator within the subexpression belongs with the operands in that subexpression. The parentheses tell the rest of the expression

> *You can have the value of this subexpression after it is evaluated; simply ignore the operators and operands inside.*

Parentheses, operator precedence, and left-to-right association determine where to place operators in the postfix expression

Parentheses are thus one of the factors that determine the placement of the operators in the postfix expression. The other factors are precedence and left-to-right association.

If the infix expression were always fully parenthesized, the conversion to postfix form would be conceptually straightforward. Because each operator would correspond to a pair of parentheses, you would simply move the operator to the position marked by the ")"—this position follows the operands of the operator. All parentheses would then be removed. For example, consider the infix expression

$$((A + B) * C)$$

First, you move each operator to the position marked by its corresponding ")":

Converting a fully parenthesized infix expression to postfix form is simple

```
((A B) C )
      +  *
```

Next, you remove the parentheses:

$$A\,B + C *$$

The actual problem is more difficult, however, because the infix expression is not always fully parenthesized. Instead, the problem allows precedence and left-to-right association, which requires a more complex algorithm. The following is a high-level description of what you must do when you encounter each character as you read the infix string from left to right.

Five steps in the conversion process

1. When an operand is encountered, append it to the output string `PE`. *Justification*: The order of the operands in the postfix expression agrees with the order in the infix expression, and the operands that appear to the left of an operator in the infix expression also appear to its left in the postfix expression.
2. Push each "(" onto the stack.
3. When you encounter a ")", you pop operators off the stack, appending them to the end of `PE` until you encounter the matching "(". *Justification*: Within a "( )" grouping, precedence and left-to-right association determine the order of the operators, and Step 4, which follows, has already ordered the operators in accordance with these rules.
4. When you encounter an operator, if the stack is empty, push the operator onto the stack. However, if the stack is not empty, pop operators of greater or equal precedence from the stack, appending them to `PE`. You stop when you encounter either a "(" or an operator of lower precedence or when the stack becomes empty. You then push the new operator onto the stack. Thus, this step orders the operators by precedence and in accordance with left-to-right association. Notice that you continue popping from the stack until you encounter an operator of strictly lower precedence than the current operator in the infix expression. You do not stop on equality, because the left-to-right association

rule says that in case of a tie in precedence, the leftmost operator is applied first—and this operator is the one that is already on the stack.

5. When you reach the end of the string, you append the remaining contents of the stack to `PE`.

For example, Figure 8-7 traces the action of the algorithm on the infix expression $A-(B+C*D)/E$, assuming that the stack `S` and the string `PE` are initially empty. `PE` contains the resulting postfix expression $ABCD*+E/-$.

You can use the previous five-step description of the algorithm to develop a fairly concise pseudocode solution. Both the stack `S` and the postfix expression `PE` are empty initially. In the pseudocode that follows, the symbol · means concatenate (append), so `PE · x` means concatenate the string currently in `PE` and the character `x`—that is, follow the string in `PE` with the character `x`.

A pseudocode algorithm that converts an infix expression to postfix form

```
for each character Ch in the infix expression do
   case Ch of
      operand :  PE := PE · Ch
      '(' :      Push(S, Ch)
      ')' :      begin { pop down to the matching open
                         parenthesis}
                    while StackTop(S) <> '(' do
                    begin
                       PE := PE · StackTop(S)
                       Pop(S)
                    end  { while }

                    Pop(S)  { remove the open parenthesis }
                 end  { ')' }

      operator :
         begin
            while not StackIsEmpty(S)
                  Cand ((StackTop(S) <> '(') and
                     (Precedence(StackTop(S)) >=
                                          Precedence(Ch))) do
            begin
               PE := PE · StackTop(S)
               Pop(S)
            end  { while }

            Push(S, Ch)
         end  { operator }
   end  { case }

{ append to PE the operators remaining on the stack }
while not StackIsEmpty(S) do
begin
   PE := PE · StackTop(S)
   Pop(S)
end  { while }
```

Ch	S	PE	
A		A	
-	-	A	
(	-(	A	
B	-(	AB	
+	-(+	AB	
C	-(+	ABC	
*	-(+*	ABC	
D	-(+*	ABCD	
)	-(+	ABCD*	{ move operators }
	-(	ABCD*+	{ from stack }
	-	ABCD*+	{ to PE until "(" }
/	-/	ABCD*+	
E	-/	ABCD*+E	
		ABCD*+E/-	{ copy operators from stack to PE }

Figure 8-7

A trace of the algorithm that converts the infix expression $A - (B + C * D)/E$ to postfix form

A complete Pascal program follows. Notice that auxiliary subprograms are hidden within the procedure *ConvToPost*.

The program uses a unit *StackOps* that contains the stack operations for a stack of characters. (That is, *itemType* in the previous implementations of the ADT stack is *char* instead of *integer*.)

```
program InfixToPostfix;
{ ********************************************************
  INFIX TO POSTFIX CONVERSION

  Input: A legal infix expression.

  Output: The equivalent postfix expression.

  Assumptions:

  1. The input string is a legal infix expression, which can
     contain parentheses. Because expressions are legal, the
     program can ignore the boolean variable Success that
     the stack operations return.
  2. The operators are the binary operators +, -, *, and /.
  3. Every character that is not an operator or a
     parenthesis is a legal operand. Blanks are legal.
  4. The stack operations are available.
  ******************************************************** }

uses  StackOps;    { operations for stack of characters; }
                   { unit defines the data type stackType }

const MaxStringLength = 20;

type  expressionType = string[MaxStringLength];

      { classes of characters }
      classType = (Operand, Operator, OpenParen, CloseParen);
```

```
procedure ConvToPost(IEin : expressionType;
                     var PEout : expressionType);
{ -----------------------------------------------------------
  Converts an infix expression to postfix form.
  Precondition: The input expression IEin is a string
  that represents a legal infix expression as follows:
       operators are +, -, *, or /
       open and close parentheses
       operands, which are any other character except blank.
  Postcondition: PEout is the equivalent postfix expression.
  Calls: Stack operations and local subprograms Prec,
  TypeOfChar, ProcessOperand, ProcessCloseParen, ProcessOperator.
  ----------------------------------------------------------- }
var S : stackType;
    function Prec(Op : char) : integer;
    { -----------------------------------------------------
      Computes the precedence of an operator Op.
      Precondition: None.
      Postcondition: Returns 1 for + and -, 2 for * and
      /, and 0 for any other character.
      ----------------------------------------------------- }
    begin
       case Op of
          '+', '-' : Prec := 1;
          '*', '/' : Prec := 2;
       else
          Prec := 0;
       end  { case }
    end;  { Prec }

    function TypeOfChar(Ch : char) : classType;
    { -----------------------------------------------------
      Computes the class of a character Ch.
      Precondition: Ch is a legal character.
      Postcondition: Returns a value -- Operand, Operator,
      OpenParen, CloseParen -- according to the class of the
      character Ch.
      ----------------------------------------------------- }
    begin
       case Ch of
          '+', '-', '*', '/' : TypeOfChar := Operator;
          '(' :                TypeOfChar := OpenParen;
          ')' :                TypeOfChar := CloseParen;
       else
          TypeOfChar := Operand;
       end  { case }
    end;  { TypeOfChar }
```

```
procedure ProcessOperand(Ch : char;
                         var PEout : expressionType);
{ -----------------------------------------------------
  Processes operands.
  Precondition: Ch is an operand. PEout is either empty
  or contains the first part of the postfix expression.
  Postcondition: Operand Ch is appended to the
  end of postfix expression PEout.
  ----------------------------------------------------- }
begin
    PEout := PEout + Ch { concatenate }
end;  { ProcessOperand }

procedure ProcessCloseParen(var PEout : expressionType);
{ -----------------------------------------------------
  Processes right parentheses.
  Precondition: Stack S is not empty.
  Postcondition: Pops operators from stack S and appends
  them to the end of postfix expression PEout until a
  matching open paren is found.
  Calls: Stack operations.
  ----------------------------------------------------- }
var Top : char;
    Success : boolean;

begin
    GetStackTop(S, Top, Success);
    while Top <> '(' do
    begin
        PEout := PEout + Top;    { concatenate }
        Pop(S, Success);
        GetStackTop(S, Top, Success)
    end; { while }

    Pop(S, Success)
end;  { ProcessCloseParen }

procedure ProcessOperator(Ch : char;
                          var PEout : expressionType);
{ -----------------------------------------------------
  Processes operators.
  Precondition: Ch is an operator; PEout is either empty
  or contains the first part of the postfix expression.
  Stack S is not empty.
  Postcondition: Pops operators from stack S whose
  precedence is >= present operator Ch and appends them
  to the end of postfix expression PEout.
  Calls: Stack operations.
  ----------------------------------------------------- }
```

```
    var Top : char;
        Done, Success : boolean;

    begin
        Done := false;
        while (not StackIsEmpty(S)) and (not Done) do
        begin
           GetStackTop(S, Top, Success);
           if (Top <> '(') and (Prec(Top) >= Prec(Ch))
              then
              begin
                 PEout := PEout + Top;  { concatenate }
                 Pop(S, Success)
              end { then }

              else Done := true
        end;  { while }
        Push(S, Ch, Success)
    end;  { ProcessOperator }

var Success : boolean;
    Ch, Top : char;
    I : integer;

begin { ConvToPost }
    CreateStack(S);   { create a stack }
    PEout := '';      { output string is empty }

    { process each character in the expression }
    for I := 1 to length(IEin) do
    begin
       Ch := IEin[I];
       case TypeOfChar(Ch) of
          { operand - concatenate to the output string }
          Operand: ProcessOperand(Ch, PEout);

          { open paren - push onto the stack }
          OpenParen: Push(S, Ch, Success);

          { close paren - pop operators until a matching
            open paren is found }
          CloseParen: ProcessCloseParen(PEout);

          { operator - pop operators of >= precedence }
          Operator: ProcessOperator(Ch, PEout);
       end  { case }
    end;  { for }

    { move the rest of the stack to the output string }
    while not StackIsEmpty(S) do
```

```
    begin
       GetStackTop(S, Top, Success);
       Pop(S, Success);
       PEout := PEout + Top      { concatenate }
    end  { while }
end;  { ConvToPost }

procedure ReadExpr(var IEin : expressionType);
{ ------------------------------------------------------
  Reads an expression from standard input.
  Precondition: None.
  Postcondition: IEin contains the expression.
  ------------------------------------------------------ }
begin
    write('Enter infix expression of no more than ');
    writeln(MaxStringLength, ' characters: ');
    readln(IEin)
end;  { ReadExpr }

var IEin  : expressionType; { infix expression - input }
    PEout : expressionType; { postfix expression - output }

begin  { Main Program - demonstrate procedure ConvToPost }
    ReadExpr(IEin); { read infix expression }

    { convert the infix expression to postfix form }
    ConvToPost(IEin, PEout);

    { write out the infix and postfix expressions }
    writeln('Infix expression: ', IEin);
    writeln('Postfix expression: ', PEout)
end.  { Program }
```

The following are samples of the program's output:

```
Infix expression: A
Postfix expression: A

Infix expression: (A)
Postfix expression: A

Infix expression: A+B
Postfix expression: AB+

Infix expression: (A+B)
Postfix expression: AB+

Infix expression: A+B*C
Postfix expression: ABC*+

Infix expression: A*B+C
Postfix expression: AB*C+
```

```
Infix expression: A*(B+C)
Postfix expression: ABC+*

Infix expression: (A+B)*C
Postfix expression: AB+C*

Infix expression: A-B+C
Postfix expression: AB-C+

Infix expression: A-(B+C)
Postfix expression: ABC+-
```

A Search Problem

Our final application of stacks is designed to give you the flavor of a general type of problem for which stacks are very useful. This type of problem, known as a **search problem**, requires that you find a way to perform a given task such as getting from some point of origin to some destination point. We shall solve this problem first by using stacks and then by using recursion. The recursive solution will bring to light the close relationship between stacks and recursion.

The particular search problem here is to write a program that will act as a simple travel agent for the High Planes Airline Company (HPAir). Given all of the flight information for HPAir, the program will process customer requests to fly from some origin city to some destination city. So that you can focus on the issue at hand—the use of stacks as a problem-solving tool—the program will produce only a yes or no answer for each customer request. That is, the program will indicate whether there exists a sequence of HPAir flights from the origin city to the destination city. The more realistic problem of actually producing an itinerary—that is, the sequence of flights—is considered in Project 20 at the end of this chapter.

Determine whether HPAir flies from one city to another

INPUT There are three input textfiles as follows:

`CityFile`	Each line contains the name of a city that HPAir serves. The names are in alphabetical order.
`FlightFile`	Each line contains a pair of city names that represents the origin and destination of one of HPAir's flights.
`RequestFile`	Each line contains a pair of city names that represents a request to fly from some origin to some destination

OUTPUT For each customer request, a message indicates whether a sequence of HPAir flights can satisfy the request.

ASSUMPTIONS

1. Each city name contains at most 15 characters. Pairs of city names are separated by a comma.

2. HPAir serves at most 20 cities.
3. The input data is correct.

EXAMPLE

Input Files

```
CityFile:      Albuquerque
               Chicago
               San Diego
FlightFile:    Chicago,       San Diego
               Chicago,       Albuquerque
               Albuquerque,   Chicago
RequestFile:   Albuquerque,   San Diego
               Albuquerque,   Paris
               San Diego,     Chicago
```

Corresponding Output

```
Request is to fly from Albuquerque to San Diego.
HPAir has service from Albuquerque to San Diego.

Request is to fly from Albuquerque to Paris.
Sorry. HPAir does not serve Paris.

Request is to fly from San Diego to Chicago.
Sorry. HPAir does not have service from San Diego to Chicago.
```

Representing the flight data. The flight map in Figure 8-8 represents the routes that HPAir flies. There is an arrow from city C_1 to city C_2 if there is a flight from C_1 to C_2. In this case C_2 is **adjacent** to C_1 and the path from C_1 to C_2 is called a **directed path**. Notice that if C_2 is adjacent to C_1, it does not follow that C_1 is adjacent to C_2. For example, in Figure 8-8, there is a flight from city *R* to city *X*, but not from city *X* to city *R*. As you will see in Chapter 11, the map in Figure 8-8 is called a **graph**.

C_2 is adjacent to C_1 if there is a directed path from C_1 to C_2

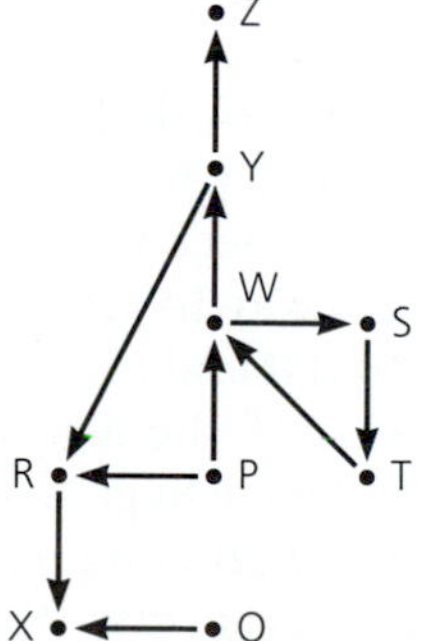

Figure 8-8
Flight map for HPAir

Searching a flight map by using a stack. When processing a customer's request to fly from some origin city to some destination city, you must determine from the flight map whether there is a route from the origin to the destination. For example, by examining the flight map in Figure 8-8, you can see that a customer could fly from city P to city Z by flying first to city W, then to city Y, and finally to city Z; that is, there is a directed path from P to Z: $P \rightarrow W$, $W \rightarrow Y$, $Y \rightarrow Z$. Thus, you must develop an algorithm that searches the flight map for a directed path from the origin city to the destination city. Such a path might involve either a single flight or a sequence of flights. The solution developed here performs an **exhaustive search**. That is, beginning at the origin city, the solution will try every possible sequence of flights until either it finds a sequence that gets to the destination city or it determines that no such sequence exists. You will see that the ADT stack is useful in organizing this search.

Use a stack to organize an exhaustive search

First consider how you might perform the search by hand. One approach is to start at the origin city C_0 and select an arbitrary path to travel—that is, select an arbitrary flight departing from the origin city. This flight will lead you to a new city, C_1. If city C_1 happens to be the destination city, you are done; otherwise, you must attempt to get from C_1 to the destination city. To do this, you select a path to travel out of C_1. This path will lead you to a city C_2. If C_2 is the destination, you are done; otherwise, you must attempt to get from C_2 to the destination city, and so on.

Consider the possible outcomes of applying the previous strategy:

Possible outcomes of the exhaustive search strategy

1. You eventually reach the destination city and can conclude that it is possible to fly from the origin to the destination.
2. You reach a city C from which there are no departing flights.
3. You go around in circles. For example, from C_1 you go to C_2, from C_2 you go to C_3, and from C_3 you go back to C_1. You might continue this tour of the three cities forever; that is, the algorithm is in an infinite loop.

If you always obtained the first outcome, everyone would be happy. However, because HPAir does not fly between all pairs of cities, you certainly cannot expect that the algorithm will always find a path from the origin city to the destination. For example, if city P in Figure 8-8 is the origin city and city Q is the destination city, the algorithm could not possibly find a path from city P to city Q.

Even if there were a sequence of flights from the origin city to the destination, it would take a bit of luck for the previous strategy to discover it—the algorithm would have to select a "correct" flight at each step. For example, even though there is a way to get from city P to city Z in Figure 8-8, the algorithm might not find it and instead would reach outcome 2 or 3. That is, suppose that from city P the algorithm chose to go to city R. From city R the algorithm would have to go to city X, from which there are no flights out (outcome 2). On the other hand, suppose that the algorithm chose to go to city W from city P. From city W the algorithm might choose to go to city *S*. It would then have to go to city *T* and then back to *W*. From *W* it might once again choose to go to city *S* and continue to go around in circles (outcome 3).

You thus need to make the algorithm more sophisticated, so that it always finds a path from the origin to the destination, if such a path exists, and otherwise terminates with the conclusion that there is no such path. Suppose that the earlier strategy results in outcome 2: You reach a city *C* from which there are no departing flights. This certainly does not imply that there is no way to get from the origin to the destination; it implies only that there is no way to get from city *C* to the destination. In other words, it was a mistake to go to city *C*. After discovering such a mistake, the algorithm can retrace its steps, or *backtrack*, to the city *C'* that was visited just before city *C* was visited. Once back at city *C'*, the algorithm can select a flight to some city other than *C*. Notice that it is possible that there are no other flights out of city *C'*. If this were the case, it would mean that it was a mistake to visit city *C'*, and thus you would want to backtrack again, this time to the city that was visited just before city *C'*.

Use backtracking to recover from a wrong choice

For example, you saw that, in trying to get from city *P* to city *Z* in Figure 8-8, the algorithm might first choose to go from city *P* to city *R* and then on to city *X*. As there are no departing flights from city *X*, the algorithm must backtrack to city *R*, the city visited before city *X*. Once back at city *R*, the algorithm would attempt to go to some city other than city *X*, but would discover that this is not possible. The algorithm would thus backtrack once more, this time to city *P*, which was visited just before city *R*. From city *P* the algorithm would choose to go to city *W*, which is a step in the right direction!

For the algorithm to implement this new strategy, it must maintain information about the order in which it visits the cities. First notice that when the algorithm backtracks from a city *C*, it must retreat to the city that it visited most recently before *C*. This observation suggests that you maintain the sequence of visited cities in a stack. That is, each time you decide to visit a city, you push its name onto the stack. You select the next city to visit from those adjacent to the city on the top of the stack. When you need to backtrack from the city *C* at the top of the stack (for example, because there are no flights out of the city), you simply pop a city from the stack. After the pop, the city on the top of the stack is the city on the current path that you visited most recently before *C*.

The algorithm as developed so far is as follows:

The search algorithm with backtracking

```
CreateStack(S)
{ push the origin city onto the stack }
Push(S, Origin)

while it is unknown whether there is a sequence of
       flights from the origin to the destination do
begin
   if you need to backtrack from the city on the stack's top
       then Pop(S)
```

```
      else
      begin
          Select a destination city C for a flight from
              the city on the top of the stack
          Push(S, C)
      end  { if }
end  { while }
```

Notice that at any point in the algorithm, the contents of the stack correspond to the sequence of flights currently under consideration. The city on the top of the stack is the city you are visiting currently, directly "below" it is the city visited previously, and so forth down to the bottom city, which is the first city visited in the sequence, or the origin city. In other words, an *invariant* of the `while` loop is that *the stack contains a directed path from the origin city at the bottom of the stack to the city at the top of the stack.* You can, therefore, always retrace your steps as far back through the sequence as needed.

Now consider the question of when to

```
Backtrack from the city on the top of the stack
```

You have already seen one case when backtracking is necessary. You must backtrack from the city on the top of the stack when there are no flights out of that city. Another time when you need to backtrack is related to the problem of going around in circles, described previously as the third possible outcome of the original strategy.

A key observation that will tell you when to backtrack is, *You never want to visit a city that the search has already visited.* As a consequence, you must backtrack from a city whenever there are no more unvisited cities to fly to. To see why you never want to visit a city a second time, consider two cases:

Two reasons for not visiting a city more than once

- If you have visited city C and it is still somewhere in the stack—that is, it is part of the sequence of cities that you are exploring currently—you do not want to visit C again. Any sequence that goes from C through $C_1, C_2, \cdots, C_k$, back to C, and then to C' might just as well skip the intermediate cities and go from C directly to C'.

  For example, suppose that the algorithm starts at P in Figure 8-8 and, in trying to find a path to Y, visits W, S, and T. There is now no reason for the algorithm to consider the flight from T to W because W is already on the stack. Anywhere you could fly to by going from W to S, from S to T, and then back to W, such as city Y, you could fly to directly from W without first going through S and T. Because you do not allow the algorithm to visit W a second time, it will backtrack from S and T to W and then go from W directly to Y. Figure 8-9 shows how the stack would appear if revisits were allowed and how it looks after backtrack-

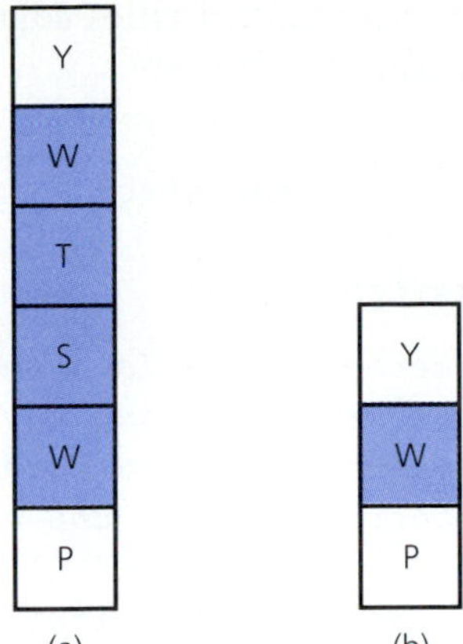

Figure 8-9

The stack of cities (a) allowing revisits and (b) after backtracking when revisits are not allowed

ing when revisits are not allowed. Notice that backtracking to *W* is very different from visiting *W* for a second time.

- If you have visited city *C*, but it is no longer in the stack—because you backtracked from it and popped it from the stack—you do not want to visit *C* again. This situation is subtle; consider two cases that depend on why you backtracked from the city.

  If you backtracked from *C* because there were no flights out of it, then you certainly do not ever want to try going through *C* again. For example, if, starting at *P* in Figure 8-8, the algorithm goes to *R* and then to *X*, it will backtrack from *X* to *R*. At this point, although *X* is no longer on the stack, you certainly do not want to visit it again, because you know there are no flights out of *X*.

  Now suppose that you backtracked from *C* because all cities adjacent to it had been visited. This implies that you have already tried all possible flights from *C* and have failed to find a way to get to the destination city. There is thus no reason to go to *C* again. For example, suppose that starting from *P* in Figure 8-8, the algorithm executes the following sequence: Visit *R*, visit *X*, backtrack to *R* (because there are no flights out of *X*), backtrack to *P* (because there are no more unvisited cities adjacent to *R*), visit *W*, visit *Y*. At this point the stack contains *P*-*W*-*Y*, with *Y* on top, and you need to choose a flight out of *Y*. You do not want to fly from *Y* to *R*, because you have visited *R* already and tried all possible flights out of *R*.

  In both cases, visiting a city a second time does not gain you anything, and in fact it may cause you to go around in circles.

Mark the visited cities

To implement the rule of not visiting a city more than once, you simply mark a city when it has been visited. When choosing the next city to visit, you restrict consideration to unmarked cities adjacent to the city on the top of the stack. The algorithm thus becomes

```
CreateStack(S)
{ push the origin city onto the stack }
Push(S, Origin)
Mark the origin as visited

while it is unknown whether there is a sequence of
      flights from the origin to the destination do
{ loop invariant: stack S contains a directed path from the
  origin city at the bottom of S to the city at the top of S }
begin
    if there are no flights to unvisited cities
       from the city on the top of the stack

       then Pop(S) { backtrack }

       else
       begin
           Select an unvisited destination city C for a
              flight from the city on the top of the stack
           Push(S, C)
           Mark C as visited
       end  { if }
end  { while }
```

Finally, you need to refine the condition in the *while* statement. That is, you need to refine the algorithm's final determination of whether there exists a path from the origin to the destination. The loop invariant, which states that the stack contains a directed path from the origin city to the city on the top of the stack, implies that the algorithm can reach an affirmative conclusion if the city at the top of the stack is the destination city. On the other hand, the algorithm can reach a negative conclusion only after it has exhausted all possibilities—that is, after the algorithm has backtracked to the origin and there remain no unvisited cities to fly to from the origin. At this point, the algorithm will pop the origin city from the stack and the stack will become empty.

With this refinement, the final version of the algorithm appears as follows:

The final version of the search algorithm

```
SearchS(Origin, Destination)

    CreateStack(S)
    { push the origin city onto the stack }
    Push(S, Origin)
    Mark the origin as visited

    while (not StackIsEmpty(S))
           Cand (StackTop(S) <> Destination) do
```

```
{ loop invariant: stack S contains a directed path from
  the origin city at the bottom of S to the city at the
  top of S}
begin
   if there are no flights to unvisited cities
       from the city on the top of the stack

       then Pop(S) { backtrack }

       else
       begin
          Select an unvisited destination city C for a
            flight from the city on the top of the stack
          Push(S, C)
          Mark C as visited
       end  { if }
end  { while }
```

Notice that the algorithm does not specify the order of selection for the unvisited cities. It really does not matter what selection criteria the algorithm uses, because the choice will not affect the final outcome: Either a sequence of flights exists or it does not. The choice, however, will affect your trace of the algorithm's action by affecting the specific sequence of flights. For the sake of the example, suppose that the algorithm always flies to the alphabetically earliest unvisited city from the city on the top of the stack.

Figure 8-10 contains a trace of the algorithm's action, given the map in Figure 8-8 and assuming that *P* is the origin city and *Z* is the destination city. The algorithm terminates with success.

Now consider the operations that the algorithm must perform on the flight map. The algorithm marks cities as it visits them, determines whether a city has been visited, and determines which cities are adjacent to a given city. You can treat the flight map as an ADT that has at least these

Action	Reason	Contents of stack
Push P	Initialize	P
Push R	Next unvisited adjacent city	PR
Push X	Next unvisited adjacent city	PRX
Pop X	No unvisited adjacent city	PR
Pop R	No unvisited adjacent city	P
Push W	Next unvisited adjacent city	PW
Push S	Next unvisited adjacent city	PWS
Push T	Next unvisited adjacent city	PWST
Pop T	No unvisited adjacent city	PWS
Pop S	No unvisited adjacent city	PW
Push Y	Next unvisited adjacent city	PWY
Push Z	Next unvisited adjacent city	PWYZ

Figure 8-10

A trace of the search algorithm, given the flight map in Figure 8-8

operations. In addition, when you read *FlightFile* and create the flight map, you must be able to insert a city adjacent to another city, and when you display the flight map, you must be able to display all cities that are adjacent to a given city. Thus, the ADT flight map could have the following operations:

*ADT **FlightMap** operations*

```
CreateMap(FlightMap)
{ Creates an empty flight map. }

MarkVisited(City, FlightMap)
{ Marks a city as visited. }

IsVisited(City, FlightMap)
{ Determines whether a city was visited. }

InsertAdjacent(City, AdjCity, FlightMap)
{ Inserts a city adjacent to another city in a flight
  map. }

GetNextCity(FlightMap, FromCity, NextCity)
{ Determines the next unvisited city, if any, that is
  adjacent to a given city. }

DisplayAdjacentCities(City, FlightMap)
{ Displays all cities that are adjacent to a given city. }
```

GetNextCity is the primary operation that the algorithm must perform on the flight map. Thus, to represent the flight map you should choose a data structure that will enable an efficient determination of cities that are adjacent to a given city. If there are N cities numbered 1, 2, ··· , N, you can use N linked lists to represent the flight map. You place a node on list i for city j if and only if there is a directed path from city i to city j. Such a data structure is called an **adjacency list**; Figure 8-11 illustrates an adjacency list for the flight map in Figure 8-8. Chapter 11 discusses adjacency lists further when it presents ways to represent graphs. At that time, you will learn why an adjacency list is a good choice for the present program.

Represent the flight map by using an adjacency list

The program associates each city name with an integer as follows. As the program reads in the names of the cities that HPAir serves, it places them in the array *CityNames* such that the ith city read is in *CityNames[i]*. The program refers to *CityNames[i]* as city i. If you require that the cities in the input file be in alphabetical order, the array *CityNames* will be sorted. This requirement allows you to perform a binary search on the array for a given name and then to associate the name with the correct city number. This scheme allows you to place integers rather than strings on the stack.

The following is a Pascal program that implements the solution to the HPAir problem. Note that the procedure *IsPath* implements the *SearchS* algorithm.

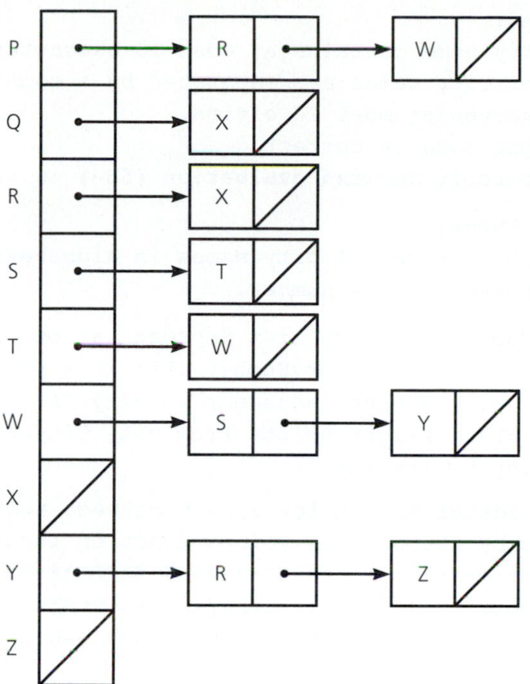

Figure 8-11

Adjacency list for the flight map in Figure 8-8

```
program HPAir;
{ *******************************************************
  HPAIR - TRAVEL AGENT

  Given data describing all of the flights operated by HPAir,
  this program determines whether a sequence of flights from
  city A to city B exists.

  Input: There are three input textfiles:

  CityFile     -  Each line contains the name of a city that
                  HPAir serves. The names are in alphabetical
                  order.

  FlightFile   -  Each line contains a pair of city names
                  that represents the origin and destination
                  of one of HPAir's flights.

  RequestFile  -  Each line contains a pair of city names
                  that represents a request to fly from some
                  origin to some destination.

  Output: For each customer request, a message indicates
          whether a sequence of HPAir flights can satisfy
          the request.
```

```
  Assumptions:
  1. Each city name contains at most 15 characters.
     Pairs of city names are separated by a comma.
  2. HPAir serves at most 20 cities.
  3. The input data is correct.
  4. Short-circuit boolean evaluation ($B-) is in effect.

  Data Structures:
  1. CityNames - array of city names in alphabetical order
     and indexed by city number.

  2. FlightMap - adjacency list representation of HPAir's
     flights. FlightMap[CityNumber].Ptr is a pointer to the
     list of city numbers adjacent to city CityNumber (that
     is, an HPAir flight exists from city CityNumber to
     each city on its list).

  Note: The actual search for a path between two cities is
        done by the boolean-valued function IsPath.
  ******************************************************** }
uses  StackOps;            { array-based stack of integers }
{ This unit defines the constant MaxStack, which is the
  maximum stack size. }

const MaxCities = 20; { max number of cities <= MaxStack }
      NameSize  = 15; { max length of city name }

type  nameType     = string[NameSize];
      nameListType = array[1..MaxCities] of nameType;

      { nodes for the adjacency list }
      adjPtrType      = ^adjNodeType;
      adjNodeType     = record
         Number : integer; { city number }
         Next : adjPtrType { pointer to next city }
      end; { record }

      { head records for adjacency list }
      adjListHeadType = record
         Ptr : adjPtrType; { pointer to adjacent city }
         Visited : boolean { true if city was visited,
                             else false }
      end; { record }

      adjListType = array[1..MaxCities] of adjListHeadType;
      mapType = adjListType;
```

ADT FlightMap operations

```
{ ********** ADT flight map operations ****************** }

procedure CreateMap(var FlightMap : mapType);
{ ------------------------------------------------------
  Initializes the flight map.
  Precondition: None.
```

```
  Postcondition: Head pointers are nil and Visited
  fields are false.
  ---------------------------------------------------------- }
var Index : integer;
begin
    for Index := 1 to MaxCities do
    begin
       FlightMap[Index].Ptr := nil;
       FlightMap[Index].Visited := false
    end  { for }
end;  { CreateMap }

procedure MarkVisited(City : integer;
                      var FlightMap: mapType);
{ ----------------------------------------------------------
  Marks a city as visited.
  Precondition: City is the number of a city,
  FlightMap is the flight map, CreateMap(FlightMap) has been
  called.
  Postcondition: The Visited field that corresponds to
  City is true.
  ---------------------------------------------------------- }
begin
    FlightMap[City].Visited := true
end;  { MarkVisited }

function IsVisited(City : integer;
                   FlightMap : mapType): boolean;
{ ----------------------------------------------------------
  Determines whether a city was visited.
  Precondition: City is the number of a city,
  FlightMap is the flight map, CreateMap(FlightMap) has been
  called.
  Postcondition: Returns true if City was visited, else
  returns false.
  ---------------------------------------------------------- }
begin
    IsVisited := (FlightMap[City].Visited = true)
end;  { IsVisited }

procedure InsertAdjacent(City, AdjCity : integer;
                         var FlightMap : mapType);
{ ----------------------------------------------------------
  Inserts a city adjacent to another city in a flight map.
  Precondition: City is the number of the origin city,
  AdjCity is the number of a city adjacent to City,
  FlightMap is the flight map, CreateMap(FlightMap) has been
  called.
  Postcondition: AdjCity is adjacent to City in FlightMap.
  ---------------------------------------------------------- }
```

```
var CityPtr : adjPtrType;
begin
   new(CityPtr);
   CityPtr^.Number := AdjCity;
   CityPtr^.Next := FlightMap[City].Ptr;
   FlightMap[City].Ptr := CityPtr
end;  { InsertAdjacent }

procedure GetNextCity(FlightMap : mapType;
              FromCity : integer; var NextCity : integer;
              var Success : boolean);
{ ---------------------------------------------------------
  Determines the next unvisited city, if any, that is
  adjacent to a given city.
  Precondition: FlightMap is the flight map, FromCity is
  the number of the origin city, CreateMap(FlightMap) has
  been called.
  Postcondition: If a city adjacent to FromCity exists
  and is unvisited, NextCity is the number of that city and
  Success is true; otherwise Success is false and NextCity
  is unchanged.
  Implementation note: The search starts at the beginning
  of the adjacency list each time. (See Exercise 16.)
  --------------------------------------------------------- }
var CityPtr : adjPtrType;
begin
   CityPtr := FlightMap[FromCity].Ptr;
   while (CityPtr <> nil) and
               IsVisited(CityPtr^.Number, FlightMap) do
      CityPtr := CityPtr^.Next;

   if CityPtr = nil
      then Success := false
      else NextCity := CityPtr^.Number
end;  { GetNextCity }

procedure DisplayAdjacentCities(City: integer;
              CityNames : nameListType; FlightMap : mapType);
{ ---------------------------------------------------------
  Displays all cities that are adjacent to a given city.
  Precondition: City is the number of a city, CityNames
  is an array of city names, FlightMap is the flight map,
  CreateMap(FlightMap) has been called.
  Postcondition: City's name and the names of all cities
  that are adjacent to City are displayed.
  --------------------------------------------------------- }
var CityPtr : adjPtrType;
begin
   CityPtr := FlightMap[City].Ptr;
   while CityPtr <> nil do
```

```
    begin
       writeln('  From ', CityNames[City],
                          ' to ', CityNames[CityPtr^.Number]);
       CityPtr := CityPtr^.Next
    end  { while }
end;  { DisplayAdjacentCities }

{ ********** end of ADT flight map operations ************ }

function IsPath(OriginCity, DestCity : integer;
                FlightMap : mapType) : boolean;
{ ---------------------------------------------------------
  Determines whether a sequence of flights between two
  cities exists. Nonrecursive stack version.
  Precondition: OriginCity and DestCity are the city
  numbers of the origin and destination cities,
  respectively. FlightMap is defined.
  Postcondition: Returns true if a sequence of flights
  exists from OriginCity to DestCity, otherwise returns
  false. Parameters are unchanged.
  Calls: Stack operations, MarkVisited, GetNextCity.
  Note: Uses a stack S for the city numbers of a potential
  path.
  --------------------------------------------------------- }
var S : stackType;
    TopCity, NextCity : integer;
    Success : boolean;
begin
    { initialize stack for the search }
    CreateStack(S);

    { push origin city onto stack, mark it visited }
    Push(S, OriginCity, Success);
    MarkVisited(OriginCity, FlightMap);

    GetStackTop(S, TopCity, Success);
    while (not StackIsEmpty(S)) and (TopCity <> DestCity) do
    { loop invariant: stack S contains a directed path from
      the origin city at the bottom of S to the city at the
      top of S}
    begin
       { find an unvisited city adjacent to the city on the
         top of the stack }
       GetNextCity(FlightMap, TopCity, NextCity, Success);
       if not Success
          then Pop(S, Success) { no city found; backtrack}

          else                 { visit city }
          begin
             Push(S, NextCity, Success);
             MarkVisited(NextCity, FlightMap)
          end;  { if }
```

The search function

```
      GetStackTop(S, TopCity, Success);
   end;  { while }

   IsPath := not StackIsEmpty(S)
end;  { IsPath }

procedure TestSolution(CityNames: nameListType;
         var FlightMap : mapType; FromNum, ToNum : integer);
{ -----------------------------------------------------------
  Tests for a solution.
  Precondition: CityNames is a list of cities that HPAir
  serves, FlightMap is the adjacency list, FromNum and ToNum
  are the city numbers of the origin and destination cities.
  FromNum and ToNum cannot exceed the number of cities in
  CityNames.
  Postcondition: Indicates whether a flight between the
  two cities exists by printing a message.
  Calls: IsPath.
  ----------------------------------------------------------- }
begin
   { test for a solution }
   if IsPath(FromNum, ToNum, FlightMap)
     then write('HPAir has service ')
     else write('Sorry. HPAir does not have service ');
   writeln('from ', CityNames[FromNum], ' to ',
                                    CityNames[ToNum], '.')
end;  { TestSolution }

procedure TrimBlanks(var CharStr : string);
{ -----------------------------------------------------------
  Removes leading and trailing blanks from a string.
  Precondition: CharStr is a string that might have
  leading or trailing blanks.
  Postcondition: CharStr has no leading or trailing
  blanks, although it may have embedded blanks. CharStr's
  dynamic length is correct.
  ----------------------------------------------------------- }
begin
    { trim leading blanks }
    while CharStr[1] = ' ' do
       CharStr := copy(CharStr, 2, pred(length(CharStr)));

    { trim trailing blanks }
    while CharStr[length(CharStr)] = ' ' do
       CharStr := copy(CharStr, 1, pred(length(CharStr)));
end;  { TrimBlanks }

procedure ReadTwoNames(var F : text;
                       var Name1, Name2 : nameType);
```

```
{ -------------------------------------------------------
  Reads two city names from a line of a textfile.
  Precondition: F represents a textfile of city names
  that is open for input. Each line in the file contains
  two names that are separated by a comma. $B- is in effect.
  Postcondition: Name1 and Name2 contain the names that
  are in the next line read. Both Name1 and Name2 have no
  leading or trailing blanks and both strings have correct
  dynamic lengths. F remains open for input; the file window
  is at the start of the next line or, if no next line
  exists, is at the end-of-file symbol.
  Calls: TrimBlanks.
  ------------------------------------------------------- }
var InputString, TempString : string;
    CommaPosition : integer;

begin
    readln(F, InputString);          { read entire line }
    CommaPosition := pos(',', InputString);

    { extract names from the line just read }

    { extract first name }
    TempString := copy(InputString,1,pred(CommaPosition));
    TrimBlanks(TempString);
    Name1 := TempString;

    { extract second name }
    TempString := copy(InputString, succ(CommaPosition),
                       length(InputString)-CommaPosition);
    TrimBlanks(TempString);
    Name2 := TempString
end;  { ReadTwoNames }

procedure ReadCities(var CityFile : text;
                     var CityNames : nameListType;
                     var NumCities : integer);
{ -------------------------------------------------------
  Reads and counts city names that HPAir serves.
  Precondition: CityFile is a textfile of city names.
  Postcondition: The array CityNames contains NumCities
  names. CityFile is closed.
  Calls: TrimBlanks.
  ------------------------------------------------------- }
var InputString : string;

begin
    reset(CityFile);
    NumCities := 0;
```

```
   while not eof(CityFile) do
   begin
      inc(NumCities);
      readln(CityFile, InputString);
      TrimBlanks(InputString);
      CityNames[NumCities] := InputString
   end;  { while }

   close(CityFile);
end;  { ReadCities }

procedure DisplayCities(CityNames : nameListType;
                        NumCities : integer);
{ ---------------------------------------------------------
  Displays city names that HPAir serves.
  Precondition: The array CityNames contains NumCities
  names.
  Postcondition: The names are displayed.
  --------------------------------------------------------- }
var CityNumber : integer;
begin
   writeln('******* HPAir FLIGHT INFORMATION *******');
   writeln;
   writeln('Cities served by HPAir:');
   writeln;
   for CityNumber := 1 to NumCities do
        writeln('  ', CityNames[CityNumber])
end;  { DisplayCities }

function CityIndex(CityNames: nameListType;
           NumCities: integer; ACity: nameType): integer;
{ ---------------------------------------------------------
  Searches a list of city names for a particular city.
  Precondition: The NumCities names in CityNames must be
  sorted alphabetically. ACity is the name of the desired
  city.
  Postcondition: Returns the index of ACity in CityNames,
  or returns 0 if the city is not found.
  Implementation note: An iterative binary search is
  used.
  --------------------------------------------------------- }
var First, Last, Mid : integer;
begin
   First := 1;
   Last := NumCities;
   while First < Last do
   begin
      Mid := (First + Last) div 2;
```

```
        if CityNames[Mid] < ACity
            then First := succ(Mid)
            else Last := Mid
    end;  { while }

    { test termination conditions }
    if CityNames[First] = ACity
        then CityIndex := First
        else CityIndex := 0
end;  { CityIndex }

procedure ReadFlightMap(var FlightFile: text;
              CityNames: nameListType; NumCities: integer;
              var FlightMap: mapType);
{ -----------------------------------------------------------
  Reads flight information and creates the flight map.
  Precondition: FlightFile is a textfile of city pairs,
  CityNames is a list of NumCities cities that HPAir serves.
  Postcondition: FlightMap is the adjacency list.
  FlightFile is closed.
  Calls: CreateMap, ReadTwoNames, CityIndex, InsertAdjacent.
  ----------------------------------------------------------- }
var Origin, Destination : nameType;  { city names }
    FromNum, ToNum : integer;         { city numbers }
begin
    CreateMap(FlightMap);  { initialize map }

    { read in all of the flight information }
    reset(FlightFile);
    while not eof(FlightFile) do
    begin
        ReadTwoNames(FlightFile, Origin, Destination);
        FromNum := CityIndex(CityNames, NumCities, Origin);
        ToNum := CityIndex(CityNames, NumCities, Destination);

        { add ToNum to FromNum's adjacency list }
        if (ToNum = 0) or (FromNum = 0)
          then writeln('Warning. Bad input Data.')
          else InsertAdjacent(FromNum, ToNum, FlightMap);
    end;  { while }

    close(FlightFile)
end;  { ReadFlightMap }

procedure DisplayFlightMap(FlightMap : mapType;
           CityNames : nameListType; NumCities : integer);
{ -----------------------------------------------------------
  Displays flight information.
  Precondition: FlightMap specifies HPAirs's flights.
  CityNames is a list of NumCities cities that HPAir serves.
```

```
  Postcondition: HPAir's flights are displayed.
  Calls: DisplayAdjacentCities.
  ---------------------------------------------------------- }
var CityNumber : integer;
begin
    writeln;
    writeln('Flights operated by HPAir:');
    writeln;

    { display cities adjacent to city CityNumber }
    for CityNumber := 1 to NumCities do
       DisplayAdjacentCities(CityNumber, CityNames, FlightMap)
end;  { DisplayFlightMap }

procedure WriteErrorMessage(Origin, Destination: nameType;
                            FromNum, ToNum : integer);
{ ----------------------------------------------------------
  Writes appropriate messages for an illegal request.
  Precondition: Origin and Destination are the names of
  the origin and destination cities. FromNum and ToNum are
  the corresponding city numbers.
  Postcondition: Prints a message that indicates an
  illegal request.
  ---------------------------------------------------------- }
begin
    if FromNum = 0 { unknown city of origin }
       then writeln('Sorry. HPAir does not serve ',
                                       Origin, '.');

    if ToNum = 0 { unknown destination city }
       then writeln('Sorry. HPAir does not serve ',
                                       Destination, '.');

    if FromNum = ToNum { origin equals destination }
       then writeln('Walk!!!')
end;  { WriteErrorMessage }

procedure ProcessRequests(var RequestFile: text;
          var CityNames: nameListType; NumCities: integer;
          var FlightMap: mapType);
{ ----------------------------------------------------------
  Processes flight requests that are in the textfile
  RequestFile.
  Precondition: CityNames is a list of NumCities cities
  that HPAir serves, FlightMap is the adjacency list,
  RequestFile is a textfile of flight requests.
  Postcondition: Prints messages about the feasibility of
  flight requests. Parameters are unchanged. RequestFile is
  closed.
```

```
  Calls: ReadTwoNames, CityIndex, TestSolution,
  WriteErrorMessage.
  ---------------------------------------------------------- }
var Origin, Destination : nameType;  { city names }
    FromNum, ToNum : integer;        { city numbers }

begin  { ProcessRequests }
    reset(RequestFile);

    { write heading }
    writeln;
    writeln('******* ITINERARY REQUESTS *******');
    writeln;

    { process each request until end of file }
    while not eof(RequestFile) do
    begin
      { read a request }
      ReadTwoNames(RequestFile, Origin, Destination);

      { write the request }
      write('Request is to fly from ');
      writeln(Origin, ' to ', Destination, '.');

      { process the request }
      FromNum := CityIndex(CityNames, NumCities, Origin);
      ToNum := CityIndex(CityNames, NumCities, Destination);

      { test for legal origin and destination cities }
      if (FromNum <> 0) and (ToNum <> 0)
                               and (FromNum <> ToNum)
        then TestSolution(CityNames, FlightMap,
                                 FromNum, ToNum)
        else WriteErrorMessage(Origin, Destination,
                                 FromNum, ToNum);

      writeln
    end;  { while }

    close(RequestFile)
end;   { ProcessRequests }

var CityNames : nameListType;    { cities served by HPAir }
    NumCities : integer;         { number of cities served }
    FlightMap : mapType;         { flight information }
    CityFile, FlightFile, RequestFile: text; { input files }

begin  { Main Program }
    { assign actual files to file variables }
    assign(CityFile, 'CITIES.DAT');
    assign(FlightFile, 'FLIGHTS.DAT');
    assign(RequestFile, 'REQUESTS.DAT');
```

```
    { read in, count, and write city names }
    ReadCities(CityFile, CityNames, NumCities);
    DisplayCities(CityNames, NumCities);

    { read in and write out all of the flight information
      and create the adjacency list }
    ReadFlightMap(FlightFile, CityNames, NumCities,
                                                FlightMap);
    DisplayFlightMap(FlightMap, CityNames, NumCities);

    { Look for solution for each request }
    ProcessRequests(RequestFile, CityNames, NumCities,
                                                 FlightMap)
end.  { Program }
```

Searching a flight map by using recursion. Recall the initial attempt at a solution to the HPAir problem of searching for a sequence of flights from some origin city to some destination city. Consider how you might perform the search "by hand." One approach is to start at the origin city and select an arbitrary flight that departs from the origin city. This flight will lead you to a new city, C_1. If city C_1 happens to be the destination city, you are done; otherwise, you must attempt to get from C_1 to the destination city by selecting a flight out of C_1. This flight will lead you to city C_2. If C_2 is the destination, you are done; otherwise, you must attempt to get from C_2 to the destination city, and so on. There is a distinct recursive flavor to this search strategy, which can be restated as follows:

A recursive search strategy

```
To fly from the origin to the destination:

    Select a city C adjacent to the origin
    Fly from the origin to city C
    if C is the destination city
        then terminate--the destination is reached
        else fly from city C to the destination
```

This statement of the search strategy makes its recursive nature very apparent. The first step in flying from the origin city to the destination city is to fly from the origin city to city C. Once at city C, you are confronted with another problem of the same type—you now must fly from city C to the destination.

This recursive formulation is nothing more than a restatement of the initial (incomplete) strategy developed previously. As such it has the same three possible outcomes:

Possible outcomes of the recursive search strategy

1. You eventually reach the destination city and can conclude that it is possible to fly from the origin to the destination.
2. You reach a city C from which there are no departing flights.
3. You go around in circles.

The first of these outcomes corresponds to a degenerate case of the recursive algorithm. If you ever reach the destination city, no additional problems of the form "fly from city *C* to the destination" are generated, and the algorithm terminates. However, as was observed previously, there is no guarantee that the algorithm will produce this outcome, that is, that it will reach this degenerate case. The algorithm might reach a city *C* from which there are no departing flights (notice that the algorithm does not specify what to do if you reach a city *C* from which there are no departing flights—in this sense the algorithm is incomplete), or it might repeatedly cycle through the same sequence of cities and thus never terminate.

You can resolve these problems by mirroring what you did in the previous solution. Consider the following refinement, in which you mark visited cities and never fly to a city that has been visited already:

A refinement of the recursive search algorithm

```
SearchR(Origin, Destination)
{ Search for a sequence of flights from
  Origin to Destination. }

    Mark Origin as visited

    if Origin is the destination city
       then terminate--the destination is reached

       else
          for each unvisited city C adjacent to Origin do
             SearchR(C, Destination)
```

Now consider what happens when the algorithm reaches a city that has no unvisited city adjacent to it. For example, consider the piece of a flight map in Figure 8-12. When `SearchR` reaches city *X*—that is, when the parameter `Origin` has the value *X*—the `for` loop will not be entered, because there are no unvisited cities adjacent to *X*. Hence, the procedure `SearchR` returns. This return has the effect of backtracking to city *W*, from which the flight to *X* originated. In terms of the previous pseudocode, the return is made to the point from which the call `SearchR(X, Destination)` occurred. This point is within the `for` loop, which iterates through the unvisited cities adjacent to *W*; that is, the parameter `Origin` has the value *W*.

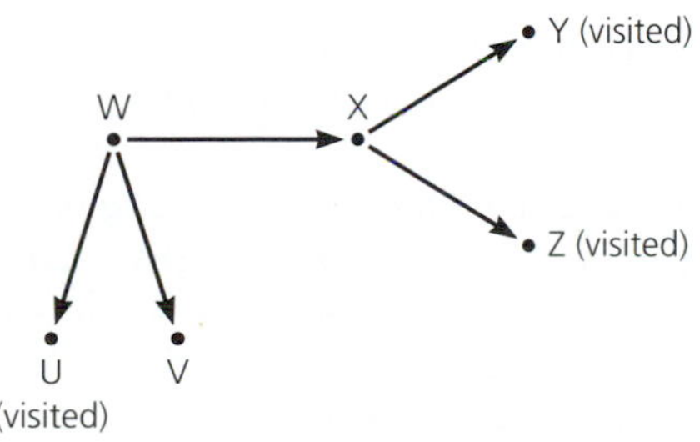

Figure 8-12
A piece of a flight map

After backtracking from *X* to *W*, the *for* loop will again execute; this time the loop chooses city *V*, resulting in the recursive call *SearchR(V, Destination)*. From this point, the algorithm either will eventually reach the destination city and terminate, or it will backtrack once again to city *W*. If it backtracks to *W*, the *for* loop will terminate because there are no more unvisited cities adjacent to *W*, and a return from *SearchR* will occur. The effect is to backtrack to the city where the flight to *W* originated. If the algorithm ever backtracks to the origin city and there remain no unvisited cities adjacent to it, the algorithm will terminate, and you can conclude that there is no sequence of flights from the origin to the destination. Notice that the algorithm will always terminate in one way or another, because it will either reach the destination city or run out of unvisited cities to try.

You can transform the previous program, which implements the stack-based search, to one that implements this recursive search simply by omitting the *uses* statement for the unit of stack operations and by replacing the function *IsPath* with the following version. The new function is a nonrecursive shell around the local recursive function *Try*. As you learned in Chapter 5, the nonrecursive shell avoids multiple copies of *FlightMap*.

*You can replace the **IsPath** function in the previous program with this recursive function*

```
function IsPath(OriginCity, DestCity : integer;
                FlightMap : mapType) : boolean;
{ ---------------------------------------------------------
  Determines whether a sequence of flights between two
  cities exists. Recursive version.
  Precondition: OriginCity and DestCity are the city
  numbers of the origin and destination cities,
  respectively. FlightMap is defined.
  Postcondition: Returns true if a sequence of flights
  exists from OriginCity to DestCity, otherwise returns
  false. Parameters are unchanged.
  Note: The local recursive function Try performs the
  search.
  --------------------------------------------------------- }
  function Try(OriginCity : integer) : boolean;
  { ------------------------------------------------------
    Performs the recursive search.
    Precondition: DestCity and FlightMap are global.
    Postcondition: Returns true if a sequence of flights
    from OriginCity to DestCity exists, otherwise returns
    false.
    Note: For each city that has a flight from OriginCity,
    tries to find a sequence of flights to DestCity.
    ------------------------------------------------------ }
  var NextCity : integer;
      Success, Done : boolean;
```

```
   begin
      { mark the current city as visited }
      MarkVisited(OriginCity, FlightMap);

      { degenerate case: the destination is reached }
      if OriginCity = DestCity
         then Try := true

         else { try a flight to each unvisited city }
         begin
            Done := false;
            GetNextCity(FlightMap, OriginCity, NextCity,
                                                    Success);
            while Success and (not Done) do
               Done := Try(NextCity);

            Try := Done
         end;  { if }
   end;  { Try }

begin  { IsPath }
   IsPath := Try(OriginCity)
end;  { IsPath }
```

You have probably noticed a close parallel between this recursive algorithm and the earlier stack-based algorithm *SearchS(Origin, Destination)*. (Compare the function *Try* with the stack-based function *IsPath*.) In fact, the two algorithms simply employ different mechanisms to implement the identical search strategy. The next section will elaborate on the relationship between the two algorithms.

THE RELATIONSHIP BETWEEN STACKS AND RECURSION

The previous section solved the HPAir problem once by using the ADT stack and again by using recursion. The goal of this section is to relate the way that the stack organizes the search for a sequence of flights to the way a recursive algorithm organizes the search. You will see that the ADT stack has a hidden presence in the concept of recursion and, in fact, that stacks have an active role in most computer implementations of recursion.

Consider how the two search algorithms implement three key aspects of their common strategy.

A comparison of key aspects of two search algorithms

- **Visiting a new city.** The recursive algorithm *SearchR* visits a new city *C* by making the call *SearchR(C, Destination)*. The algorithm *SearchS* visits city *C* by pushing *C* onto a stack.

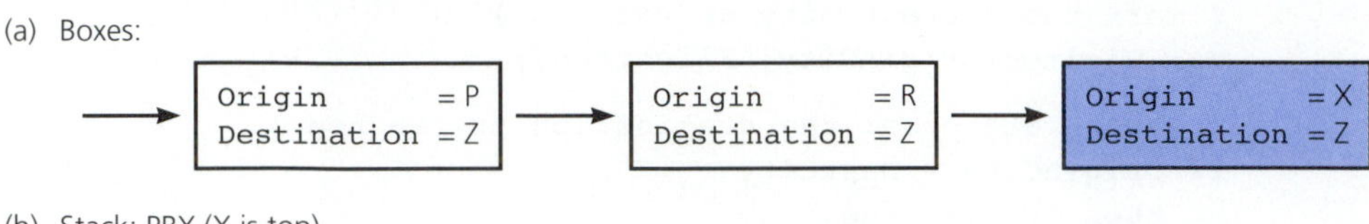

Figure 8-13

Visiting a new city: (a) box trace versus (b) stack

Notice that if you were to use the box method to trace the execution of `SearchR`, the call `SearchR(C, Destination)` would generate a box in which the city *C* is associated with the formal parameter `Origin` of `SearchR`.

For example, Figure 8-13 shows both the state of the box trace for `SearchR` and the stack for `SearchS` at corresponding points of their search for a path from city *P* to city *Z* in Figure 8-8.

- **Backtracking.** Both search algorithms attempt to visit an unvisited city that is adjacent to the current city. Notice that this current city is the value associated with the formal parameter `Origin` in the deepest (rightmost) box of `SearchR`'s box trace. Similarly, the current city is on the top of `SearchS`'s stack. In Figure 8-13, this current city is *X*. If there are no unvisited cities adjacent to the current city, the algorithms must backtrack to the previous city. The algorithm `SearchR` backtracks by returning from the current recursive call. You represent this action in the box method by crossing off the deepest box. The algorithm `SearchS` backtracks by explicitly popping from its stack. For example, from the state depicted in Figure 8-13, both algorithms backtrack to city *R* and then to city *P*, as Figure 8-14 illustrates.
- **Termination.** The search algorithms terminate either when they reach the destination city or when they exhaust all possibilities. All possibilities are exhausted when, after backtracking to the origin city, there remain no unvisited adjacent cities. This situation occurs for `SearchR` when all boxes have been crossed off in the box trace and a return occurs to the point of the original call, which, for example, occurred in the main program. For `SearchS` there remain no unvisited cities adjacent to the origin when the stack becomes empty.

Figure 8-14

Backtracking: (a) box trace versus (b) stack

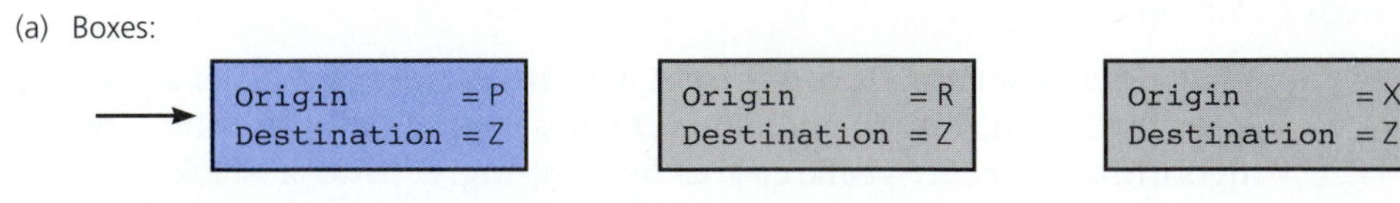

Thus, the two search algorithms really do perform the identical action. In fact, provided that they use the same rule to select an unvisited city—for example, traverse the current city's list of adjacent cities alphabetically—they will always visit the identical cities in the identical order. The similarities between the algorithms are far more than coincidence. In fact, it is always possible to capture the actions of a recursive subprogram by using a stack.

An important context in which the close tie between stacks and recursion is explicitly utilized is a compiler's implementation of a recursive subprogram. It is common for a compiler to use a stack to implement a recursive subprogram in a manner that greatly resembles the box method. When a recursive call to a subprogram occurs, the implementation must remember certain information. This information consists essentially of the same local environment that you place in the boxes—values of both parameters and local variables, and a reference to the point from which the recursive call was made.

Typically, stacks are used to implement recursive subprograms

During execution, the compiled program must manage these boxes of information, or **activation records**, just as you must manage them on paper. As the HPAir example has indicated, the operations needed to manage the activation records are those that a stack provides. When a recursive call occurs, a new activation record is created and pushed onto a stack. This action corresponds to the creation of a new box at the deepest point in the sequence. When a return is made from a recursive call, the stack is popped, bringing the activation record that contains the appropriate local environment to the top of the stack. This action corresponds to crossing off the deepest box and following the arrow back to the preceding box. Although we have greatly simplified the process, most implementations of recursion are based on stacks of activation records.

Each recursive call generates an activation record that is pushed onto a stack

Programmers use a similar strategy when implementing a nonrecursive version of a recursive algorithm. You might need to recast a recursive algorithm into a nonrecursive form to make it more efficient, as mentioned in Chapter 5. The previous discussion should give you a taste of the techniques for removing recursion from a program. You will encounter recursion removal as a formal topic in more advanced courses, such as compiler construction.

You can use stacks when implementing a nonrecursive version of a recursive algorithm

SUMMARY

1. **The ADT stack operations have a last-in, first-out (LIFO) behavior.**
2. **Algorithms that operate on algebraic expressions are an important application of stacks. The LIFO nature of stacks is exactly what the algorithm that evaluates postfix expressions needs to organize the operands. Similarly, the algorithm that transforms infix expressions to postfix form uses a stack to organize the operators in accordance with precedence rules and left-to-right association.**

3. **You can use a stack to determine whether a sequence of flights exists between two cities. The stack keeps track of the sequence of visited cities and enables the search algorithm to backtrack easily. Because the origin city is at the bottom of the stack and the destination is at the top, it is awkward to print the sequence of cities in their normal order from origin to destination.**
4. **There is a strong relationship between recursion and stacks. Most implementations of recursion maintain a stack of activation records in a manner that resembles the box method.**

COMMON PITFALLS / DEBUGGING

1. **Operations such as `StackTop` and `Pop` must take reasonable action when the data structure is empty. One possibility is to return a boolean flag whose value is `false` in this event.**
2. **Algorithms that evaluate an infix expression or transform one to postfix form must determine to which operands a given operator applies. Doing so allows for precedence and left-to-right association so that you can omit parentheses.**
3. **When searching for a sequence of flights between cities, you must take into account the possibility that the algorithm will make wrong choices. For example, the algorithm must be able to backtrack when it hits a dead end, and you must eliminate the possibility that the algorithm will cycle.**

SELF-TEST EXERCISES

1. If you push the letters A, B, C, and D in order onto a stack of characters and then pop them, in what order will they be deleted from the stack?
2. What do the stacks *S* and *T* "look like" after the following sequence of operations:

```
CreateStack(S)
Push(S, 1)
Push(S, 2)
CreateStack(T)
Push(T, 3)
Push(T, 4)
Pop(S)
Push(S, StackTop(T))
Push(S, 5)
Pop(T)
Push(T, 6)
```

3. Under what conditions in the line-reversal problem would you choose an array-based implementation for the stack? Under what conditions would you choose a pointer-based implementation?

4. For each of the following strings, trace the execution of the balanced-parentheses algorithm and show the contents of the stack at each step.

   a. `x((yz)))`
   b. `(x(y((z)))`
   c. `(((x)))`

5. Use the stack algorithms in this chapter to evaluate the postfix expression $AB-C+$. Assume the following values for the identifiers: $A = 7$; $B = 3$; $C = -2$. Show the status of the stack after each step.

6. Use the stack algorithms in this chapter to convert the infix expression $A/B*C$ to postfix form. Be sure to account for left-to-right association. Show the status of the stack after each step.

7. Explain the significance of the precedence tests in the infix-to-postfix conversion algorithm. Why is a $\geq$ test used rather than a $>$ test?

8. Execute the HPAir algorithm with the map in Figure 8-15 for the following requests. Show the state of the stack after each step.

   a. Fly from *A* to *D*
   b. Fly from *A* to *B*
   c. Fly from *C* to *G*

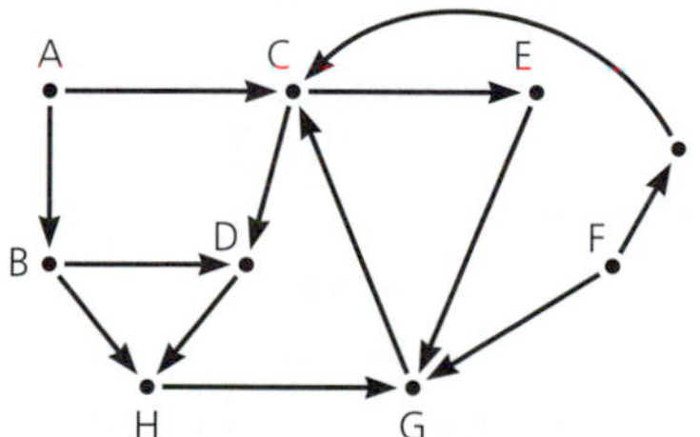

Figure 8-15

Flight map for Self-Test Exercise 8 and Exercise 12

EXERCISES

1. For the following input line, trace the execution of the `LineReverse` pseudocode and show the contents of the stack at each step:

   `abc#de##fg#h`

2. Revise the solution to the balanced-parentheses problem so that the expression can contain three types of parentheses: ( ), [ ], and { }. Thus, {*ab*(*c*[*d*])*e*} is valid, but {*ab*(*c*)) is not.

3. The diagram of a railroad switching system in Figure 8-16 is commonly used to illustrate the notion of a stack. Identify three stacks in

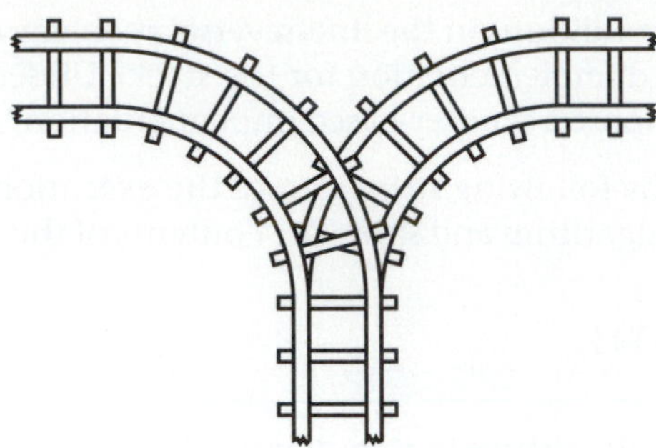

Figure 8-16

Railroad switching system

the figure and show how they relate to one another. How can you use this system to construct any possible permutation of railroad cars?

4. List the changes that you must make to convert a program that uses an array-based implementation of a stack to one that uses a pointer-based implementation of a stack.

5. Suppose that you have a stack `S` and an empty auxiliary stack `T`. Show how you can do each of the following tasks by using the ADT stack operations:

a. Print the contents of `S` in reverse order.
b. Count the number of items in `S`, leaving `S` unchanged.
c. Delete every occurrence of a specified item from `S`, leaving the order of the remaining items unchanged.

6. For each of the following strings, trace the execution of the language-recognition algorithm described in the section "Recognizing Strings in a Language," and show the contents of the stack at each step.

a. `xy$xy`
b. `xy$x`
c. `y$yx`
d. `xx$xx`
e. `xy$y`

7. Implement in Pascal the line-reversal problem described in the section "The Stack As an Example of an ADT in Program Development."

8. Evaluate the following postfix expressions. Assume the following values for the identifiers: $A = 7$; $B = 3$; $C = -2$; $D = -5$; $E = 1$.

a. $ABC+-$
b. $ABC-D*+$
c. $AB+C-DE*+$

9. Convert the following infix expressions to postfix form. Do not forget to account for the precedence rules and left-to-right association.

a. $A-B+C$
b. $A/(B*C)$
c. $(A+B)*C$
d. $A-(B+C)$
e. $A-(B/C*D)$
f. $A/B/C-(D+E)*F$
g. $A*(B/C/D)+E$
h. $A-(B+C*D)/E$

10. Repeat Exercises 8 and 9, but this time use the algorithms given in this chapter. Show the status of the stack after each step.

11. Implement the algorithm that evaluates postfix expressions in Pascal. For illustrative purposes, recognize only the operands *A, B, C, D,* and *E,* and write a procedure that assigns values to the operands as follows: $A = 5, B = 7, C = -1, D = 11$, and $E = 25$. Assign the value zero to any other operand. Although the pseudocode treats `StackTop` as a function, you may want to implement it as a procedure.

12. Execute the HPAir algorithm with the map in Figure 8-15 (see Self-Test Exercise 8) for the following requests. Show the state of the stack after each step.

a. Fly from *A* to *G*
b. Fly from *F* to *H*
c. Fly from *E* to *I*
d. Fly from *I* to *G*

13. Consider a popular variation of the ADT stack. Instead of the `Pop` and `StackTop` operations, define `Pop` to both retrieve and remove the top element from a stack. Modify the pointer-based and array-based implementations of the original ADT stack accordingly.

How does this new definition of the ADT stack affect the infix-to-postfix conversion program and the HPAir program? How does it affect the postfix evaluation program that you wrote in Exercise 11?

14. You can implement two stacks in one array by having them grow toward each other from the opposite ends of the array, as shown in Figure 8-17. What are the advantages of one array rather than two separate arrays of half the size? Work out the details of an implementation. How are the limiting conditions (empty and full) recognized? Note that it is important that the two stacks do not run into each other.

15. Suppose that you redefine the `Pop` operation for a stack as follows:

```
Pop(S, n)
{ Removes from stack S the n items that were most
  recently added. It is an error if there are fewer
  than n items on S. }
```

Modify the pointer-based and array-based implementations of the original `Pop` operation to reflect this change. Could you define the new operation in terms of the old operations? Which implementation of the new operation would be more efficient?

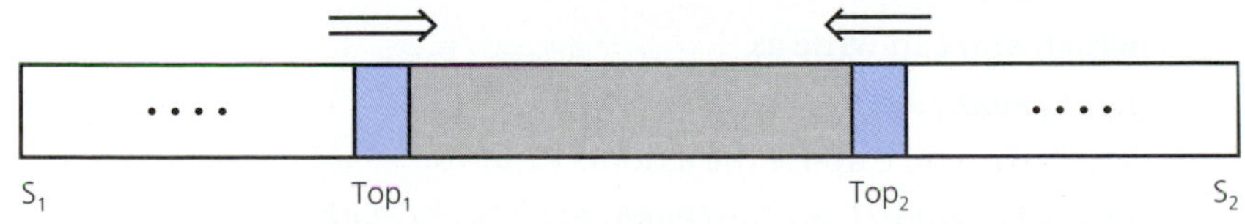

Figure 8-17
Two stacks implemented in a single array

16. In the implementation of the HPAir program, the search for the next unvisited city adjacent to a city *i* always starts at the beginning of the ith linked list in the adjacency list. This approach is actually a bit inefficient, because a city can never become unvisited after it has already been visited by the search. Modify the program so that the search for the next city begins where the last search left off. That is, maintain an array of `TryNext` pointers into the adjacency list.

17. Using stacks, write nonrecursive versions of the procedures `Towers`, as defined in Chapter 6, and `Quicksort`, as defined in Chapter 7.

***18.** As Chapter 4 pointed out, you can define ADT operations in a mathematically formal way by using axioms. For example, you can formally define the ADT stack by using the following axioms, where `S` is an arbitrary stack and `Item` an arbitrary stack item. Note that `CreateStack` is treated as a constant that represents a "newly created empty stack."

`StackIsEmpty(CreateStack) = true` (A new stack is empty.)

`StackIsEmpty(Push(S, Item)) = false`

`Pop(CreateStack) = CreateStack` (or an error.)

`Pop(Push(S, Item)) = S`

`StackTop(CreateStack) = error`

`StackTop(Push(S, Item)) = Item`

You can use the axioms, for example, to prove that the stack defined by the sequence of operations

```
Create an empty stack
Push a 5
Push a 7
Push a 3
Pop (the 3)
Push a 9
Push a 4
Pop (the 4)
```

which you can write as

```
Pop(Push(Push(Pop(Push(Push(Push(CreateStack,5),7),3)),9),4))
```

is exactly the same as the stack defined by the sequence

```
Create an empty stack
Push a 5
Push a 7
Push a 9
```

which you can write as

```
Push(Push(Push(CreateStack,5),7),9)
```

Similarly, you can use the axioms to show

```
StackIsEmpty(Pop(Pop(Push(Pop(Push(Push
(CreateStack,1),2)),3)))) = true
```

a. The representation of a stack as a sequence *Push(Push(· · · Push(CreateStack, · · ·)* without any *Pop* operations is called a **canonical form.** Prove that any stack is equal to a stack that is in canonical form.

b. Prove that the canonical form is unique. That is, a stack is equal to exactly one stack that is in canonical form.

c. Use the axioms to formally show the following:

```
StackTop(Pop(Push(Push(Pop(Push(Push(Pop(Pop(Push
(CreateStack,6))),9),2)),3),1))) = 3
```

19. Exercise 14 of Chapter 4 asked you to revise the object type `ordListType` so that each item on the ordered list is a dynamically allocated object. Revise the object type `stackType`, which descends from `ordListType`, so that the items on the stack are dynamically allocated objects that descend from `genericObjectType`, as defined in Chapter 4. Write a small program that demonstrates how to allocate, use, and deallocate your new object. Include a procedure that allocates objects that descend from `genericObjectType`.

PROJECT

20. Consider an expanded statement of the HPAir problem. In addition to the "from" and "to" cities, each line of input contains a flight number (an integer) and the cost of the flight (an integer). Modify the HPAir program so that it will produce a complete itinerary for each request, including the flight number of each flight, the cost of each flight, and the total cost of the trip.

EXAMPLE

Input Files

```
CityFile:          Albuquerque
                   Chicago
                   San Diego

FlightFile:        Chicago,          San Diego    703     125
                   Chicago,          Albuquerque  111     450
                   Albuquerque,      Chicago      178     450

RequestFile:       Albuquerque,      San Diego
                   Albuquerque,      Paris
                   San Diego,        Chicago
```

Corresponding Output

```
Request is to fly from Albuquerque to San Diego.
Flight #178 from Albuquerque  to Chicago   Cost: $450
Flight #703 from Chicago      to San Diego Cost: $125
Total Cost ............  $575
```

```
Request is to fly from Albuquerque to Paris.
Sorry. HPAir does not serve Paris.

Request is to fly from San Diego to Chicago
Sorry. HPAir does not have service from San Diego to Chicago.
```

When the HPAir program in this chapter finds a sequence of flights from the origin city to the destination city, its stack contains the corresponding path of cities. The stumbling block to reporting this path is that the cities appear on the stack in reverse order; that is, the destination city is at the top of the stack and the origin city is at the bottom. For example, if you use the program to find a path from city *P* to city *Z* in Figure 8-8, the final contents of the stack will be *P-W-Y-Z*, with *Z* on top. You want to print the origin city *P* first, but it is at the bottom of the stack. If you restrict yourself to the stack operations, the only way that you can print the path in its correct order is first to reverse the stack by popping it onto a temporary stack and then to print the cities as you pop them off the temporary stack. Note that this approach requires that you process each city on the path twice.

Evidently a stack is not the appropriate ADT for the problem of printing the path of cities in the correct order; the appropriate ADT is a **traversable stack**. In addition to the five standard stack operations, `CreateStack`, `StackIsEmpty`, `Push`, `Pop`, and `StackTop`, a traversable stack includes the operation `Traverse`. `Traverse` begins at one end of the stack and *visits* each item in the stack until it reaches the other end of the stack. For this project, you want `Traverse` to begin at the bottom of the stack and move toward the top.

What modifications are required to find a least-cost trip for each request? How can you incorporate time considerations into the problem?

CHAPTER 9

Queues

PREVIEW The operations that define a queue give this ADT a behavior opposite from that of a stack. While a stack's behavior is characterized as last in, first out, a queue's behavior is characterized as first in, first out. This chapter defines the queue's operations and discusses strategies for implementing them. Queues are important in simulation, a technique for analyzing the behavior of complex systems. As an example of this application of queues, this chapter presents a simulation of people waiting in line at a bank. The first-in, first-out behavior of a queue makes this ADT an appropriate model for the behavior of people in a line.

THE ABSTRACT DATA TYPE QUEUE

You can think of a stack as having only one end, because all operations are performed at the top of the stack. This characteristic of the operations gives a stack its last-in, first-out behavior. A **queue**, on the other hand, has two ends: a **rear**, where new items are inserted, and a **front**, from which items are deleted. This characteristic gives a queue its **first-in, first-out** (FIFO) behavior, which makes it appropriate for modeling real-world structures such as a line of customers.

FIFO: The first item inserted into a queue is the first item out

The abstract data type queue is defined by five operations:

KEY CONCEPTS

ADT Queue Operations

```
CreateQueue(Q)
{ Creates an empty queue Q. }

QueueIsEmpty(Q)
{ Determines whether queue Q is empty. }

Add(Q, NewItem)
{ Adds NewItem to queue Q. }

Remove(Q)
{ Removes from queue Q the item that was added earliest. }

QueueFront(Q)
{ Retrieves from queue Q the item that was added earliest,
  leaving Q unchanged. }
```

Figure 9-1 illustrates these operations with a queue of integers. Notice that *Add* inserts an item at the rear of the queue and that *QueueFront*

Operation	Queue after operation
	Front ↓
`CreateQueue(Q)`	
`Add(Q, 5)`	5
`Add(Q, 2)`	5 2
`Add(Q, 7)`	5 2 7
`QueueFront(Q)`	5 2 7 (returns 5)
`Remove(Q)`	2 7

Figure 9-1

Some queue operations

looks at the item at the front of the queue, whereas ***Remove*** deletes the item at the front of the queue.

Consider how you might formalize the FIFO property of a queue by using axioms. For example, you need an axiom that indicates that after a series of ***Add*** operations, ***QueueFront*** returns the item I_1 added earliest. Intuitively, you want the axiom to say

$$QueueFront(Add(\cdots Add(Add(empty\ queue,\ I_1),\ I_2),\cdots,I_n)) = I_1$$

This attempt at an axiom is not completely rigorous, however, because the meaning of the dots, ⋯ , is not well defined. Exercise 8 at the end of this chapter discusses further the formal axioms that define the ADT queue.

A SIMPLE APPLICATION OF THE ADT QUEUE

Recall from Chapter 6 that a palindrome is a string of characters that reads the same from left to right as it does from right to left. In the previous chapter, you learned that you can use a stack to reverse the order of occurrences. You should realize now that you can use a queue to preserve the order of occurrences. Thus, you can use both a queue and a stack to determine whether a string is a palindrome.

You can use a queue in conjunction with a stack to recognize palindromes

As you traverse the character string from left to right, you can insert each character into both a queue and a stack. Figure 9-2 illustrates the result of this action for the string "abcbd." You can see that the first character in the string is at the front of the queue and at the bottom of the stack. Likewise, the last character in the string is at the rear of the queue but at the top of the stack.

Thus, you can compare the characters at the top of the stack and the front of the queue. If the characters are the same, you can delete them. You can repeat this process until either the ADT's become empty, in which case the original string is a palindrome, or the two characters are not the same, in which case the string is not a palindrome.

Figure 9-2

The results of inserting a string into both a queue and a stack

String: abcbd

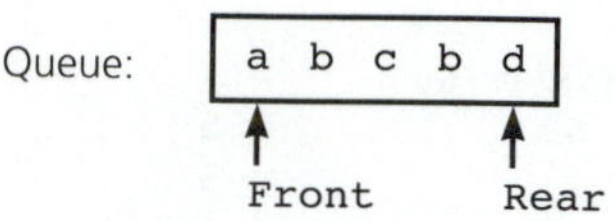

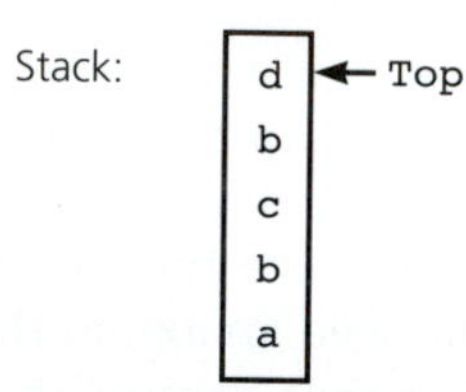

The following is a pseudocode version of a nonrecursive recognition algorithm for the language of palindromes:

A nonrecursive recognition algorithm for palindromes

```
function IsPal(Str) : returns a boolean value
{ Determines whether the string Str is a palindrome. }

   CreateQueue(Q)        { create a queue }
   CreateStack(S)        { create a stack }

   { insert each character into both the queue and the stack }
   for I := 1 to length(Str) do
   begin
      NextChar := Str[I]
      Add(Q, NextChar)
      Push(S, NextChar)
   end  { for }

   { compare the queue characters with the stack characters }
   IsPal := true
   while (not QueueIsEmpty(Q)) and IsPal do
   begin
      if (QueueFront(Q) = StackTop(S))
         then
         begin
            Remove(Q)
            Pop(S)
         end  { if }
         else IsPal := false
   end  { while }
```

IMPLEMENTATIONS OF THE ADT QUEUE

As with stacks, there are array-based and pointer-based implementations of queues. The choice between the two implementations once again depends on whether or not your problem can use the fixed-size queue that an array-based implementation provides.

For queues, the pointer-based implementation is a bit more straightforward than the array-based one, so we start with it.

A Pointer-Based Implementation of the ADT Queue

You might expect a pointer-based implementation to use two external pointers, one to the front and one to the rear, as Figure 9-3a illustrates. However, as Figure 9-3b shows, you can actually get by with a single external pointer—to the rear—if you make the queue circular.

When a circular linked list represents a queue, the node at the rear of the queue points to the node at the front. Thus,

A circular linked list can represent a queue

> `Q` points to the node at the rear of the queue, and
>
> `Q^.Next` points to the node at the front

Insertion at the rear and deletion from the front are straightforward. Figure 9-4 illustrates the addition of an item to a nonempty queue. Inserting the new node, to which *p* points, at the rear of the queue requires three pointer changes: the next pointer in the new node, the next pointer in the

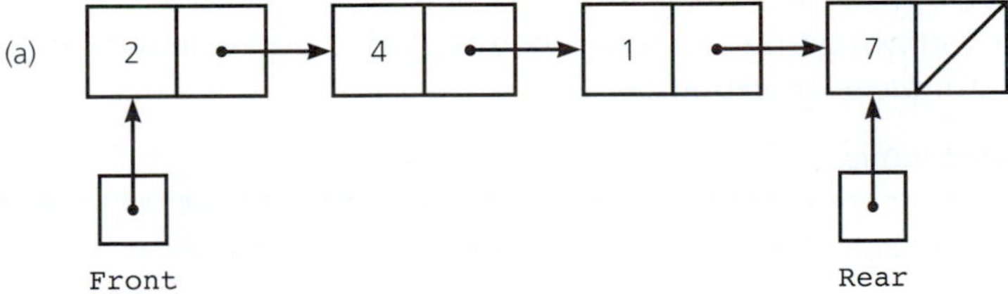

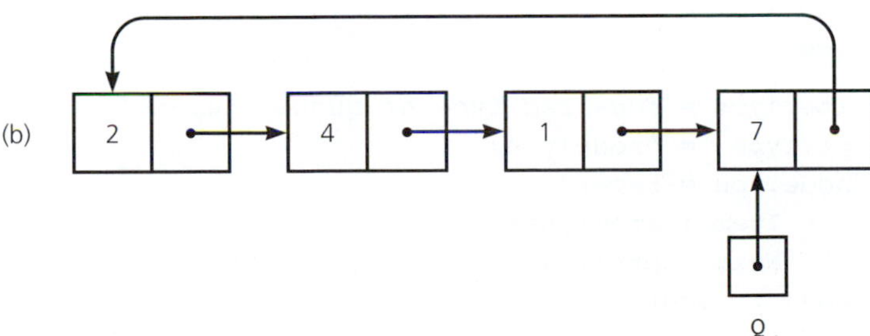

Figure 9-3

A pointer-based implementation of a queue: (a) with two external pointers; (b) circular

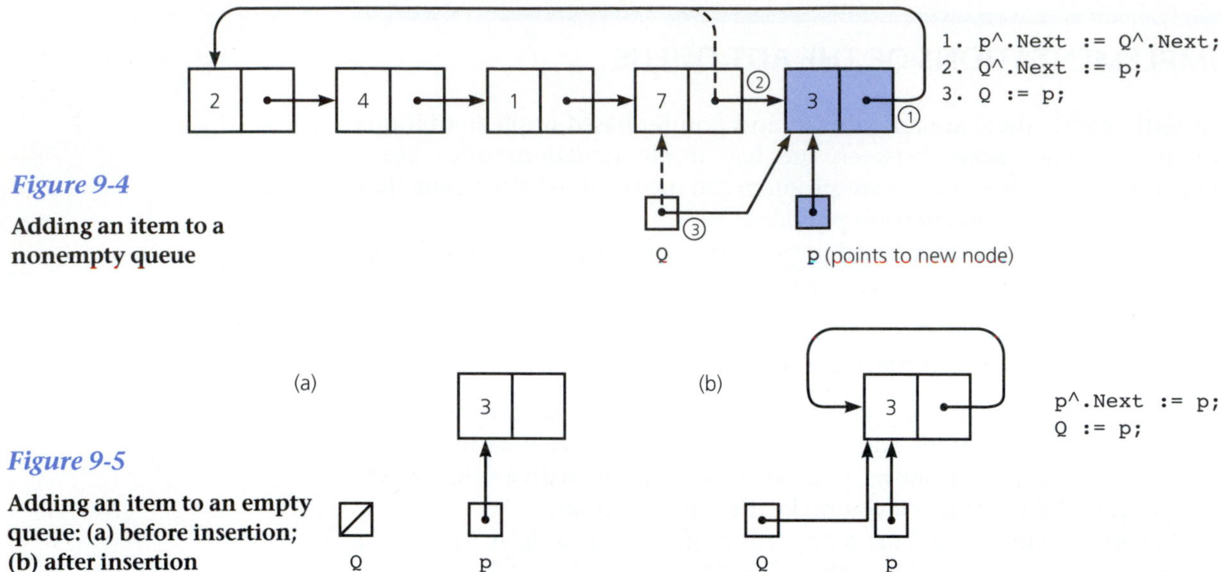

Figure 9-4

Adding an item to a nonempty queue

Figure 9-5

Adding an item to an empty queue: (a) before insertion; (b) after insertion

rear node, and the external pointer *Q*. Figure 9-4 depicts these changes and indicates the order in which they must occur. (The dashed lines indicate pointer values before the changes.) The addition of an item to an empty queue is a special case, as Figure 9-5 illustrates.

Deletion from the front of the queue is simpler than insertion at the rear. Figure 9-6 illustrates the removal of the front of a queue that contains more than one item. Notice that you need to change only one pointer. Deletion from a queue of one item is a special case that sets the external pointer *Q* to *nil*.

The following unit contains a pointer-based implementation in Pascal of the ADT queue operations:

```
unit QueueOps;
{ ***********************************************************
  BASIC QUEUE OPERATIONS - Pointer-based implementation

    CreateQueue, QueueIsEmpty, Add, Remove, GetQueueFront
  *********************************************************** }

interface

type itemType = <desired type of queue item>;
      ptrType   = ^nodeType;
      nodeType = record
          Item : itemType;
          Next : ptrType
      end; { record }

      queueType = ptrType;
```

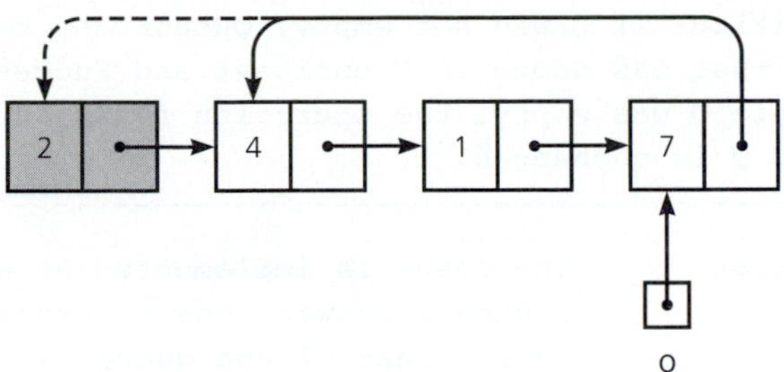

Figure 9-6

Removing an item from a queue of more than one item

```
procedure CreateQueue(var Q : queueType);
{ ---------------------------------------------------------
  Creates an empty queue.
  Precondition: None.
  Postcondition: The queue Q is empty.
  --------------------------------------------------------- }
function QueueIsEmpty(Q : queueType) : boolean;
{ ---------------------------------------------------------
  Determines whether a queue is empty.
  Precondition: CreateQueue(Q) has been called.
  Postcondition: Returns true if Q was empty, else returns
  false.
  --------------------------------------------------------- }
procedure Add(var Q : queueType; NewItem : itemType;
              var Success : boolean);
{ ---------------------------------------------------------
  Adds an item to the rear of a queue.
  Precondition: CreateQueue(Q) has been called.
  Postcondition: NewItem is at the rear of queue and
  Success is true.
  --------------------------------------------------------- }
procedure Remove(var Q : queueType;
                 var Success : boolean);
{ ---------------------------------------------------------
  Removes the item at the front of a queue.
  Precondition: CreateQueue(Q) has been called.
  Postcondition: If Q was not empty, the item that was
  added to Q earliest is removed and Success is true.
  However, if Q was empty, removal is impossible and Success
  is false.
  --------------------------------------------------------- }
procedure GetQueueFront(Q : queueType;
         var QueueFront: itemType; var Success : boolean);
{ ---------------------------------------------------------
  Retrieves the item at the front of a queue.
  Precondition: CreateQueue(Q) has been called.
```

```
  Postcondition: If Q was not empty, QueueFront contains
  the item that was added to Q earliest and Success is true.
  However, if Q was empty, the operation fails and Success
  is false. Q is unchanged.
  ----------------------------------------------------------- }
implementation     { The queue is implemented as a circular
                     linked list with one external pointer
                     to the rear of the queue. }

procedure CreateQueue(var Q : queueType);
begin
    Q := nil
end;  { CreateQueue }

function QueueIsEmpty(Q : queueType) : boolean;
begin
    QueueIsEmpty := (Q = nil)
end;  { QueueIsEmpty }

procedure Add(var Q : queueType; NewItem : itemType;
              var Success : boolean);
var NewFrontPtr : ptrType;
begin
    { get a new node }
    new(NewFrontPtr);
    NewFrontPtr^.Item := NewItem;

    { insert the new node }
    if QueueIsEmpty(Q)
          then         { insertion into empty queue }
             NewFrontPtr^.Next := NewFrontPtr
          else
          begin        { insertion into nonempty queue }
             NewFrontPtr^.Next := Q^.Next;
             Q^.Next := NewFrontPtr
          end; { if }
    Q := NewFrontPtr;
    Success := true
end;  { Add }

procedure Remove(var Q : queueType;
                 var Success : boolean);
var FrontPtr : ptrType;
begin
    Success := not QueueIsEmpty(Q);

    if Success
          then
          begin
             FrontPtr := Q^.Next;
```

```
            if FrontPtr = Q { special case? }
               then Q := nil     { yes, one node in Q }
               else Q^.Next := FrontPtr^.Next;

            dispose(FrontPtr);
            Success := true
         end  { if }
end;  { Remove }

procedure GetQueueFront(Q : queueType;
         var QueueFront: itemType; var Success : boolean);
begin
    Success := not QueueIsEmpty(Q);

    if Success
          then { queue is not empty }
          begin
             QueueFront := Q^.Next^.Item;
             Success := true
          end  { if }
end;  { GetQueueFront }

end.   { unit }
```

A program that uses this unit could begin as follows:

```
program DemonstrateQueue;
uses QueueOps;     { pointer-based queue operations }

var Q : queueType;
    Entry : itemType;
    Success : boolean;

begin
    CreateQueue(Q);
    readln(Entry);
    Add(Q, Entry, Success);
    . . .
```

An Array-Based Implementation of the ADT Queue

An array-based implementation is appropriate for applications in which a fixed-sized queue does not present a problem. As Figure 9-7a illustrates, a naive array-based implementation might define a queue as follows:

A naive array-based implementation of a queue suffers from rightward drift

```
const  MaxQueue = <maximum size of queue>;
type   itemType = <desired type of queue item>;
       queueType = record
           Front : 1..MaxQueue;
           Rear  : 0..MaxQueue;
           Items : array[1..MaxQueue] of itemType
       end;  { record }

var    Q : queueType
```

Figure 9-7

(a) A naive array-based implementation of a queue; (b) rightward drift

(a)

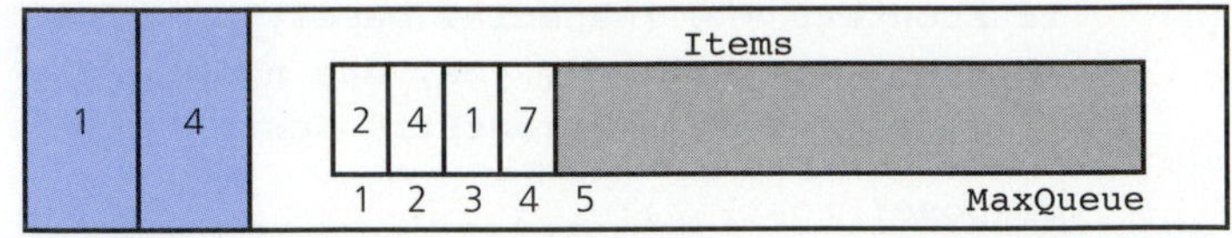

(b)

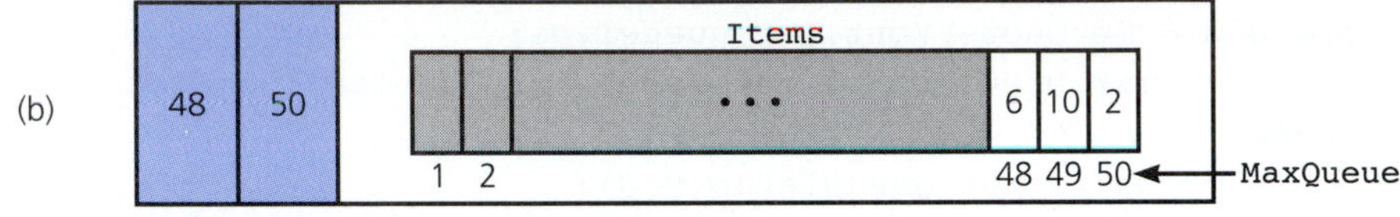

The queue is initialized with `Front` = 1 and `Rear` = 0. When a new item is added to the queue, `Rear` is incremented and the item is placed in the position that the new value of `Rear` references. When an item is removed, `Front` is incremented. The queue is empty whenever `Rear < Front`. The queue is full when `Rear = MaxQueue`.

Rightward drift can cause a queue-full condition even though the queue contains few entries

The problem with this strategy is **rightward drift**—that is, after a sequence of additions and removals, the items in the queue will drift down to the high end of the array, and `Rear` could equal `MaxQueue` even when there are only a few items currently in the queue. Figure 9-7b illustrates this situation.

Shifting elements to compensate for rightward drift is expensive

One possible solution to this problem is to shift array elements to the left, either after each deletion or whenever `Rear = MaxQueue`. This solution guarantees that the queue can always contain up to `MaxQueue` items. Shifting is not really satisfactory, however, as it would dominate the cost of the implementation.

A circular array eliminates rightward drift

A much more elegant solution is possible by viewing the array as circular, as Figure 9-8 illustrates. You advance the queue indexes `Front`—to remove an item—and `Rear`—to add an item—by moving them clockwise around the array. Figure 9-9 illustrates the effect of a sequence of three queue operations on `Front`, `Rear`, and the array. When either `Front` or `Rear` advances past location `MaxQueue`, it wraps around to location 1. This

Figure 9-8

A circular implementation of a queue

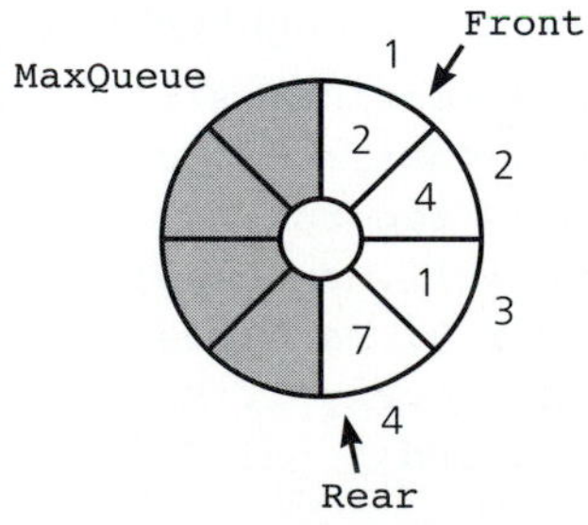

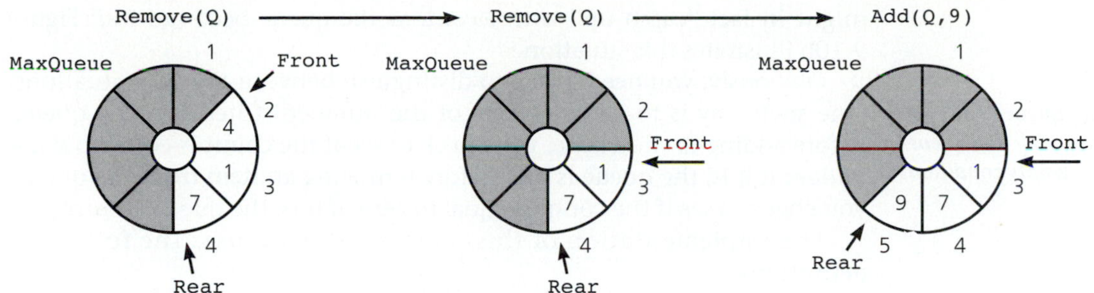

Figure 9-9

No drifting

wraparound eliminates the problem of rightward drift, which occurred in the previous implementation, because here the circular array has no end.

The only difficulty with this scheme is the detection of the queue-empty and queue-full conditions. It seems reasonable to select as the queue-empty condition

Front and Rear cannot be used to distinguish between queue-full and queue-empty conditions

`Front` is one slot ahead of `Rear`

since this appears to indicate that `Front` "passes" `Rear` when the queue becomes empty, as Figure 9-10a depicts. However, it is also possible that this condition signals a full queue: Because the queue is circular, `Rear`

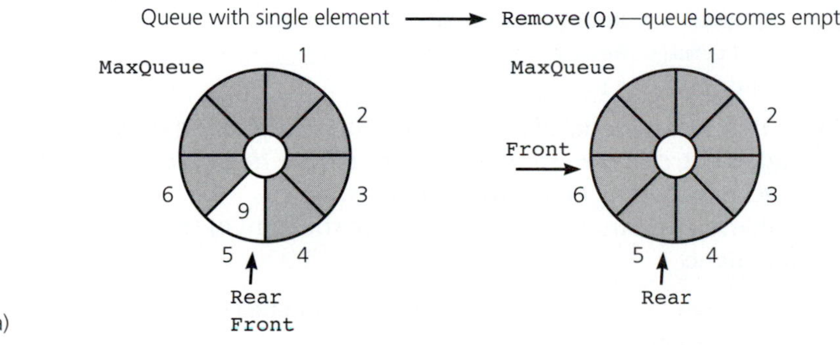

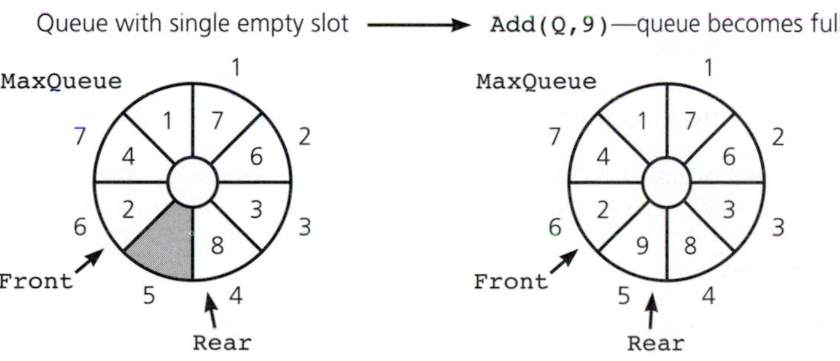

Figure 9-10

(a) `Front` passes `Rear` when the queue becomes empty; (b) `Rear` catches up to `Front` when the queue becomes full

might in fact "catch up" with *Front* as the queue becomes full; Figure 9-10b illustrates this situation.

By counting queue items, you can detect queue-full and queue-empty conditions

Obviously, you need a way to distinguish between the two situations. One such way is to keep a count of the number of items in the queue. Before adding to the queue, you check to see if the count is equal to *MaxQueue*; if it is, the queue is full. Before removing an item from the queue, you check to see if the count is equal to zero; if it is, the queue is empty.

The implementation of this scheme in Pascal uses the following definitions:

An array-based queue

```
const  MaxQueue = <maximum size of queue>;

type   itemType = <desired type of queue item>;
       queueType = record
            Items : array[1..MaxQueue] of itemType;
            Front, Rear : 1..MaxQueue;
            Count : 0..MaxQueue
       end;  { record }

var    Q : queueType
```

*Initialize **Front**, **Rear**, and **Count***

The queue is initialized with *Front* = 1, *Rear* = *MaxQueue*, and *Count* = 0. You obtain the wraparound effect of a circular queue by using modulo arithmetic (that is, Pascal's *mod* operator) when incrementing *Front* and *Rear*. For example, you can add *NewItem* to the queue by using the statements

Adding to the rear of a queue

```
Q.Rear := succ(Q.Rear mod MaxQueue);
Q.Items[Q.Rear] := NewItem;
inc(Q.Count)
```

Notice that if *Rear* equaled *MaxQueue* before the addition of *NewItem*, the first statement, *Q.Rear := succ(Q.Rear mod MaxQueue)*, would have the effect of wrapping *Rear* around to location 1.

Similarly, you can remove an item from the front of the queue by using the statements

Removing from the front of a queue

```
Q.Front := succ(Q.Front mod MaxQueue);
dec(Q.Count)
```

The following Pascal unit contains an array-based implementation of the ADT queue that uses a circular array as just described.

```
unit QueueOps;
{ ********************************************************
  BASIC QUEUE OPERATIONS - Array-based implementation

    CreateQueue, QueueIsEmpty, Add, Remove, GetQueueFront
  ******************************************************** }

interface

const MaxQueue = <maximum size of queue>;
```

```
type  itemType = <desired type of queue item>;
      queueType = record
          Items : array[1..MaxQueue] of itemType;
          Front, Rear : 1..MaxQueue;
          Count : 0..MaxQueue
      end;  { record }

procedure CreateQueue(var Q : queueType);
{ ------------------------------------------------------
  Creates an empty queue.
  Precondition: None.
  Postcondition: The queue Q is empty.
  ------------------------------------------------------ }
function QueueIsEmpty(Q : queueType) : boolean;
{ ------------------------------------------------------
  Determines whether a queue is empty.
  Precondition: CreateQueue(Q) has been called.
  Postcondition: Returns true if Q was empty, else returns
  false.
  ------------------------------------------------------ }
procedure Add(var Q : queueType; NewItem : itemType;
              var Success : boolean);
{ ------------------------------------------------------
  Adds an item to the rear of a queue.
  Precondition: CreateQueue(Q) has been called.
  Postcondition: If Q was not full, NewItem is at the
  rear of queue and Success is true; otherwise Success
  is false.
  Note: The queue is full if it contains MaxQueue items.
  ------------------------------------------------------ }
procedure Remove(var Q : queueType;
                 var Success : boolean);
{ ------------------------------------------------------
  Removes the item at the front of a queue.
  Precondition: CreateQueue(Q) has been called.
  Postcondition: If Q was not empty, the item that was
  added to Q earliest is removed and Success is true.
  However, if Q was empty, removal is impossible and Success
  is false.
  ------------------------------------------------------ }
procedure GetQueueFront(Q : queueType;
         var QueueFront: itemType; var Success : boolean);
{ ------------------------------------------------------
  Retrieves the item at the front of a queue.
  Precondition: CreateQueue(Q) has been called.
  Postcondition: If Q was not empty, QueueFront contains
  the item that was added to Q earliest and Success is true.
```

```
  However, if Q was empty, the operation fails and Success
  is false. Q is unchanged.
  ---------------------------------------------------------- }

implementation

{ The array is circular. Front and Rear are indexes to the
  front and rear, respectively, of the queue. Count is the
  number of items currently in the queue. }

procedure CreateQueue(var Q : queueType);
begin
    Q.Front := 1;
    Q.Rear := MaxQueue;
    Q.Count := 0
end;  { CreateQueue }

function QueueIsEmpty(Q : queueType) : boolean;
begin
    QueueIsEmpty := (Q.Count = 0)
end;  { QueueIsEmpty }

procedure Add(var Q : queueType; NewItem : itemType;
              var Success : boolean);
begin
    Success := not (Q.Count = MaxQueue);

    if Success
          then   { queue is not full }
          begin  { insert item }
             Q.Rear := succ(Q.Rear mod MaxQueue);
             Q.Items[Q.Rear] := NewItem;
             inc(Q.Count)
          end  { if }
end; { Add }

procedure Remove(var Q : queueType;
                 var Success : boolean);
begin
    Success := not QueueIsEmpty(Q);

    if Success
          then   { queue is not empty }
          begin  { remove item }
             Q.Front := succ(Q.Front mod MaxQueue);
             dec(Q.Count)
          end  { if }
end; { Remove }

procedure GetQueueFront(Q : queueType;
         var QueueFront: itemType; var Success : boolean);
```

```
begin
    Success := not QueueIsEmpty(Q);

    if Success
          then   { queue is not empty; retrieve item }
             QueueFront := Q.Items[Q.Front]
end; { GetQueueFront }

end. { unit }
```

There are several variations of this scheme in common use that do not require a count of the number of items in the queue. In our opinion, however, these implementations are not quite as clean as the one just presented. Exercises 3 and 4 at the end of this chapter consider two of the alternative schemes.

The Queue As an Object (Optional)

You can implement the ADT queue as an object. This section presents two possible approaches. The first approach closely models the pointer-based implementation of the ADT queue discussed earlier in this chapter. The second approach defines the queue as a descendent of the object *ordListType*, which Chapter 4 defined on page 216.

A pointer-based queue. The following pointer-based implementation of a queue object has many similarities with the pointer-based implementation of the ADT queue that you saw earlier in this chapter:

```
unit QueueObj;
interface

type  itemType = <desired type of queue item>;
      ptrType = ^nodeType;

      nodeType = record
          Item : itemType;
          Next : ptrType
      end; { record }

      queueType = object

        constructor Init;
        { ---------------------------------------------
          Creates an empty queue.
          Precondition: None.
          Postcondition: The queue is empty.
          --------------------------------------------- }
        destructor Done; virtual;
        { ---------------------------------------------
          Deallocates a queue.
          Precondition: Init has been called.
```

```
      Postcondition: All storage associated with
      the queue is deallocated. The queue is empty.
      ---------------------------------------------- }
    function QueueIsEmpty : boolean;
    { ----------------------------------------------
      Determines whether a queue is empty.
      Precondition: Init has been called.
      Postcondition: Returns true if the queue was
      empty, else returns false.
      ---------------------------------------------- }
    procedure Add (NewItem : itemType;
                   var Success : boolean);
    { ----------------------------------------------
      Adds an item to the rear of a queue.
      Precondition: Init has been called.
      Postcondition: NewItem is at the rear
      of the queue and Success is true.
      ---------------------------------------------- }

    procedure Remove(var Success : boolean);
    { ----------------------------------------------
      Removes the item at the front of a queue.
      Precondition: Init has been called.
      Postcondition: If the queue was not empty, the
      item that was added earliest is removed and
      Success is true. However, if the queue was empty,
      removal is impossible and Success is false.
      ---------------------------------------------- }

    procedure GetQueueFront(var QueueFront : itemType;
                            var Success : boolean);
    { ----------------------------------------------
      Retrieves the item at the front of a queue.
      Precondition: Init has been called.
      Postcondition: If the queue was not empty,
      QueueFront contains the item that was added
      earliest and Success is true. However, if the
      queue was empty, the operation fails and Success
      is false. The queue is unchanged.
      ----------------------------------------------- }
  private
    Rear : ptrType;
  end; { object }

implementation
{ The queue is implemented as a circular linked list.
  The single pointer Rear points to the rear of the queue. }
```

```
constructor queueType.Init;
begin
   Rear := nil
end; { queueType.Init }

destructor queueType.Done;
var Cur, Temp : ptrType;
begin
    if Rear <> nil
       then
       begin
          Cur := Rear^.Next;    { point to first node }
          Rear^.Next := nil;    { mark the last node }
          Rear := nil;

          while Cur <> nil do
          begin
             Temp := Cur;
             Cur := Cur^.Next;
             dispose(Temp)
          end { while }
       end { if }
end;  { queueType.Done }

function queueType.QueueIsEmpty : boolean;
begin
    QueueIsEmpty := (Rear = nil)
end; { queueType.QueueIsEmpty }

procedure queueType.Add(NewItem : itemType;
                        var Success: boolean);
var NewFrontPtr : ptrType;
begin
    { get a new node }
    new(NewFrontPtr);
    NewFrontPtr^.Item := NewItem;

    { insert the new node }
    if QueueIsEmpty
       then           { insertion into empty queue }
          NewFrontPtr^.Next := NewFrontPtr
       else
       begin         { insertion into nonempty queue }
          NewFrontPtr^.Next := Rear^.Next;
          Rear^.Next := NewFrontPtr
       end; { if }
    Rear := NewFrontPtr;
    Success := true
end;  { queueType.Add }
```

```
procedure queueType.Remove(var Success : boolean);
var FrontPtr : ptrType;
begin
    Success := not QueueIsEmpty;

    if Success
      then
      begin
         FrontPtr := Rear^.Next;
         if FrontPtr = Rear      { special case? }
            then Rear := nil     { yes, one node in queue }
            else Rear^.Next := FrontPtr^.Next;

         dispose(FrontPtr);
         Success := true
      end  { if }
end;  { queueType.Remove }

procedure queueType.GetQueueFront(var QueueFront : itemType;
                                  var Success : boolean);
begin
    Success := not QueueIsEmpty;

    if Success
      then   { queue is not empty }
      begin
         QueueFront := Rear^.Next^.Item;
         Success := true
      end  { if }
end;  { queueType.GetQueueFront }

end.  { unit }
```

Compare the implementation of this object with the previous pointer-based implementation of the ADT queue. The differences are as follows: *queueType* qualifies each method name (for example, *queueType.Add*), *QueueIsEmpty* replaces each occurrence of *QueueIsEmpty(Q)*, and *Rear* replaces each instance of *Q*.

The following statements demonstrate how to use this object:

```
var AnItem    : itemType;
    Q         : queueType;
    Success   : boolean;

begin  { Main Program }
    Q.Init;

    readln(AnItem);
    Q.Add(AnItem, Success);
```

A queue that descends from *ordListType*. You can implement a queue as an ordered list. If you let the item in position 1 of an ordered list represent the front of the queue, you can implement the queue operation *Remove* as *OrderedListDelete(1)* and the queue operation *GetQueueFront(QueueFront)* as *OrderedListRetrieve(1, QueueFront)*. Similarly, if the item at the end of the ordered list represents the rear of the queue, you can implement the queue operation *Add* as *OrderedListInsert(ListLength+1, NewItem)*.

Recall that Chapter 4 presented the ordered list as the object *ordListType*. Object inheritance allows you to conveniently define a queue as an object that descends from *ordListType*. The queue object uses its ancestor's methods to implement its own methods, as the following unit demonstrates. Pre- and postconditions are omitted to save space but are the same as those given in the previous object definition.

```
unit QueueObj;
{$R+}
{Queue based on ordered list object}

interface

uses ULists;  { contains definition of ordListType }

type itemType = <desired type of queue item>;
     queueType = object(ordListType)
        { constructor, destructor inherited }
        function QueueIsEmpty : boolean;
        procedure Add(NewItem : itemType;
                      var Success : boolean);
        procedure Remove(var Success : boolean);
        procedure GetQueueFront(var QueueFront : itemType;
                                var Success : boolean);
     end;  { object }

implementation

function queueType.QueueIsEmpty : boolean;
begin
   QueueIsEmpty := (ListLength = 0)
end;  { queueType.QueueIsEmpty }

procedure queueType.Add(NewItem : itemType;
                        var Success : boolean);
begin
   OrderedListInsert(succ(ListLength), NewItem, Success)
end;  { queueType.Add }

procedure queueType.Remove(var Success : boolean);
begin
   if QueueIsEmpty
      then Success := false
      else OrderedListDelete(1, Success)
end;  { queueType.Remove }
```

```
procedure queueType.GetQueueFront(var QueueFront : itemType;
                                  var Success : boolean);
begin
   if QueueIsEmpty
      then Success := false
      else OrderedListRetrieve(1, QueueFront, Success)
end;  { queueType.GetQueueFront }

end.  { unit }
```

Notice how simple it is to implement a queue object, once you have implemented the ordered list.

Exercise 14 of Chapter 4 asked you to revise the object *ordListType* so that each item on the ordered list is a dynamically allocated object. Notice that once you make that change, enabling *queueType* to contain dynamically allocated objects is straightforward. Exercise 9 at the end of this chapter asks you to make this revision.

SIMULATION AS AN APPLICATION OF THE ADT QUEUE

Simulation models the behavior of systems

Simulation is a major application area for computers. It is a technique for modeling the behavior of both natural and human-made systems. Generally, the goal of a simulation is to generate statistics that summarize the performance of an existing system or to predict the performance of a proposed system. In this section we present a simple example that illustrates one important type of simulation.

Consider the following problem. Ms. Drysdale, president of the First City Bank of Shiprock, has heard her customers complain about how long they have to wait for service. Because she fears that they may move their accounts to another bank, she is considering whether to hire a second teller.

Before Ms. Drysdale hires another teller, she would like an approximation of the average time that a customer has to wait for service from First City's only teller. How can Ms. Drysdale obtain this information? She could stand with a stopwatch in the bank's lobby all day, but she does not find this prospect particularly exciting. Besides, she would like to use a method that also allows her to predict how much improvement she could expect if the bank hired a given number of additional tellers. She certainly does not want to hire the tellers on a trial basis and monitor the bank's performance before making a final decision.

Ms. Drysdale concludes that the best way to obtain the information she wants is to simulate the behavior of her bank. The first step in simulating a system such as a bank is to construct a mathematical model that captures the relevant information about the system. For example, how many tellers does the bank employ? How often do customers arrive? If the model accurately describes the real-world system, you can use a simulation to derive accurate predictions about the system's overall performance. For example, a simulation could predict the average time a customer has to wait before receiving service. You can also use a simulation to evaluate proposed changes to the real-world system. For example, to evaluate an increase in the number of tellers in the bank, you could make the appropriate changes in the model and use the simulation to predict the behavior of this hypothetical system. A large decrease in the time predicted for the average wait of a customer might justify the cost of hiring additional tellers.

Simulated time

Central to a simulation is the concept of simulated time. Envision a stopwatch that measures elapsed time as the simulation mimics the behavior of the system under study. For example, suppose that the model of the bank specifies that there is one teller. At *Time* = 0, which is the start of the banking day, the simulated system would be in its initial state with no customers. As the simulation runs, the stopwatch ticks away units of time—perhaps minutes—and certain events occur. At *Time* = 12 the bank's first customer arrives. Since there is no line, the customer goes directly to the teller and begins her transaction. At *Time* = 20, a second customer arrives. Because the first customer has not yet completed her transaction, the second customer must wait in line. At *Time* = 38, the first customer completes her transaction and the second customer can begin his. Figure 9-11 illustrates these four times in the simulation.

To gather the information you need, you run this simulation for a specified period of simulated time. During the course of the run, you need to keep track of certain statistics, such as the average time a customer has to wait for service. Notice that in the small example of Figure 9-11, the first customer had to wait 0 minutes to begin a transaction and the second customer had to wait 18 minutes to begin a transaction—an average wait of 9 minutes.

One point not addressed in the previous discussion is how to determine when certain events occur. For example, why did we say that the first customer arrived at *Time* = 12 and the second at *Time* = 20? After studying real-world systems like our bank, mathematicians learned to model events such as the arrival of people by using techniques from probability theory. This statistical information is incorporated into the mathematical model of the system and is used to generate events in a way that reflects the real world. The simulation uses these events and is thus called an **event-driven simulation**. Note that the goal is to reflect long-term average behavior of the system rather than to predict occurrences of specific events. This goal is sufficient for the needs of the simulation.

Although the techniques for generating events to reflect the real world are interesting and important, they require a good deal of mathematical sophistication. Therefore, simply assume that you already have a list of events available for your use. In particular, for the bank problem, assume

Figure 9-11

(a) *Time* = 0; (b) *Time* = 12; (c) *Time* = 20; (d) *Time* = 38

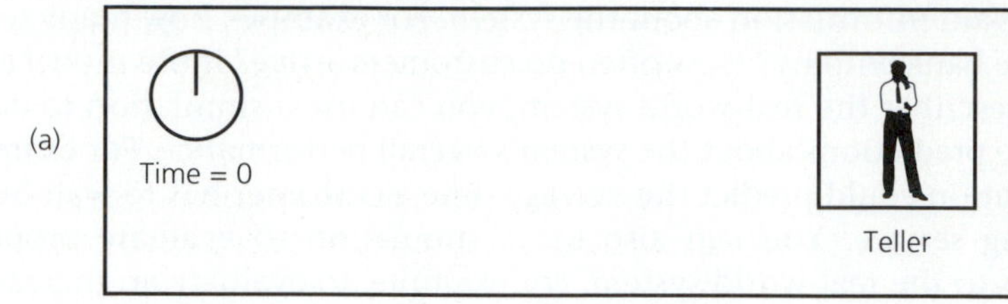

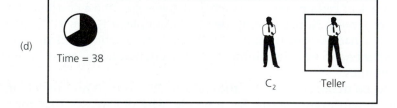

that a file contains the time of each customer's arrival—an **arrival event**—and the duration of that customer's transaction once the customer reaches the teller. For example, the data

Sample arrival and transaction times

20	3
22	9
30	6

indicates that the first customer arrives 20 minutes into the simulation and that the transaction—once begun—requires 3 minutes; the second customer arrives 22 minutes into the simulation and the transaction requires 9 minutes; and the third customer arrives 30 minutes into the simulation and the transaction requires 6 minutes. Assume that the input file is ordered by arrival time.

Notice that there are no **departure events** in the data; the data does not specify when a customer will complete the transaction and leave. It is the job of the simulation to determine when departures occur. By using the arrival time and the transaction length, the simulation easily can determine the time at which a customer departs. To see how to make this determination, you can conduct a simulation by hand with the previous data as follows:

The results of a simulation

Time	*Event*
20	Customer 1 enters bank and begins transaction
22	Customer 2 enters bank and stands at end of line
23	Customer 1 departs; customer 2 begins transaction
30	Customer 3 enters bank and stands at end of line
32	Customer 2 departs; customer 3 begins transaction
38	Customer 3 departs

Notice that the amount of time that elapses between a customer's arrival in the bank and the time that the customer reaches the front of the line and begins a transaction is the amount of time the customer has to wait. It is the average of this wait time over all the customers that you want to obtain.

To summarize, this simulation is concerned with two types of events:

- **Arrival events (A).** These events indicate the arrival at the bank of a new customer. The input file specifies the times at which the arrival events occur. As such, they are **external events**. When a customer arrives at the bank, one of two things happens. If the teller is idle when the customer arrives, the customer begins the transaction immediately. If the teller is busy, the new customer must stand at the end of the line and wait for service.
- **Departure events (D).** These events indicate the departure from the bank of a customer who has completed a transaction. The simulation determines the times at which the departure events occur. As such, they are **internal events**. When a customer completes the transaction, he or she departs and the next person in line—if there is one—begins a transaction.

You now must develop an algorithm to perform the simulation. The main task of the algorithm is to determine the times at which the events occur and to process the events when they do occur. The algorithm is stated at a high level as follows:

A first attempt at a simulation algorithm

```
{ initialize }
Time := 0
Initialize the line to "no customers"
```

```
while Time ≤ time of the final event do
begin
   if an arrival event occurs at time Time
      then process the arrival event

   if a departure event occurs at time Time
      then process the departure event

   { when an arrival event and departure event occur at the
     same time, arbitrarily process the arrival event first }

   Time := Time + 1
end
```

A time-driven simulation simulates the ticking of a clock

Do you really want to increment `Time` by 1? You would for a **time-driven simulation**, where you would determine arrival and departure times randomly and compare those times to `Time`. In such a case, you would increment `Time` by 1 to simulate the ticking of a clock. Recall, however, that this simulation is **event driven**, so you have a file of arrival times and transaction times. Because you are interested only in those times at which arrival and departure events occur, and as no action is required at the time steps between the occurrences of events, you can advance `Time` from the time of one event directly to the time of the next.

An event-driven simulation considers only times of certain events, in this case, arrivals and departures

Thus, you can revise the pseudocode solution as follows:

First revision of the simulation algorithm

```
{ initialize }
Initialize the line to "no customers"

while there remain events to be processed do
begin
   Time := time of next event

   if an arrival event occurs
      then process the arrival event
      else process the departure event { the other possibility}

   { when an arrival event and departure event occur at the
     same time, arbitrarily process the arrival event first }
end
```

You must determine the time of the next arrival or departure event so that you can implement the statement

```
Time := time of next event
```

An event list contains all future events

This determination entails the maintenance of an **event list.** An event list contains all arrival and departure events that will occur but have not occurred yet. The times of the events in the event list are in ascending order, and thus the next event to be processed is always at the head of the list. The algorithm simply gets the event from the head of the list, advances to the time specified, and processes the event. The difficulty lies in successfully managing such an event list.

For this particular problem you can manage the event list so that it always contains at most one event of each kind. Recall that the arrival events are specified in the input file and that they appear in ascending time order. You thus never need to worry about an arrival event until you have processed all the arrival events that precede it in the file. You simply keep the earliest unprocessed arrival event on the event list. When you eventually process this event—that is, when it is time for this customer to arrive—you replace it on the event list with the next unprocessed arrival event, which is the next item in the input file.

The particular event list here contains at most one arrival event and one departure event

Similarly, you need to place only the next departure event to occur on the event list. But how can you determine the times for the departure events? Observe that the next departure event always corresponds to the customer that the teller is currently serving. As soon as a customer begins service, you can determine the time of his or her departure. This time is simply

time of next departure = time service begins + length of customer's transaction

Recall that the length of the customer's transaction is in the input file along with the arrival time. Thus, as soon as a customer begins service, you place a departure event corresponding to this customer on the event list. Figure 9-12 illustrates a typical instance of the event list for this particular simulation.

Now consider how you can process an event when it is time for the event to occur. You must perform two general types of actions:

Two tasks are required to process each event

- **Update the line:** Add or remove customers.
- **Update the event list:** Add or remove new events.

Notice that as customers arrive, they are added to the rear of the line. The current customer, who is at the front of the line, is receiving service, and it is this customer that you remove from the system next. It is thus natural to use a queue to manage the customers in the system. For this problem, the only information that you store in the queue about each customer is the time of arrival and the length of the transaction.

A queue represents the customers in line

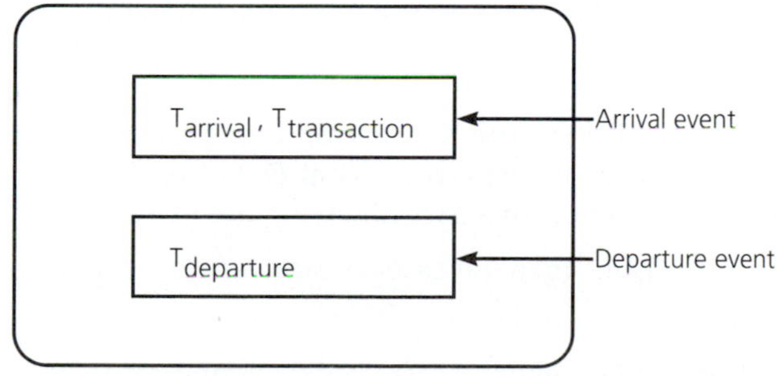

Figure 9-12

A typical instance of the event list

To summarize, you process an event as follows:

The event-processing algorithm

```
TO PROCESS AN ARRIVAL EVENT FOR CUSTOMER C

Update the line:

   Add the new customer C to the queue

Update the event list:

   Remove the arrival event for customer C from
     the event list
   if not at the end of the input file
        then add a new arrival event to the event list
               (time of event = time specified in file)

   if the new customer C began service immediately
   { i.e., the queue was empty so customer C went directly
     to the teller }
      then add a departure event for customer C to the
             event list (time of event = current time +
             transaction length)

TO PROCESS A DEPARTURE EVENT

Update the line:

   Remove the first customer from the queue
   { if the queue does not become empty, then the new first
     customer begins service }

Update the event list:

   Remove the departure event from the event list
   if the queue has not become empty
       then add to the event list the departure event for
         the person now at the front of the queue (time of
         event = current time + transaction length)
```

Examining the event list more closely will help explain the workings of the algorithm. Although the event list has no general form among various simulations, for this particular simulation, it has four possible configurations as follows. Initially, the event list contains an arrival event *A* after you read the first arrival event from the input file but before you process it:

Event List: *A*

Generally, the event list for this simulation contains exactly two events: one arrival event *A* and one departure event *D*. Either the departure event is first or the arrival event is first as follows:

Event List: *D A* (general case—next event is a departure),

or

Event List: *A D* (general case—next event is an arrival)

If the departure event is first and that event leaves the teller's line empty, a new departure event does not replace the just-processed event. Thus, in this case, the event list appears as

Event List: *A* (a departure leaves the teller's line empty)

Notice that this instance of the event list is the same as its initial state.

If the arrival event is first and if, after it is processed, there are no more arrival events in the input file, the event list contains only a departure event:

Event List: *D* (the input has been exhausted)

Also notice that new events may be inserted either at the beginning of the event list or at the end, depending on the relative times of the new event and the event currently on the list. For example, suppose that the event list contains only an arrival event *A* and that you generate a departure event *D* for the customer who is now at the front of the line and beginning a transaction. If the customer's departure time is before the time of the arrival event *A*, then you must insert the departure event *D* before the event *A* in the event list. However, if the departure time is after the time of the arrival event, you must insert the departure event *D* after the arrival event *A*. In the case of a tie, you need a rule to determine which event should take precedence. In this solution we have arbitrarily chosen to place the departure event after the arrival event.

You can now combine and refine the pieces of the solution into an algorithm that performs the simulation. The following algorithm uses the ADT queue operations to manage the bank line. Notice that the procedure *ProcessArrival* updates the event list before it updates the line. This ordering allows the use of the function *QueueIsEmpty* to determine whether the new arrival begins service immediately; if so, then you must add a departure event for the new arrival to the event list. Also, before calling procedures *ProcessArrival* and *ProcessDeparture*, the procedure *Simulate* removes from the event list the event that is about to be processed. This removal is thus not performed by procedures *Process-Arrival* and *ProcessDeparture*. The other refinements to the algorithm should be self-explanatory.

The final pseudocode for the event-driven simulation

```
ProcessArrival(Event)
{ Procedure to process an arrival event. }

   { update the event list }
   if QueueIsEmpty(Q)
      then { the line is empty, so the customer
                goes directly to the teller }

         Add to the event list a departure event that
           corresponds to the new customer and has Time =
           Time + transaction length

   if not at the end of the input file
      then
```

```
      begin
         Get the next arrival event from the input file
         Add the event--with time as specified in the input
            file--to the event list
      end

   { update the line by adding the new customer to the queue }
   Item := information about new customer
   Add(Q, Item, Success)

ProcessDeparture(Event)
{ Procedure to process a departure event. }

   { update the line by removing the first customer }
   Remove(Q, Success)

   { update the event list }
   if not QueueIsEmpty(Q)
      then add to the event list a departure event that
         corresponds to the customer now at the front of the
         line and has Time = Time + transaction length

Simulate
{ Procedure to perform the simulation. }

   { initialize the event list }
   Get the first arrival event from the input file
   Place event on the event list

   { initialize the bank line }
   CreateQueue(Q)

   while the event list is not empty do
   begin
      { get next event from the beginning of the event list }
      NewEvent := the first event on the event list
      Delete the first event from the event list

      Time := time specified by NewEvent

      if NewEvent is an arrival event
          then ProcessArrival(NewEvent)
          else ProcessDeparture(NewEvent)
   end  { while }
```

A Pascal implementation of the simulation follows. The program uses a unit *QueueOps* that contains the queue operations for a queue of records. Each such record contains two integer fields: the transaction time and the arrival time. Note that the program also uses a record to count customers and to keep track of their cumulative waiting time. These statistics are sufficient to compute the average waiting time after the last event has been processed.

```
program SimulationDemo;
{ *********************************************************
  SAMPLE EVENT-DRIVEN SIMULATION

  Simulation of a single waiting line of people.

  There are two kinds of events:
    A : arrival - enter the line
    D : departure - complete transaction and leave the line

  Input:    The textfile InputFile. Each line contains the
            arrival time and required transaction time for
            a customer.

  Assumption:   The arrival times in the input file are
                ordered by increasing time.

  Output:    A trace of the events executed.
             Summary statistics (total number of arrivals,
             average time spent waiting in line).

  Data Structures:
    Line of people - a queue of records defined by

       type itemType = record
               TransTime,                (transaction time)
               ArrivalTime : integer     (arrival time)
            end; ( record )

    Event list - a linked list of two kinds of event nodes:
      arrival event: an arrival time and a transaction time
      departure event: a departure time

  Subprograms:
    InsertEvent      - inserts event node into event list
    GetArrival       - reads arrival event from input file,
                       inserts it into event list
    ProcessArrival   - executes an arrival event
    ProcessDeparture - executes a departure event
    Simulate         - performs the simulation
    ADT Queue operations

  Major Variables:
    Line         - line of people waiting (a queue)
    EL           - event list
    Statistics   - a record with two fields as follows:
      TotalNum   - total number of arrivals (customers)
      TotalWait  - cumulative time spent waiting in line
  ********************************************************* }
```

```
uses QueueOps; { pointer-based implementation of ADT queue;
                 unit defines data types itemType and
                 queueType }
    { event list }
type eType = (A, D);                { arrival and departure }
     eventPtrType = ^eventType;
     eventType = record
        Next : eventPtrType;            { next event }
        Time : integer;                 { time of event }
        case WhichEvent: eType of       { kind of event }
           A : (TransTime: integer);    { transaction time}
           D : ()
     end; { record }

     statType = record
        TotalNum : integer;  { total no. of customers }
        TotalWait : integer; { cumulative waiting time }
     end; { record }

procedure InsertEvent(var EL : eventPtrType;
                          NewPtr : eventPtrType);
{ ---------------------------------------------------------
  Inserts an event node into the event list ordered by time.
  Precondition: Event list EL is empty or has 1 node.
  NewPtr points to the node to be added to EL.
  Postcondition: Node to which NewPtr points is added to
  EL such that times are ordered. (If nodes have the same
  times, arrival events come before departure events.)
  --------------------------------------------------------- }
begin
    { if the event list is empty }
    if EL = nil then
       EL := NewPtr

    { if the event list is not empty, then insert new node
      at front or end of list according to time }

    { new node has earliest time or has same time, but is
      arrival event - insert at front of list }
    else if (NewPtr^.Time < EL^.Time) or
                ((NewPtr^.Time = EL^.Time) and
                            (NewPtr^.WhichEvent = A))
       then
       begin
          NewPtr ^.Next := EL;
          EL := NewPtr
       end

    { new node has later time or has same time, but is
      departure event - insert at end of the list }
```

```
    else
    begin
       NewPtr^.Next := nil;
       EL^.Next := NewPtr
    end
end;  { InsertEvent }

procedure GetArrival(var InputFile : text;
                     var EL : eventPtrType);
{ ---------------------------------------------------------
  Reads data for the next arrival event, and inserts the
  new arrival node into the event list.
  Precondition: InputFile is a textfile, which is open
  for input, of arrival and transaction times. EL is the
  current event list.
  Postcondition: Event is read from InputFile and is
  inserted into EL. At end-of-file, EL is unchanged.
  InputFile is open for input.
  Calls: InsertEvent.
  --------------------------------------------------------- }
var NewPtr : eventPtrType;
begin
    if not eof(InputFile)
       then
       begin
          { create a new event node }
          new(NewPtr);        { get pointer to new node }
          NewPtr^.WhichEvent := A;   { arrival event }
          NewPtr^.Next := nil;
          readln(InputFile, NewPtr^.Time,
                            NewPtr^.TransTime);

          { insert the node into the event list }
          InsertEvent(EL, NewPtr)
       end   { if }
end;  { GetArrival }

procedure ProcessArrival(Arrival : eventType;
       var InputFile : text; var EL : eventPtrType;
       var Line : queueType; var Statistics : statType);
{ ---------------------------------------------------------
  Executes an arrival event.
  Precondition: Arrival contains the arrival event node,
  InputFile of arrival events is open for input, EL is the
  event list, the queue Line has been created,
  Statistics.TotalNum is the total number of arrivals.
  Postcondition: If Line is empty, a departure event is
  inserted into event list EL. A new arrival event is read
  from InputFile and is inserted into EL and Arrival is
```

```
  added to Line (the queue). Statistics.TotalNum is updated
  (total no. of arrivals). InputFile is open for input.
  Calls: InsertEvent, GetArrival, QueueIsEmpty, Add.
  -------------------------------------------------------- }
var CurrentTime: integer;{ arrival time of current person }
    PersonInLine: itemType;{ data about person in queue }
    EventPtr: eventPtrType;{ ptr to event in event list }
    Success: boolean;
begin
    { update the statistics }
    inc(Statistics.TotalNum);

    { get current time }
    CurrentTime := Arrival.Time;
    writeln('Processing an arrival event at time: ',
                                            CurrentTime:4);

    { update the event list }

    { if the line is empty, the person starts transaction }
    if QueueIsEmpty(Line)
       then
       begin
          { create a departure event }
          new(EventPtr);       { get pointer to new node }
          EventPtr^.WhichEvent := D; { departure event }
          EventPtr^.Next := nil;
          EventPtr^.Time := CurrentTime + Arrival.TransTime;

          { insert the node into the event list }
          InsertEvent(EL, EventPtr)
       end;   { if }

    { get the next arrival event from input file }
    GetArrival(InputFile, EL);

    { person arrives: update the waiting line (queue) }
    PersonInLine.TransTime := Arrival.TransTime;
    PersonInLine.ArrivalTime := CurrentTime;
    Add(Line, PersonInLine, Success)
end;  { ProcessArrival }

procedure ProcessDeparture(Departure : eventType;
                var EL : eventPtrType; var Line : queueType;
                var Statistics : statType);
{ --------------------------------------------------------
  Executes a departure event.
  Precondition: Departure contains the departure event
  node, EL is the event list, the queue Line has been
  created, Statistics.TotalWait is the total waiting time.
```

```
  Postcondition: A person is removed from the queue. The
  event list is updated by adding a departure event for the
  next customer, if any. Statistics.TotalWait (total
  waiting time) is updated.
  Calls: InsertEvent, QueueIsEmpty, Remove, GetQueueFront.
  ----------------------------------------------------------- }
var CurrentTime: integer;{ arrival time of current person }
    PersonInLine : itemType;{ data about person in queue }
    EventPtr : eventPtrType;{ ptr to event in event list }
    Success : boolean; { flag for queue ops - ignored }
begin
    CurrentTime := Departure.Time;
    writeln('Processing a departure event at time: ',
                                              CurrentTime:3);

    { person departs - update the line (queue) }
    Remove(Line, Success);      { remove person from queue }

    { update the event list }

    { if the line is not empty, then the next person starts
      a transaction }
    if not QueueIsEmpty(Line)
       then
       begin
          { create a departure node }
          GetQueueFront(Line, PersonInLine, Success);
          new(EventPtr);       { get pointer to new node }
          EventPtr^.WhichEvent := D; { departure event }
          EventPtr^.Next := nil;
          EventPtr^.Time := CurrentTime +
                                PersonInLine.TransTime;

          { insert the node into the event list }
          InsertEvent(EL, EventPtr);

          { update the statistics }
          Statistics.TotalWait := Statistics.TotalWait +
                  (CurrentTime - PersonInLine.ArrivalTime)
       end { if }
end;  { ProcessDeparture }

procedure Simulate(var InputFile : text;
                   var Statistics: statType);
{ ----------------------------------------------------------
  Simulates a line of people.
  Precondition: InputFile is associated with a textfile
  of arrival events.
  Postcondition: Statistics.TotalWait is the total
  cumulative waiting time of all customers.
```

```
  Statistics.TotalNum is the total number of customers.
  InputFile is closed.
  Calls: GetArrival, CreateQueue, ProcessArrival,
  ProcessDeparture.
  ------------------------------------------------------------ }
var EL : eventPtrType;          { the event list }
    NewEvent : eventType;       { the current event node }
    Line : queueType;           { the waiting line }

begin
    writeln('Simulation Begins');
    reset(InputFile);
    EL := nil;

    { get the first arrival event and place on event list }
    GetArrival(InputFile, EL);

    CreateQueue(Line);
    { process events until the event list is empty }
    while EL <> nil do
    begin
       NewEvent := EL^; { get next event from beginning of
                          event list }
       EL := EL^.Next;  { delete event from event list }

       if NewEvent.WhichEvent = A
           then    { process arrival event }
              ProcessArrival(NewEvent, InputFile, EL, Line,
                                                  Statistics)
           else { process departure event }
              ProcessDeparture(NewEvent, EL, Line,
                                                  Statistics)
    end;  { while }

    close(InputFile);
    writeln('Simulation Ends')
end;  { Simulate }

var InputFile : text;           { input data }
    Statistics: statType;       { summary statistics }

begin  { Main Program }
    assign(InputFile, 'PEOPLE.DAT');

    { initialize statistics record }
    Statistics.TotalNum := 0;
    Statistics.TotalWait := 0;

    { perform the simulation }
    Simulate(InputFile, Statistics);

    { write out the final statistics }
    writeln;
```

```
   writeln('Final Statistics:');
   writeln(' Total number of people processed: ',
                                   Statistics.TotalNum:3);
   write(' Average amount of time spent waiting: ');
   if Statistics.TotalNum = 0
      then writeln(' 0.0')
      else writeln((Statistics.TotalWait/
                                   Statistics.TotalNum):5:1)
end.  { Program }
```

If this program were run with the input file shown in the left columns of the following table, it would produce the output shown in the right column:

Input file		*Output*
1	5	Simulation Begins
2	5	Processing an arrival event at time: 1
4	5	Processing an arrival event at time: 2
20	5	Processing an arrival event at time: 4
22	5	Processing a departure event at time: 6
24	5	Processing a departure event at time: 11
26	5	Processing a departure event at time: 16
28	5	Processing an arrival event at time: 20
30	5	Processing an arrival event at time: 22
88	3	Processing an arrival event at time: 24
		Processing a departure event at time: 25
		Processing an arrival event at time: 26
		Processing an arrival event at time: 28
		Processing an arrival event at time: 30
		Processing a departure event at time: 30
		Processing a departure event at time: 35
		Processing a departure event at time: 40
		Processing a departure event at time: 45
		Processing a departure event at time: 50
		Processing an arrival event at time: 88
		Processing a departure event at time: 91
		Simulation Ends
		Final Statistics:
		Total number of people processed: 10
		Average amount of time spent waiting: 5.6

A SUMMARY OF POSITION-ORIENTED ADT'S

So far, we have introduced three abstract data types—the ordered list, the stack, and the queue—that have a common theme: All of their operations are defined in terms of the positions of their data items. Stacks and queues

Operations for the ADT's ordered list, stack, and queue reference the position of items

greatly restrict the positions that their operations can affect; their operations apply only to the end positions of their structures. The ordered list removes this restriction.

There is really a great deal of similarity between stacks and queues. This similarity becomes apparent if you pair off their operations, as follows:

A comparison of stack and queue operations

- ***CreateStack(S)*** **and** ***CreateQueue(Q)***. These operations create an empty structure of the appropriate type.
- ***StackIsEmpty(S)*** **and** ***QueueIsEmpty(Q)***. These operations tell whether there are any items in the structure. Notice that in both cases the operations do not look beyond the ends of their structures to see how many items are present. Rather, the operations tell only if there is an item present at one of the ends.
- ***Push(S, NewItem)*** **and** ***Add(Q, NewItem)***. These operations insert a new item into one end (the top and rear) of their structures.
- ***Pop(S)*** **and** ***Remove(Q)***. *Pop* deletes the last item, which is at the top of the stack, and *Remove* deletes the first item, which is at the front of the queue.
- ***StackTop(S)*** **and** ***QueueFront(Q)***. *StackTop* retrieves the last item, which is at the top of the stack, and *QueueFront* retrieves the first item, which is at the front of the queue.

The ADT ordered list, introduced in Chapter 4, allows you to insert into, delete from, and inspect the item at any position of the structure. Thus, it has the most flexible operations of the three position-oriented ADT's. You can view the ordered list operations as generalizing the stack and queue operations to the logical extreme as follows:

Ordered list operations generalize stack and queue operations

- ***OrderedListLength(OL)***. If you remove the restriction that *StackIsEmpty* and *QueueIsEmpty* can tell only when an item is present at the ends of their structures, you obtain an operation that can count the number of items that are present.
- ***OrderedListInsert(OL, Position, NewItem)***. If you remove the restriction that *Push* and *Add* can insert new items only into one position, you obtain an operation that can insert a new item into any position of the list.
- ***OrderedListDelete(OL, Position)***. If you remove the restriction that *Pop* and *Remove* can delete items only from one position, you obtain an operation that can delete an item from any position of the list.
- ***OrderedListRetrieve(OL, Position, DataItem)***. If you remove the restriction that *StackTop* and *QueueFront* can retrieve items only from one position, you obtain an operation that can retrieve the item from any position of the list.

Because each of these three ADT's defines its operations in terms of an item's position in the structure, we have presented implementations for them that can provide easy access to specified positions. For example, both of the stack implementations allow the first position (top) to be accessed quickly, while both of the queue implementations allow the first position (front) and the last position (rear) to be accessed quickly.

In the remainder of this book, you will study ADT's that organize their data by value. That is, rather than asking for the ith item on a list, the operations of these ADT's will ask, for example, for the item with name John Smith. To support these types of operations efficiently, you will need new and more complex data structures.

SUMMARY

1. **The definition of the queue operations gives this ADT first-in, first-out (FIFO) behavior.**
2. **As is the case for the other ADT's that you have studied, the primary criterion for choosing between an array-based and a pointer-based implementation of a queue is the issue of fixed versus dynamic size.**
3. **Models of real-world systems often use queues. The event-driven simulation in this chapter used a queue to model a line of customers.**
4. **Central to a simulation is the notion of simulated time. In a time-driven simulation, simulated time is advanced by a single time unit, whereas in an event-driven simulation, simulated time is advanced to the time of the next event. To implement an event-driven simulation, you maintain an event list that contains events that have not yet occurred. The list is ordered by the time of the events so that the next event to occur is always at the head of the list.**

COMMON PITFALLS / DEBUGGING

1. **The pointer-based queue implementation is straightforward, but a linear array-based implementation has to overcome the problem of rightward drift of the elements in the array. This problem can lead to a queue-full condition even though only a few items are present.**
2. **You can solve the problem of rightward drift by viewing the array as circular. However, you must be able to distinguish between the queue-full and queue-empty conditions. One way to make this distinction is to maintain a count of the number of items in the queue. Other ways are suggested in Exercises 3 and 4.**

3. The management of an event list in an event-driven simulation typically is more difficult than it was in the example presented in this chapter. For instance, if there were more than one line in the bank, the structure of the event list would be much more complex.

SELF-TEST EXERCISES

1. If you add the letters A, B, C, and D in order to a queue of characters and then remove them, in what order will they be deleted from the queue?

2. What do the queues *Q* and *T* "look like" after the following sequence of operations?

```
CreateQueue(Q)
Add(Q, 1)
Add(Q, 2)
CreateQueue(T)
Add(T, 3)
Add(T, 4)
Remove(Q)
Add(Q, QueueFront(T))
Add(Q, 5)
Remove(T)
Add(T, 6)
```

   Compare these results with Self-Test Exercise 2 in Chapter 8.

3. Trace the palindrome-recognition algorithm described in the section "A Simple Application of the ADT Queue" for each of the following strings:

   a. `abcda`
   b. `radar`

4. For each of the following situations, which of these ADT's

   (1) a queue; (2) a stack; (3) an ordered list; (4) none of these

   would be most appropriate?

   a. The customers at the deli counter who take numbers to mark their turn
   b. An alphabetic list of names
   c. Integers that need to be sorted
   d. The boxes in a box trace of a recursive function
   e. A grocery list ordered by the occurrence of the items in the store
   f. The items on a cash register tape
   g. A word processor that allows you to correct typing errors by using the Backspace key

h. A program that uses backtracking
i. A list of ideas in chronological order
j. Airplanes that stack above a busy airport, waiting to land
k. People who are put on hold when they call an airline to make reservations
l. An employer who fires the most recently hired person

EXERCISES

1. Consider the language

   $L = \{w\$w' : w \text{ is string of characters other than } \$, w' = \text{reverse}(w)\}$

   as defined in Chapter 8. Write a recognition algorithm for this language that uses both a queue and a stack. Thus, as you traverse the input string, you insert each character of w into a queue and each character of w' into a stack. Assume that each input string contains exactly one $.

2. Revise the infix-to-postfix conversion algorithm of Chapter 8 so that it uses a queue instead of an array to represent the postfix expression.

3. Consider the array-based implementation of a queue described in the text. Instead of counting the number of items in the queue, you could maintain a boolean flag `IsFull` to distinguish between the full and empty conditions. Revise the array-based implementation by using the `IsFull` flag.

4. Another popular array-based implementation of a queue uses no special data field—such as `Count` or `IsFull` (see Exercise 3)—to distinguish between the full and empty conditions. In this implementation, you declare the array `Items` to be `[0..MaxQueue]` instead of `[1..MaxQueue]` and sacrifice one of the array locations as follows. By convention, `Front` will always point to the array location that precedes the location holding the item that is at the front of the queue. That is, the front item of the queue is always at the location one past the location that `Front` points to. (Note that location 0 follows location `MaxQueue`.) Before adding to the queue, you check to see if `Rear` + 1 is equal to `Front`. If this is the case, you disallow the insertion because it would violate the rule that at least one array location be empty. How does this allow you to distinguish between the full and empty conditions? Revise the array-based implementation by using this convention.

5. a. Consider a slight variation of the ADT queue. In this variation, new items can be added to and deleted from either end. This ADT is commonly called a **doubly ended queue**, or **deque**. Construct array-based and pointer-based implementations of the deque. Organize the implementations as units.
   b. Implement the deque as an object.

6. With the following data, hand-trace the execution of the bank-line simulation that this chapter describes. Show the state of the queue and the event list at each step.

5	9
7	5
14	5
30	5
32	5
34	5

Note that at *Time* = 14 there is a tie between the execution of an arrival event and a departure event.

7. Consider the stack-based search of the flight map in the HPAir problem of Chapter 8. You can replace the stack that the search uses with a queue. That is, you can replace every call to `Push` with a call to `Add`, every call to `Pop` with a call to `Remove`, and every call to `GetStackTop` with a call to `GetQueueFront`. Trace the resulting algorithm when you fly from *P* to *Z* in the flight map in Figure 8-8. Indicate the contents of the queue after every operation on it.

***8.** As Chapter 4 pointed out, you can define ADT operations in a mathematically formal way by using axioms. Consider the following axioms for the ADT queue, where `Q` is an arbitrary queue and `x` is an arbitrary queue item.

```
QueueIsEmpty(CreateQueue) = true   (A new queue is empty.)
QueueIsEmpty(Add(Q, x)) = false
Remove(CreateQueue) = error
Remove(Add(CreateQueue, x)) = CreateQueue
QueueIsEmpty(Q) = false ⇒
                 Remove(Add(Q, x)) = Add(Remove(Q), x)
QueueFront(CreateQueue) = error
QueueFront(Add(CreateQueue, x)) = x
QueueIsEmpty(Q) = false ⇒
                 QueueFront(Add(Q, x)) = QueueFront(Q)
```

a. Note the recursive nature of the definition of the operation `QueueFront`. What is the degenerate case? What is the recursive step? What is the significance of the `QueueIsEmpty` test? Why is `QueueFront` recursive in nature while the operation `StackTop` for the ADT stack is not?

b. The representation of a stack as a sequence

```
Push(Push( ··· Push(CreateStack, ··· )
```

without any `Pop` operations was called a canonical form. (See Exercise 18 in Chapter 8.) Is there a canonical form for the ADT queue that uses only `Add` operations? That is, is every queue equal to a queue that can be written with only `Adds`? Prove your answer.

9. Exercise 14 of Chapter 4 asked you to revise the object type `ordListType` so that each item on the list is a dynamically allocated object. Revise the object type `queueType`, which descends from `ordListType`, so that the items on the queue are dynamically allocated objects that descend from `genericObjectType`, as defined in Chapter 4. Write a small program that demonstrates how to allocate, use, and deallocate your new object. Include a procedure that allocates objects that descend from `genericObjectType`.

PROJECTS

10. Modify and expand the event-driven simulation program that this chapter describes. Here are a few suggestions:

a. Add some statistics to the simulation. For example, compute the maximum wait in line, the average length of the line, and the maximum length of the line.

b. Modify the simulation so that it accounts for three tellers, each with a distinct line. You should keep in mind that there should be

- Three queues, one for each teller
- A rule that chooses a line when processing an arrival event (for example, enter the shortest line)
- Three distinct departure events, one for each line
- Rules for breaking ties in the event list

Run both this simulation and the original simulation on several sets of input data. How do the statistics compare?

c. The bank is considering the following change: Instead of having three distinct lines (one for each teller), there will be a single line for the three tellers. The person at the front of the line will go to the first available teller. Modify the simulation of part *b* to account for this variation. Run both simulations on several sets of input data. How do the various statistics compare (averages and maximums)? What can you conclude about having a single line as opposed to having distinct lines?

11. The people that run the Motor Vehicle Department (MVD) have a problem. They are concerned that people do not spend enough time waiting in lines to appreciate the privilege of owning and driving an automobile. The current arrangement is as follows:

- When people walk in the door, they must wait in a line to sign in.
- Once they have signed in, they are told either to stand in line for

registration renewal or to wait until they are called for license renewal.

- Once they have completed their desired transaction, they must go and wait in line for the cashier.
- When they finally get to the front of the cashier's line, if they expect to pay by check, they are told that all checks must get approved. To do this, it is necessary to go to the check-approver's table and then reenter the cashier's line at the end.

The object of this problem is to write an event-driven simulation to help the Motor Vehicle Department gather statistics.

INPUT

Each line of input will contain

- An arrival time (integer).
- A name. To simplify reading in the data, you can assume that every name will contain exactly eight characters, possibly ending in blanks.
- A desired transaction code (L for license renewal, R for registration renewal).
- A method-of-payment code ($ for cash, C for check).

OUTPUT

Write out the details of each event (when, who, what, and so on).

FINAL STATISTICS

Licenses—total number and average time spent in MVD (arrival until completion of payment)

Registrations—total number and average time spent in MVD (arrival until completion of payment)

DETAILS OF THE SIMULATION

a. Define the following events: arrive, sign in, renew license, renew registration, and cope with the cashier (make a payment or find out about check approval).

b. In case of ties, let the order be determined by the order of the events just given—that is, arrivals have the highest priority.

c. Assume that the various transactions take the following amounts of time:

Sign in	10 seconds
Renew license	90 seconds
Register automobile	60 seconds
See cashier (payment)	30 seconds
See cashier (check not approved)	10 seconds

d. As ridiculous as it may seem, the people waiting for license renewal are called in alphabetical order. Note, however, that people are not pushed back once their transactions have started.

e. For the sake of this simulation, you can assume that checks are approved instantly. Therefore, the rule for arriving at the front of the cashier's line with a check that has not been approved is to go to the rear of the cashier's line with a check that has been approved.

CHAPTER 10

Tables and Trees

PREVIEW The ADT's presented in earlier chapters are appropriate for problems that must manage data by position. This chapter considers the ADT table, which is appropriate for problems that must manage data by value.

Several implementations of a table will be presented, along with their advantages and disadvantages. These implementations range from familiar data structures based on arrays and linked lists to new and important data structures based on trees. Thus, this chapter also discusses general trees, binary trees, and binary search trees.

To make an intelligent choice among the various possible table implementations, you must analyze the efficiency with which each of the implementations supports the table operations. For example, this chapter analyzes the efficiency of array-based and pointer-based table implementations and concludes that, in many applications, the implementations do not support the table operations as efficiently as possible. This conclusion motivates the use of a more sophisticated table implementation based on the binary search tree.

INTRODUCTION

In a broad sense, the following operations are what the management of data is all about:

General categories of data-management operations

- Operations that insert data into a data structure
- Operations that delete data from a data structure
- Operations that ask questions about the data in a data structure

The operations of the ADT's presented in the previous chapters each fit into at least one of these categories. The ADT's ordered list, stack, and queue are all **position oriented.** The operations of these ADT's have the form

The form of operations on position-oriented ADT's

- Insert a data item into the ith position of a data structure.
- Delete a data item from the ith position of a data structure.
- Ask a question about the data item in the ith position of a data structure.

As you have seen, the ADT ordered list places no restriction on the value of *i*, while the other ADT's do impose some restrictions. For example, the operations of the ADT stack are restricted to inserting into, deleting from, and asking a question about one end of the data structure (the top of the stack). Thus, although they differ with respect to the flexibility of their operations, all the previous ADT's manage an association between data items and *positions.*

This chapter introduces **value-oriented** ADT's whose operations are of the form

The form of operations on value-oriented ADT's

NOT POSITION
∴ SEARCH ON KEY!

- Insert a data item containing the *value x* into a data structure.
- Delete a data item containing the *value x* from a data structure.
- Ask a question about a data item containing the *value x*.

Although these operations, like position-oriented operations, fit into the three general categories of operations listed at the beginning of this section—they insert data, delete data, and ask questions about data—the operations are based upon *values* of data items instead of *positions*. Applications that require such value-oriented operations are extremely prevalent, as you might imagine. For example, the tasks

- *Find the phone number of John Smith*
- *Delete all the information about the employee with ID number 12908*

involve values instead of positions. The next section presents an example of a value-oriented ADT.

THE ADT TABLE

The name of an ADT often suggests images of familiar objects that possess properties resembling those of the ADT. For example, the name "stack" might remind you of a stack of dishes. What does the name "table" bring to mind? If you had heard the question before you began reading this chapter, you might have answered, "My favorite mahogany coffee table." However, your answer now should be something more like, "A table of the major cities of the world," such as the following one:

An ordinary table

City	*Country*	*Population*
Athens	Greece	2,500,000
Barcelona	Spain	1,800,000
Cairo	Egypt	9,500,000
London	England	9,400,000
New York	U.S.A.	7,300,000
Paris	France	2,200,000
Rome	Italy	2,800,000
Toronto	Canada	3,200,000
Venice	Italy	300,000

This table of cities contains several pieces of information about each city. Its design allows you to look up this information. For example, suppose that you want to know the population of London. You could scan the column of city names, starting at the top, until you came to London. However, because the cities are listed in alphabetical order, you could also mimic a binary search. You could begin the search near the middle of the table, determine in which half London lies, and recursively apply the binary search to the appropriate half. As you know, a binary search is far more efficient than scanning the entire table from the beginning.

Now suppose that you want to find which of the major cities are in Italy. To answer this question, you have no choice but to scan the entire table. The fact that the city names are in alphabetical order does not help you for this problem at all. The table's arrangement facilitates the search for a given city, but other types of questions require a complete scan of the table.

ADT table

The ADT **table** also allows you to look up information easily and has a special operation for this purpose. Frequently, the ADT table contains several pieces of information—that is, the items of a table are often records. Other ADT's that you saw earlier also allowed the items to be records. In the implementations of ordered lists, stacks, and queues, you could define `itemType` to be a record, and the operations would still make sense without modification. Because the ADT table is value oriented, however, there is greater significance to the fact that its items are records.

Search-key field

By designating one of the record's fields as the **search key**, you can facilitate the retrieval of items based on a specified value for this field. In the table of cities, for example, you could designate `City` as the search key if you often needed to retrieve the information about a city. You can devise implementations of a table that allow the rapid retrieval of the item(s) whose search key matches some specified value. However, if you need to retrieve the item(s) whose non-search-key field matches some specified value, you will have to inspect the entire table. Therefore, by designating a given field to be a search key, the problem solver sends the ADT implementer the following message:

> *Arrange the data in a way that facilitates the search for an item that has a specified value in its search key.*

The basic operations that define the ADT table are as follows:

ADT Table Operations

KEY CONCEPTS

```
CreateTable(T)
{ Creates an empty table T. }

TableIsEmpty(T)
{ Determines whether table T is empty. }

TableInsert(T, NewItem, Success)
{ Inserts NewItem into table T, if T is not already full,
  and sets Success to true. Otherwise sets Success to
  false. It is assumed that no two table items have the
  same search key and that no item in the table has the
  same search key as NewItem's search key. (Note that if
  the table items are records, NewItem is also a record
  with a value for each field.) }
```

```
TableDelete(T, SearchKey, Success)
{ Deletes from table T the item whose search key equals
  SearchKey. The operation fails if no such item exists.
  The flag Success indicates whether the operation
  succeeded. }

TableRetrieve(T, SearchKey, TableItem, Success)
{ Retrieves into TableItem the item in table T whose search
  key equals SearchKey. The operation fails if no such item
  exists. The flag Success indicates whether the operation
  succeeded. }

TraverseTable(T, Visit)
{ Traverses the table T and calls the procedure Visit once
  for each item. }
```

Various sets of table operations are possible

You should realize that these operations are only one possible set of table operations. The problem solver may require either a subset of these operations or other operations not listed here to fit the application at hand. It also may be convenient to modify the definitions of some of the operations. For example, these operations assume that no two table items have the same values in their search keys. In addition, `TableInsert` assumes that no table item has the same search key as the item to be inserted. However, in many applications it is quite reasonable to expect duplicate search-key values. If this is the case, you must redefine several of the operations to eliminate the ambiguity that would arise from duplicate search-key values. For example, which item should `TableRetrieve` return if several items have the specified value in their search keys? The point is that you should tailor your definition of the ADT table to the problem at hand. (The problem of duplicate search-key values is the subject of Exercises 8 through 10 at the end of this chapter.)

Although the operations `TableInsert`, `TableDelete`, and `Table-Retrieve` in the previous set of operations are sufficient for some applications, you cannot do several significant things without additional operations. For instance, you cannot perform an important task such as

```
Print out all the items that are in the table
```

because you cannot retrieve a data item unless you know the value of its search key. Thus, you cannot print out all the items that are in the table unless you can *traverse* the table.

`TraverseTable` visits all table items in a specified order

The definition of the `TraverseTable` operation is intuitively simple: The operation *visits* each item in the table once. In defining the `TraverseTable` operation, you must specify the order in which `TraverseTable` should visit the items. One common specification is to visit the items sorted by search key. It is also possible that you do not care in what order `TraverseTable` visits the items. As you will see, the way you define *TraverseTable*—if you request it at all—may affect the way that you implement the table.

The notion of traversing an ADT is quite important and is actually more difficult than you might imagine. Although traversal means to visit each item in the ADT, it can be difficult because you do something with each item when you visit it. You might simply print each item or you might copy it into another data structure or even alter the items.

The details of *TraverseTable* are thus very application dependent, which makes it difficult to define the operation within the ADT framework. You could have a different traversal operation for each task that you wanted to do as you visited items. Or *TraverseTable* could call a user-defined procedure, whose name you passed as a parameter, for each item in the table. The header of such a traversal operation is

```
procedure TraverseTable(T: tableType; Visit: procType);
{ Traverses table T and calls procedure Visit for each item. }
```

where *procType* is defined as

```
type procType = procedure(T: tableType; AnItem: itemType);
```

When you define the actual procedure whose name corresponds to the parameter *Visit*, you must specify the *far* directive. Simply follow the procedure header with *far*, as in

```
procedure Display(T: tableType; AnItem: itemType); far;
```

Note that if *Visit* alters the table items it visits, *T* must be a variable parameter.

Because you can define the *Visit* procedure to do any number of things—including access the table via the ADT operations—*TraverseTable* is a versatile operation. This versatility is illustrated with three brief examples, which represent the previous table of major cities as an ADT table.

Suppose that the items in the table are records of the form

```
type  itemType = record
          City ··· ;       { city's name }
          Country ··· ;    { city's country }
          Pop ···          { city's population }
      end;
```

Three tasks that you could perform on this table are

Tasks that use **City** *as the search key*

- *Print, in alphabetical order, the name of each city and its population*
- *Increase the population of each city by 10 percent*
- *Delete all cities with a population of less than 1,000,000*

Each task suggests that you designate the *City* field as the search key.

The first task requires you to print the city names in alphabetical order. Thus, `TraverseTable` must visit items alphabetically by search key.

To perform the first task, you pass to `TraverseTable` the name of the procedure `PrintInfo`, which appears in pseudocode as follows:

First task

```
PrintInfo(T, Item)

    Print(Item.City, Item.Pop)
```

`TraverseTable`'s visitation order is immaterial for the other two tasks. To perform the second task, you pass to `TraverseTable` the name of the procedure `UpdatePop`:

Second task

```
UpdatePop(T, Item)

    Item.Pop := Item.Pop + Round(0.1 * Item.Pop)
    TableDelete(T, Item.City, Success)
    TableInsert(T, Item, Success)
```

Note that to update the population of a city, you must delete the old item and insert a new one that contains the updated field. Because `UpdatePop` is on the user's side of the wall, you must use the ADT operations; that is, you cannot update the record directly. If an application frequently requires a replace operation such as this, it would be wise to include `TableReplace` as one of the ADT table operations. (See Exercise 2 at the end of this chapter.)

To perform the third task, you pass to `TraverseTable` the name of the procedure `DeleteSmall`:

Third task

```
DeleteSmall(T, Item)

    if Item.Pop < 1,000,000
        then TableDelete(T, Item.City, Success)
```

However, this task is not as simple as it may seem. By deleting an item, you alter the table during the traversal. Which item will `TraverseTable` visit next? Clearly it should visit the one after the deleted item, but will `TraverseTable` skip that item? Notice that during the second task (update), the deletion is followed by an insertion, so that the number and order of the items are unchanged in the table. Thus, for the update task, `TraverseTable` visits the correct next item. However, when deletion is the only task, you must ensure that `TraverseTable` does not skip a node. The traversal of a table while deleting parts of it is left as a difficult exercise.

Despite the fact that the ADT operation `TraverseTable` calls a user-supplied procedure, the sanctity of the wall between the program and the implementation of the ADT has not been violated. Because `Visit` is on the user's side of the wall, the procedure can access the data only through the ADT operations.

Selecting an Implementation

A major goal of this chapter is to indicate how the requirements of a particular application influence the selection of an implementation. The five operations given earlier make table a powerful ADT. Some applications will require all the operations; others only a subset of them. It is important that, before requesting the implementation of a set of table operations, the problem solver carefully analyze which operations are really needed for the application at hand. It is tempting always to request that all the operations be supported. This strategy, however, is a poor one. The sections that follow discuss the trade-offs between various implementations of a table. You will see that frequently one implementation supports some of the operations more efficiently than another implementation. Therefore, if you request an operation that you never use, the implementer of the ADT might select an implementation that is not best suited for what you are really doing.

What operations are needed?

In addition to knowing what operations you need for a given application, it is often important that the ADT implementer know approximately how frequently the application will perform each of the operations. Although some applications may require many occurrences of every operation, other applications may not. For example, if you maintained a table of major cities such as the one given earlier in this chapter, you would expect to perform far more retrieval operations than insertions or deletions. Other applications may require many more insertions and deletions than retrievals. Thus, if you seldom retrieve items, you can tolerate a table implementation that results in an inefficient *`TableRetrieve`* operation, as long as the operations that you will use frequently are efficient. The mix of operations is therefore one of the factors that influences which implementation of table you should select for a particular application.

How often is each operation required?

The next section presents several different application scenarios. Each of these scenarios involves an application that requires a particular mix of the table operations. The scenarios will present successively more challenging problems. For the first scenarios, adequate table implementations are possible through the use of arrays and linked lists. The later scenarios require a new type of data structure. The analysis of various implementations of the ADT table will illustrate some of the basic concerns of the analysis of algorithms. Given an application, you will see how to select an implementation that supports in a reasonably efficient manner the required mix of table operations. You should, however, remain conscious of factors other than efficiency, as was discussed in Chapter 7 in the section "Keeping Your Perspective."

LINEAR IMPLEMENTATIONS OF THE ADT TABLE

Linear implementation is a generic term that covers both array-based and pointer-based implementations. A linear implementation represents items one after another in the data structure and thus mirrors the flat, listlike appearance of the table of cities that was presented earlier in this chapter. Linear implementations are less sophisticated and less efficient than other implementations that you will see later in this chapter, but they are nevertheless appropriate for many applications. Because linear implementations are easy to understand conceptually, they are appropriate for tables that will contain only a small number of items. In such cases efficiency is not as great a concern as simplicity and clarity.

Even when a table is large, a linear implementation may still be appropriate. Whether or not it is appropriate depends upon the mix of operations that the given application requires. As a first step in examining this issue, observe that the linear implementations fall into four categories:

Four categories of linear implementations

- Unsorted, array-based
- Unsorted, pointer-based
- Sorted (by search key), array-based
- Sorted (by search key), pointer-based

Whether sorted or unsorted, the array-based and pointer-based implementations have the basic structures shown in Figure 10-1.

Under the array-based implementation, the table *T* is a record with two fields:

```
Size : 0..MaxItems; { number of items currently in the table }
Items : array[1..MaxItems] of itemType; { table items }
```

Under the pointer-based implementation, *T* is a pointer to the first node of a linked list. Each node contains both an item of data type `itemType` and a pointer to the next node. Note that the items in either implementation can be records with several fields.

The unsorted implementations store the items in no particular order; they can insert a new item into any convenient location. The sorted implementations must insert a new item into its proper position as determined by the value of its search key. You should review the techniques for inserting into and deleting from a sorted linked list that were first presented in Chapter 3. As you will see, the unsorted and sorted implementations have their relative advantages and disadvantages.

Next, we analyze the effectiveness of the linear table implementations for four application scenarios. The analysis of the last two scenarios leads to the development of a nonlinear implementation, the binary search tree.

Figure 10-1

Linear implementations of the ADT table: (a) array based; (b) pointer based

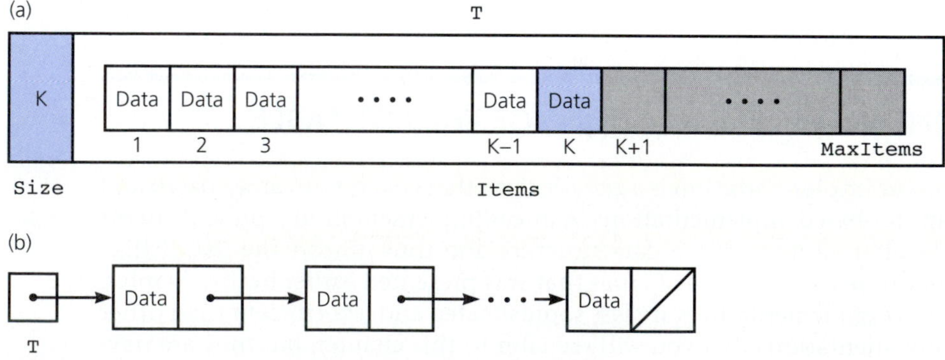

Scenario A: Insertion and Traversal in No Particular Order

Consider an application where the predominant tasks are to insert a new item into a table and print out a report of the items currently present. Suppose that the organization of the report is irrelevant: The items can be sorted or unsorted. If the application needs to perform a retrieval, deletion, or traversal in sorted order, it does so infrequently enough in this scenario that these operations should not influence your choice of an implementation.

An unsorted order is efficient

For this application there is no advantage to maintaining the items in a sorted order. In fact, by not maintaining a sorted order, the `TableInsert` operation can be quite efficient: Under either unsorted implementation, you can insert a new item into any convenient location. Under the unsorted array-based implementation, it is convenient to insert a new item at the end of the used portion of the array—that is, at location `Items[Size + 1]` in Figure 10-1a. Figure 10-2a shows the result of this insertion after `Size` has been updated. Under the pointer-based implementation, it is convenient to insert a new item at the beginning of the linked list—that is, `T` points to the new item and the new item points to the item previously first in the list. (See Figure 10-2b.) Thus, not only can you insert a new item quickly into either unsorted implementation of a table, but also the `TableInsert` operation requires a constant time for either implementation regardless of the table size.

Array based versus pointer based

As for whether you should choose the array-based or pointer-based implementation, there is really only one significant issue, given this particular mix of operations. As you have seen with other ADT's, the dynamic nature of a pointer-based implementation makes it appropriate if you do not have a good estimate of the maximum possible size of the table. In other situations, the choice is mostly a matter of style. The space requirements of the array-based implementation are slightly less than for the pointer-based implementation—because no explicit pointer is stored—but in most situations the difference is not likely to be significant.

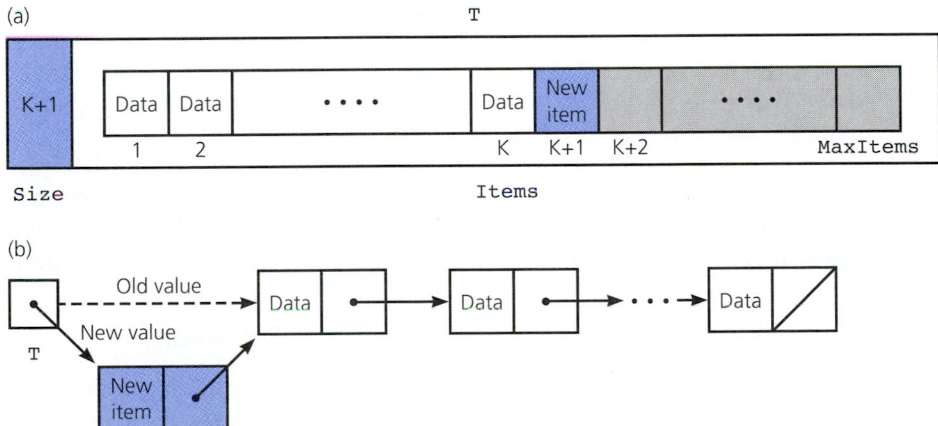

Figure 10-2

Insertion for unsorted linear implementations: (a) array based; (b) pointer based

Scenario B: Traversal in Sorted Order

It is perhaps most common for an application to traverse a table's items in sorted order according to their search keys. Consider an application where such a traversal is the predominant operation, and the insertion and deletion operations occur only infrequently. Suppose that your local library has computerized its catalog of the books currently in its collection. Furthermore, suppose that the library's computer prints this catalog for each person who enters the library. This task will thus occur much more frequently than updates to the catalog. In addition, the catalog will be of greatest use to the patron if the books' titles appear in alphabetical order. Therefore, the most frequently required task is a sorted `TraverseTable` operation.

Order the table items by their search keys

This application obviously requires that you choose the book title as the search key and order the table items by their search keys. Now the question becomes, should you use a sorted implementation that is array based or pointer based? In general, there are three issues to consider:

Issues that affect the implementation choice

1. Do you require the dynamic nature of a pointer-based implementation?
2. How quickly can you locate an item with a given value in its search key?
3. How quickly can you insert and delete a given item?

For the present library problem, the second and third issues are not of great importance, because insertions and deletions are infrequent and there is no mention of a retrieval operation. Thus, if you do not have a good idea of the maximum number of books that the library can contain, the pointer-based implementation is necessary.

What if you do know the maximum capacity of the library? For this mix of operations (many sorted traversals, few insertions and deletions), the two implementations do not differ significantly in their efficiency, because the time required to traverse the table under the two implementations is roughly the same.

Array-based and pointer-based implementations are comparable here

To summarize, the array-based and pointer-based implementations have approximately the same efficiency when the predominant operation is traversal in sorted order. The choice is thus mostly one of personal taste, unless the lack of a good estimate of the maximum size of the table mandates that you choose a pointer-based implementation because of its dynamic nature.

In fact, it is possible to do quite a bit better than either of these implementations. If the table is large, neither the array-based nor the pointer-based implementation would be satisfactory. For a large table you should use a different implementation—one that you will see later in this chapter.

Scenario C: Traversal in Sorted Order and Retrieval

Suppose that the librarian from the previous scenario has realized that frequently a patron wants only information about a particular title rather than the entire catalog. Therefore, to the environment of Scenario *B*—frequent sorted traversals, infrequent insertions and deletions—add frequent retrievals. The addition of frequent retrieval operations requires a table implementation that allows you to search efficiently for an item that has a specified value in its search key.

Under an array-based implementation, you can use a binary search to retrieve a particular title. On the other hand, under a pointer-based implementation, you must traverse the list from its beginning until you encounter the title on the list. The binary search performs this retrieval in significantly less time than the time required to traverse a linked list. Two questions come to mind at this point:

Questions

1. Is a binary search possible under a linear pointer-based implementation?
2. How much more efficient is a binary search under an array-based implementation than the linear pointer-based implementation's traversal from the beginning of a linked list?

A binary search is impractical with a pointer-based implementation

Can you perform a binary search under a pointer-based implementation? Yes, but too inefficiently to be practical. Consider the very first step of the binary search algorithm:

```
Look at the "middle" item in the table
```

If the items are in a linked list, how can you possibly get to the middle item on the list? The only way that comes to mind (for now) is to traverse the list from the beginning until you have visited `N div 2` items. But, as you will see in the answer to the second question, the time required to do just this first step often will be more than the time required to perform the entire binary search algorithm on an array. Further, you would have the same problem of finding the "middle" element at each recursive step. It is thus not practical to perform a binary search under the pointer-based implementation. This observation is extremely significant.

On the other hand, if the items are in an array `Items[1..N]`, then the middle item is at location `N div 2` and can be accessed directly. Thus, a binary search of an array requires considerably less time than an algorithm that must inspect every item in the table. What does "considerably less time" mean? As you know, without the ability to perform a binary search, you may have to inspect every item in the table, either to locate an item with a particular value in its search key or to determine that such an item is not present. In other words, if a table has size N, then you will have to inspect as many as N items; thus, such a search is $O(N)$. How much better can you do with a binary search? Recall from Chapter 7 that a binary search is $O(\log_2 N)$ in its worst case and that an $O(\log_2 N)$ algorithm is substantially more efficient than an $O(N)$ algorithm. For example, $\log_2 1024 = 10$ and $\log_2 1{,}048{,}576 = 20$. For a large table, the binary search has an enormous advantage.

What impact will this discussion have on the implementation decisions for Scenario *C*? Because retrieval is one of the predominant operations, unless you know that the library's catalog is quite small, you must choose an implementation under which a binary search is practical. As you have just seen, this decision eliminates both the sorted and unsorted linear pointer-based implementations and leaves only the sorted array-based implementation. This choice is fine if you have a good estimate of the maximum size of the table. Unfortunately, a good estimate is not always possible, and you will thus require the dynamic nature offered by a pointer-based implementation.

This situation seems to be irreconcilable. The requirement that a binary search be used mandates an array-based implementation, yet most applications will require the dynamic storage allocation available only to a pointer-based implementation. Thus, for this problem, the linear implementations are not suitable. A satisfactory solution requires a new type of implementation. Later in this chapter, we introduce a nonlinear pointer-based implementation on which you can perform a binary search-like algorithm. First, however, there is one more scenario to discuss. This scenario also finds the linear implementations unsatisfactory.

Linear implementations are not suitable here

Scenario D: Traversal in Sorted Order, Insertion, and Deletion

Scenario *B* introduced the library catalog problem. In that scenario the predominant operation was traversal in sorted order, with occasional insertions and deletions. The linear implementations were satisfactory for this mix of operations. Scenario *C* required, in addition, frequent retrievals, which made the linear implementations inadequate. If, instead of adding the retrieval operation to Scenario *B*, you add frequent insertions and deletions, the same inadequacy will result, as you will now see.

To insert into the table an item that has the value *X* in its search key, you must first determine where the item belongs in the table's sorted order. Similarly, to delete from the table an item that has the value *X* in its search key, you must first locate the item. Thus, both the `TableInsert` and `TableDelete` operations perform the following steps:

Both insertion and deletion perform these two steps

1. Find the appropriate position in the table.
2. Insert into (or delete from) this position.

Use an array-based implementation for Step 1

Step 1 is accomplished far more efficiently under an array-based implementation than it is under a pointer-based implementation. Under an array-based implementation, you can use a binary search to determine—in the case of insertion—where the new item *X* belongs and—in the case of deletion—where the item is located. On the other hand, under a pointer-based implementation, you know from the discussion in Scenario *C* that a binary search is impractical, and so you must traverse the list from its beginning until you encounter the appropriate location on the list. You also saw in Scenario *C* that an array-based implementation's binary search performs this step in significantly less time than the time required to traverse a linked list.

Use a pointer-based implementation for Step 2

Thus, because it facilitates a binary search, the array-based implementation is superior with respect to Step 1 of `TableInsert` and `TableDelete`. However, as you may have guessed, the pointer-based implementation is better for Step 2, which is the actual insertion or deletion of the item at the located position in the table. Under the array-based implementation, `TableInsert` must shift array items to make room for the new item, while `TableDelete` must shift array items to fill in the gap created when the item is removed. (See Figure 10-3a.) The worst case would require that every array item be shifted. On the other hand, under the pointer-based implementation, you can accomplish this second step simply by changing at most two pointers, as Figure 10-3b illustrates.

When you take Steps 1 and 2 together, you will find that both the sorted array-based and sorted pointer-based implementations of `TableInsert` or `TableDelete` require roughly the same amount of time. However, neither implementation supports these operations particularly well. Once again you find yourself in what seems to be an irreconcilable position. If the table is large, the speed of a binary search in performing Step 1 is desirable, and thus an array-based implementation is required. On the other hand, a pointer-based implementation avoids shifting array elements in Step 2. Once again, what is really needed is a pointer-based structure on which you can perform a binary search.

You have seen scenarios in which the linear table implementations are adequate and other scenarios in which they are not. Those latter scenarios provide the motivation to develop a different type of implementation for a table, one that combines the best features of the linear implementations. Such an implementation is the topic of much of the remainder of this chapter. However, we first conclude this section by presenting the sorted array-based implementation of the ADT table.

The Sorted Array-Based Implementation of the ADT Table

A Pascal version of the sorted array-based implementation follows. Exercise 1 at the end of this chapter asks you to write the other linear implementations.

Recall that the given ADT table operations assume that no two table items contain the same search key. Furthermore, `TableInsert` assumes

Figure 10-3

Insertion for sorted linear implementations: (a) array based; (b) pointer based

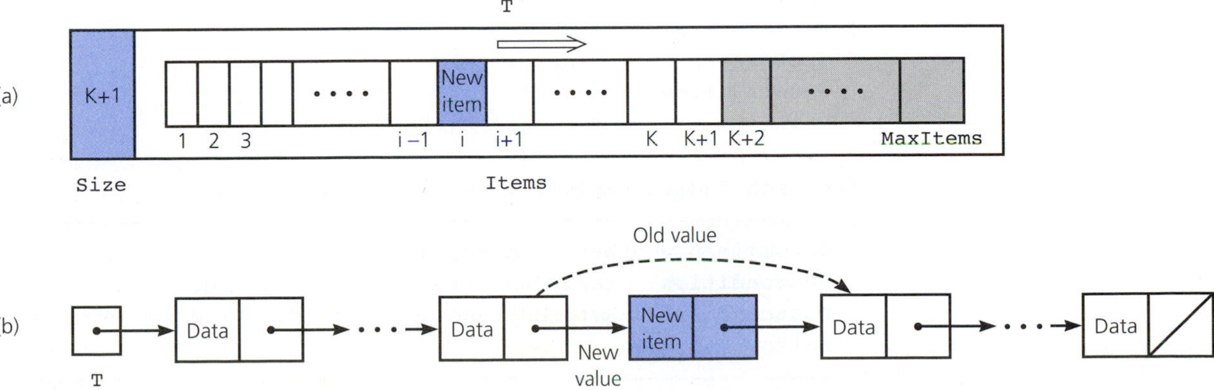

that no item already in the table has a search key equal to that of the new item to be inserted. Exercises 8, 9, and 10 at the end of this chapter ask you to remove these assumptions.

```
unit TableOps;
{ ******************************************************
  BASIC TABLE OPERATIONS--Sorted Array-Based Implementation

    CreateTable, TableIsEmpty, TableInsert, TableDelete,
    TableRetrieve, and TraverseTable

  Assumptions:
    1. A table contains at most one item with a given
       search key at any time. (See Exercises 8 - 10.)
    2. $B- is in effect.

  Notes: If T is of type tableType,
    1. 0 <= T.Size <= MaxItems
    2. T.Items[1..T.Size] contains the current table items
    3. If 0 <= I < J <= T.Size, T.Items[I] < T.Items[J]
  ****************************************************** }
interface

const MaxItems = <maximum size of table>;

type  keyType = <desired type of search key>;

      itemType = record
         Key : keyType;
         < ... and possibly other fields>
      end; { record }

      tableType = record
         Size : 0..MaxItems;
         Items : array[1..MaxItems] of itemType
      end; { record }

      procType = procedure(var T : tableType;
                               AnItem : itemType);

procedure CreateTable(var T : tableType);
{ ------------------------------------------------------
  Creates an empty table.
  Precondition: None.
  Postcondition: The empty table T is created.
  ------------------------------------------------------ }
function TableIsEmpty(T : tableType) : boolean;
{ ------------------------------------------------------
  Determines whether a table is empty.
  Precondition: CreateTable(T) has been called.
  Postcondition: Returns true if T was empty; else returns
  false.
  ------------------------------------------------------ }
```

```
procedure TableInsert(var T: tableType; NewItem: itemType;
                                    var Success: boolean);
{ ---------------------------------------------------------
  Inserts an item into a table in its proper sorted order
  according to the item's search key.
  Precondition: CreateTable(T) has been called and no two
  items of T have the same search key. T's items are sorted
  by search key. The item to be inserted into T is NewItem,
  whose search key differs from all search keys presently
  in T.
  Postcondition: If T was not already full, NewItem is in
  its proper order in T and Success is true. Otherwise, T
  is unchanged and Success is false.
  Calls: Position.
  --------------------------------------------------------- }
procedure TableDelete(var T: tableType;
             SearchKey: keyType; var Success: boolean);
{ ---------------------------------------------------------
  Deletes an item with a given search key from a table.
  Precondition: CreateTable(T) has been called and no two
  items of T have the same search key. T's items are sorted
  by search key. SearchKey is the search key of the item to
  be deleted. $B- is in effect.
  Postcondition: If the item whose search key equals
  SearchKey existed in T, the item is deleted and Success is
  true. Otherwise, T is unchanged and Success is false.
  Calls: Position.
  --------------------------------------------------------- }
procedure TableRetrieve(T: tableType; SearchKey: keyType;
        var TableItem: itemType; var Success : boolean);
{ ---------------------------------------------------------
  Retrieves an item with a given search key from a table.
  Precondition: CreateTable(T) has been called and no two
  items of T have the same search key. T's items are sorted
  by search key; SearchKey is the search key of the item to
  be retrieved. $B- is in effect.
  Postcondition: If the retrieval was successful,
  TableItem contains the retrieved item and Success is
  true. If no such item exists, TableItem and T are
  unchanged and Success is false.
  Calls: Position.
  --------------------------------------------------------- }
procedure TraverseTable(var T:tableType; Visit: procType);
{ ---------------------------------------------------------
  Traverses a table in sorted order, calling procedure
  Visit once for each item.
  Precondition: CreateTable(T) has been called and no two
  items of T have the same search key. T's items are sorted
```

```
  by search key. The procedure represented by Visit exists
  outside of the ADT implementation and is defined with the
  far directive.
  Postcondition: Visit's action occurs once for each item
  in T. (var allows Visit to alter T.)
  ----------------------------------------------------------- }

implementation

function Position(T: tableType; SearchKey: keyType) : integer;
{ -----------------------------------------------------------
  Finds the position of a table item or its insertion point
  by using a binary search.
  Precondition: CreateTable(T) has been called and no two
  items of T have the same search key. T's items are sorted
  by search key. SearchKey is the value of the search key
  sought in the table.
  Postcondition: Returns the index (between 1 and T.Size)
  of the item in T whose search key equals SearchKey. If no
  such item exists, returns the position (between 1 and
  T.Size + 1) that the item would occupy if inserted. T is
  unchanged.
  Calls: Local recursive function KeyIndex.
  ----------------------------------------------------------- }

   { local function for the recursive binary search }
   function KeyIndex(First, Last : integer;
                     SearchKey : keyType): integer;
   var Mid : integer;
   begin
      if First > Last
         then KeyIndex := First

         else
         begin
            Mid := (First + Last) div 2;
            if SearchKey = T.Items[Mid].Key then
               KeyIndex := Mid
            else if SearchKey < T.Items[Mid].Key then
               KeyIndex := KeyIndex(First, pred(Mid),
                                            SearchKey)
            else KeyIndex := KeyIndex(succ(Mid), Last,
                                            SearchKey)
         end  { if }
   end;  { KeyIndex }

begin  { Position }
    Position := KeyIndex(1, T.Size, SearchKey)
end;  { Position }
```

```
procedure CreateTable(var T : tableType);
begin
   T.Size := 0 { set count field to 0 }
end;  { CreateTable }

function TableIsEmpty(T : tableType) : boolean;
begin
   TableIsEmpty := (T.Size = 0)
end;  { TableIsEmpty }

procedure TableInsert(var T: tableType; NewItem: itemType;
                      var Success : boolean);
var Spot, Index : integer;
begin
   Success := not (T.Size = MaxItems);

   if Success
      then   { insert in proper order }
      begin
         { locate the position where NewItem belongs }
         Spot := Position(T, NewItem.Key);

         { shift up to make room for the new item }
         for Index := T.Size downto Spot do
            T.Items[succ(Index)] := T.Items[Index];

         T.Items[Spot] := NewItem;
         inc(T.Size)
      end  { if }
end;  { TableInsert }

procedure TableDelete(var T: tableType;
               Searchkey: keyType; var Success : boolean);
var Spot, Index : integer;
begin
   { locate the position where SearchKey exists/belongs }
   Spot := Position(T, SearchKey);

   Success := (Spot <= T.Size)
                    and (T.Items[Spot].Key = SearchKey);

   if Success { delete if present }
      then
      begin
         dec(T.Size); { delete the item }

         { shift down to fill the gap }
         for Index := Spot to T.Size do
            T.Items[Index] := T.Items[succ(Index)]
      end { if }
end;  { TableDelete }
```

```
procedure TableRetrieve(T: tableType; SearchKey: keyType;
           var TableItem: itemType; var Success: boolean);
var Spot : integer;
begin
    Spot := Position(T, SearchKey); { locate the item }

    Success := (Spot <= T.Size)
                      and (T.Items[Spot].Key = SearchKey);

    if Success    { retrieve if present }
       then TableItem := T.Items[Spot]
end;  { TableRetrieve }

procedure TraverseTable(var T:tableType; Visit: procType);
var Index : integer;
begin
    for Index := 1 to T.Size do
          Visit(T, T.Items[Index])
end; { TraverseTable }

end. { unit }
```

BINARY TREES

The desired nonlinear implementation of the ADT table requires a new data structure, which this section presents. You will learn about general trees, binary trees, and binary search trees. Although they are treated here as data structures, some people think of trees as ADT's, just as you can think of a linked list either as a data structure or as an ADT. Exercise 24 at the end of this chapter considers this issue.

Tree Terminology

Computer scientists use **general trees** to represent relationships. Previous chapters informally used tree diagrams to represent the relationships between the calls of a recursive algorithm. Recall, for example, Figure 5-12 of Chapter 5 for the *Rabbit* algorithm. The diagram is actually a tree. Each call to *Rabbit* is represented by a box, or a **node** in the tree. The lines between the nodes (boxes) are called **directed edges**. For this tree, the directed edges indicate recursive calls. For example, the directed edges from *Rabbit*(7) to *Rabbit*(6) and *Rabbit*(5) indicate that subproblem *Rabbit*(7) makes calls to *Rabbit*(6) and *Rabbit*(5).

Trees are hierarchical

All trees are **hierarchical** in nature. Intuitively, hierarchical means that there is a "parent-child" relationship between the nodes in the tree. If there is a directed edge from node *n* to node *m*, then *n* is the **parent** of *m*, and *m* is a **child** of *n*. In the tree in Figure 10-4, nodes *B* and *C* are children

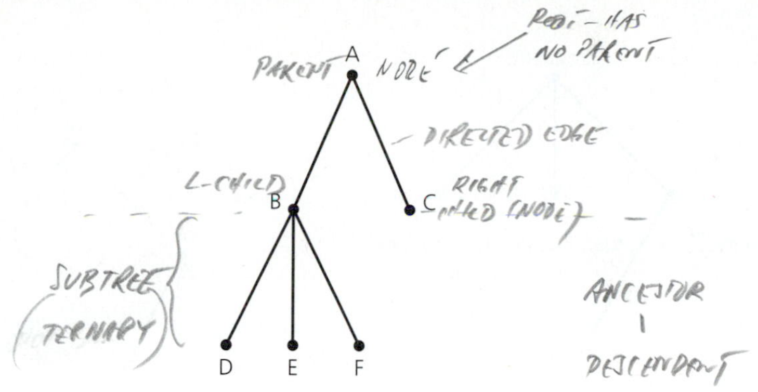

Figure 10-4

A general tree

of node *A*. Children of the same parent—for example, *B* and *C*—are called **siblings**. Each node in a tree has at most one parent, and there is exactly one node, called the **root** of the tree, which has no parent. Node *A* is the root of the tree in Figure 10-4. A node that has no children is called a **leaf** of the tree. The leaves of the tree in Figure 10-4 are *C, D, E,* and *F*.

The parent-child relationship between the nodes is generalized to the relationships **ancestor** and **descendent**. In Figure 10-4, *A* is an ancestor of *D,* and thus *D* is a descendent of *A*. Notice that not all nodes are related by the ancestor or descendent relationship: *B* and *C,* for instance, are not so related. However, the root of any tree is an ancestor of every node in that tree. A **subtree** of a tree is any node in the tree together with all of its descendents. A **subtree of a node** *n* is a subtree rooted at a child of *n*. For example, Figure 10-5 shows a subtree of the tree in Figure 10-4. This subtree has *B* as its root and is a subtree of the node *A*.

A subtree is any node and its descendents

Because trees are hierarchical in nature, you can use them to represent information that itself is hierarchical in nature—for example, organization charts and family trees, as Figure 10-6 depicts. It may be disconcerting to discover, however that the nodes in the family tree in Figure 10-6b that represent Caroline's parents are the children of the node that represents Caroline! That is, the nodes in the family tree that represent Caroline's ancestors are the descendents of Caroline's node. It's no wonder that computer scientists often seem to be confused by reality.

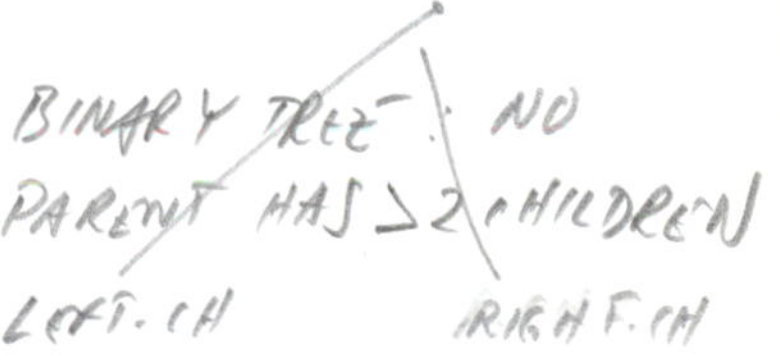

A **binary tree** is a tree in which each node has no more than two children. Thus, the trees in Figures 5-12 and 10-6b are binary, but the trees in Figures 10-4 and 10-6a are not; they are general trees. The remainder of this chapter will focus on binary trees.

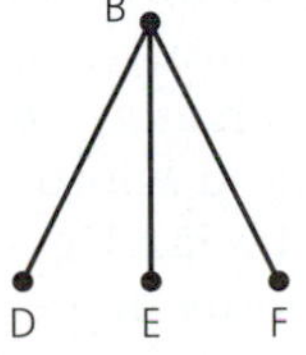

Figure 10-5

A subtree of the tree in Figure 10-4

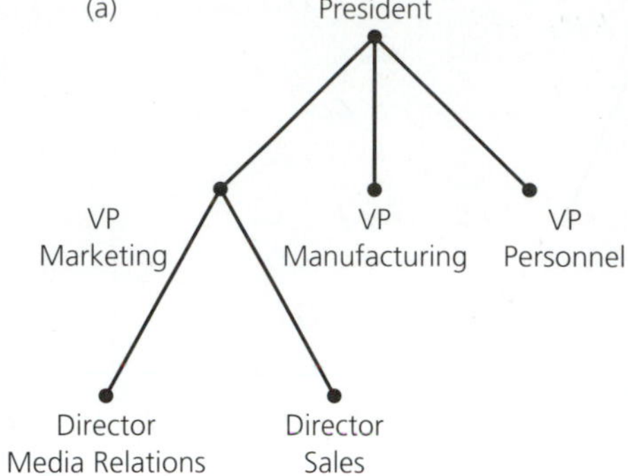

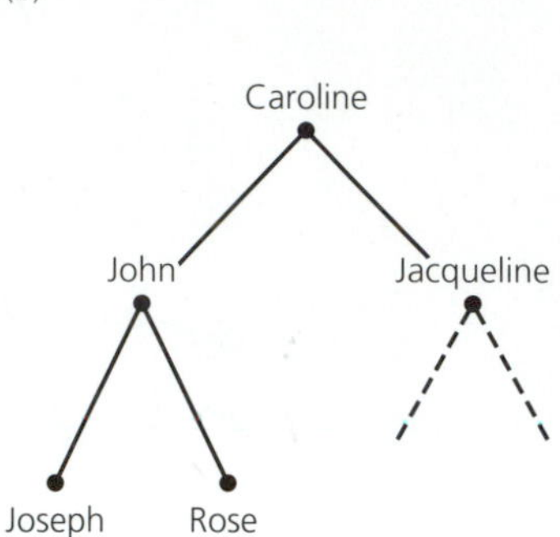

Figure 10-6

(a) An organization chart; (b) a family tree

A formal, recursive definition of a binary tree follows:

Formal definition of a binary tree

A set T of elements—called nodes—is a binary tree if either

1. T is empty, or
2. T is partitioned into three disjoint sets:
   - A single element r, its root
   - Two sets that are binary trees, called **left and right subtrees** of r

It is useful to have the following intuitive restatement of the definition of a binary tree:

Intuitive definition of a binary tree

T is a binary tree if either

1. T has no nodes, or
2. T is of the form

$$\begin{array}{ccc} & r & \\ T_L & & T_R \end{array}$$

where r is a node and T_L and T_R are both binary trees.

Notice that the formal definition agrees with this intuitive one: If r is the root of T, then the binary tree T_L is the left subtree of node r and T_R is the right subtree of node r. If T_L is not empty, its root is the **left child** of r, and if T_R is not empty, its root is the **right child** of r. Notice that if both subtrees of a node are empty, that node is a leaf.

As an example of how you can use a binary tree to represent data in a hierarchical form, consider Figure 10-7. The binary trees in this figure represent algebraic expressions that involve the binary operators +, −, *, and /. To represent an expression such as $a - b$, you place the operator in the root node and the operands a and b into left and right children, respectively, of the root. (See Figure 10-7a.) Figure 10-7b represents the expression $a - b/c$. Notice that a subtree represents the subexpression b/c. A

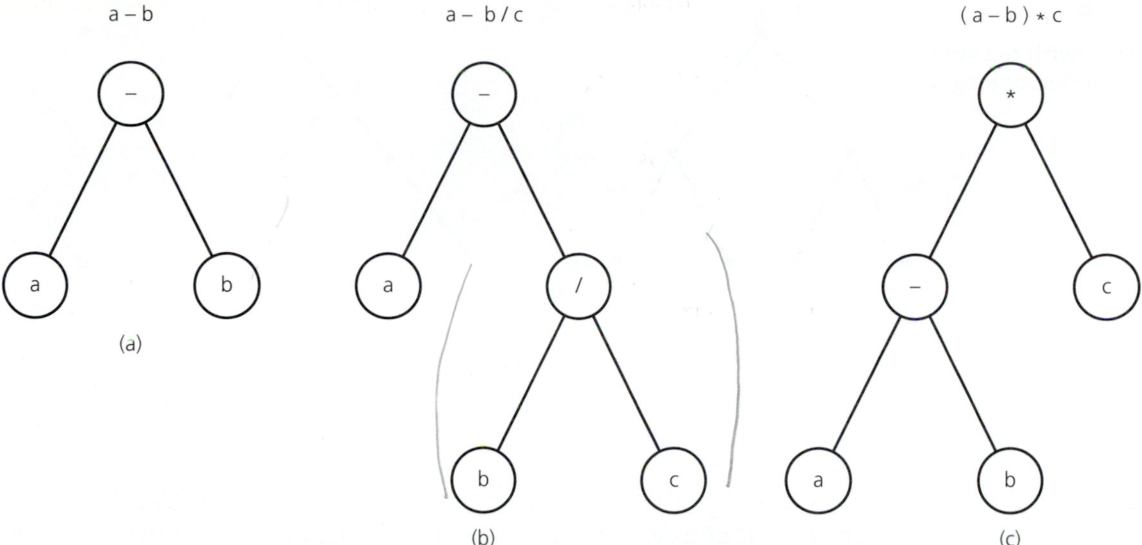

Figure 10-7

Binary trees that represent algebraic expressions

similar situation exists in Figure 10-7c, which represents $(a - b) * c$. Notice that parentheses do not appear in the tree. Also notice that the leaves of the tree contain the expression's operands, while other tree nodes contain the operators. The binary tree provides a hierarchy for the operations—that is, the tree specifies an unambiguous order for evaluating an expression.

The nodes of a tree typically contain values. A **binary search tree** is a binary tree that is in a sense sorted according to the values in its nodes. For each node n, a binary search tree satisfies the following three properties:

Properties of a binary search tree

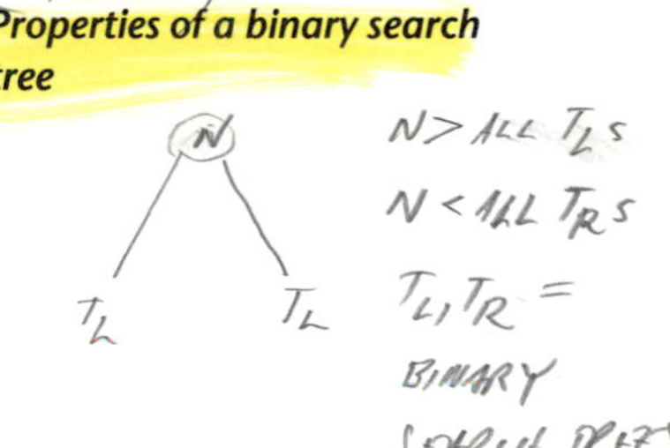

- n's value is greater than all values in its left subtree T_L.
- n's value is less than all values in its right subtree T_R.
- Both T_L and T_R are binary search trees.

Figure 10-8 is an example of a binary search tree. As its name suggests, a binary search tree organizes data in a way that facilitates searching it for a particular data item. As you will see later, the binary search tree will solve the difficulties with the linear implementations of the ADT table.

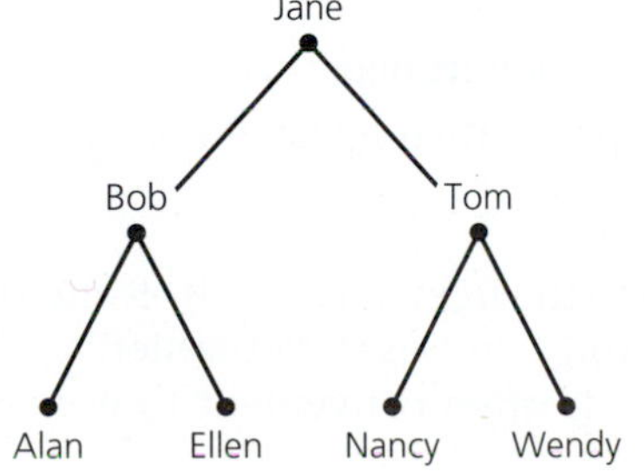

Figure 10-8

A binary search tree of names

Figure 10-9

Binary trees with the same nodes but different heights

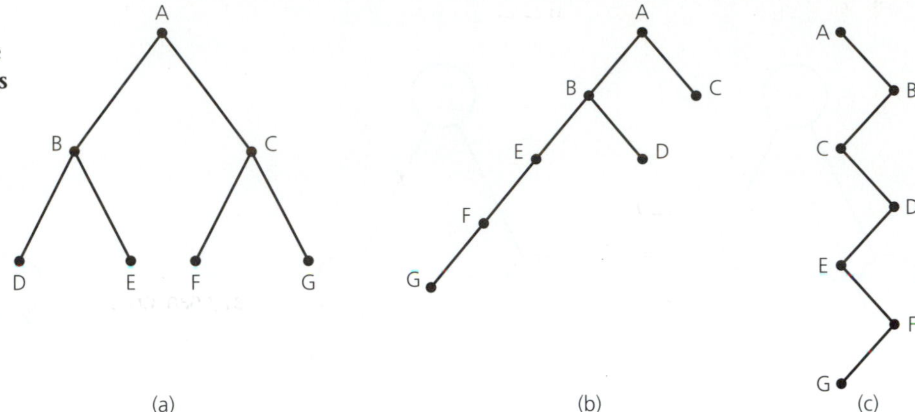

The height of trees. Trees come in many shapes. For example, although the binary trees in Figure 10-9 all contain the same nodes, their structures are quite different. Although each of these trees has seven nodes, some are "taller" than others. Intuitively, the **height** of any general tree is the distance from its root to its farthest leaf. More precisely, the height is the number of nodes on the longest path from the root to a leaf. For example, the trees in Figure 10-9 have respective heights of 3, 5, and 7. Many people's intuitive notion of height of would lead them to say that these trees have heights of 2, 4, and 6. Indeed, many authors define height to agree with this intuition. However, the definition of height given here leads to a cleaner statement of many algorithms and properties of trees.

There are other equivalent ways to define the height of a general tree *T*. One way uses the following definition of the **level** of a node *n*:

Level of a node

- If *n* is the root of *T*, then it is at level 1.
- If *n* is not the root of *T*, then its level is 1 greater than the level of its parent.

For example, in Figure 10-9a, node *A* is at level 1, node *B* is at level 2, and node *D* is at level 3.

Now the **height** of a general tree *T* in terms of the levels of its nodes is defined as follows:

Height of a tree in terms of levels

- If *T* is empty, then its height is 0.
- If *T* is not empty, then its height is equal to the maximum level of its nodes.

Apply this definition to the trees in Figure 10-9 and show that their heights are respectively 3, 5, and 7, as was stated earlier.

For binary trees, it is often convenient to use an equivalent recursive definition of height:

- If T is empty, its height is 0.
- If T is a nonempty binary tree, then because T is of the form

  r

  T_L T_R

  the height of T can be defined as 1 greater than the height of its root's taller subtree; that is,

  $$height(T) = 1 + max\{\ height(T_L),\ height(T_R)\ \}$$

Recursive definition of height

Later, when we discuss the efficiency of searching a binary search tree, it will be necessary to determine the maximum and minimum heights of a binary tree of N nodes.

Full, complete, and balanced binary trees. A **full binary tree** of height h has all its leaves at level h, and all nodes that are at a level less than h each have two children. Figure 10-10 depicts a full binary tree of height 3.

When proving properties about full binary trees—such as how many nodes they have—it is convenient to use the following recursive definition of a full binary tree:

- If T is empty, then T is a full binary tree of height 0.
- If T is not empty and has height $h > 0$, then T is a full binary tree if its root's subtrees are both full binary trees of height $h - 1$.

A full binary tree

Notice that this definition closely reflects the recursive nature of a binary tree.

A **complete binary tree** of height h is a binary tree that is full down to level $h - 1$, with level h filled in from left to right, as Figure 10-11 illustrates. More formally, a binary tree T of height h is complete

1. If all nodes at level $h - 2$ and above have two children each
2. If, when a node has a right descendent at level h (that is, a descendent at level h in its right subtree) all leaves in its left subtree are at level h

A complete binary tree

Notice that part 2 of this definition formalizes the requirement that level h be filled in from left to right. Also notice that *if a binary tree is full, it is necessarily complete.*

Full binary trees are complete

Figure 10-10

A full binary tree of height 3

Figure 10-11

A complete tree

Finally, a binary tree is **height balanced**, or simply **balanced**, if the height of any node's right subtree differs from the height of the node's left subtree by no more than 1. A binary tree is **completely balanced** if the left and right subtrees of every node have the same height. The binary tree in Figure 10-11 is balanced, and the binary tree in Figure 10-9a is completely balanced, but the other trees in Figure 10-9 are not balanced. Notice that a complete binary tree is balanced, whereas a full binary tree is completely balanced.

The following is a summary of the major tree terminology presented so far.

KEY CONCEPTS

Summary of Tree Terminology

Parent of node *n*	The node directly above node *n* in the tree
Child of node *n*	A node directly below node *n* in the tree
Root	The only node in the tree with no parent
Leaf	A node with no children
Siblings	Nodes with a common parent
Ancestor of node *n*	A node on the path from the root to *n*
Descendent of node *n*	A node on a path from *n* to a leaf
Empty tree	A tree with no nodes
Subtree of node *n*	A tree that consists of a child (if any) of *n* and the child's descendents
Height	The number of nodes on the longest path from the root to a leaf
General tree	A set of nodes that is either empty or has a root node and zero or more subtrees of the root

Binary tree	A tree in which each node has at most two children, the **left child** and the **right child**
Left (right) subtree of node *n*	In a binary tree, the left (right) child (if any) of node *n* plus its descendents
Binary search tree	A binary tree where the value in any node *n* is greater than the value in every node in *n*'s left subtree, but less than the value of every node in *n*'s right subtree
Full binary tree	A binary tree of height *h* whose leaves are all at level *h* and whose nonleaves each have two children
Complete binary tree	A binary tree of height *h* that is full to level $h - 1$ and has level *h* filled from left to right
Balanced binary tree	A binary tree in which the left and right subtrees of any node have heights that differ by at most 1
Completely balanced binary tree	A binary tree in which the left and right subtrees of any node have the same height

Implementations of a Binary Tree

There are two common ways in which you can implement a binary tree by using the constructs of Pascal. One way uses pointers and the other uses arrays. Suppose that you want to implement the binary tree of names in Figure 10-8. Each node in this tree contains a name and, because the tree is a binary tree, each node is followed by at most two descendent nodes.

Pointer-based implementation. You can use Pascal pointers to link the nodes in the tree. Thus, you can represent a tree by using the following Pascal statements:

```
const MaxLength = 20;            { maximum length of name }
type  nameType = string[MaxLength];
      ptrType =  ^nodeType;

      nodeType = record
          Name   : nameType;
          LChild : ptrType;      { pointer to left child }
          RChild : ptrType       { pointer to right child }
      end; { record }

      binTreeType = ptrType;

var   T: binTreeType;            { pointer to tree's root }
```

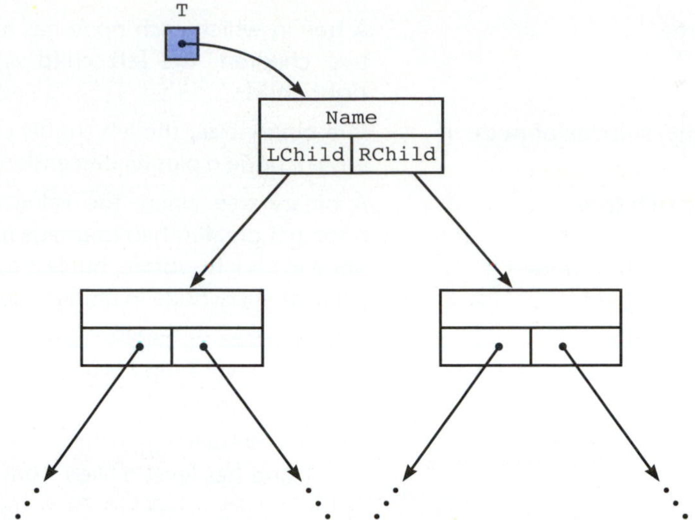

Figure 10-12

A pointer-based implementation of a binary tree

The external pointer *T* points to the tree's root. If the tree is empty, *T* is *nil*. Figure 10-12 illustrates this implementation.

Recall from the recursive definition of a binary tree that every nonempty binary tree consists of a left subtree and a right subtree, each of which is a binary tree. Under the pointer-based implementation, if *T* points to the root *r* of a binary tree, then *T^.LChild* points to the root of the left subtree of *r* and *T^.RChild* points to the root of the right subtree of *r*.

Array-based implementation. Another way to represent the nodes in a tree is by using an array of records. Array indexes can indicate a node's children, as the following Pascal statements indicate:

```
const MaxNodes = 100;            { maximum number of nodes }
      MaxLength = 20;            { maximum length of name }
type  nameType = string[MaxLength];
      indexType = 0..MaxNodes;

      nodeType = record
          Name   : nameType;
          LChild : indexType;    { index to the left child }
          RChild : indexType     { index to the right child }
      end; { record }

      binTreeType = array[1..MaxNodes] of nodeType;

var   Tree : binTreeType;
      T    : indexType;          { index of root }
      Free : indexType;          { index of free list }
```

The variable *T* is an index to the tree's root within the array *Tree*. If the tree is empty, *T* is 0. Both *LChild* and *RChild* within a node are indexes to the children of that node. A zero value for either index indicates that there is no child.

As the tree changes due to insertions and deletions, its nodes may not be in consecutive elements of the array. Therefore, this implementation requires you to establish a list of available nodes, which is called a **free list**. To insert a new node into the tree, you first obtain an available node from the free list. If you delete a node from the tree, you place it into the free list so that you can reuse the node at a later time. The variable `Free` is the index to the first node in the free list and, arbitrarily, the field `RChild` of each node in the free list is the index of the next node in the free list. Figure 10-13 illustrates this array-based implementation for the binary tree in Figure 10-8. Note that `Free` points to the next available node in the array—the first node in the free list—and that the `RChild` field of that node points to next node in the free list.

A free list keeps track of available nodes

Under this array-based implementation, if `T` points to the root *r* of a binary tree, then `Tree[T].LChild` points to the root of the left subtree of *r* and `Tree[T].RChild` points to the root of the right subtree of *r*.

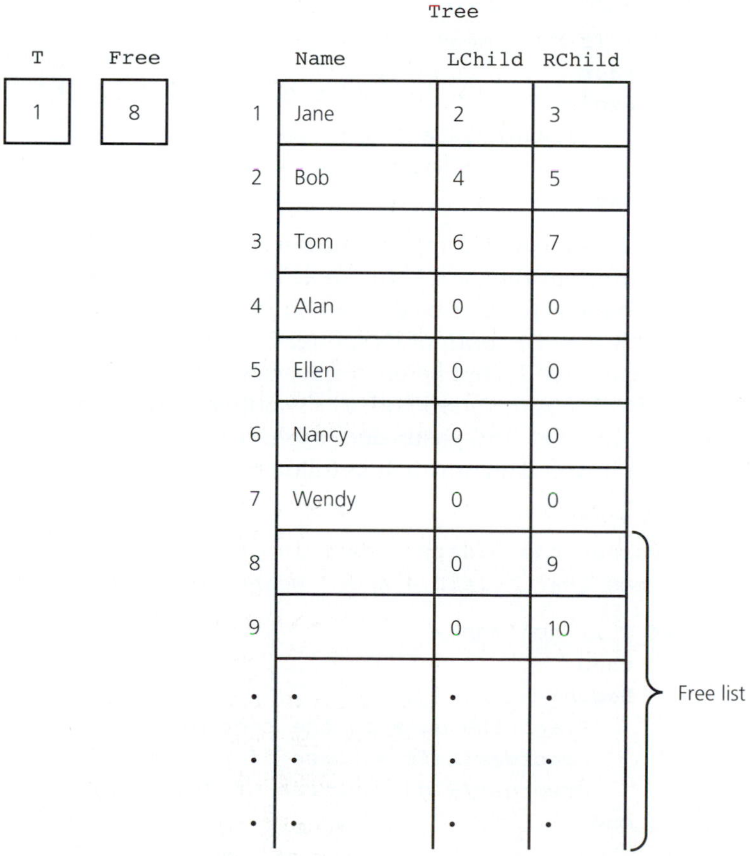

T: 1   Free: 8

Tree

	Name	LChild	RChild
1	Jane	2	3
2	Bob	4	5
3	Tom	6	7
4	Alan	0	0
5	Ellen	0	0
6	Nancy	0	0
7	Wendy	0	0
8		0	9
9		0	10
.	.	.	.
.	.	.	.
.	.	.	.

(Rows 8 onward: Free list)

Figure 10-13

An array-based implementation of the binary tree in Figure 10-8

Traversals of Binary Trees

The definitions of a binary tree make apparent its recursive nature, which is reflected in many algorithms. As an illustration, consider algorithms for traversing a binary tree *T*—that is, for visiting each node in *T* once. These algorithms will be useful later. For illustrative purposes, assume that visiting a node simply means printing the data portion of the node.

With the recursive definition of a binary tree in mind, you can construct a recursive traversal algorithm as follows. According to the definition, the binary tree *T* is either empty or is of the form

$$\begin{array}{ccc} & r & \\ T_L & & T_R \end{array}$$

If *T* is empty, then the traversal algorithm takes no action—an empty tree is the degenerate case. If *T* is not empty, then the traversal algorithm must perform three tasks: It must print the data in the root *r*, and it must traverse the two subtrees T_L and T_R, each of which is a binary tree smaller than *T*.

Thus, the general form of the recursive traversal algorithm is

A recursive traversal algorithm

```
Traverse(T)
{ Traverses the binary tree T. }

   if T is not empty
      then
      begin
          Traverse(Left subtree of T's root)
          Traverse(Right subtree of T's root)
      end
```

This algorithm is not quite complete, however. What is missing is the instruction to print out the data in the root. When traversing any binary tree, the algorithm has three choices of when to process the root *r*. It can process *r* before it traverses both of *r*'s subtrees, it can process *r* after it has traversed *r*'s left subtree T_L, but before it traverses *r*'s right subtree T_R, or it can process *r* after it has traversed both of *r*'s subtrees. These traversals are called **preorder**, **inorder**, and **postorder**, respectively.

The preorder traversal algorithm is as follows:

Preorder traversal

```
Preorder(T)
{ Traverses the binary tree T in preorder.
  Assumes that "visit a node" means to print its data. }

   if T is not empty
      then
      begin
         Print the data in the root of T
         Preorder(Left subtree of T's root)
         Preorder(Right subtree of T's root)
      end
```

The preorder traversal of the tree in Figure 10-14a visits the nodes in this order: 60, 20, 10, 40, 30, 50, 70. If you apply preorder traversal to a binary tree that represents an algebraic expression, such as any tree in Figure 10-7, you will obtain the prefix form of the expression.

The inorder traversal algorithm is as follows:

Inorder traversal

```
Inorder(T)
{ Traverses the binary tree T in inorder.
  Assumes that "visit a node" means to print its data. }

    if T is not empty
       then
       begin
          Inorder(Left subtree of T's root)
          Print the data in the root of T
          Inorder(Right subtree of T's root)
       end
```

The result of the inorder traversal of the tree in Figure 10-14b is 10, 20, 30, 40, 50, 60, 70. If you apply inorder traversal to a binary search tree, you will visit the nodes in order according to their data values. Such is the case for the tree in Figure 10-14b.

Finally, the postorder traversal algorithm is as follows:

Postorder traversal

```
Postorder(T)
{ Traverses the binary tree T in postorder.
  Assumes that "visit a node" means to print its data. }

    if T is not empty
       then
       begin
          Postorder(Left subtree of T's root)
          Postorder(Right subtree of T's root)
          Print the data in the root of T
       end
```

The result of the postorder traversal of the tree in Figure 10-14c is 10, 30, 50, 40, 20, 70, 60. If you apply postorder traversal to a binary tree that represents an algebraic expression, such as any tree in Figure 10-7, you will obtain the postfix form of the expression.

You can easily implement each of these traversals as a recursive Pascal procedure. For example, if you have a pointer-based implementation of a binary tree, as was described previously, the inorder traversal appears in Pascal as follows. (The two points from which a recursive call is made are marked for future reference.)

Inorder traversal in Pascal for a pointer-based implementation

```
procedure Inorder(T : binTreeType);
{ Traverses the binary tree T in inorder.
  Assumes that "visit a node" means to print its data. }
```

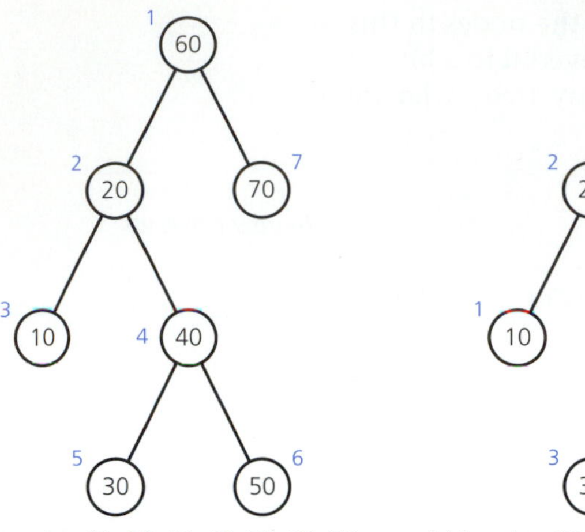

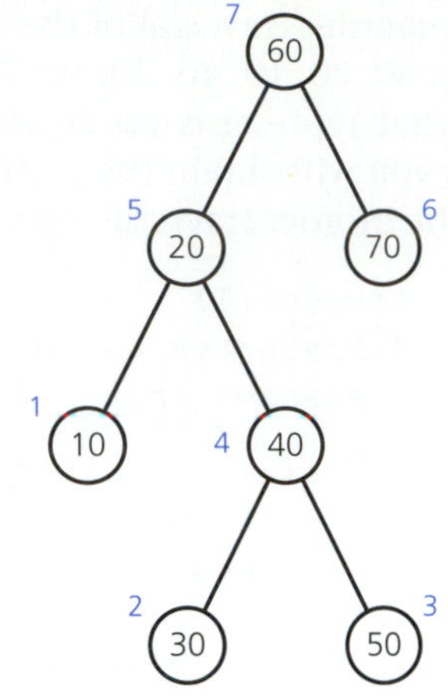

(a) Preorder: 60, 20, 10, 40, 30, 50, 70 (b) Inorder: 10, 20, 30, 40, 50, 60, 70 (c) Postorder: 10, 30, 50, 40, 20, 70, 60

Figure 10-14

Traversals of a binary tree: (a) preorder; (b) inorder; (c) postorder

```
begin
   if T <> nil
      then
      begin
         Inorder(T^.LChild);   { Point 1 }
         writeln(T^.Name);
         Inorder(T^.RChild)    { Point 2 }
      end; { if }
end; { Inorder }
```

Nonrecursive traversal. Before leaving the topic of traversals, it will be instructive to develop a *nonrecursive* traversal algorithm. The process will illustrate further the relationship between stacks and recursion that was first discussed in Chapter 8.

As an example of nonrecursive traversal techniques, consider a nonrecursive *inorder* traversal for the pointer-based implementation of a binary tree. The conceptually difficult part of the nonrecursive traversal is determining where to go next after a particular node has been visited. To gain some insight into this problem, consider how the recursive inorder traversal works. Notice that the preceding `Inorder` procedure has its recursive calls marked as points 1 and 2.

In the course of the traversal's execution, the current value of the pointer `T` actually marks the position in the tree. Each time `Inorder` makes a recursive call (from either point 1 or point 2), the effect is to descend the tree. In terms of the stack that is implicit to recursive subprograms, a call to `Inorder` pushes a pointer to the new current node—that is, the new value of `T`—onto the stack. At any given time, the stack contains pointers to the nodes along the path from the tree's root to the current node *n*, with the pointer to *n* at the top of the stack and the pointer to the root at the bottom, as Figure 10-15 illustrates.

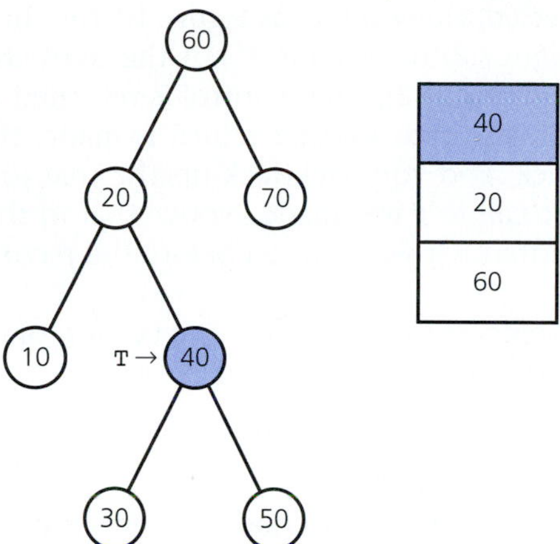

Figure 10-15

Inorder traversal using a stack

Now consider what happens when `Inorder` returns from a recursive call. The effect of the return is to backtrack up the tree from a node *n* to its parent *p*, from which the recursive call to *n* was made. (Note that *n* is possibly "empty"—that is, is indicated by a `nil` value for *T* at the top of the stack.) A pointer to *p* comes to the top of the stack when, as the return is made from the recursive call, the pointer to *n* is popped from the stack.

What happens next depends on which subtree of *p* has just been traversed. If, as Figure 10-16a illustrates, the process has just finished traversing *p*'s left subtree (that is, if *n* is the left child of *p* and thus the return is made to point 1 in the `Inorder` procedure), then control is returned to the `writeln` statement that prints out the data in node *p*. After the data in *p* has been printed, a recursive call is made from point 2 and the right

Figure 10-16

Traversing (a) the left and (b) the right subtrees of 20

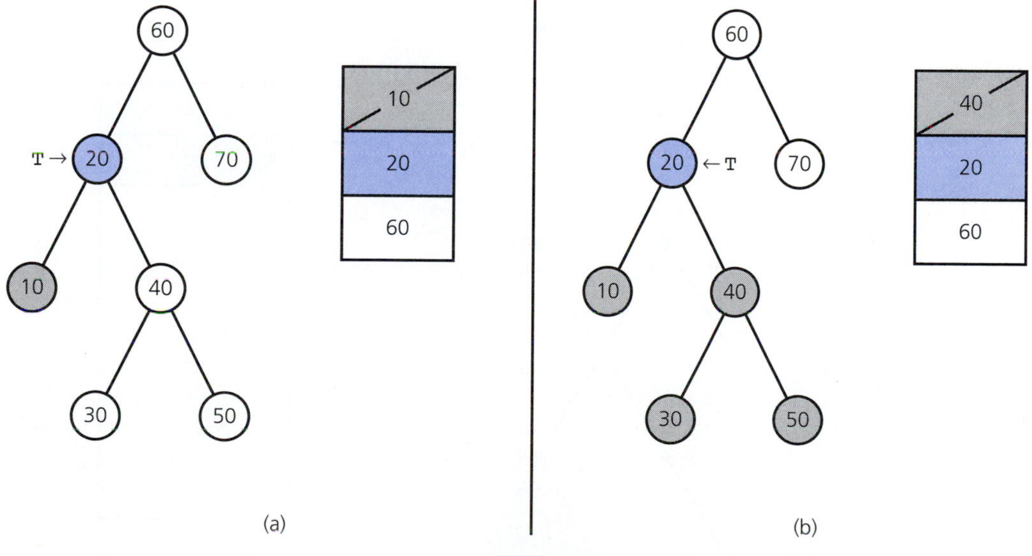

subtree of p is traversed. However, if, as Figure 10-16b illustrates, you have just traversed p's right subtree (that is, if n is the right child of p and thus the return is made to point 2), then control is returned to the end of the procedure. As a consequence another return is made, the pointer to p is popped off the stack, and you backtrack up the tree to p's parent, from where the recursive call to p was made. Notice that in this latter case, the data in p is not printed—it was printed before the recursive call to n was made from point 2.

Thus, two facts emerge from the recursive version of the `Inorder` procedure when a return is made from a recursive call:

Actions at a return from a recursive call to `Inorder`

1. The implicit recursive stack of pointers is used to find the node p to which the traversal must backtrack.
2. Once the traversal backtracks to node p, it either visits p (for example, prints out its data) or backtracks further up the tree. It visits p if p's left subtree has just been traversed; it backtracks if its right subtree has just been traversed. The appropriate action is taken simply as a consequence of the point—1 or 2—to which control is returned.

You could directly mimic this action by using an iterative procedure and an explicit stack, as long as some bookkeeping device kept track of which subtree of a node had just been traversed. However, you can use the following observation both to eliminate the need for the bookkeeping device and to speed up the traversal somewhat. Consider the subtree in Figure 10-17. After you have finished traversing the subtree rooted at node R, there is no need to return to nodes B and C, because the right subtrees

Figure 10-17

A subtree with a stack

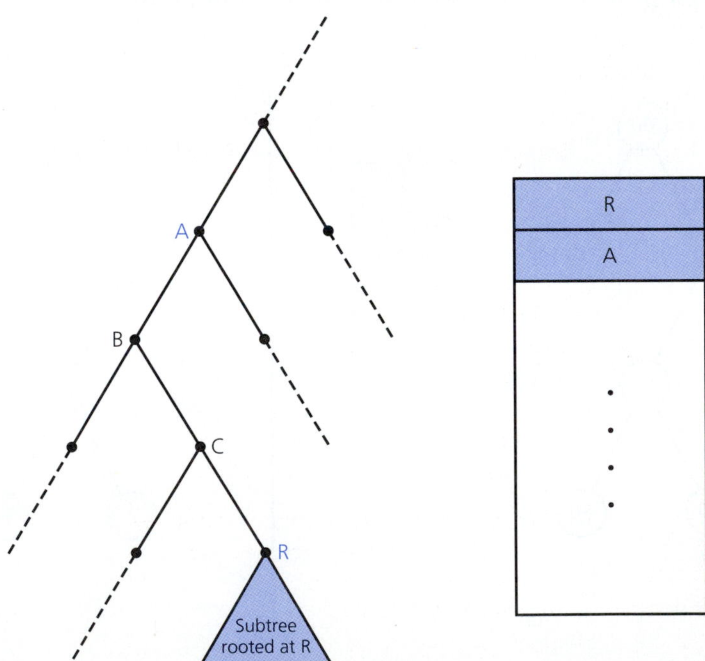

of these nodes have already been traversed. You can instead return directly to node *A*, *which is the nearest ancestor of R whose right subtree has not yet been traversed.*

It is a simple matter to implement this strategy of not returning to a node after its right subtree has been traversed. All that is required is that you place a pointer to a node on the stack only before the node's left subtree is traversed, and not before its right subtree is traversed. Thus, in Figure 10-17, when you are at node *R* the contents of the stack are *A*-*R* (with *R* on top). Nodes *B* and *C* are not on the stack because you are currently traversing their right subtrees; on the other hand, *A* is on the stack because you are currently traversing its left subtree. When you return from node *R*, nodes *B* and *C* are thus bypassed because you have finished with their right subtrees and do not need to return to these nodes. Thus, you go directly to node *A*, whose left subtree has just been traversed. You then visit *A*, pop its pointer from the stack, and traverse *A*'s right subtree.

This nonrecursive traversal strategy is captured by the following pseudocode:

Nonrecursive inorder traversal

```
{ initialize }
CreateStack(S)
Cur := Root
Push(S, Cur)
Done := false

while not Done do
begin
    if Cur <> nil
       then  { traverse the left subtree }
       begin
          Cur := Cur^.LChild
          Push(S, Cur)
       end

       else  { backtrack from the empty subtree }
       begin
          Pop(S)  { pop the nil pointer }
          { Visit the node at the top of the stack.
            However, if the stack is empty, you are done. }
          if not StackIsEmpty(S)
                then
                begin
                   Cur := StackTop(S)
                   Pop(S)
                   Visit(Cur)

                   { traverse the right subtree
                     of the node just visited }
                   Cur := Cur^.RChild
                   Push(S, Cur)
                end  { then }
```

```
            else Done := true
        end  { else backtrack }
end  { while }
```

You should note that eliminating recursion can be more complicated than the example given here. However, the general case is beyond the scope of this book.

A NONLINEAR IMPLEMENTATION OF THE ADT TABLE

A nonlinear implementation of the ADT table that uses a binary search tree provides the best features of the linear implementations of the ADT table that were presented earlier in this chapter. You can insert and delete data items by changing either pointers or indexes, without shifting data. You can locate data items by using a binary search-like algorithm, a technique you previously could apply only to an array-based implementation. Finally, in its pointer-based form, the binary search tree allows you to take advantage of dynamic storage allocation.

Despite certain difficulties, linear implementations of a table can be appropriate

If all of these claims are indeed true, you might wonder why you studied the linear implementations of the ADT table at all. There are three main reasons why it is appropriate to discuss the linear table implementations before introducing the nonlinear implementation. The first and foremost reason is perspective. Chapter 7 spoke of the dangers of overanalyzing a problem. If the size of the problem is small, it is unlikely that there will be a significant difference in efficiency among the possible solutions. In particular, if the size of the table is small, you should select a linear implementation because it is simple to understand.

The second reason is that there actually are scenarios for which a linear implementation is quite efficient. Recall that a linear implementation was adequate for Scenario *A*, where the predominant operations are insertion and traversal in no particular order; Scenario *B*, where the predominant operation is traversal in sorted order; and, if the maximum number of items is known, Scenario *C*, where the predominant operations are traversal in sorted order and retrieval. For these situations, a concern for simplicity suggests that you use a linear implementation and not a binary search tree, even for large tables.

The third reason is motivation. By seeing scenarios for which the linear implementations are not adequate, you can appreciate binary search trees more fully. Recall that in these scenarios there seemed to be conflicting needs that could not be reconciled. For the task of locating a table item for both the retrieval operation and the first steps of the insertion and deletion operations, a binary search is desirable. Thus, an array-based implementation is preferable. On the other hand, the need for dynamic storage allocation and the desire not to shift items during the insertion and deletion operations make a pointer-based implementation equally desirable. The binary search tree reconciles this conflict.

The recursive definition of a binary search tree, whose nodes each contain one field designated as the search key, can be restated as follows:

> For each node n, a **binary search tree** satisfies the following three properties:
>
> - n's search key is greater than all search keys in n's left subtree T_L.
> - n's search key is less than all search keys in n's right subtree T_R.
> - Both T_L and T_R are binary search trees.

A recursive definition of a binary search tree

The sorted nature of a binary search tree allows efficient retrieval, insertion, deletion, and traversal operations.

For example, suppose that you want to locate the name Ellen in the binary search tree of Figure 10-18. Beginning with Jane, which is in the root node of the tree, you know that if the name Ellen is present in the tree, it must be in Jane's left subtree because Ellen is before Jane alphabetically. From the recursive definition, you know that Jane's left subtree is also a binary search tree, so you use exactly the same strategy to search this subtree for Ellen. The name Bob is in the root of this binary search tree, and because Ellen is greater than Bob it must be in Bob's right subtree. Bob's right subtree is also a binary search tree, and it happens that Ellen is in the root node of this tree. Thus, the search has located the name.

This search strategy for the pointer-based implementation of the binary search tree is formalized as follows. Let each node in the tree be a record whose search key is a person's name, as the following Pascal statements describe:

```
const  MaxLength = 20;     { maximum length of name }
type   keyType = string[MaxLength];

       itemType = record
          Key : keyType;
          <... and possibly other fields>
       end;   { record }

       ptrType = ^nodeType;

       nodeType = record
          Item   : itemType;
          LChild : ptrType;
          RChild : ptrType
       end;   { record }

       binTreeType = ptrType;

var    T : binTreeType;
```

Assume that figures such as Figure 10-18 show only the search keys. The search algorithm for this implementation is

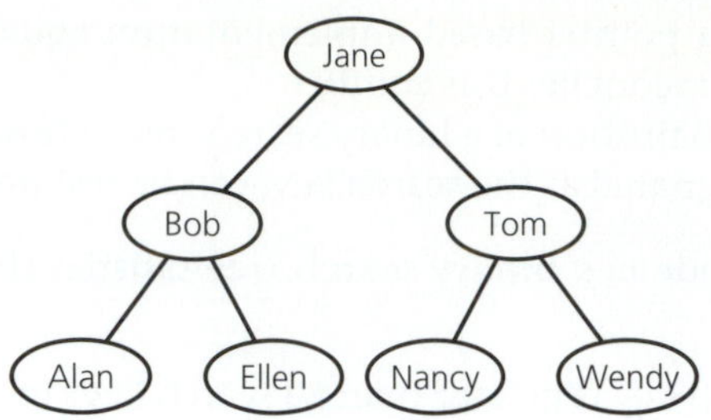

Figure 10-18

A binary search tree

A search algorithm for a pointer-based binary search tree

```
Find(T, X)
{ Searches the binary search tree T for the name X. }

  if T = nil then
     Print 'X is not present' { empty tree }

  else if X = T^.Item.Key then
     Print 'X is present'      { name is found }

  else if X < T^.Item.Key then
     Find(T^.LChild, X)        { search the left subtree }

  else Find(T^.RChild, X)      { search the right subtree }
```

As you will see, this `Find` algorithm is the basis of the operations `TableInsert`, `TableDelete`, and `TableRetrieve`.

Several different binary search trees are possible for the same data

Many different binary search trees can contain the names Alan, Bob, Ellen, Jane, Nancy, Tom, and Wendy. For example, in addition to the tree in Figure 10-18, each tree in Figure 10-19 is a valid binary search tree for these names. Although these trees have different shapes, the shape of the tree in no way affects the validity of the `Find` algorithm. The only property that `Find` needs is that a tree be a binary search tree.

`Find` works more efficiently on some trees than on others, however. For example, with the tree in Figure 10-19c, the `Find` algorithm inspects every node before locating Wendy. In fact, this binary tree really has the same structure as a sorted linear list. In contrast, with the full tree in Figure 10-18, the `Find` algorithm inspects only the nodes that contain the names Jane, Tom, and Wendy. Notice that these are exactly the same names that a binary search of the sorted array in Figure 10-20 would inspect. Later in this chapter, you will learn more about how the shape of a binary search tree affects efficiency and how the `TableInsert` and `TableDelete` operations affect this shape.

Now consider traversal in sorted order. The inorder traversal that you saw earlier in this chapter will visit the nodes of a binary search tree in sorted order. Recall that the inorder traversal algorithm appears as follows:

```
Inorder(T)
{ Traverses the binary tree T in inorder. }

  if T is not empty
     then
```

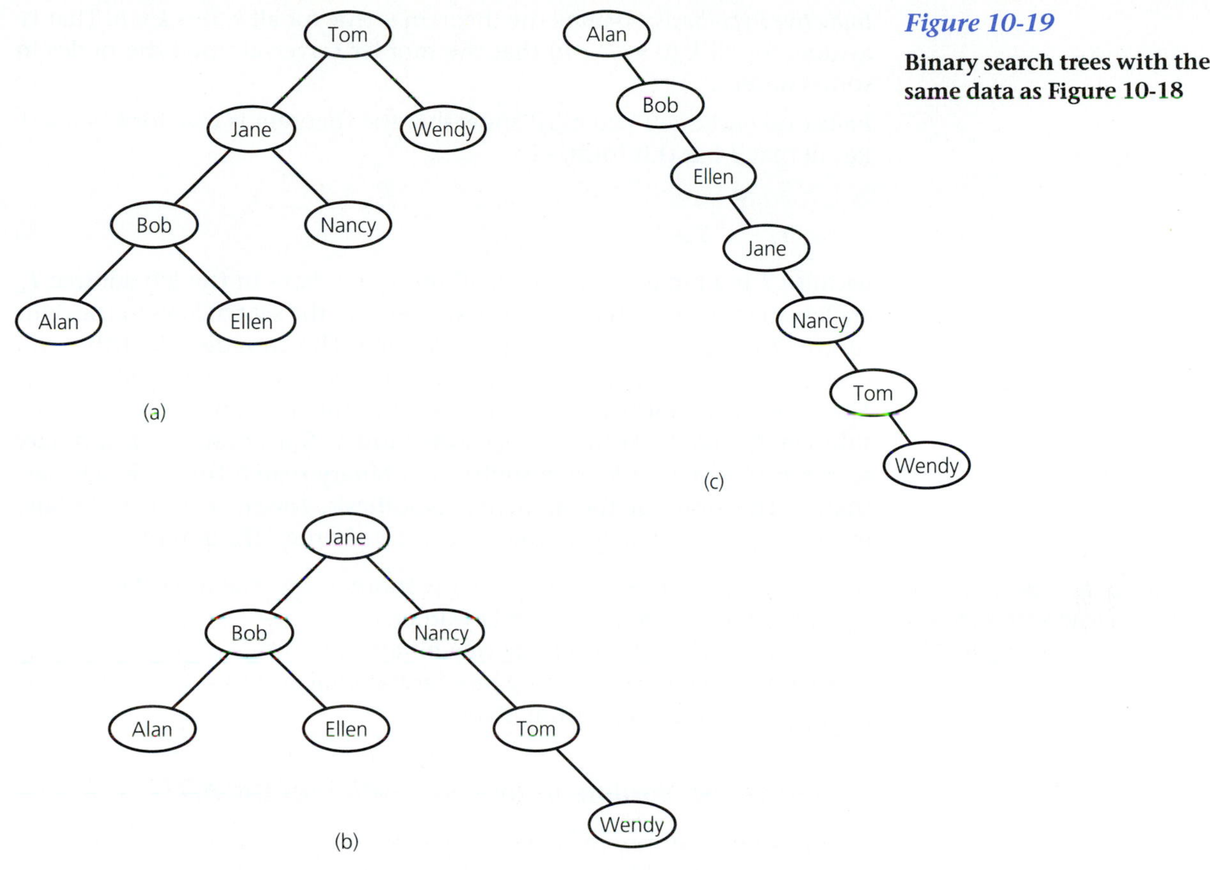

Figure 10-19

Binary search trees with the same data as Figure 10-18

```
begin
   Inorder(Left subtree of T's root)
   Visit the root of T
   Inorder(Right subtree of T's root)
end
```

THEOREM 10-1. The inorder traversal of a binary search tree *T* will visit its nodes in sorted search-key order.

PROOF. The proof is by induction on *h*, the height of *T*.

Basis: $h = 0$. When *T* is empty, the algorithm does not visit any nodes. This is the proper sorted order for the zero names that are in the tree!

Alan	Bob	Ellen	Jane	Nancy	Tom	Wendy
1	2	3	4	5	6	7

Figure 10-20

An array of names in sorted order

Inductive hypothesis: Assume the theorem is true for all k, $0 \leq k < h$. That is, assume for all k $(0 \leq k < h)$ that the inorder traversal visits the nodes in sorted order.

Inductive conclusion: You must show that the theorem is true for $k = h > 0$. Recall that T has this form:

$$\begin{array}{ccc} & r & \\ T_L & & T_R \end{array}$$

Because T is a binary search tree, all the search keys in the left subtree T_L are less than the search key in the root r, and all the search keys in the right subtree T_R are greater than the search key in r. The `Inorder` algorithm will visit all the nodes in T_L, then visit r, and then visit all the nodes in T_R. Thus, the only concern is that `Inorder` visit the nodes within each of the subtrees T_L and T_R in the correct sorted order. But because T is a binary search tree of height h, each subtree is a binary search tree of height less than h. Therefore, by the inductive hypothesis, `Inorder` visits the nodes in each subtree T_L and T_R in the correct sorted order. **(End of proof.)**

Use inorder traversal to visit nodes of a binary search tree in search-key order

As a result of this theorem, you can use inorder traversal to visit the nodes of a binary search tree in search-key order.

To summarize, the structure of a binary search tree allows you to traverse it in sorted order by using inorder traversal and to search it by using a binary search-like algorithm, `Find`.

Details of the Nonlinear Implementation of the ADT Table

This section examines the details of a pointer-based nonlinear implementation of the ADT table that uses a binary search tree. A binary search tree is recursive by nature, and it is thus natural to formulate the algorithms recursively. Chapter 6 examined a recursive implementation of the linked list operations, which this section will now use.

Insertion. Suppose that you want to insert the name Frank into the binary search tree of Figure 10-18. As a first step, imagine that you instead want to *find* the item with a search key of Frank. The `Find` algorithm first searches the tree rooted at Jane, then the tree rooted at Bob, and then the tree rooted at Ellen. It then searches the tree rooted at the right child of Ellen. Because this tree is empty, as Figure 10-21 illustrates, the `Find` algorithm has reached a degenerate case and will terminate with the report that Frank is not present. What does it mean that `Find` looked for Frank in the right subtree of Ellen? For one thing, it means that if Frank were the right child of Ellen, `Find` would have found Frank there.

This observation indicates that a good place to insert Frank is as the right child of Ellen. Because Ellen has no right child, the insertion is simple, requiring only that Ellen's `RChild` pointer field be set to point to Frank. More importantly, Frank belongs in this location—`Find` will look for Frank here. Specifically, inserting Frank as the right child of Ellen will

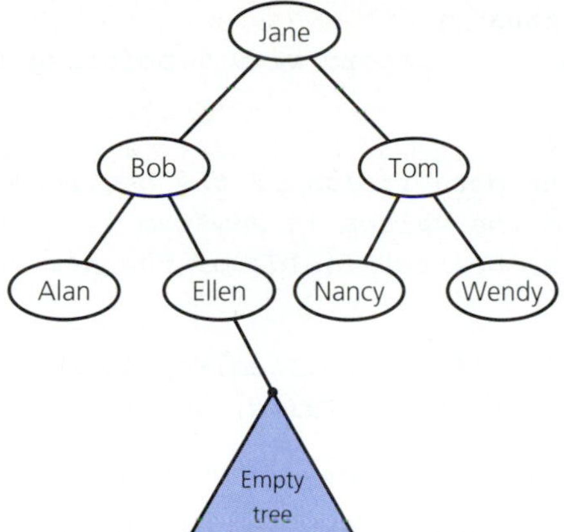

Figure 10-21

Empty subtree where *Find* terminates

preserve the tree's binary search tree property. Because *Find*, when searching for Frank, would follow a path that leads to the right child of Ellen, you are assured that Frank is in the proper relation to the names above it in the tree.

Use Find to determine the insertion point

Notice that the use of *Find* to determine the insertion point in the tree for the new name always leads to an easy insertion. No matter what new name you insert into the tree, *Find* will always terminate at an empty subtree, and thus it will always indicate that you should insert the name as a new leaf. Because adding a leaf requires only that you set the appropriate pointer field in the parent, the work required for an insertion is virtually the same as that for the corresponding find.

The following high-level pseudocode describes this insertion process:

Insertion algorithm at a high level

```
TableInsert(T, NewItem)
{ Inserts NewItem into table T, where no item
  in T has the same search key as that of NewItem. }

    { X is the search key of NewItem }
    Let N be the parent of the empty subtree
     at which Find(T, X) terminates

    if the empty subtree is the left subtree of N
       then set LChild of N to point to NewItem
       else set RChild of N to point to NewItem
```

Observe that the appropriate pointer (*LChild* or *RChild*) of node N must be set to point to the new node. The recursive nature of the algorithm provides an elegant means of setting the pointer, provided that you pass *T* as a variable parameter. Thus, *TableInsert* is refined as follows:

Refinement of the insertion algorithm

```
TableInsert(T, NewItem)
{ Inserts NewItem into table T, where no item
  in T has the same search key as that of NewItem. }
```

```
if T = nil then
   { create a new record with T pointing to it }
   begin
      new(T)
      Set the data fields of the new record
          to the values in NewItem
      Set the pointer fields of the new record to nil
   end

else if NewItem.Key < T^.Item.Key then
       TableInsert(T^.LChild, NewItem)

else TableInsert(T^.RChild, NewItem)
```

Does this procedure really set the appropriate pointer variable to point to the new node? The situation is quite similar to the recursive insertion procedure for the sorted linked list that you saw in Chapter 6. If the tree was empty before the insertion, the external pointer to the root of the tree would be `nil` and the procedure would not make a recursive call. In this case the actual parameter is therefore the external pointer to the root of the tree. Because `T` is a variable parameter, when it is set to point to the new record, the effect is to set the external pointer to point to the new record. Figure 10-22a illustrates insertion into an empty tree.

The general case of `TableInsert` is similar to the special case when the tree is empty. When the formal parameter `T` becomes `nil`, the corresponding actual parameter is the `LChild` or `RChild` pointer field of the parent of the empty subtree; that is, this pointer field has the value `nil`. This pointer field was passed to the `TableInsert` procedure by one of the recursive calls

```
TableInsert(T^.LChild, NewItem)
```

or

```
TableInsert(T^.RChild, NewItem)
```

Thus, when `T` is set to point to the new record, the effect is to set the actual parameter, which is the appropriate pointer field of the parent, to point to the new record. Parts *b* and *c* of Figure 10-22 illustrate the general case of insertion.

You can create a binary search tree by using `TableInsert`. For example, beginning with an empty tree, if you insert the names Jane, Bob, Alan, Ellen, Tom, Nancy, and Wendy in order, you will get the binary search tree in Figure 10-18. It is interesting to note that the inserted names Jane, Bob, Alan, Ellen, Tom, Nancy, and Wendy constitute the preorder traversal of the tree in Figure 10-18. Thus, if you take the output of a preorder traversal of a binary search tree and use it with `TableInsert` to create a binary search tree, you will obtain a duplicate tree.

By inserting the previous names in a different order, you will get a different binary search tree. For example, by inserting the previous names in alphabetic order, you will get the binary search tree in Figure 10-19c.

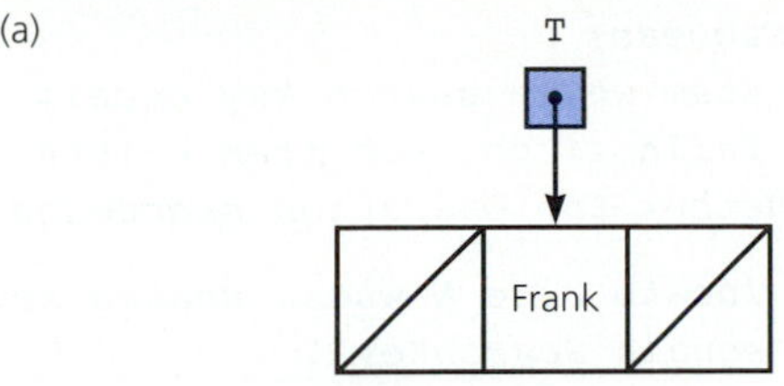

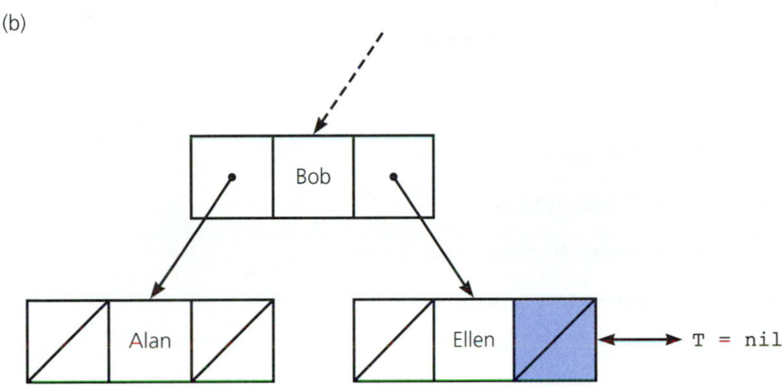

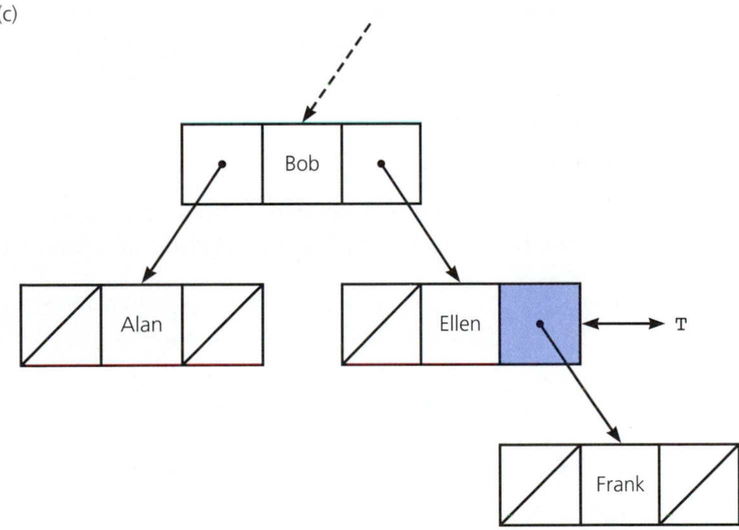

Figure 10-22

(a) Insertion into an empty tree; (b) search terminates at a leaf; (c) insertion at a leaf

Deletion. The deletion operation is a bit more involved than insertion. First, you use the *`Find`* algorithm to locate the node with the specified search key and then, if it is found, you must remove the node from the tree. A first draft of the algorithm follows:

First draft of the deletion algorithm

```
TableDelete(T, SearchKey, Success)
{ Deletes from table T the item whose search key equals
  SearchKey. The operation fails if no such item exists. The
  flag Success indicates whether the operation succeeded. }

   Find(T, SearchKey)    { locate node N whose search key
                            equals SearchKey }
   if node N is found
      then
      begin
         Remove node N from the tree
         Success := true
      end

      else Success := false
```

The essential task here is

```
Remove node N from the tree
```

There are three cases to consider:

Three cases for the node, N, *to be deleted*

1. *N* is a leaf.
2. *N* has only one child.
3. *N* has two children.

Case 1: Set the pointer in a leaf's parent to `nil`

The first case is the easiest. To remove a leaf, you need only set the pointer field of its parent to `nil`. The second case is a bit more difficult. If *N* has only one child, there are really two possibilities:

Case 2: Two possibilities for N

- *N* has only a left child.
- *N* has only a right child.

The two possibilities are symmetrical, so it is sufficient to illustrate the solution for a left child. In Figure 10-23a *L* is the left child of *N*, and *P* is the

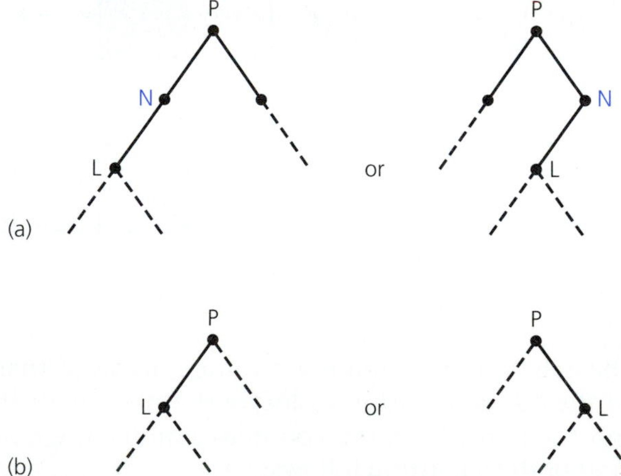

Figure 10-23

(a) *N* with only a left child—*N* can be either the left or right child of *P*; (b) after deleting node *N*

parent of *N*. Notice that *N* can be either the left or right child of *P*. If you deleted *N* from the tree, *L* would be without a parent, and *P* would be without one of its children. Suppose you let *L* take the place of *N* as one of *P*'s children, as in Figure 10-23b. Does this adoption preserve the binary search tree property?

Let N*'s parent adopt* N*'s child*

If *N* is the left child of *P*, for example, then all the search keys in the subtree rooted at *N* are less than the search key in *P*. Thus, all the search keys in the subtree rooted at *L* are less than the search key in *P*. Therefore, after *N* is removed and *L* is adopted by *P*, all the search keys in *P*'s left subtree are still less than the search key in *P*. This deletion strategy thus preserves the binary search tree property. A parallel argument holds if *N* is a right child of *P*, and therefore the binary search tree property is preserved in either case.

Case 3: N *has two children*

The most difficult of the three cases occurs when the node *N* to be deleted has two children, as in Figure 10-24. Recall that when *N* has one child, the child replaces *N*; that is, *N*'s parent adopts the child. However, when *N* has two children, these children cannot both replace *N*: *N*'s parent has room for only one of *N*'s children as a replacement for *N*. A different strategy is necessary.

In fact, you will not delete *N* at all. You can find another node that is easier to delete and delete it instead of *N*. That may sound like cheating. After all, the programmer who requests

```
TableDelete(T, SearchKey, Success)
```

expects that the item whose search key equals *SearchKey* will be deleted from the tree. However, the programmer expects only that the *item* will be deleted and has no right, because of the wall between the program and the ADT implementation, to expect a particular *node* in the tree to be deleted. In fact, because of the wall, the programmer has no right to even expect that there is a tree at all!

Consider, then, an alternate strategy. To delete from a binary search tree an item that resides in a node *N* that has two children, take the following steps:

Deleting an item whose node has two children

1. Locate another node *M* that is easier to remove from the tree than is the node *N*.
2. Copy the item that is in *M* to *N*, thus effectively deleting from the table the item originally in *N*.
3. Remove the node *M* from the tree.

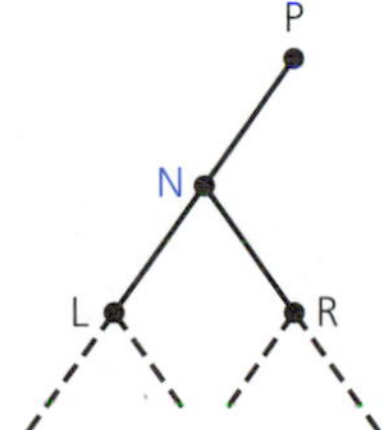

Figure 10-24

N with two children

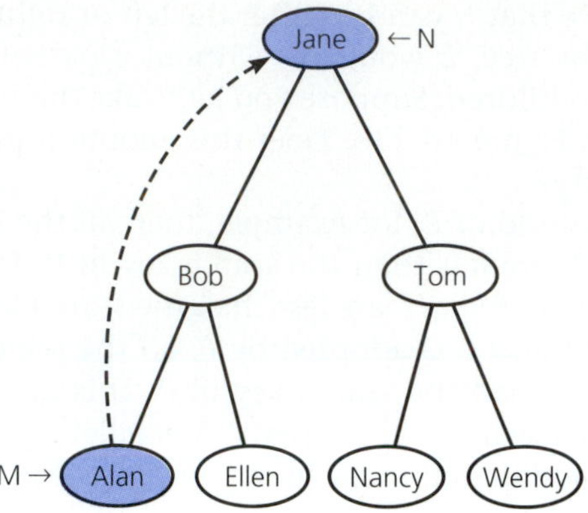

Figure 10-25
Not any node will do

What kind of node *M* is easier to remove than the node *N*? Because you know how to delete a node that has no children or one child, *M* could be such a node. You have to be careful, though. Can you choose any node and copy its value into *N*? No, because you must preserve the tree's status as a binary search tree. For example, if in the tree of Figure 10-25, you copied the value from *M* to *N*, the result would no longer be a binary search tree.

What value, when copied into the node *N*, will preserve the tree's status as a binary search tree? All search keys in the left subtree of *N* are less than the search key in *N*, and all the search keys in the right subtree of *N* are greater than the search key in *N*. You must retain this property when you replace the search key *X* in node *N* with the search key *Y*. There are two suitable possibilities for the value *Y*: It can come immediately after or immediately before *X* in the sorted order of search keys. If *Y* comes immediately after *X*, then clearly all search keys in the left subtree of *N* are smaller than *Y*, because they are all smaller than *X*, as Figure 10-26 illustrates. Further, all search keys in the right subtree of *N* are greater than or equal to *Y*, because they are greater than *X* and, by assumption, there are

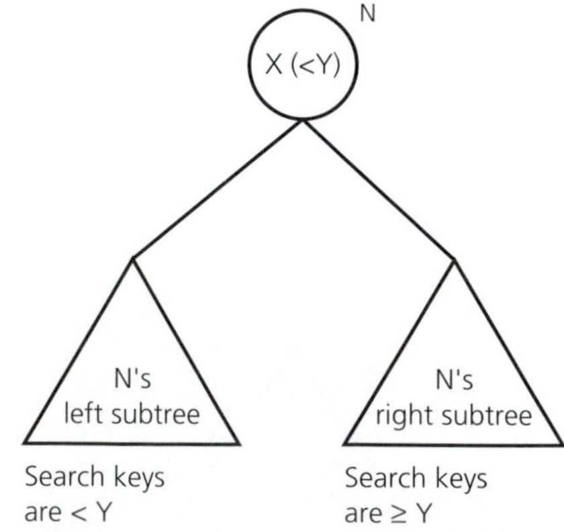

Figure 10-26
Search key *X* can be replaced by *Y*

no search keys in the tree between *X* and *Y*. A similar argument illustrates that if *Y* comes immediately before *X* in the sorted order, then it is greater than or equal to all search keys in the left subtree of *N* and smaller than all search keys in the right subtree of *N*.

You can thus copy into *N* either of the two items whose search keys are the two values of *Y*, as just described. How can you locate one of these items? Suppose that, arbitrarily, you decide to locate the search key *Y* that comes immediately after *X*. Recall that the inorder traversal will visit the search keys of a binary search tree in proper sorted order. Therefore, search key *Y* is contained in the node that the inorder traversal visits immediately after node *N*. This node is called *N*'s **inorder successor**. Given that *N* has two children, its inorder successor is the leftmost node of *N*'s right subtree. That is, to find the node that contains *Y*, you follow *N*'s `RChild` pointer to its right child *R*, which must be present because *N* has two children. You then descend the tree rooted at *R* by taking left branches at each node until you encounter a node *M* with no left child. You copy the value of the item in this node *M* into node *N* and, because *M* has no left child, you can remove *M* from the tree as one of the two easy cases (see Figure 10-27).

Inorder successor of* N*: the leftmost node in* N*'s right subtree

A more detailed high-level description of the deletion algorithm follows:

Second draft of the deletion algorithm

```
TableDelete(T, SearchKey, Success)
{ Deletes from table T the item whose search key equals
  SearchKey. The operation fails if no such item exists. The
  flag Success indicates whether the operation succeeded. }

    Find(T, SearchKey)  { locate node N whose search key
                          equals SearchKey }
    if node N is found
       then
       begin
          DeleteItem(N) { DeleteItem is defined next }
          Success := true
       end

       else Success := false

DeleteItem(N)
{ Deletes the item in the node N of a binary search tree. }

    if N is a leaf then
       Remove N from the tree

    else if N has only one child C then
       begin
          if N was a left child of its parent P
               then make C the left child of P
               else make C the right child of P
       end
```

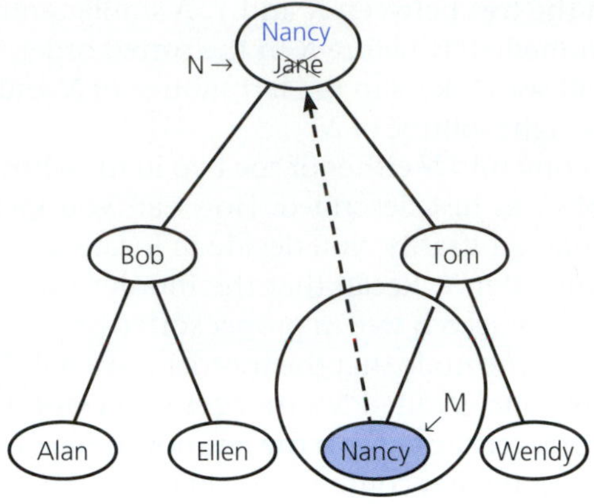

Figure 10-27

Copying *N*'s inorder successor to *N*

```
else  { N has two children }
begin
   Find N's inorder successor M
   Copy the item from M into N
   Remove M from the tree by using the previous
        technique for a leaf or a node with one child
end
```

In the following refinement, `Find`'s algorithm is adapted and inserted directly into `TableDelete`. Also, the procedure `DeleteItem` uses the procedure `ProcessLeftmost` to find the node that contains the inorder successor of the item in *N*. `ProcessLeftmost` deletes this node from the tree and returns the inorder successor. This item then replaces in node *N* the item to be deleted from the binary search tree.

Final draft of the deletion algorithm

```
TableDelete(T, SearchKey, Success)
{ Deletes from table T the item whose search key equals
  SearchKey. The operation fails if no such item exists. The
  flag Success indicates whether the operation succeeded. }

   if T = nil then
      Success := false

   else if SearchKey = T^.Item.Key then
      begin    { item is in the root of some subtree }
         DeleteItem(T)        { delete the item }
         Success := true
      end

   else if SearchKey < T^.Item.Key then
      { search the left subtree }
      TableDelete(T^.LChild, SearchKey, Success)

   else { search the right subtree }
      TableDelete(T^.RChild, SearchKey, Success)
```

```
DeleteItem(NPtr)
{ Deletes the item in the node N to which NPtr points. }

   if N is a leaf then
      { remove from the tree }
      begin
         dispose(NPtr)
         NPtr := nil
      end

   else if N has only one child C then
      { C replaces N as the child of N's parent }
      begin
         DelPtr := NPtr
         if C is the left child of N
            then NPtr := NPtr^.LChild
            else NPtr := NPtr^.RChild
         dispose(DelPtr)
      end

   else    { N has two children }
   begin
      { find the inorder successor of value in N: it is in
        the leftmost node of the subtree rooted at N's
        right child }
      ProcessLeftmost(NPtr^.RChild, ReplacementItem)
      Put ReplacementItem in node N
   end

ProcessLeftmost(NodePtr, TableItem)
{ Retrieves into TableItem the item in the leftmost
  descendent of the node to which NodePtr points. Deletes
  the node that contains this item. }

   if NodePtr^.LChild = nil
      then
      { this is the node you want - it has no left
        child, but it might have a right subtree }
      begin
         TableItem := NodePtr^.Item
         DelPtr := NodePtr

         { notice that the actual parameter corresponding
           to NodePtr is a child-pointer field of
           NodePtr's parent - thus, the following
           correctly "moves up" NodePtr's right subtree }
         NodePtr := NodePtr^.RChild

         dispose(DelPtr)
      end

      else ProcessLeftmost(NodePtr^.LChild, TableItem)
```

Figure 10-28

Recursive deletion of node *N*

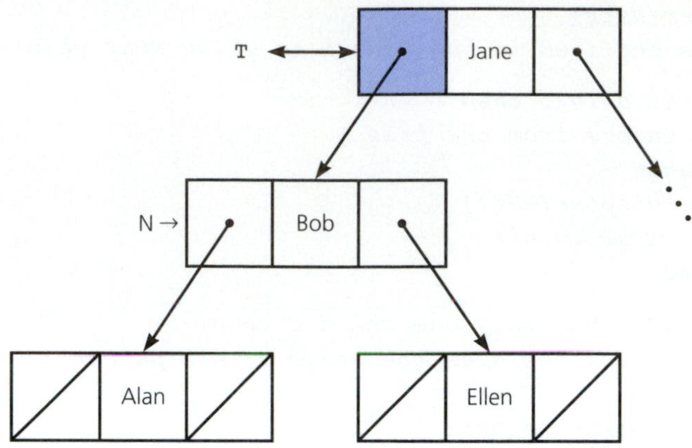

Any change to `T` while deleting node N (Bob) changes `LChild` of Jane

Observe that, as in the case of the *`TableInsert`* procedure, the actual parameter that corresponds to *`T`* is either one of the pointer fields of the parent of *N*, as Figure 10-28 depicts, or is the external pointer to the root in the case where *N* is the root of the original tree. Thus, any change you make to *`T`*, which points to node *N*, by calling the procedure *`DeleteItem`* with actual parameter *`T`* changes the pointer field of the parent of *N*. The recursive procedure *`ProcessLeftmost`*, which is called by *`DeleteItem`* if *N* has two children, also uses this strategy to remove the node that contains the inorder successor of the item to be deleted.

Exercise 22 at the end of this chapter discusses an easier deletion algorithm. However, that algorithm tends to increase the height of the tree and, as you will see later, an increase in height can decrease the efficiency of searching the tree.

Retrieval. By refining the *`Find`* algorithm, you can implement the *`TableRetrieve`* operation. Recall that the *`Find`* algorithm is

```
Find(T, X)
{ Searches the binary search tree T for the name X. }

   if T = nil then
      Print 'X is not present' { empty tree }

   else if X = T^.Item.Key then
      Print 'X is present'     { name is found }

   else if X < T^.Item.Key then
      Find(T^.LChild, X)       { search the left subtree }

   else Find(T^.RChild, X)     { search the right subtree }
```

`TableRetrieve` must return the item with the desired search key if it exists, and otherwise it must return the boolean flag *`Success`* with the value *`false`*. These actions replace the *`Print`* statements in the *`Find`* algorithm.

The *TableRetrieve* procedure, therefore, appears as follows:

TableRetrieve **is a refinement of** *Find*

```
TableRetrieve(T, SearchKey, TableItem, Success)
{ Retrieves into TableItem the item in table T whose search
  key equals SearchKey. The operation fails if no such item
  exists. The flag Success indicates whether the operation
  succeeded. }

    if T = nil then
       Success := false      { T is empty }

    else if SearchKey = T^.Item.Key then
       begin    { item is in the root of some subtree }
           TableItem := record to which T points
           Success := true
       end

    else if SearchKey < T^.Item.Key then
       { search the left subtree }
       TableRetrieve(T^.LChild, SearchKey, TableItem, Success)

    else { search the right subtree }
    TableRetrieve(T^.RChild, SearchKey, TableItem, Success)
```

Pascal implementation. The Pascal nonlinear implementation of the ADT table follows.

```
unit TableOps;
{ *******************************************************
  BASIC TABLE OPERATIONS
    Pointer-Based Binary Search Tree Implementation

    CreateTable, TableIsEmpty, TableInsert, TableDelete,
    TableRetrieve, and TraverseTable

  Assumption:
    A table contains at most one item with a given search
    key at any time. (See Exercises 8 through 10.)
  ******************************************************* }
interface

type   keyType = <desired type of search key>;

       itemType = record
           Key : keyType;
           < ... and possibly other fields>
       end; { record }

       treePtrType = ^nodeType;

       nodeType = record
           Item : itemType;
           LChild, RChild : treePtrType
       end; { record }
```

```
     tableType = treePtrType;

     procType = procedure(var T : tableType;
                          Item : itemType);

procedure CreateTable(var T : tableType);
{ ---------------------------------------------------------
  Creates an empty table.
  Precondition: None.
  Postcondition: The empty table T is created.
  ----------------------------------------------------- }
function TableIsEmpty(T : tableType) : boolean;
{ -------------------------------------------------------
  Determines whether a table is empty.
  Precondition: CreateTable(T) has been called.
  Postcondition: Returns true if T was empty; else returns
  false.
  ------------------------------------------------------- }
procedure TableInsert(var T: tableType; NewItem: itemType;
                      var Success: boolean);
{ ---------------------------------------------------------
  Inserts an item into a table in its proper sorted order
  according to the item's search key.
  Precondition: CreateTable(T) has been called and no two
  items of T have the same search key. T's items are sorted
  by search key. The item to be inserted into T is NewItem,
  whose search key differs from all search keys presently
  in T.
  Postcondition: NewItem is in its proper order in T and
  Success is true.
  ------------------------------------------------------- }
procedure TableDelete(var T: tableType;
              SearchKey: keyType; var Success: boolean);
{ ---------------------------------------------------------
  Deletes an item with a given search key from a table.
  Precondition: CreateTable(T) has been called and no two
  items of T have the same search key. T's items are sorted
  by search key. SearchKey is the search key of the item to
  be deleted.
  Postcondition: If the item whose search key equals
  SearchKey existed in T, the item is deleted and Success is
  true. Otherwise, T is unchanged and Success is false.
  Calls: Local procedure DeleteItem, which calls
  ProcessLeftmost.
  ------------------------------------------------------- }
procedure TableRetrieve(T: tableType; SearchKey: keyType;
          var TableItem: itemType; var Success : boolean);
```

```
{ ---------------------------------------------------------
  Retrieves an item with a given search key from a table.
  Precondition: CreateTable(T) has been called and no two
  items of T have the same search key. T's items are sorted
  by search key; SearchKey is the search key of the item to
  be retrieved.
  Postcondition: If the retrieval was successful,
  TableItem contains the retrieved item and Success is
  true. If no such item exists, TableItem and T are
  unchanged and Success is false.
  --------------------------------------------------------- }
procedure TraverseTable(var T: tableType; Visit: procType);
{ ---------------------------------------------------------
  Traverses a table in sorted order, calling procedure
  Visit once for each item.
  Precondition: CreateTable(T) has been called and no two
  items of T have the same search key. T's items are sorted
  by search key. The procedure represented by Visit exists
  outside of the ADT implementation and is defined with the
  far directive.
  Postcondition: Visit's action occurs once for each item
  in T.
  Note: var allows Visit to alter T.
  --------------------------------------------------------- }

implementation

procedure CreateTable(var T : tableType);
begin
    T := nil
end; { CreateTable }

function TableIsEmpty(T : tableType) : boolean;
begin
    TableIsEmpty := (T = nil)
end; { TableIsEmpty }

procedure TableInsert(var T: tableType; NewItem: itemType;
                      var Success: boolean);
begin
    if T = nil then
       { the position has been found - insert after leaf }
       begin
          new(T);
          T^.Item := NewItem;
          T^.LChild := nil;
          T^.RChild := nil
       end
```

```
      { else search for the position }
      else if NewItem.Key < T^.Item.Key then
         { search the left subtree }
         TableInsert(T^.LChild, NewItem, Success)

      else { search the right subtree }
         TableInsert(T^.RChild, NewItem, Success)
end;  { TableInsert }

procedure TableDelete(var T: tableType;
               SearchKey: keyType; var Success: boolean);

   procedure ProcessLeftmost(var NodePtr : treePtrType;
                             var TableItem : itemType);
   { ---------------------------------------------------
     Retrieves and deletes the leftmost descendent of a
     given node.
     Precondition: NodePtr points to a node in a binary
     search tree. This tree contains at most one item with
     a given search key.
     Postcondition: TableItem contains the item in the
     leftmost descendent of the node to which NodePtr
     points. The leftmost descendent of NodePtr is
     deleted.
     --------------------------------------------------- }
   var DelPtr : treePtrType;
   begin
       if NodePtr <> nil
          then
          begin
             if NodePtr^.LChild = nil
                then
                begin
                   TableItem := NodePtr^.Item;
                   DelPtr := NodePtr;
                   NodePtr := NodePtr^.RChild;
                   dispose(DelPtr)
                end

                else ProcessLeftmost(NodePtr^.LChild,
                                              TableItem)
          end { if }
   end;  { ProcessLeftmost }

   procedure DeleteItem(var RootPtr : treePtrType);
   { ---------------------------------------------------
     Deletes the item in the root of a given tree.
     Precondition: RootPtr points to the root of a
     binary search tree. This tree contains at most one
     item with a given search key.
```

```
  Postcondition: The item in the root of the given
  tree is deleted.
  Algorithm note: There are four cases to consider:
      1. The root is a leaf.
      2. The root has no left child.
      3. The root has no right child.
      4. The root has two children.
  Calls: ProcessLeftmost.
  ------------------------------------------------ }
var DelPtr : treePtrType;
    ReplacementItem : itemType;
begin
    if RootPtr <> nil
       then
       begin
          { test for a leaf }
          if (RootPtr^.LChild = nil) and
                (RootPtr^.RChild = nil) then
             begin
                dispose(RootPtr);
                RootPtr := nil
             end

          { test for no left child }
          else if RootPtr^.LChild = nil then
             begin
                DelPtr := RootPtr;
                RootPtr := RootPtr^.RChild;
                dispose(DelPtr)
             end

          { test for no right child }
          else if RootPtr^.RChild = nil then
             begin
                DelPtr := RootPtr;
                RootPtr := RootPtr^.LChild;
                dispose(DelPtr)
             end

          { there are two children - delete and
            retrieve the inorder successor }
          else
          begin
             ProcessLeftmost(RootPtr^.RChild,
                                  ReplacementItem);
             RootPtr^.Item := ReplacementItem
          end
       end { if RootPtr <> nil }
end; { DeleteItem }
```

```
begin { TableDelete }
    if T = nil then
       Success := false { empty tree }

    else if SearchKey = T^.Item.Key then
       begin   { item is in the root of some subtree }
          DeleteItem(T);  { delete the item }
          Success := true
       end

    { else search for the item }
    else if SearchKey < T^.Item.Key then
       { search the left subtree }
       TableDelete(T^.LChild, SearchKey, Success)

    else { search the right subtree }
       TableDelete(T^.RChild, SearchKey, Success)
end; { TableDelete }

procedure TableRetrieve(T: tableType; SearchKey: keyType;
         var TableItem: itemType; var Success : boolean);
begin
    if T = nil then
       Success := false { empty tree }

    else if SearchKey = T^.Item.Key then
       begin   { item is in the root of some subtree }
          TableItem := T^.Item;
          Success := true
       end

    else if SearchKey < T^.Item.Key then
       { search the left subtree }
       TableRetrieve(T^.LChild, SearchKey, TableItem, Success)
    else { search the right subtree }
       TableRetrieve(T^.RChild, SearchKey, TableItem, Success)
end; { TableRetrieve }

procedure TraverseTable(var T: tableType; Visit: procType);
begin
    { inorder traversal }
    if T <> nil
          then
          begin
             TraverseTable(T^.LChild, Visit);
             Visit(T, T^.Item);
             TraverseTable(T^.RChild, Visit)
          end
end; { TraverseTable }

end. { unit }
```

The Table As an Object (Optional)

You can implement the ADT table as an object. The following implementation of a table object has many similarities with the pointer-based implementation of the ADT table that you just saw. Unlike previous objects that this book has considered, the implementation of the table object is recursive. Notice how the recursion is hidden within local procedures that the table methods invoke. Also notice the postorder traversal that the destructor uses to deallocate the object.

```
unit TableObj;

interface

type  keyType = <desired type of table item>;

      itemType = record
          Key : keyType;
          <... and possibly other fields>
      end; { record }

      treePtrType = ^nodeType;
      nodeType = record
          Item : itemType;
          LChild, RChild : treePtrType
      end;   { record }

      procType = procedure(Item : itemType);

      tableType = object

         constructor Init;
         { -----------------------------------------------
           Creates an empty table
           Precondition: None.
           Postcondition: An empty table is created.
           ----------------------------------------------- }
         destructor Done; virtual;
         { -----------------------------------------------
           Deallocates a table.
           Precondition: Init has been called.
           Postcondition: All storage associated with the
           table is deallocated.
           Calls: Local procedure PostorderTraverse.
           ----------------------------------------------- }
         function TableIsEmpty : boolean;
         { -----------------------------------------------
           Determines whether a table is empty.
           Precondition: Init has been called.
           Postcondition: Returns true if table was empty;
           else returns false.
           ----------------------------------------------- }
```

```
procedure TableInsert(NewItem : itemType;
                      var Success : boolean);
{ -----------------------------------------------
  Inserts an item into a table in its proper sorted
  order according to the item's search key.
  Precondition: Init has been called. No two
  items of the table have the same search key. The
  table items are sorted by search key. The item to
  be inserted is NewItem, whose search key differs
  from all search keys presently in the table.
  Postcondition: NewItem is in its proper order
  in the table and Success is true.
  Calls: Local procedure TreeInsert.
  ----------------------------------------------- }
procedure TableDelete(SearchKey: keyType;
                      var Success : boolean);
{ -----------------------------------------------
  Deletes an item with a given search key from a
  table.
  Precondition: Init has been called. No two
  items of the table have the same search key. The
  table items are sorted by search key. SearchKey
  is the search key of the item to be deleted.
  Postcondition: If the item whose search key
  equals SearchKey existed in the table, the item is
  deleted and Success is true. Otherwise, the table
  is unchanged and Success is false.
  Calls: Local procedure TreeDelete, which calls
  DeleteItem, which calls ProcessLeftmost.
  ----------------------------------------------- }
procedure TableRetrieve(SearchKey: keyType;
  var TableItem: itemType; var Success : boolean);
{ -----------------------------------------------
  Retrieves an item with a given search key from a
  table.
  Precondition: Init has been called. No two
  items of the table have the same search key. The
  table items are sorted by search key. SearchKey
  is the search key of the item to be retrieved.
  Postcondition: If retrieval was successful,
  TableItem contains the retrieved item and Success
  is true. If no such item exists, TableItem is
  unchanged and Success is false.
  Calls: Local procedure TreeRetrieve.
  ----------------------------------------------- }
```

```
      procedure TraverseTable(Visit : procType);
      { ------------------------------------------------
        Traverses a table in sorted order, calling
        procedure Visit once for each item.
        Precondition: Init has been called. No two
        items of the table have the same search key. The
        table items are sorted by search key. The
        procedure represented by Visit exists outside of
        the ADT implementation and is defined with the
        far directive.
        Postcondition: Visit's action occurs once for
        each item in the table.
        Calls: Local procedure InorderTraverse.
        ------------------------------------------------ }

   private
      Root : treePtrType;
   end; { object }

implementation
{ Pointer-Based Binary Search Tree Implementation }

constructor tableType.Init;
begin
   Root := nil
end; { tableType.Init }

destructor tableType.Done;

   procedure PostorderTraverse(var TreePtr : treePtrType);
   begin { PostorderTraverse }
      if TreePtr <> nil
         then
         begin
            PostorderTraverse(TreePtr^.LChild);
            PostorderTraverse(TreePtr^.RChild);
            dispose(TreePtr);
         end
   end; { PostorderTraverse}

begin { tableType.Done }
   PostorderTraverse(Root);
   Root := nil
end;  { tableType.Done }

function tableType.TableIsEmpty : boolean;
begin
   TableIsEmpty := (Root = nil)
end; { tableType.TableIsEmpty }
```

```
procedure tableType.TableInsert(NewItem : itemType;
                               var Success : boolean);

   procedure TreeInsert(var TreePtr : treePtrType;
                         NewItem : itemType);
   begin
      if TreePtr = nil then
         { the position has been found - insert after leaf }
         begin
            new(TreePtr);
            TreePtr^.Item := NewItem;
            TreePtr^.LChild := nil;
            TreePtr^.RChild := nil
         end

      { else search for the position }
      else if NewItem.Key < TreePtr^.Item.Key then
         { search the left subtree }
         TreeInsert(TreePtr^.LChild, NewItem)
      else { search the right subtree }
         TreeInsert(TreePtr^.RChild, NewItem)
   end; { TreeInsert }

begin { tableType.TableInsert }
   TreeInsert(Root, NewItem)
end; { tableType.TableInsert }

procedure tableType.TableDelete(SearchKey : keyType;
                               var Success : boolean);

   procedure ProcessLeftmost(var NodePtr : treePtrType;
                             var TableItem : itemType);
   { declarations and procedure body same as those in the
     previous section }
   end; { ProcessLeftmost }

   procedure DeleteItem(var RootPtr : treePtrType);
   { declarations and procedure body same as those in the
     previous section }
   end; { DeleteItem }

   procedure TreeDelete(var TreePtr : treePtrType;
                 SearchKey : keyType; var Success:boolean);
   begin { TreeDelete }
      if TreePtr = nil then
         Success := false { empty tree }

      else if SearchKey = TreePtr^.Item.Key then
         begin  { item is in the root of some subtree }
            DeleteItem(TreePtr);
            Success := true
         end
```

```
      { else search for the item }
      else if SearchKey < TreePtr^.Item.Key then
          { search the left subtree }
          TreeDelete(TreePtr^.LChild, SearchKey, Success)

      else { search the right subtree }
          TreeDelete(TreePtr^.RChild, SearchKey, Success)
   end; { TreeDelete }

begin { tableType.TableDelete }
   TreeDelete(Root, SearchKey, Success)
end; {tableType.TableDelete }

procedure tableType.TableRetrieve(SearchKey : keyType;
       var TableItem : itemType; var Success : boolean);

   procedure TreeRetrieve(var TreePtr : treePtrType;
         SearchKey : keyType; var TableItem : itemType;
         var Success : boolean);
   begin
      if TreePtr = nil then
         Success := false { empty tree }

      else if SearchKey = TreePtr^.Item.Key then
         begin   { item is in the root of some subtree }
            TableItem := TreePtr^.Item;
            Success := true
         end

      else if SearchKey < TreePtr^.Item.Key then
         { search the left subtree }
         TreeRetrieve(TreePtr^.LChild, SearchKey,
                                     TableItem, Success)

      else { search the right subtree }
         TreeRetrieve(TreePtr^.RChild, SearchKey,
                                      TableItem, Success)
   end; { TreeRetrieve }

begin { tableType.TableRetrieve }
   TreeRetrieve(Root, SearchKey, TableItem, Success)
end; { tableType.TableRetrieve }

procedure tableType.TraverseTable(Visit : procType);

   procedure InorderTraverse(var TreePtr : treePtrType;
                                       Visit : procType);
   begin
      if TreePtr <> nil
         then
         begin
            InorderTraverse(TreePtr^.LChild, Visit);
            Visit(TreePtr^.Item);
```

```
            InorderTraverse(TreePtr^.RChild, Visit)
         end
      end; { InorderTraverse}
begin { tableType.TraverseTable}
   InorderTraverse(Root, Visit)
end; {tableType.TraverseTable}

end. { unit }
```

The following statements demonstrate how to use this object:

```
var T         : tableType;
    AnItem    : itemType;
    Success   : boolean;

begin   { Main Program }
   T.Init;

   with AnItem do
      readln(Key, <and other fields>);
   T.TableInsert(AnItem, Success);
```

The Efficiency of the Nonlinear Implementation of the ADT Table

An analysis of this nonlinear implementation of the ADT table will show whether it succeeds where the linear implementations failed. You saw binary search trees in many shapes. For example, even though the binary search trees in Figures 10-18 and 10-19c have seven nodes each, they have radically different shapes and heights. You saw that to locate Wendy in Figure 10-19c, you would have to inspect all seven nodes, but to locate Wendy in Figure 10-18 would require you to inspect only three nodes (Jane, Tom, and Wendy). Consider now the relationship between the height of a binary search tree and the efficiency of the operations *`TableRetrieve`*, *`TableInsert`*, and *`TableDelete`*.

Each of these operations compares the specified value *`SearchKey`* to the search keys in the nodes along a **path** through the tree. This path always starts at the root of the tree and, at each node *n*, follows the left or right branch, depending on the comparison of *`SearchKey`* to the search key in *n*. The path terminates at the node that contains *`SearchKey`* or, in the case that *`SearchKey`* is not present, at an empty subtree. The number of comparisons that each operation requires is thus equal to the number of nodes along this path.

The number of comparisons that *`TableRetrieve`*, *`TableInsert`*, and *`TableDelete`* require therefore depends on the location in the tree of the node (or empty subtree) at which the path terminates. This location in turn depends on both the value *`SearchKey`* and the values in the tree. Thus, the maximum number of comparisons that the operations can require is the number of nodes on the longest path through the tree. In

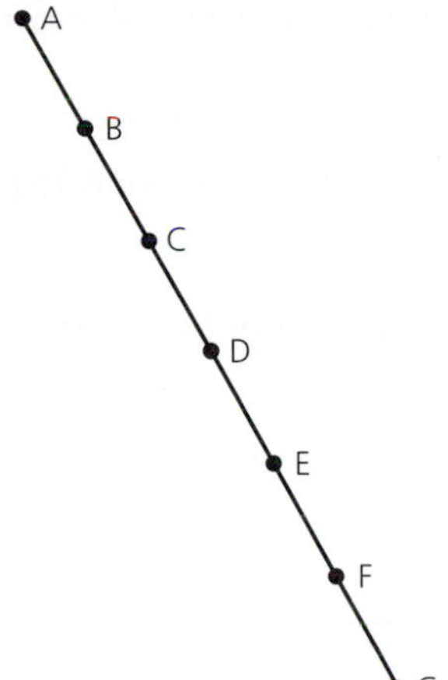

Figure 10-29

A maximum-height binary tree with seven nodes

other words, the *maximum number of comparisons that these operations can require is equal to the height of the binary search tree.* What then are the maximum and minimum heights of a binary search tree of N nodes?

The maximum number of comparisons for a retrieval, insertion, or deletion is the height of the tree

The maximum and minimum heights of a binary search tree. You can maximize the height of a binary tree with N nodes simply by giving each internal node (nonleaf) exactly one child, as shown in Figure 10-29. This process will result in a tree of height N. Notice that an N-node tree with height N strikingly resembles a linear list.

N is the maximum height of a binary tree with N nodes

A minimum-height binary tree with N nodes is a bit more difficult to obtain. It is useful first to consider the number of nodes that binary trees with a given height h can have. For example, if $h = 3$, the possible binary trees include those in Figure 10-30. Thus, binary trees of height 3 can have between 3 and 7 nodes. In addition, Figure 10-30 shows that 3 is the minimum height for a binary tree with 4, 5, 6, or 7 nodes. Similarly, binary trees with more than 7 nodes require a height greater than 3.

Intuitively, to minimize the height of a binary tree given N nodes, you must fill each level of the tree as completely as possible. That is, you want a complete tree. Notice that the trees b, c, d, and e of Figure 10-30 are complete trees. If a complete binary tree of a given height h is to have the maximum possible number of nodes, it should be full (as in Figure 10-30e).

(a)

(b)

(c)

(d)

(e)

Figure 10-30

Binary trees of height 3

Figure 10-31 counts these nodes by level and shows the following:

THEOREM 10-2. A full binary tree of height h ($h \geq 0$) has $2^h - 1$ nodes.

A formal proof by induction of this theorem is left as an exercise.

It follows then that

THEOREM 10-3. The maximum number of nodes that a binary tree of height h can have is $2^h - 1$.

The formal proof of this theorem, which closely parallels that of Theorem 10-2, is left as an exercise.

The following theorem uses Theorems 10-2 and 10-3 to determine the minimum height of a binary tree that contains some given number of nodes.

THEOREM 10-4. The minimum height of a binary tree with N nodes is $\lceil \log_2(N + 1) \rceil$.

PROOF. Let h be the smallest integer such that $N \leq 2^h - 1$. To find the minimum height of a binary tree with N nodes, first establish the following facts:

1. *A binary tree whose height is* $\leq h-1$ *has* $< N$ *nodes.*
   By Theorem 10-3, a binary tree of height $h-1$ has at most $2^{h-1}-1$ nodes. If it is possible that $N \leq 2^{h-1}-1 < 2^h-1$, then h is not the smallest integer such that $N \leq 2^h-1$. Therefore, N must be greater than $2^{h-1}-1$ or, equivalently, $2^{h-1}-1 < N$. Because a binary tree of height $h-1$ has at most $2^{h-1}-1$ nodes, it must have fewer than N nodes.

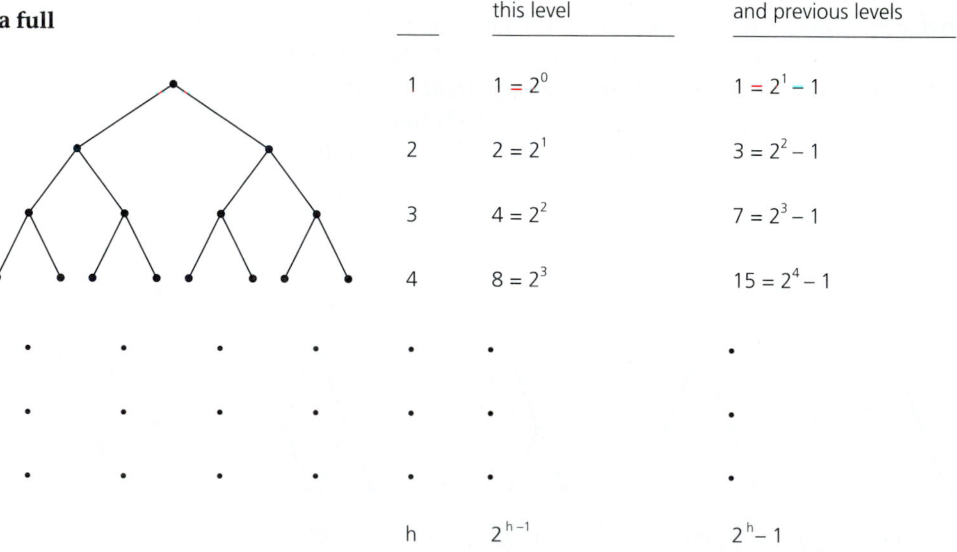

Level
Number of nodes at this level
Number of nodes at this and previous levels
1
1 = 2^0
1 = 2^1 – 1
2
2 = 2^1
3 = 2^2 – 1
3
4 = 2^2
7 = 2^3 – 1
4
8 = 2^3
15 = 2^4 – 1
h
2^h–1
2^h – 1

Figure 10-31

Counting the nodes in a full binary tree of height *h*

2. *There exists a complete binary tree of height h that has exactly N nodes.* Consider the full binary tree of height $h-1$. By Theorem 10-2, it has $2^{h-1}-1$ nodes. As you just saw, $N > 2^{h-1}-1$ because h was selected so that $N \leq 2^h-1$. You can thus add nodes to the full tree from left to right until you have N nodes, as Figure 10-32 illustrates. Because $N \leq 2^h-1$ and a binary tree of height h cannot have more than 2^h-1 nodes, you will reach N nodes by the time level h is filled up.
3. *The minimum height of a binary tree with N nodes is the smallest integer h such that $N \leq 2^h-1$.*
   If h is the smallest integer such that $N \leq 2^h-1$, and if a binary tree has height $\leq h-1$, then by fact 1 it has fewer than N nodes. Because by fact 2 there is a binary tree of height h that has exactly N nodes, h must be as small as possible.

The previous discussion implies that

$$2^{h-1} - 1 < N \leq 2^h - 1$$
$$2^{h-1} < N + 1 \leq 2^h$$
$$h - 1 < \log_2(N + 1) \leq h$$

If $\log_2(N + 1) = h$, the theorem is proven. Otherwise, $h-1 < \log_2(N + 1) < h$ implies that $\log_2(N + 1)$ cannot be an integer. Therefore, *round* $\log_2(N + 1)$ *up* to get h. The standard way of writing X rounded up is $\lceil X \rceil$, which is read the **ceiling of X**. (For example, $\lceil 6 \rceil = 6$, $\lceil 6.1 \rceil = 7$, and $\lceil 6.8 \rceil = 7$.)

Thus, $h = \lceil \log_2(N + 1) \rceil$ is the minimum height of a binary tree with N nodes. **(End of proof.)**

Complete trees and full trees have minimum height

Complete trees and full trees with N nodes thus have heights of $\lceil \log_2(N + 1) \rceil$, which, as you just saw, is the theoretical minimum. Notice that this minimum height agrees with the maximum number of comparisons a

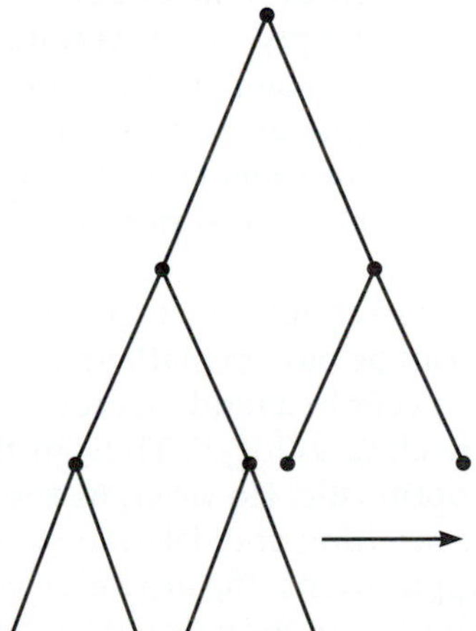

Figure 10-32

Filling in the last level of a tree

binary search must make to search an array with N elements. Therefore, if a binary search tree is complete and therefore balanced, the time it takes to search it for a value is about the same as is required by a binary search of an array. On the other hand, as you go from balanced trees toward trees with a linear structure, the height approaches the number of nodes N. This number agrees with the maximum number of comparisons that you must make when searching a linked list of N nodes.

The height of an N-node binary search tree ranges from $\lceil \log_2(N + 1) \rceil$ to N

Given that the height of an N-node binary search tree can vary from a maximum of N to a minimum of approximately $\log_2 N$, what height should you use when comparing the linear and nonlinear implementations of the ADT table? Suppose that the height of the binary search tree is close to the theoretical minimum of $\lceil \log_2(N + 1) \rceil$. Although this height may seem overly optimistic, you will soon see that the optimism is quite justified.

If the height of the binary search tree is $\lceil \log_2(N + 1) \rceil$, the nonlinear implementation of the ADT table certainly succeeds where the linear implementations failed. By using a binary search tree, you can, with efficiency comparable to that of a binary search, locate an item in both the retrieval operation and the first steps of the insertion and deletion operations. In addition, the pointer-based implementation of the binary search tree permits dynamic allocation of its nodes, so that it can handle a table whose maximum size is unknown. This implementation also efficiently performs the second step of the insertion and deletion operations: The actual insertion and removal of a node is accomplished via a few pointer changes (plus a short traversal to the inorder successor if the node to be removed has two children) rather than via the possible shifting of all the table items, as the array-based implementations require. The nonlinear implementation of the ADT table therefore combines the best aspects of the two linear implementations.

However, the outstanding efficiency of the nonlinear implementation hinges on the assumption that the height of the binary search tree is $\lceil \log_2(N + 1) \rceil$. What will the height of a binary search tree actually be? The factor that determines the height of a binary search tree is the order in which you perform the insertion and deletion operations on the tree. Recall that, starting with an empty tree, if you insert names in the order Alan, Bob, Ellen, Jane, Nancy, Tom, Wendy, you would obtain a binary search tree of maximum height, as shown in Figure 10-19c. On the other hand, if you insert names in the order Jane, Bob, Tom, Alan, Ellen, Nancy, Wendy, you would obtain a binary search tree of minimum height, as shown in Figure 10-18.

Insertion in search-key order produces a maximum-height binary search tree

Which of these situations should you expect to encounter in the course of a real application? It can be proven mathematically that if the insertion and deletion operations occur in a random order, the height of the binary search tree will be quite close to $\log_2 N$. Thus, in this sense, the previous analysis is not unduly optimistic. However, in a real-world application, is it realistic to expect the insertion and deletion operations to occur in random order? In many applications, the answer is yes. There are, however, applications in which this assumption would be dubious. For example, the

Insertion in random order produces a near-minimum-height binary search tree

	Sorted array based	Sorted pointer based	Nonlinear
Retrieval	O(log *N*) comparisons	O(*N*) comparisons	O(log *N*) comparisons
Insertion	O(log *N*) comparisons O(*N*) item shifts	O(*N*) comparisons O(1) pointer changes	O(log *N*) comparisons O(1) pointer changes
Deletion	O(log *N*) ccomparisons O(*N*) item shifts	O(*N*) comparisons O(1) pointer changes	O(log *N*) comparisons O(1) pointer changes

Figure 10-33

The order of the retrieval, insertion, and deletion operations for three implementations of the ADT table

person preparing the previous sequence of names for the insertion operations might well decide to "help you out" by arranging the names to be inserted into sorted order. This arrangement, as has been mentioned, would lead to a tree of maximum height. Thus, while in many applications you can expect the behavior of a binary search tree to be excellent, you should be wary of the possibility of poor performance due to some characteristic of a given application.

Is there anything you can do if you suspect that the operations might not occur in a random order? Similarly, is there anything you can do if you have an enormous number of items and need to ensure that the height of the tree is close to $\log_2 N$? Chapter 13 presents a variation of the basic binary search tree, called a **2-3 tree**, which is guaranteed always to remain balanced. The fact that you can, if need be, always keep the height of a binary search tree near $\log_2 N$ justifies the claim that it provides the best aspects of the two linear implementations of the ADT table.

Figure 10-33 summarizes the order of the retrieval, insertion, and deletion operations for the three implementations discussed in this chapter.

Saving a Table in a File

Suppose that you want to save in a file an ADT table whose implementation is nonlinear, as described previously. To save such a table and later restore it, you must consider this question: How can you save a binary search tree's data in a file so that you can later restore the tree? Two different algorithms for saving and restoring a tree will be considered here. The first algorithm will restore a tree to its original shape. The second will restore a tree to a shape that is balanced.

Saving a tree and then restoring it to its original shape. The first algorithm restores a tree to exactly the same shape it had before it was saved. For example, consider the tree in Figure 10-34a. If you save the tree in preorder, you get the sequence 60, 20, 10, 40, 30, 50, 70. If you then use `TableInsert` to insert these values into a tree that is initially empty, you will get the original tree. Figure 10-34b shows this sequence of insertion operations.

Saving a tree and then restoring it to a balanced shape. Can you do better than the previous algorithm? That is, do you necessarily want the

Figure 10-34

(a) A binary search tree; (b) the sequence of insertions that result in this tree

(a)

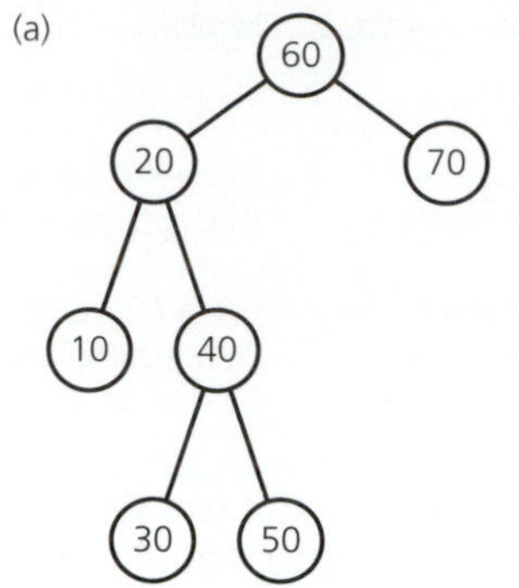

(b)

```
TableInsert(T, 60)
TableInsert(T, 20)
TableInsert(T, 10)
TableInsert(T, 40)
TableInsert(T, 30)
TableInsert(T, 50)
TableInsert(T, 70)
```

A balanced tree increases the efficiency of the nonlinear implementation of the ADT table

restored tree to have its original shape? Recall that you can organize a given set of data items into binary search trees with many different shapes. Although the shape of a binary search tree has no effect whatsoever on the correctness of the ADT table operations, it will affect the efficiency of those operations. What is needed is an algorithm that will restore a tree to a shape that is balanced. It turns out that this algorithm is surprisingly simple. In fact, you can even guarantee that the restored tree will be of minimum height—a condition stronger than balanced.

To see how you can design an algorithm that will restore a binary search tree to a balanced shape, first recall that the whole purpose of a balanced binary search tree is to facilitate a binary search of a structure that can have a pointer-based implementation. That is, each node of the tree represents the middle item of a subproblem that the binary search algorithm could encounter. This observation tells you exactly how to build a balanced binary search tree from a fixed set of data: Let the middle item be the root of the tree, and make the root's left and right subtrees be balanced binary search trees.

Consider, for example, a full tree with exactly $N = 2^h - 1$ nodes for some height *h,* as Figure 10-35 illustrates. Note that, as a consequence of the definition of a full tree, the root contains the exact middle of the data items, and the left and right subtrees of the root are full trees of $2^{h-1} - 1$ nodes each (that is, half of $N - 1$, since N is odd, or equivalently, N `div` 2). Thus, you can use the following recursive algorithm to restore a full tree T with N nodes, provided that you had saved it in sorted order (by using an inorder traversal) and you either know or can determine N beforehand. It

Figure 10-35

Building a full tree from a file

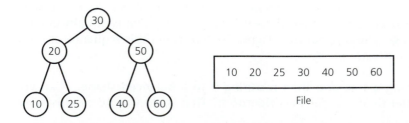

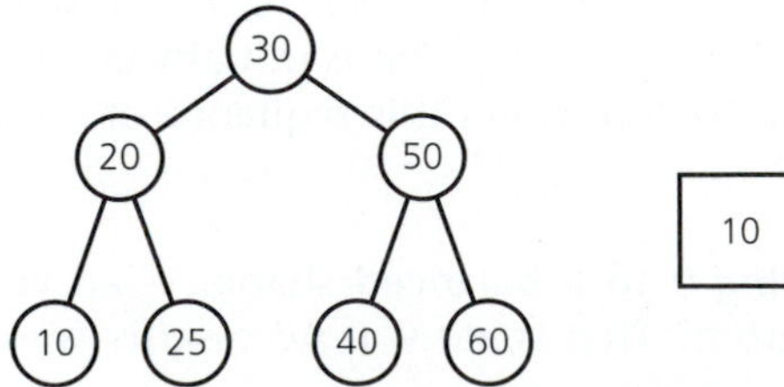

10 20 25 30 40 50 60

File

may be surprising that you can construct the tree directly by reading the sorted data from left to right from the file.

Building a full binary search tree

```
ReadFull(T, N)
{ Builds a full binary search tree T from N sorted values
  in a file. }

  if N > 0
     then
     begin
        { construct the left subtree }
        ReadFull(left subtree of T's root, N div 2)

        { get the root }
        read(item for root of T)

        { construct the right subtree }
        ReadFull(right subtree of T's root, N div 2)
     end
```

This algorithm for restoring a full binary search tree is simple, but what can you do if the tree to be restored is not full (that is, if it does not have $N = 2^h - 1$ nodes for some h)? The first thing that comes to mind is that the restored tree should be complete—full up to the last level, with the last level filled in from left to right. Actually, because you care only about minimizing the height of the restored tree, it does not matter where the nodes on the last level go, as Figure 10-36 shows.

Procedure `ReadFull` is essentially correct even if the tree is not full. However, you do have to be a bit careful when computing the sizes of the left and right subtrees of the tree's root. If N is odd, both subtrees are of size N `div` 2, as before. (The root is automatically accounted for.) If N is even, however, you have to account for the root and the fact that one subtree will have one more node than the other. In this case, you can arbitrarily choose to put the extra node in the left subtree. The following algorithm makes these compensations:

Building a minimum-height binary search tree

```
ReadTree(T, N)
{ Builds a minimum-height binary search tree T from N
  sorted values in a file.}

  if N > 0
     then
     begin
        { construct the left subtree }
        ReadTree(left subtree of T's root, N div 2)

        { get the root }
        read(item for root of T)

        { construct the right subtree }
        ReadTree(right subtree of T's root, (N-1) div 2)
     end
```

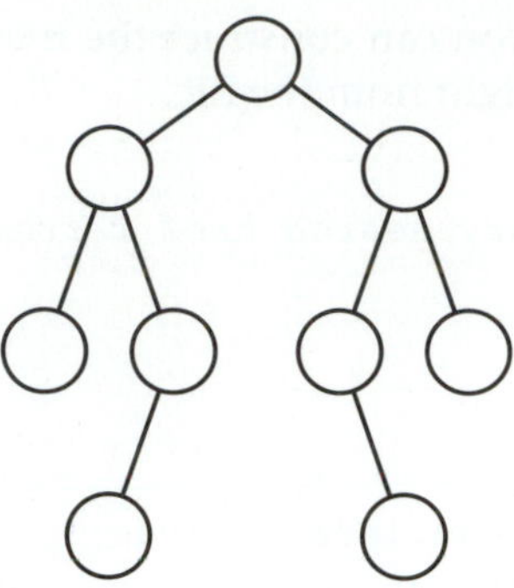

Figure 10-36

A tree of minimum height that is not complete

You should trace this algorithm and convince yourself that it is correct for both even and odd values of *N*.

To summarize, you can easily restore a tree as a balanced binary search tree if the data is sorted—that is, if it has been produced from the inorder traversal—and you know the number *N* of nodes in the tree. You need *N* so that you can determine the middle item and, in turn, the number of nodes in the left and right subtrees of the tree's root. Knowing these numbers is a simple matter of counting nodes as you traverse the tree and then saving the number in a file that the restore operation can read.

SUMMARY

1. **The ADT table supports value-oriented operations, such as `Retrieve all the information about John Smith`.**
2. **The linear implementations (array based and pointer based) of a table are adequate only in limited situations, such as when the table is small or for certain operations. The fundamental problem with the linear implementation is this paradox: A binary search, which you use to locate either a specified value or the point of insertion, requires an array-based implementation; however, insertions and deletions can avoid the shifting of items only under a pointer-based implementation.**
3. **A nonlinear (pointer-based binary search tree) implementation of the ADT table provides the best aspects of the two linear implementations. The pointer-based implementation allows the table to grow dynamically and allows insertions and deletions of data to occur through pointer changes instead of data movement. In addition, the binary search tree allows you to use a binary search-like algorithm when searching for an item with a specified value. These characteristics make a nonlinear table implementation far superior to the linear implementations in many applications.**

4. **Traversing an ADT is an important concept. Intuitively, traversing an ADT means to visit every item in the ADT. If you need to traverse an ADT table, you should include a *TraverseTable* operation in the ADT's definition. Because the meaning of "visit" is application dependent, you can pass a user-defined *Visit* procedure to the *TraverseTable* operation.**

5. **Binary search trees come in many shapes. The height of a binary search tree with N nodes can range from a minimum of $\lceil \log_2(N + 1) \rceil$ to a maximum of N. The shape of a binary search tree determines how efficiently it is able to support the table operations. The closer a binary search tree is to a balanced tree (and the further it is from a linear structure), the closer will be the behavior of the *Find* algorithm to a binary search (and the further will it be from the behavior of a linear search).**

6. **If you save a binary search tree's data in a file so that it is sorted (by using an inorder traversal), you can restore the tree as a binary search tree of minimum height.**

COMMON PITFALLS / DEBUGGING

1. **When defining an ADT to solve a particular problem, do not request unnecessary operations. The proper choice of an implementation depends on the mix of requested operations, and if you request an operation that you do not need, you might get an implementation that does not best support what you are really doing.**

2. **Although a linear pointer-based implementation of the ADT table eliminates the need to shift data, it does not support the insertion and deletion operations any more efficiently than does an array-based implementation, because you cannot perform a binary search in a reasonable fashion.**

3. **Usually a binary search tree can support the ADT table operations quite efficiently. However, in the worst case, when the tree approaches a linear shape, the performance of the table operations is comparable to that of a linear pointer-based implementation. If you must avoid such a situation for a given application, you should use the balancing methods presented in Chapter 13.**

SELF-TEST EXERCISES

1. Consider the tree in Figure 10-37. What node or nodes are
   a. The tree's root
   b. Parents

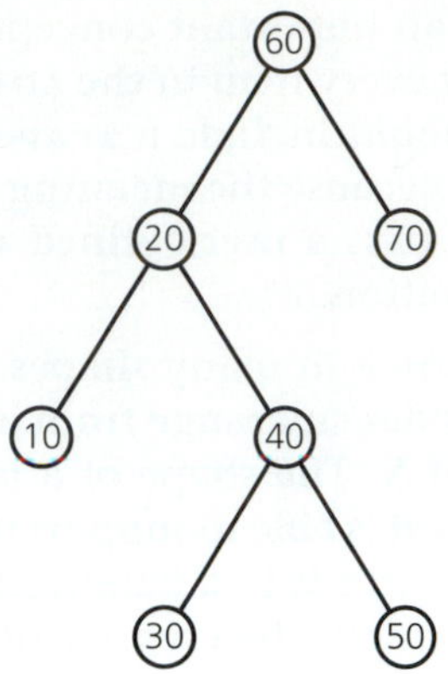

Figure 10-37

A tree for Self-Test Exercises 1, 3, and 9 and Exercise 6

c. Children of the parents in Part *b*
d. Siblings
e. Ancestors of 50
f. Descendents of 20
g. Leaves

2. What are the levels of all nodes in the tree in

a. Figure 10-9b
b. Figure 10-9c

3. What is the height of the tree in Figure 10-37?

4. Consider the binary trees in Figure 10-30. Which are complete? Which are full? Which are balanced?

5. What are the preorder, inorder, and postorder traversals of the binary tree in Figure 10-9a?

6. Is the tree in Figure 10-38 a binary search tree?

7. Beginning with an empty binary tree, what binary search tree is formed when you insert the following values in the order given: J, N, B, A, W, E, T?

8. By using the ADT table operations, write pseudocode for a `TableReplace` operation that replaces the table item whose search key is *X* with another item whose search key is also *X*.

9. Trace the algorithm that searches a binary search tree when the tree is the one in Figure 10-37 and the search key is

a. 30
b. 15

In each case, list the nodes in the order in which the search visits them.

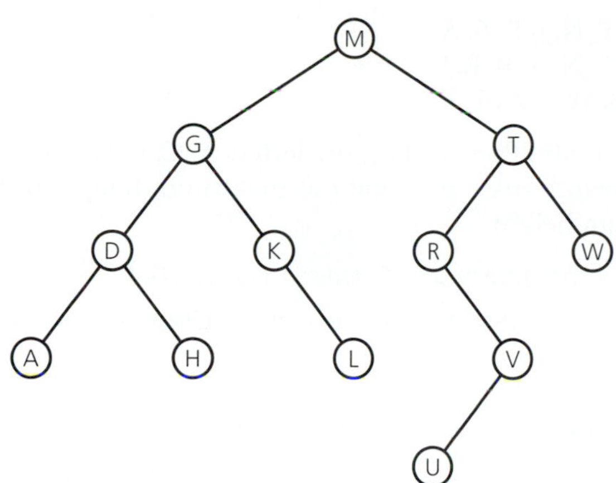

Figure 10-38

A tree for Self-Test Exercise 6 and Exercise 3a

10. **a.** What binary tree results when you execute `ReadTree` with a file of the six integers 2, 4, 6, 8, 10, 12?

b. Is the resulting tree's height a minimum? Is the tree complete? Is it full?

EXERCISES

1. **a.** Complete the sorted pointer-based, unsorted array-based, and unsorted pointer-based implementations of the ADT table described in this chapter.

b. Define each of the linear implementations of the ADT table as an object.

2. Many applications require a `TableReplace` operation in the definition of the ADT table. Although you can simulate this operation by using other ADT operations, it is more efficient to implement the operation directly. Write implementations of `TableReplace` for the five implementations (four linear and the binary search tree) of the ADT table described in this chapter.

3. What are the preorder, inorder, and postorder traversals of the binary trees in

a. Figure 10-38
b. Figure 10-9b
c. Figure 10-9c

4. Beginning with an empty binary tree, what binary search tree is formed when you insert the following values in the order given?

a. W, T, N, J, E, B, A
b. W, T, N, A, B, E, J
c. A, B, W, J, N, T, E

5. Arrange nodes that contain the letters A, C, E, F, L, V, and Z into two binary search trees: one that has maximum height and one that has minimum height.

6. Consider the binary search tree in Figure 10-37.
   a. What tree results after you insert the nodes 80, 65, 75, 45, 35, and 25?
   b. After inserting the nodes mentioned in Part *a*, what tree results when you delete the nodes 50 and 20?

7. Does the sequence of operations `TableDelete(T, X)` followed by `TableInsert(T, X)` ever change the shape of the binary search tree `T`?

Exercises 8 through 10 discuss the problem of duplicates in an ADT or data structure. Duplicates could mean either items that are identical in all fields or, more subtly, items that have identical search keys but differ in other fields.

8. The implementations of the ADT table given in this chapter make the following assumption: At any time, a table contains at most one item with a given search key. Although the ADT definition required for a specific application may not allow duplicates, it is probably wise to test for them rather than simply to assume that they will not occur. Why? What are the implications of a user inserting duplicate items? What are the implications of a user inserting items that have the same search key but that have other data fields that differ? Specifically, what would the implementations of `TableInsert`, `TableDelete`, and `TableRetrieve` do?

   Modify the table implementations so that they test for—and disallow—any duplicates. What table operations are affected? What are the implications for the unsorted linear implementations?

9. Although disallowing duplicates (see Exercise 8) is reasonable for some applications, it is just as reasonable to have an application that will allow duplicates. What are the implications of allowing duplicates for the definitions of the ADT table operations? In particular, how can the retrieval and deletion operations be defined?

***10.** If duplicates are allowed in a binary search tree, it is important to have a convention that determines the relationship between the duplicates in the data structure. Items that duplicate the root of a tree should either all be in the left subtree or all be in the right subtree, and, of course, this property must hold for every subtree. Why is this convention critical to the effective use of the binary search tree?

   This chapter stated that you can delete an item from a binary search tree by replacing it with either its inorder successor or its inorder predecessor. If duplicates are allowed, however, the choice between inorder predecessor and inorder successor is no longer arbitrary. How does the convention of putting duplicates in either the left or right subtree affect this choice?

11. The following procedure constructs a binary tree from two binary trees and a data item for its root:

```
type   ptrType = ^nodeType;

       nodeType = record
           Data : itemType;
           LChild, RChild : ptrType
       end;    { record }

       binTreeType = ptrType;

var    P, Q, R, S, T : binTreeType;

procedure MakeTree(var Tree : binTreeType;
                       RootValue : integer;
                       LeftTree, RightTree : binTreeType);
begin
   new(Tree);
   with Tree^ do
   begin
      Data := RootValue;
      LChild := LeftTree;
      RChild := RightTree
   end
end;  { MakeTree }
```

What tree(s) would the following sequence of statements produce?

```
MakeTree(T, 1, nil, nil);
MakeTree(T^.LChild, 2, nil, nil);
MakeTree(T^.RChild, 3, nil, nil);
MakeTree(T^.LChild^.RChild, 4, nil, nil);
MakeTree(T^.LChild, 5, nil, nil); { subtree is "lost" }
MakeTree(P, 6, nil, nil);
MakeTree(Q, 7, nil, nil);
MakeTree(R, 8, P, Q);
MakeTree(R, 9, nil, R);
new(R^.LChild);
S := R^.LChild;
S^.Data := 10;
S^.LChild := T;
S^.RChild := nil;
```

12. Consider an array-based implementation of a binary search tree. Figure 10-13 illustrates such a representation for the binary search tree in Figure 10-8.

a. Depict the arrays in an array-based implementation for the binary search tree in Figure 10-19a.

b. Show the effect of each of the following sequential operations on the arrays in Part *a* of this exercise.

```
TableInsert(T, Doug)
TableDelete(T, Nancy)
TableDelete(T, Bob)
TableInsert(T, Sarah)
```

c. Repeat Parts *a* and *b* of this exercise for the tree in Figure 10-19b.

13. Given the recursive nature of the tree, a good strategy for writing a Pascal subprogram that operates on a binary tree is often first to write a recursive definition of the task. For example, suppose that the task is to count the number of nodes in a binary tree. An appropriate recursive definition for the number of nodes $C(T)$ of binary tree T is

$$C(T) = \begin{cases} 0 & \text{if } T \text{ is the empty tree} \\ C(\text{left subtree of } T) + C(\text{right subtree of } T) + 1 & \text{otherwise} \end{cases}$$

Given such a recursive definition, a Pascal implementation is often straightforward.

Write recursive definitions that perform the following tasks on arbitrary binary trees. Implement the definitions in Pascal. For simplicity, assume that a tree data item is a single integer and that there are no duplicates.

a. Compute the height of a tree.

b. Find the maximum element.

c. Find the sum of the elements.

***d.** Find the average of the elements.

e. Find a specific item.

f. Determine whether one item is an ancestor of another (that is, whether one item is in the subtree rooted at the other item).

g. Determine the highest level that is full (that is, has the maximum number of nodes for that level [see Exercise 18]).

***h.** Dispose of all of the nodes.

14. Consider a nonempty binary tree with two types of nodes: **min** nodes and **max** nodes. Each node has an integer value initially associated with it. You can define the **value** of such a tree as follows:

- If the root is a min node, then the value of the tree is equal to the *minimum* of

  The integer stored in the root

  The value of the left subtree, but only if it is nonempty

  The value of the right subtree, but only if it is nonempty

- If the root is a max node, then the value of the tree is equal to the *maximum* of the above three values.

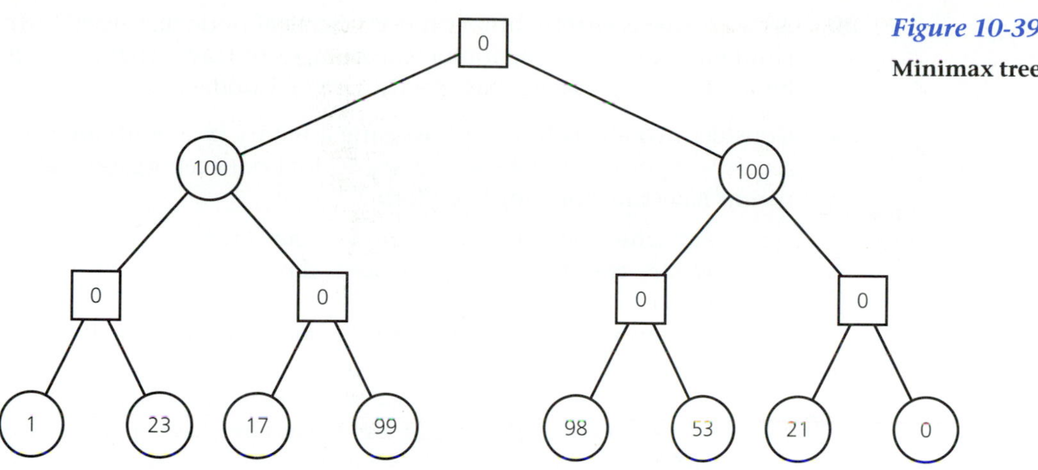

Figure 10-39
Minimax tree

a. Compute the value of the tree in Figure 10-39. Each node is labeled with its initial value.
b. Write a general solution for representing and evaluating these trees in Pascal.

***15.** Recall that a binary search tree with a given set of data items can have several different structures that conform to the definition of a binary search tree. Suppose that you are given a list of data items. Is there always at least one binary search tree whose preorder traversal matches the order of the items on your list? Is there ever more than one binary search tree that has the given preorder traversal?

***16.** How many different (in shape) binary trees are there with N nodes? How many different binary search trees are there with N nodes? (Write recursive definitions.)

17. Prove Theorems 10-2 and 10-3 by induction.

18. What is the maximum number of nodes that can exist at level N of a binary tree? Prove your answer by induction. Use this fact to do the following:

a. Rewrite the formal definition of a complete tree of height h.
b. Derive a closed form for the formula

$$\sum_{i=1}^{h} 2^{i-1}$$

What is the significance of this sum?

19. Prove by induction that a binary tree with N nodes has exactly $N + 1$ empty subtrees (or, in Pascal terms, $N + 1$ `nil` pointers).

20. A binary tree is **strictly binary** if every nonleaf node has exactly two children. Prove by induction on the number of leaves that a strictly binary tree with N leaves has exactly $2 * N - 1$ nodes.

21. Consider two algorithms for traversing a binary tree. Both are nonrecursive algorithms that use an extra list for bookkeeping. Both algorithms have the following basic form:

```
Put the root of the tree on the list
while the list is not empty do
begin
   Remove a node from the list and call it N
   Visit N
   Put the left child of N on the list (if it exists)
   Put the right child of N on the list (if it exists)
end
```

The difference between the two algorithms is the method for choosing a node N to remove from the list.

Algorithm *X:* Remove the newest (most recently added) node from the list.

Algorithm *Y:* Remove the oldest (earliest added) node from the list.

a. In what order would each algorithm visit the nodes of the tree in Figure 10-18?

b. For each algorithm, describe an ADT that is appropriate for maintaining the bookkeeping list. What should the list item be? Do not use extra memory unnecessarily for the bookkeeping list. Also, note that the traversal of a tree should not alter the tree in any way.

22. Design another algorithm to delete nodes from a binary search tree. This algorithm differs from the one described in this chapter when the node N has two children. First let N's right child take the place of the deleted node N in the same manner in which you delete a node with one child. Next reconnect N's left child (along with its subtree, if any) to the left side of N's inorder successor.

23. Write an iterative procedure to insert a node into a binary search tree.

24. Some people define a binary tree as an ADT instead of a data structure. List and implement the operations that are suitable for such an ADT.

25. Suppose that you want to support table deletion operations for two different search keys (for example, `TableDeleteN` [delete by name] and `TableDeleteS` [delete by Social Security number]). Describe an efficient implementation.

26. Repeat Exercise 25, but instead organize one of the search keys with a binary search tree and the other with a sorted linked list.

27. Recall that the motivation for a doubly linked list is the need to locate and delete a node on a list without traversing the list. The analogy for a binary search tree is to maintain parent pointers. That is, every node except the root will have a pointer to its parent in the tree. Write insertion and deletion operations for this structure.

28. In the object definition `tableType`, which appears in the section "The Table As an Object," how can you hide the data type `treePtrType` from the user of the table?

29. Revise the object type `tableType`, which appears in the section "The Table As an Object," so that the items in the table are dynamically allocated objects that descend from `genericObjectType`, as defined in Chapter 4. Write a small program that demonstrates how to allocate, use, and deallocate your new object. Include a procedure that allocates objects that descend from `genericObjectType`. Consider both linear and nonlinear implementations.

***30.** A node in a general tree, such as the one in Figure 10-4, can have an arbitrary number of children.

a. Describe a Pascal implementation of a general tree in which every node contains an array of child pointers. What are the advantages and disadvantages of this implementation?

b. What happens if you replace the array of children with a linked list of children? Observe that every node will have two pointers: a pointer to its oldest child—that is, to the first node on its linked list of children—and a pointer to its next sibling, which follows this node on its parent's list of children. Consider a tree *T* in which every node has at most two children. Compare the oldest-child/next-sibling representation of *T* to the left-child/right-child representation described in this chapter. Are the two representations ever the same?

***31.** Implement a `TraverseTable` operation that permits `Visit` to delete the node visited.

CHAPTER 11

Graphs

PREVIEW Graphs are an important mathematical concept that have significant applications in computer science. You can view a graph as a mathematical construct, a data structure, or an abstract data type. This chapter provides an introduction to graphs that allows you to view a graph in any of these three ways. It also presents the major operations and applications of graphs that are relevant to the computer scientist.

TERMINOLOGY

You are undoubtedly familiar with graphs: Line graphs, bar graphs, and pie charts are in common use. The simple line graph in Figure 11-1 is illustrative of the type of graph that this chapter considers: a set of points that are joined by lines. Clearly, graphs provide a way to illustrate data. However, graphs also represent the relationships between data, and it is this feature of graphs that is important here.

G = {V, E}

Formally, a **graph** *G* consists of two sets: a set *V* of **vertices**, or **nodes**, and a set *E* of **edges** that connect the vertices. For example, the campus map in Figure 11-2 is a graph whose vertices represent buildings and whose edges represent the sidewalks between the buildings. This definition of a graph is more general than the definition of a line graph. In fact, a line graph, with its points and lines, is a special case of the general definition of a graph.

Adjacent vertices

Path, cycle

A **subgraph** consists of a subset of a graph's vertices and a subset of its edges. Figure 11-3 shows a subgraph of the graph in Figure 11-2. Two vertices of a graph are **adjacent** if they are joined by an edge. In Figure 11-3, the Library and the Student Union are adjacent. A **path** between two vertices is a sequence of edges that begins at one vertex and ends at another vertex. For example, there is a path that begins at the Dormitory, leads first to the Library, then to the Student Union, and finally back to the Library. Although a path may pass through the same vertex more than once, as the path just described does, a **simple path** may not. The path Dormitory-

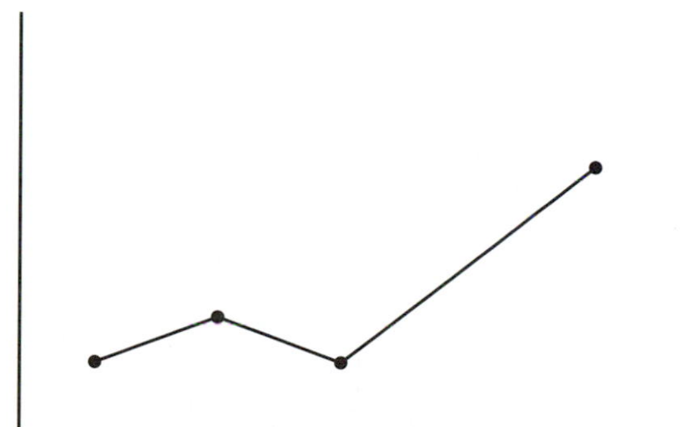

Figure 11-1

An ordinary line graph

Figure 11-2

A campus map

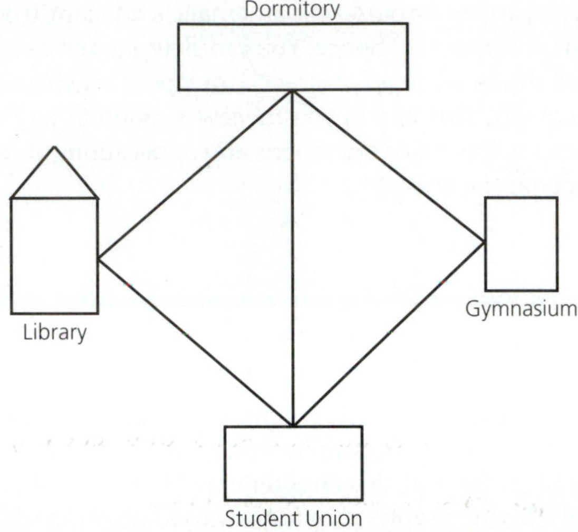

Library-Student Union is a simple path. A **cycle** is a path that begins and ends at the same vertex but does not pass through other vertices more than once. The path Library-Student Union-Gymnasium-Dormitory-Library is a cycle in the graph in Figure 11-2. A graph is **connected** if there is a path between every pair of vertices. Figure 11-4a shows a connected graph, while Figure 11-4b shows a **disconnected** graph. A graph is **complete** if there is an edge between every pair of vertices. The graph in Figure 11-4c is complete. Clearly, a complete graph is also connected, but the converse is not true; notice that the graph in Figure 11-4a is connected but is not complete.

Connected, disconnected

PATH-ORIENTED, G={V,E}

A complete graph is connected

You can label the edges of a graph. When these labels represent numeric values, the graph is called a **weighted graph**. The graph in Figure

Weighted

Figure 11-3

A subgraph of the graph in Figure 11-2

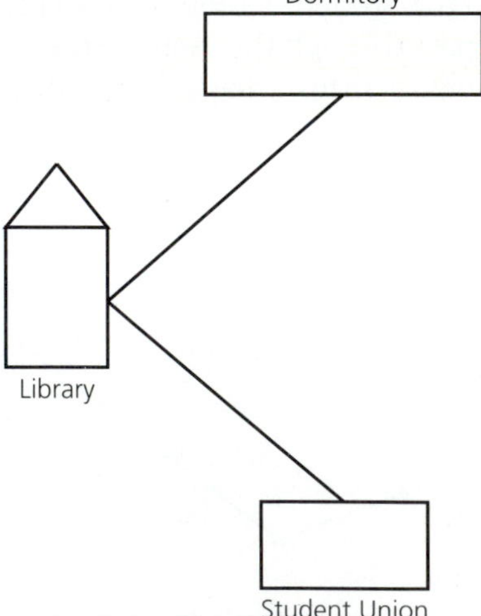

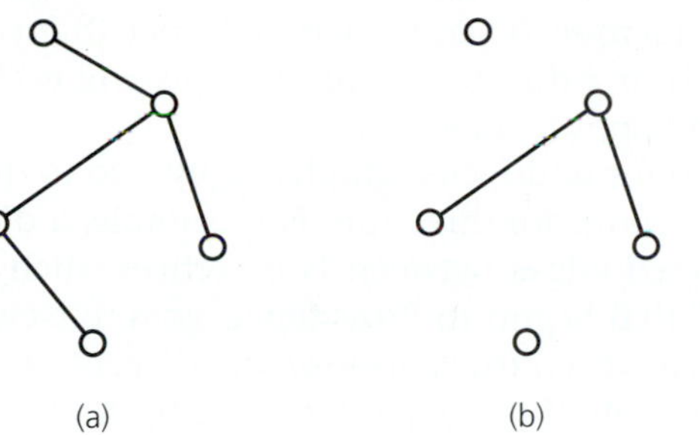

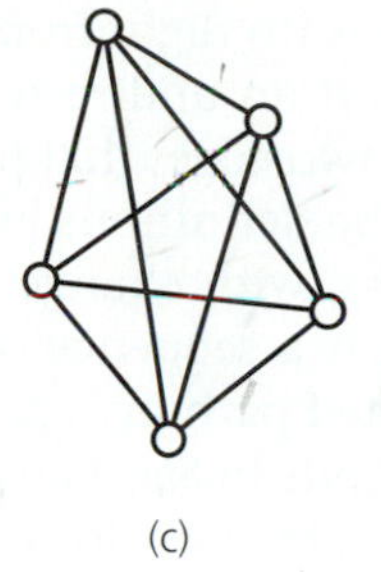

Figure 11-4

Graphs that are (a) connected; (b) disconnected; and (c) complete

11-5 is a weighted graph whose edges are labeled with the distances between cities.

Undirected, directed

All of the previous graphs are examples of **undirected** graphs because there is at most one edge between any two vertices and the edges do not indicate a direction. That is, you can travel in either direction along the edges between the vertices of an undirected graph. In contrast, each edge in a **directed graph**, or **digraph**, has a direction and is called a **directed edge**. Although there can be only one edge between two vertices of an undirected graph, a directed graph can have two edges between a pair of vertices. For example, the airline flight map in Figure 11-6 is a directed graph. There are flights in both directions between Providence and New York but, although there is a flight from San Francisco to Albuquerque,

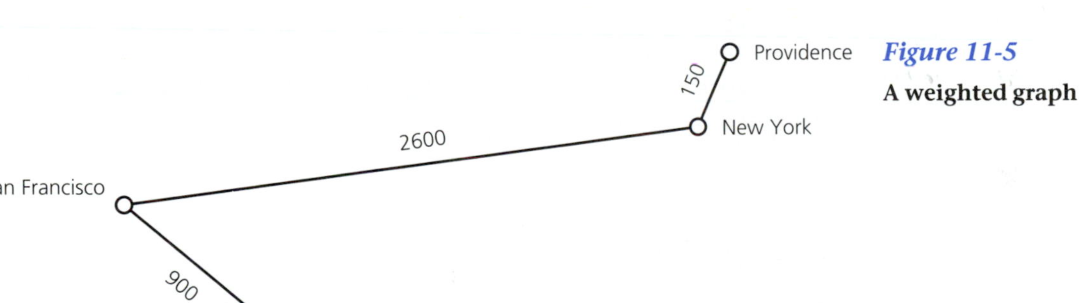

Figure 11-5

A weighted graph

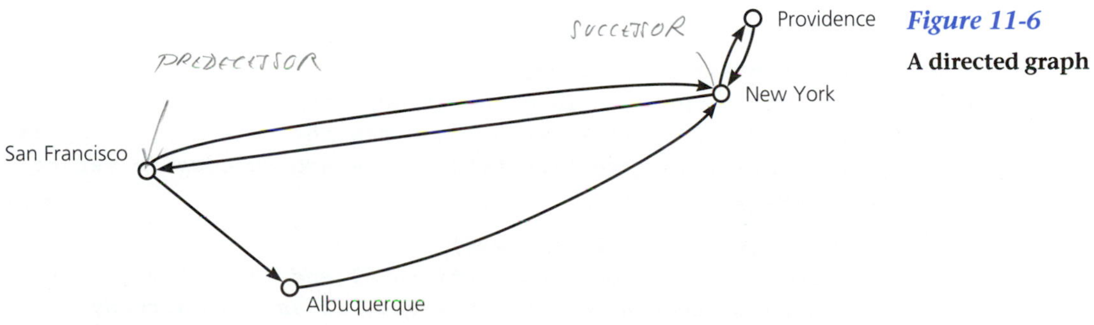

Figure 11-6

A directed graph

there is no flight from Albuquerque to San Francisco. Notice that you can convert an undirected graph to a directed graph by replacing each edge with two edges that point in opposite directions.

The definitions just given for undirected graphs apply also to directed graphs, with changes that account for direction. For example, a **directed path** is a sequence of **directed edges** between two vertices, such as the directed path in Figure 11-6 that begins in Providence, goes to New York, and ends in San Francisco. However, the definition of adjacent vertices is not quite as obvious for a digraph. If there is a directed edge from vertex *x* to vertex *y*, then *y* is **adjacent** to *x*. (Alternatively, *y* is a **successor** of *x*.) It does not necessarily follow, however, that *x* is adjacent to *y*. Thus, in Figure 11-6, Albuquerque is adjacent to San Francisco, but San Francisco is not adjacent to Albuquerque.

GRAPHS AS ADT'S

You can treat graphs as abstract data types. Insertion and deletion operations are somewhat different for graphs than for other ADT's that you have studied in that they apply to either vertices or edges. You can define the ADT graph so that its vertices either do or do not contain values. A graph whose vertices do not contain values represents the relationships only between vertex positions. It is not unusual for a graph problem to involve only the relationships between vertex positions and to have no need for vertex values. However, the following ADT graph operations assume that the graph's vertices contain values.

KEY CONCEPTS

ADT Graph Operations

```
CreateGraph(G)
{ Creates an empty graph G. }

GraphIsEmpty(G)
{ Returns true if the graph G is empty; otherwise returns
  false. }

InsertVertex(G, v, Success)
{ Inserts a vertex v into the graph G and sets Success to
  true. However, if a vertex in G has the same search key as
  that of v, no insertion takes place and Success is set to
  false. }

InsertEdge(G, v1, v2, Success)
{ Inserts an edge between vertices v1 and v2 in the graph G
  and sets Success to true. However, if an edge already
```

```
  exists between the specified vertices, sets Success to
  false. }

DeleteVertex(G, v, Success)
{ Deletes the vertex v from the graph G, deletes any edges
  between v and other vertices of G, and sets Success to
  true. However, if no such vertex exists, sets Success to
  false. }

DeleteEdge(G, v1, v2, Success)
{ Deletes the edge between vertices v1 and v2 in the graph G
  and sets Success to true. However, if no edge exists
  between the specified vertices, sets Success to false. }

RetrieveVertex(G, SearchKey, v, Success)
{ Copies into v the vertex, if any, of G that contains
  SearchKey. Sets Success to true if vertex is found;
  otherwise sets it to false. }

ReplaceVertex(G, SearchKey, v, Success)
{ Replaces the vertex that contains SearchKey with v. Sets
  Success to true if vertex is found; otherwise sets it to
  false. }

IsEdge(G, v1, v2)
{ Returns true if an edge between the vertices v1 and v2
  exists; otherwise returns false. }
```

Several variations of this ADT are possible. For example, if the graph is directed, you can replace instances of "edges" in the previous specifications with "directed edges." You can also add traversal operations to the ADT. This chapter will discuss graph-traversal algorithms shortly.

Implementing Graphs

Adjacency matrix

The two most common implementations of a graph are the adjacency matrix and the adjacency list. In both implementations, it is convenient to imagine that the vertices are numbered 1, 2, and so on to *N*. An **adjacency matrix** for a graph with *N* vertices is an *N* by *N* boolean array `A` such that `A[i, j]` is `true` if and only if there is an edge from vertex *i* to vertex *j*. Figure 11-7 shows a directed graph and its adjacency matrix. Notice that `A[i, i]` is `false`. However, there may be times when it is preferable to set the diagonal entries of the adjacency matrix to `true`. You should choose the value that is most convenient for your application. Finally, note that the adjacency matrix for an undirected graph is symmetric, that is, `A[i, j] = A[j, i]`.

When the graph is weighted, it is convenient to let `A[i, j]` be the weight that labels the edge from vertex *i* to vertex *j*, instead of the boolean

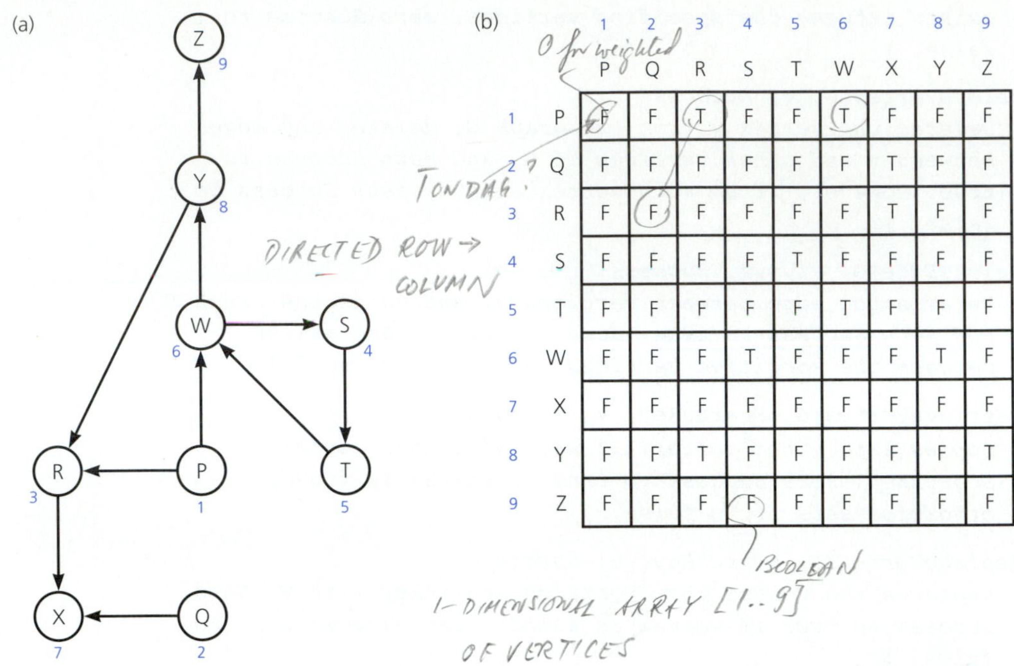

		1 P	2 Q	3 R	4 S	5 T	6 W	7 X	8 Y	9 Z
1	P	F	F	T	F	F	T	F	F	F
2	Q	F	F	F	F	F	F	T	F	F
3	R	F	F	F	F	F	F	T	F	F
4	S	F	F	F	F	T	F	F	F	F
5	T	F	F	F	F	F	T	F	F	F
6	W	F	F	F	T	F	F	F	T	F
7	X	F	F	F	F	F	F	F	F	F
8	Y	F	F	T	F	F	F	F	F	T
9	Z	F	F	F	F	F	F	F	F	F

Figure 11-7

(a) A directed graph and (b) its adjacency matrix

value `true`, and to let `A[i, j]` equal ∞ instead of `false` when there is no edge from vertex *i* to vertex *j*. In addition, the diagonal entries `A[i, i]` are zero, which implies that there is no distance between a vertex and itself. For example, Figure 11-8 contains a weighted undirected graph and its adjacency matrix.

Vertices can have values

Notice that with an adjacency matrix, there is no mention of the value in a vertex. However, if you do need to associate values with vertices, you can use a one-dimensional array `Values` of *N* items that represent vertex values; that is, `Values[i]` is the value in vertex *i*.

Adjacency list

An **adjacency list** for a graph with *N* vertices numbered 1, 2, ⋯ , *N* consists of *N* linked lists. There is a node in the ith linked list for vertex *j* if and only if there is an edge from vertex *i* to vertex *j*. Figure 11-9 shows the adjacency list for the graph in Figure 11-7a.

Figure 11-8

(a) A weighted undirected graph and (b) its adjacency matrix

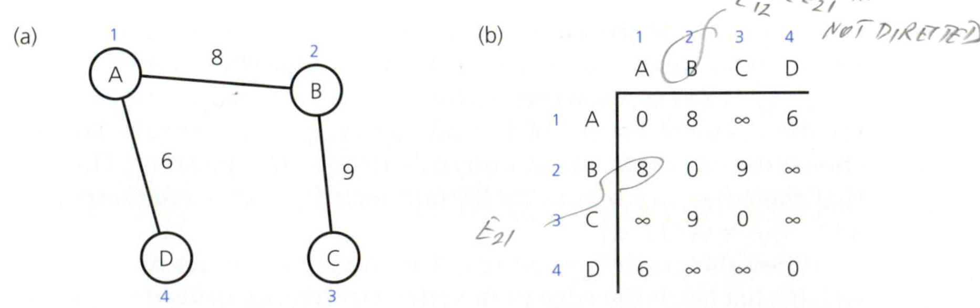

		1 A	2 B	3 C	4 D
1	A	0	8	∞	6
2	B	8	0	9	∞
3	C	∞	9	0	∞
4	D	6	∞	∞	0

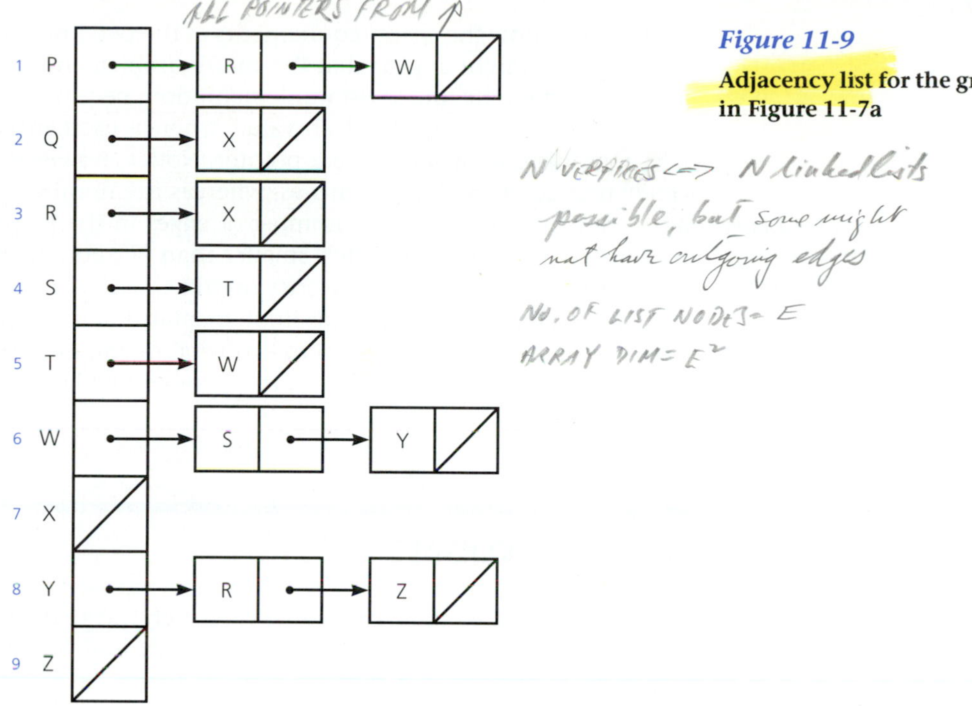

Figure 11-9

Adjacency list for the graph in Figure 11-7a

Which of these two implementations of a graph—the adjacency matrix or the adjacency list—is better? The answer depends on how your particular application uses the graph. For example, the two most commonly performed graph operations are

Two common operations on graphs

1. Given two vertices *i* and *j*, determine whether there is an edge from *i* to *j*.
2. Find all vertices adjacent to a given vertex *i*.

An adjacency matrix supports operation 1 more efficiently

The adjacency matrix supports the first operation somewhat more efficiently than does the adjacency list. To determine whether there is an edge from *i* to *j* by using an adjacency matrix, you need only examine the value of `A[i, j]`. If you use an adjacency list, however, you must traverse the ith linked list to determine whether a vertex corresponding to vertex *j* is present.

An adjacency list supports operation 2 more efficiently

The second operation, on the other hand, is supported more efficiently by the adjacency list. To determine all vertices adjacent to a given vertex *i* given the adjacency matrix, you must traverse the ith row of the array; however, given the adjacency list, you must traverse the ith linked list. For a graph with *N* vertices, the ith row of the adjacency matrix always has *N* entries, whereas the ith linked list has only as many nodes as there are vertices adjacent to vertex *i*, a number typically far less than *N*. Notice that the HPAir problem of Chapter 8 used an adjacency list because its most frequent operation was to find all vertices adjacent to a given vertex.

Consider now the space requirements of the two implementations. On the surface it might appear that the matrix implementation requires less space than does the linked list implementation, because each entry in the matrix is simply a single boolean value, whereas each entry in the linked lists contains both a value and a pointer. Notice, however, that the adjacency matrix always has N^2 entries, whereas the number of entries in an adjacency list is equal to the number of edges in the graph. Because the number of edges is often much smaller than N^2, an adjacency list often requires less space than an adjacency matrix.

An adjacency list usually requires less space than an adjacency matrix

Thus, when choosing a graph implementation for a particular application, you must consider such factors as what operations you will perform most frequently on the graph and the number of edges that the graph is likely to contain.

GRAPH TRAVERSALS

Chapter 8 presented the HPAir problem, which was to determine whether an airline provided a sequence of flights from an origin city to a destination city. The flight map for that problem is in fact a directed graph and appeared earlier in this chapter in Figure 11-7a. The solution to the HPAir problem involved an exhaustive search of an adjacency list to determine a directed path from the origin vertex (city) to the destination vertex (city). The algorithm `SearchS` started at a given vertex and traversed edges to other vertices until it either found the desired vertex or determined that no directed path existed between the two vertices.

What distinguishes `SearchS` from a standard graph traversal is that `SearchS` stops when it first encounters the designated destination vertex. A **graph-traversal algorithm**, on the other hand, will not stop until it has visited *all the vertices that it can reach*. That is, a graph traversal that starts at vertex v will visit all vertices w for which there is a path between v and w. Notice that unlike a tree traversal, which always visits *all* the nodes in a tree, a graph traversal does not necessarily visit all the vertices in the graph unless the graph is connected. In fact, a graph traversal visits every vertex in the graph if and only if the graph is connected, regardless of where the traversal starts. (See Exercise 12.) If a graph is not connected, then a graph traversal that begins at vertex v will visit only a subset of the graph's vertices. This subset is called the **connected component** containing v.

A graph traversal visits only the vertices that it can reach

Two basic graph-traversal algorithms are presented next. These algorithms visit the vertices in different orders, but if they both start at the same vertex, they will visit the same set of vertices.

Depth-First Search

DFS traverses as far as possible from a vertex before backtracking

From a given vertex v, the **depth-first search** (DFS) strategy of graph traversal goes as deep into the graph as it can before backtracking. That is, after visiting vertex v, DFS visits, if possible, an unvisited vertex u adjacent to *v*. The algorithm then visits an unvisited vertex adjacent to *u* and continues as far as possible before returning to *v* to visit the next unvisited vertex adjacent to *v*. An iterative version of this algorithm follows.

Iterative* DFS *traversal algorithm

```
DFS(v)
{ Traverses a graph beginning at vertex v by using depth-
  first search – Iterative version. }

    CreateStack(S)

    { push v onto the stack and mark it }
    Push(S, v)
    Mark v as visited

    { loop invariant: there is a path from vertex v at the
      bottom of the stack S to the vertex at the top of S }
    while (not StackIsEmpty(S)) do
    begin
       if there are no unvisited vertices adjacent to the
           vertex on the top of the stack

           then Pop(S) { backtrack }

           else
           begin
              Select an unvisited vertex u adjacent to
                  the vertex on the top of the stack
              Push(S, u)
              Mark u as visited
           end  { if }
    end  { while }
```

Notice that `DFS` is similar to `SearchS` of Chapter 8, but the `while` statement in `SearchS` terminates when `StackTop(S) = Destination`.

Order in which adjacent vertices are visited

The depth-first search algorithm does not completely specify the order in which it should visit the vertices adjacent to *v*. One possibility is to visit the vertices adjacent to *v* in sorted (that is, alphabetic or numerically increasing) order. This possibility is natural either when an adjacency matrix represents the graph or when the nodes in each linked list of an adjacency list are linked in sorted order.

As an example of DFS traversal, consider the graph in Figure 11-10. Figure 11-11 shows the contents of the stack as the procedure `DFS` visits vertices in this graph beginning at vertex *a*. Because the graph is connected, `DFS` will visit every vertex. In fact, the traversal visits the vertices in this order: *a, b, c, d, g, e, f, h, i*.

A recursive version of `DFS` is also possible:

Recursive* DFS *traversal algorithm

```
DFS(v)
{ Traverses a graph beginning at vertex v by using depth-
  first search – Recursive version. }

    Mark v as visited
```

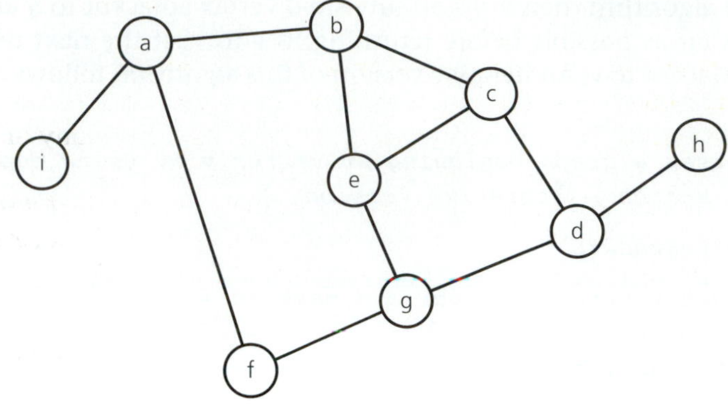

Figure 11-10

A connected graph with cycles

```
for each unvisited vertex u adjacent to v do
   DFS(u)
```

Notice that the vertex from which *DFS* embarks is the vertex that it visited most recently. This *last visited, first explored* strategy is reflected both in the explicit stack of vertices that the iterative *DFS* uses and in the implicit stack of vertices that the recursive *DFS* generates with its recursive calls.

Figure 11-11

The results of a depth-first traversal, beginning at vertex *a*, of the graph in Figure 11-10

Node visited	Stack (bottom → top)
a	a
b	a b
c	a b c
d	a b c d
g	a b c d g
e	a b c d g e
(backtrack)	a b c d g
f	a b c d g f
(backtrack)	a b c d g
(backtrack)	a b c d
h	a b c d h
(backtrack)	a b c d
(backtrack)	a b c
(backtrack)	a b
(backtrack)	a
i	a i
(backtrack)	a
(backtrack)	*(empty)*

Breadth-First Search

After visiting a given vertex *v*, the **breadth-first search** (BFS) strategy of graph traversal visits every vertex adjacent to *v* that it can before visiting any other vertex. Thus, the traversal will not embark from any of the vertices adjacent to *v* until it has visited all possible vertices adjacent to *v*. Whereas DFS is a *last visited, first explored* strategy, BFS is a *first visited, first explored* strategy. It is not surprising, then, that a breadth-first search uses a queue. An iterative version of this algorithm follows.

BFS visits all vertices adjacent to a vertex before going forward

Iterative BFS traversal algorithm

```
BFS(v)
{ Traverses a graph beginning at vertex v by using breadth-
  first search — Iterative version. }

    CreateQueue(Q)

    { add v to queue and mark it }
    Add(Q, v)
    Mark v as visited

    while (not QueueIsEmpty(Q)) do
    begin
       w := QueueFront(Q)
       Remove(Q)

       { loop invariant: there is a path from vertex w to
             every vertex in the queue Q }
       for each unvisited vertex u adjacent to w do
       begin
             Mark u as visited
             Add(Q, u)
       end  { for }
    end  { while }
```

Figure 11-12 shows the contents of the queue as the procedure `BFS` visits vertices in the graph in Figure 11-10 beginning at vertex *a*. `BFS` will visit the same vertices as `DFS`: all of them, in this example. The traversal visits the vertices in this order: *a, b, f, i, c, e, g, d, h*.

A recursive version of `BFS` is not as simple as the recursive version of `DFS`. Exercise 13 at the end of this chapter asks you to think about why this is so.

Recall that a connected component of a vertex *v* contains all vertices that a traversal algorithm visits when it begins at *v*. You can generate all the connected components of a graph by repeatedly starting a traversal at an unvisited vertex.

Generating connected components

APPLICATIONS OF GRAPHS

There are many useful applications of graphs. This section surveys some of these common applications.

Figure 11-12

The results of a breadth-first traversal, beginning at vertex *a*, of the graph in Figure 11-10

Node visited	Queue (front → rear)
a	a
	(empty)
b	b
f	b f
i	b f i
	f i
c	f i c
e	f i c e
	i c e
g	i c e g
	c e g
	e g
d	e g d
	g d
	d
	(empty)
h	h
	(empty)

Topological Sorting

There is a natural order in a directed graph without cycles, such as the one in Figure 11-13. For example, vertex *a* precedes *b*, which precedes *c*. Such a graph has significance in ordinary life. Suppose that the vertices represent academic courses and that the graph represents the prerequisite structure for the courses. For example, course *a* is a prerequisite to course *b*, which is a prerequisite to course *c*. In what order should you take all five courses so that you will satisfy all prerequisites? There is a linear order, called the **topological order**, of the vertices in a directed graph without cycles that answers this question. In a list of vertices in topological order, vertex *x* precedes vertex *y* if there is a directed edge from *x* to *y* in the graph. There may be several topological orders for a given graph; Figure 11-14 shows two possible topological orders for the vertices in the graph in Figure

Figure 11-13

A directed graph without cycles

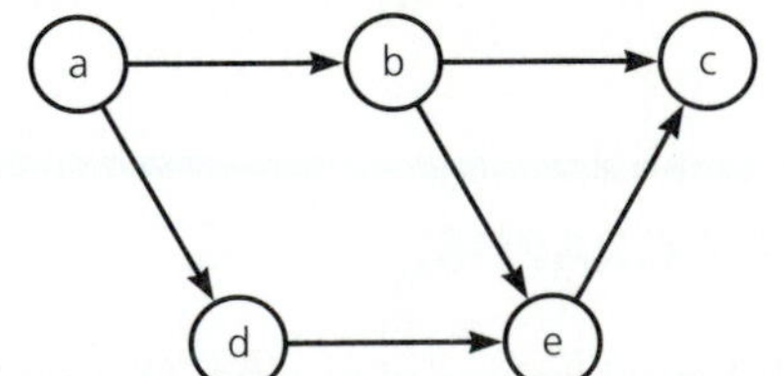

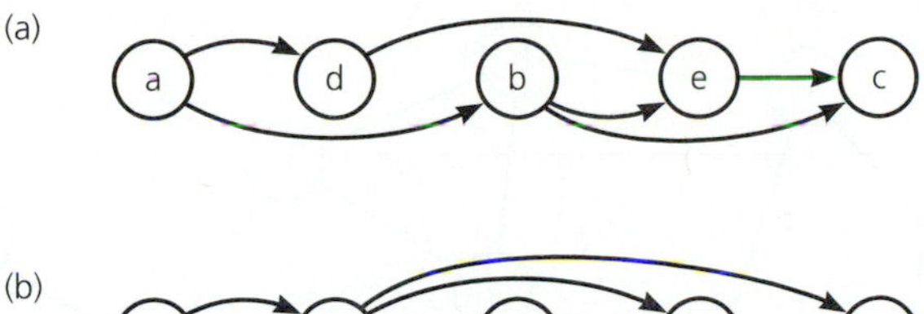

Figure 11-14

Two topological orders for the graph in Figure 11-13

11-13. Note that arranging the vertices into a topological order is called **topological sorting**.

A simple topological sorting algorithm

There are several simple algorithms for finding a topological order. First, you could find a vertex that has no successor, remove it from the graph, and add it to the beginning of an ordered list of vertices. You add each subsequent vertex that has no successor to the beginning of the ordered list. When the graph is empty, the ordered list of vertices will be in topological order. By applying this algorithm to the graph in Figure 11-13, you get one of the topological orders in Figure 11-14.

The DFS topological sorting algorithm

Another algorithm is a simple modification of the iterative depth-first search algorithm *DFS*. Each time you pop a vertex from the stack, you add it to the beginning of an ordered list of vertices. When the traversal ends, the ordered list of vertices will be in topological order. Figure 11-15 traces this algorithm for the graph in Figure 11-13. The resulting topological order is shown in Figure 11-14a.

Spanning Trees

A tree is an undirected, connected graph without cycles

A **tree** is a special kind of undirected graph, one that is connected but has no cycles. The graph in Figure 11-4a is a tree. Although all trees are graphs, not all graphs are trees. The nodes (vertices) of a tree are arranged in a hierarchy that is not required of all graphs.

Action	Stack (bottom → top)	Ordered list
Push a	a	
Push b	a b	
Push c	a b c	
Pop c	a b	c
Push e	a b e	c
Pop e	a b	e c
Pop b	a	b e c
Push d	a d	b e c
Pop d	a	d b e c
Pop a	*(empty)*	a d b e c

Figure 11-15

A trace of the DFS topological-sorting algorithm for the graph in Figure 11-13

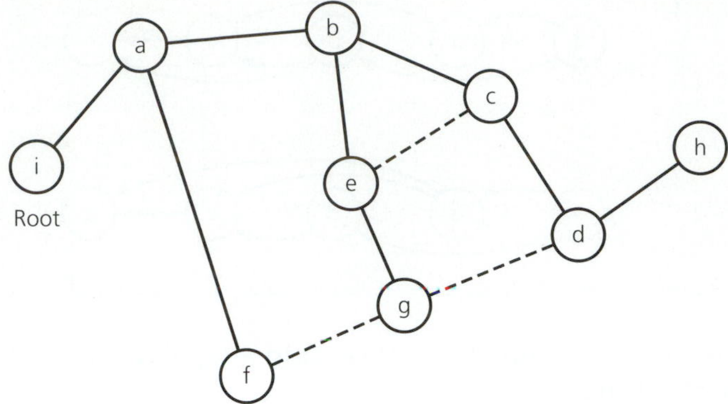

Figure 11-16

A spanning tree for the graph in Figure 11-10

A **spanning tree** of a connected undirected graph *G* is a subgraph of *G* that contains all of *G*'s vertices and enough of its edges to form a tree. For example, Figure 11-16 shows a spanning tree for the graph in Figure 11-10. The dashed lines in Figure 11-16 indicate edges that were omitted from the graph to form the tree. There may be several spanning trees for a given graph.

If you have a connected undirected graph with cycles and you remove edges until there are no cycles, you will obtain a spanning tree for the graph. It is relatively simple to determine whether a graph contains a cycle. One way to make this determination is based on the following observations about undirected graphs:

Observations about undirected graphs

1. **A connected undirected graph that has *N* vertices must have at least *N* − 1 edges.** To establish this fact, recall that a connected graph has a path between every pair of vertices. Suppose that, beginning with *N* vertices, you choose one vertex and draw an edge between it and any other vertex. Next, draw an edge between this second vertex and any other unattached vertex. If you continue this process, you will get a connected graph like the one in Figure 11-1. Notice that if there are *N* vertices, there are *N* − 1 edges. In addition, if you remove an edge, the graph will not be connected.

2. **A connected undirected graph with *N* vertices and *N* − 1 edges cannot contain a cycle.** To see this, begin with the previous observation: To be connected, a graph with *N* vertices must have at least *N* − 1 edges. If a connected graph did have a cycle, you could remove any edge along that cycle and still have a connected graph. Thus, if a connected graph with *N* vertices and *N* − 1 edges did contain a cycle, removing an edge along the cycle would leave you with a connected graph with only *N* − 2 edges, which is impossible.

3. **A connected undirected graph with *N* vertices and more than *N* − 1 edges must contain at least one cycle.** This fact is harder to establish and is left as an exercise. (See Exercise 11 at the end of this chapter.)

Thus, you can determine whether a connected graph contains a cycle simply by counting its vertices and edges.

It follows, then, that a tree, which is a connected undirected graph without cycles, must connect its N nodes with $N - 1$ edges. Thus, to obtain the spanning tree of a connected graph of N vertices, you must remove edges along cycles until there are $N - 1$ edges left.

Two algorithms for determining a spanning tree of a graph are based on the previous traversal algorithms and are presented next. In general, these algorithms will produce different spanning trees for any particular graph.

The DFS spanning tree. One way to determine a spanning tree for a connected undirected graph is to traverse the graph's vertices by using a depth-first search. As you traverse the graph, mark the edges that you follow. After the traversal is complete, the graph's vertices and the marked edges form a spanning tree, which is called the **depth-first search (DFS) spanning tree.** (Alternatively, you can remove the unmarked edges from the graph to form the spanning tree.) Simple modifications to the previous iterative and recursive versions of the procedure *DFS* result in algorithms to create a DFS spanning tree. For example, the recursive algorithm follows:

DFS spanning tree algorithm

```
DFSTree(v)
{ Forms a spanning tree for a connected undirected graph
  beginning at vertex v by using depth-first search.
  Recursive version. }

    Mark v as visited

    for each unvisited vertex u adjacent to v do
    begin
       Mark the edge from u to v
       DFSTree(u)
    end
```

Figure 11-17 shows the DFS spanning tree rooted at vertex *a* for the graph in Figure 11-10. The figure indicates the order in which the procedure visits vertices and marks edges.

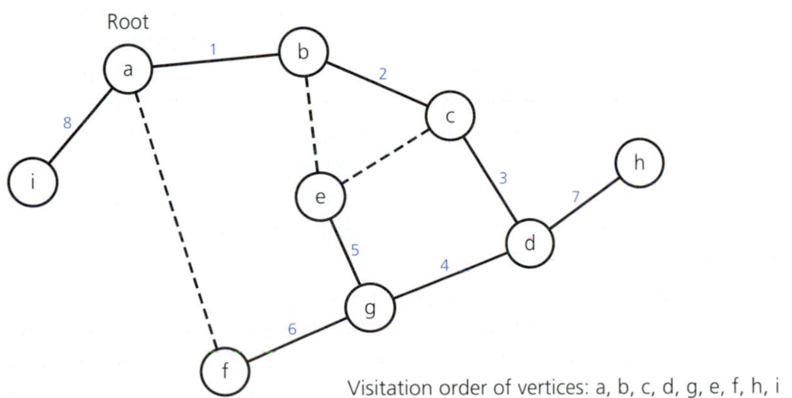

Figure 11-17

The DFS spanning tree rooted at vertex *a* for the graph in Figure 11-10

Figure 11-18

The BFS spanning tree rooted at vertex *a* for the graph in Figure 11-10

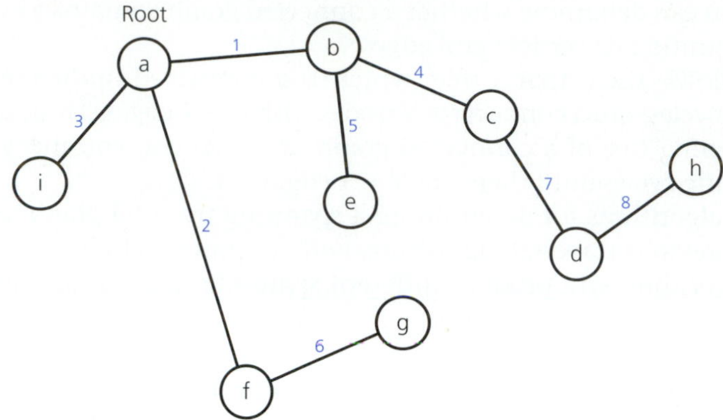

Visitation order of vertices: a, b, f, i, c, e, g, d, h

The BFS spanning tree. Another way to determine a spanning tree for a connected undirected graph is to traverse the graph's vertices by using a breadth-first search. As you traverse the graph, mark the edges that you follow. After the traversal is complete, the graph's vertices and the marked edges form a spanning tree, which is called the **breadth-first search (BFS) spanning tree**. (Alternatively, you can remove the unmarked edges from the graph to form the spanning tree.) You can modify the previous iterative procedure *BFS* by marking the edge between *w* and *u* before you add *u* to the queue. The result will be an algorithm to create a BFS spanning tree.

Figure 11-18 shows the BFS spanning tree rooted at vertex *a* for the graph in Figure 11-10. The figure indicates the order in which the procedure visits vertices and marks edges.

Minimum Spanning Trees

Suppose that a developing country has hired you to design its telephone system to allow all the cities in the country to call one another. Obviously, one solution is to place telephone lines between every pair of cities. However, your engineering team has determined that due to the country's mountainous terrain, it is impossible to put lines between certain pairs of cities. The team's report contains the weighted undirected graph in Figure 11-19. The vertices in the graph represent *N* cities. An edge between two vertices indicates that it is feasible to place a telephone line between the cities that the vertices represent, and each edge's weight represents the installation cost of the telephone line. Note that if this graph is not connected, you will be unable to link all of the cities with a network of telephone lines. The graph in Figure 11-19 is connected, however, making the problem feasible.

If you install a telephone line between each pair of cities that is connected by an edge in the graph, you will certainly solve the problem. However, this solution may be too costly. From observation 1 in the previous section, you know that $N - 1$ is the minimum number of edges necessary

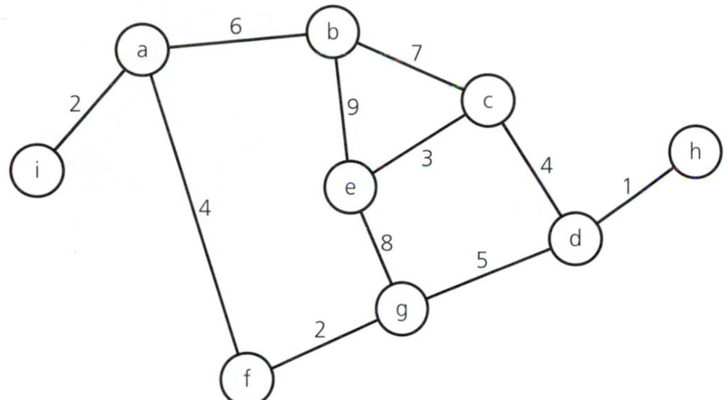

Figure 11-19

A weighted, connected, undirected graph

for a graph of N vertices to be connected. Thus, $N - 1$ is the minimum number of lines that can connect N cities.

If the cost of installing each line is the same, the problem is reduced to one of finding any spanning tree of the graph. The total installation cost, that is, the **cost of the spanning tree**, is the sum of the costs of the edges in the spanning tree. However, suppose that the cost of installing each line varies. Because there may be more than one spanning tree, and because the cost of different trees may vary, you can solve the problem by selecting a spanning tree with the least cost; that is, you select a spanning tree for which the sum of the edge costs is minimal. Such a tree is called the **minimum spanning tree**, and it need not be unique. Although there may be several minimum spanning trees for a particular graph, their costs are equal.

Minimum spanning tree of a connected undirected graph

One simple algorithm that finds a minimum spanning tree begins at any vertex and moves to an unvisited vertex along a least-cost edge. At each stage, the algorithm selects a least-cost edge from among those that begin with a visited node and end with an unvisited node. The following pseudocode describes this algorithm:

Minimum spanning tree algorithm

```
MST(v)
{ Determines a minimum spanning tree for a weighted
  connected undirected graph, whose weights are nonnegative,
  beginning with any vertex v. }

   Mark vertex v as visited and include it in the minimum
     spanning tree

   while there are unvisited vertices do
   begin
      Find the least-cost edge (v, u) from a visited vertex
        v to some unvisited vertex u
      Mark u as visited
      Add the vertex u and the edge (v, u) to the minimum
        spanning tree
   end
```

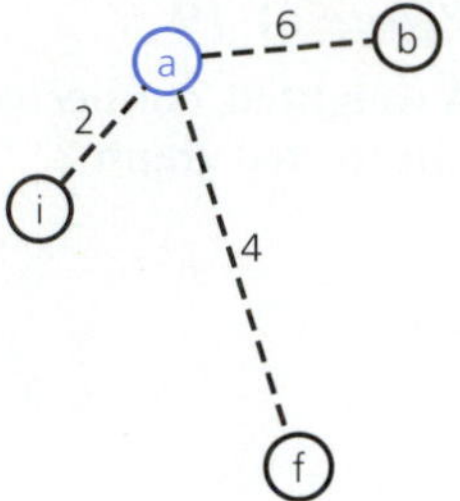

(a) Mark a, consider edges from a

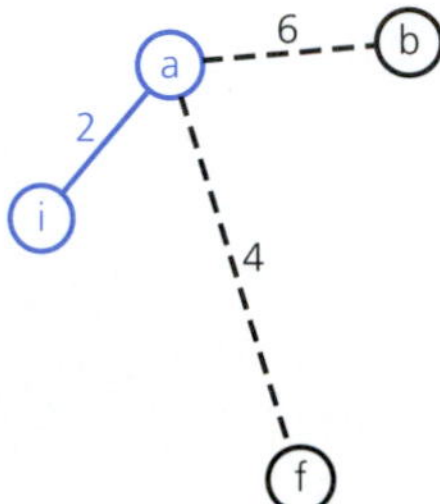

(b) Mark i, include edge (a, i)

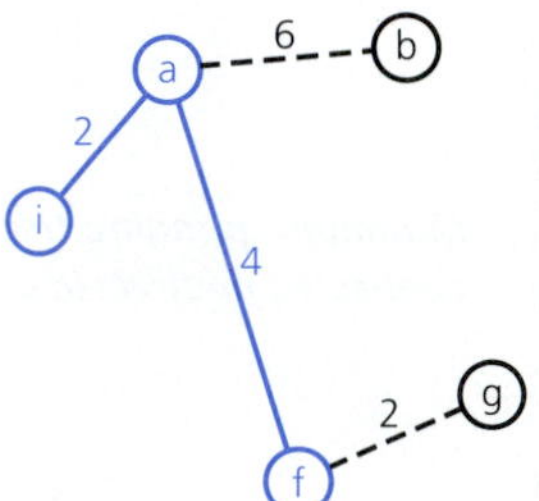

(c) Mark f, include edge (a, f)

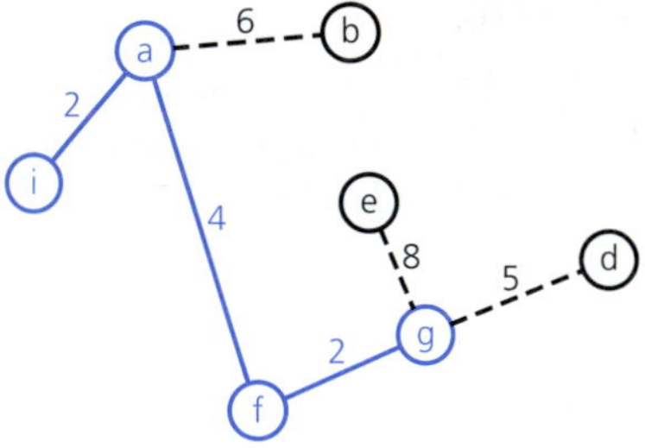

(d) Mark g, include edge (f, g)

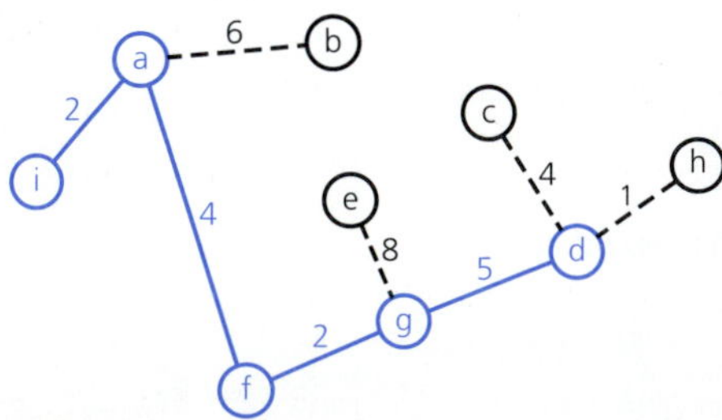

(e) Mark d, include edge (g, d)

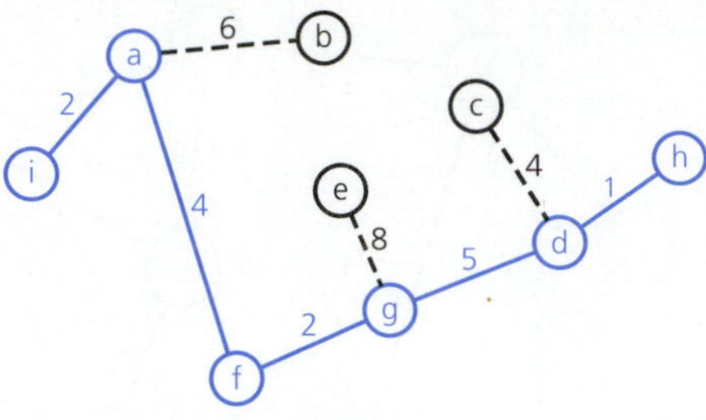

(f) Mark h, include edge (d, h)

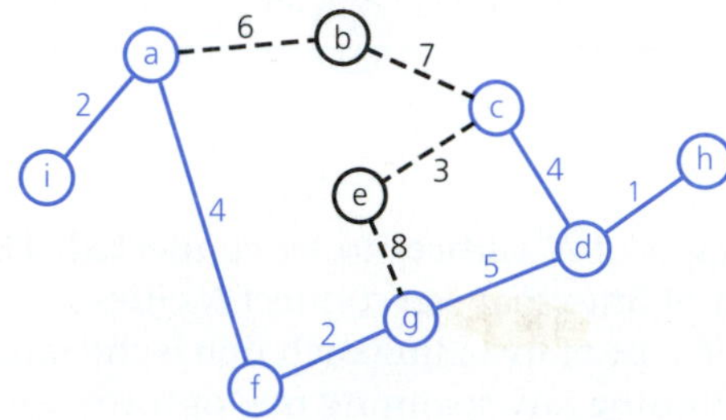

(g) Mark c, include edge (d, c)

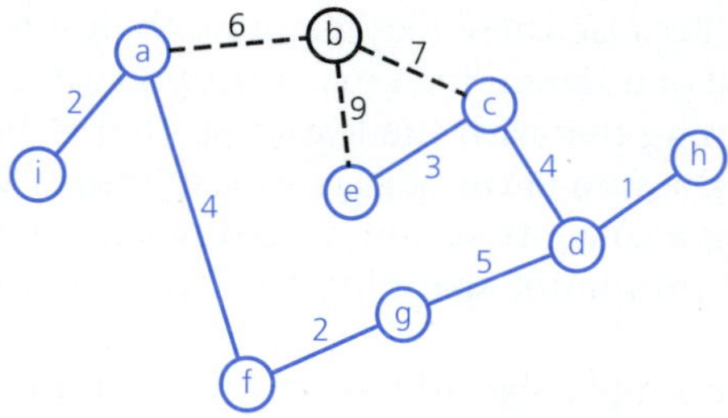

(h) Mark e, include edge (c, e)

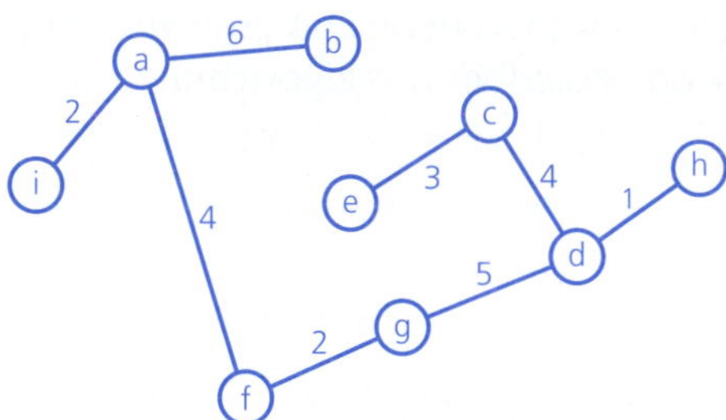

(i) Mark b, include edge (a, b)

Figure 11-20

A trace of the *MST* algorithm for the graph in Figure 11-19 beginning at vertex *a*

Figure 11-20 traces `MST` for the graph in Figure 11-19 beginning at vertex *a*. Edges added to the tree appear as solid lines, while edges under consideration appear as dashed lines.

The fact that `MST` selects a least-cost edge from among those that begin with a visited node and end with an unvisited node does not necessarily imply that the spanning tree will be minimal. However, the proof that `MST` is correct is beyond the scope of this book.

Shortest Paths

Suppose that a weighted directed graph represents a map of airline routes: The vertices are cities, and the edges indicate existing flights between cities. The edge weights represent the mileage between cities (vertices); as such, the weights are not negative. For example, you could combine the graphs in Figures 11-5 and 11-6 to get such a weighted directed graph.

Often for weighted directed graphs you need to know the shortest path between two particular vertices. The **shortest path** between two given vertices in a weighted graph is the path that has the smallest sum of its edge weights. Although we use the term "shortest," realize that the weights could be a measure other than distance, such as the cost of each flight in dollars or the duration of each flight in hours. The sum of the weights of the edges of a path is called the path's **length**, or **weight**, or **cost**.

It turns out that the algorithm to determine the shortest path between two given vertices actually determines the shortest paths between a given vertex—the origin—and *all* other vertices. The algorithm is attributed to E. Dijkstra. For convenience, let the given vertex be vertex 1, and number the other vertices in the graph from 2 to N, as in the graph in Figure 11-21a. Notice the graph's adjacency matrix A in Figure 11-21b.

Finding the shortest paths between vertex 1 and all other vertices

The algorithm uses a set S of selected vertices and an array W, where $W[v]$ is the weight of the shortest (cheapest) path from vertex 1 to vertex v that passes through vertices in S. If v is in S, then the shortest path involves only vertices in S. However, if v is not in S, then v is the only vertex along the path that is not in S. That is, the path ends with an edge from a vertex in S to v. Initially, S contains only vertex 1, and W contains the weights of the single-edge paths from vertex 1 to v for all v. That is, $W[v]$ equals $A[1, v]$ for all v. Thus, initially W is simply the first row of the adjacency matrix A.

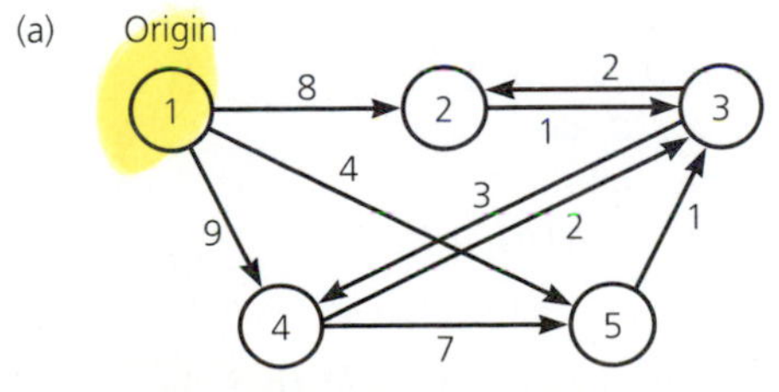

(b)

	1	2	3	4	5
1	0	8	∞	9	4
2	∞	0	1	∞	∞
3	∞	2	0	3	∞
4	∞	∞	2	0	7
5	∞	∞	1	∞	0

Figure 11-21

(a) A weighted directed graph and (b) its adjacency matrix *A*

After this initialization step, you select vertices from those that you have not selected, add them to S, and adjust W as follows. You select a vertex v from among those not in S such that $W[v]$ is a minimum. After adding v to S, you check the values $W[u]$ for all unselected vertices u, that is, for those vertices not in S, to ensure that these values are indeed minimums. In other words, you must determine whether it is possible to reduce $W[u]$—the weight of a path from vertex 1 to vertex u—by passing through the newly selected vertex v.

To make this determination, break the path from 1 to u into two pieces and find their weights as follows:

$W[v]$ = weight of the shortest path from 1 to v

$A[v, u]$ = weight of the edge from v to u

Then compare $W[u]$ with $W[v] + A[v, u]$ and let

$W[u]$ = the smaller of the values $W[u]$ and $W[v] + A[v, u]$

The pseudocode for **Dijkstra's shortest-path algorithm** is as follows:

The shortest-path algorithm

Loop invariant

```
ShortestPath(G, W)
{ Finds the minimum-cost path between vertex 1 and all other
  vertices in a weighted directed graph G of N vertices.
  G's weights are nonnegative. }

    { Step 1: initialization }
    S := [1]
    for v := 1 to N do
       W[v] := A[1, v]

    { Steps 2 through N }
    { Invariant : For v not in S, W[v] is the smallest
      weight of all paths from 1 to v that pass through only
      vertices in S before reaching v. For v in S, W[v] is
      the smallest weight of all paths from 1 to v
      (including paths outside S), and the shortest path
      from 1 to v lies entirely in S. }
    for Step := 2 to N do
    begin
       Find the smallest W[v] such that v is not in S
       S := S + [v]    { Add v to S }

       { Check W[u] for all u not in S }
       for all vertices u not in S do
          if W[u] > W[v] + A[v, u]
             then W[u] := W[v] + A[v, u]
    end  { for }
```

The loop invariant states that once a vertex v is placed in S, $W[v]$ is the weight of the absolutely shortest path from 1 to v and will not change.

Step	v	S	W[1]	W[2]	W[3]	W[4]	W[5]
1	–	[1]	0	8	∞	9	4
2	5	[1, 5]	0	8	5	9	4
3	3	[1, 5, 3]	0	7	5	8	4
4	2	[1, 5, 3, 2]	0	7	5	8	4
5	4	[1, 5, 3, 2, 4]	0	7	5	8	4

Figure 11-22

A trace of the shortest-path algorithm applied to the graph in Figure 11-21a

Figure 11-22 traces the algorithm for the graph in Figure 11-21a. The algorithm takes the following steps:

A trace of the shortest-path algorithm

Step 1. S is initialized to 1 and W is initialized to the first row of the graph's adjacency matrix, shown in Figure 11-21b.

Step 2. $W[5] = 4$ is the smallest value in W, ignoring $W[1]$ because 1 is in S. Thus, $v = 5$, so add 5 to S. For vertices not in S, that is, for u = 2, 3, and 4, check whether it is shorter to go from 1 to 5 and then along an edge to u instead of directly from 1 to u along an edge. For vertices 2 and 4, it is not shorter to include vertex 5 in the path. However, for vertex 3 notice that $W[3] = \infty > W[5] + A[5, 3] = 4 + 1 = 5$. Therefore, replace $W[3]$ with 5. You can also verify this conclusion by examining the graph directly, as Figure 11-23a shows.

Step 3. $W[3] = 5$ is the smallest value in W, ignoring $W[1]$ and $W[5]$ because 1 and 5 are in S. Thus, $v = 3$, so add 3 to S. For vertices not in S, that is, for $u = 2$ and 4, check whether it is shorter to go from 1 to 3 and then along an edge to u instead of directly from 1 to u along an edge. (See parts b and c of Figure 11-23.) Notice that

$W[2] = 8 > W[3] + A[3, 2] = 5 + 2 = 7$. Therefore, replace $W[2]$ with 7.

$W[4] = 9 > W[3] + A[3, 4] = 5 + 3 = 8$. Therefore, replace $W[4]$ with 8.

Step 4. $W[2] = 7$ is the smallest value in W, ignoring $W[1]$, $W[3]$, and $W[5]$ because 1, 3, and 5 are in S. Thus, $v = 2$, so add 2 to S. For vertex 4, which is the only vertex not in S, notice that

$W[4] = 8 < W[2] + A[2, 4] = 7 + \infty$

as Figure 11-23d shows. Therefore, leave $W[4]$ as it is.

Step 5. The only remaining vertex not in S is 4, so add it to S and stop.

Does this algorithm work? That is, are the weights in W the smallest possible? The answer to both questions is yes as long as the loop invariant is true. The proof that the loop invariant is true is by induction on `Step`, and is left as a difficult exercise. (See Exercise 16.)

Some Difficult Problems

The next three applications of graphs have solutions that are beyond the scope of this book.

Figure 11-23

Checking *W*[*u*] by examining the graph: (a) *W*[3] in Step 2; (b) *W*[2] in Step 3; (c) *W*[4] in Step 3; (d) *W*[4] in Step 4

(a)

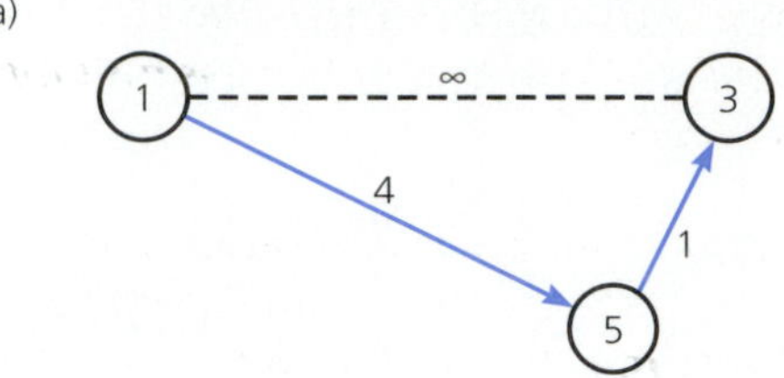

Step 2. The path (1, 5, 3) is shorter than (1, 3)

(b)

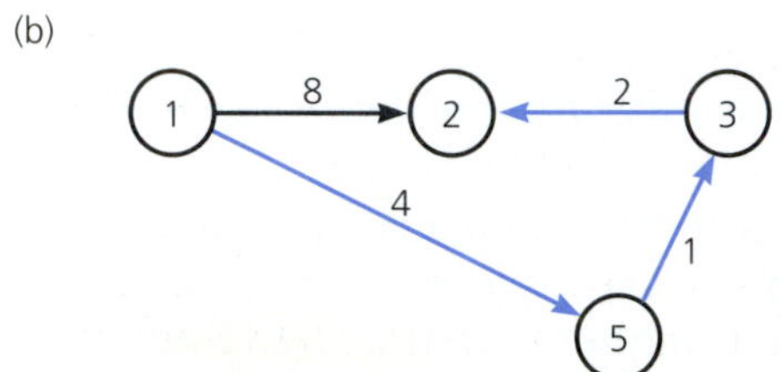

Step 3. The path (1, 5, 3, 2) is shorter than (1, 2)

(c)

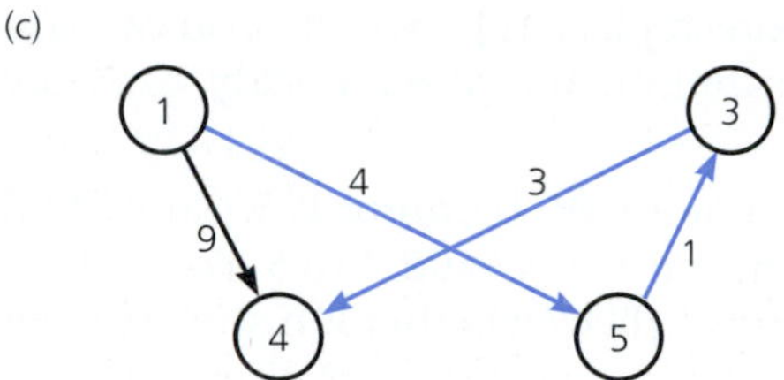

Step 3 continued. The path (1, 5, 3, 4) is shorter than (1, 4)

(d)

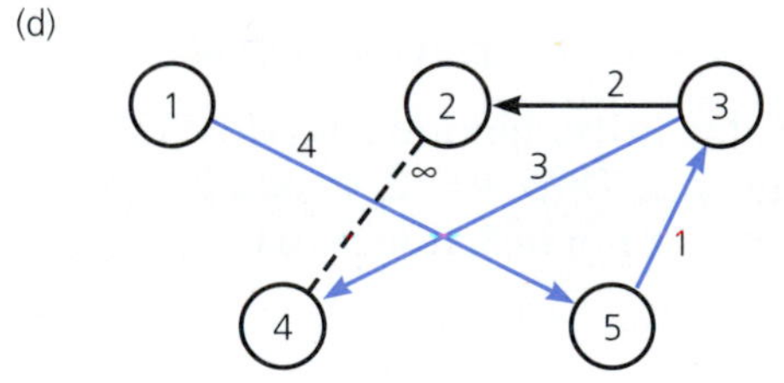

Step 4. The path (1, 5, 3, 4) is shorter than (1, 5, 3, 2, 4)

Circuit **The traveling salesperson problem.** A **circuit** is a path that begins at a vertex *v*, passes through every vertex in the graph exactly once, and terminates at *v*. Obviously, a graph that is not connected cannot contain a circuit. However, determining whether or not an arbitrary graph contains a circuit can be difficult. A well-known variation of this problem—the traveling salesperson problem—involves a weighted graph that represents a road map. Each edge has an associated cost, such as the mileage between cities or the time required to drive from one city to the next. The salesperson must begin at an origin city, visit every other city exactly once, and return to the origin city. However, the circuit traveled must be the least expensive. Unfortunately for this traveler, solving the problem is no easier than determining whether a circuit exists.

The three utilities problem. Suppose that there are three houses *A*, *B*, and *C* and three utilities *X*, *Y*, and *Z* (such as telephone, water, and electricity). If the houses and the utilities are vertices in a graph, is it possible to connect each house to each utility with edges that do not cross one another? The answer to this question is no.

Planar graph

A graph is **planar** if you can draw it in a plane in at least one way so that no two edges cross. The generalization of the three utilities problem determines whether or not a given graph is planar. Making this determination has many important applications. For example, a graph can represent an electronic circuit where the vertices represent components and the edges represent the connections between components. Is it possible to design the circuit so that the connections do not cross? The solutions to these problems are also beyond the scope of this book.

The four-color problem. Given a planar graph, can you color the vertices so that no adjacent vertices have the same color, if you use at most four colors? For example, the graph in Figure 11-10 is planar because none of its edges cross. You can solve the coloring problem for this graph by using only three colors. Color vertices *a*, *c*, *g*, and *h* red, color vertices *b*, *d*, *f*, and *i* blue, and color vertex *e* green.

The answer to our question is yes, but it is difficult to prove. In fact, this problem was posed more than a century before it was proven in the 1970s with the use of a computer.

SUMMARY

1. **Graph searching is an important application of stacks. Depth-first search is a graph-traversal algorithm that uses a stack to keep track of the sequence of visited vertices. It goes as deep into the graph as it can before backtracking. Breadth-first search uses a queue to keep track of the sequence of visited vertices. It visits all possible adjacent vertices before traversing further into the graph.**
2. **The two most common implementations of a graph are the adjacency matrix and the adjacency list. Each has its relative advantages and disadvantages. The choice should depend on the needs of the given application.**
3. **Topological sorting produces a linear order of the vertices in a directed graph without cycles. Vertex *x* precedes vertex *y* if there is a directed edge from *x* to *y* in the graph.**
4. **Trees are connected undirected graphs without cycles. A spanning**

tree of a connected undirected graph is a subgraph that contains all the graph's vertices and enough of its edges to form a tree. DFS and BFS traversals produce DFS and BFS spanning trees.

5. **A minimum spanning tree is a spanning tree for a weighted undirected graph whose edge-cost sum is minimal. There may be several minimum spanning trees for a particular graph. However, their edge-cost sums will be equal.**
6. **The shortest path between two vertices in a weighted directed graph is the path that has the smallest sum of its edge weights.**

COMMON PITFALLS / DEBUGGING

1. **When searching a graph, realize that the algorithm might take wrong turns. For example, you must eliminate the possibility of cycling within the algorithm; the algorithm must be able to backtrack when it hits a dead end.**

SELF-TEST EXERCISES

1. Describe the graphs in Figure 11-24. For example, are they directed? Connected? Complete? Weighted?
2. Use the depth-first strategy and the breadth-first strategy to traverse the graph in Figure 11-24a, beginning with vertex 1. List the vertices in the order in which each traversal visits them.
3. Write the adjacency matrix for the graph in Figure 11-24a.
4. Add an edge to the directed graph in Figure 11-13 that runs from vertex *d* to vertex *b*. Write all possible topological orders for the vertices in this new graph.

Figure 11-24

Graphs for Self-Test Exercises 1, 2, and 3

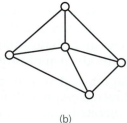

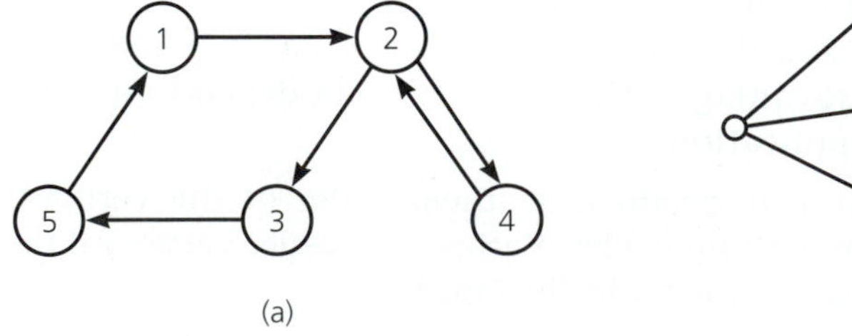

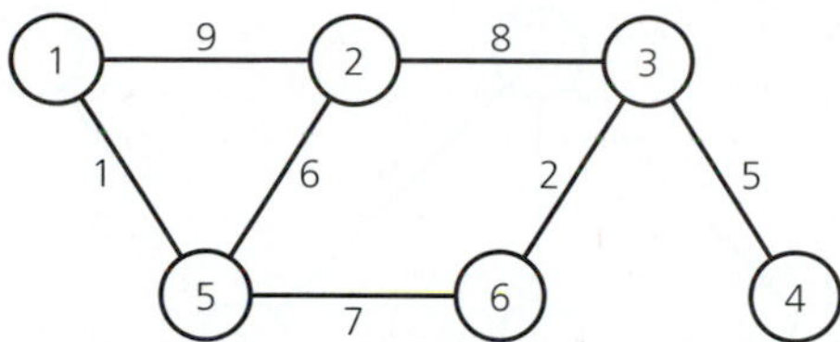

Figure 11-25

A graph for Self-Test Exercises 6 and 7 and Exercises 1 and 3

5. Is it possible for a connected undirected graph with 5 vertices and 4 edges to contain a cycle? Explain.

6. Draw the DFS spanning tree whose root is 1 for the graph in Figure 11-25.

7. Draw the minimum spanning tree whose root is 1 for the graph in Figure 11-25.

8. What are the shortest paths from vertex 1 to each vertex of the graph in Figure 11-21a? (Note the weights of these paths in Figure 11-22.)

EXERCISES

When given a choice of vertices to visit, the traversals in the following exercises should visit vertices in sorted order.

1. Write the adjacency matrix for the weighted graph in Figure 11-25.

2. Consider the directed graph in Figure 11-26. Give the adjacency matrix and adjacency list representations of the graph.

3. Use both the depth-first strategy and the breadth-first strategy to traverse the graph in Figure 11-25, beginning with the vertex 1, and the graph in Figure 11-27, beginning with the vertex *a*. List the vertices in the order in which each traversal visits them.

4. Trace the DFS topological sorting algorithm and indicate the resulting topological order of the vertices for each graph in Figure 11-28.

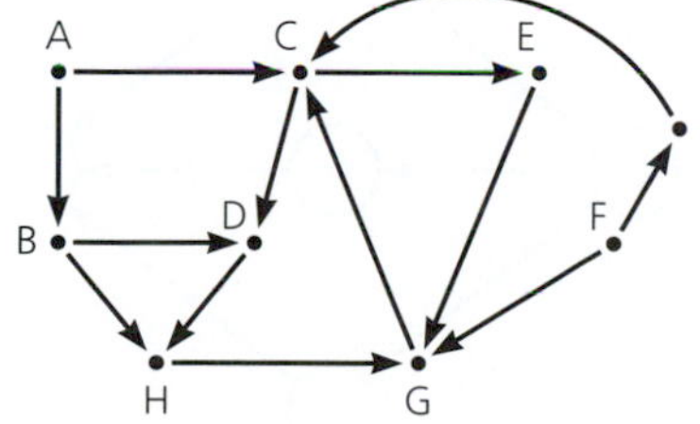

Figure 11-26

A graph for Exercise 2

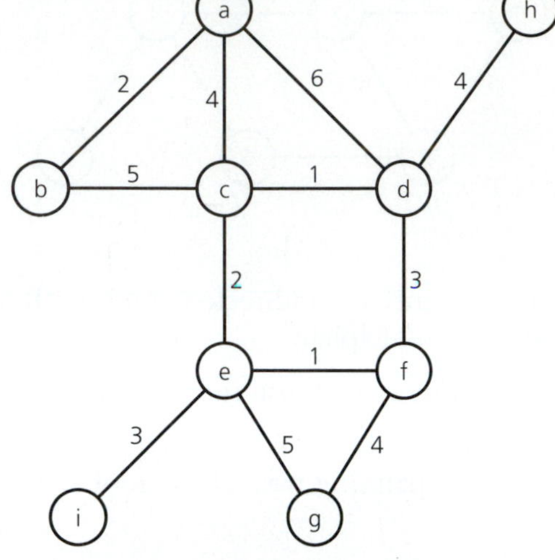

Figure 11-27
A graph for Exercises 3 and 6

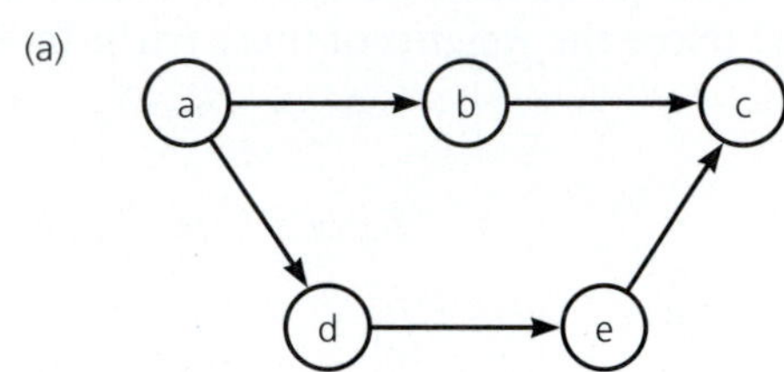

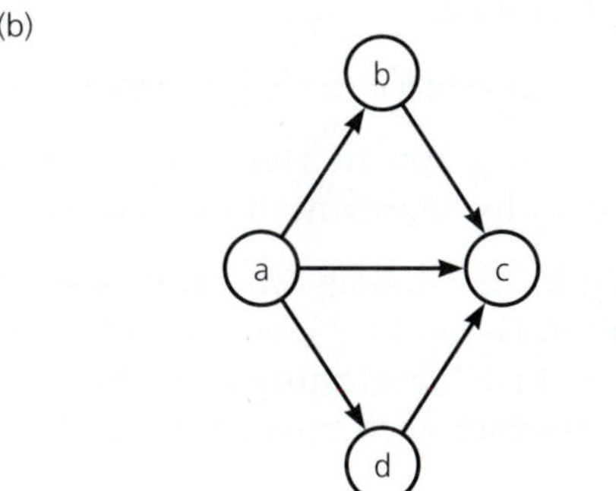

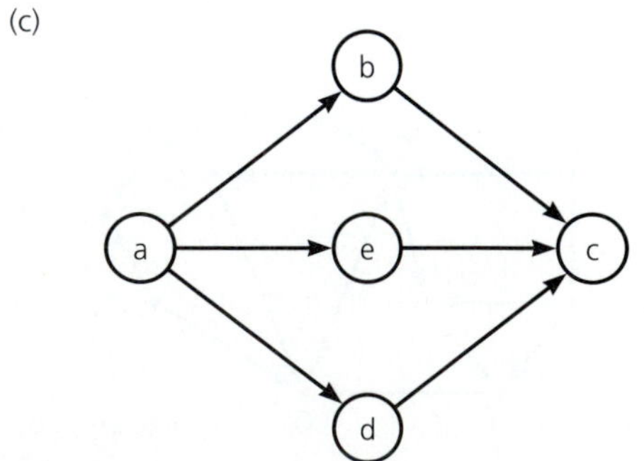

Figure 11-28
Graphs for Exercise 4

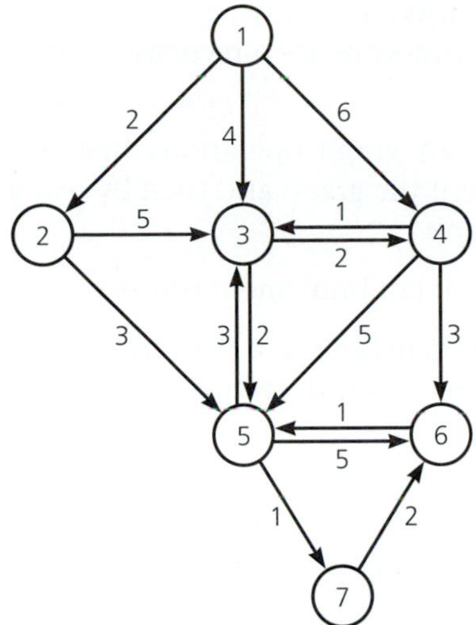

Figure 11-29

A graph for Exercise 8

5. Trace the DFS and BFS spanning tree algorithms, beginning with vertex *a* of the graph in Figure 11-10, and show that the spanning trees are the trees in Figures 11-17 and 11-18, respectively.

6. Draw the DFS and BFS spanning trees rooted at *a* for the graph in Figure 11-27. Then draw the minimum spanning tree rooted at *a* for this graph.

7. Draw the minimum spanning tree for the graph in Figure 11-19 when you start with (a) vertex *g* and (b) vertex *c*.

8. Trace the shortest-path algorithm for the graph in Figure 11-29.

9. Write Pascal procedures that determine the DFS and BFS spanning trees for a connected graph.

10. Implement the shortest-path procedure in Pascal. How can you modify this procedure so that any vertex can be the origin?

11. Prove that a connected undirected graph with N vertices and more than $N - 1$ edges must contain at least one cycle. *Hint:* Take an arbitrary connected undirected graph with N vertices and $N - 1$ edges, which, because of observation 2 in the section "Spanning Trees," you know cannot contain a cycle, and add any edge.

***12.** Prove that a graph-traversal algorithm visits every vertex in the graph if and only if the graph is connected, regardless of where the traversal starts.

***13.** Although the DFS traversal algorithm has a simple recursive form, a recursive BFS traversal algorithm is not straightforward.

a. Explain why this fact is true.
b. Write the pseudocode for a recursive version of the BFS traversal algorithm.

14. Implement the ADT graph operations first by using an adjacency matrix to represent the graph and then by using an adjacency list to represent the graph.

15. Repeat Exercise 14, but implement the ADT graph as an object.

*16. Prove that the loop invariant of Dijkstra's shortest-path algorithm is true by using a proof by induction on `Step`.

CHAPTER 12

Priority Queues and Heaps

PREVIEW This chapter introduces an important variation of the ADT table, the priority queue. This ADT supports operations that allow the item with the largest value to be retrieved and deleted easily. Although you can implement a priority queue by using a binary search tree, a simpler tree structure, known as a heap, is often more appropriate for this purpose. The case study in this chapter is an enhancement of the case study in Chapter 3.

The table is one of the most useful abstract data types that you have studied. In addition to the basic table presented in Chapter 10, there are several classical variations of the ADT table. This chapter presents one of these variants, the ADT priority queue.

The chapter contains two main sections. The first defines a priority queue and develops implementations for it. The second section presents a case study that illustrates modifications to the videocassette inventory system originally developed in Chapter 3. One of the modifications to the system serves to illustrate an application of the ADT priority queue.

A VARIATION OF THE ADT TABLE: THE ADT PRIORITY QUEUE

ENTRIES ORDERED BY PRIORITY

The **priority queue** is an abstract data type whose operations make it useful in the solution to many problems. For example, it is desirable to enhance the videocassette inventory system developed in Chapter 3 so that it manages the repair of cassettes. If a cassette in the inventory is in need of repair, it is placed on a *repair queue*. When a worker becomes available to fix a cassette, a cassette is selected from the repair queue, as Figure 12-1 illustrates. The videocassette dealer wants the tapes that are most important to the inventory to be repaired as quickly as possible. That is, the dealer does not necessarily want the *first in, first out* rule of a standard queue to govern the behavior of the repair queue. Rather, the dealer would like to assign some measure of importance, or **priority**, to the cassettes awaiting repair and to select for repair the tape with the highest priority.

A priority queue is not FIFO

A priority queue orders by priority values

When a cassette first enters the repair queue, the videocassette dealer assigns a **priority value** *P*, which reflects the urgency with which the tape should be repaired. What quantity should the dealer use for this priority

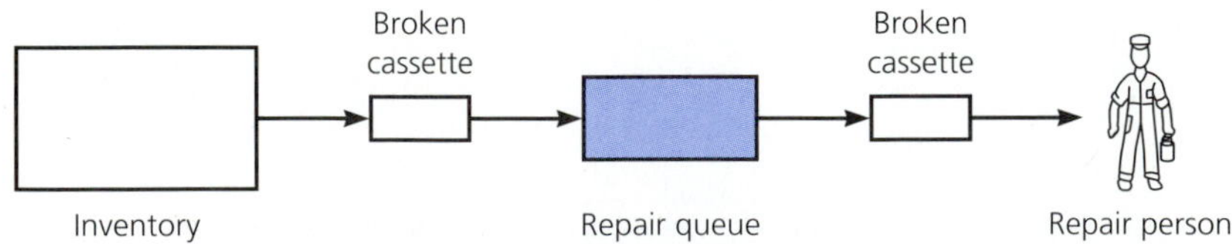

Figure 12-1
A repair queue

value? There are many reasonable possibilities, including those that take into account the title's popularity, its selling price, and the number of copies of the title currently in the inventory. Recall from the case study in Chapter 3 that the inventory system maintains a *have value* and a *want value* for each title. The have value of a title is the number of copies of the title currently in stock. The want value is the number of copies that should be in stock. The want value, which presumably reflects the popularity of a title, is used to determine how many new copies should be ordered—enough are ordered so that the have value is brought up to the want value. Thus, you could use, for example, the following ratio for a cassette's priority value:

$$P = \frac{\text{want value of title}}{\text{have value of title}}$$

To summarize, when a defective cassette is found, the dealer assigns it a priority value and places it on the repair queue. The next available worker selects the cassette with the highest priority value from the repair queue. This management of the repair queue describes an ADT known as a priority queue. More formally, a priority queue is an abstract data type that supports the following operations:

KEY CONCEPTS

ADT Priority Queue Operations

```
CreatePQueue(PQ)
{ Creates an empty priority queue PQ. }

PQueueIsEmpty(PQ)
{ Determines whether priority queue PQ is empty. }

PQueueInsert(PQ, NewItem)
{ Adds NewItem to priority queue PQ. }

PQueueRemove(PQ, PriorityItem)
{ Removes and retrieves from priority queue PQ the item with
  the highest priority value. }
```

***`PQueueRemove`* is the difference between a priority queue and a table**

These operations resemble a subset of the ADT table operations. The significant difference is the `PQueueRemove` operation. While the sequence `TableRetrieve-TableDelete` of table operations allows you to retrieve and delete an item that has a specified value in its search key, `PQueue-Remove` allows you to retrieve and delete the item with the highest priority value. Notice that `PQueueRemove`, unlike `TableRetrieve` and `Table-Delete`, is not told the value in question. Since in general you will not know what the highest priority value is, `TableRetrieve` and `Table-`

`Delete` could not easily perform this task. On the other hand, you could not use `PQueueRemove` to retrieve and delete an item with some specified value.

The ADT priority queue and the ADT table are thus both similar and dissimilar, a fact that is reflected in their implementations. A binary search tree implementation is good for both a table and a priority queue. On the other hand, this chapter develops an implementation that, for many applications, is the most appropriate one for a priority queue but that is not at all appropriate as an implementation of a table.

Possible implementations

To begin, consider some of the table implementations as implementations for a priority queue. The sorted linear implementations are appropriate if the number of items in the priority queue is small. The array-based implementation would maintain the items sorted in ascending order of priority value, so that the item with the highest priority value would be at the end of the array, as Figure 12-2a illustrates. Thus, `PQueueRemove` sim-

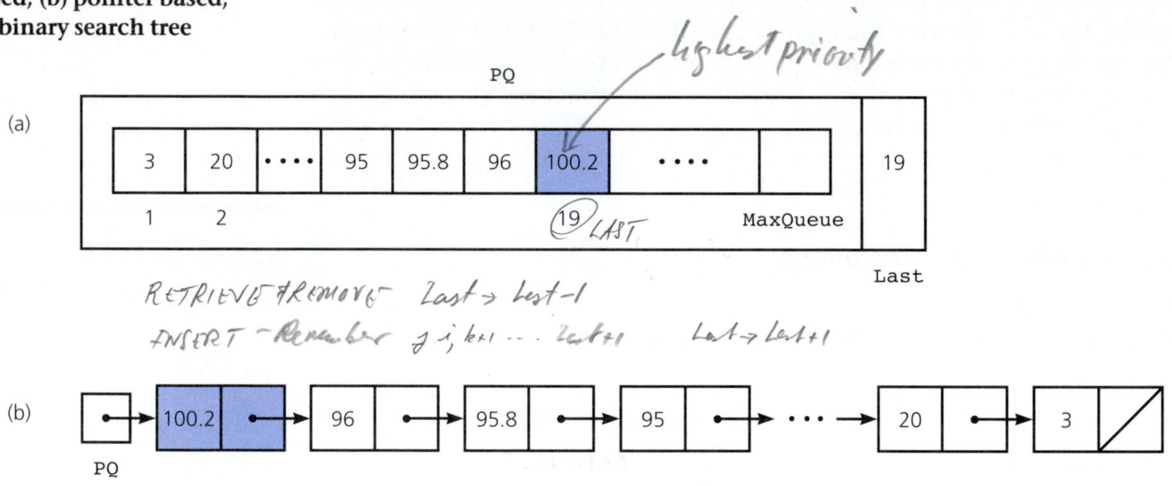

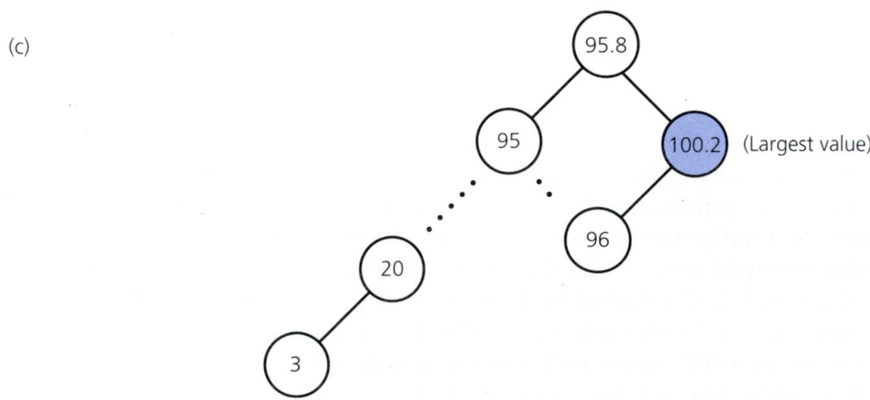

Figure 12-2

Implementations of the ADT priority queue: (a) array based; (b) pointer based; (c) binary search tree

ply returns the item in `PQ[Last]` and decrements `Last`. However, the `PQueueInsert` operation, after using a binary search to find the correct position for the insertion, must shift the array elements to make room for the new item.

The pointer-based implementation (Figure 12-2b) maintains the items sorted in descending order of priority value, so that the item with the highest priority value is at the beginning of the list. Thus, `PQueueRemove` simply returns the item pointed to by `PQ` and changes `PQ` to point to the next item. The `PQueueInsert` operation, however, must traverse the list to find the correct position for the insertion. Thus, the linear implementations of priority queues suffer from the same problems as the linear implementations of tables.

Instead, consider a binary search tree as an implementation of a priority queue, as Figure 12-2c illustrates. Although the `PQueueInsert` operation is the same as `TableInsert`, the `PQueueRemove` operation has no direct analogue among the table operations. `PQueueRemove` must locate the item with the highest priority value, without knowing what this value is. The task is not difficult, however, because this item is always in the rightmost node of the tree. (Why?) You thus need only follow `RChild` pointers until you encounter a node with a `nil RChild` pointer. (A procedure analogous to the binary search tree's `ProcessLeftmost` can accomplish this task.) The removal of this node from the tree is particularly easy because it has at most one child.

The binary search tree is thus a good implementation of a priority queue. For some applications, however, you can do even better. A **heap** is an important array-based implementation of a priority queue. Because it is array based, a heap is appropriate only for applications in which a fixed-size data structure is not a problem.

An Array-Based Representation of Complete Trees

Chapter 10 discussed both array-based and pointer-based representations of a binary tree. There is another array-based representation of a binary tree that is useful, provided that the tree is complete. As you will see, a heap is a binary tree that happens to be complete.

Recall the definition of a complete binary tree from Chapter 10:

Reminder: a complete binary tree

> A binary tree T of height h is **complete**
>
> 1. If all nodes at level $h-2$ and above have two children each
> 2. If, when a node has a right descendent at level h, all leaves in its left subtree are at level h

Recall that criterion 2 of this definition formalizes the requirement that level h be filled in from left to right.

Figure 12-3 shows a complete tree with nine nodes. The nodes are numbered according to a standard level-by-level numbering scheme. The root is numbered 1, and the children of the root (the next level of the tree) are

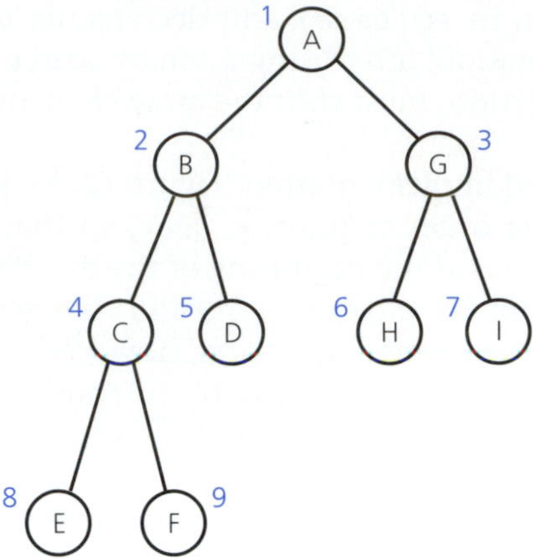

Figure 12-3

Level-by-level numbering of a complete binary tree

numbered left to right 2 and 3. The nodes at the next level are numbered left to right 4, 5, 6, and 7, and so forth. This level-by-level numbering scheme for a complete tree allows you to conveniently develop a simple array-based implementation.

The array-based representation of a complete binary tree is rather elegant. If *Tree* is an array that represents the tree, then *Tree[1]* contains node 1 (the root), *Tree[2]* contains node 2, and so forth, as Figure 12-4 illustrates. The key observation is that, given any node, you can easily locate both of its children and its parent. If you study the tree in Figure 12-3, you will observe that for any node i, its left child (if it exists) is node $2 * i$, and its right child (if it exists) is node $2 * i + 1$. Further, the parent of node i (assuming the node is not the root) is node *i div* 2. Because the array representation stores node i in *Tree[i]*, it is quite simple to go from any node to either of its children or to its parent.

An array can represent a complete binary tree, if you know the maximum number of nodes in the tree

For this array-based representation to be appropriate for a binary tree, two conditions must occur. First, the tree must be complete. If nodes were missing from the middle of the tree, the numbering scheme would be thrown off, and there would be ambiguity as to who was the child of whom. In addition, because the representation is array based, you must know the maximum number of nodes.

Figure 12-4

An array representation of the complete binary tree in Figure 12-3

1	A
2	B
3	G
4	C
5	D
6	H
7	I
8	E
9	F

Heaps

A heap differs from a binary search tree in two ways

A **heap** is a data structure similar to a binary search tree, although it differs from a binary search tree in two significant ways. First, while you can view a binary search tree as sorted, a heap is ordered in a much weaker sense. However, the manner in which a heap is ordered is sufficient for the efficient performance of the priority queue operations (`CreatePQueue`, `PQueueIsEmpty`, `PQueueInsert`, and `PQueueRemove`). The second significant difference is that while binary search trees come in many different shapes, heaps are always complete binary trees. As a consequence, if you know the maximum size of a heap, you can use the array-based implementation that was just described.

Heap

A **heap** is a complete binary tree

1. That is empty

or

2a. In which the priority value in the root is greater than or equal to the priority value in each of its children, and

2b. In which both subtrees of the root are themselves heaps

For example, Figure 12-5 shows a heap along with its array representation. Notice that, unlike the node values in a binary search tree, the value of each node in a heap is greater than or equal to the value in each of its children. Further, in a heap there is no relationship between the values of the children; that is, you do not know which child contains the larger value.

A Heap As an Implementation of a Priority Queue

Consider how you can use a heap to implement the priority-queue operations `PQueueRemove` and `PQueueInsert`. Let the priority queue `PQ` be a record with two fields:

Priority queue as a record with two fields

- `Items`: an array of priority-queue items
- `Last`: an integer that indicates the number of items in the priority queue

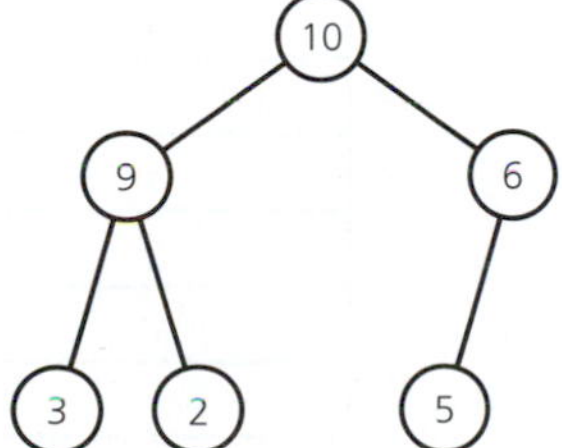

1	10
2	9
3	6
4	3
5	2
6	5

Figure 12-5

A heap with its array representation

The array *Items* corresponds to the array-based representation of a tree, as was described earlier. (To simplify the following examples, assume that the priority-queue items are integers.)

First consider the *PQueueRemove* operation. Where is the largest value in the heap? Because the value of every node is greater than or equal to that of either of its children, the largest value must be in the root of the tree. Thus, the first step of the *PQueueRemove* operation is

***PQueueRemove*'s first step**

```
{ return the item in the root }
Return the item in PQ.Items[1]
```

That was easy, but you must do more.

When you remove the largest value, you are left with two disjoint heaps, as Figure 12-6a indicates. Therefore, you need to transform the nodes that remain after the root is removed back into a heap. To begin this transformation, you take the item in the last node of the tree and place it in the root as follows:

***PQueueRemove*'s second step produces a semiheap**

```
{ copy the item from the last node into the root }
PQ.Items[1] := PQ.Items[Last]
```

Figure 12-6

(a) Disjoint heaps; (b) a semiheap

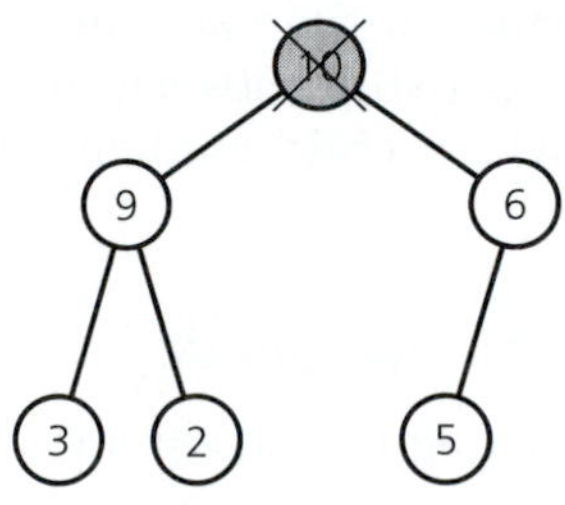

1	~~10~~
2	9
3	6
4	3
5	2
6	5

(a)

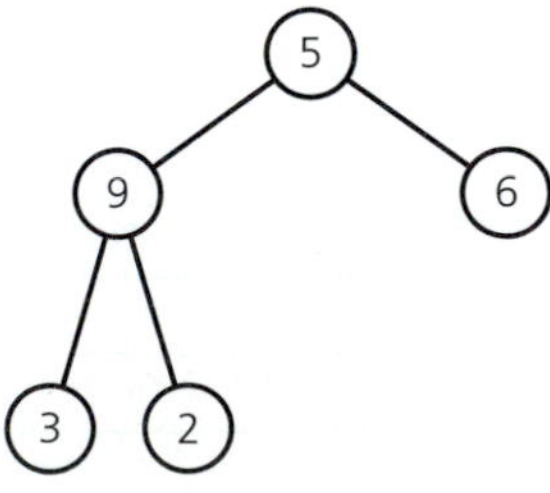

1	5
2	9
3	6
4	3
5	2

(b)

```
  { remove the last node }
  PQ.Last := PQ.Last - 1
```

As Figure 12-6b suggests, the result of this step is *not* necessarily a heap. It is, however, a complete binary tree whose left and right subtrees are both heaps. The only problem is that the item in the root may be (and usually is) out of place. Such a structure is called a **semiheap**. You thus need a way to transform a semiheap into a heap. One strategy allows the value in the root to *trickle down* the tree until it reaches a node in which it will not be out of place; that is, the value will come to rest in the first node where it would be greater than (or equal to) the value of each of its children. To accomplish this, you first compare the value in the root of the semiheap to the values in its children. If the root's value is smaller than the values of both of its children, you swap the item in the root with that of the larger child. (By larger child, we mean the child whose value is greater than the value of the other child.)

Figure 12-7 illustrates the `PQueueRemove` operation. Although the value 5 trickles down to its correct position after only one swap, in general, more swaps may be necessary. In fact, once the values in the root and the larger child *C* have been swapped, *C* becomes the root of a semiheap. (Notice that node *C* does not move; only its value changes.) This strategy suggests the following recursive algorithm:

`PQueueRemove`'s final step transforms the semiheap into a heap

```
Adjust(H, Root)
{ Converts the semiheap H rooted at position Root into a
  heap. }

  { Recursively trickle the item at position Root down to
    its proper position by swapping it with its larger
    child, if the child is larger than the item. If (2 *
    Root) > H.Last, then the item is at a leaf and nothing
    needs to be done. }

  if (root is not a leaf, i.e. 2 * Root <= H.Last) and
     ((the value in the root, stored in H.Items[Root]) <
     (the value of its children, stored in H.Items[2*Root]
     and H.Items[2*Root + 1]))

     then
     begin
       Let Child indicate the larger of the two children nodes

       { swap value in node Child with value in the root }
       Swap(H.Items[Root], H.Items[Child])

       { recursively call Adjust on the semiheap
           rooted at node Child }
       Adjust(H, Child)
     end

     else the value is in the correct place and you are done
```

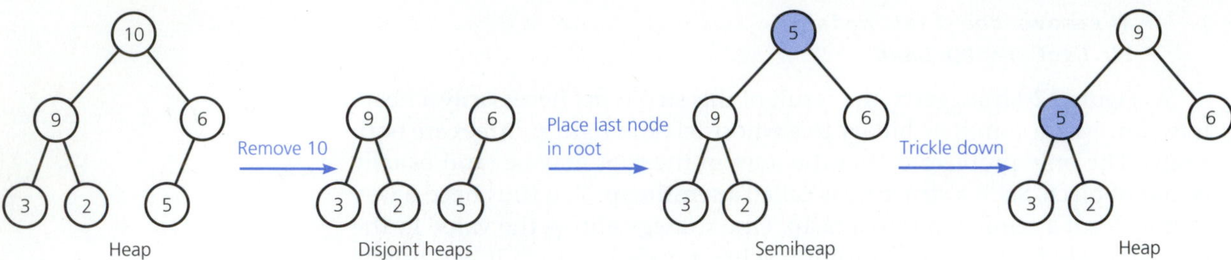

Figure 12-7

Removal from a heap

Figure 12-8 illustrates the recursive calls to the procedure `Adjust`. The entire `PQueueRemove` operation uses `Adjust` as follows:

```
PQueueRemove(PQ)

  { return the item in the root }
  Return the item in PQ.Items[1]

  { copy the item from the last node into the root }
  PQ.Items[1] := PQ.Items[PQ.Last]

  { remove the last node }
  PQ.Last := PQ.Last - 1

  { transform the semiheap back into a heap }
  Adjust(PQ, 1)
```

`PQueueRemove`'s efficiency

Before developing the insertion algorithm, consider briefly the efficiency of `PQueueRemove`. Because the tree is stored in an array, the removal of a node requires that you swap array elements rather than simply change a few pointers. These swaps may concern you, but they do not necessarily indicate that the algorithm is inefficient. You must ask, what is the largest number of array elements that you might have to swap? `PQueueRemove` first copies the item in the last node of the tree into the root. `Adjust` then trickles this item down the tree until its appropriate

Figure 12-8

Recursive calls to the procedure `Adjust`

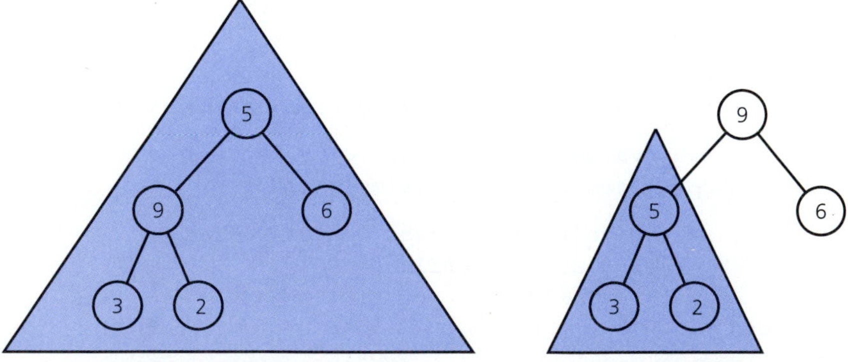

place is found. The key observation is that this item travels down a single path from the root to, at worst, a leaf. Therefore, the number of array items that `Adjust` must swap is no greater than the height of the tree. Because the height of a complete binary tree with N nodes is always approximately $\log_2 N$, `PQueueRemove` is in fact quite efficient.

`PQueueRemove` swaps at most $\lceil \log_2(N + 1) \rceil$ items

The strategy for the `PQueueInsert` algorithm is the opposite of that for `PQueueRemove`. A new item is inserted at the bottom of the tree, and it trickles up to its proper place, as Figure 12-9 illustrates. It is easy to trickle up a node, because the parent of node *i*—other than a root—is always stored in `PQ.Items[i div 2]`. The pseudocode for `PQueueInsert` follows.

Insertion strategy

```
PQueueInsert(PQ, NewItem)

   { insert the new item into the last position of the tree }
   PQ.Last := PQ.Last + 1
   PQ.Items[PQ.Last] := NewItem

   { trickle the item up to the appropriate spot in the tree }
   Place := PQ.Last
   Parent := Place div 2
   while (Parent > 0) Cand
                            (PQ.Items[Place] > PQ.Items[Parent]) do
   begin
        Swap(PQ.Items[Place], PQ.Items[Parent])
        Place := Parent
        Parent := Place div 2
   end
```

The efficiency of `PQueueInsert` is like that of `PQueueRemove`. `PQueueInsert`, at worst, has to swap array elements on a path from a leaf to the root. The number of swaps, therefore, cannot exceed the height of the tree. Because the height of the tree, which is complete, is always approximately $\log_2 N$, `PQueueInsert` is also very efficient.

`PQueueInsert` swaps at most $\lceil \log_2(N + 1) \rceil$ items

A heap is thus an efficient implementation of a priority queue. How does a heap compare to a binary search tree as an implementation of a priority queue? As was stated earlier, because a heap has an array-based implementation, it is appropriate only if you know the maximum number of items that the priority queue can contain. If you know this number, a

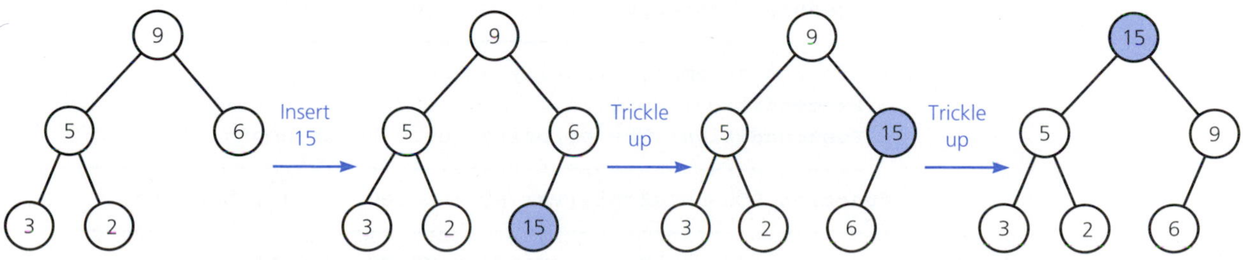

Figure 12-9
Insertion into a heap

heap has several advantages over a binary search tree. For one thing, because a heap does not store explicit pointers, it requires slightly less space than a binary search tree. In most settings, however, this is not a major issue.

A heap is always balanced

The real advantage of a heap is that it is always balanced. (Recall that complete is a stronger condition than balanced.) As you know, the height of a binary search tree can greatly exceed $\log_2 N$. The operations that keep a binary search tree balanced are far more complex than the heap operations. Do not think, however, that a heap can replace a binary search tree as a table implementation; as was stated earlier, a heap is not appropriate in this role. If this fact is not apparent to you, try to perform the table operation *TableRetrieve(T, X)* on a heap, or try to traverse a heap in sorted order.

A Turbo Pascal unit for the heap implementation of the ADT priority queue follows:

```
unit PQops;
{ *********************************************************
  BASIC PRIORITY QUEUE OPERATIONS (Heap Implementation):

    CreatePQueue, PQueueIsEmpty, PQueueInsert, and
    PQueueRemove

  Assumption: $B- is in effect.
  ******************************************************** }
interface

const MaxQueue = <maximum size of priority queue>;

type  keyType = <desired type of search key>;

      itemType = record
          Key : keyType;
          < ... and possibly other fields>
      end; { record }

      heapType = record
          Items : array[1..MaxQueue] of itemType;
          Last : 0..MaxQueue
      end; { record }

      pqueueType = heapType;

procedure CreatePQueue(var PQ : pqueueType);
{ ---------------------------------------------------------
  Creates an empty priority queue.
  Precondition: None.
  Postcondition: The priority queue PQ is empty.
  --------------------------------------------------------- }
function PQueueIsEmpty(var PQ : pqueueType) : boolean;
{ ---------------------------------------------------------
  Determines whether a priority queue is empty.
```

```
  Precondition: CreatePQueue(PQ) has been called.
  Postcondition: Returns true if PQ is empty; else
  returns false.
  ---------------------------------------------------------- }
procedure PQueueInsert(var PQ : pqueueType;
              NewItem : itemType; var Success : boolean);
{ ----------------------------------------------------------
  Inserts an item into a priority queue.
  Precondition: CreatePQueue(PQ) has been called.
  $B- is in effect.
  Postcondition: If PQ was not full, NewItem is in its
  proper position in PQ and Success is true; otherwise
  Success is false.
  ---------------------------------------------------------- }
procedure PQueueRemove(var PQ : pqueueType;
                       var PriorityItem : itemType;
                       var Success : boolean);
{ ----------------------------------------------------------
  Retrieves and deletes the item with the largest priority
  value from a priority queue.
  Precondition: CreatePQueue(PQ) has been called.
  Postcondition: If PQ was not empty, PriorityItem is the
  retrieved item, the item is deleted from PQ, and Success
  is true. However, if PQ was empty, removal is impossible
  and Success is false.
  Calls: Local procedure Adjust.
  ---------------------------------------------------------- }

implementation

{ local procedure Adjust helps maintain a heap. }
procedure Adjust(var H : heapType; Root : integer);
{ ----------------------------------------------------------
  Converts a semiheap into a heap.
  Precondition: H is a semiheap rooted at position Root.
  $B- is in effect.
  Postcondition: H is a heap rooted at position Root.
  Method: Recursively trickles the item at position Root
  down to its proper position by swapping it with its larger
  child, if the child is larger than the item. If (2 * Root)
  > H.Last, the item is at a leaf and nothing needs to be
  done.
  ---------------------------------------------------------- }
var Child, RightChild : integer;
    Temp : itemType;
begin
   if (2 * Root) <= H.Last
      then            { root is not a leaf }
```

```
      begin
      { find index of larger child of root }
         Child := 2 * Root;{ index of root's left child }
         RightChild := succ(Child);{ right child, if any}

         { if there is a right child, find larger child }
         if (RightChild <= H.Last) and
           (H.Items[RightChild].Key > H.Items[Child].Key)
             then Child := RightChild;
         { Child is the index of larger child of root }

      { if the value at position Root is smaller than
        the value in the larger child, swap values }
         if H.Items[Root].Key < H.Items[Child].Key
             then
             begin
                { swap }
                Temp := H.Items[Root];
                H.Items[Root] := H.Items[Child];
                H.Items[Child] := Temp;

                { adjust the new subtree }
                Adjust(H, child)
             end  { if }
      end { if }
      { if root is a leaf, do nothing }

end; { Adjust }

procedure CreatePQueue(var PQ : pqueueType);
begin
   PQ.Last := 0
end; { CreatePQueue }

function PQueueIsEmpty(var PQ : pqueueType) : boolean;
begin
   PQueueIsEmpty := (PQ.Last = 0)
end;  { PQueueIsEmpty }

procedure PQueueInsert(var PQ : pqueueType;
              NewItem : itemType; var Success : boolean);
{ Method: Inserts the new item after the last item in the
  heap and trickles it up to its proper position. The
  priority queue is full when it contains MaxQueue items. }
var Parent, Place : integer;
    Temp : itemType;
begin
   if PQ.Last = MaxQueue
      then Success := false       { PQ is full }
```

```
      else
      begin
         { place the new item at the end of the heap }
         inc(PQ.Last);
         PQ.Items[PQ.Last] := NewItem;

         { trickle it up to its proper position }
         Place := PQ.Last;
         Parent := Place div 2;
         while (Parent > 0) and (PQ.Items[Place].Key >
                                 PQ.Items[Parent].Key) do
         begin
            Temp := PQ.Items[Parent];
            PQ.Items[Parent] := PQ.Items[Place];
            PQ.Items[Place] := Temp;
            Place := Parent;
            Parent := Place div 2
         end; { while }

         Success := true
      end  { if }
end; { PQueueInsert }

procedure PQueueRemove(var PQ : pqueueType;
                       var PriorityItem : itemType;
                       var Success : boolean);
{ Method: Swaps the last item in the heap with the root
  and trickles it down to its proper position.}
begin
   if PQ.Last = 0
      then Success := false

      else
      begin
         PriorityItem := PQ.Items[1];
         PQ.Items[1] := PQ.Items[PQ.Last];
         dec(PQ.Last);
         Adjust(PQ, 1);
         Success := true
      end  { if }
end; { PQueueRemove }

end. { unit }
```

Finite distinct priority values. Suppose that you have a finite number of distinct priority values, such as the integers 1 through 10. In such cases, it is likely that many items will have the same priority value, and therefore you probably will need to order these items.

A heap of queues

A heap of queues accommodates this situation. Each priority value appears in the heap only once. To insert an item into the priority queue, you add its priority value to the heap, if it is not already there, and then add the item to the corresponding queue. To delete an item, you remove the item at the front of the queue that corresponds to the highest priority value in the heap. If this deletion leaves the queue empty, you remove the corresponding priority value from the heap.

Exercise 8 at the end of this chapter treats distinct priority values further.

The Priority Queue As an Object (Optional)

You can implement the ADT priority queue as an object. The following implementation of such an object has many similarities with the heap implementation of the ADT priority queue that you just saw. Like the table object of Chapter 10, this priority queue object uses recursion. Notice that the recursive procedure `Adjust` is local to the method `PQueueRemove`.

```
unit PQobj; { priority queue of records }
{ Assumes $B- is in effect. }
interface

const MaxQueue = <maximum size of priority queue>;

type  keyType = <desired type of search key>;

      itemType = record
          Key : keyType;
          < ... and possibly other fields>
      end;  { record }

      heapType = record
          Items : array[1..MaxQueue] of itemType;
          Last : 0..MaxQueue
      end;  { record }

      pqueueType = object

        constructor Init;
        { -----------------------------------------------
          Creates an empty priority queue.
          Precondition: None.
          Postcondition: The priority queue is empty.
          ----------------------------------------------- }
        destructor Done; virtual;
        { -----------------------------------------------
          Deallocates a priority queue.
          Precondition: Init has been called.
          Postcondition: All storage associated with the
```

```
            priority queue is deallocated. The priority queue
            is empty.
            Note: The destructor is unnecessary for static
            objects, but having one is desirable for future
            use.
            ------------------------------------------------- }
          function PQueueIsEmpty : boolean;
          { -------------------------------------------------
            Determines whether a priority queue is empty.
            Precondition: Init has been called.
            Postcondition: Returns true if the priority
            queue is empty; else returns false.
            ------------------------------------------------- }
          procedure PQueueInsert(NewItem : itemType;
                                 var Success : boolean);
          { -------------------------------------------------
            Inserts an item into a priority queue.
            Precondition: Init has been called. $B- is in
            effect.
            Postcondition: If the priority queue was not
            full, NewItem is in its proper position and
            Success is true; otherwise Success is false.
            ------------------------------------------------- }
          procedure PQueueRemove(var PriorityItem:itemType;
                                 var Success : boolean);
          { -------------------------------------------------
            Retrieves and deletes the item with the largest
            priority value from a priority queue.
            Precondition: Init has been called.
            Postcondition: If the priority queue was not
            empty, PriorityItem is the retrieved item, the
            item is deleted from the priority queue, and
            Success is true. However, if the priority queue
            was empty, removal is impossible and Success is
            false.
            Calls: Local procedure Adjust.
            ------------------------------------------------- }

       private
          H: heapType;
       end;  { object }

implementation  { as a heap }

constructor pqueueType.Init;
begin
   H.Last := 0
end;  { pqueueType.Init }
```

```
destructor pqueueType.Done;
begin
end;  { pqueueType.Done }

function pqueueType.PQueueIsEmpty : boolean;
begin
   PQueueIsEmpty := (H.Last = 0)
end;  { pqueueType.PQueueIsEmpty }

{ The implementations of the following procedures have the
  same bodies as in the previous section of this chapter,
  except that H replaces each instance of PQ, as in the
  preceding methods pqueueType.Init and
  pqueueType.PQueueIsEmpty. }

procedure pqueueType.PQueueInsert(NewItem : itemType;
                                  var Success : boolean);
{ ---------------------------------------------------------
  Method: Inserts the new item after the last item in the
  heap and trickles it up to its proper position. The
  priority queue is full when it contains MaxQueue items.
  --------------------------------------------------------- }
begin

end;  { pqueueType.PQueueInsert }

procedure pqueueType.PQueueRemove(
                              var PriorityItem : itemType;
                              var Success : boolean);
{ ---------------------------------------------------------
  Method: Swaps the last item in the heap with the root
  and trickles it down to its proper position.
  --------------------------------------------------------- }

   procedure Adjust(var H : heapType; Root : integer);
   { Converts a semiheap into a heap.
     You can use Adjust as it appears in the previous
     section, or you can omit H as a parameter. (Adjust
     is called once by itself recursively and once by
     pqueueType.PQueueRemove.) }
   begin

   end; { Adjust }

begin

end;  { pqueueType.PQueueRemove }

end. { unit }
```

The following statements demonstrate how to use this object, assuming that *GetRecord* and *DisplayRecord* are available to perform record I/O:

```
program DemonstratePriorityQueueObject;

uses PQobj;

var PQ      : pqueueType; { defined in the unit }
    AnItem  : itemType;   { defined in the unit }
    Success : boolean;
    Count   : integer;

{ GetRecord and DisplayRecord are defined here }

begin { Main Program }
   PQ.Init;

   for Count := 1 to 4 do         { insert 4 items }
   begin
      GetRecord(AnItem);
      PQ.PQueueInsert(AnItem, Success)
   end;  { for }

   writeln('Removing items in priority order...');
   while not PQ.PQueueIsEmpty do
   begin
      PQ.PQueueRemove(AnItem, Success);{ retrieve,delete }
      DisplayRecord(AnItem)
   end { while }
end. { Program }
```

Heapsort

Building a heap from an array of items

As its name implies, the heapsort algorithm uses a heap to sort an array `A` of items that are in no particular order. The first step of the algorithm transforms the array into a heap. One way to accomplish this transformation is to use the priority queue's *`PQueueInsert`* procedure to insert the items into the heap one by one.

There is, however, a more efficient method of building a heap out of the items of `A`. Suppose, for example, that the initial contents of `A` are as shown in Figure 12-10a. First, you imagine the array as a binary tree by assigning the items of `A` to the tree's nodes, beginning with the root and proceeding left to right down the tree. Figure 12-10b shows the resulting tree. Next, you transform this tree into a heap by calling *`Adjust`* repeatedly. Recall that *`Adjust`* transforms a semiheap—a tree whose subtrees are both heaps but whose root may be out of place—into a heap. But are there any semiheaps in the tree for *`Adjust`* to work on? Although `A` itself is not a semiheap, if you look at the leaves you will find semiheaps—that is, each leaf is a semiheap. (In fact, each leaf is a heap, but for the sake of simplicity ignore this fact.) You first call *`Adjust`* on the leaves from right to left. You then move up the tree, knowing that by the time you reach a node *i*, its subtrees are heaps, and thus *`Adjust`* will transform the semiheap rooted at *i* into a heap.

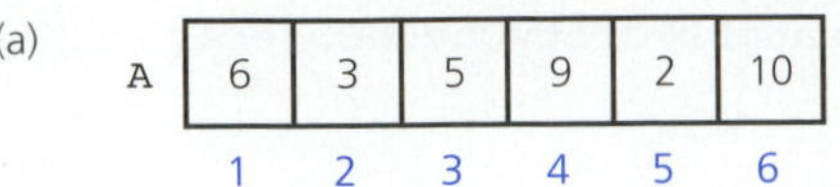

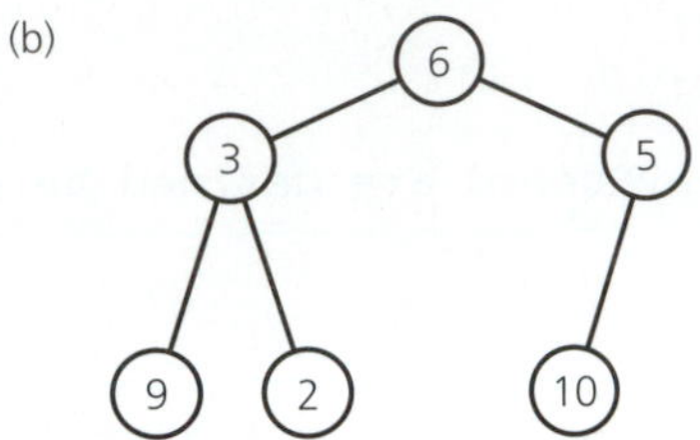

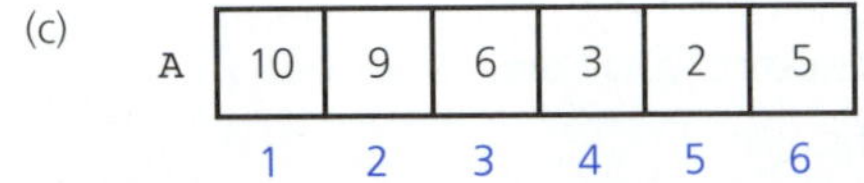

Figure 12-10

(a) The initial contents of `A`; (b) `A`'s corresponding tree; (c) the contents of `A` after `BuildHeap`

The following procedure transforms the array `A` into a heap and is the first step of the heapsort algorithm. Notice that you need to modify the previous version of `Adjust` slightly: In addition to the root of the semiheap, you must also pass `N`, the number of items in the array.

```
BuildHeap(A, N)

   for Index := N downto 1 do
      { the tree rooted at Index is a semiheap -
        call Adjust to transform it into a heap }

     Adjust(A, Index, N)
```

Now that the array of items is structured as a heap (Figure 12-10c), heapsort partitions the array into two regions: the Heap region and the Sorted region. The Heap region is in `A[1..Last]`, and the Sorted region is in `A[Last+1..N]`, as Figure 12-11 illustrates. The invariant of the heapsort algorithm is that after step *i*

Invariant for heapsort

- The Sorted region contains the *i* largest values in `A`, and they are in sorted order—that is, `A[N]` is the largest, `A[N-1]` is the second largest, and so on.
- The items in the Heap region form a heap.

After converting `A` to a heap, heapsort initializes the Heap region to be all of `A` and the Sorted region to be empty—that is, `Last` is equal to `N`. Each

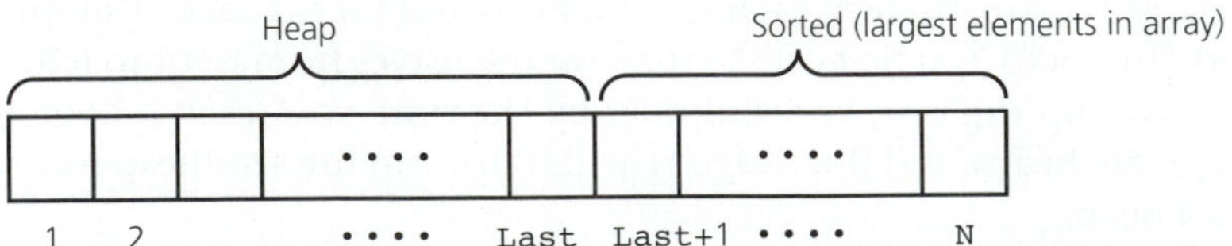

Figure 12-11

The invariant for heapsort

step of the algorithm moves an item *I* from the Heap region to the Sorted region. So that the invariant holds, *I* must be the item that has the largest value in the Heap region, and therefore *I* must be in the root of the heap. To accomplish the move, you exchange the item in the root of the heap with the last item in the heap—that is, you exchange `A[1]` with `A[Last]`—and then decrement the value of `Last`. The result is that the item that was just swapped from the root into `A[Last]` becomes the smallest item in the Sorted region (and is in the first position of the Sorted region). After the move, you must transform the Heap region back into a heap because the new root may be out of place. You can accomplish this transformation by using `Adjust`—modified as was noted earlier—to trickle down the item now in the root so that the Heap region is once again a heap.

The following algorithm summarizes the steps:

```
Heapsort(A, N)
{ Sorts A[1..N]. }

   { build initial heap }
   BuildHeap(A, N)

   { initialize the regions }
   Last := N

   { loop invariant: A[1..Last] is a heap, A[Last+1..N] is
     sorted and contains the largest elements of A }

   for Step := N downto 2 do
   begin
   { Remove the largest item from the Heap region and place
     it at the beginning of the Sorted region. Since the
     Heap region is a heap, the largest item is at the
     root. To move the largest item into the first position
     of the Sorted region, swap A[1] and A[Last] and
     decrement Last }

      Swap(A[1], A[Last])

      { expand the Sorted region, shrink the Heap region }
      Last := Last - 1

      { make the Heap region a heap again }
      Adjust(A, 1, Last)
   end
```

Heapsort is O(N * log N)

The analysis of the efficiency of heapsort is similar to that of mergesort, as given in Chapter 7. Both algorithms are $O(N * \log N)$ in both the worst and average cases. Heapsort has an advantage over mergesort in that it does not require a second array.

The following Pascal procedures implement heapsort. Note that to sort an array `A[1..N]` of integers, you would write `Heapsort(A, N)`.

```
const MaxSize = 10;

type  dataType = integer;
      heapType = array[1..MaxSize] of dataType;

procedure Adjust(var H : heapType; Root, Last : integer);
{ ---------------------------------------------------------
  Converts a semiheap into a heap.
  Precondition: H is a semiheap rooted at position Root;
  Last marks the end of the semiheap. $B- is in effect.
  Postcondition: H is a heap rooted at position Root;
  Last marks the end of the heap.
  Method: Recursively trickles the item at position Root
  down to its proper position by swapping it with its larger
  child, if the child is larger than the item. If (2 * Root)
  > Last, the item is at a leaf and nothing needs to be
  done.
  --------------------------------------------------------- }
var Child, RightChild : integer;
    Temp : dataType;
begin
    if (2 * Root) <= Last
       then           { root is not a leaf }
       begin
       { find index of larger child of root }
           Child := 2 * Root;{ index of root's left child }
           RightChild := succ(Child);{ right child, if any}

           { if there is a right child, find larger child }
           if (RightChild <= Last) and
                                  (H[RightChild] > H[Child])
              then Child := RightChild;
           { Child is the index of larger child of root }

       { if the value at position Root is smaller than
         the value in the larger child, swap values }
           if H[Root] < H[Child]
              then
              begin
                 { swap }
                 Temp := H[Root];
                 H[Root] := H[Child];
                 H[Child] := Temp;

                 { adjust the new subtree }
                 Adjust(H, Child, Last)
              end { if }
       end { if }
       { if root is a leaf, do nothing }
end; { Adjust }
```

```
procedure BuildHeap(var H : heapType; N : integer);
{ -------------------------------------------------------
  Builds the initial heap.
  Precondition: H is an array of N items.
  Postcondition: H is a heap of N items.
  ------------------------------------------------------- }
var Index : integer;
begin
    for Index := N downto 1 do
       { tree rooted at Index is a semiheap -
         transform it into a heap }
       Adjust(H, Index, N)
end; { BuildHeap }

procedure Heapsort(var A: heapType; N : integer);
{ -------------------------------------------------------
  Sorts an array by using heapsort.
  Precondition: A is an array of N items.
  Postcondition: A is sorted into ascending order.
  ------------------------------------------------------- }
var Last : integer;
    Temp : dataType;
begin
    BuildHeap(A, N);     { build the initial heap }

    for Last := N downto 2 do     { heapsort }
    { loop invariant: A[1..Last] is a heap, A[Last+1..N] is
      sorted and contains the largest elements of A }
    begin
       { swap A[1] and A[Last] }
       Temp := A[1];
       A[1] := A[Last];
       A[Last] := Temp;

       { change semiheap into a heap }
       Adjust(A, 1, pred(Last))
    end { for }
end; { Heapsort }
```

A CASE STUDY: ENHANCEMENTS TO THE VIDEOCASSETTE INVENTORY SYSTEM

The case study in this section helps to illustrate, once again, the use of ADT's in the problem-solving process. It modifies and enhances the inventory program that was presented in Chapter 3.

Although a program might meet the needs of its users at the time of the original design, those needs can change as the environment of the users changes (for example, as a company grows). Ideally, the program should evolve along with its users' needs. At least two types of changes to a program can occur:

Program changes that can occur

- The program specifications might change. For example, the program could be required to do more (perform more functions) than was previously needed or desired.
- The requirements for performance might change. When the program was originally written, the demands on computer resources may have been minimal. As the usage of the program or the size of the problem increases (for instance, as the size of an inventory grows), a simple implementation that was satisfactory before may become unsatisfactory.

One of the things that this book has stressed throughout is that a program that is properly organized into modules, with respect to both its processes and the management of its data, will be amenable to modification. Imagine that the videocassette dealership discussed in Chapter 3 has grown considerably since the design of the inventory program and that the program is no longer completely addressing its current needs. The objective of this case study is to bring the implementation up to date with these needs (and with the material that you have been studying!).

Suppose that the new requirements are classified as follows:

New requirements of the program

- **Performance**. At the time of the original program design, the dealership was quite small, and efficient management of data was not a major concern. (Also, of course, you had not yet studied the issue of efficiency.) This case study will begin by reviewing the original implementation in the context of the material you have covered since Chapter 3. As a consequence of this review, we will consider more efficient implementations of the data-management parts of the program.
- **Features**. The dealer would like the program to help keep track of the cassettes that need repair. Because the store repairperson can fix only one cassette at a time, it is important that at any time the most-needed cassette be repaired first. In particular, the program should be able to execute the following three new commands associated with the repair of cassettes:

Three new commands

B <*title*> (broken cassette) Move the specified cassette from the stock shelves to the repair area. (This decreases the corresponding value in the inventory by 1.) If the number of cassettes waiting to be repaired is at some prespecified maximum (that is, if the back-

		log is too great), send the new cassette out to be repaired somewhere else.
F	(start repairing the most-needed cassette)	The most-needed cassette in the repair area is identified (the one with the highest priority value), and the repairperson starts working on it.
P <*title*>	(put a cassette back into the inventory)	Add one copy of the specified title to the inventory. This command is executed when a repair is completed.

- Note that the B command assigns to the cassette a priority value, which determines how soon the cassette should be repaired. This value is defined to be the cassette's want value divided by its have value. That is, the more popular the cassette is (based on the want value), the sooner it should be repaired; the more copies that are on hand (based on the have value), the less urgent the repair becomes.

Make a few changes at a time

As is the case when you are designing a solution from scratch, the best approach to making changes to an existing program is to make a few related modifications at a time. The program should be fully tested and debugged with each new set of modifications before you proceed to the next set. Ideally, this strategy will ensure that you will make changes to only a few isolated modules at a time. In this spirit, the modification of the inventory program will occur in two stages that correspond to the two classes of requirements (performance and features) just described.

Improving the Performance of the Program

If you review the original implementation of the inventory program with the discussions of ADT's in mind, you can identify the key data-management operations that are performed on the inventory items. Because the operations are essentially value oriented rather than position oriented, the ADT resembles a variation of the ADT table.

For the following operations, assume that the inventory list is alphabetical by title.

Operations associated with the inventory

BASIC TABLE OPERATIONS FOR THE INVENTORY

```
InvInsert(InvList, ATitle)
{ Inserts a title into an inventory list, if it is not
  already present.
  Precondition: The inventory list InvList has been created.
  Postcondition: If ATitle is not in InvList, insert it in
  alphabetical order; otherwise do nothing.
  Called by: ProcAM and ProcD. }
```

```
InvRetrieve(InvList, ATitle, StockItem, Success)
{ Retrieves an item from the inventory list.
  Precondition: The inventory list InvList has been created.
  Postcondition: Retrieves into StockItem the inventory item
  with the specified title. The operation fails if the item
  is not present. The flag Success indicates whether the
  operation succeeded.
  Calls: Find.
  Called by: ProcI, ProcAM, ProcD, and ProcS. }

InvReplace(InvList, ReplItem, Success)
{ Replaces an item in the inventory list.
  Precondition: The inventory list InvList has been created.
  Postcondition: If found, the item in the inventory list
  whose title matches that of ReplItem is replaced by
  ReplItem and Success is true. If the item is not found,
  the operation fails and Success is false.
  Calls: Find.
  Called by: ProcAM, ProcD, ProcR, and ProcS. }

InvTraverse(InvList, Visit)
{ Traverses an inventory list in sorted order, calling
  procedure Visit once for each item.
  Precondition: The inventory list InvList has been created;
  Visit is a user-defined procedure.
  Postcondition: Visit's action occurs once for each item
  in the inventory list.
  Calls: Visit.
  Called by: ProcL, ProcO, and ProcR. }
```

OPERATIONS ON THE WAIT LIST ASSOCIATED WITH EACH INVENTORY ITEM

```
WriteWaitList(InvList, ATitle)
{ Writes out the names on the wait list for a particular
  title.
  Precondition: The inventory list InvList has been created.
  Postcondition: The wait list for ATitle is printed.
  Calls: Find.
  Called by: ProcL and ProcI. }

AddWait(InvList, ATitle, Name, Success)
{ Adds a name to the wait list associated with a given title.
  Precondition: The inventory list InvList has been created.
  Postcondition: If ATitle is in the inventory list, then
  Name is added to ATitle's wait list and Success is true;
  otherwise, Success is false.
  Calls: Find.
  Called by: ProcS. }
```

```
DeleteWait(InvList, ATitle, Name)
{(This specification changes during the subsequent
  discussion.)}
{ Deletes and retrieves the first name from the wait list
  associated with a particular inventory item.
  Precondition: The inventory list InvList has been created.
  Postcondition: Name is the first name on ATitle's wait
  list; deletes this name from the wait list. If wait list
  is empty, does nothing.
  Calls: Find.
  Called by: ProcD. }
```

OPERATIONS THAT SAVE AND RESTORE THE INVENTORY EACH DAY

```
PutInv(InvList, InvFile, SizeFile, WaitFile)
{ Saves the current inventory in specified files for use by
  the restore operation.
  Precondition: The inventory list InvList has been created.
  Postcondition: Files associated with file parameters are
  either created, if they did not exist already, or are
  rewritten so that their prior contents are lost. The
  inventory list is written to InvFile. The size of the
  structure and the associated wait lists are saved in the
  separate files SizeFile and WaitFile. Items that have zero
  have and want values and empty wait lists are eliminated.
  Files remain open for output.
  Calls: PutWait.
  Called by: The main program. }

GetInv(InvList, InvFile, SizeFile, WaitFile)
{ Restores the inventory from a sorted file into a binary
  search tree of minimum height. Restores the corresponding
  wait lists.
  Precondition: The following files, created by the save
  operation, are available but need not be open:
     InvFile - the main inventory structure
     SizeFile - the size of the inventory
     WaitFile - the associated wait lists
  Postcondition: The inventory list is read into InvList.
  Files remain open for input.
  Calls: GetWait.
  Called by: The main program. }
```

***CreateTable* and *TableDelete* are unnecessary**

Note that there are no *CreateTable* or *TableDelete* operations. There is no *CreateTable* operation because the inventory is restored from the files—that is, the table already exists. The issue of the initial execution of the program will be discussed in Exercise 15 at the end of this chapter. There is no *TableDelete* operation because the only time an item is deleted is when the inventory is written to the file. The deletion of an unwanted item is therefore handled by the *PutInv* operation.

You can rewrite the original program, which was described in Chapter 3, in terms of these ADT operations. The result is a program with a much clearer wall between the implementation of the data-management operations and the rest of the program.

The conversion to this ADT version of the program is straightforward. The ADT operations were already implemented in the original program, and all that is needed is to isolate them into separate subprograms. Here, for example, is the new version of one of the procedures (*ProcAM*) that uses the ADT operations. The rest of the transformation is left as an exercise.

An example of the ADT operations in use

```
procedure ProcAM(var InvList : stockPtrType);
{ ---------------------------------------------------------
  Adds a new title to the inventory or modifies the want
  value for a title that already exists in the inventory.
  Precondition: The inventory list InvList has been created.
  Postcondition: Modifies InvList as described previously.
  Calls: Prompt, GetString, InvInsert, InvRetrieve,
  InvReplace.
  --------------------------------------------------------- }
var OneItem : stockInfoType;
    WantVal : integer;
    NewTitle : string;
    Success : boolean;
begin
   { get the title argument }
   Prompt(TitlePrompt);
   GetString(NewTitle, input);

   { insert a new stock item if necessary }
   InvInsert(InvList, NewTitle);
   InvRetrieve(InvList, NewTitle, OneItem, Success);

   { update the want value for the stock item }
   writeln('Title: ', NewTitle);

   writeln;
   writeln('The current want value is ', OneItem.Want:1,
           '. Enter correct value:');
   readln(WantVal);
   if WantVal < 0
       then
       begin
          writeln(' Negative want value is not allowed.');
          writeln(' The want value will be set to 0.');
          OneItem.Want := 0
       end
```

```
        else OneItem.Want := WantVal;
        InvReplace(InvList, OneItem, Success)
end;  { ProcAM }
```

Notice that in the original program, the data structure is very much integrated with the rest of the program. For example, the *InvInsert* routine returned a pointer to the inserted item; you could then use the pointer to make direct changes—without using ADT operations—to that item in the data structure. Note how this approach violates the spirit of the wall between the data structure and the routines that use it.

Comparing the revised program with the original one

What is the consequence of rewriting the program in terms of the previous ADT operations? Consider, for example, the old and new versions of procedure *ProcAM* (which adds or modifies an inventory item). In the original version, a call to *InvInsert* locates or inserts an item, and *ProcAM* directly modifies the have value of the item by referencing the pointer that *InvInsert* returns. In the new version, a call to *InvInsert* is followed by a call to *InvRetrieve*, which is followed by a call to *InvReplace*. However, unless you use a clever implementation or redefine the ADT operations (see Exercise 14), you will have to search the data structure three times instead of the one time required by the original insert-modify sequence.

On the surface it seems that there is a large price to pay for the sake of clarity and the wall. Recall, however, the comments in Chapter 7 about keeping your perspective. In this spirit, a good argument can be made that this extra cost is of no real consequence.

In contrast to procedure *ProcAM*, consider the old and new versions of procedure *ProcD* (which processes a delivery). In particular, focus on the modification of the wait list associated with a newly delivered cassette. In the original version, a call to *InvInsert* inserts (or locates) an item. You modify the wait list directly by referencing the pointer that *InvInsert* returns. In the new version, however, *InvInsert* does not return a pointer, because if it did, the wall around the ADT implementation would be violated. Instead, you must make a call to the ADT operation *DeleteWait* for each name that you want to remove from the wait list. Note that *DeleteWait* must search for the item each time it is called. As a consequence, if there are several copies of a single title, you might search for the same inventory item repeatedly.

It is important to appreciate how significant the difference between the old and new versions of *ProcD* is. One search (for each delivered title) is replaced by a number of searches that depends on the size of the shipment (the quantity of each title delivered). This number can easily be large enough to make the cost of the extra searches of the inventory prohibitive. On the other hand, in *ProcAM*, the original one search of the inventory is replaced by exactly three searches (calls to *InvInsert*, *InvRetrieve*, and *InvReplace*.)

You can eliminate the redundant searching in *ProcD* by modifying the definition of the operation *DeleteWait*. Instead of deleting and retrieving one name at a time from a specified wait list, you can pass an extra argument that allows you to delete several items at once. A consequence of this modification is that the message that must be written out for each name removed from the wait list will now be defined as part of the ADT operation.

A more efficient **`DeleteWait`**

```
DeleteWait(InvList, ATitle, Count)
{ Deletes Count names from the wait list associated with the
  specified inventory item. Writes a message for each name. }
```

With this digression out of the way, we can examine the implementation of the ADT operations more closely. It is assumed that the inventory has grown quite large and that there is now a concern for the efficiency of the data-management operations. It should not be difficult to see that the original implementation of the inventory corresponds to the sorted linear implementation of the ADT table discussed in Chapter 10. Given that the inventory has grown quite large and that it may continue to grow, the binary search tree implementation should immediately come to mind.

The conversion to the binary search tree implementation of the ADT operations is straightforward and is left as an exercise. Most of the routines do not require special comment; we will discuss the only `GetInv` and `PutInv` operations for saving and restoring the inventory structure.

How can you save a binary search tree's data in a file so that you can restore the tree later? Recall that Chapter 10 presented two different algorithms for saving and restoring a tree. The first algorithm restores a tree to its original shape. The second restores a tree to a shape that is balanced. Do you necessarily want the restored tree to have its original shape? Recall that you can organize a given set of data items into binary search trees with many different shapes. All that is required for the inventory program to work correctly is that the restored tree have the binary search tree property. That is, the search key in any node must be greater than all the search keys in its left subtree and less than all of the search keys in its right subtree.

A balanced tree will increase the program's efficiency

Although the shape of a binary search tree has no effect whatsoever on the correctness of the program, it will affect the efficiency of the tree operations, and efficiency is a concern. After all, that is why we are considering a binary search tree implementation in the first place! What is needed is the algorithm that will restore a tree to a shape that is balanced.

Thus, `PutInv` should save the inventory list, which is a binary search tree, as follows:

```
Write the data items to a file in the order of the
   tree's inorder traversal, counting the number of
   nodes in the tree

Save the size of the tree
```

Likewise, `GetInv` should restore the inventory list as follows:

```
Read the size of the tree
Execute the recursive ReadTree procedure (Chapter 10)
```

So far, the primary differences between the revised program and the original program are as follows:

The program revisions so far

- The revised program uses identified ADT operations. This use further modularizes the program by separating the implementation of the data-management operations from that of the rest of the program. The implication is that if the underlying data structure changes, you need modify only the implementations of the ADT operations—behind the wall.
- The data structure that supports the inventory is a binary search tree instead of a sorted linked list. The intended outcome is to support the data-management operations more efficiently.

Adding New Features to the Program

The second major task in bringing the program up to date with the users' current needs is to add new features to the new ADT version of the program that was just described. The videocassette dealer has requested that the program help keep track of cassettes that need to be repaired. In particular, the new commands B, F, and P, which were described earlier, are desired. The addition of these new features requires the following seven subtasks:

Seven tasks that the new features require

I. Process command B (`ProcB`).
II. Process command F (`ProcF`).
III. Process command P (`ProcP`).
IV. Identify the ADT operations needed to support the repair queue.
V. Choose an implementation for the defined ADT.
VI. Modify the main program to accommodate the B, F, and P commands and the repair queue.
VII. Modify the H command (`ProcH`) to list the B, F, and P commands.

Subproblem I: Process command B. Move a specified cassette from the inventory to the repair queue.

FIRST PASS

```
ProcB(Invlist, Repair)

  Read in a title argument
  Retrieve the inventory item

  { add the title to the repair queue }
  Compute the priority value for the cassette
  Add the title to the repair queue

  { update the inventory item }
  Decrement the have value by 1
  Replace the inventory item
```

Because you are modifying an existing program, many of the implementation details have already been worked out. Therefore, the second refinement can be fairly complete.

SECOND PASS

```
ProcB(InvList, Repair)

  Prompt(TitlePrompt)
  GetString(Title, input)
  InvRetrieve(InvList, Title, OneItem, Success)
  if (not Success) Cor (OneItem.Have < 1)
     then write a message

     else
     begin
       { add the title to the repair queue }
       Priority := OneItem.Want/OneItem.Have
       Add the title to the repair queue
       if the add is not successful (repair area is full)
          then write a message (send cassette out for repair)

       { update the inventory item }
       OneItem.Have := OneItem.Have - 1
       InvReplace(InvList, OneItem, Success)
     end
```

Subproblem II: Process command F. Identify the most-needed cassette and start repairing it.

```
ProcF(InvList, Repair)

  if the repair queue is empty
     then write a message
     else remove from the repair queue the cassette with
          highest priority value
```

Subproblem III: Process command P. Put a cassette into the inventory.

FIRST PASS

```
ProcP(InvList)

  Read a title argument
  Insert a new item if necessary
  Retrieve the item
  Add 1 to the have value (call DeleteWait if necessary)
  Replace the modified item
```

SECOND PASS

```
ProcP(InvList)

  Prompt(TitlePrompt)
  GetString(ATitle, input)
  InvInsert(InvList, ATitle)
  InvRetrieve(InvList, ATitle, OneItem, Success)
  if OneItem.Have < 0
     then DeleteWait(InvList, ATitle, 1)
  OneItem.Have := OneItem.Have + 1
  InvReplace(InvList, OneItem, Success)
```

Subproblem IV: Identify the ADT operations needed to support the repair queue. So far, the following operations are necessary to support the previous subproblems:

```
RepairQInsert
{ Adds a title to the repair queue. }

RepairQRemove
{ Removes the title with highest priority value. }

RepairQIsEmpty
{ Determines whether the repair queue is empty. }
```

In addition to these operations, operations are necessary to save the repair queue along with the rest of the inventory at the end of the day. As was true for the table for the inventory structure, here a *CreateRepairQ* operation is unnecessary because the queue will be restored from a file. Notice that these operations define a variation of the classic priority queue.

Subproblem V: Choose an implementation for the repair queue. The fixed maximum size of the repair queue suggests a heap implementation of the priority queue, which was presented earlier in this chapter. The following Pascal definitions describe the repair queue:

```
const  MaxQueue = <desired size of repair queue>;

type   keyType = real;
       itemType = record
           Key : keyType;
           Title : string
       end;

       pqueueType = record
           Items : array[1..MaxQueue] of itemType;
           Last : 0..MaxQueue
       end;

var    RepairQ : pqueueType;      { repair queue }
```

This implementation, in turn, suggests an extremely simple implementation for the save and restore operations. By defining a file of type *pqueueType* as follows:

```
type   pqFileType = file of pqueueType;
var    RepairFile : pqFileType
```

you can save or restore a heap by using simple Pascal *write* or *read* statements. Thus, the pseudocode for the save and restore operations appears as follows:

```
SaveRepairQ(RepairQ, RepairFile)

     rewrite(RepairFile)
     write(RepairFile, RepairQ)

RestoreRepairQ(RepairQ, RepairFile)

     reset(RepairFile)
     read(RepairFile, RepairQ)
```

Subproblem VI: Modify the main program to accommodate the B, F, and P commands and the repair queue. You simply make the following additions to the program:

- Add B, F, and P to the list of recognized command characters.
- Add calls to *ProcB*, *ProcF*, and *ProcP* in the *case* statement.
- Add calls to *SaveRepairQ* and *RestoreRepairQ*, along with *PutInv* and *GetInv*.

Subproblem VII: Modify the H command (*ProcH*) to list the B, F, and P commands. The modification to *ProcH* is simply a matter of listing the three new commands in the help listing.

The implementation of the previous modifications is left as an exercise. The following guidelines summarize the approach to program modification used here.

KEY CONCEPTS

Modifying or Enhancing a Program

1. When making changes to a program, it is best to make a few at a time. By maintaining a modular design, you can reduce a fairly large modification to a set of small and relatively simple modifications to isolated parts of the program.
2. You can add new features to a program by applying the same techniques that you use in an original design. These techniques include the use of top-down design and data abstraction.
3. If a program is properly modularized, it is a simple matter to replace implementations of specific algorithms or data structures with new implementations.

SUMMARY

1. A priority queue is a variation of the ADT table. Its operations allow you to retrieve and remove the item in the queue with the largest priority value.
2. A heap that uses an array-based representation of a complete binary tree is a good implementation of a priority queue when you know the maximum number of items that will be stored at any one time.
3. Heapsort, like mergesort, has very good worst-case and average-case behaviors, but neither algorithm is as good in the average case as quicksort. Heapsort has an advantage over mergesort in that it does not require a second array.
4. The case study illustrated that a modular program is easy to modify and expand. It is a simple matter to replace implementations of algorithms and data structures with new ones. You should add new features to a program in accordance with the principles of top-down design and data abstraction.

COMMON PITFALLS / DEBUGGING

1. Although a heap is a good implementation of a priority queue, it is not appropriate for a table. Specifically, a heap does not support the sorted `TableRetrieve` and `TraverseTable` operations efficiently.
2. The array-based representation of a binary tree is appropriate only when the tree is complete and the maximum number of nodes is known.

SELF-TEST EXERCISES

1. Represent the full binary tree in Figure 10-35 with an array.
2. What complete binary tree does the array in Figure 12-12 represent? Is the tree a heap?
3. Is the full binary tree in Figure 10-35 a semiheap? Is it a heap?

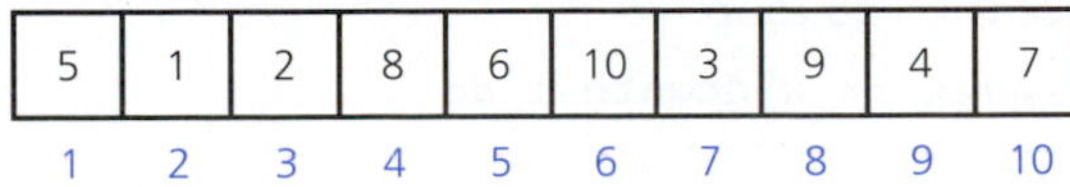

5	1	2	8	6	10	3	9	4	7
1	2	3	4	5	6	7	8	9	10

Figure 12-12

Array for Self-Test Exercises 2 and 6 and Exercise 5

4. Consider the heap in Figure 12-5. Draw the heap after you insert 12 and then remove 12.

5. What does the heap that represents the priority queue *PQ* contain after the following sequence of operations?

```
CreatePQueue(PQ)
PQueueInsert(PQ, 5)
PQueueInsert(PQ, 9)
PQueueInsert(PQ, 6)
PQueueInsert(PQ, 7)
PQueueInsert(PQ, 3)
PQueueInsert(PQ, 4)
PQueueRemove(PQ)
PQueueInsert(PQ, 9)
PQueueInsert(PQ, 2)
PQueueRemove(PQ)
```

6. Execute *BuildHeap* on the array in Figure 12-12.

EXERCISES

1. How does the order in which you insert into a heap two items that have the same priority value affect the order in which they will be deleted? What can you do if you need elements with equal priority value to be served on a first-come, first-served basis?

2. Prove that the root of a heap is the largest element in the tree.

3. The heap that this chapter described is called a **maxheap** because the largest element is at the root. (See Exercise 2.) This organization is appropriate because the *PQueueRemove* operation for the heap implementation of the priority queue deletes the element with the highest priority value. Imagine that the *PQueueRemove* operation deletes the element with the lowest priority value instead. You would then use a **minheap**. Convert the maxheap implementation to a minheap implementation.

4. Suppose that you want to maintain the index of the item with smallest priority value in a maxheap. That is, in addition to a *RemoveMax* operation, you might want to support a *RetrieveMin* operation. How difficult will it be to maintain this index under *PQueueInsert* and *RemoveMax* operations?

5. a. Show that in the *BuildHeap* procedure of *Heapsort*, you can replace the *for* loop

```
for Index := N downto 1 do
```

with

```
for Index := (N div 2) downto 1 do
```

b. Trace the action of *Heapsort* on the array in Figure 12-12.

6. As Figure 12-2 illustrates, you can use data structures other than a heap to implement the ADT priority queue.

   a. Write the Pascal declarations for a pointer-based implementation.
   b. Write the Pascal declarations for a binary search tree implementation.
   c. Implement the ADT's four operations first by using pointers and then by using a binary search tree.
   d. Implement the ADT priority queue as an object.

7. Revise the object type *pqueueType*, which appears in the section "The Priority Queue As an Object," so that the items in the priority queue are dynamically allocated objects that descend from *genericObjectType*, as defined in Chapter 4. Such objects must be able to set and retrieve their priority values, and therefore must include methods to do so.

   Write a small program that demonstrates how to allocate, use, and deallocate your new object. Include a procedure that allocates objects that descend from *genericObjectType*.

8. Suppose that you want to implement a priority queue under the assumption that there are only 10 distinct priority values.

   a. Implement the priority queue as a heap of queues, as described in this chapter.
   b. Another solution uses an array of 10 queues, one for each priority value. Use this approach to implement the priority queue.

9. Implement the ADT operations *InvInsert*, *InvRetrieve*, *InvReplace*, *InvTraverse*, *WriteWaitList*, *AddWait*, *DeleteWait*, *PutInv*, and *GetInv* as described in the case study. Note that the restore operation is part of the procedure *GetInv* and that the save operation is part of the procedure *PutInv*. The following auxiliary procedures will be helpful:

```
function Find(InvList, ATitle)
{ Finds a title in the inventory list.
  Precondition: The inventory list InvList has been
  created.
  Postcondition: Returns a pointer to the title.
  However, if the title is not found, returns nil.
  Called by: InvRetrieve, InvReplace, WriteWaitList,
  AddWait, and DeleteWait. }

PutWait(StockItem, WaitFile)
{ Writes the wait list for an inventory item into a file.
  Precondition: The file associated with WaitFile is
  open for output.
  Postcondition: The wait list for StockItem is written
  to WaitFile, which remains open for further output.
```

```
  Note: The size of the wait list is the negative of
  the have value of the inventory item.
  Called by: PutInv. }

GetWait(StockItem, WaitFile)
{ Reads the wait list for an inventory item from WaitFile.
  Precondition: The file associated with WaitFile is
  open for output.
  Postcondition: The wait list is created from the data
  in WaitFile, which remains open for output.
  Note: The wait list is a singly linked list. The size
  of the list is the negative of the have value of the
  inventory item.
  Called by: GetInv. }
```

10. Implement the procedures *ProcB*, *ProcF*, and *ProcP*, as described in the case study.

11. Rewrite the original inventory program from Chapter 3 in terms of the ADT operations described in this chapter.

12. Suppose that you want to count the total number of copies sold of each title in the inventory. Which routines in the inventory program have to be modified? How might you use this sales information to determine a priority value for the repair queue?

13. If you modify the inventory structure for an existing inventory (for example, if you add a new data field to a stock item), the restore operation that executes at the very beginning of the program will not be valid. (Why?) Write a program that will convert all the files associated with a saved inventory to a new format. Keep your conversion program as general as possible to account for future modifications to the inventory program.

14. Suppose that you know in advance that you tend to access a given item several times in a row before accessing a different item. You would like to take advantage of this knowledge to avoid searching for the same item repeatedly.

In the case study, you were faced with this problem to some extent when you had to perform *InvInsert-InvRetrieve-InvReplace* sequences for a given title. More significantly, you faced the problem with the *DeleteWait* operation when you had to delete several names at a time from a wait list associated with an inventory item. Recall that we resolved this problem by redefining the *DeleteWait* operation to include an integer argument that specified the number of names to delete. Unfortunately, it will not always be easy to address this problem by redefining a simple ADT operation.

Another way to address this problem is to add an extra bookkeeping component to your implementation. That is, you can maintain a last-accessed indicator that will always reference the last item that was accessed in the table (by any operation). Whenever you perform an operation that references the location of a specific table item, you can check the last-accessed item before starting the search.

For example, if you use this scheme with a binary search tree implementation of a table, *T* becomes a record of the following type:

```
type    tableType = record
            Root, LastAccessed : treePtrType
        end;  { record }
```

Complete the implementation of the basic ADT table operations under this scheme. Note that the operations that are currently implemented recursively cause a problem: The initial call is passed a record (of type `tableType`) as an argument, but the recursive calls are passed a pointer (of type `treePtrType`). You can resolve this problem by adding a nonrecursive shell around the recursive procedures (as you did for the binary search in Chapter 5).

15. Note that the inventory program assumes the existence of a previously saved inventory. How must you modify the program to start a new inventory from scratch?

***16.** Recall the use of the repair queue in the inventory program. Imagine that you would like to adjust the priority of an item in the queue after each sale. For example, if a title that is on the repair queue sells out, then it becomes important to repair it more quickly.

a. How can you adjust a heap if a single priority value changes?

b. How can you link the two main structures (the inventory and the repair queue) together to make updates easy?

PROJECT

17. Write an interactive program that will monitor the flow of patients in a large hospital. The program should account for patients checking in and out of the hospital and should allow access to information about a given patient. In addition, the program should manage the scheduling of three operating rooms. Doctors make a request that includes a patient's name and a priority value between 1 and 10 that reflects the urgency of the operation. Patients are chosen for the operating room by priority value, and patients with the same priority are served on a first-come, first-served basis. The basic control of the program should be with external commands (as in the inventory case studies). Although this problem is very similar in spirit to the inventory case studies that were developed previously, the object of this exercise is to design a program from scratch by incorporating the techniques of data abstraction into your problem-solving process.

That is, as you design your solution, try to identify the essential operations (excuse the pun) that will be performed on the data, and only then choose an appropriate data structure for implementation. This approach will allow you to maintain the wall between the main part of the program and the implementations. An interesting exercise would be to recast this problem as an event-driven simulation.

IV

Advanced Techniques for the Management of Data

CHAPTER 13

Advanced Implementations of the ADT Table

PREVIEW This chapter introduces several advanced implementations of the ADT table. The first topic discussed is balanced search trees. In Chapter 10 you saw that the efficiency of the binary search tree implementation of a table depends on the balance of the tree. This chapter discusses modifications to the basic binary search tree algorithms that ensure efficiency by dealing with the balance of the search tree.

This chapter then considers a completely different implementation of the ADT table that attempts to provide direct access to the data item with a given key value. In principle the algorithm, which is called hashing, calculates where to look for the data, given the search key value, rather than searching for it.

Finally, the problem of organizing data to support diverse kinds of operations simultaneously is considered. One such implementation uses doubly linked lists.

INTRODUCTION

This final part of the book looks at several fundamentally important techniques for managing data. These techniques can all be characterized as advanced methods for implementing the ADT table and its variants. Some of the techniques provide improvements to the table implementations that you have already studied, while others adopt approaches to implementing a table that are completely different from anything you have seen so far. In addition, the next chapter considers methods for implementing a table that, because of its great size, must reside on an external storage device such as a disk.

The following thumbnail description previews the major topics that you will encounter in the last two chapters.

- **Balanced search trees.** The high degree of efficiency with which a binary search tree can implement a table depends on the balance of the tree. This chapter examines a slightly different type of search tree, which remains balanced in all situations and thus can always be searched with efficiency comparable to a binary search.
- **Hashing.** Hashing is a technique that, for many applications, can provide a table implementation that is even more efficient than a search tree. Hashing locates a data item by calculating the location where it should be stored rather than by searching for it.
- **Data with multiple organizations.** Some problems require that you maintain data in different organizations simultaneously. For example, you may want to organize data according to a first in, first out order, but you may also require the data to be in sorted order. The problem is how to avoid storing the data more than once.

- **External methods.** All of the table implementations discussed so far assume that the table will reside in the computer's internal memory when the operations are performed. In many real-world applications, however, the size of a table greatly exceeds the amount of available internal memory. In such situations you must be able to operate on the table while it resides on an external device. Chapter 14 briefly examines the nature of external storage and describes methods for implementing a table that must be stored externally.

Although the details and mathematical analyses of these techniques are quite difficult, their underlying concepts are not. Therefore, by focusing on only the basic concepts, this last part of the book will present a useful introduction to material that is central to the efficient management of data.

BALANCED SEARCH TREES

Recall from the presentation of binary search trees in Chapter 10 that a tree's performance is related to its height. To perform the table operations `TableRetrieve`, `TableInsert`, and `TableDelete`, you must follow a path from the root of the tree down to the node that contains the desired item (or, in the case of the insertion operation, to the node that is to become the parent of the new item). At each node along the path, you compare the search value to the value in the node and determine which branch to follow next. Because the maximum number of nodes that can be on such a path is equal to the height of the tree, the maximum number of comparisons that the table operations can require is equal to this height.

You learned in Chapter 10 that a binary search tree of N items has a height that ranges from a maximum of N to a minimum of $\lceil \log_2(N + 1) \rceil$. As a consequence, the number of comparisons that could be required to locate a particular item in a binary search tree can be anywhere between that required by a sequential search of a linked list and that required by a binary search of an array. Because the motivation for developing the binary search tree implementation was to obtain a linked structure that could be searched with speed comparable to that of a binary search, it is certainly critical that the most optimistic behavior of a binary search tree be realized.

The height of a binary search tree is sensitive to the order of insertions and deletions

Consider the factors that determine the height of a binary search tree. The algorithms developed in Chapter 10 that maintain a binary search tree make the height of the tree very sensitive to the order in which items are inserted and deleted. For example, consider a binary search tree that contains the items 10, 20, 30, 40, 50, 60, and 70. (For simplicity, assume that each item consists solely of an integer search key.) If you inserted the items into the tree in ascending order, as was just given, you would obtain a binary search tree of maximum height, as shown in Figure 13-1a. If, on the

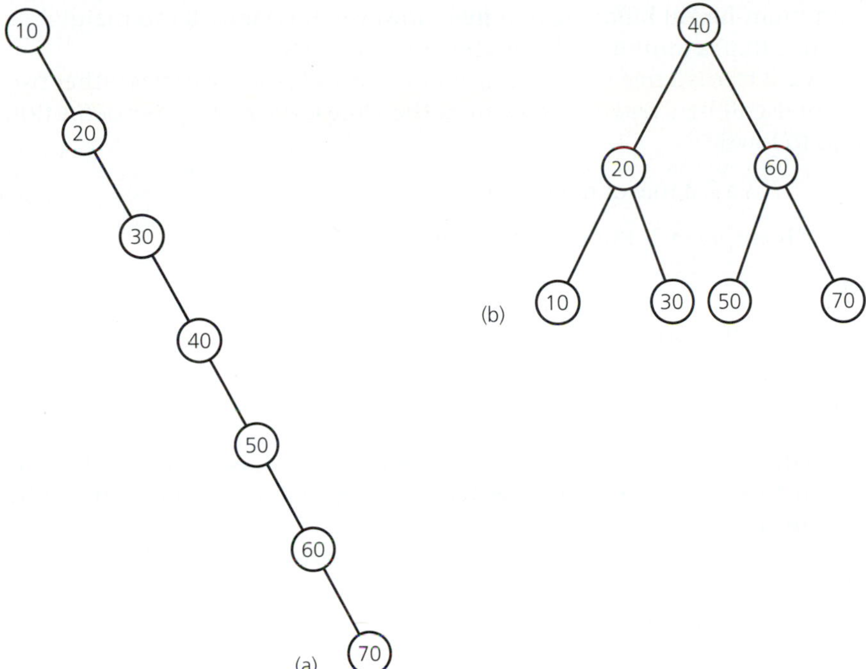

Figure 13-1

(a) A search tree of maximum height; (b) a search tree of minimum height

other hand, you inserted the items in the order 40, 20, 60, 10, 30, 50, 70, you would obtain a binary search tree of minimum height, as shown in Figure 13-1b.

Thus, if you use the algorithms in Chapter 10 to maintain a binary search tree, it is always possible that the tree will approach a linear shape and, as a consequence, that its behavior will be no better than that of a linked list. For this reason, it is desirable in many applications to use one of several variations of the basic binary search tree together with algorithms that can prevent the shape of the tree from degenerating. Two of the better-known variations are the **2-3 tree** and the **AVL tree**.

This chapter will consider 2-3 trees in greater detail than AVL trees. One reason for concentrating on the 2-3 tree is that a generalization of the 2-3 tree, the **B-tree**, is a data structure that you can use to implement a table that resides in external memory, such as on a disk. The B-tree is discussed in the next chapter.

2-3 TREES

A 2-3 tree retains its shape despite insertions and deletions

A 2-3 tree permits the number of children of an internal node to vary between two and three. As you will see, this feature allows a 2-3 tree to absorb insertions and deletions without a deterioration of the tree's shape. You can therefore search a 2-3 tree almost as efficiently as you can search a minimum-height binary search tree. However, it is far easier to maintain a 2-3 tree than a minimum-height binary search tree.

A **2-3 tree** is a tree in which each internal node (nonleaf) has either two or three children, and all leaves are at the same level. A recursive definition is as follows:

Recursive definition of a 2-3 tree

T is a 2-3 tree of height h if

1. T is empty (a 2-3 tree of height 0).

or

2. T is of the form

$$\begin{array}{ccc} & r & \\ T_L & & T_R \end{array}$$

where r is a node and T_L and T_R are both 2-3 trees, each of height $h - 1$. In this case T_L is called the **left subtree**, and T_R is called the **right subtree**.

or

3. T is of the form

$$\begin{array}{ccc} & r & \\ T_L & T_M & T_R \end{array}$$

where r is a node and T_L, T_M, and T_R are 2-3 trees, each of height $h - 1$. In this case T_L is called the **left subtree**, T_M is called the **middle subtree**, and T_R is called the **right subtree**.

For example, Figure 13-2 shows a 2-3 tree of height 3.

A 2-3 tree is not necessarily binary

The most striking feature of a 2-3 tree is that it is not necessarily a binary tree, since a node can have three children. A 2-3 tree does, nevertheless, resemble a full binary tree. If a 2-3 tree contains no node that has three children—a situation that the definition permits—then it is in fact a full binary tree, because all its internal nodes would have two children and all its leaves would be at the same level. If, on the other hand, some of the internal nodes of a 2-3 tree do have three children, then the tree will contain more nodes than a full binary tree of the same height. Therefore, a 2-3 tree of height h always has at least as many nodes as a full binary tree of height h; that is, it always has at least $2^h - 1$ nodes. To put this another

Figure 13-2

A 2-3 tree of height 3

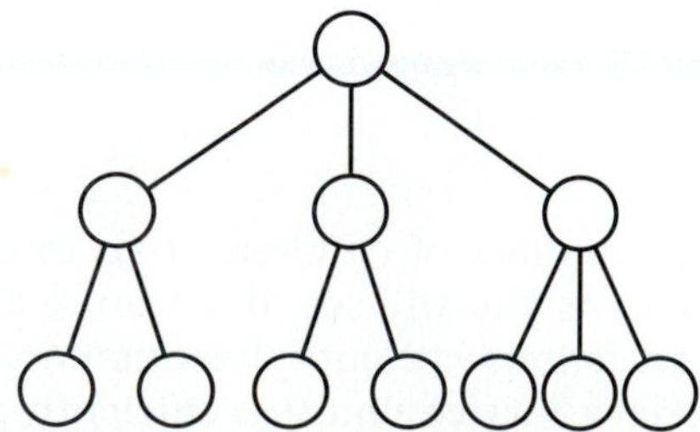

way, a 2-3 tree with N nodes never has height greater than $\lceil \log_2(N + 1) \rceil$, the minimum height of a binary tree with N nodes.

A 2-3 tree with N nodes is never taller than a minimum-height binary search tree with N nodes

Given these observations, you should suspect that a 2-3 tree is a type of balanced tree that might be useful in implementing the ADT table, and this is indeed the case. You can use a **2-3 search tree**, defined as follows, to implement the ADT table.

A 2-3 search tree

A 2-3 search tree T is a 2-3 tree such that

1. T is empty.

or

2. T is of the form

$$\begin{array}{ccc} & r & \\ T_L & & T_R \end{array}$$

and node r contains one data item. In this case, the value of the search key in r must be greater than the value of each search key in the left subtree T_L and smaller than the value of each search key in the right subtree T_R. Also, T_L and T_R must each be a 2-3 search tree.

or

3. T is of the form

$$\begin{array}{ccc} & r & \\ T_L & T_M & T_R \end{array}$$

and node r contains two data items. In this case, the value of the smaller search key in r must be greater than the value of each search key in the left subtree T_L and smaller than the value of each search key in the middle subtree T_M. The value of the larger search key in r must be greater than the value of each search key in the middle subtree T_M and smaller than the value of each search key in the right subtree T_R. In addition, T_L, T_M, and T_R must each be a 2-3 search tree.

This definition sets the following rules for how you may place data items in the nodes of a 2-3 search tree:

KEY CONCEPTS

Rules for Placing Data Items in the Nodes of a 2-3 Search Tree

1. If a node has two children, it must contain a single data item.
2. If a node has three children, it must contain two data items.
3. If a node is a leaf, it may contain either one or two data items.

Items in a 2-3 search tree are ordered

In addition to these three structural rules, the definition of a 2-3 search tree implies that its values are ordered. For example, the tree in Figure 13-3 is a 2-3 search tree whose data items are each a single integer value. Notice

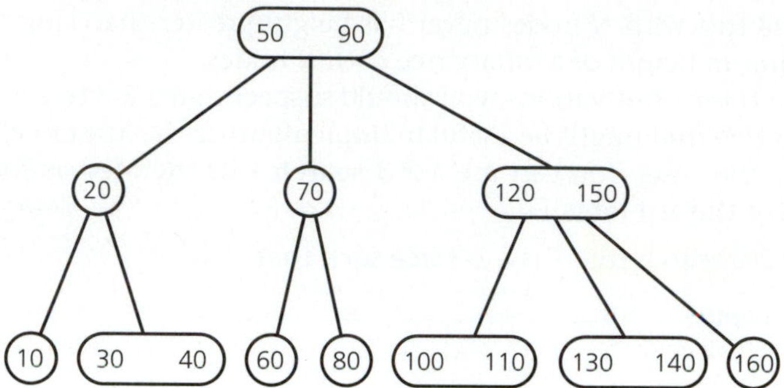

Figure 13-3
A 2-3 search tree

that if the data items were records, nodes with three children would each have to accommodate two records.

Searching a 2-3 search tree is efficient

Notice that the ordering of items in a 2-3 search tree is analogous to the ordering of values in a binary search tree. As you will see, this ordering allows you to search a 2-3 search tree efficiently for the item with a given search key. In fact, the 2-3 search tree implementation of the `TableRetrieve` operation is quite similar to a binary search tree implementation, as you can see from the following pseudocode:

```
TableRetrieve(T, SearchKey, TableItem, Success)
{ Retrieves into TableItem from a nonempty table T the item
  whose search key equals SearchKey. The operation fails if
  no such item exists. The flag Success indicates whether
  the operation succeeded. }

   Let R be the root node of T

   if SearchKey is in R then      { the item has been found }
      begin
         TableItem := the appropriate item from R
         Success := true
      end

   else if R is a leaf then     { failure }
      Success := false

   { else search the appropriate subtree }

   else if R has two data items then
      begin
         if SearchKey < smaller search key of R then
             TableRetrieve(R's left subtree, SearchKey,
                                         TableItem, Success)
         else if SearchKey < larger search key of R then
             TableRetrieve(R's middle subtree, SearchKey,
                                        TableItem, Success)
         else TableRetrieve(R's right subtree, SearchKey,
                                        TableItem, Success)
      end
```

```
   else    { R has one data item }
   begin
      if SearchKey < R's search key
         then TableRetrieve(R's left subtree, SearchKey,
                                      TableItem, Success)
         else TableRetrieve(R's right subtree, SearchKey,
                                       TableItem, Success)
   end
```

For the 2-3 search tree algorithms, it is convenient to define the degenerate case to be a leaf rather than an empty subtree. As a result, the algorithms must assume that they are not passed an empty tree as an argument. This change will allow you to avoid distracting implementation details. For example, you can traverse a 2-3 search tree in sorted order by performing the analogue of an inorder traversal:

Traversal in sorted order

```
Inorder(T)
{ Traverses the 2-3 search tree T in sorted order.
  Assumes that "visit" means "print." }

   Let R be the root node of T

   if R is a leaf then
      Print the data item(s)

   { R has two data items }
   else if R has two data items then
      begin
         Inorder(left subtree)
         Print the first data item
         Inorder(middle subtree)
         Print the second data item
         Inorder(right subtree)
      end

   { R has one data item }
   else
      begin
         Inorder(left subtree)
         Print the data item
         Inorder(right subtree)
      end
```

Consider now what you have gained by using a 2-3 tree rather than a binary search tree. (Most people use the term "2-3 tree" to mean "2-3 search tree"; we will also.) Earlier you saw that a 2-3 tree with N nodes can have a height no greater than $\lceil \log_2(N + 1) \rceil$. Thus, a 2-3 tree that represents a given table of items always has a height less than or equal to that of the *best possible* binary search tree for that same table. This fact, plus the fact that no node in a 2-3 tree has more than two items, can be shown to imply

From now on, the term "2-3 tree" will mean "2-3 search tree"

that you can search a table represented by a 2-3 tree with approximately the same efficiency as that obtained if the table is represented by a binary search tree that is *as balanced as possible.*

It may have surprised you that the efficiency of searching a 2-3 tree is not greater than the efficiency of searching a binary search tree. After all, by allowing the nodes of a 2-3 tree to have three children, it seems possible that the 2-3 tree could be shorter than the balanced binary search tree. Although the height of a 2-3 tree might indeed be less than that of a balanced binary search tree, this advantage is canceled out by the fact that, when searching a 2-3 tree for a given value *X*, at some nodes you must compare *X* with two search-key values instead of just one. In other words, although you might visit fewer nodes when searching a 2-3 tree, you might have to make more comparisons at each node. As a consequence, the number of comparisons required to search a 2-3 tree for a given value is *approximately equal* to the number of comparisons required to search a binary search tree that is as balanced as possible. This number is approximately $\log_2 N$, where *N* is the number of items in the table.

Searching a 2-3 tree is $O(\log_2 N)$

If you can search a 2-3 tree and a balanced binary search tree with approximately the same efficiency, why then should you use a 2-3 tree? The answer is that, although it is difficult to maintain the balance of a binary search tree in the face of insertion and deletion operations, it is relatively simple to maintain the shape of a 2-3 tree. For example, consider the two trees in Figure 13-4. The first tree is a binary search tree and the second is a 2-3 tree. Both trees contain the same data items. The binary search tree is as balanced as possible, and you can thus search both it and the 2-3 tree for a value with approximately the same efficiency. If, however, you perform a sequence of insertions on the binary search tree—by using the insertion algorithm of Chapter 10—the tree can quickly lose its balance, as Figure 13-5a indicates. As you will soon see, you can perform the same sequence of insertions on the 2-3 tree without a degradation in the tree's shape—it will retain its structure, as Figure 13-5b shows.

Maintaining the shape of a 2-3 tree is relatively easy

Notice that the new values (32 through 39) that were inserted into the binary search tree of Figure 13-4a appear along a single path in Figure

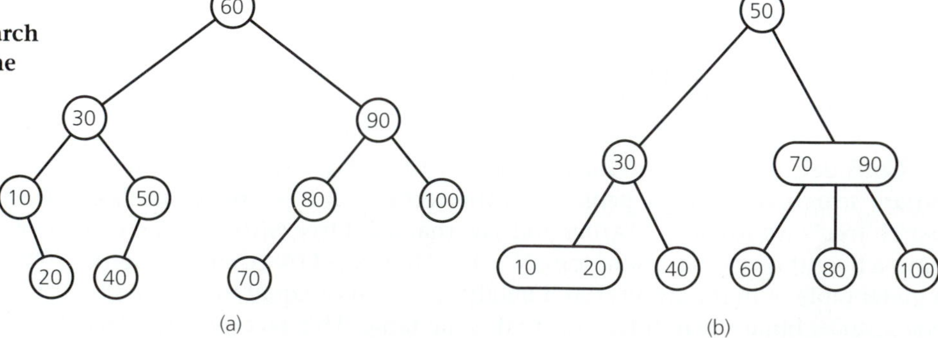

Figure 13-4

(a) A balanced binary search tree; (b) a 2-3 tree with the same elements

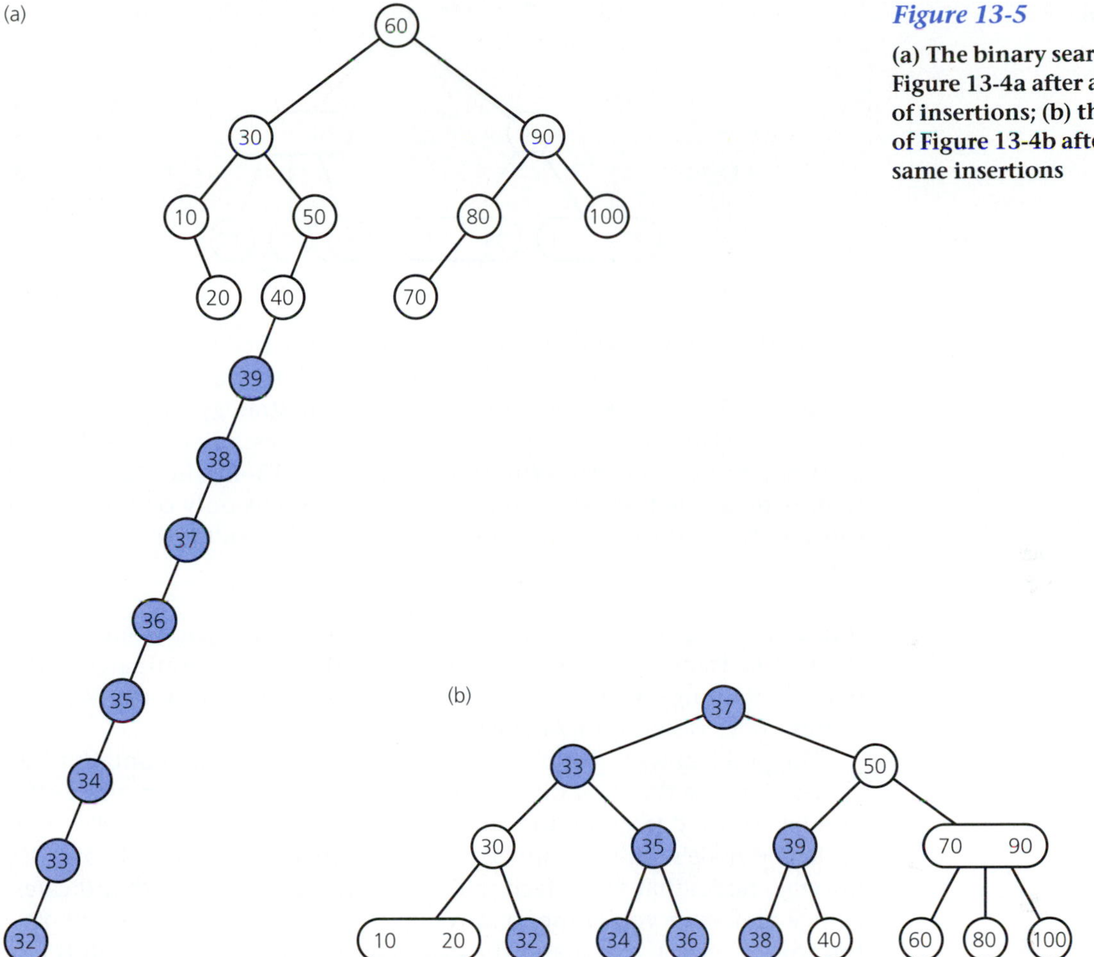

Figure 13-5

(a) The binary search tree of Figure 13-4a after a sequence of insertions; (b) the 2-3 tree of Figure 13-4b after the same insertions

13-5a. The insertions increased the height of the binary search tree from 4 to 12—an increase of 8. On the other hand, the new values have been spread throughout the 2-3 tree in Figure 13-5b. As a consequence, the height of the resulting tree is only 1 greater than the height of the original 2-3 tree in Figure 13-4b. The next section demonstrates these insertions into the original 2-3 tree.

Insertion into a 2-3 Tree

The fact that the nodes of a 2-3 tree can have either two or three children and can contain one or two values allows you to insert items into the tree while maintaining its shape. Suppose you were to make the same sequence of insertions that Figure 13-5a indicates into the 2-3 tree in Figure 13-4b. Consider an informal description of these insertions.

Figure 13-6

Insert 39

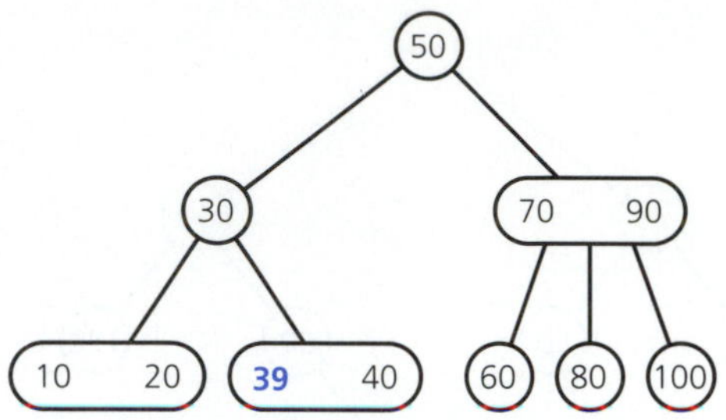

Insert 39. As is true with a binary search tree, the first step in inserting a node into a 2-3 tree is to locate the node at which the search for 39 would terminate. To do this, you can use the search strategy of the *`TableRetrieve`* algorithm given previously; an unsuccessful search will then always terminate at a leaf. With the tree in Figure 13-4b, the search for 39 terminates at the leaf <40>. Since this node contains only one item, you can simply insert the new item into this node. The result is the 2-3 tree in Figure 13-6.

Insert 38. In a manner similar to that just described, you would search the tree in Figure 13-6 for 38 and find that the search terminates at the node containing <39 40>. As a conceptual first step, you should place 38 in this node, as Figure 13-7a illustrates.

The problem with this placement is that a node cannot contain three values. Suppose that you divide these three values into the smallest (38), middle (39), and largest (40) values. You can move the middle value (39) up to the node's parent *P* and separate the remaining values, 38 and 40, into two nodes that you attach to *P* as children, as Figure 13-7b indicates. Notice that since you chose to move up the middle value of <38 39 40>, the parent correctly separates the values of its children; that is, 38 is less than 39, which is less than 40. The result of the insertion is the 2-3 tree in Figure 13-7c.

Insert 37. The insertion of 37 into the tree in Figure 13-7c is easy because 37 belongs in a leaf that currently contains only one value, 38. The result of this insertion is the 2-3 tree in Figure 13-8.

Figure 13-7

Insert 38

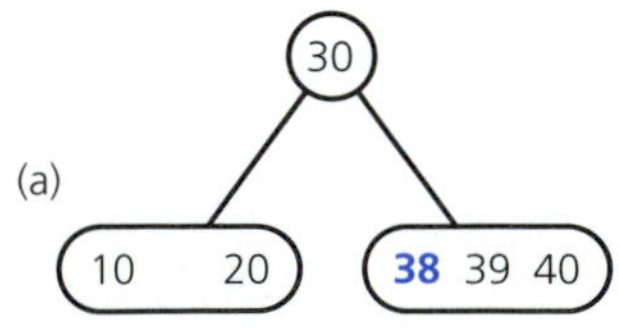

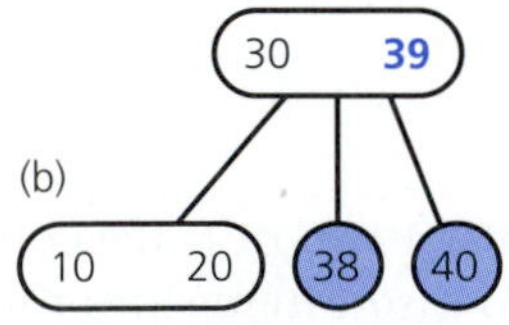

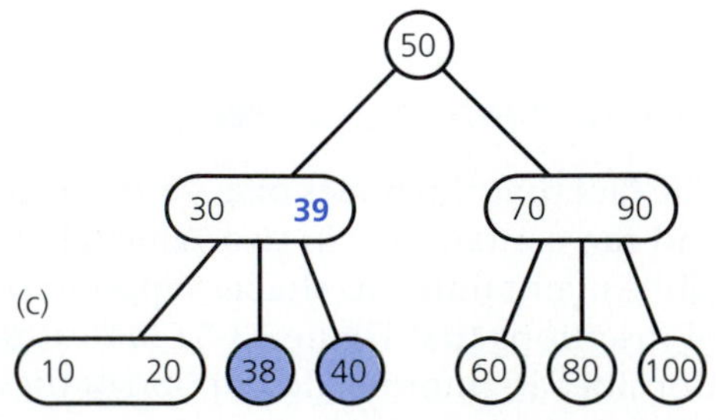

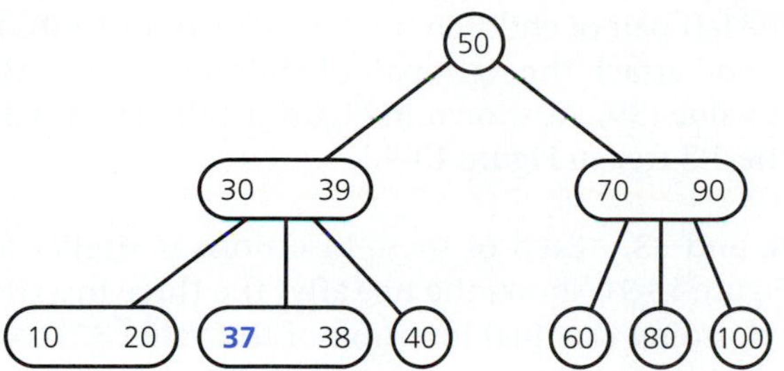

Figure 13-8
Insert 37

Insert 36. The search strategy determines that 36 belongs in the node <37 38>. Again, as a conceptual first step, place it there, as Figure 13-9a indicates.

Because the node <36 37 38> now contains three values, you divide it—as you did previously—into the smallest (36), middle (37), and largest (38) values. You then move the middle value (37) up to the node's parent *P*, and attach to *P*—as children—nodes that contain the smallest (36) and largest (38) values, as Figure 13-9b illustrates.

This time, however, you are not finished: You have a node <30 37 39> that contains three values and has four children. What should you do next? (*Hint*: Think recursively.) This situation is familiar, with the slight difference that the overcrowded node is not a leaf but rather has four children. As you did before, you divide the node into the smallest (30), middle (37), and largest (39) values, and then move the middle value up to the node's parent. Because you are splitting an internal node, you now must account for its four children; that is, what happens to nodes <10 20>, <36>, <38>, and <40>, which were the children of node <30 37 39>? The solution

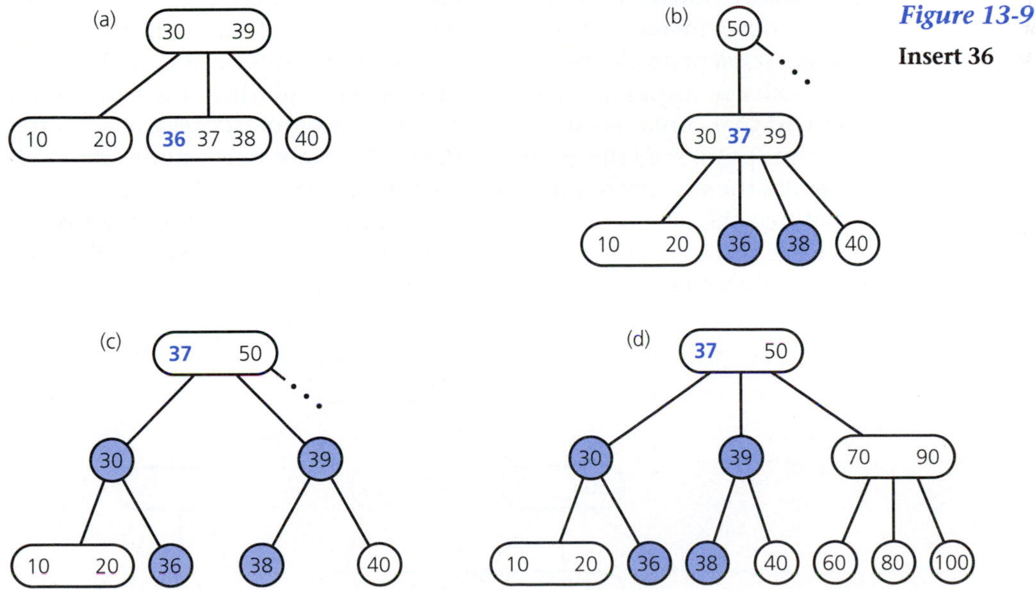

Figure 13-9
Insert 36

is to attach the left pair of children (nodes <10 20> and <36>) to the smallest value (30) and attach the right pair of children (nodes <38> and <40>) to the largest value (39), as shown in Figure 13-9c. The final result of this insertion is the 2-3 tree in Figure 13-9d.

Insert 35, 34, and 33. Each of these insertions is similar to those done previously. Figure 13-10 shows the tree after the three insertions.

Before performing the final insertion of the value 32, consider the 2-3 tree's insertion strategy.

The insertion algorithm. To insert the value X into a 2-3 tree, you first locate the leaf L at which the search for X would terminate. You insert the new value X into L, and if L now contains only two values, you are done.

Splitting a leaf

However, if L contains three values, you must split it into two nodes, L_1 and L_2. L_1 gets the smallest of the three values in L, L_2 gets the largest of the values, and the middle value is moved up to L's parent P. Nodes L_1 and L_2 then become children of P, as Figure 13-11a illustrates.

Splitting an internal node

If P now has only three children (and contains two values), you are finished. If, on the other hand, P now has four children (and contains three values), you must split P. You split the internal node P as you just split the leaf L, except that you must also take care of P's four children. As Figure 13-11b illustrates, you split P into P_1 and P_2, give P_1 the smallest value in P, attach P's two leftmost children to P_1, move the middle value of P up to its parent, give P_2 the largest value in P, and attach P's two rightmost children to P_2.

After this, the process of splitting a node and moving a value up to the parent continues recursively until a node is reached that had only one value before the insertion and thus has only two values after it takes on a new value. Notice in the previous sequence of insertions that the tree's height never increased from its original value of 3. In general, *an insertion will not result in an increase in the height of the tree* as long as there is at least one node on the path from the root to the leaf into which the new value is inserted that contains only one value. The insertion strategy of a 2-3 tree has thus postponed the growth of the tree's height much more effectively than did the strategy of a basic binary search tree.

When the height of a 2-3 tree does grow, it does so from the top. An increase in the height of a 2-3 tree will occur if every node on the path from the root of the tree to the leaf into which the new value is inserted

Figure 13-10

The tree after the insertion of 35, 34, and 33

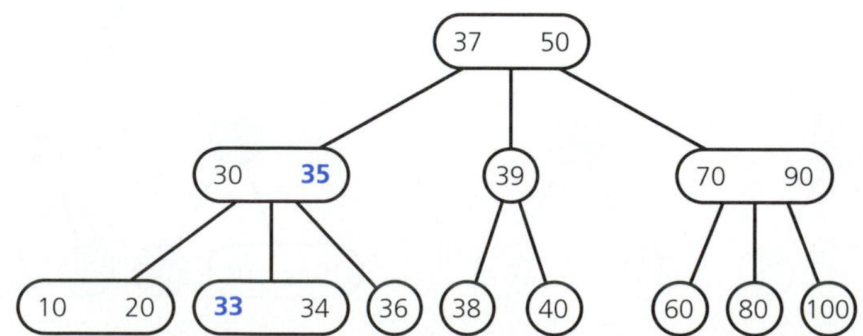

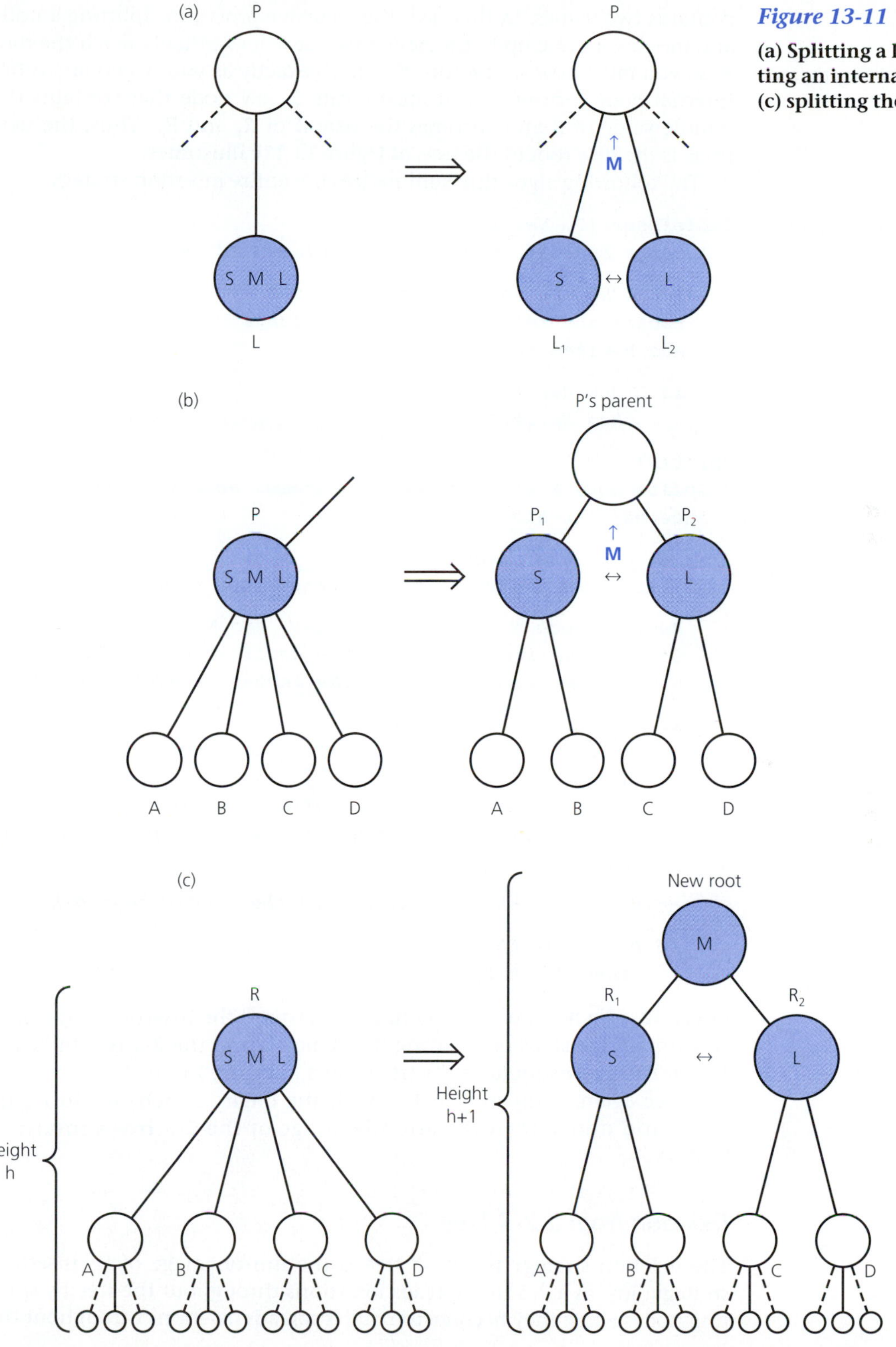

Figure 13-11

(a) Splitting a leaf; (b) splitting an internal node; (c) splitting the root

contains two values. In this case, the recursive process of splitting a node and moving a value up to the node's parent will eventually reach the root *R*, so you must now split *R* into R_1 and R_2 exactly as you would any other internal node. However, you must create a new node that contains the middle value of *R* and becomes the parent of R_1 and R_2. Thus, the new node is the new root of the tree, as Figure 13-11c illustrates.

Splitting the root

The following algorithm summarizes the entire insertion strategy:

2-3 tree insertion algorithm

```
TableInsert(T, NewItem)
{ Inserts NewItem into table T implemented as a 2-3 tree. }

   Let X be the search key of NewItem
   Locate the leaf L in which X belongs
   Add NewItem to L

   if L now has three items
       then Split(L)

Split(N)
{ Splits node N which contains 3 items. Note that if N is
  internal, it has 4 children. }

   Let P be the parent of N
     (if N is the root, then create a new node P)

   Replace node N with two nodes, N1 and N2
   Give N1 the item in N with the smallest search-key value
   Give N2 the item in N with the largest search-key value

   if N is an internal node
       then
       begin
          N1 becomes the parent of N's two leftmost children
          N2 becomes the parent of N's two rightmost children
       end

   Move up to P the item in N with the middle search-key value

   if P now has three items
       then Split(P)
```

Insert 32. To be sure that you fully understand the insertion algorithm, go through the steps of inserting the value 32 into the 2-3 tree in Figure 13-10. The result should be the tree shown in Figure 13-5b.

Once again, compare this tree with the binary search tree in Figure 13-5a and notice the dramatic advantage of the 2-3 tree's insertion strategy.

Deletion from a 2-3 Tree

The deletion strategy for a 2-3 tree is the mirror image of its insertion strategy. Just as a 2-3 tree spreads insertions throughout the tree by splitting nodes when they become too full, it spreads deletions throughout the tree by merging nodes when they become empty. As an illustration of the 2-3 tree's deletion strategy, consider the deletion of 70, 100, and 80 from the tree in Figure 13-4b.

Delete 70. By searching the tree, you will discover that the value 70 is in the node <70 90>. Because you always want to begin the deletion process at a leaf, the first step is to swap the value 70 with its inorder successor—the value that follows it in the sorted order. Because 70 is the smaller of the two values in the node, its inorder successor (80) is the smallest value in the node's middle subtree. (The inorder successor of an item in an internal node will always be in a leaf.) After the swap, the tree appears as shown in Figure 13-12a. The value 80 is in a legal position of the search tree,

Swap the value to be deleted with its inorder successor

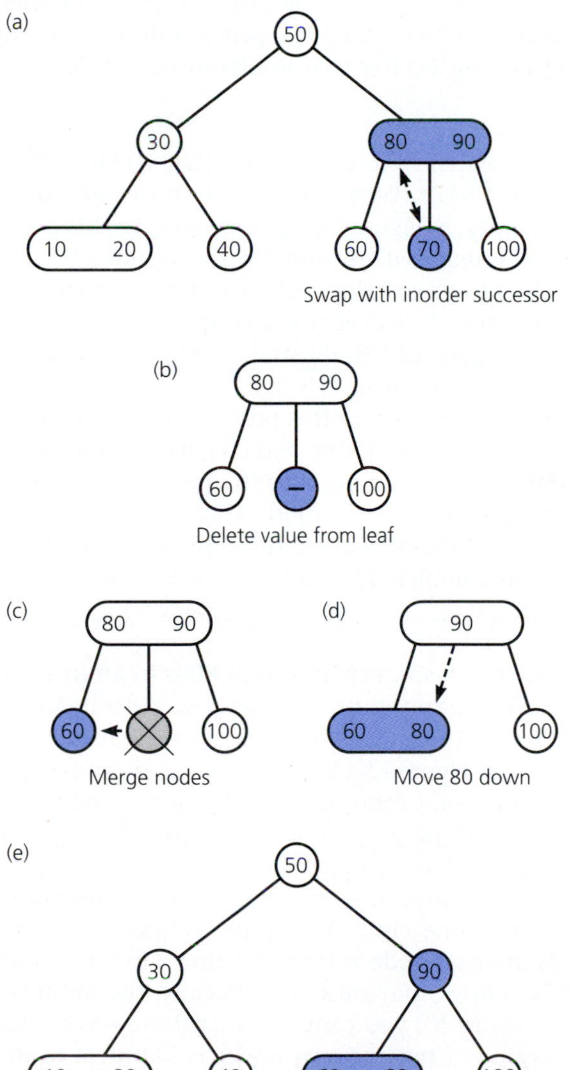

Figure 13-12
Delete 70

because it is larger than all the values in its node's left subtree and smaller than all the values in its node's right subtree. The value 70, however, is not in a legal position, but this is of no concern, because the next step is to delete this value from the leaf.

In general, after you delete a value from a leaf, another value may remain in the leaf (because the leaf contained two values before the deletion). If this is the case, you are done, because a leaf of a 2-3 tree may contain a single value. In this example, however, once you delete 70 from the leaf, the node is left without a value, as Figure 13-12b indicates. You then delete the node by merging it with one of its siblings, as Figure 13-12c illustrates.

Empty node

At this point you see that the parent of the deleted node contains two values (80 and 90) but has two children (60 and 100). This situation is not allowed in a 2-3 tree. (See rule 1.) You can remedy the problem by moving the smaller value (80) down from the parent into the left child, as Figure 13-12d illustrates. The 2-3 tree that results from this deletion is shown in Figure 13-12e.

Moving a value down

Delete 100. The search strategy discovers that 100 is in the leaf <100> of the tree in Figure 13-12e. When you delete the value from this leaf, the node becomes empty, as Figure 13-13a indicates. In this case, however, no merging of nodes is required, because the sibling <60 80> can spare a value. That is, the sibling has two values, whereas a 2-3 tree requires only that it have at least one value. However, if you simply move the value 80 into the empty node—as Figure 13-13b illustrates—you find that the search-tree order is destroyed: The value in 90's right child is 80, whereas it should be greater than 90. The solution to this problem is to redistribute the values among the empty node, its sibling, and its parent. Here you can move the larger value (80) from the sibling into the parent and move the value 90 down from the parent into the node that had been empty, as Figure 13-13c shows. Notice that this distribution preserves the search-tree order, and you have thus completed the deletion. The resulting 2-3 tree is shown in Figure 13-13d.

Redistribution of values

Delete 80. The search strategy finds that 80 is in an internal node of the tree in Figure 13-13d. You must thus swap 80 with its inorder successor, 90, as Figure 13-14a illustrates. When you delete 80 from the leaf, the node becomes empty. (See Figure 13-14b.) Because the sibling of the empty node has only one value, you cannot redistribute as you did in the deletion of 100. Instead you must merge the nodes, bringing the value 90 down from the parent, as Figure 13-14c indicates.

You are not yet finished, however, because the parent now contains no values and has only one child. You must recursively apply the deletion strategy to this internal node without a value. First, you should check to see if the node's sibling can spare a value. Because the sibling <30> contains only the single value 30, you cannot redistribute—you must merge the nodes. The merging of two internal nodes is identical to the merging of

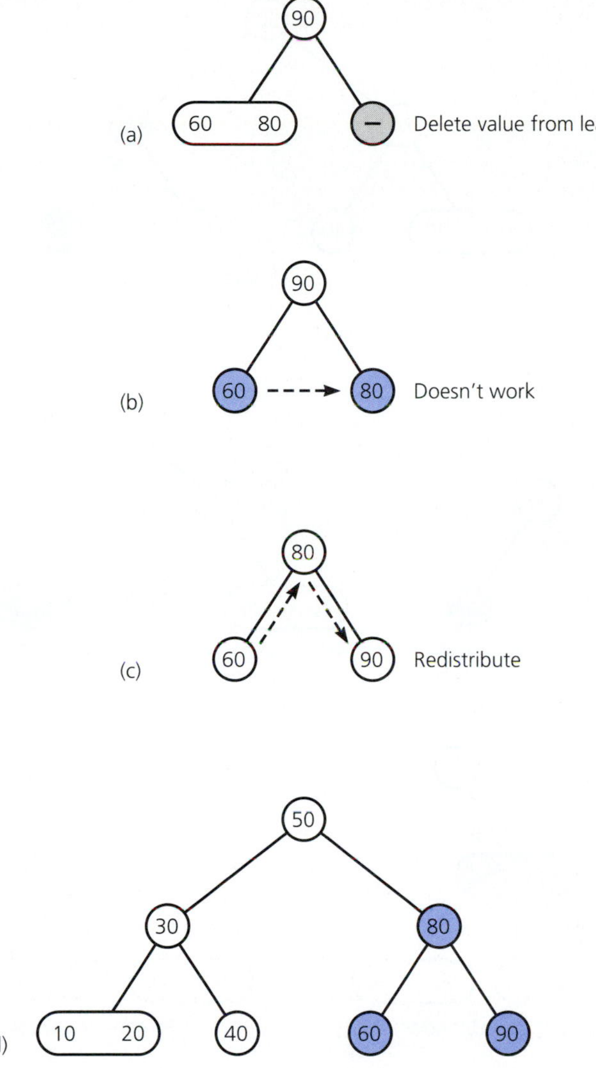

Figure 13-13
Delete 100

leaves, except that the child <60 90> of the empty node must be adopted. Because the sibling of the empty node contains only one value (and hence can have only two children, as stated in rule 1), it can become the parent of <60 90> if you bring the value 50 down from the sibling's parent. The tree now appears as shown in Figure 13-14d. Note that this operation preserves the search property of the tree.

Now the parent of the merged nodes is left with no values and only a single child. You would usually simply apply the recursive deletion strategy to this node, but this is a special case because the node is the root. Because the root is empty and has only one child, you can simply delete it, allowing <30 50> to become the root of the tree, as Figure 13-14e illustrates. This deletion has thus caused the height of the tree to shrink by 1.

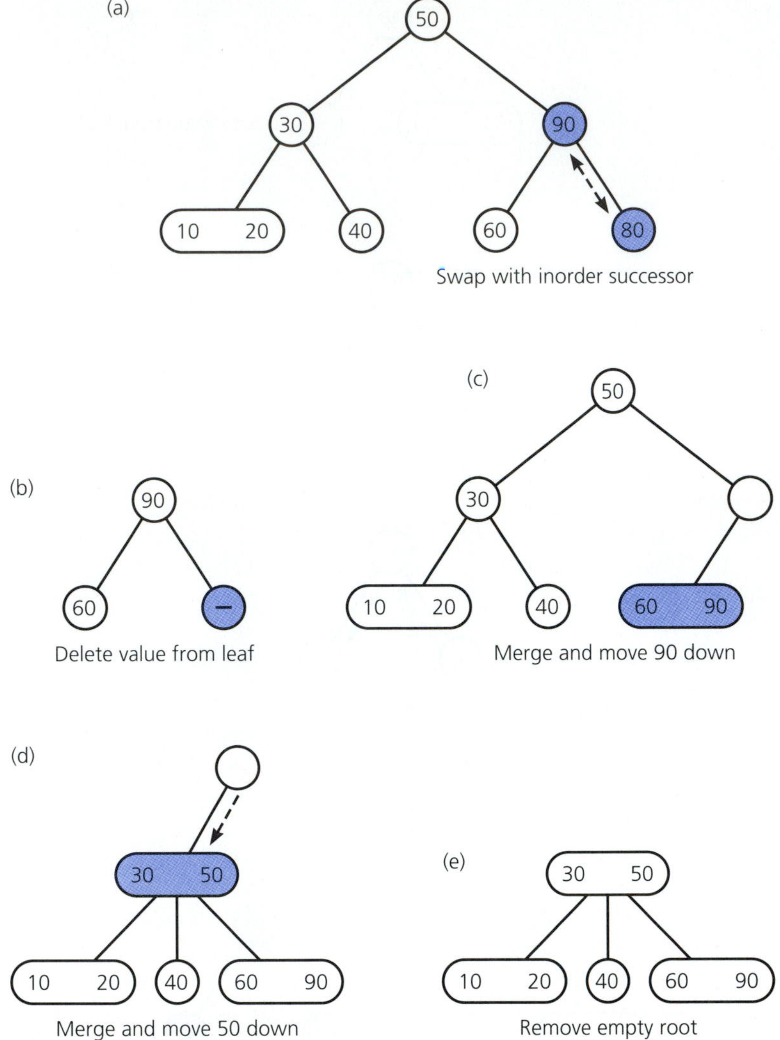

Figure 13-14

Delete 80

In contrast, consider the same deletions from the balanced binary search tree in Figure 13-4a. After deleting 70, 100, and 80 from the binary search tree, you are left with the tree in Figure 13-15. Notice that the deletions affected only one part of the tree, causing it to lose its balance. The left subtree has not been affected at all, and thus the overall height of the tree has not been diminished.

The deletion algorithm. The deletion procedure is summarized as follows: To delete *X* from a 2-3 tree, you first locate the node *N* that contains it. If *N* is an internal node, you find *X*'s inorder successor and swap it with *X*. As a result of the swap, the deletion always begins at a leaf *L*. If *L* contains a value in addition to *X*, you simply delete *X* from *L* and you are done. On the other hand, if *L* contains only *X*, then deleting it would leave

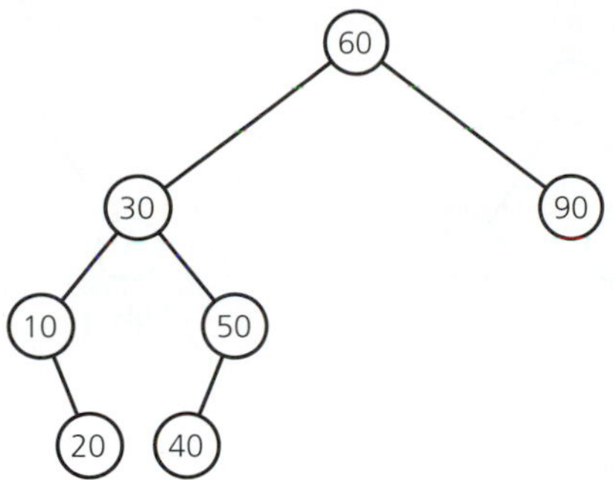

Figure 13-15

The binary search tree of Figure 13-4a after the deletion of 70, 100, and 80

L without a value. In this case you must perform some additional work to complete the deletion.

You first check the siblings of the now-empty leaf *L*. If a sibling has two values, you redistribute the values among *L*, *L*'s sibling, and *L*'s parent, as Figure 13-16a illustrates. If no sibling of *L* has two values, you merge *L* with an adjacent sibling and bring down a value from *L*'s parent. (The sibling had only one value before, so it has room for another.) This case is shown in Figure 13-16b.

The merging of *L* may have caused its parent *P* to be left without a value and with only one child. If so, you recursively apply the deletion procedure to *P*. If *P* has a sibling with two values (and three children), you redistribute the values among *P*, the sibling, and *P*'s parent. You also give *P* one of its sibling's children, as Figure 13-16c indicates.

If *P* has no sibling with two values, you merge *P* with a sibling (Figure 13-16d). You move a value down from the parent and let the sibling adopt *P*'s one child. (At this point you know that the sibling previously had only one value and two children.) If the merge causes *P*'s parent to be without a value, you recursively apply the deletion process to it.

If the merging continues so that the root of the tree is without a value (and has only one child), you simply delete the root. When this step occurs, the height of the tree is reduced by 1, as Figure 13-16e illustrates.

The following is a high-level statement of the algorithm for deleting from a 2-3 tree:

2-3 tree deletion algorithm

```
TableDelete(T, SearchKey, Success)
{ Deletes from table T, which is implemented as a 2-3 tree,
  the item whose search key equals SearchKey. The operation
  fails if no such item exists. The flag Success indicates
  whether the operation succeeded. }

    Attempt to locate item I whose search key equals SearchKey

    if I is present
       then
       begin
          Swap item I with its inorder successor, which will
             be in a leaf L
```

Figure 13-16

(a) Redistributing values; (b) merging a leaf; (c) redistributing values and children; (d) merging internal nodes; (e) deleting the root

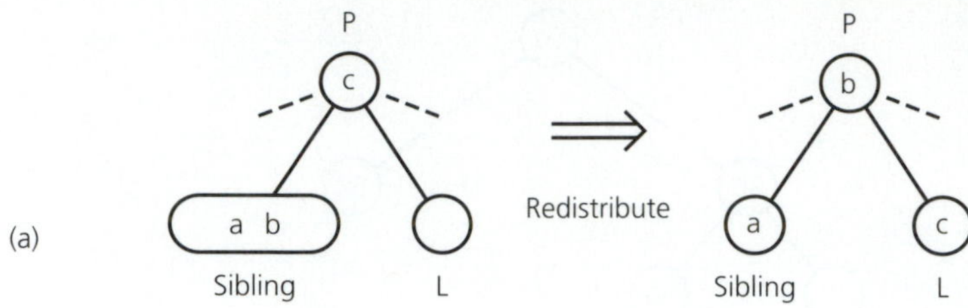

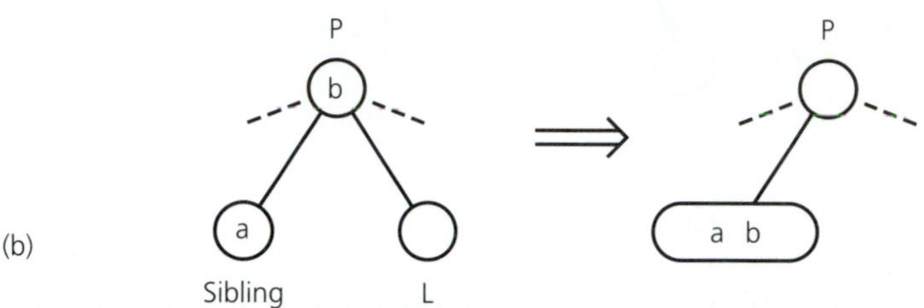

Merge and bring down value

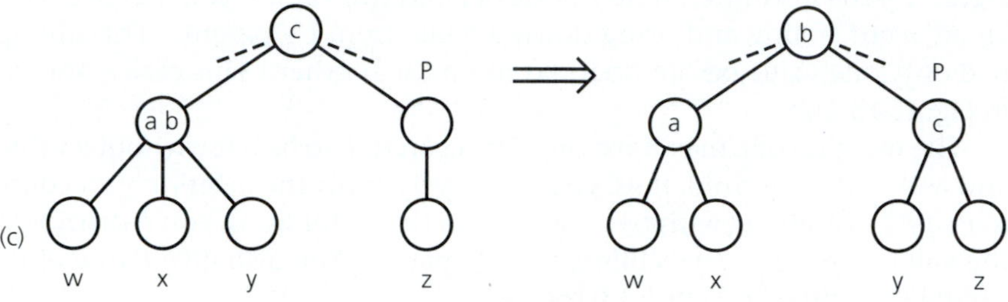

Redistribute among P, its parent, and its sibling

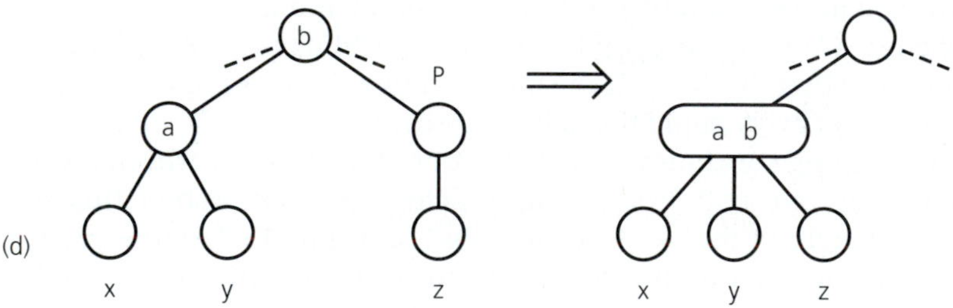

Merge and bring down value

(e)

Root

h

a b

x y z

h−1

a b

x y z

Remove empty root

```
        { the deletion always begins at a leaf }
         Delete item I from leaf L

         if L now has no items
            then Fix(L)
         Success := true
      end

      else Success := false

Fix(N)
{ Completes the deletion when node N is empty. Note that if
  N is internal, it has one child. }

    Let P be the parent of N--if N is the root, delete it and return
    if some sibling of N has two items
      then
      begin
         Distribute items appropriately among N, the sibling,
            and P

         if N is internal
             then move the appropriate child from sibling to N
      end

      else   { must merge the node }
      begin
         Choose an adjacent sibling S of N

         Bring the appropriate item down from P into S

         if N is internal
            then move N's child to S

         Delete node N

         if P is now empty
            then Fix(P)
      end
```

The details of the Pascal implementation of the preceding insertion and deletion algorithms for 2-3 trees are rather involved. The implementation is left as a challenging programming project.

Concluding Remarks About 2-3 Trees

The algorithms for inserting into and deleting from a 2-3 tree have just been described. Given that a 2-3 tree is always balanced, you can search it in all situations with the logarithmic efficiency of a binary search.

A 2-3 tree is always balanced

You might be concerned that the insertion and deletion algorithms incur some overhead in the course of maintaining the 2-3 structure of the tree. That is, after the search strategy locates either the item or the position for the new item, the insertion and deletion algorithms sometimes have to perform extra work, such as splitting and merging nodes. However, this extra work is not a real concern. A rigorous mathematical analysis would show that the extra work required to maintain the structure of a 2-3 tree after an insertion or a deletion is not significant. In other words, when analyzing the efficiency of the `TableInsert` and `TableDelete` algorithms, it is sufficient to consider only the time required to locate the item (or the position for the insertion). As you have seen, this step is highly efficient in all situations. Thus, the 2-3 tree implementation of the ADT table is guaranteed to support all the table operations in logarithmic time.

A 2-3 implementation of a table is O($\log_2 N$) for all table operations

Before leaving the topic of 2-3 trees, consider one final question: If a 2-3 tree is so good, are trees whose nodes can have more than three children even better? Recall that the advantage of a 2-3 tree is that it is a balanced structure that is easy to maintain, not that it might be shorter than a balanced binary search tree. The reduction in height of a 2-3 tree is offset by the fact that at each node the search algorithm may require more comparisons to determine which branch to take than those necessary if you use a balanced binary search tree. Similarly, although a tree whose nodes can have 100 children would be shorter than a 2-3 tree, its search algorithm would require more comparisons at each node in order to determine the appropriate subtree to search. It can be shown, in fact, that a binary search tree that is as balanced as possible minimizes the amount of work required to support the ADT table operations. The problem with a binary search tree is, of course, that its balance is difficult to maintain. A 2-3 tree is a compromise—although searching it may not be quite as efficient as searching a binary search tree of minimum height, it is relatively simple to maintain. Allowing the nodes of a tree to have more than three children would be counterproductive because searches would require more comparisons.

Allowing nodes with more than three children is counterproductive

Although searching a tree whose nodes have more than three children requires more comparisons than does searching a 2-3 tree, there are contexts in which you should use them. In the next chapter, for example, you will see that when a search tree is implemented in external storage, it is desirable to reduce its height, even at the expense of additional comparisons. The justification is that when a search tree is implemented externally, it is far more expensive to go from node to node than it is to perform comparisons with the data values in a node. As a consequence, you will want a search tree with the minimum possible height, even if it means that you will have to perform several comparisons at each node. Chapter 14 will discuss this point further and introduce an external search tree known as a **B-tree**.

AVL TREES

An AVL tree is a balanced binary search tree

An AVL **tree**—named for its inventors, Adel'son-Vel'skii and Landis—is a balanced binary search tree. Recall that the heights of the left and right subtrees of any node in a balanced binary tree differ by no more than 1.

Like a 2-3 tree, an AVL tree can be searched almost as efficiently as a minimum-height binary search tree. This section will simply introduce you to the notion of an AVL tree and leave the details for another course.

It is, in fact, possible to rearrange any binary search tree to obtain a binary search tree with the minimum possible height, that is, $\lceil \log_2(N + 1) \rceil$ for a tree with N nodes. Recall, for example, the algorithm developed in Chapter 10 and used in the case study of Chapter 12. The algorithm starts with an arbitrary binary search tree, saves its values in a file, and then constructs a new binary search tree of minimum height that contains these same values. Although this approach was appropriate in the context of the inventory system (since the rebuilding was performed only once a day), it requires too much work to be performed every time an insertion or deletion leaves the tree unbalanced. The cost of repeatedly rebuilding the tree could very well outweigh the benefit of searching a tree of minimum height.

An AVL tree maintains a height close to the minimum

The AVL method is a compromise. It maintains a binary search tree with a height close to the minimum, but it is able to do so with far less work than would be necessary to keep the height of the tree exactly equal to the minimum. The basic strategy of the AVL method is to monitor the shape of the binary search tree. You insert or delete nodes just as you would for any binary search tree, but after each insertion or deletion, you check that the tree is still an AVL tree. That is, you determine whether any node in the tree has left and right subtrees that differ in height by more than 1. For example, suppose that the binary search tree in Figure 13-17a is the result of a sequence of insertions and deletions. The heights of the left and right subtrees of the root 30 differ by 2. You can restore this tree's AVL property, that is, its balance, by rearranging its nodes. For instance, you can **rotate** the tree so that the node 20 becomes the root with left child 10 and right child 30, as in Figure 13-17b. Notice that you cannot arbitrarily rearrange the tree's nodes, because you must take care not to destroy the search tree's ordering property in the course of the rebalancing.

Rotations restore the balance

Rotations are not necessary after every insertion or deletion. For example, you can insert 40 into the AVL tree in Figure 13-17b and still have an AVL tree. (See Figure 13-17c.) However, when a rotation is necessary to restore a tree's AVL property, the rotation will be one of two possible types. We will demonstrate these rotations by example.

Suppose that you have the tree in Figure 13-18a after the insertion or deletion of a node. (Perhaps you obtained this tree by inserting 60 into an AVL tree.) An imbalance occurs at the node 20; that is, 20's left and right subtrees differ in height by more than 1. A **single rotation** to the left is

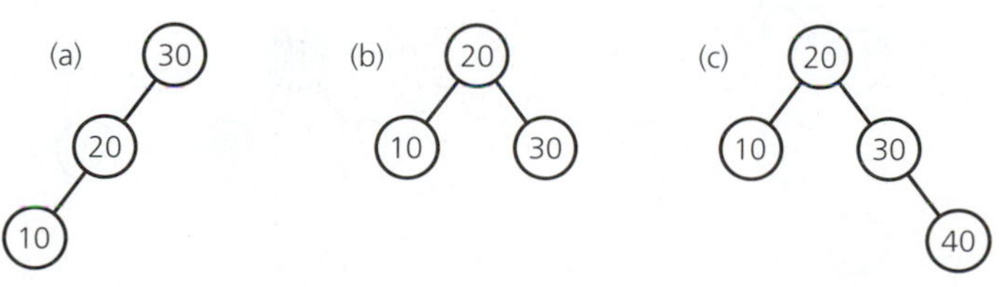

Figure 13-17

(a) An unbalanced binary search tree; (b) a balanced tree after rotation; (c) a balanced tree after insertion

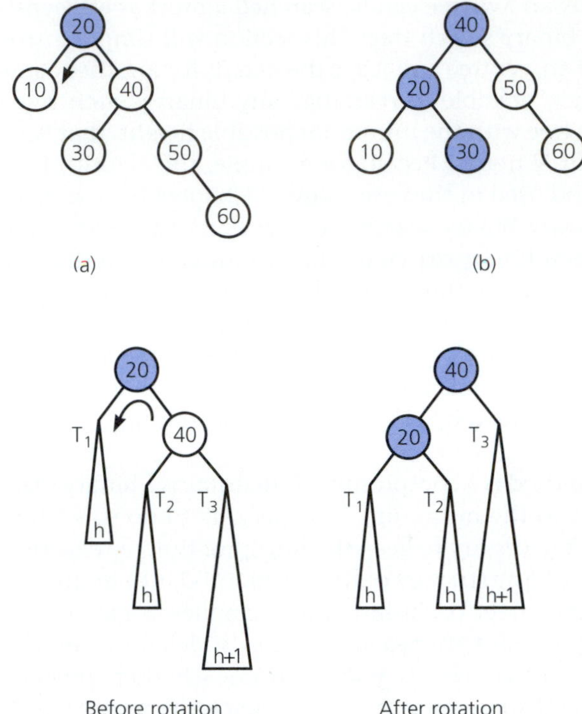

Figure 13-18

(a) An unbalanced binary search tree; (b) a balanced tree after a single left rotation

Figure 13-19

Before and after a single left rotation that decreases the tree's height

necessary to obtain the balanced tree in Figure 13-18b: 40 becomes the parent of 20, which adopts 30 as its right child. Figure 13-19 shows this rotation in a more general form. It shows, for example, that before the rotation the left and right subtrees of the node 40 have heights h and $h + 1$, respectively. After the rotation the tree is balanced and, in this particular case, has decreased in height from $h + 3$ to $h + 2$. Figures 13-20 and 13-21 show examples of a single left rotation that restores a tree's balance but does not affect its height. An analogous single right rotation would produce a mirror image of these examples.

A more complex rotation may be necessary. For example, consider the tree in Figure 13-22a, which is the result of nodes being added to or deleted from an AVL tree. The left and right subtrees of 20 differ in height by more than 1. A **double rotation** is necessary to restore this tree's balance. Figure 13-22b shows the result of a left rotation about 20, and Figure 13-22c

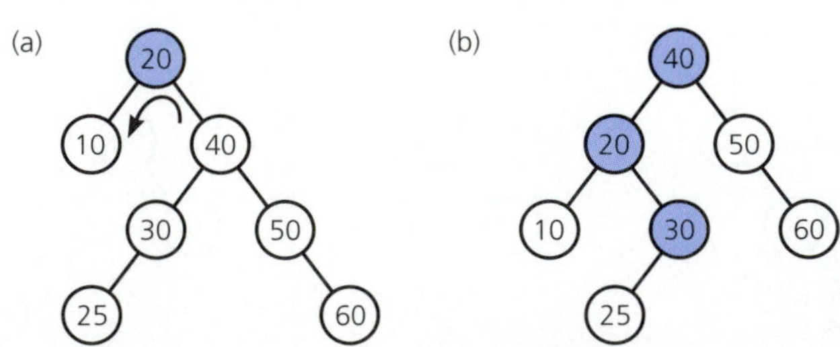

Figure 13-20

(a) An unbalanced binary search tree; (b) a balanced tree after a single left rotation

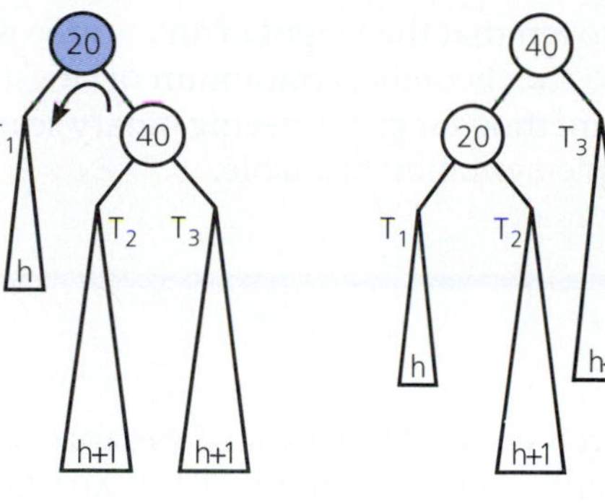

Figure 13-21

Before and after a single left rotation that does not affect the tree's height

Figure 13-22

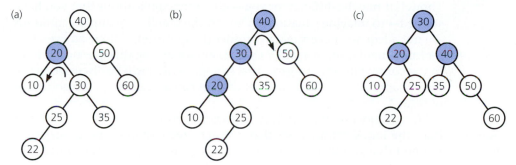

(a) Before; (b) during; and (c) after a double rotation

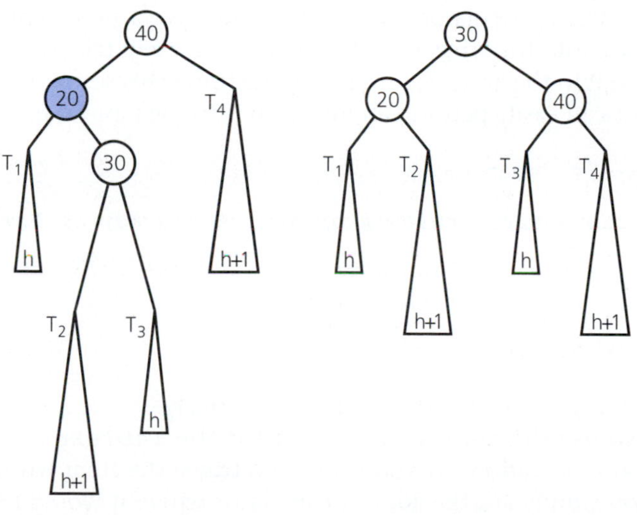

Figure 13-23

Before and after a double rotation that decreases the tree's height

shows the result of a right rotation about 40. Figure 13-23 illustrates this double rotation in a more general form. Mirror images of these figures provide examples of other possible double rotations.

It can be proven that the height of an AVL tree with N nodes will always be very close to the theoretical minimum of $\lceil \log_2(N + 1) \rceil$. The AVL tree is, therefore, one method for guaranteeing binary search-like efficiency in the search-tree implementation of a table.

HASHING

The binary search tree and its balanced variants, such as 2-3 and AVL trees, provide excellent implementations of the ADT table. They allow you to perform all the table operations quite efficiently. If, for example, a table contains 10,000 items, the operations `TableRetrieve`, `TableInsert`, and `TableDelete` each require approximately $\log_2 10{,}000 \approx 13$ steps. Though it may be difficult for you—given the applications that you have studied—to imagine situations in which the search-tree implementations are not adequate, nevertheless consider the question, is there an even better implementation of a table? One reason for asking this question is that, in the context of searching external storage, which will be discussed in the next chapter, even a small number of steps can actually require a good deal of time.

Table operations without searches

A radically different strategy is necessary to locate an item with fewer than the $\log_2 N$ comparisons that a search tree requires. Try to imagine a method that would allow you to locate (and insert or delete) an item virtually instantaneously.

Suppose that you have an array `T[0..N-1]`, with each array slot capable of holding a single table item. You also have a seemingly magical box called an "address calculator." Whenever you have a new item that you want to insert into the table, the address calculator will tell you where you should place it in the array. Figure 13-24 illustrates this scenario.

You thus can easily perform an insertion into the table as follows:

```
TableInsert(T, NewItem)

    Tell the address calculator the search key of NewItem

    Let I be the location where the address calculator
      tells you to put the new item

    T[I] := NewItem
```

An insertion is performed virtually instantaneously.

You also use the address calculator for the `TableRetrieve` and `TableDelete` operations. If you want to retrieve the item whose search key is `X`, you simply ask the address calculator where it would tell you to insert such an item. Because you would have inserted the item earlier by using the `TableInsert` algorithm just given, if the desired item is present in the table, it would be in the array location that the address calculator specifies. Thus, the retrieval operation appears as follows:

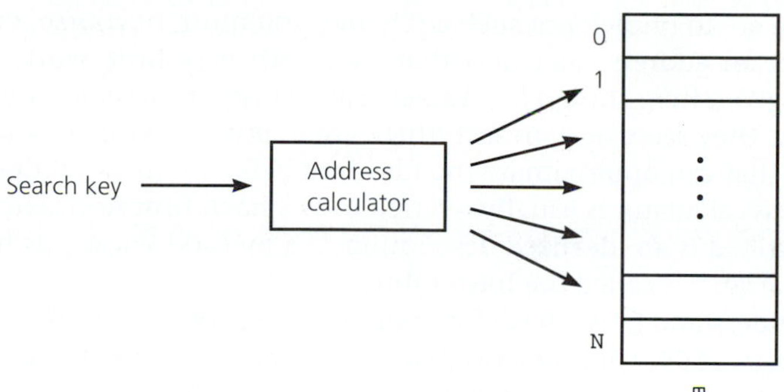

Figure 13-24

Address calculator

```
TableRetrieve(T, SearchKey, TableItem, Success)

    Let I be the location where the address calculator
      would put an item whose search key equals SearchKey

    if T[I].Key = SearchKey
       then
       begin
           TableItem := T[I]
           Success := true
       end

       { the item is not in the table }
       else Success := false
```

Similarly, the pseudocode for the deletion operation is

```
TableDelete(T, SearchKey, Success)

    Let I be the location where the address calculator
      would put an item whose search key equals SearchKey

    if T[I].Key = SearchKey
       then
       begin
           Delete the item from T[I]
           Success := true
       end

       { the item is not in the table }
       else Success := false
```

It thus appears that you can perform the operations `TableRetrieve`, `TableInsert`, and `TableDelete` virtually instantaneously. You never have to search for an item; instead, you simply let the address calculator determine where the item should be. The amount of time required to carry out the operations depends only on how quickly the address calculator can perform this computation.

If you are to implement such a scheme, you must, of course, be able to construct an address calculator that can, with very little work, tell you where a given item should be. Address calculators are actually not as mysterious as they seem and, in fact, there are many well-known address calculators that can approximate the idealized behavior just described. Such an address calculator is usually referred to as a **hash function**. The scheme just described is an idealized description of a method known as **hashing**, and the array `T` is called the **hash table.**

To understand how a hash function works, suppose that the array `T` has locations `0..100`. Suppose also that the search keys of the table items are positive integers, such as employee ID numbers. Then a hash function h must take an arbitrary positive integer x and map it into an integer in the range 0 through 100; that is, h is a function such that for any positive integer x,

A hash function

$$h(x) = n, \text{ where } n \text{ is an integer in the range } 0, \cdots, 100$$

Once you have selected a hash function h, the table operations are easy to write. For example in the `TableRetrieve` procedure, the step

```
Let I be the location where the address calculator
  would put an item whose search key equals SearchKey
```

is implemented simply as

```
I := h(SearchKey)
```

The table operations appear to be virtually instantaneous. But is hashing really as good as it sounds? If it really were this good, there would have been little reason for developing all those other table implementations. Hashing would beat them hands down!

Why is hashing not quite as simple as it seems? You might first notice that since the hashing scheme stores the items in an array, it would appear to suffer from the familiar problems associated with a fixed-size implementation. Obviously, the hash table must be large enough to contain all items that you want to store. This requirement, however, is not the crux of the implementation's difficulty, for—as you will see later—there are ways to allow the table to grow dynamically. There is, however, a major pitfall in the implementation, even given the assumption that the number of items in the table will never exceed the size of the hash table.

A perfect hash function is possible if you know all the search keys

Ideally, you want the hash function to map each x into a unique integer n. The hash function in the ideal situation is called a **perfect hash function.** In fact, it is possible to construct perfect hash functions, if you know all possible search keys. Although as you will see, this requirement is not impossible, you usually will not know the values of the search keys in advance.

Typically, collisions occur

Typically, a hash function will map two or more search keys x and y into the *same* integer n. That is, the hash function tells you to store two or more items in the same array location `T[I]`. This occurrence is called a **collision**. Thus, even if fewer than 101 items are present in the hash table

T[0..100], *h* could very well tell you to place more than one item into the same array location. For example, if two items have search keys 123445678 and 123445779, and if

$$h(123445678) = h(123445779) = 44$$

then *h* will tell you to place the two items into the same array location, *T[44]*. That is, the search keys 123445678 and 123445779 have collided.

Even if the number of items that can be in the array at any one time is small, the only way to avoid collisions completely is for the hash table to be large enough so that each possible search-key value can have its own location. If, for example, Social Security numbers were the search keys, you would need an array location for each integer in the range 000000000 through 999999999. This situation would certainly require a good deal of storage! Because reserving vast amounts of storage is usually not practical, collision-resolution schemes are necessary to make hashing a viable method. Such resolution schemes usually require that the hash function place items evenly throughout the hash table.

To summarize, a typical hash function must

Requirements for a hash function

- Be easy and fast to compute
- Place items evenly throughout the hash table

In addition, the hash table must be large enough to allow the hash function to distribute the items evenly throughout the table.

Consider now several hash functions and collision-resolution schemes.

Hash Functions

It is sufficient for hash functions to operate on integers

It is sufficient to consider hash functions that operate on search keys that are arbitrary integers. Why? If a search key is not an integer, there are simple ways to map the search key into an integer, which you then hash. If, for example, the search key is a character string—such as a name—you could convert it into an integer in one of several ways. The simplest way is first to assign each character in the string an integer value. For example, you could use the character's ASCII value—by using Pascal's *ord* function—or simply assign arbitrary values such as A = 1, B = 2, and so on. You could then add the values of the characters in the string. For example, you could convert the word "THE" either into the integer 2,085 by adding the ASCII values of the letters T, H, and E or into the integer 33 because T = 20, H = 8, and E = 5, and 20 + 8 + 5 = 33.

There are many ways to convert an arbitrary integer *x* into an integer within a certain range, such as 0 through 100. Here are several simple hash functions that assume that the search keys are positive integers.

Selecting digits. Suppose that your search key is the nine-digit employee ID number 001364825. You could select the fourth digit and the last digit to obtain 35 as the index to the hash table. That is,

$$h(001364825) = 35 \quad \{\text{select the fourth and last digits}\}$$

Therefore, you would store the item whose search key is 001364825 in `T[35]`.

You do need to be careful about which digits you choose in a particular situation. For example, the first three digits of a Social Security number are based on geography. If you select only these digits, you will map all people from the same state into the same location of the hash table.

Digit selection does not distribute items evenly in the hash table

Digit-selection hash functions are simple and fast, but generally they do not evenly distribute the items in the hash table.

Folding. One way to improve upon the previous method of selecting digits is to add the digits. For example, you can add all the digits in 001364825 to obtain

$$0 + 0 + 1 + 3 + 6 + 4 + 8 + 2 + 5 = 29 \qquad \{\text{add the digits}\}$$

Therefore, you would store the item whose search key is 001364825 in `T[29]`. Notice that if you add all digits from a nine-digit search key,

$$0 \leq h(\text{search key}) \leq 81$$

That is, you would use only `T[0]` through `T[81]` of the hash table. To change this situation or to increase the size of the hash table, you can group the digits in the search key and add the groups. For example, you could form three groups of three digits from the search key 001364825 and add them as follows:

$$001 + 364 + 825 = 1{,}190$$

For this hash function,

$$0 \leq h(\text{search key}) \leq 3 * 999 = 2{,}997$$

Clearly, if 2,997 is larger than the size of the hash table that you want, you can alter the groups that you choose. Perhaps not as obvious is that you can apply more than one hash function to a search key. For example, you could select some of the digits from the search key before adding them, or you could either select digits from the previous result 2,997 or apply folding to it once again by adding 29 and 97.

Applying more than one hash function to a single search key

Modulo arithmetic. Modulo arithmetic provides a simple and effective hash function. For example, consider the function

$$h(x) = x \bmod \mathit{TableSize}$$

where the hash table `T` has *TableSize* elements. In particular, $h(x) = x \bmod 101$ maps any integer x into the range 0 through 100. This hash function maps 001364825, for example, into array location 12 (001364825 mod 101).

There are many x's that map into `T[0]` because $x \bmod \mathit{TableSize} = 0$, many x's that map into `T[1]` because $x \bmod \mathit{TableSize} = 1$, and so on. However, you can distribute the table items evenly over all of `T`—thus reducing collisions—by choosing a prime number as *TableSize*. For instance, 101 in the previous example is prime.

The table size should be prime

Resolving Collisions

Consider the problems caused by a collision. Suppose that you want to insert an item whose search key is 123445678 into the hash table `T`, as was described previously. If you apply the hash function $h(x) = x$ `mod` 101 to 123445678, you will find that you should place the new item in `T[44]`. Suppose, however, that `T[44]` already contains an item, as Figure 13-25 illustrates. That is, earlier you had placed 123445779 into `T[44]` because 123445779 `mod` 101 equals 44. The question is, what do you do with the new item? You certainly do not want to disallow the insertion on the grounds that the table is full: You could have a collision even when inserting into a table containing only a single item!

There are two general approaches to collision resolution. One approach allocates another location *within* the hash table to the new item. A second approach changes the structure of the hash table so that each location `T[I]` can accommodate more than one item. The four collision-resolution schemes that appear next exemplify these two approaches.

Two approaches to collision resolution

Linear probing. Some commonly used methods for resolving collisions are based on the notion of **open addressing.** That is, during an attempt to insert a new item into a table, if the hash function indicates a location in the hash table that is already occupied, you **probe** for some other empty, or *open,* location in which to place the item. The concern, of course, is that you must be able to find a table item efficiently after you have inserted it. That is, the insertion-probe sequence must be reproducible by the `TableDelete` and `TableRetrieve` operations.

The difference among the various open-addressing schemes is the method used to probe for an empty location. One common scheme is called **linear probing.** In this scheme, you search the hash table sequentially, starting from the original hash location. More specifically, if

Begin at the hash location and search the table sequentially

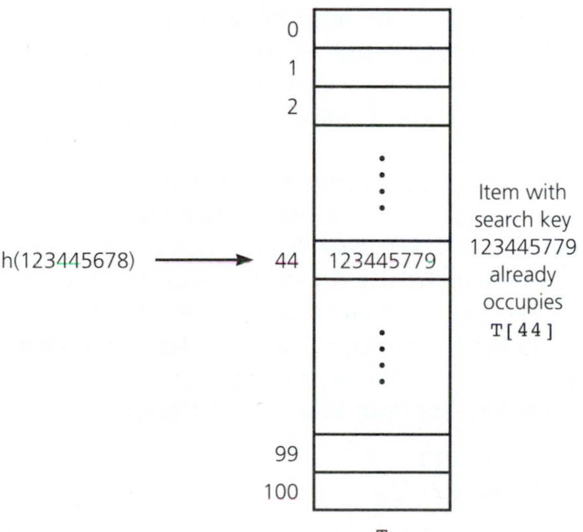

Figure 13-25

A collision

`T[h(SearchKey)]` is occupied, you check `T[h(SearchKey) + 1]`, `T[h(SearchKey) + 2]`, and so on until you find an available location. Typically you *wrap around* from the last table location to the first table location if necessary.

In the absence of deletions, it is straightforward to implement the `TableRetrieve` operation under this scheme. You need only follow the same probe sequence that the `TableInsert` operation used until you either find the item you are searching for; reach an empty location, which indicates that the item is not present; or visit every table location.

The presence of deletions, however, adds a slight complication. The `TableDelete` operation itself is no problem. You merely find the desired item, as in the `TableRetrieve` operation, and delete it, making the location empty. But what happens to the `TableRetrieve` operation after deletions? The new empty locations that `TableDelete` created along a probe sequence could cause the `TableRetrieve` operation to stop prematurely, incorrectly indicating a failure. You can resolve this problem by allowing a table location to be in one of three states: *occupied* (currently in use), *empty* (has not been used), or *deleted* (was once occupied, but is now available). You then modify the `TableRetrieve` operation to continue probing when it encounters a location in the deleted state. Similarly, you modify the `TableInsert` operation to insert into either empty or deleted locations.

Three states: occupied, empty, deleted

Efficiency

How efficient is linear probing? As the hash table fills, the chance of collision increases. As collisions increase, the probe sequences increase in length, causing increased search times. An unsuccessful search requires more time in general than a successful search. For example, for a table that is two-thirds full, an average unsuccessful search might require at most five comparisons, or probes, while an average successful search might require at most two comparisons. To maintain efficiency, it is important to prevent the hash table from filling up.

Clustering

One of the problems with the linear-probing scheme is that table items tend to **cluster** together in the hash table. That is, one part of the table might be quite dense, even though another part has relatively few items. It can be shown that this form of clustering is detrimental to the overall efficiency of hashing because it causes long probe searches.

Double hashing. Double hashing, which is a second open-addressing scheme, drastically reduces clustering. Notice that the **probe sequence** that linear probing uses is *key independent*. That is, linear probing inspects the table locations sequentially no matter what the hash key is. Double hashing defines *key-dependent* probe sequences. In this scheme the probe sequence still searches the table in a linear order, but a second hash function determines the size of the steps taken. For example, let h_1 and h_2 be the primary and secondary hash functions defined as

A hash address and a step size determine the probe sequence

$$h_1(key) = key \bmod 11$$
$$h_2(key) = key \bmod 7$$

where we assume a hash table of only 11 items, so that you can readily see the effect of these functions on the hash table. If *key* = 25, then h_1 indicates that *key* hashes to table location 3 (25 mod 11), and h_2 indicates that the probe sequence should take steps of size 4 (25 mod 7). In other words, the probe sequence will be 3, 7, 0 (wraps around), 4, 8, 1 (wraps around), 5, 9, 2, 6, 10, 3. On the other hand, if *key* = 9, then h_1 indicates that *key* hashes to table location 9 (9 mod 11), and h_2 indicates that the probe sequence should take steps of size 2 (9 mod 7), and so the probe sequence would be 9, 0, 2, 4, 6, 8, 10, 1, 3, 5, 7, 9.

Note that each of these probe sequences visits *all* the table locations. This phenomenon always occurs if the size of the table and the size of the probe step are relatively prime, that is, if their greatest common divisor is 1. Because the size of a hash table is commonly a prime number, it will be relatively prime to all step sizes.

On the average, double hashing requires fewer comparisons than linear probing. As a result, you can use a smaller hash table for double hashing than you can for linear probing. However, because they are open-addressing schemes, both linear probing and double hashing suffer when you are unable to predict the number of insertions and deletions that will occur. If your hash table is too small, it will fill up, and search efficiency will decrease.

Buckets. Another method commonly used to resolve a collision is to change the structure of the array `T`—the hash table—so that it can accommodate more than one item in the same location. You could, for example, change `T` so that each location `T[I]` is itself an array—called a **bucket**—capable of holding *B* items. The problem with this approach, of course, is choosing *B*. If *B* is too small, you will only have postponed the problem of collisions until *B* + 1 items map into some array location. If you attempt to make *B* large enough so that each array location can accommodate the largest number of items that might map into it, you are likely to waste a good deal of storage.

Accommodate more than one item per hash-table location

Separate chaining. An approach that is better than using buckets is to design the hash table as an array of linked lists. In this collision-resolution method, known as **separate chaining**, each entry `T[I]` is a pointer to a linked list—the **chain**—of items that the hash function has mapped into location `I`, as Figure 13-26 illustrates. The following Pascal statements describe such a hash table:

Each hash-table location is a linked list

```
const  TableSize = <maximum size of hash table>;

type   keyType = <desired type of search key>;

       itemType = record
           Key : keyType;
           <... and possibly other fields>
       end;   { record }
```

```
         ptrType = ^nodeType;
         nodeType = record
            Item : itemType;
            Next : ptrType
         end;  { record }

         hashTableType = array[0..TableSize-1] of ptrType;

var      T : hashTableType;
```

When you insert a new item into the table, you simply place it at the beginning of the linked list that the hash function indicates. The following pseudocode describes the insertion algorithm for a linked hash table:

```
TableInsert(T, NewItem)

   SearchKey := the search key of NewItem
   I := h(SearchKey)
   new(p)
   p^.Item := NewItem
   p^.Next := T[I]
   T[I] := p
```

When you want to retrieve an item, you search the linked list that the hash function indicates. The following pseudocode describes the retrieval algorithm:

```
TableRetrieve(T, SearchKey, TableItem, Success)

   I := h(SearchKey)
   p := T[I]

   while (p <> nil) Cand (p^.Key <> SearchKey) do
      p := p^.Next
   if p <> nil
      then
```

Figure 13-26

Separate chaining

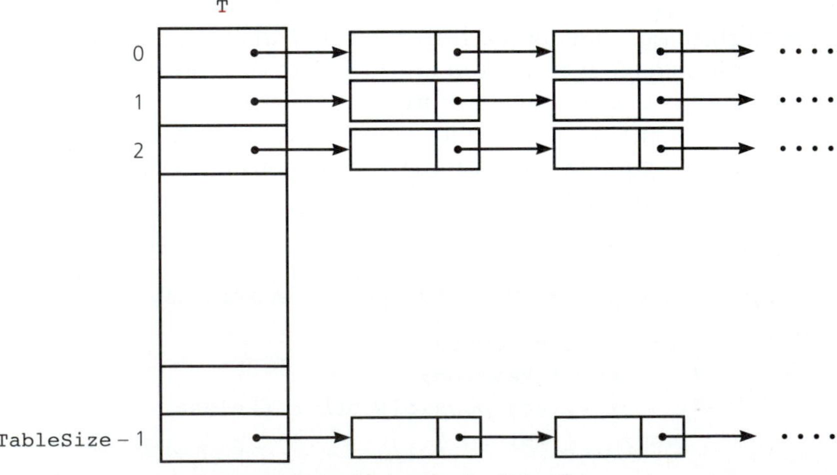

Each table location is a linked list

```
begin
    TableItem := p^.Item
    Success := true
end

else Success := false
```

The `TableDelete` algorithm is very similar to `TableRetrieve` and is left as an exercise.

Separate chaining successfully resolves collisions

Separate chaining is thus a successful method of resolving collisions. Notice also that the total size of the table is now dynamic, since each linked list can be as long as necessary. This observation leads to the next question: How efficient are the table operations under this scheme? While the `TableInsert` operation is still instantaneous, the `TableRetrieve` and `TableDelete` operations are not. They require a search of the linked list of items.

Efficiency

To analyze the efficiency of the retrieval and deletion operations under the separate-chaining approach, you must estimate the length of the linked lists that you need to search. If your array `T` has `TableSize` entries—that is, if it is an array `T[0..TableSize-1]`—and there are `N` items in the table, then the average length of a linked list is `N/TableSize`. In choosing the size of the array `T`, you should estimate the largest possible `N` and select an array size `TableSize` so that `N/TableSize` is small. For example, you could select `TableSize` to be near `N`, the expected maximum number of items in the table. If you are successful at this selection, it is likely that the linked lists that `TableRetrieve` and `TableDelete` must search will be quite short.

Even if it is likely that the linked lists are short, you still should ask, in the worst case, how long can a list be? If you seriously underestimate the maximum size of the table or if you are extremely unlucky and most of the table items happen to hash into the same location, the number of items on a linked list could be quite large. (Shortly you will see circumstances that might make you appear to be unlucky.) In fact, in the worst case, all `N` items in the table could be on the same linked list!

As you can see, the time that a retrieval or deletion operation requires can range between almost nothing—if the linked list to be searched has only one or two items on it—to the time required to search a linked list that contains all the items in the table, if all the items hashed into the same location. Therefore, although the hashing implementation might often be faster than a search-tree implementation, in the worst case it can be much slower. If so, you should either change your hashing function or increase the size of the hash table; you should not use complex collison-resolution schemes.

Table Traversal: An Operation That Hashing Does Not Support Well

For many applications, hashing provides the most efficient implementation of the ADT table. There is, however, one important table operation not yet considered that the hashing schemes do not support well at all: the operation of traversing the table in *sorted order*. A hash function scatters the items randomly throughout the array, so that there is no ordering relationship between the search keys that hash into `T[I]` and those that hash into `T[I+1]`. (In fact, as you will see, a good hash function necessarily scatters the search keys as randomly as possible.) As a consequence, if you must traverse the table in sorted order—for example, to print it out—you would first have to perform a sort on the items. If this operation were required frequently, hashing would be a far less attractive implementation than a search tree.

Items hashed into `T[I]` and `T[I+1]` have no ordering relationship

Traversing a table in sorted order is really just one example of a whole class of operations that hashing does not support well. Many similar operations that you often wish to perform on a table require the items to be ordered. For example, consider an operation that must find the table item with the smallest or largest value in its search key. If you use a search-tree implementation, then these items are in the leftmost and rightmost nodes of the tree, respectively. If you use a hashing implementation, however, there is no way of knowing where these items are—you would have to search the entire table. A similar type of operation is a **range query**, which requires that you retrieve all items that have a search key that falls into a given range of values. For example, you might want to retrieve all of the items whose search keys are in the range 129 to 755. This task is relatively easy to perform by using a binary search tree (see Exercise 1), but if you use hashing, there is no efficient way to answer the range query.

Hashing versus balanced search trees

In general, if an application requires any of these ordered operations, you should probably use a search tree. Although hashing does support the `TableRetrieve`, `TableInsert`, and `TableDelete` operations somewhat more efficiently than does a balanced search tree, the balanced search tree supports these operations so efficiently itself that, in most contexts, the difference in speed for these operations is negligible (whereas the advantage of the search tree over hashing for the ordered operations is significant). In the context of external storage, however, the story is different. For data that is stored externally, the difference in speed between hashing's implementation of `TableRetrieve` and a search tree's implementation may well be significant. As you will see in Chapter 14, in an external setting it is not uncommon to see a hashing implementation used to support the `TableRetrieve` operation and a search-tree implementation used simultaneously to support the ordered operations.

What Constitutes a Good Hash Function?

Before concluding this introduction to hashing, consider in more detail the issue of choosing a hash function to perform the address calculations for a given application. A great deal has been written on this subject, most of which is beyond the mathematical level of this book. However, this section will present a brief summary of the major concerns.

- **A hash function should be easy and fast to compute.** If a hashing scheme is to perform table operations almost instantaneously, you certainly must be able to calculate the hash function rapidly. Most of the common hash functions require only a single division (like the modulo function), a single multiplication, or some kind of "bit-level" operation on the internal representation of the search key. In all these cases, the requirement that the hash function be easy and fast to compute is satisfied.

- **A hash function should evenly scatter the data throughout the hash table.** No matter what hash function you use, there is in general no way to avoid collisions entirely. (Of course, a perfect hashing function avoids collisions.) For example, to achieve the best performance from a separate chaining scheme, each entry `T[I]` should contain approximately the same number of items on its chain; that is, each chain should contain approximately `N/TableSize` items (and thus no chain should contain significantly more than `N/TableSize` items). To accomplish this goal, your hash function should scatter the search keys evenly throughout the hash table.

You cannot avoid collisions entirely

There are two issues to consider with regard to how evenly a hash function scatters the search keys.

- **How well does the hash function scatter random data?** If every search-key value is equally likely, will the hash function scatter the search keys evenly? For example, consider the following scheme for hashing nine-digit ID numbers:

  `T[0..39]` is the hash table, and
  the hash function is $h(x)$ = (first two digits of x) mod 40

  The question is, given the assumption that all employee ID numbers are equally likely, does a given ID number x have equal probability of hashing into any one of the 40 array locations? For this hash function, the answer is no. Notice that three different ID *prefixes*—that is, the first two digits of an ID number—map into each array location `0..19`, while only two different prefixes map into each array location `20..39`. For example, ID numbers that start with 19, 59, and 99 map into `T[19]`, while only ID numbers that start with 20 and 60 map into `T[20]`. Given that all ID numbers are equally likely—and thus that all prefixes 00 through 99 are equally likely—a given ID number is 50 percent more likely to hash into one of the locations `0..19` than it is to hash into one of the locations `20..39`. As a result, each array location `0..19` would contain, on average, 50 percent more items than each location `20..39`.

  Thus, the hash function

  $h(x)$ = (first two digits of x) mod 40

  A function that does not scatter random data evenly

  does not scatter random data evenly throughout the array `T[0..39]`. On the other hand, it can be shown that the hash function

A function that does scatter random data evenly

$h(x) = x \bmod 101$

does, in fact, scatter random data evenly throughout the array `T[0..100]`.

- **How well does the hash function scatter nonrandom data?** Even if a hash function scatters random data evenly, it may have trouble with nonrandom data. In general, no matter what hash function you select, it is always possible that the data will have some unlucky pattern that will result in uneven scattering. Although there is no way to guarantee that a hash function will scatter all data evenly, there are hashing techniques that can greatly increase the likelihood of uniformity.

  As an example, consider the following scheme:

  `T[0..99]` is the hash table, and
  the hash function is $h(x)$ = first two digits of x

  If every ID number is equally likely, then it is apparent that h will scatter the search keys evenly throughout the array. But what if every ID number is not equally likely? A company might assign employee ID's according to department. For instance, suppose that ID numbers are assigned according to the following convention:

10xxxxx	Sales
20xxxxx	Customer Relations
. . .	
90xxxxx	Data Processing

  Under this assignment, only 9 out of the 100 array locations would contain any items at all. Further, those locations corresponding to the largest departments (Sales, for example, which corresponds to `T[10]`) would contain more items than those locations corresponding to the smallest departments. This scheme certainly does not scatter the data evenly. A large body of theoretical results describes the types of hash functions that you should use to guard against various types of patterns in the data. These results are really in the province of more advanced courses, but two general principles can be noted here:

General requirements of a hash function

1. The calculation of the hash function should *involve the entire search key*. Thus, for example, computing a modulo of the entire ID number is much safer than using only its first two digits.
2. If a hash function uses modulo arithmetic, *the base should be prime;* that is, if h is of the form

   $h(x) = x \bmod TableSize$

   then *TableSize* should be a prime number. This selection of *TableSize* is a safeguard against many subtle kinds of patterns in the data (for example, search keys whose digits are likely to be multiples of one another). Although each application can have its own particular kind of patterns and thus should be analyzed on an individual basis, choosing *TableSize* to be prime is an easy way to safeguard against some common types of patterns in the data.

To summarize, hashing is a table implementation that in many cases can support the operations `TableRetrieve`, `TableInsert`, and `TableDelete` even faster than a balanced search tree. Although hashing does not efficiently support operations that require the table items to be ordered—for example, traversing the table in sorted order—it is nevertheless the most efficient table implementation for many types of applications. The next chapter uses hashing in a discussion of external searching techniques.

DATA WITH MULTIPLE ORGANIZATIONS

Many applications require a data organization that simultaneously supports several different data-management tasks. As a simple example, suppose that you must maintain a waiting list of customers, that is, a queue of customer records. Suppose that in addition to requiring the standard queue operations `QueueIsEmpty`, `Add`, `Remove`, and `QueueFront`, the application frequently requires a listing of the records of the customers in the queue. This listing is more useful if the records appear sorted by customer name. You thus need a `Traverse` operation that visits the customer records in sorted order.

This scenario presents an interesting problem. If you simply store the customer records in a queue, they will not, in general, be sorted by name. If, on the other hand, you simply store the records in sorted order, you will not be able to perform the queue operations; that is, you will be unable to process the customers on a first-come, first-served basis. Apparently, this problem requires you to organize the data in two different ways.

One solution is to maintain two independent data structures, one organized to support the sorted traversal and the other organized to support the queue operations. Figure 13-27 depicts a sorted linked list of customer records and a pointer-based implementation of the queue. The pointer-based data structures are a good choice because there is no good estimate of the maximum number of customer records that must be stored.

Several independent data structures waste space

One obvious disadvantage of this scheme is the space that it requires to store two copies of each customer record. In addition, not all of the required operations are supported as efficiently as possible. How well does this scheme support the required operations?

The operations that require you only to *retrieve* data—sorted `Traverse` and `QueueFront`—are easy to perform. You can obtain a sorted listing of customer records by traversing the sorted linked list, and you can perform

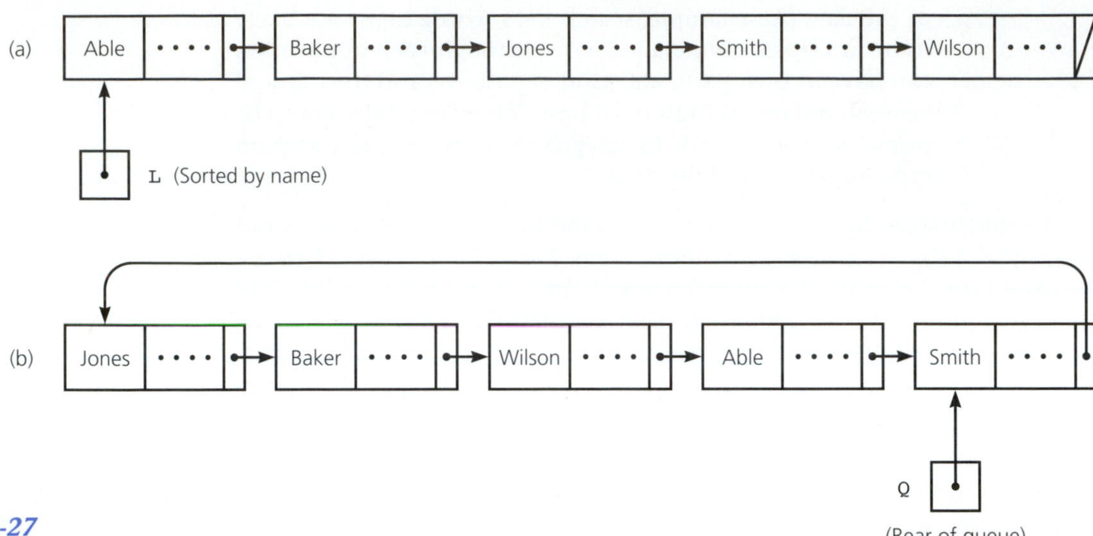

Figure 13-27

Independent data structures: (a) a sorted linked list; (b) a pointer-based queue

the `QueueFront` operation by inspecting the record at the front of the queue. The operations `Add` and `Remove` are, however, more difficult to perform because they must *modify* the data.

The `Add` operation has two steps:

1. Insert a copy of the new customer record at the rear of the queue. This step requires only a few pointer changes.
2. Insert a copy of the new customer record into its proper position in the sorted linked list. This step requires a traversal of the sorted linked list.

Similarly, the `Remove` operation has two steps:

1. Delete the customer at the front of the queue, but retain a copy of the name. This step requires only a few pointer changes.
2. Search the sorted linked list for the name just removed from the queue, and delete from the list the customer record containing this name. This step requires a traversal of the sorted linked list.

Several independent data structures do not support all operations efficiently

Thus, although the scheme efficiently supports the `Traverse` and `QueueFront` operations, `Add` and `Remove` require a traversal of the sorted linked list (whereas in a queue alone `Add` and `Remove` require only a small, constant number of steps). Is there any way to improve this scheme? One possibility is to store the customer records in a binary search tree rather than a sorted linked list. This approach would allow you to perform the second steps of the `Add` and `Remove` operations much more efficiently. While the binary search tree strategy is certainly an improvement over the original scheme, the `Add` and `Remove` operations would still require significantly more work than they would for a normal queue.

In fact, a different kind of scheme, one that supports the `Remove` operation almost as efficiently as if you were maintaining only a queue, is possible by allowing the data structures to communicate with each other.

This concept is demonstrated here first with a sorted linked list and a queue, and then with more complex structures, such as a binary search tree.

A better way

In the data structure shown in Figure 13-28, the sorted linked list still contains customer records, but the queue now contains only pointers to customer records. That is, each entry of the queue points to the record in the sorted linked list of the customer at the given queue position. An obvious advantage of storing only pointers in the queue is that the storage requirements are reduced, since a pointer is likely to be much smaller than a customer record (which could contain a large number of fields). As you will soon see, this scheme also significantly improves the efficiency of the `Remove` operation.

The efficiency of the `Traverse`, `QueueFront`, and `Add` operations does not differ significantly from the original scheme that Figure 13-27 depicts. You still perform the `Traverse` operation by traversing the sorted linked list. However, you perform `QueueFront` and `Add` as follows:

```
QueueFront(Q)

    Let p be the pointer stored at the front of the queue

    { p points to the record in the sorted linked list
      corresponding to the customer at the front of the
      queue }

    Return the record pointed to by p

Add(Q, NewItem)

    Find the proper position for NewItem in the sorted
      linked list
    Insert a record containing NewItem into this position
    Add to the rear of the queue a pointer to the new record
```

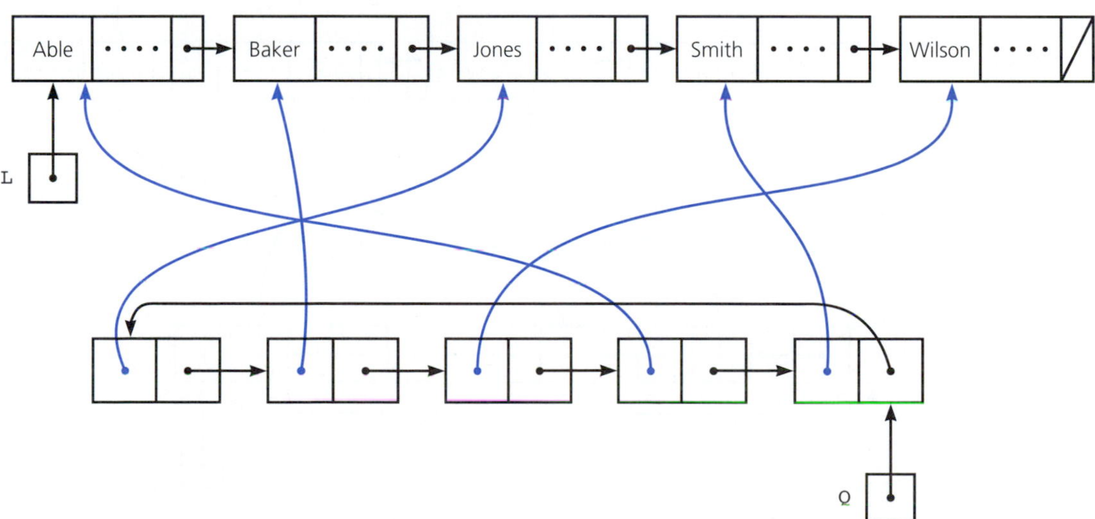

Figure 13-28

A queue pointing into a sorted linked list

The real benefit of the new scheme is in the implementation of the `Remove` operation.

```
Remove(Q)

  Remove the item at the front of the queue and retain its
    value p

  { p points to the customer record to be deleted }
  Delete from the sorted linked list the customer record to
    which p points
```

Because the front of the queue contains a pointer to the customer record *R* that you want to delete, there is no need to search the sorted linked list. You have a pointer to the appropriate record, and all you need to do is delete it.

There is one big problem, however. Because you are able to go directly to *R* without traversing the linked list from its beginning, you have no trailing pointer to the record that precedes *R* on the list! Recall that you must have a trailing pointer to delete the record. As the scheme now stands, the only way to obtain the trailing pointer is to traverse the linked list from its beginning, but this requirement negates the advantage gained by having the queue point into the linked list. However, as you saw in Chapter 3, you can solve this problem by replacing the singly linked list in Figure 13-28 with a doubly linked list, as shown in Figure 13-29. (See Project 12.)

A doubly linked list is required

To summarize, you have seen a fairly good scheme for supporting the queue operations plus a sorted traversal. The only operation whose efficiency you might improve significantly is `Add`. Recall that to perform the

Figure 13-29

A queue pointing into a doubly linked list

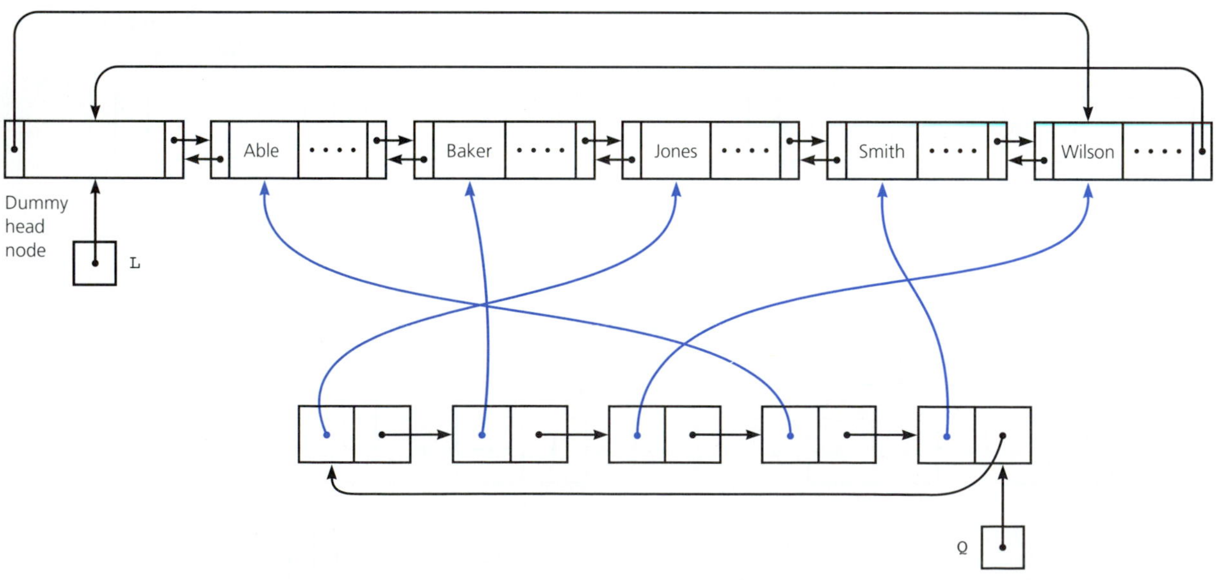

`Add` operation, you still must traverse the linked list to find the proper place to insert a new customer record.

The choice to store the customer records in a linear linked list was made to simplify the discussion. A more efficient scheme has the queue point into a binary search tree rather than a linked list. This data structure allows you to perform the `Add` operation in logarithmic time, assuming that the tree remains balanced. Notice, however, that you need the analogue of a doubly linked tree to support the `Remove` operation efficiently. That is, each node in the tree must point to its parent so that you can easily delete the node to which the front of the queue points. Figure 13-30 illustrates this data structure; its implementation, which is somewhat difficult, is the subject of Project 13.

Figure 13-30

A queue pointing into a doubly linked binary search tree

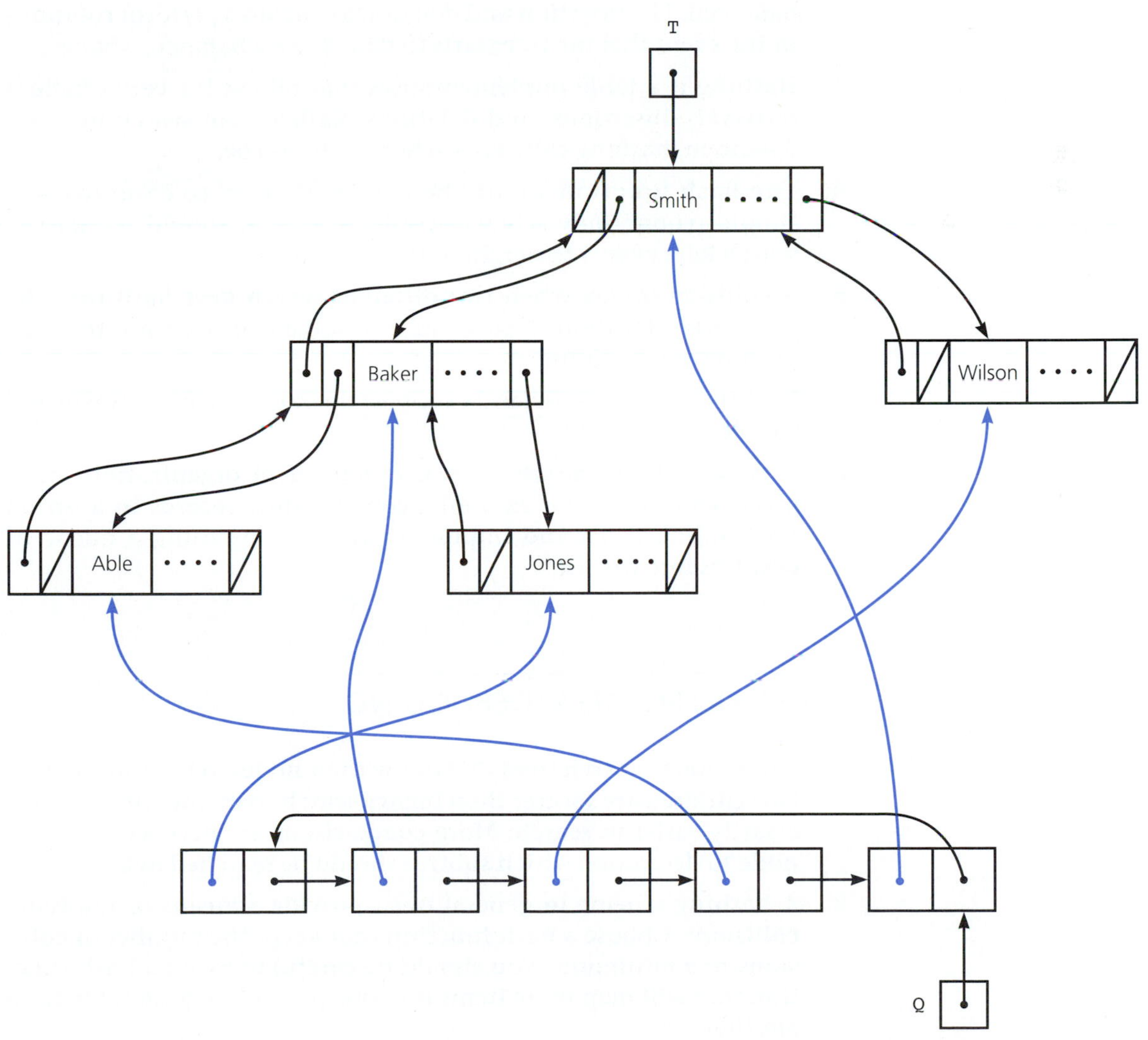

In general, it is possible to impose several different organizations simultaneously on a set of data items. This concept is discussed further in Chapter 14 in the context of indexing external storage.

SUMMARY

1. **A 2-3 tree is a variant of a binary search tree. The internal nodes of a 2-3 tree can have either two or three children. By allowing the number of children to vary, the insertion and deletion algorithms can easily maintain the balance of the tree.**
2. **An AVL tree is a binary search tree that is guaranteed to remain balanced. The insertion and deletion algorithms perform rotations in the event that the tree starts to stray from a balanced shape.**
3. **Hashing is a table implementation that allows for very efficient retrievals, insertions, and deletions. Rather than searching for a data item, hashing calculates where it should be.**
4. **The hash function should be extremely easy to compute—it should require only a few operations—and it should scatter the search keys evenly throughout the hash table.**
5. **A collision occurs when two different search keys hash into the same array location. Two ways to resolve collisions are through probing and chaining.**
6. **Hashing does not efficiently support operations such as traversing a table in sorted order.**
7. **It is possible to impose several independent organizations on a given set of data. For example, you can store records in a sorted doubly linked list and impose a FIFO order by using a queue of pointers into the list.**

COMMON PITFALLS / DEBUGGING

1. **Even though search trees that allow their nodes to have more than two children are shorter than binary search trees, they are not necessarily easier to search: More comparisons are necessary at each node to determine which subtree should be searched next.**
2. **A hashing scheme in general must provide a means of resolving collisions. Choose a hash function that keeps the number of collisions to a minimum. You should be careful to avoid a hash function that will map more items into one part of the hash table than another.**

3. **Hashing is not a good table implementation if you frequently require operations that depend on some order of the table's items. For example, if you frequently need to either traverse the table in sorted order or find the item with the largest search-key value, you probably should not use hashing.**

SELF-TEST EXERCISES

1. What is the result of inserting 5, 40, 10, 20, 15, and 30—in the order given—into an initially empty 2-3 tree? Note that insertion of an item into an empty 2-3 tree will create a single node that contains the inserted item.
2. What is the result of deleting the 10 from the 2-3 tree that you created in Self-Test Exercise 1?
3. Write the pseudocode for the `TableDelete` operation when linear probing is used to implement the hash table.
4. What is the probe sequence that double hashing uses when $h_1(key) = key \bmod 11$, $h_2(key) = key \bmod 7$, and $key = 19$.
5. If $h(x) = x \bmod 7$ and separate chaining resolves collisions, what does the hash table look like after the following insertions occur: 8, 10, 24, 15, 32, 17? Assume that each table item contains only a search key.

EXERCISES

1. Write a procedure to implement a **range query** for a binary search tree. That is, write a procedure that will visit all items that have a search key in a given range of values (such as all values between 100 and 1,000).
2. Write the pseudocode for a range-query procedure for a 2-3 tree. (See Exercise 1.)
3. What are the advantages of implementing the ADT table with a 2-3 tree instead of a binary search tree? Why do you not, in general, maintain a completely balanced binary search tree?
4. Execute the following sequence of operations on an initially empty ADT table that is implemented as
   a. A binary search tree
   b. A 2-3 tree
   c. An AVL tree

```
TableInsert(10)
TableInsert(100)
TableInsert(30)
TableInsert(80)
TableInsert(50)
TableDelete(10)
TableInsert(60)
TableInsert(70)
TableInsert(40)
TableDelete(80)
TableInsert(90)
TableInsert(20)
TableDelete(30)
TableDelete(70)
```

5. Write the pseudocode for the `TableDelete` operation when separate chaining resolves collisions.

6. Consider search keys that are English words instead of integers.

  a. Write a program that will implement a hash table for English words by using the following scheme: Let A = 1, B = 2, and so on, and let *h*(*key*) be the value of the first character of the search key. Thus, "THE" maps to 20. Resolve collisions by separate chaining with unsorted linked lists.

  b. How appropriate is the hash function in Part *a* if you are entering random strings into a table? What if the words come from English text?

  c. Experiment with other hashing schemes. Experiment with other implementations of chaining (for example, binary search trees, 2-3 trees, and other hash functions).

7. Modify the hash implementation of the ADT table described in Exercise 6a to check for duplicates on insertion. That is, you should add an item to a table only if it is not already present. Does this change affect the amount of time required to perform an insertion?

8. Repeat Exercise 6, but this time use linear probing as the collision-resolution scheme.

9. Repeat Exercise 6, but this time use double hashing as the collision-resolution scheme.

10. The success of a hash-table implementation of the ADT table is related to the choice of a good hash function. A good hash function is one that is easy to compute and will evenly distribute the possible data. Comment on the appropriateness of the following hash functions. What patterns would hash to the same location?

  a. The hash table has size 2,048. The search keys are identifier names in Pascal. The hash function is

  h(*key*) = (position of first letter of *key* in alphabet) mod 2048

b. The hash table is 10,000 entries long. The search keys are integers in the range *0..9999*. The hash function is

h(*key*) = (*key* * *random*) truncated to an integer

where *random* represents a sophisticated random-number generator that returns a real value between 0 and 1.

c. The search keys are integers in the range *0..9999*. The hash function is given by the following Pascal function:

```
function Hash(X : integer) : 0..TableSize;
var I : integer;
begin
   for I := 1 to 1000000 do
       X := (X * X) mod TableSize;
   Hash := X
end;
```

d. The keys are English words. The hash function is

h(*key*) = (sum of positions in alphabet of *key*'s letters) mod *TableSize*

PROJECTS

***11.** Implement the ADT table by using a 2-3 tree.

12. Implement the ADT queue operations as well as a sorted traversal operation for a queue that points into a doubly linked list, as shown in Figure 13-29.

***13.** Implement the ADT queue operations as well as a sorted traversal operation for a queue that points into a doubly linked binary search tree, as shown in Figure 13-30. You will need the insertion and deletion operations for a binary search tree that contains parent pointers, as discussed in Exercise 27 of Chapter 10.

14. Repeat Project 11, 12, or 13, but implement the ADT as an object.

15. Revise the object type that you wrote in Project 14 so that the items in the object are dynamically allocated objects that descend from *genericObjectType*, as defined in Chapter 4. Write a small program that demonstrates how to allocate, use, and deallocate your new object. Include a procedure that allocates objects that descend from *genericObjectType*.

CHAPTER 14

External Methods

PREVIEW This chapter considers a table that is so large you must store it in an external file. By using a direct access file as a model of external storage, the chapter shows how you can modify the mergesort algorithm to sort data that resides in a file. Finally, you will see how to search an external file by using generalizations of the hashing and search-tree schemes developed previously.

A LOOK AT EXTERNAL STORAGE

This chapter considers the problem of data management in a different type of environment. Whereas previous tables of data items were stored in the internal memory of the computer, assume now that the table resides on an external storage device such as a disk.

Until now, your only contact with external storage involved reading data from and writing data to Pascal files. For example, recall the videocassette inventory program developed in the case studies of Chapters 3 and 12. At the end of each business day, the program saves the current inventory in a Pascal file so that at the beginning of the next day, it can restore the inventory by reading the file. This scenario illustrates one of the advantages of external storage: It exists beyond the execution period of a program.

External storage exists after program execution

Another advantage of external storage is that, in general, it is available in a far greater quantity than is internal memory. If you have a table of 1,000,000 data items, each of which is a record of moderate size, it is not likely that you will be able to store the entire table in internal memory at one time. On the other hand, this much data can easily reside on an external disk. As a consequence, when dealing with tables of this magnitude, you cannot simply read the entire table into memory when you want to operate on it, and write it out when you are finished. Instead, you must devise ways to operate on data—for example, sort it and search it—while it resides externally.

Generally, there is more external storage than internal memory

Recall that Turbo Pascal enables you to access a general file either sequentially or directly. To access the data stored at a given position in a **sequential access file**, you must advance the file window beyond all the intervening data. In this sense, a sequential access file resembles a linked list. To access a particular node on the list, you must traverse the list from its beginning until you reach the desired node. In contrast, a **direct access file** allows you to access the data at a given position directly. A direct access file resembles an array in that you can access the element at `A[i]` without first accessing the elements before `A[i]`.

Without direct access files, it would be impossible to support the table operations efficiently in an external environment. Many programming languages, including Turbo Pascal, support direct access files. However, to permit a language-independent discussion, we will construct a model of direct access files that illustrates how a programming language that does

Direct access files are essential for external tables

not support such files might implement them. This model will be a simplification of reality, but will include the features necessary for this discussion.

Imagine that a computer's memory is divided into two parts: internal memory and external memory, as Figure 14-1 illustrates. Assume that an executing program, along with its nonfile data, resides in the computer's internal memory; the permanent files of a computer system reside in the external memory. Further assume that the external storage devices have the characteristics of a disk (though some systems use other devices).

A file consists of **data records**. A data record can be anything from a simple value, such as an integer, to a multifield Pascal-like record, such as an employee record. For simplicity, assume that the data records in any one file are all of the same type.

A file contains records that are partitioned into blocks

The records of a file are partitioned into one or more **blocks**, each of which typically contains many data records, as Figure 14-2 shows. The size of a block, that is, the number of bits of data it can contain, is determined by both the hardware configuration and the system software of the computer. In general, an individual program has no control over this size. Therefore, the number of records that can fit per block is a function of the size of the records in the file. For example, a file of integer records will have more records per block than a file of employee records.

Much as you number the elements of an array, you can number the blocks of a file linearly. With a direct access file, a program can read a given block from the file by specifying its block number, and similarly, it can write data out to a particular block. In this regard a direct access file resembles an array of arrays, with each block of the file analogous to a single array entry, which is itself an array that contains several records.

Direct access I/O involves blocks instead of records

Notice that in this direct access model, *all input and output is at the block level rather than at the record level.* That is, you can read and write a block of records, but you cannot read or write an individual record. It is interesting to note that several programming languages, including Turbo Pascal, have commands that make it *appear* that you can access records one at a time. In general, however, the system actually performs I/O (input and output) at the block level and perhaps hides this fact from the program. For example, if a programming language includes the command

```
ReadRecord(F, i, R)
{ Reads the ith record of file F into variable R. }
```

the system probably accesses the entire block that contains the ith record. The previous model of I/O therefore approximates reality reasonably well.

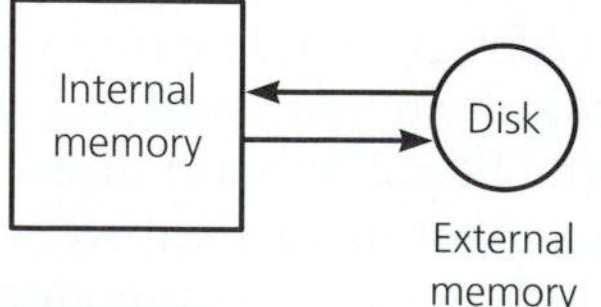

Figure 14-1
Internal and external memory

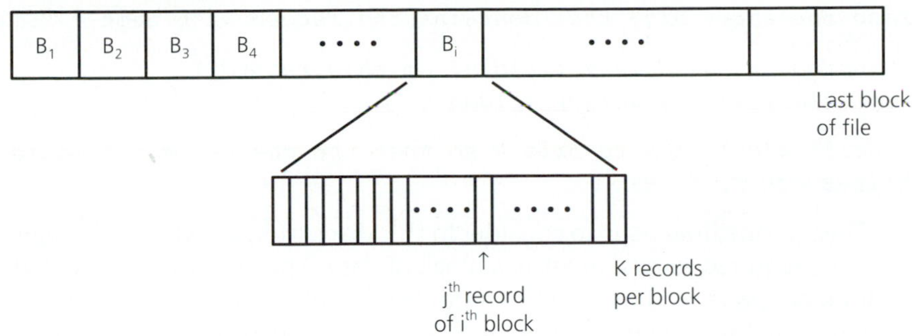

Figure 14-2
A file partitioned into blocks of records.

In the algorithms that this chapter presents, you should assume that your programming language has two commands for performing block I/O. The statement

```
ReadBlock(F, i, B)
```

will read the ith block of file *F* and place it in program variable *B*. Notice that variable *B* must accommodate the many records that each block of file *F* contains. For example, if each block contains 100 employee records, program variable *B* must be an array, such as *B[1..100]*, of employee records. *B* is called a **buffer**, which is a location that temporarily stores data as it makes its way from one process or location to another.

Once the system has read a block into *B*, the program can process—for example, inspect or modify—the records in the block. It is important to note that you can process data only after you have copied (read) it from the file into the internal memory of the computer. Also, because the records in the program variable *B* are only copies of the records in the file *F*, if a program does modify the records in *B*, the program must write *B* back out to *F*, so that the file also reflects the modifications. You can use the statement

```
WriteBlock(F, i, B)
```

to write the contents of *B* to the ith block of the file *F*. If *F* contains *N* blocks, you can use the statement

```
WriteBlock(F, N+1, B)
```

to append a new block to *F*, and thus the file can grow dynamically, just like a Pascal file.

Again, realize that these I/O commands allow you to read and write only entire blocks. As a consequence, even if you need to operate on only a single record of the file, you must access an entire block. For example, suppose that you want to give employee Smith a $1,000 raise. If Smith's record is in block *i* (how to determine the correct block is discussed later in the chapter), you would perform the following steps:

Updating a field within a record within a block

```
{ read block i from file F into array B }
ReadBlock(F, i, B)
```

```
Find the entry B[j] that contains the record with Name = "Smith"

{ increment the Salary field of Smith's record }
B[j]Salary := B[j]Salary + 1000

{ write block back to file F so that the change is reflected }
WriteBlock(F, i, B)
```

There is one final issue to consider in this discussion of external storage: the time required to read or write a block of data. The amount of time that a **block access** (a read or write) requires is typically much longer than the time required to operate on the block's data once it is in the computer's internal memory. For example, it is reasonable to assume that the time necessary to inspect every record in a block is less than the time required to read or write that block. In this case, data enters and leaves the buffer B at different rates. (Hence, a buffer between two processes compensates for the difference in the rates at which they operate on data.)

File access time is the dominant factor when considering an algorithm's efficiency

In most external data-management applications, the time required for block accesses typically dominates all other factors. As a consequence, in the next two sections, which devise schemes to sort and search data that is stored externally, *the goal will be to reduce the number of required block accesses*. You should pay little attention to the time required to operate on a block of data once it has been read into internal memory.

SORTING DATA IN AN EXTERNAL FILE

This section considers the following problem of sorting data that resides in an external file:

A sorting problem

> An external file contains 1,600 employee records. You want to sort these records by the Social Security number field. Each block contains 100 records, and thus the file contains 16 blocks of records B_1, B_2, and so on to B_{16}. Suppose that the program can only access enough internal memory to manipulate about 300 records (three blocks' worth) at one time.

Sorting the file might not sound like a difficult problem, because you have already seen several sorting algorithms in earlier chapters. There is, however, a fundamental difference here in that the file is far too large to fit into internal memory all at once. This restriction creates somewhat of a difficulty because the sorting algorithms presented earlier assume that all the data to be sorted is available at one time in internal memory (for example, that it is all in an array). Fortunately, however, a mergesort can be modified so that this assumption is not necessary.

The basis of the mergesort algorithm is that you can easily merge two sorted segments—such as arrays—of data records into a third sorted segment that is the combination of the two. What makes a mergesort appropriate for the problem of sorting external files is that the merge step needs to look only at the *leading edge* of each of the segments. For example, if S_1 and S_2 are sorted segments of records, the first step of the merge is to compare the first record of each segment and select the record with the smaller search key. If the record from S_1 is selected, the next step is to compare the second record of S_1 to the first record of S_2. This process is continued until all the records are exhausted. The key observation is that at any step, the merge never needs to look beyond the leading edge of either segment.

Now consider the details of modifying the mergesort algorithm so that you can use it for external files. Suppose that the 1,600 records to be sorted are in the file F_1 and that you are not permitted to alter this file. You have two work files, F_2 and F_3. One of the work files will contain the sorted records when the algorithm terminates. The algorithm has two phases: Phase 1 sorts each block of records, and Phase 2 performs a series of merges.

External mergesort

> **Phase 1.** Read a block from F_1 into internal memory, sort its records by using an internal sort, and write the sorted block out to F_2 before you read the next block from F_1. After you process all 16 blocks of F_1, F_2 contains 16 **sorted runs** R_1, R_2, and so on to R_{16}; that is, it contains 16 groups of records, with the records within each group sorted among themselves, as Figure 14-3a illustrates.
>
> **Phase 2.** Phase 2 is a sequence of merge steps. Each merge step merges pairs of sorted runs to form larger sorted runs. Each merge step doubles the number of blocks in each sorted run and thus halves the total number of sorted runs. For example, as Figure 14-3b shows, the first merge step merges eight pairs of sorted runs from F_2 (R_1 with R_2, R_3 with R_4, $\cdots$, R_{15} with R_{16}) to form eight sorted runs, each two blocks long, which are written to F_3. The next merge step merges four pairs of sorted runs from F_3 (R_1 with R_2, R_3 with R_4, $\cdots$, R_7 with R_8) to form four sorted runs, each four blocks long, which are written to F_2, as Figure 14-3c illustrates. The next step merges the two pairs of sorted runs from F_2 to form two sorted runs, which are written to F_3. (See Figure 14-3d.) The final step merges the two sorted runs into one, which is written to F_2. At this point, F_2 will contain all of the records of the original file in sorted order.

Merging sorted runs in Phase 2

Given this overall strategy, how can you merge the sorted runs at each step of Phase 2? The statement of the problem specifies that there is only sufficient internal memory to manipulate at most 300 records at once. However, the later steps of Phase 2 require that you merge runs that contain more than 300 records, so you must merge the runs a piece at a time. To accomplish this merge, you must divide the program's internal memory into three arrays, `In1`, `In2`, and `Out`, each capable of holding 100 records (the block size). You read block-sized pieces of the runs into the two `In` arrays and merge them into the `Out` array. Whenever an `In` array is exhausted—that is, when all its elements have been copied to `Out`—you

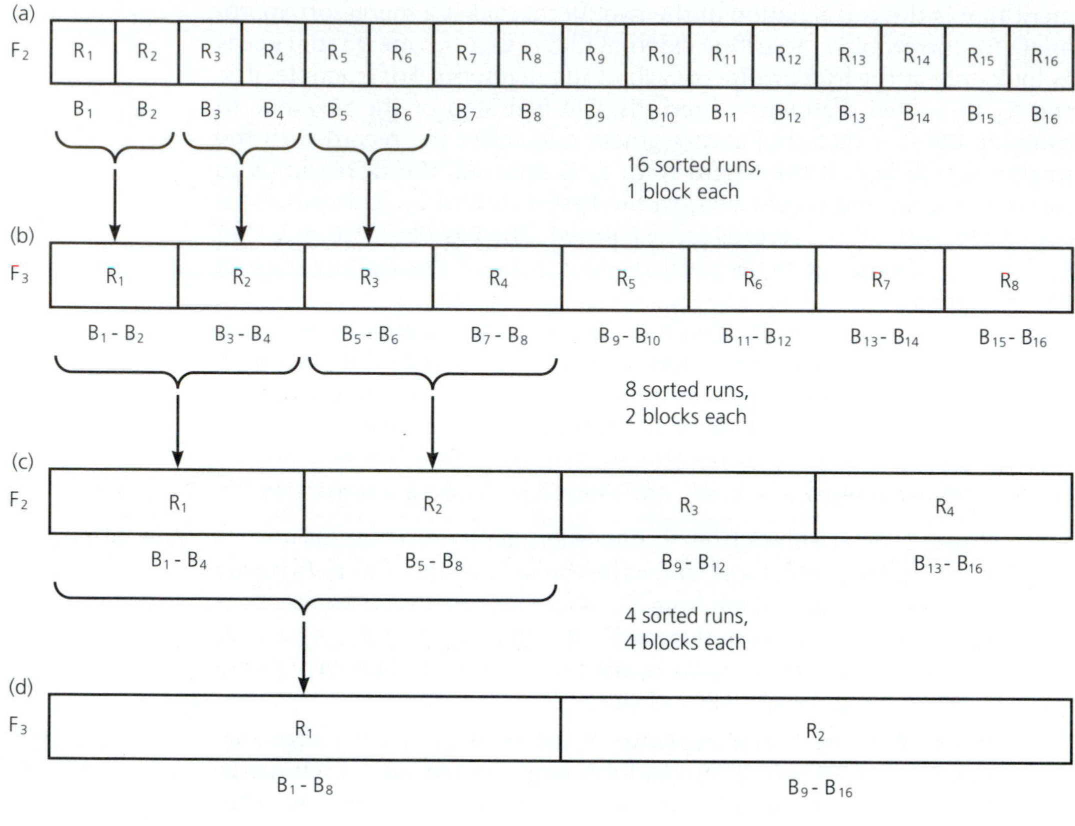

Figure 14-3

(a) 16 sorted runs, 1 block each, in file F_2; (b) 8 runs, 2 blocks each, in file F_3; (c) 4 runs, 4 blocks each, in file F_2; (d) 2 runs, 8 blocks each, in file F_3

read the next piece of the run into the `In` array; whenever the `Out` array becomes full, you write this completed piece of the new sorted run to one of the files.

Consider how you can perform the first merge step. You start this step with the pair of runs R_1 and R_2, which are in the first and second blocks, respectively, of the file F_2. (See Figure 14-3a.) Because at this first merge step each run contains only one block, an entire run can fit into one of the `In` arrays. You can thus read R_1 and R_2 into the arrays `In1` and `In2`, and then merge `In1` and `In2` into `Out`. However, although the result of merging `In1` and `In2` is a sorted run two blocks long (200 records), `Out` can hold only one block (100 records). Thus, when in the course of the merge `Out` becomes full, you write its contents to the first block of F_3, as Figure 14-4a illustrates. The merging of `In1` and `In2` into `Out` then resumes. The array `Out` will become full for a second time only after all the records in `In1` and `In2` are exhausted. At that time, write the contents of `Out` to the second block of F_3. You merge the remaining seven pairs from F_1 in the same manner and append the resulting runs to F_3.

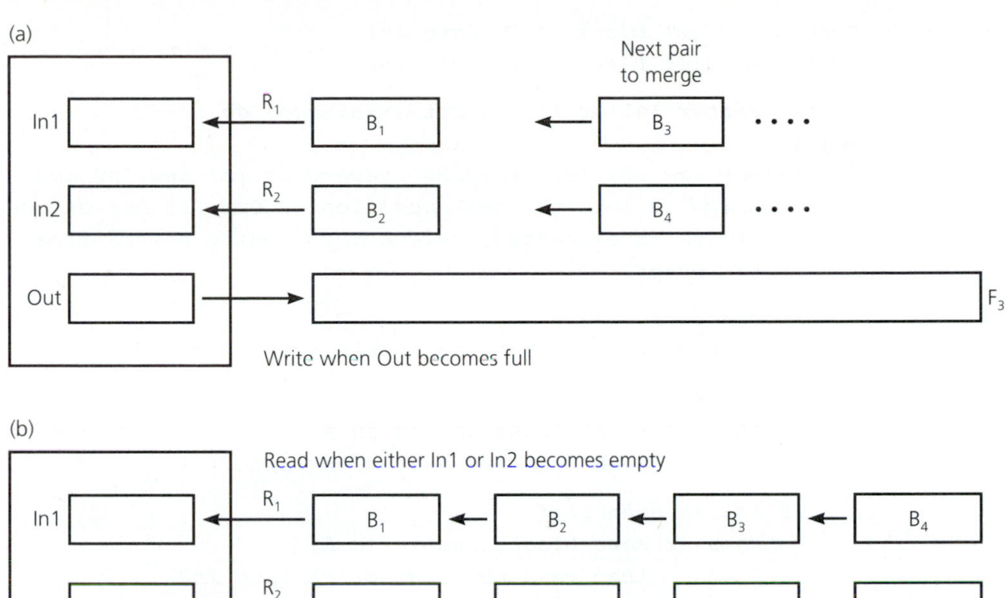

Figure 14-4

(a) Merging single blocks; (b) merging long runs

This first merge step is conceptually a bit easier than the others because the initial runs are only one block in size, and thus each can fit in its entirety into one of the `In` arrays. What do you do in the later steps when the runs to be merged are larger than a single block? Consider, for example, the merge step in which you must merge runs of four blocks each to form runs of eight blocks each. (See Figure 14-3c.) The first pair of these runs to be merged is in blocks 1 through 4 and 5 through 8 of F_2.

The algorithm will read the first block of R_1—which is the first block B_1 of the file—into `In1` and the first block of R_2—which is B_5—into `In2`, as Figure 14-4b illustrates. Then, as it did earlier, the algorithm merges `In1` and `In2` into `Out`. The complication here is that as soon as you finish moving all of the records from either `In1` or `In2`, you must read the next block from the corresponding run. For example, if you finish `In2` first, you must read the next block of R_2—which is B_6—into `In2` before the merge can continue. The algorithm thus must detect when the `In` arrays become exhausted as well as when the `Out` array becomes full.

A high-level description of the algorithm for merging arbitrary-sized sorted runs R_i and R_j from F_2 into F_3 is as follows:

Pseudocode to merge sorted runs

```
Read the first block of Ri into In1
Read the first block of Rj into In2

while (either In1 or In2 is not exhausted) do
begin
   Select the smaller "leading" record of In1 and In2 and
      place it into the next position of Out (if one of the
      arrays is exhausted, select the leading record from
      the other)

   if Out is full
      then write its contents to the next block of F3

   if In1 is exhausted
      then if more blocks remain in Ri
              then read the next block into In1

   if In2 is exhausted
      then if more blocks remain in Rj
              then read the next block into In2
end
```

A pseudocode version of the external sorting algorithm follows. Notice that it uses the procedures `ReadBlock` and `WriteBlock`, introduced in the previous section, and assumes a procedure `CopyFile` that copies a file. To avoid further complications, the solution assumes that the number of blocks in the file is a power of 2. This assumption allows the algorithm always to pair off the sorted runs at each step of the merge phase. Also note that the algorithm uses two scratch files and copies the final sorted scratch file to the designated output file.

A pseudocode mergesort procedure

```
ExternalMergesort(UnsortedFileName, SortedFileName);
{ ---------------------------------------------------------
  Sorts a file by using an external mergesort.
  Precondition: UnsortedFileName is the name of an external
  file to be sorted. SortedFileName is the name that the
  procedure will give to the resulting sorted file.
  Postcondition: The new file named SortedFileName is
  sorted. The original file is unchanged. Both files are
  closed.
  Calls: BlockSort, MergeFile, and CopyFile.
  Simplifying Assumption: The number of blocks in the
  unsorted file is an exact power of 2. Without this
  assumption, you would need special end-of-file testing
  that would obscure the algorithm that this procedure
  illustrates.
  --------------------------------------------------------- }
begin
   Associate UnsortedFileName with the file variable InFile
     and SortedFileName with the file variable OutFile
```

```
    { Phase I: sort the file block by block and count the blocks }
    BlockSort(InFile, TempFile1, NumBlocks)

    { Phase II: merge runs of Size 1, 2, 4, ... , NumBlocks/2
      (uses two temporary files and a toggle that keeps track
       of the source and destination files for each merge step) }
    Size := 1
    Toggle := 1
    while Size < NumBlocks do
    begin
       if Toggle = 1
           then MergeFile(TempFile1, TempFile2, Size, NumBlocks)
           else MergeFile(TempFile2, TempFile1, Size, NumBlocks)
       Size := 2 * Size
       Toggle := - Toggle
    end    { while }

    { copy the current temporary file to OutFile }
    if Toggle = 1
        then CopyFile(TempFile1, OutFile)
        else CopyFile(TempFile2, OutFile)
end    { ExternalMergesort }
```

ExternalMergesort calls *BlockSort* and *MergeFile*, which calls *MergeRuns*. The pseudocode for these procedures follows.

```
BlockSort(InFile, OutFile, NumBlocks)
{ ----------------------------------------------------------
  Sorts each block of records in a file.
  Precondition: InFile is available.
  Postcondition: OutFile contains the blocks of InFile.
  Each block is sorted; NumBlocks is the number of blocks
  processed. Both files are closed.
  Calls: ReadBlock and WriteBlock to perform direct access
  input and output, and Sort to sort an array.
  ---------------------------------------------------------- }
begin
    reset(InFile)
    rewrite(OutFile)

    NumBlocks := 0
    while not eof(InFile) do
    begin
       NumBlocks := NumBlocks + 1
       ReadBlock(InFile, NumBlocks, Buffer)

       Sort(Buffer)    { sort with some internal sort }

       WriteBlock(OutFile, NumBlocks, Buffer)
    end    { while }
```

```
    close(InFile)
    close(OutFile)
end   { BlockSort }

MergeFile(InFile, OutFile, RunSize, NumBlocks)
{ --------------------------------------------------------
  Merges blocks from one file to another.
  Precondition: InFile is an external file that contains
  NumBlocks sorted blocks organized into runs of RunSize
  blocks each.
  Postcondition: OutFile contains the merged runs of
  InFile. Both files are closed.
  -------------------------------------------------------- }
begin
    reset(InFile)
    rewrite(OutFile)

    Next := 1
    while Next <= NumBlocks do
    { Invariant: runs in OutFile are ordered }
    begin
       MergeRuns(InFile, OutFile, Next, RunSize)
       Next := Next + (2 * RunSize)
    end    { while }

    close(InFile)
    close(OutFile)
end   { MergeFile }

MergeRuns(FromFile, ToFile, Start, Size)
{--------------------------------------------------------
 Merges two consecutive sorted runs in a file.
 Precondition: FromFile is an external file of sorted runs
 open for input. ToFile is an external file of sorted runs
 open for output. Start is the block number of the first
 run on FromFile to be merged; this run contains Size blocks.
    Run 1: block Start to block Start + Size - 1
    Run 2: block Start + Size to Start + (2 * Size) - 1
 Postcondition: The merged runs from FromFile are appended
 to ToFile. The files remain open.
 -------------------------------------------------------- }
begin
    { initialize the input buffers for runs 1 and 2 }
    ReadBlock(FromFile, first block of Run 1, In1)
    ReadBlock(FromFile, first block of Run 2, In2)

    { Merge until one of the runs is finished. Whenever an
      input buffer is exhausted, the next block is read in.
      Whenever the output buffer is full, it is written out.}
```

```
    while neither run is finished do
    begin
       { Invariant: Out and each block in ToFile are ordered.}
       Select the smaller "leading edge" of In1 and In2, and
         place it in the next position of Out

       if Out is full
           then WriteBlock(ToFile, next block of ToFile, Out)

       if In1 is exhausted
           then if more blocks remain in Run 1
               then ReadBlock(FromFile, next block of Run 1, In1)

       if In2 is exhausted
           then if more blocks remain in Run 2
               then ReadBlock(FromFile, next block of Run 2, In2)
    end   { while }

{ Assertion: exactly one of the runs is complete }

{ append the remainder of the unfinished input buffer to
  the output buffer and write it out }

    while In1 is not exhausted do
       { Invariant: Out is ordered }
       Place the next item of In1 into the next position of
         Out

    while In2 is not exhausted do
       { Invariant: Out is ordered }
       Place the next item of In2 into the next position of
         Out

    WriteBlock(ToFile, next block of ToFile, Out)

{ finish off the remaining complete blocks }

    while blocks remain in Run 1 do
    { Invariant: each block in ToFile is ordered }
    begin
       ReadBlock(FromFile, next block of Run 1, In1)
       WriteBlock(ToFile, next block of ToFile, In1)
    end   { while }

    while blocks remain in Run 2 do
    { Invariant: Each block in ToFile is ordered }
    begin
       ReadBlock(FromFile, next block of Run 2, In2)
       WriteBlock(ToFile, next block of ToFile, In2)
    end   { while }
end   { MergeRuns }
```

SEARCHING EXTERNAL TABLES

This section discusses techniques for organizing records in external storage so that you can perform ADT table operations such as retrieval, insertion, deletion, and traversal efficiently. Although this discussion will only scratch the surface of this topic, you do have a head start: Two of the most important external table implementations are variations of the 2-3 tree and hashing, which you studied in Chapter 13.

A simple external table implementation: records stored in search-key order

Suppose you have a direct access file of records that are to be table items. The file is partitioned into blocks, as was described earlier in this chapter. One of the simplest table implementations stores the records in order by their search key, perhaps sorting the file by using the external sorting algorithm developed in the previous section. Once it is sorted, you can easily traverse the file in sorted order by using the following algorithm:

Sorted-order traversal

```
TraverseTable(F, Visit)
{ Traverses in sorted order the sorted file F, calling
  procedure Visit for each item. }

    { read each block of file F into an internal array B }
    for BlockNumber := 1 to NumberOfBlocks do
    begin
       ReadBlock(F, BlockNumber, B)

       { visit each record in the block }
       for RecdNumber := 1 to RecordsPerBlock do
           Visit(B[RecdNumber])
    end
```

To perform the *TableRetrieve* operation on the sorted file, you can use a binary search algorithm as follows:

Retrieval by using a binary search

```
TableRetrieve(F, First, Last, SearchKey, TableItem, Success)
{ Searches blocks First through Last of file F and retrieves
  into TableItem the record whose search key equals
  SearchKey. The operation fails if no such item exists. The
  flag Success indicates whether the operation succeeded. }

     if (First > Last) or eof(F)
        then Success := false

        else
        begin
            { read the middle block of file F into internal
              array B }
            Mid := (First + Last) div 2
            ReadBlock(F, Mid, B)
```

```
    if (SearchKey >= B[1].Key) and
          (SearchKey <= B[RecordsPerBlock].Key) then
        begin    { desired block is found }
            Search array B for record B[j] whose
              search key equals SearchKey
            if record is found
                 then
                 begin
                     TableItem := B[j]
                     Success := true
                 end

                 else Success := false
        end

    { else search appropriate half of the file }
    else if SearchKey < B[1].Key then
        TableRetrieve(F, First, Mid-1, SearchKey,
                                      TableItem, Success)

    else TableRetrieve(F, Mid+1, Last, SearchKey,
                                      TableItem, Success)
end
```

The previous *TableRetrieve* algorithm recursively splits the file in half and reads the middle block into the internal array *B*. Note that splitting a file segment requires that you know the numbers of the first and last blocks of the segment. You would pass these values as parameters, along with the file name, to the *TableRetrieve* procedure.

Once you have read the middle block of the file segment into *B*, you determine if a record whose search key equals *SearchKey* could be in this block. You can make this determination by comparing *SearchKey* to the smallest search key in *B*—which is in *B[1]*—and to the largest search key in *B*—which is in *B[RecordsPerBlock]*. If *SearchKey* does not lie between the values of the smallest and largest search keys in *B*, you must recursively search one of the halves of the file (which half to search depends on whether *SearchKey* is less than or greater than the search keys in the block you just examined). If, on the other hand, *SearchKey* does lie between the values of the smallest and largest search keys of the block in *B*, you must search *B* for the record. Notice that because the records within the block *B* are sorted, you could use a binary search on the records within this block. However, the number of records in the block *B* is typically small, and thus the time required to scan the block sequentially is insignificant compared to the time required to read the block from the file. It is therefore common simply to scan the block sequentially.

This external implementation of the ADT table is not very different from the internal sorted array-based implementation. As such, it has many of the same advantages and disadvantages. Its main advantage is that

Figure 14-5

Shifting across block boundaries

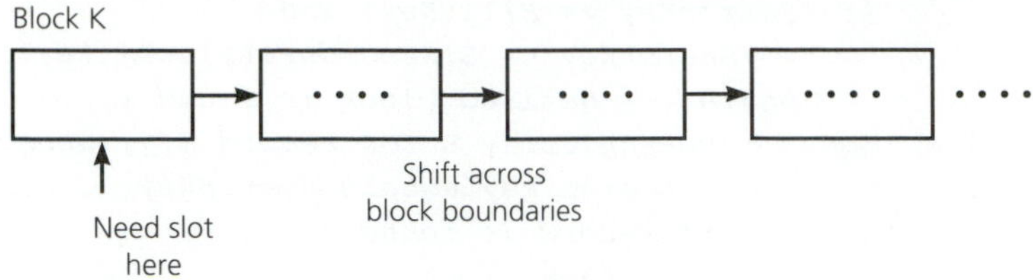

`TableInsert` and `TableDelete` for an external implementation of the ADT table can require many costly file accesses due to shifting records

because the records are sorted sequentially, you can use a binary search to locate the block that contains a given search key. The main disadvantage of the implementation is that, as is the case with an array-based implementation, the *`TableInsert`* and *`TableDelete`* operations must shift table items. Shifting records in an external file is, in general, far more costly than shifting array items. A file may contain an enormous number of large records, which are organized as several thousand blocks. As a consequence, the shifting could require a prohibitively large number of block accesses.

Consider, for example, Figure 14-5. If you insert a new record into block *K,* you must shift the records not only in block *K,* but also in every block after it. Note that you must shift some records across block boundaries. Thus, for each of these blocks, you must read the block into internal memory, shift its records by using an assignment such as

```
B[i+1] := B[i]
```

and write the block to the file so that the file reflects the change. This large number of block accesses makes the external sorted array-based implementation practical only for tables where insertions and deletions are rare. (See Exercise 1 at the end of this chapter.)

Indexing an External File

Two of the best external table implementations are variations of the internal hashing and search-tree schemes. The biggest difference between the internal and external versions of these implementations is that in the external versions, it is often advantageous to organize an **index** to the data file rather than to organize the data file itself. An index to a data file is conceptually similar to other indexes with which you are familiar. For example, consider a card catalog in a library. Rather than looking all over the library for a particular title, you can simply search the card catalog. The catalog is typically organized alphabetically by title (or by author), so it is a simple matter to locate the appropriate entry. The entry for each book contains a *pointer* (for example, a Library of Congress number), which indicates where on the shelves you can find the book.

There are at least three benefits to using a card catalog to index the books in a library:

Advantages of a library card catalog

- The library can organize the books on the shelves in any way, without regard to how easy it will be for a patron to scan the shelves for a particular book. To locate a particular book, the patron searches the card catalog for the appropriate entry.

- Because each catalog entry is small (for example, a 3-inch by 5-inch index card), the entire catalog for a large library can fit into a small area. A patron can thus locate a particular book without running all over the library.
- The library can have different types of catalogs to facilitate different types of searches. For example, it can have one catalog organized by title and another organized by author.

Now consider how you can use an index to a data file to much the same advantage as the card catalog. As Figure 14-6 illustrates, you can leave the data file in a disorganized state and maintain an index to it. When you need to locate a particular record in the data file, you search the index for the corresponding entry, which will tell you where to find the desired record in the data file.

An index to a data file

An index to the data file is simply a file, called the **index file**, that contains an **index record** for each record in the data file, just as a card catalog contains an entry for each book in the library. An index record has two fields: a **key field**, which contains the same value as the search key of its corresponding record in the data file, and a **pointer field**, which shows the number of the block in the data file that contains this data record. (Despite its name, the pointer field contains an integer, not a Pascal pointer.) You can thus determine which block of the data file contains the record whose search key field equals `SearchKey` by searching the index file for the index record whose key field equals `SearchKey`. (This type of index is often called a **dense index** to distinguish it from other types of indexes.)

Maintaining an index to a data file has benefits analogous to those provided by the library's card catalog:

Advantages of an index file

- Because you do not need to maintain the data file in any particular order, you can insert new records in any convenient location, such as at the end of the file. As you will see, this flexibility

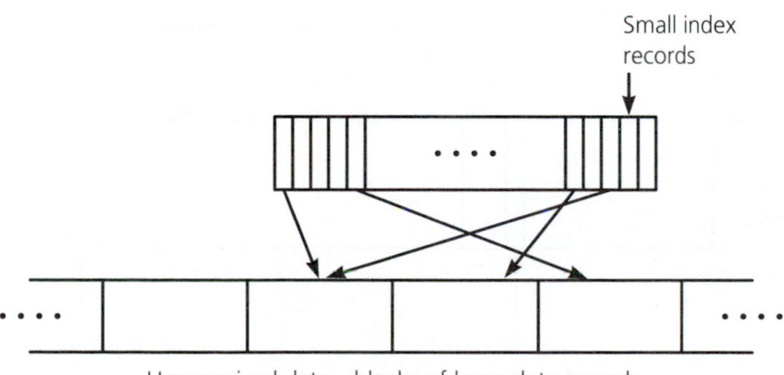

Figure 14-6

A data file with an index

eliminates the need for shifting the data records during insertions and deletions.

- In general, an index record will be much smaller than a data record. While the data record may contain many fields, an index record contains only two fields: the search key, which is also one of the fields of the data record, and a single integer pointer, which is the block number. Thus, just as the library's card catalog occupies only a small fraction of the space occupied by the books it indexes, an index file is only a fraction of the size of the data file. As you will see, the small size of the index file often allows you to manipulate it with fewer block accesses than would be required to manipulate the data file.
- You can maintain several indexes simultaneously. Just as a library can have one card catalog organized by title and another organized by author, you can have one index file that indexes the data file by one search key (for example, an index file that consists of <`Name, Pointer`> records), and a second index file that indexes the data file by another search key (for example, an index file that consists of <`SocSec, Pointer`> records). Such **multiple indexing** is discussed briefly at the end of this chapter.

Organize the index file but not the data file

Although you do not organize the data file, you must organize the index file so that you can search and update it rapidly. Before considering how to organize an index file by using either hashing or search-tree schemes, first consider a less complex organization that illustrates the concepts of indexing. Suppose that the index file simply stores the index records sequentially, sorted by their key fields, as shown in Figure 14-7. Because the index records are far smaller than the data records, the index file contains far fewer blocks than the data file. For example, if the index records are one-tenth the size of the data records and the data file contains

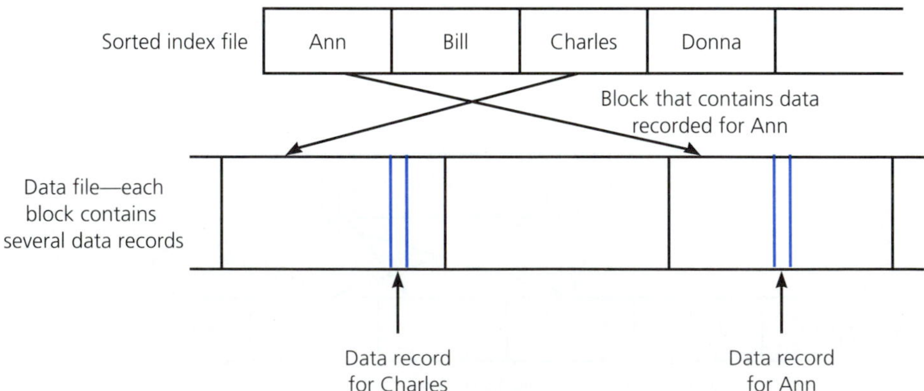

Figure 14-7

A data file with a sorted index file

1,000 blocks, the index file will require only about 100 blocks. As a result, you can perform the operations *TableRetrieve*, *TableInsert*, and *TableDelete* with fewer block accesses.

For example, to perform the *TableRetrieve* operation, you can use a binary search on the index file as follows:

Retrieval by searching an index file

```
TableRetrieve(TIndex, TData, SearchKey, TableItem, Success)
{ Retrieves into TableItem the record whose search key
  equals SearchKey, where TIndex is the index file and
  TData is the data file. The operation fails if no such
  record exists. The flag Success indicates whether the
  operation succeeded. }

     if eof(TIndex)
        then Success := false
        else
        begin
            { read the middle block of index file into
              internal array B }
           Mid := middle block of index file TIndex
           ReadBlock(TIndex, Mid, B)

           if (SearchKey >= B[1].Key) and
            (SearchKey <= B[IndexRecordsPerBlock].Key) then
               begin  { desired block of index file found }
                   Search array B for index file record B[j]
                     whose key value equals SearchKey

                   if index record B[j] is found
                        then
                        begin
                             BlockNum := block number of data
                                         file to which B[j]
                                         points
                             ReadBlock(TData, BlockNum, D)
                             Find data record D[k] whose
                               search key equals SearchKey
                             TableItem := D[k]
                             Success := true
                        end   { then }

                        else Success := false

               end   { then }

           else if TIndex is one block in size then
               Success := false   { no more blocks in file }
```

```
        { else search appropriate half of index file }
        else if SearchKey < B[1].Key then
            TableRetrieve(first half of TIndex, TData,
                          SearchKey, TableItem, Success)
        else TableRetrieve(second half of TIndex, TData,
                          SearchKey, TableItem, Success)
    end  { else }
```

An index file reduces the number of required block accesses for table operations

For the previous example, the use of an index cuts the number of block accesses down from about $\log_2 1000 = 10$ to about $1 + \log_2 100 = 8$. (The one additional block access is into the data file once you have located the appropriate index record.)

The reduction in block accesses is far more dramatic for the `TableInsert` and `TableDelete` operations. In the implementation of an external table that was discussed earlier in this section, if you insert a record into or delete a record from the first block of data, for example, you have to shift records in every block, requiring that you access all 1,000 blocks of the data file. (See Figure 14-5.)

Shift index records instead of data records

However, when you perform an insertion or a deletion by using the index scheme, you have to shift only index records. When you use an index file, you do not keep the data file in any particular order, so you can insert a new data record into any convenient location in the data file. This flexibility means that you can simply insert a new data record at the end of the file or at a position left vacant by a previous deletion (as you will see). As a result, you never need to shift records in the data file. However, you do need to shift records in the index file to create an opening so that you can insert the corresponding index entry into its proper sorted position. Because the index file contains many fewer blocks than the data file (100 versus 1,000 in the previous example), the maximum number of block accesses that are necessary is greatly reduced. A secondary benefit of shifting index records rather than data records is that, because the records themselves are smaller, the amount of time required for a single shift is diminished; that is, the time required for the assignment `B[i + 1] := B[i]` is decreased.

Deletions under the index scheme reap similar benefits. Once you have searched the index file and located the data record to be deleted, you can simply leave its location vacant in the data file, and thus you need not shift any data records. You can keep track of the vacant locations in the data file (see Exercise 2), so that you can insert new data records into the vacancies, as was mentioned earlier. The only shifting required is in the index file to fill the gap created when the index record that corresponds to the deleted data record is removed.

An unsorted data file with a sorted index is more efficient than a sorted data file, but other schemes are even better

Even though this scheme is an improvement over maintaining a sorted data file, in many applications it is far from satisfactory. The 100 block accesses that could be required to insert or delete an index record would often be prohibitive. Far better implementations are possible when you use either hashing or search trees to organize the index file.

External Hashing

The external hashing scheme is quite similar to the internal scheme described in Chapter 13. Recall that in the internal hashing scheme each entry of the array `T[0..TableSize-1]` contains a pointer to the beginning of the list of items that hash into that location. In the external hashing scheme, each entry of `T` still contains a pointer to the beginning of a list, but here each list consists of *blocks of index records*. In other words, you hash an index file rather than the data file, as Figure 14-8 illustrates. (In many applications the array `T` is itself so large that you must keep it in external storage—for example, in the first *K* blocks of the index file. To avoid this extra detail, you can assume that the array `T` is an internal array.)

Hashed index file

In Figure 14-8, you see that associated with each entry `T[i]` is a linked list of blocks of the index file. Each block of `T[i]`'s linked list contains index records whose keys (and thus whose corresponding data-records' search keys) hash into location `i`. To form the linked lists, you must reserve space in each block for a block pointer—the integer block number of the next block in the chain—as Figure 14-9 illustrates. That is, in this linked list the pointers are integers, not Pascal pointers. By convention, the value

Figure 14-8

A hashed index file

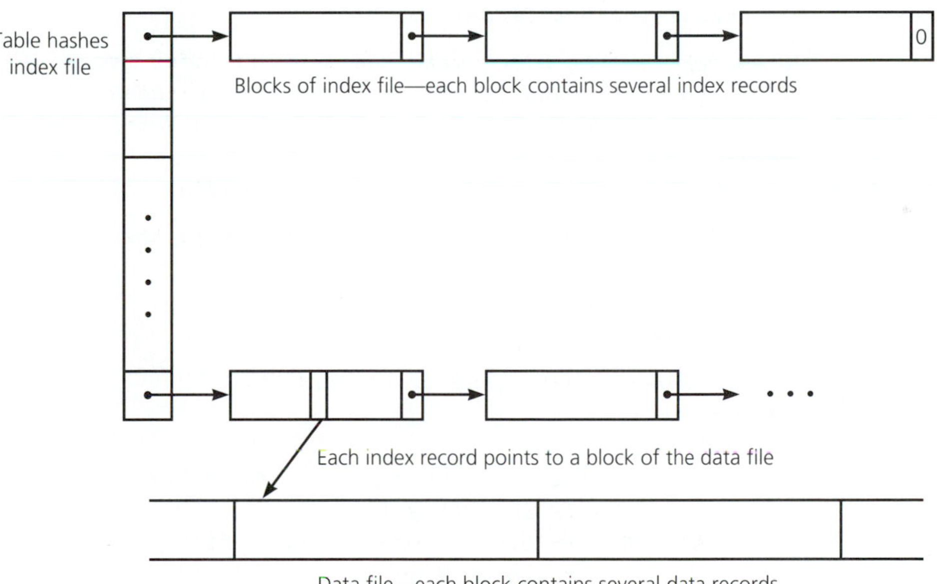
Table hashes index file
0
Blocks of index file—each block contains several index records
Each index record points to a block of the data file
Data file—each block contains several data records

Figure 14-9

A single block with a pointer

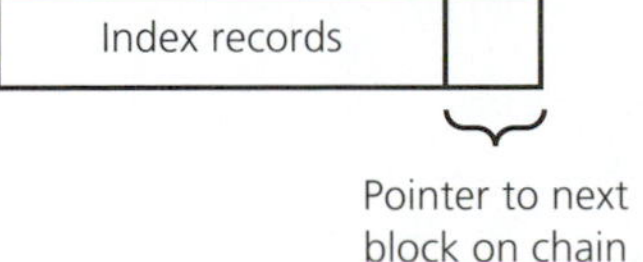
Index records
Pointer to next block on chain

zero is placed in the last block on the chain (which is analogous to setting a Pascal pointer to `nil`).

The following is a high-level description of the *TableRetrieve* algorithm that uses external hashing:

Retrieval under external hashing of an index file

```
TableRetrieve(TIndex, TData, SearchKey, TableItem, Success)
{ Retrieves into TableItem the item whose search key equals
  SearchKey, where TIndex is the index file, which is
  hashed, and TData is the data file. The operation fails if
  no such record exists. The flag Success indicates whether
  the operation succeeded. }

   { apply the hash function to the search key }
   i := h(SearchKey)

   { find the first block on the chain of index blocks -
     these blocks contain index records that hash into
     location i }
   p := T[i]

   { if p = 0, no values have hashed into location i }
   if p <> 0
      then ReadBlock(TIndex, p, B)

   { search for the block with the desired index record }
   while (p <> 0) Cand (B does not contain an index
                 record whose key value equals SearchKey) do
   begin
      p := block number of next block on chain

      { if p = 0, you are at the last block in the chain }
      if p <> 0
          then ReadBlock(TIndex, p, B)
   end  { while }

   { retrieve the data item if present }
   if p <> 0
      then
      begin { B[j] is the index record whose key value
              equals SearchKey }
         BlockNum := block number of data file pointed
                     to by B[j]
         ReadBlock(TData, BlockNum, D)
         Find data record D[k] whose search key
           equals SearchKey
         TableItem := D[k]

         Success := true
      end  { then }

      else Success := false
```

The `TableInsert` and `TableDelete` algorithms are also similar to those for internal hashing. The major difference is that, in the external environment, you must insert or delete both a data record and the corresponding index record. First consider the steps of the insertion algorithm.

INSERT A NEW DATA RECORD WHOSE SEARCH KEY EQUALS `SearchKey`

Insertion under external hashing of an index file

1. **Insert the data record into the data file.** Because the data file is not ordered, the new record can go anywhere you want. If a previous deletion has left a free slot in the middle of the data file, you can insert it there. (See Exercise 2.)

   If there are no free slots, you insert the new data record at the end of the last block or, if necessary, you append a new block to the end of the data file and store the record there. In either case, let `p` denote the number of the block that contains this new data record.

2. **Insert a corresponding index record into the index file.** You need to insert into the index file an index record that has key value `SearchKey` and pointer value `p`. (Recall that `p` is the number of the block in the data file into which you inserted the new data record.) Because the index file is hashed, you first apply the hash function to `SearchKey`, letting

   ```
   i := h(SearchKey)
   ```

   You then insert the index record `<SearchKey, p>` into the chain of blocks pointed to by the entry `T[i]`. You can insert this record into any block on the chain that contains a free slot or, if necessary, you can allocate a new block and link it to the beginning of the chain.

The steps for a deletion are as follows:

DELETE A DATA RECORD WHOSE SEARCH KEY EQUALS `SearchKey`

Deletion under external hashing of an index file

1. **Search the index file for the corresponding index record.** You apply the hash function to `SearchKey`, letting

   ```
   i := h(SearchKey)
   ```

   You then search the chain of index blocks pointed to by entry `T[i]` for an index record whose key value equals `SearchKey`. If you do not find such a record, you can conclude that there is no record in the data file whose search key equals `SearchKey`. However, if you find an index record `<SearchKey, p>`, you delete it from the index file after noting the block number `p`, which indicates where in the data file you can find the data record to be deleted.

2. **Delete the data record from the data file.** You know that the data record is in block `p` of the data file. You simply access this block, search the block for the record, delete the record, and write the block back to the file.

Observe that for each of the operations `TableRetrieve`, `TableInsert`, and `TableDelete`, the number of block accesses is very low. You never have to access more than one block of the data file, and at worst you have to access all of the blocks along a single hash chain of the index file. Like internal hashing, with external hashing you can take measures to keep the length of each of the chains quite short (for example, one or two blocks long). You should make the size of the array `T` large enough so that the average length of a chain is near one block, and the hash function should scatter the keys evenly. If necessary, you can even structure each chain as an external search tree—a **B-tree**—by using the techniques described next.

Choose external hashing for **`TableRetrieve`**, **`TableInsert`**, *and* **`TableDelete`** *operations*

The hashing implementation is the one to choose when you need to perform the operations `TableRetrieve`, `TableInsert`, and `TableDelete` on a large external table. As is the case with internal hashing, however, there are operations that this implementation does not support well. These are operations such as sorted traversal, retrieval of the smallest or largest item, and range queries that require ordered data. When these types of operations are added to the basic table operations `TableRetrieve`, `TableInsert`, and `TableDelete`, a search-tree implementation may be more appropriate than hashing.

B-Trees

Another way to search an external table is to organize it as a search tree. Just as you applied external hashing to the index file, you organize the index file, not the data file, as an external search tree. The implementation developed here is a generalization of the 2-3 tree of Chapter 13.

Observe that you can organize the blocks of an external file into a tree structure by using block numbers for child pointers. In Figure 14-10, for example, the blocks are organized into a 2-3 tree. Each block of the file is a node in the tree and contains three child pointers, each of which is the integer block number of the child. A child pointer value of zero plays the role of a `nil` pointer, and thus, for example, a leaf will contain three child pointers with the value zero.

Organize the index file as an external 2-3 tree

If you organized the index file into a 2-3 tree, each node (block of the index file) would contain either one or two index records, each of the form <`Key, Pointer`>, along with three child pointers. It is important to remember that the pointer field of the record <`SearchKey, p`> indicates the block (of the data file) that contains the data record whose search key equals `SearchKey` and has nothing to do with the tree structure of the index file. To help avoid confusion, the term **child pointers** is used here to refer to the pointers that are used to maintain the tree structure of the index file.

You must organize the index records in the tree so that their keys obey the same search-tree ordering property as an internal 2-3 tree. This organization allows you to retrieve the data record with a given value in its search key as follows:

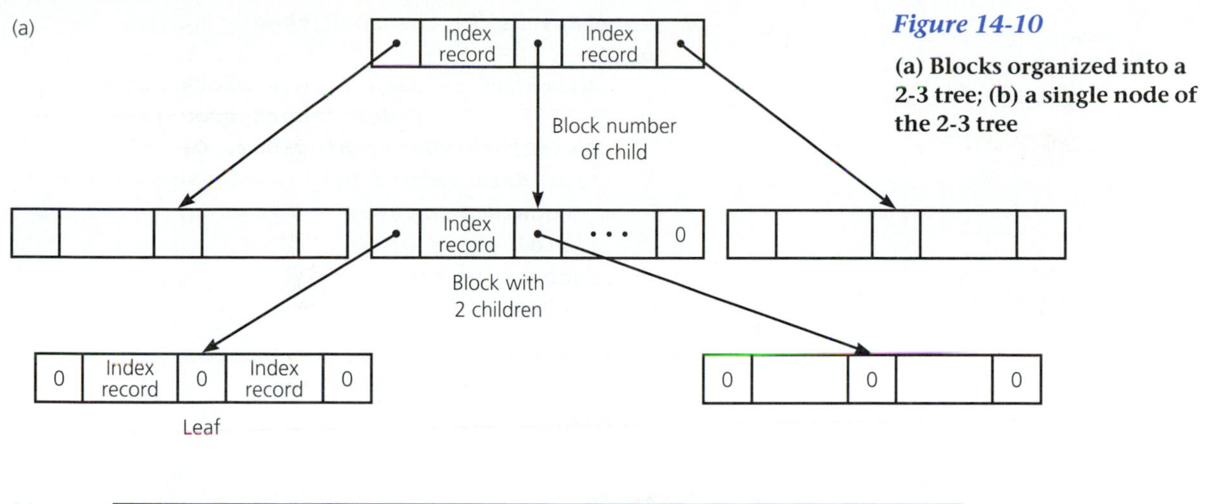

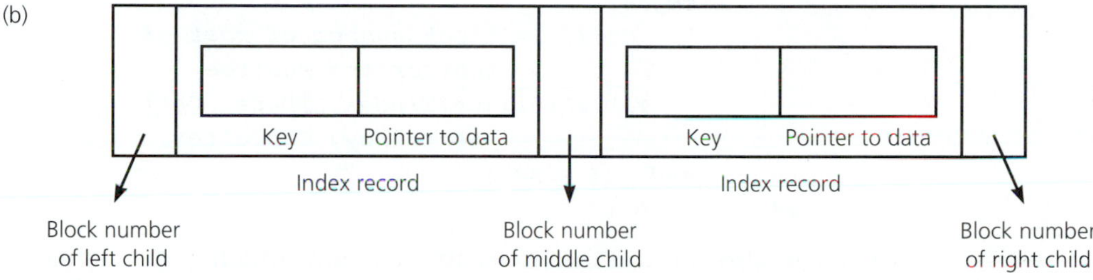

Figure 14-10

(a) Blocks organized into a 2-3 tree; (b) a single node of the 2-3 tree

Retrieval when the index file is a 2-3 tree

```
TableRetrieve(TIndex, TData, RootNum, SearchKey,
                                   TableItem, Success)
{ Retrieves into TableItem the record whose search key
  equals SearchKey. TIndex is the index file, which is
  organized as a 2-3 tree. RootNum is the block number (of
  the index file) that contains the root of the tree. TData
  is the data file. The operation fails if no such record
  exists. The flag Success indicates whether the operation
  succeeded. }

    if eof(TIndex)
      then Success := false

      else
      begin
         { read from index file into internal array B the
           block that contains the root of the 2-3 tree }
         ReadBlock(TIndex, RootNum, B)

         { search for the index record whose key value
           equals SearchKey }
```

```
      if SearchKey is in the root then
         begin
            BlockNum := data file's block number that
                        index record specifies
            ReadBlock(TData, BlockNum, D)
            Find data record D[k] whose search key
              equals SearchKey
            TableItem := D[k]
            Success := true
         end { then }

      { else search the appropriate subtree }
      else if the root is a leaf then
         Success := false

      else
         begin
            Child := block number of root of
                     appropriate subtree
           TableRetrieve(TIndex, TData, Child,
                         SearchKey, TableItem, Success)
         end   { else }
   end   { else }
```

You can also perform insertions and deletions in a manner similar to the internal version, with the addition that you must insert records into and delete records from both the index file and the data file (as was the case in the external hashing scheme described earlier). In the course of insertions into and deletions from the index file, you must split and merge nodes of the tree just as you do for the internal version. You perform insertions into and deletions from the data file—which, recall, is not ordered in any way—exactly as described for the external hashing implementation.

An external 2-3 tree is adequate, but an improvement is possible

You can thus support the table operations fairly well by using an external version of the 2-3 tree. However, you can generalize the 2-3 tree to a structure that is even more suitable for an external environment. Recall the discussion in Chapter 13 about search trees that allow their nodes to have more than three children. You saw that any reduction in the height of the search tree obtained by allowing its nodes to have more than three children is offset by the fact that, in the course of searching for a value, more comparisons are necessary at each node visited. In an external environment, however, the advantage of keeping a search tree short far outweighs the disadvantage of performing extra work at each node.

Keep an external search tree short

In an external environment, as you traverse the search tree you must perform a block access for each node visited. Because the time required to access a block of an external file is, in general, far greater than the time required to operate on that block once it has been read in (for example, the time required to inspect its data), the overriding concern is to reduce the number of block accesses required. This fact implies that you should attempt to reduce the height of the tree, even at the expense of requiring more comparisons at each node. In an external search tree, you should thus allow each node to have as many children as possible, with only the block size as a limiting factor.

How many children can a block of some fixed size accommodate? If a node is to have *m* children, then clearly you must be able to fit *m* child pointers in the node. In addition to child pointers, however, the node must also contain index records.

Before you can answer the question of how many children a block can accommodate, you must first consider this related question: If a node *N* in a search tree has *m* children, how many key values—and thus how many index records—must it contain?

Binary search tree: the number of records and children per node

In a binary search tree, if the node *N* has two children, then it must contain one key value, as Figure 14-11a indicates. You can think of the key value in node *N* as separating the key values in *N*'s two subtrees—all the key values in *N*'s left subtree are less than *N*'s key value, and all the key values in *N*'s right subtree are greater than *N*'s key value. When you are searching the tree for a given key value, the key value in *N* tells you which branch to take.

2-3 tree: the number of records and children per node

Similarly, if a node *N* in a 2-3 tree has three children, it must contain two key values. (See Figure 14-11b.) These two values separate the key values in *N*'s three subtrees—all the key values in the left subtree are less than *N*'s smaller key value, all the key values in *N*'s middle subtree lie between *N*'s two key values, and all the key values in *N*'s right subtree are greater than *N*'s larger key value. As is the case with a binary search tree, this requirement allows a search algorithm to know which branch to take at any given node.

General search tree: the number of records and children per node

In general, if a node *N* in a search tree is to have *m* children, then it must contain $m - 1$ key values to separate the values in its subtrees correctly. (See Figure 14-11c.) Suppose that you denote the subtrees of *N* as S_0,

(a)

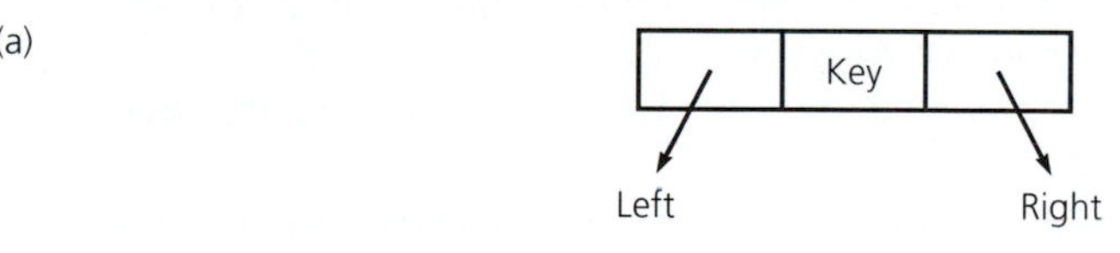

(b)

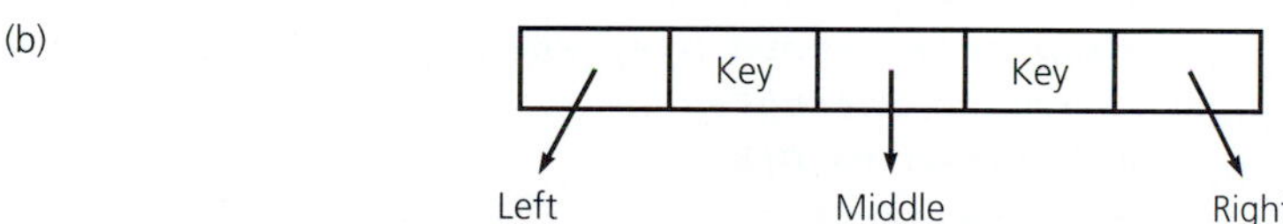

(c)

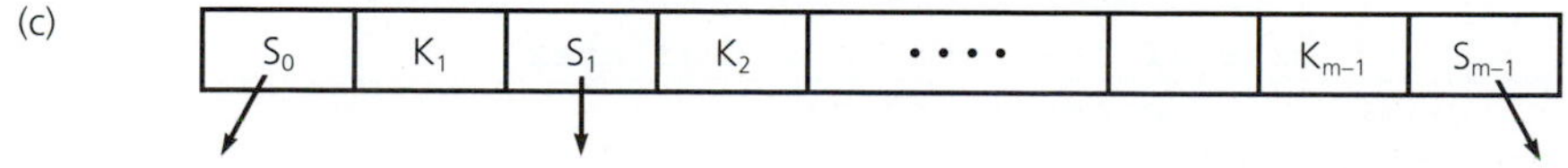

Figure 14-11

(a) A node with two children; (b) a node with three children; (c) a node with *m* children

S_1, and so on to S_{m-1} and denote the key values in N as K_1, K_2, and so on to K_{m-1} (with $K_1 < K_2 < \cdots < K_{m-1}$). The key values in N must separate the values in its subtrees as follows:

- All the values in subtree S_0 must be less than the key value K_1.
- For all i, $1 \leq i \leq m - 2$, all the values in subtree S_i must lie between the key values K_i and K_{i+1}.
- All the values in subtree S_{m-1} must be greater than the key value K_{m-1}.

If every node in the tree obeys this property, you can search the tree by using the following generalized version of a search tree's retrieval algorithm:

Retrieval with a general external search tree

```
TableRetrieve(TIndex, TData, RootNum, SearchKey,
                                  TableItem, Success)
{ Retrieves into TableItem the record whose search key
  equals SearchKey. TIndex is the index file, which is
  organized as a search tree. RootNum is the block number
  (of the index file) that contains the root of the tree.
  TData is the data file. The operation fails if no such
  record exists. The flag Success indicates whether the
  operation succeeded. }

   if eof(TIndex)
      then Success := false

      else
      begin
         { read from index file into internal array B the
           block that contains the root of the tree }
         ReadBlock(TIndex, RootNum, B)

         { search for the index record whose key value
           equals SearchKey }
         if SearchKey is one of the K_i in the root then
            begin
               BlockNum := data file's block number that
                             index record specifies
               ReadBlock(TData, BlockNum, D)
               Find data record D[k] whose search key
                  equals SearchKey
               TableItem := D[k]
               Success := true
            end { then }

         { else search the appropriate subtree }
         else if the root is a leaf then
              Success := false
```

```
      else
         begin
            Determine which subtree Si to search
            Child := block number of the root of Si
            TableRetrieve(TIndex, TData, Child,
                          SearchKey, TableItem, Success)
         end   { else }
   end   { else }
```

Now return to the question of how many children the nodes of the search tree can have—that is, how big can *m* be? If you wish to organize the index file into a search tree, then the items that you store in each node will be records of the form `<Key, Pointer>`. Thus, if each node in the tree (which, recall, is a block of the index file) is to have *m* children, it must be large enough to accommodate *m* child pointers and $m - 1$ records of the form `<Key, Pointer>`. You should choose *m* to be the largest integer such that *m* child pointers (which, recall, are integers) and $m - 1$ `<Key, Pointer>` records can fit into a single block of the file. Actually, the algorithms are somewhat simplified if you always choose *m* to be odd. That is, you should choose *m* to be the largest odd integer such that *m* child pointers and $m - 1$ index records can fit into a single block.

Number of children per node

Ideally, then, you should structure the external search tree so that every internal node has *m* children, where *m* is chosen as just described, and all leaves are at the same level, as is the case with full trees and 2-3 trees. For example, Figure 14-12 shows a full tree whose internal nodes each have five children. Although this structure would give you the search tree with the minimum possible height, it is too difficult to maintain in the face of insertions and deletions. As a consequence, you must make a compromise.

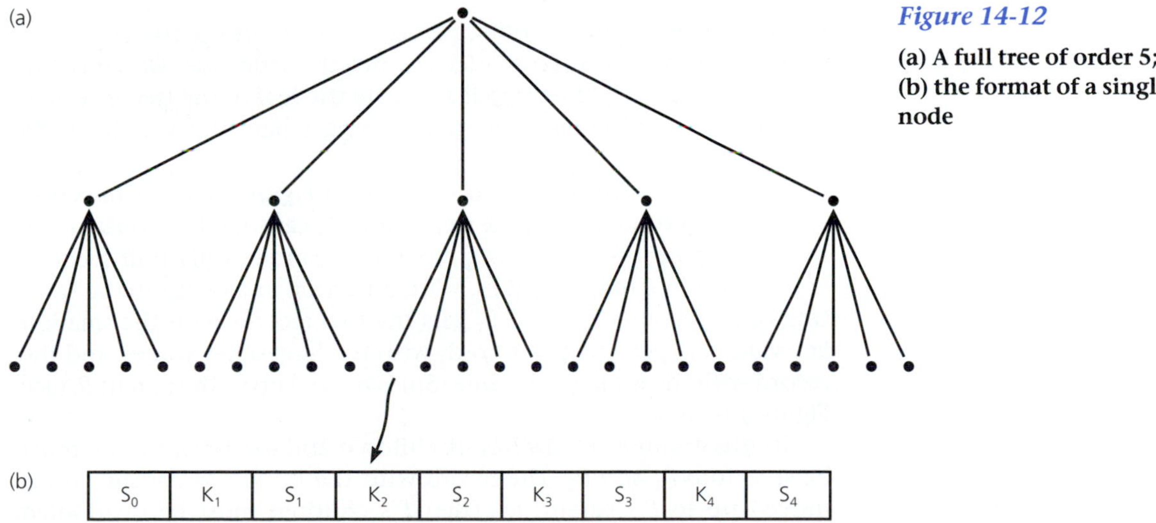

Figure 14-12

(a) A full tree of order 5; (b) the format of a single node

You can still insist that all the leaves of the search tree be at the same level—that is, that the tree be balanced—but you must allow each internal node to have between m and (m `div` 2) + 1 children.

B-tree of degree m

This type of search tree is known as a **B-tree of degree m**. A B-tree of degree m is a search tree such that

- All leaves are at the same level.
- Each node contains between $m - 1$ and (m `div` 2) records, and each internal node has one more child than it has records. An exception to this rule is that the root of the tree can contain as few as one record and can have as few as two children. This exception is necessitated by the insertion and deletion algorithms described next.

Notice that a 2-3 tree is a B-tree of degree 3. Furthermore, the manner in which the B-tree insertion and deletion algorithms maintain the structure of the tree is a direct generalization of the 2-3 tree's strategy of splitting and merging nodes.

The B-tree insertion and deletion algorithms are illustrated next by means of an example. Suppose that the index file is organized into a B-tree of degree 5—that is, 5 is the maximum and 3 is the minimum number of children that an internal node (other than the root) in the tree can have. (Typically, a B-tree will be of a higher degree, but the diagrams would get out of hand!)

Insertions into a B-tree. The steps that insert a data record with search key 55 into the tree of Figure 14-13 are as follows:

1. **Insert the data record into the data file.** First you find block *p* in the data file into which you can insert the new record. As was true with the external hashing implementation, block *p* is either any block with a vacant slot or is a new block.
2. **Insert a corresponding index record into the index file.** You now must insert the index record <55, *p*> into the index file, which is a B-tree of degree 5. The first step is to locate the leaf of the tree in which this index record belongs by determining where the search for 55 would terminate.

   Suppose that this is the leaf L shown in Figure 14-14a. Conceptually, you insert the new index record into L, causing it to contain five records (Figure 14-14b). Since a node can contain only four records, you must split L into L_1 and L_2. With an action analogous to the splitting of a node in a 2-3 tree, L_1 gets the two records with the smallest key values, L_2 gets the two records with the largest key values, and the record with the middle key value (56) is moved up to the parent P. (See Figure 14-14c.)

   In this example, P now has six children and five records, so it must be split into P_1 and P_2. The record with the middle key value (56) is moved up to P's parent, Q. Then P's children must be distributed

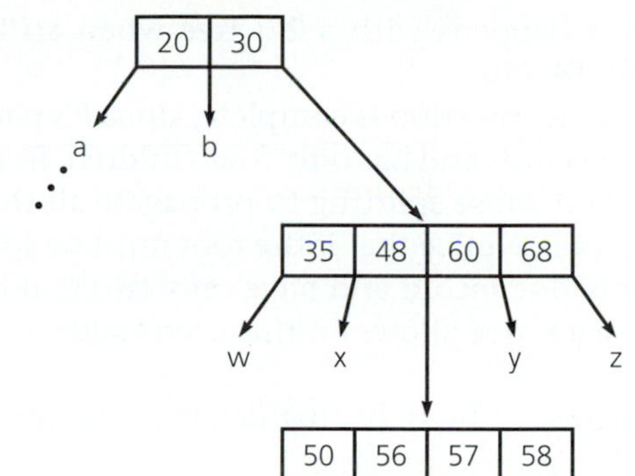

Figure 14-13

A B-tree

(a)

20 30

a b

35 48 60 68 P

w x y z

50 56 57 58 L Leaf found

(b)

20 30

a b

35 48 60 68 P

w x y z

50 55 56 57 58 L Record inserted

(c)

20 30 Q

a b

35 48 56 60 68 P

w x y z

50 55 57 58 Split leaf

L_1 L_2

(d)

20 30 56 Q

a b

35 48 P_1 60 68 P_2

w x y z

50 55 57 58

L_1 L_2

Split internal node

(e)

10 15 35 45 55 Root

u v w x y z

Height h

35 New root

10 15 45 55 Height h+1

u v w x y z

Splitting can propagate to the root

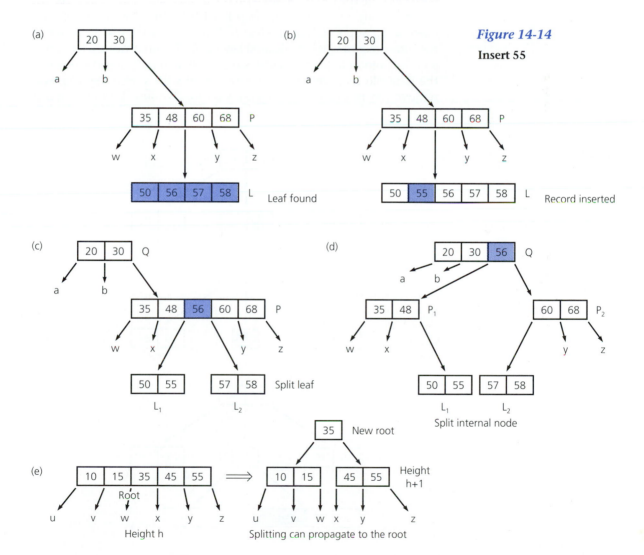

Figure 14-14

Insert 55

appropriately, as happens with a 2-3 tree when an internal node is split. (See Figure 14-14d.)

At this point the insertion is complete, since *P*'s parent Q now contains only three records and has only four children. In general, though, an insertion might cause splitting to propagate all the way up to the root (Figure 14-14e). Notice that if the root must be split, the new root will contain only one record and have only two children. (Recall that the definition of a B-tree allows for this eventuality.)

Deletions from a B-tree. The steps that delete a data record with a given search key from a B-tree are as follows:

1. **Locate the index record in the index file.** You use the search procedure to locate the index record with the desired key value. If this record is not already in a leaf, you swap it with its inorder successor. (See Exercise 5.) Suppose that the leaf *L* shown in Figure 14-15a contains the index with the desired key value, 73. After noting the value *p* of the pointer field of this index record (which indicates the block of the data file that contains the data record with search key 73), you remove the record from *L* (Figure 14-15b). Because *L* now contains

Figure 14-15
Delete 73

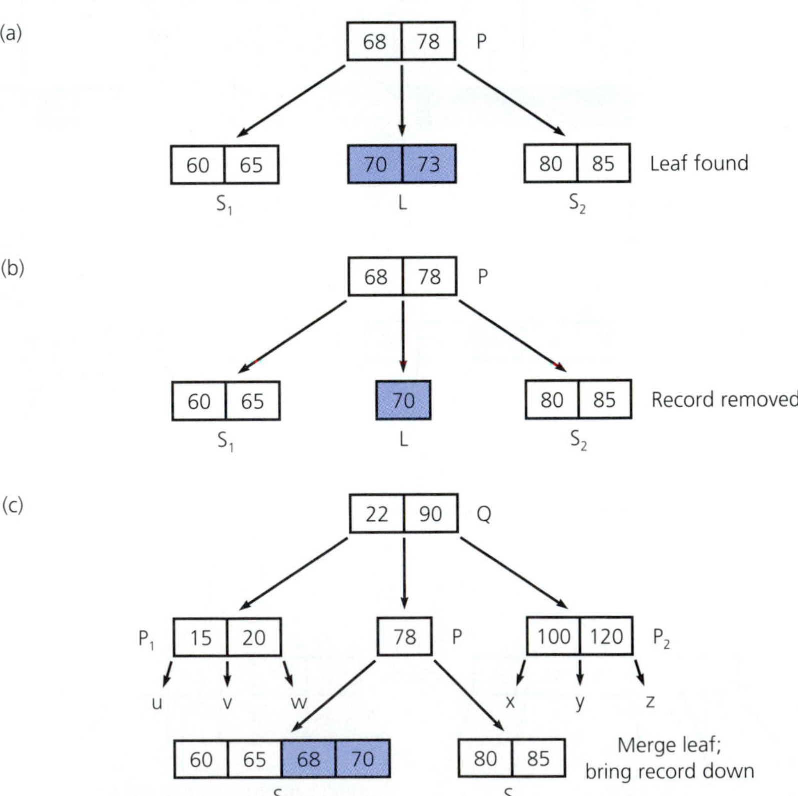

only one value (recall that two is the minimum number of values that a node is permitted to contain), and since *L*'s siblings cannot spare a value, you merge *L* with one of the siblings and bring down a record from the parent *P* (Figure 14-15c). Notice that this step is analogous to the merge step for a 2-3 tree. However, *P* now has only one value and two children, and since its siblings cannot spare a record and child, you must merge *P* with its sibling P_1 and bring a record down from *P*'s parent, *Q*. Since *P* is an internal node, its children must be adopted by P_1. (See Figure 14-15d.)

After this merge, *P*'s parent *Q* is left with only two children and one record. In this case, however, *Q*'s sibling Q_1 can spare a record and a child, so you redistribute children and records among Q_1, *Q*, and the parent *T* to complete the deletion. (See Figure 14-15e.) Notice that if a deletion ever propagates all the way up to the root so that it has only

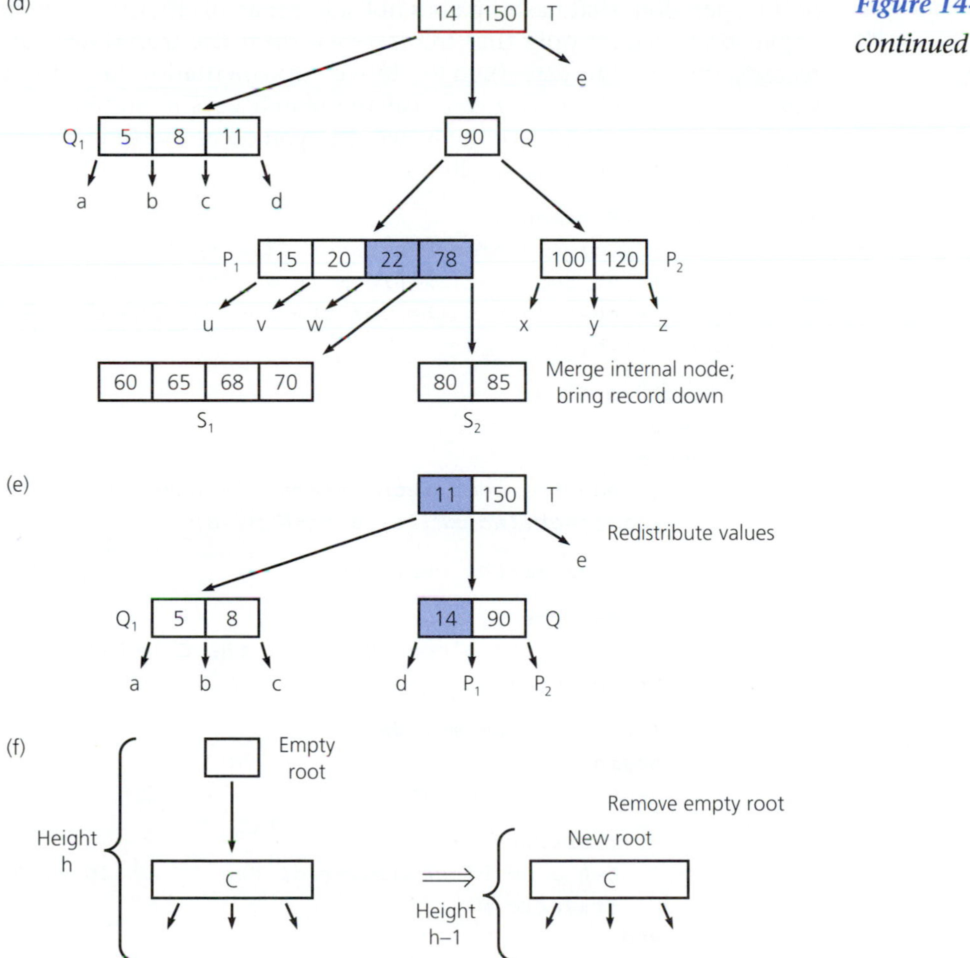

Figure 14-15 *continued*

two children and contains only one record, you simply let this situation stand. Recall that this eventuality is accounted for in the definition of a B-tree. If a future deletion causes the root to have a single child and no records, you remove the root so that the tree's height decreases by 1, as Figure 14-15f illustrates. The deletion of the index record is complete and you now must delete the data record.

2. **Delete the data record from the data file.** Prior to deleting the index record, you noted the value *p* of its pointer field. Thus, you know that the data record is in block *p* of the data file. You simply access this block, delete the record, and write the block back to the file. The high-level pseudocode for the insertion and deletion algorithms parallels that of the 2-3 tree and is left as an exercise.

Traversals

Accessing only the search key of each record, but not the data file

Now consider the operation *TraverseTable* in sorted order, which is one of the operations that hashing does not support at all efficiently. Often an application requires only that the traversal print the search keys of the records. If such is the case, then the B-tree implementation can efficiently support the operation. You can visit the search keys in sorted order by using an inorder traversal of the B-tree, and you do not have to access the data file. The algorithm is as follows:

Inorder traversal of a B-tree index file

```
TraverseTable(BlockNum)
{ Traverses in sorted order an index file that is organized
  as a B-tree of degree m, where m is a global constant.
  BlockNum is the block number of the root of the B-tree in
  the index file. }

   if BlockNum <> 0
      then
      begin
         { read the root into internal array B }
         ReadBlock(IndexFile, BlockNum, B)

         { traverse the children }

         { traverse S0 }
         Let p be the block number of the 0th child of B
         Traverse(p)

         for i := 1 to m-1 do
         begin
            Print key Ki of B

            { traverse Si }
            Let p be block number of the ith child of B
            Traverse(p)
         end
      end
```

This traversal accomplishes the task with the minimum possible number of block accesses because each block of the index file is read only once. Notice, however, that this algorithm assumes that there is enough internal memory to accommodate a recursive stack that contains *h* blocks, where *h* is the height of the tree. In many situations this assumption is reasonable—for example, a 255-degree B-tree that indexes a file of 16 million data records has a height of no more than 3. When internal memory cannot accommodate *h* blocks, you must use a different algorithm. (See Exercise 9.)

Accessing the entire data record

If the traversal must print the entire data record (and not just the search key), then the B-tree implementation is less attractive. In this case, as you traverse the B-tree, you must access the appropriate block of the data file. The traversal becomes

Sorted-order traversal of a data file indexed with a B-tree

```
TraverseTable(BlockNum)
{ Traverses in sorted order a data file that is indexed with
  a B-tree of degree m, where m is a global constant.
  BlockNum is the block number of the root of the B-tree. }

   if BlockNum <> 0
      then
      begin
         { read the root into internal array B }
         ReadBlock(IndexFile, BlockNum, B)

         { traverse S0 }
         Let p be the block number of the 0th child of B
         Traverse(p)

         for i := 1 to m-1 do
         begin
            Let p_i be the pointer in the ith index
               record of B
            ReadBlock(DataFile, p_i, D)
            Extract from D the data record whose search
               key equals Ki
            Print the data record

            { traverse Si }
            Let p be block number of the ith child of B
            Traverse (p)
         end
      end
```

Generally, the previous traversal is unacceptable

Notice that this traversal requires you to read a block of the data file before you print each data record; that is, the number of data-file block accesses is equal to the number of data records. In general, such a large number of block accesses would not be acceptable. If you must perform this type of traversal frequently, you probably would modify the B-tree scheme so that the data file itself was kept nearly sorted.

Multiple Indexing

There is one final point to make before we conclude the discussion of external implementations. This point concerns the multiple indexing of a data file. Chapter 13 presented a problem where you had to support multiple organizations for data stored in internal memory. Such a problem is also common for data stored externally. For example, suppose that a data file contains a collection of employee records on which you need to perform two types of retrievals:

```
RetrieveN(AName)
{ Retrieves the item whose Name field contains the value
  AName. }

RetrieveS(SS)
{ Retrieves the item whose SocSec field contains the value
  SS. }
```

Multiple index files allow multiple data organizations

One solution to this problem is to maintain two independent index files to the data file. For example, you could have one index file that contains index records of the form <`Name, Pointer`> and a second index file that contains index records of the form <`SocSec, Pointer`>. These index files could both be hashed, could both be B-trees, or could be one of each, as Figure 14-16 indicates. The choice would depend on the operations you wanted to perform with each search key. (Similarly, if an application requires extremely fast retrievals on `SocSec` and also requires operations such as traverse in sorted `SocSec` order and range queries on `SocSec`, it might be reasonable to have two `SocSec` index files—one hashed, the other a B-tree.)

Figure 14-16

Multiple index files

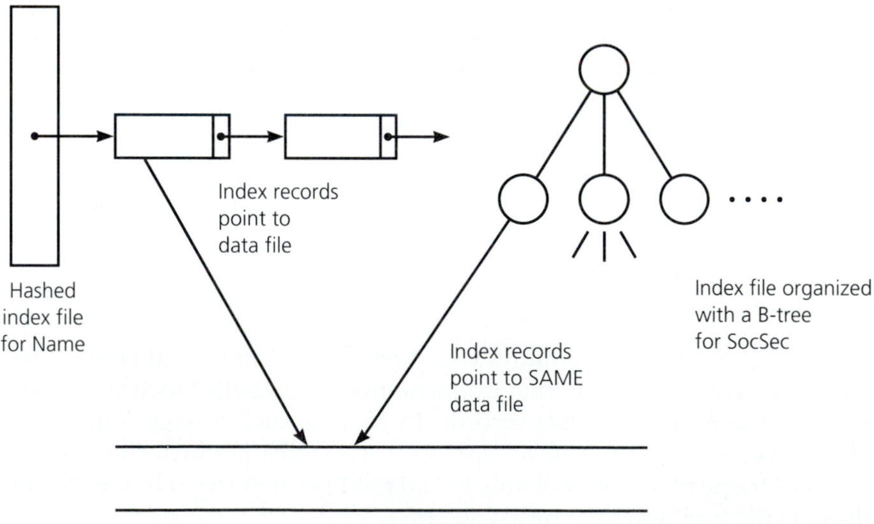

Notice that while you can perform each retrieval operation by using only one of the indexes (that is, use the `Name` index for `RetrieveN` and the `SocSec` index for `RetrieveS`), insertion and deletion operations must update both indexes. For example, the delete-by-name operation `DeleteN(Jones)` requires that you

1. Search the `Name` index file for Jones and delete the index record.
2. Delete the appropriate data record from the data file, noting the `SocSec` value `SS` of this record.
3. Search the `SocSec` index file for `SS` and delete this index record.

In general, the price paid for multiple indexing is more storage space and an additional overhead for updating each index whenever you modify the data file.

This chapter has presented at a very high level the basic principles of managing data in external storage. The details of implementing the algorithms are quite complex and depend heavily on the specific computing system. Particular situations often mandate either variations of the methods described here or completely different approaches. In future courses and work experience, you will undoubtedly learn much more about these techniques.

SUMMARY

1. **An external file is partitioned into blocks. Each block typically contains many data records, and a block is generally the smallest unit of transfer between internal and external memory. That is, to access a record, you must access the block that contains it.**
2. **You can access the ith block of a direct access file without accessing the blocks that precede it. In this sense direct access files resemble arrays.**
3. **`Mergesort` (Chapter 7) can be modified so that it can sort a file of records without requiring all the records to be in internal memory at one time.**
4. **A dense index to a data file is a file that contains an index record for each record in the data file. An index record contains both the search key of the corresponding data record and the number of the block that contains that record.**
5. **You can organize the index file by using either hashing or B-trees. These schemes allow you to perform the basic table operations by using only a few block accesses.**
6. **It is possible to have several index files for the same data file. Such multiple indexing allows you to perform different types of operations efficiently, such as retrieve by name and retrieve by Social Security number.**

COMMON PITFALLS / DEBUGGING

1. **Before you can process (for example, inspect or update) a record, you must read it from an external file into internal memory. Once you modify a record, you must write it back to the file.**
2. **Block accesses are typically quite slow when compared to other computer operations. Therefore, you must carefully organize a file so that you can perform tasks by using only a few block accesses. Otherwise, response time can be very poor.**
3. **If a record is inserted into or deleted from a data file, you must make the corresponding change to the index file. If a data file has more than one index file, you must update each index file. Thus, multiple indexing has an overhead.**
4. **Although external hashing generally supports retrievals, insertions, and deletions more quickly than does a B-tree, it does not support such operations as sorted traversals or range queries. This deficiency is one motivation for multiple indexing.**

SELF-TEST EXERCISES

1. Consider two files of 1,600 employee records each. The records in each file are organized into sixteen 100-record blocks. One file is sequential access and the other is direct access. Describe how you would append one record to the end of each file.
2. Trace the `ExternalMergesort` algorithm with an external file of 16 blocks. Assume that the arrays `In1`, `In2`, and `Out` are each one block long. List the calls to the various procedures in the order in which they occur.
3. Trace the `TableRetrieve` algorithm for an indexed external file when the search key is less than all keys in the index. Assume that the index file is sorted by its search key, the data file contains 100 blocks, and each block contains 10 employee records. The index file contains 20 blocks of 50 records each. List the calls to the various procedures in the order in which they occur.
4. Repeat Self-Test Exercise 3, but this time assume that the search key equals the key field of record 26 in block 12 of the index. Also assume that record 26 of the index points to block 98 of the data file.

EXERCISES

1. Assuming the existence of `ReadBlock` and `WriteBlock` procedures, write a pseudocode program for shifting data to make a gap at some specified location of a sorted file. Pay particular attention to the

details of shifting the last item out of one block and into the first position of the next block. You can assume that the last record of the file is in record `LastRec` of block `LastBlock` and that `LastBlock` is not full. (Note that this assumption permits shifting without allocating a new block to the file.)

2. The problem of managing the blocks of an external data file indexed by a B-tree or external hashing scheme is similar to that of managing memory for internal structures. When an external structure such as a data file needs more memory (for example, to insert a new record), it gets a new block from a **free list** that the system manages. That is, if the file contains N blocks, the system can allocate to it an $(N + 1)^{st}$ block. When the file no longer needs a block, you can deallocate it and return it to the system.

The complication in the management of external storage is that a block allocated to a file may have available space interspersed with data. For example, after you delete a record from the middle of a data file, the block that contained that record now has space available for at least one record, even though it may not be completely empty. Therefore, you must be able to keep track of blocks that have space available for one or more records as well as recognize when blocks are completely empty (so that you can return them to the system).

Assuming the existence of `AllocateBlock` and `ReturnBlock` procedures that get empty blocks from and return empty blocks to the system, write pseudocode implementations of the following external memory-management procedures:

```
GetSlot(F, BlockNum, RecNum)
{ Determines the block number (BlockNum) and record
  number (RecNum) of an available slot in file F. A new
  block is allocated to the file from the system if
  necessary. }
FreeSlot(F, BlockNum, RecNum)
{ Makes record RecNum in block BlockNum of file F
  available. The block is returned to the system if it
  becomes empty. }
```

What data structure is appropriate to support these operations? You may assume that you can distinguish slots of a block that do not contain a record from those that do. You can make this distinction either by having a convention for `nil` values in the fields of a record or by adding an empty/full boolean field.

3. Describe pseudocode algorithms for insertion into and deletion from a table implemented externally with a hashed index file.

4. Execute the following sequence of operations on an initially empty ADT table that is implemented as a B-tree of order 5. Note that insertion into an empty B-tree will create a single node that contains the inserted item.

```
TableInsert(10)
TableInsert(100)
TableInsert(30)
TableInsert(80)
TableInsert(50)
TableDelete(10)
TableInsert(60)
TableInsert(70)
TableInsert(40)
TableDelete(80)
TableInsert(90)
TableInsert(20)
TableDelete(30)
TableDelete(70)
```

5. Describe a pseudocode algorithm for finding an item's inorder successor in an external B-tree.

6. Describe pseudocode algorithms for insertion into and deletion from an ADT table implemented with an index file organized as a B-tree.

7. Write a `RangeQuery` procedure for a B-tree in pseudocode. (See Exercises 1 and 2 of Chapter 13.) Assume that only the key values are needed (as opposed to the entire data record).

8. Integrate calls to the appropriate memory-management procedures (see Exercise 2) into the pseudocode for `TableInsert` and `TableDelete` under both the B-tree and hashing schemes. (See Exercises 3 and 6.)

9. The B-tree traversal algorithm presented in this chapter assumes that internal memory is large enough to accommodate the recursive stack that contains up to h blocks, where h is the height of the B-tree. Suppose that you are in an environment where this assumption is not true. Modify the traversal algorithm so that the recursive stack contains block numbers rather than the actual blocks. How many block accesses does your algorithm have to perform?

10. a. Suppose that traversals and range queries need to access entire data records, not simply the search key. Write pseudocode implementations of such operations against a B-tree. How many block accesses do your procedures require?

    b. To reduce the number of block accesses required by these operations, various modifications of the basic B-tree structure are frequently used. The central idea behind such structures is to keep the data file itself sorted. First, assume that you can keep the data file in sequential sorted order—that is, so that the records are sorted within each block and the records in B_{i-1} are less than the records in B_i for $i = 2$, 3, and so on to the number of blocks in the file. Rewrite your implementations of the traversal and range-query operations to take advantage of this fact. How many block accesses do these operations now require?

c. Because it is too inefficient to maintain a sequentially sorted data file in the face of frequent insertions and deletions, a compromise scheme is often employed. One such possible compromise is as follows. If a data record belongs in block *B* and *B* is full, a new block is allocated and linked to *B*, allowing the new record to be inserted into its proper sorted location. The difficulty is that you must now view each index record in the B-tree as indicating the first of possibly several blocks on a chain of blocks that might contain the corresponding data record. Rewrite the `TableInsert`, `TableDelete`, `TableRetrieve`, `TraverseTable`, and `RangeQuery` operations in terms of this implementation. What is the effect on their efficiency?

11. Write an iterative (nonrecursive) version of internal `Mergesort`, as given in Chapter 7, that is based on the external version that this chapter describes. That is, merge sorted runs that double in size at each pass of the array.

PROJECT

***12.** a. Implement the `ExternalMergesort` algorithm in Turbo Pascal by using the `seek` procedure. Assume that the file to be sorted is a file of type `integer` and that each block contains one integer. Further assume that the file contains 2^N integers for some integer N.

b. Now assume that each block contains many integers. Write Turbo Pascal procedures that simulate `ReadBlock` and `WriteBlock`. Implement the `ExternalMergesort` by using these procedures.

c. Extend your implementation of `ExternalMergesort` by removing the restriction that the file contains 2^N blocks.

APPENDIX A

Mathematical Induction

Many proofs of theorems or invariants in computer science use a technique called **mathematical induction**, or simply **induction**. Induction is a principle of mathematics that is like a row of dominoes stood on end. If you push the first domino, all the dominoes will fall one after another. What is it about the dominoes that allows us to draw this conclusion? If you know that when one domino falls the next domino will fall, then pushing the first domino will cause them all to fall in succession. More formally, you can show that all the dominoes will fall if you can show that the following two facts are true:

- The first domino falls.
- For any $k \geq 1$, if the kth domino falls, the $(k + 1)^{st}$ domino will fall.

The principle of mathematical induction is an axiom that is stated as follows:

AXIOM A-1. The principle of mathematical induction. A property $P(n)$ that involves an integer n is true for all $n \geq 0$ if the following are true:

1. $P(0)$ is true.
2. If $P(k)$ is true for any $k \geq 0$, then $P(k + 1)$ is true.

A **proof by induction on *n*** is one that uses the principle of mathematical induction. Such a proof consists of the two steps given in Axiom A-1. The first step is called the **basis,** or **base case.** The second step is the **induc-**

tive step. We usually break the inductive step into two parts: the **inductive hypothesis** ("if $P(k)$ is true for any $k \geq 0$") and the **inductive conclusion** ("then $P(k + 1)$ is true").

Example 1

Chapter 5 presented the following recursive function that computes x^n:

```
function Pow2(x, n)

  if n = 0
     then Pow2 := 1
     else Pow2 := x * Pow2(x, n-1)
```

You can prove that `Pow2` returns x^n for all $n \geq 0$ by using the following proof by induction on n:

Basis. ***Show that the property is true when n = 0.*** That is, you must show that `Pow2(x, 0)` returns x^0, which is 1. However, as you can see from the definition of `Pow2`, `Pow2(x, 0)` is 1.

Now you must establish the inductive step. By assuming that the property is true when $n = k$ (the inductive hypothesis), you must show that the property is true when $n = k + 1$ (the inductive conclusion).

Inductive hypothesis. ***Assume that the property is true when n = k.*** That is, assume that

`Pow2(x, k)` $= x^k$

Inductive conclusion. ***Show that the property is true when n = k + 1.*** That is, you must show that `Pow2(x, k + 1)` returns the value x^{k+1}. By definition of the function `Pow2`,

`Pow2(x, k + 1)` $=$ `x * Pow2(x, k)`

By the inductive hypothesis, `Pow2(x, k)` returns the value x^k, so

`Pow2(x, k + 1)` $= x * x^k$
$= x^{k+1}$

which is what you needed to show to establish the inductive step.

The inductive proof is thus complete. We demonstrated that the two steps in Axiom A-1 are true, so the principle of mathematical induction guarantees that `Pow2` returns x^n for all $n \geq 0$. (**End of proof.**)

Example 2

Prove that

$$1 + 2 + \cdots + n = \frac{n(n+1)}{2} \text{ when } n \geq 1$$

It will be helpful to let S_n represent the sum $1 + 2 + \cdots + n$.

Basis. Sometimes the property to be proven is trivial when $n = 0$, as is the case here. You can use $n = 1$ as the basis instead. (Actually, you can use any value of $n \geq 0$ as the basis, but a value of 0 or 1 is typical.)

You need to show that the sum S_1, which is simply 1, is equal to $1(1 + 1)/2$. This fact is obvious.

Inductive hypothesis. Assume that the formula is true when $n = k$; that is, assume that $S_k = k(k + 1)/2$.

Inductive conclusion. Show that the formula is true when $n = k + 1$. To do so, you can proceed as follows:

$$\begin{aligned} S_{k+1} &= (1 + 2 + \cdots + k) + (k + 1) && \text{(definition of } S_{k+1}\text{)} \\ &= S_k + (k + 1) && \text{(definition of } S_k\text{)} \\ &= k(k + 1)/2 + (k + 1) && \text{(inductive hypothesis)} \\ &= (k(k + 1) + 2(k + 1))/2 && \text{(common denominator)} \\ &= (k + 1)(k + 2)/2 && \text{(factorization)} \end{aligned}$$

The last expression is $n(n + 1)/2$ when n is $k + 1$. Thus, if the formula for S_k is true, the formula for S_{k+1} is true. Therefore, by the principle of mathematical induction, the formula is true when $n \geq 1$. (**End of proof.**)

Example 3

Prove that $2^n > n^2$ when $n \geq 5$.

Basis. Here is an example where the base case is not $n = 0$ or 1, but instead is $n = 5$. It is obvious that the relationship is true when $n = 5$ because

$$2^5 = 32 > 5^2 = 25$$

Inductive hypothesis. Assume that the relationship is true when $n = k \geq 5$; that is, assume that $2^k > k^2$ when $k \geq 5$.

Inductive conclusion. Show that the relationship is true when $n = k + 1$; that is, show that $2^{k+1} > (k + 1)^2$ when $k \geq 5$. To do so, you can proceed as follows:

$$\begin{aligned} (k + 1)^2 &= k^2 + (2k + 1) && \text{(square } k + 1\text{)} \\ &< k^2 + k^2 \text{ when } k \geq 5 && (2k + 1 < k^2)^* \\ &< 2^k + 2^k \text{ when } k \geq 5 && \text{(inductive hypothesis)} \\ &= 2^{k+1} \end{aligned}$$

Therefore, by the principle of mathematical induction, $2^n > n^2$ when $n \geq 5$. (**End of proof.**)

Sometimes, the inductive hypothesis in Axiom A-1 is not sufficient. That is, you may need to assume more than $P(k)$. The following axiom is a stronger form of the principle of mathematical induction:

---

*See Exercise 3.

AXIOM A-2. The principle of mathematical induction (strong form). A property $P(n)$ that involves an integer n is true for all $n \geqslant 0$ if the following are true:

1. $P(0)$ is true.
2. If $P(0), P(1), \cdots, P(k)$ are true for any $k \geqslant 0$, then $P(k + 1)$ is true.

Notice that the inductive hypothesis of Axiom A-2 ("If $P(0), P(1), \cdots, P(k)$ are true for any $k \geqslant 0$") includes the inductive hypothesis of Axiom A-1 ("If $P(k)$ is true for any $k \geqslant 0$").

Example 4

Prove that every integer greater than 1 can be written as a product of prime integers.

Recall that a prime number is one that is divisible only by 1 and itself. The inductive proof is as follows:

Basis. The statement that you must prove involves integers greater than 1. Thus, the base case is $n = 2$. However, 2 is a prime number and, therefore, it trivially is a product of prime numbers.

Inductive hypothesis. Assume that the property is true for each of the integers $2, 3, \cdots, k$, where $k \geqslant 2$.

Inductive conclusion. Show that the property is true when $n = k + 1$; that is, show that $k + 1$ can be written as a product of prime numbers.

If $k + 1$ is a prime number, then there is nothing more to show. However, if $k + 1$ is not a prime number, it must be divisible by an integer x such that $1 < x < k + 1$. Thus,

$$k + 1 = x * y$$

where $1 < y < k + 1$. Notice that x and y are each less than or equal to k, so the inductive hypothesis applies. That is, x and y can each be written as a product of prime numbers. Clearly $x * y$, which is equal to $k + 1$, must be a product of prime numbers. Because the formula holds for $n = k + 1$, it holds for all $n \geqslant 2$ by the principle of mathematical induction. (**End of proof.**)

Example 5

Chapter 5 discusses the following recursive definition:

$$Rabbit(1) = 1$$
$$Rabbit(2) = 1$$
$$Rabbit(n) = Rabbit(n - 1) + Rabbit(n - 2) \text{ when } n > 2$$

Prove that

$$Rabbit(n) = (a^n - b^n)/\sqrt{5}$$

where $a = (1 + \sqrt{5})/2$ and $b = (1 - \sqrt{5})/2 = 1 - a$.

Basis. *Rabbit*(0) is undefined, so begin at $n = 1$. Some algebra shows that *Rabbit*(1) $= (a^1 - b^1)/\sqrt{5} = 1$. However, notice that *Rabbit*(2) is also a special case. That is, you cannot compute *Rabbit*(2) from *Rabbit*(1) by using the recurrence relationship given here. Therefore, the basis in this inductive proof must include $n = 2$.

When $n = 2$, some more algebra will show that *Rabbit*(2) $= (a^2 - b^2)/\sqrt{5} = 1$. Thus, the formula is true when n is either 1 or 2.

Inductive hypothesis. Assume that the formula is true for all n such that $1 \leq n \leq k$, where k is at least 2.

Inductive conclusion. Show that the formula is true for $n = k + 1$. To do so, you can proceed as follows:

$$\begin{aligned} Rabbit(k+1) &= Rabbit(k) + Rabbit(k-1) && \text{(recurrence relation)} \\ &= [(a^k - b^k) + (a^{k-1} - b^{k-1})]/\sqrt{5} && \text{(inductive hypothesis)} \\ &= [a^{k-1}(a+1) - b^{k-1}(b+1)]/\sqrt{5} && \text{(factorization)} \\ &= [a^{k-1}(a^2) - b^{k-1}(b^2)]/\sqrt{5} && (a + 1 = a^2;\ b + 1 = b^2) \\ &= (a^{k+1} - b^{k+1})/\sqrt{5} \end{aligned}$$

Because the formula holds for $n = k + 1$, it holds for all $n > 2$ by the principle of mathematical induction. (**End of proof.**)

Note that the previous proof requires that you show that $a + 1 = a^2$ and $b + 1 = b^2$. Although simple algebra will demonstrate the validity of these equalities, exactly how did we discover them after the factorization step? Some experience with inductive proofs will give you the confidence to determine and verify the auxiliary relationships—such as $a + 1 = a^2$—that are necessary in a proof. Here, after we introduced the factors $(a + 1)$ and $(b + 1)$, we observed that if these factors were equal to a^2 and b^2, respectively, we could finish the proof. Thus, we tried to show that $a + 1 = a^2$ and $b + 1 = b^2$; indeed, we were successful. Inductive proofs often require adventurous algebraic manipulations!

SELF-TEST EXERCISES

Answers on next page

1. Prove that $1 + 2^1 + 2^2 + \cdots + 2^m = 2^{m+1} - 1$ for all $m \geq 0$.
2. Prove that the sum of the first n odd positive integers is n^2.
3. Prove that *Rabbit*(n) $\geq a^{n-2}$ when $n \geq 2$ and $a = (1 + \sqrt{5})/2$.

EXERCISES

1. Prove that the sum of the first n even positive integers is $n(n + 1)$.
2. Prove that $1^2 + 2^2 + \cdots + n^2 = n(n + 1)(2n + 1)/6$ for all $n \geq 1$.
3. Prove that $2n + 1 < n^2$ for all $n \geq 3$.

4. Prove that $n^3 - n$ is divisible by 6 for all $n \geqslant 0$.

5. Prove that $2^n > n^3$ when $n \geqslant 10$.

6. Prove that $n! > n^3$ when n is large enough.

7. Recall the following recursive definition from Chapter 5:

   $C(n, 0) = 1$
   $C(n, n) = 1$
   $C(n, k) = C(n - 1, k - 1) + C(n - 1, k)$ when $0 < k < n$

   a. Prove that $C(n, 0) + C(n, 1) + \cdots + C(n, n) = 2^n$.
      Hint: Use $C(n + 1, 0) = C(n, 0)$ and $C(n + 1, n) = C(n, n)$.

   b. Prove that $(x + y)^n = \sum_{k=0}^{n} C(n, k)\, x^k y^{n-k}$

8. Prove that *Rabbit*(n) $\leqslant a^{n-1}$ when $n \geqslant 1$ and $a = (1 + \sqrt{5})/2$.

9. Suppose that the rabbit population doubles every year. If you start with two rabbits, find and prove a formula that predicts the rabbit population after n years.

Answers to Self-Test Exercises in Appendix A

1. Proof by induction on m. When $m = 0$, $2^0 = 2^1 - 1$. Now assume that the statement is true for $m = k$; that is, assume that $1 + 2^1 + 2^2 + \cdots + 2^k = 2^{k+1} - 1$. Show that the statement is true for $m = k + 1$, as follows:

$$\begin{aligned}(1 + 2^1 + 2^2 + \cdots + 2^k) + 2^{k+1} &= (2^{k+1} - 1) + 2^{k+1} \\ &= 2^{k+2} - 1\end{aligned}$$

2. Proof by induction on n. When $n = 1$, the first odd integer is 1 and the sum is trivially 1, which is equal to 1^2. Now assume that the statement is true for $n = k$; that is, assume that $1 + 3 + \cdots + (2k - 1) = k^2$. Show that the statement is true for $n = k + 1$, as follows:

$$\begin{aligned}[1 + 3 + \cdots + (2k - 1)] + (2k + 1) &= k^2 + (2k + 1) \\ &= (k + 1)^2\end{aligned}$$

3. Proof by induction on n. When $n = 2$, *Rabbit*(2) $= 1 = a^0$. Now assume that the statement is true for all $n \leqslant k$; that is, assume that *Rabbit*(n) $\geqslant a^{n-2}$ for all $n \leqslant k$. Show that the statement is true for $n = k + 1$, as follows:

$$\begin{aligned}\mathit{Rabbit}(k + 1) &= \mathit{Rabbit}(k) + \mathit{Rabbit}(k - 1) \\ &\geqslant a^{k-2} + a^{k-3} \\ &= a^{k-3}\,(a + 1) \\ &= a^{k-3}\,(a^2) \\ &= a^{k-1}\end{aligned}$$

APPENDIX B

Conditional And, Conditional Or

When either you use Standard Pascal or you specify the *$B+* compiler directive in Turbo Pascal, both operands of the *and* and *or* operators are evaluated, even when the value of the first operand determines the value of the entire boolean expression. For example, both relational expressions in

```
(I <= N) and (A[I] <> Target)
```

are evaluated, even when *I* is greater than *N*, which implies that the entire expression is *false* regardless of the value of *A[I] <> Target*.

In Chapter 2, we defined the pseudocode operator *Cand* (conditional and), which does not evaluate its second operand if its first operand is *false*. Similarly, we defined the *Cor* (conditional or) operator, which does not evaluate its second operand if its first operand is *true*.

Even though this notation simplifies algorithms greatly, how do you implement these conditional operators in Standard Pascal? When your pseudocode contains a loop such as

```
while <x> Cand <y> do
   <S> { body of the loop }
```

replace it with the following statements, where *Done* is a boolean variable, *<x>* and *<y>* are boolean expressions, and *<S>* is the body of the loop:

```
Done := false;
while <x> and (not Done) do
begin
   if <y>
      then <S> { body of loop }
      else Done := true
end; { while }
```

Thus, the algorithm

```
Index := 1
while (Index <= N) Cand (A[Index] <> Target) do
    Index := Index + 1
```

which searches an array sequentially for a given value, is implemented in Standard Pascal as

```
Index := 1;
Done := false;
while (Index  <= N) and (not Done) do
begin
   if A[Index] <> Target
      then Index  := Index + 1
      else Done := true
end;  { while }
```

When *Cand* occurs in an *if* statement in your pseudocode, such as

```
if <x> Cand <y>
   then <S1>
   else <S2>
```

you implement it in Standard Pascal by using statements of the following form:

```
if not <x> then
   <S2>
else if not <y> then
   <S2>
else <S1>
```

When *Cor* occurs in an *if* statement in your pseudocode, such as

```
if <x> Cor <y>
   then <S1>
   else <S2>
```

you write the following Standard Pascal statements instead:

```
if <x> then
   <S1>
else if <y> then
   <S1>
else <S2>
```

The case in which *Cor* occurs in a *while* statement is left as an exercise.

SELF-TEST EXERCISES

1. Implement the following pseudocode in Standard Pascal by removing the *Cand* operator:

```
{ locate the first (if any) nonzero element in the
  array A of N integers }
Index := 1
while (Index <= N) Cand (A[Index] = 0) do
   Index := Index + 1
if Index > N
   then all elements are zero
   else the first nonzero element is A[Index]
```

2. What does the Standard Pascal implementation of the following pseudocode look like when you remove the `Cor` operator? *Hint:* Use a boolean variable.

```
while <x> Cor <y> do
   <S>  { body of the loop }
```

Answers to Self-Test Exercises in Appendix B

1.

```
Index := 1;
Done := false;
while (Index <= N) and (not Done) do
begin
   if A[Index] = 0
       then Index := succ(Index)
       else Done := true
end;  { while }

if Index > N
    then writeln('All elements are zero.')
    else writeln('The first nonzero element is ', A[Index])
```

2.

```
{ while <x> Cor <y> do }
Done := false
while <x> or (not Done) do
begin
   if <y>
        then <S>  { body of the loop }
        else Done := true
end;  { while }
```

APPENDIX C

Turbo Pascal Reserved Words and Standard Identifiers

Reserved Words

You may not redefine reserved words. Items in color are not defined in Standard Pascal.

and	div	goto	nil	record	type
array	do	if	not	repeat	unit
asm	downto	implementation	object	set	until
begin	else	in	of	shl	uses
case	end	inline	or	shr	var
const	file	interface	packed	string	while
constructor	for	label	procedure	then	with
destructor	function	mod	program	to	xor

Standard Identifiers and Directives

You may redefine standard identifiers and standard directives, but you will lose the item's original capability and confuse people who read your program, including yourself. Items in color are not defined in Standard Pascal.

Constants	false, maxint, maxlongint, true
Directives	absolute, assembler, external, far, forward, interrupt, near, private, virtual
Files	input, output

Functions	*arithmetic:*	abs, arctan, cos, exp, frac, int, ln, pi, sin, sqr, sqrt
	dynamic allocation:	maxavail, memavail
	input/output:	eof, eoln, filepos, filesize, ioresult, seekeof, seekeoln
	miscellaneous:	hi, lo, paramcount, paramstr, random, sizeof, swap, upcase
	ordinal:	odd, pred, succ
	pointer and address:	addr, cseg, dseg, ofs, ptr, seg, sptr, sseg
	string:	concat, copy, length, pos
	transfer:	chr, ord, round, trunc
Procedures	*dynamic allocation:*	dispose, freemem, getmem, mark, new, release
	flow control:	exit, halt, runerror
	input/output:	append, assign, blockread, blockwrite, chdir, close, erase, flush, getdir, mkdir, read, readln, rename, reset, rewrite, rmdir, seek, settextbuf, truncate, write, writeln
	miscellaneous:	fillchar, move, randomize
	ordinal:	dec, int
	string:	delete, insert, str, val

Types	*ordinal:*	boolean, byte, char, integer, longint, shortint, word
	real:	comp, double, extended, real, single
	structured:	text

Units: crt, dos, graph, overlay, printer, system

APPENDIX D

Turbo Pascal Operators

Operators

Address: @

Arithmetic: +, −, *, /, div, mod

Assignment: :=

Boolean: and, or, not, xor

Relational: <, <=, =, <>, >=, >

Set: in, =, <>, <=, >=, *, +, −

Shift: shl, shr

String: +, <, <=, =, <>, >=, >

Operator Precedence

In the absence of parentheses, which override operator precedence, operators are executed in the following order:

1. @, not, unary +, unary −
2. *, /, div, mod, and, shl, shr
3. +, −, or, xor
4. <, <=, =, <>, >=, >, in

Operators of equal precedence are executed in left-to-right order.

APPENDIX E

ASCII Character Codes

0	^@	NUL	32	(blank)	64	@	96	‘ (reverse quote)
1	☺	SOH	33	!	65	A	97	a
2	☻	STX	34	"	66	B	98	b
3	♥	ETX	35	#	67	C	99	c
4	♦	EOT	36	$	68	D	100	d
5	♣	ENQ	37	%	69	E	101	e
6	♠	ACK	38	&	70	F	102	f
7	●	BEL	39	' (apostrophe)	71	G	103	g
8	◘	BS	40	(	72	H	104	h
9	○	TAB	41	)	73	I	105	i
10	◙	LF	42	*	74	J	106	j
11	♂	VT	43	+	75	K	107	k
12	♀	FF	44	, (comma)	76	L	108	l
13	♪	CR	45	−	77	M	109	m
14	♫	SO	46	.	78	N	110	n
15	¤	SI	47	/	79	O	111	o
16	►	DLE	48	0	80	P	112	p
17	◄	DC1	49	1	81	Q	113	q
18	↕	DC2	50	2	82	R	114	r
19	!!	DC3	51	3	83	S	115	s
20	¶	DC4	52	4	84	T	116	t
21	§	NAK	53	5	85	U	117	u
22	■	SYN	54	6	86	V	118	v
23	↨	ETB	55	7	87	W	119	w
24	↑	CAN	56	8	88	X	120	x
25	↓	EM	57	9	89	Y	121	y
26	→	SUB	58	:	90	Z	122	z
27	←	ESC	59	;	91	[	123	{
28	∟	FS	60	<	92	\	124	|
29	↔	GS	61	=	93	]	125	}
30	▲	RS	62	>	94	^	126	~
31	▼	US	63	?	95	_ (underscore)	127	⌂

APPENDIX F

Standard Functions

You may redefine standard functions, but you will lose the function's original capability and confuse people who read your program, including yourself. Items in color are not defined in Standard Pascal.

Name	Parameter Type	Result Type	Returns
`abs(x)`	*integer* or *real*	same as parameter	absolute value of *x*
`addr(x)`	*object*	pointer	address of object *x*
`arctan(x)`	*integer* or *real*	*real*	arctangent of *x* (*x* in radians)
`chr(x)`	*integer*	*char*	character whose ordinal value is *x*
`concat(`S_1`[, `S_2`, ..., `S_n`])`	*string*	*string*	concatenates listed strings
`copy(S, Index, Count)`	*S* is a *string*, *Index* and *Count* are integers	*string*	substring of *Count* characters of *S* beginning with *S[Index]*
`cos(x)`	*integer* or *real*	*real*	cosine of *x* (*x* in radians)
`cseg`		*word*	current value of the CS register
`dseg`		*word*	current value of the DS register
`eof(x)`	*file* or *text*	*boolean*	*true* if end of file, *false* otherwise
`eoln(x)`	*text*	*boolean*	*true* if end of line or end of file, *false* otherwise
`exp(x)`	*integer* or *real*	*real*	e to the power *x*

filepos(F)	*file*	*longint*	current file position of *F*
filesize(F)	*file*	*longint*	current size of file *F*
frac(x)	*real*	*real*	fractional part of *x*
hi(x)		*byte*	high-order byte of *x*
int(x)	*real*	*real*	integer part of *x*
ioresult		*word*	status of last I/O operation
length(S)	*string*	*integer*	length of *S*
ln(x)	*integer* or *real*	*real*	natural logarithm of *x*
lo(x)		*byte*	low-order byte of *x*
maxavail		*longint*	size of largest dynamic variable that can be allocated now
memavail		*longint*	number of free bytes of heap storage
new(T[, Init])	pointer type	pointer	pointer to a newly allocated memory cell
odd(x)	*integer*	*boolean*	*true* if *x* is odd, *false* if *x* is even
ofs(x)		*word*	offset of *x*
ord(x)	ordinal	*integer*	ordinal position of *x*
paramcount		*word*	number of parameters passed to program on command line
paramstr(i)	*integer*	*string*	i^{th} command-line parameter
pi		*real*	π (3.1415926535897932385)
pos(Sub, S)	*string*	*byte*	position in *S* that substring *Sub* occurs, otherwise 0
pred(x)	ordinal	same as parameter	predecessor of *x*, unless *x* is first
ptr(Seg, Ofs)	*word*	pointer	pointer formed from a segment base and an offset address
random		*real*	random number r, $0 \leq r < 1$
random(Max)	*integer*	*integer*	random number r, $0 \leq r < Max$
round(x)	*real*	*integer*	*x* rounded to an integer
seekeof(F)	*text*	*boolean*	*false* if nonblank characters exist between the current position of the file window and the end-of-file symbol, *true* otherwise
seekeoln(F)	*text*	*boolean*	*false* if nonblank characters exist between the current position of the file window and the end-of-line character, *true* otherwise

`seg(x)`	*object*	*word*	segment of specified object
`sin(x)`	*integer* or *real*	*real*	sine of *x* (*x* in radians)
`sizeof(x)`		*integer*	number of bytes that *x* occupies
`sptr`		*word*	current value of the SP register
`sqr(x)`	*integer* or *real*	same as parameter	*x* squared
`sqrt(x)`	*integer* or *real*	*real*	square root of *x*
`sseg`		*word*	current value of the SS register
`succ(x)`	ordinal	same as parameter	successor of *x*, unless *x* is last
`swap(x)`		same as parameter	swaps high- and low-order bytes of *x*
`trunc(x)`	*real*	*integer*	*x* truncated to an integer
`typeof`	*object*	pointer	pointer to object type's VMT
`upcase(Ch)`	*char*	*char*	uppercase of `Ch`, if `Ch` is a lower-case letter; otherwise `Ch`

APPENDIX G

Standard Procedures

You may redefine standard procedures, but you will lose the procedure's original capability and confuse people who read your program, including yourself. Items in color are not defined in Standard Pascal.

Name	***Action***
`append(F)`	Opens an existing textfile for appending.
`assign(F, Name)`	Associates the file variable *F* with an external file name.
`blockread(F, Buff, BufSize, NumRead)`	Reads one or more records from file *F* into *Buff*, whose length is *BufSize*. *NumRead* is the number of records read.
`blockwrite(F, Buff, NumRecds, NumWritten)`	Writes *NumRecds* records in *Buff* to file *F*. *NumWritten* is the number of records written.
`chdir(Name)`	Changes the current directory to *Name*.
`close(F)`	Closes an open file.
`dec(x, n)`	Decrements *x* by *n*. (If *n* is omitted, decrements by 1.)
`delete(S, i, Count)`	Deletes *Count* characters from string *S*, beginning at the ith character.
`dispose(p)`	Frees memory to which pointer *p* points.
`erase(F)`	Erases an external file *F*.
`exit`	Exits the current block immediately.
`fillchar(x, n, Value)`	Fills *n* contiguous bytes of *x* with *Value*.
`flush(F)`	Flushes the buffer of a textfile *F* that is open for output.
`freemem(p, Size)`	Disposes a dynamic variable *p* of a given size.

Name	*Action*
`getdir(Drive, Name)`	Gets the name of the current directory of the specified drive.
`getmem(p, Size)`	Creates a dynamic variable of a given size and sets pointer *p* to point to it.
`halt`	Stops program execution and returns to the operating system.
`inc(x, n)`	Increments *x* by *n*. (If *n* is omitted, increments by 1.)
`insert(Sub, S, i)`	Inserts a substring *Sub* into string *S* after the ith character.
`mark(p)`	Records heap state in pointer *p*.
`mkdir(Name)`	Creates a subdirectory.
`move(Source, Dest, n)`	Copies *n* contiguous bytes from *Source* to *Dest*.
`new(p)`	Allocates a new memory cell and sets pointer *p* to point to it.
`randomize`	Initializes the function *random*.
`read(F, <variable_list>)`	Reads values from file *F* and assigns them to variables in *<variable_list>*. (Assumes standard output file, if *F* is omitted.)
`readln(F, <variable_list>)`	Same as *read*, but then advances file window beyond the next end-of-line character. Valid only with textfiles.
`release(p)`	Returns heap state to that indicated by *p*.
`rename(F, NewName)`	Renames an external file to *NewName*.
`reset(F)`	Opens file *F* for input and positions file window at the beginning of the file.
`rewrite(F)`	Opens file *F* for output. If *F* exists already, it is erased; otherwise a new file is created.
`rmdir(Name)`	Removes the empty subdirectory *Name*.
`runerror(n)`	Stops program execution and generates an error numbered *n*.
`seek(F, n)`	Moves the file window of a general file *F* to the nth component.
`settextbuf(F, Buff, Size)`	Assigns an I/O buffer to a textfile *F*.
`str(i, S)`	Converts a numeric value *i* to a string *S*.
`truncate(F)`	Truncates the general file *F* at current position of file window.
`val(S, V, ErrorPos)`	Converts a string *S* of characters that represent a number to internal form, as if they were read from a textfile, and places the result into the variable *V*. Returns *ErrorPos* = 0 if all characters are legal; otherwise *ErrorPos* indicates the position of the illegal character.
`write(F, <variable_list>)`	Writes values specified in *<variable_list>* to the file *F*. (Assumes standard output file, if *F* is omitted.)
`writeln(F, <variable_list>)`	Same as *write*, but then writes an end-of-line character and advances file window beyond it. Valid only with textfiles.

APPENDIX H

Compiler Directives

You can control some of Turbo Pascal's compiler features either by using the Options|Compiler menu or by including compiler directives in your program. Such directives have precedence over choices made in the Options|Compiler menu.

Compiler directives look like special comments and can appear anywhere that a comment can. Here are some examples.

`{$B-}`	Switch directive
`{$R+ enable range checking}`	Switch directive with comment
`{$B-,$R+}`	Two switch directives
`{$I StackOps.Pas}`	Parameter directive
`{$IFDEF Debug}`	Conditional directive

Within the braces, all compiler directives begin with a `$` followed by the directive name. (No blanks are permitted before or after the `$`.) What follows the name depends on the type of directive. Three types of directives are available.

- **Switch directives** enable or disable certain compiler features. You specify + to enable a feature and – to disable it. The first three examples of directives just given are switch directives. Notice the optional comment in the second example. The third example indicates how to specify several directives in one statement: no spaces are allowed.
- **Parameter directives** require parameters that affect the compilation. At least one blank must separate the directive name and

its parameter. The fourth example given previously is a parameter directive.

- **Conditional directives** affect the compilation according to certain conditions, which you specify. One blank must separate the directive name and its parameter, as in the last example given previously.

Some switch and parameter directives affect the entire compilation, that is, are global. They must appear before the first occurrence of a `uses`, `const`, `type`, `procedure`, `function`, `begin`, or `label` statement. Other switch and parameter directives are local and can appear anywhere in the program. They affect the portion of the program that follows the directive.

Switch Directives

Turbo Pascal assumes a default value for any switch directive that you do not specify. The following list of switch directives specifies the syntax and default value for each directive and indicates whether the directive is global or local.

A (Align data) — *Type: Global*

Default	`{$A+}`	Aligns all variables and typed constants larger than one byte on an even-numbered address.
	`{$A-}`	No alignment occurs.

B (Boolean evaluation) — *Type: Local*

	`{$B+}`	Evaluates each boolean expression entirely.
Default	`{$B-}`	Evaluation of each boolean expression stops as soon as its value is apparent. (This short-circuit evaluation implements *Cand* and *Cor*.)

D (Debug information) — *Type: Global*

Default	`{$D+}`	Generates information that enables you to use the Turbo Pascal debugger. Usually used with *$L+*.
	`{$D-}`	Disables the debugger.

E (Emulation) — *Type: Global*

Default	`{$E+}`	Emulates the 8087 numeric coprocessor for real numeric computations, if the coprocessor is not present on your computer, by using a run-time library.
	`{$E-}`	No emulation. Real numeric computations require your computer to have an 8087 numeric coprocessor.

F* (Force far calls)** ***Type: Local

	`{$F+}`	Procedures and functions use the far call model.
Default	`{$F-}`	Procedures and functions declared in the interface section of a unit use the far call model; otherwise they use the near model.

G* (Generate 80286 code)** ***Type: Local

	`{$G+}`	Uses the 80286 instruction set. Such programs will not run on an 8088 or 8086.
Default	`{$G-}`	Uses only 8086 instructions. Such programs will run on any 80*x*86 processor.

I* (Input and output checking)** ***Type: Local

Default	`{$I+}`	Enables automatic I/O error checking that produces error messages when one occurs.
	`{$I-}`	Disables automatic I/O error checking. You must use the *`IOResult`* function to check for I/O errors.

L* (Local symbol information)** ***Type: Global

Ignored if *$D–* is in effect.

Default	`{$L+}`	Generates local symbol information for the debugger.
	`{$L-}`	No local symbol information is generated.

N* (Numeric processing)** ***Type: Global

	`{$N+}`	Uses 8087 instructions to perform real arithmetic. Variables of type *`real`*, *`single`*, *`double`*, *`extended`*, and *`comp`* are permitted.
Default	`{$N-}`	Performs real numeric computations by using a run-time library. Only variables of type *`real`* are permitted. (Variables of type *`single`*, *`double`*, *`extended`*, and *`comp`* are not allowed.) Ignores the *$E* compiler directive.

O* (Overlay code generation)** ***Type: Global

	`{$O+}`	Allows you to overlay units.
Default	`{$O-}`	Disables overlay code generation.

R (Range checking) ***Type: Local***

	`{$R+}`	Checks the range of all array and string indexes, the range of all scalar and subrange variables, and the initialization of any object making a call to a virtual method.
Default	`{$R-}`	Disables range checking.

S (Stack overflow checking) ***Type: Local***

Default	`{$S+}`	Checks for sufficient stack space for local variables and temporary storage. If insufficient space is available, the program will terminate with an error message.
	`{$S-}`	If insufficient space is available for local variables and temporary storage, the system will probably crash.

V (Var string checking) ***Type: Local***

Default	`{$V+}`	Requires a string passed as a variable parameter to have a type identical to that of its corresponding formal parameter.
	`{$V-}`	A string passed as a variable parameter can have a string type that differs from the string type of its corresponding formal parameter.

X (Extended syntax) ***Type: Global***

	`{$X+}`	Allows you to call a function as you would a procedure, effectively ignoring its output. This directive does not apply to built-in functions.
Default	`{$X-}`	Disallows calling functions as procedures.

Parameter Directives

I (Include file) ***Type: Local***

`{$I` *filename*`}`	Effectively inserts the source file *filename* at the point where this directive occurs in the program. This directive cannot occur within a statement, including a compound statement.

L (Link object file) ***Type: Local***

{$L *filename*}

Links the named object file with the current program or unit.

M (Memory allocation sizes) ***Type: Global***

{$M *stacksize, heapmin, heapmax*}

Specifies the memory allocated to the program. The default is *{$M 16384, 0, 655360}*. The parameters must be within the following ranges:

1,024 ≤ *stacksize* ≤ 65,520
0 ≤ *heapmin* ≤ 655,360
heapmin ≤ *heapmax* ≤ 655,360

$M has no effect within units.

O (Overlay unit name) ***Type: Local***

{$O *unitname*}

Specifies the units that should be overlays. *$O* must appear after the program's *uses* statements. *$O* has no effect within units.

Conditional Directives

Conditional directives allow you to compile certain portions of your source program if a given condition is met. For example, you could specify that a Turbo Pascal version 6.0 feature be used only if the version 6.0 compiler is used.

The **conditional constructs** resemble Pascal *if/then/else* statements. These constructs examine **conditional symbols,** which are analogous to Pascal boolean variables.

Conditional symbols. Conditional symbols look exactly like Pascal identifiers, but they have no relation to the particular identifiers in your program. Conditional symbols are either *true* (defined) or *false* (undefined). You define a conditional symbol and make it *true* by writing

{$DEFINE *symbol*}

You can make a previously defined conditional symbol *false* by writing

{$UNDEF *symbol*}

The following are standard (built-in) conditional symbols:

VER60	*true* if you are using version 6.0 of Turbo Pascal. Similar symbols exist to indicate other versions of Turbo Pascal.
MSDOS	*true* if the operating system is MS-DOS or PC-DOS.
CPU86	*true* if the CPU belongs to the 80*x*86 family.
CPU87	*true* if an 80*x*87 numeric coprocessor is installed.

Conditional compilation constructs. Two forms of the conditional compilation constructs are possible, as follows:

```
{$IFxxx yyyyyy} ··· {$ENDIF}
```

or

```
{IFxxx yyyyyy} ··· {$ELSE} ··· {$ENDIF}
```

`{$IFxxx yyyyyy}` has three possibilities, as follows:

`{$IFDEF` *symbol*`}`	Compiles the source statements that follow if the conditional symbol *symbol* is `true` (defined).
`{$IFNDEF` *symbol*`}`	Compiles the source statements that follow if the conditional symbol *symbol* is `false` (undefined).
`{$IFOPT` *switch*`}`	Compiles the source statements that follow if the indicated switch directive is in the state specified. Here, *switch* is the single-letter name of a switch directive followed by a + or – state.

You use `{$ELSE}` to indicate a substitute compilation when `{$IFxxx yyyyyy}` indicates that the statements that follow it are not compiled.

The following examples demonstrate the conditional compilation constructs:

```
{$DEFINE Debugging}
{$IFDEF CPU87} {$N+} {$ELSE} {$N-} {ENDIF}
  . . .
type Round = object
     {$IFNDEF VER60}
       Radius : real;
     {$ENDIF}
       procedure Init(R: real);
         ...
     {$IFDEF VER60}
     private
       Radius : real;
     {$ENDIF}
     end;
   . . .
{$IFDEF Debugging}
     writeln('Debugging on: Name = ', Name)
{$ENDIF}
```

GLOSSARY

abstract data type (ADT) A collection of data values together with a set of well-specified operations on that data.

abstract object type An object type that is the basis of a family of other object types that descend from it. An abstract object type has no instances but rather defines characteristics for its descendents to inherit and augment.

access time The time required to access a particular item in a data structure such as an array, a linked list, or a file.

activation record A record that contains a subprogram's local environment at the time of and as a result of the call to the subprogram.

actual parameter A variable or expression that is passed to a subprogram. An actual parameter appears in a call to a subprogram and corresponds to a formal parameter in the heading of the subprogram's definition. See also *value parameter* and *variable parameter*.

address A number that labels a location in a computer's memory.

adjacency list N linked lists that implement a graph of N vertices numbered 1, 2, ⋯ , N such that there is a node in the ith linked list for vertex j if and only if there is an edge from vertex i to vertex j.

adjacency matrix An N-by-N boolean array `A` that implements a graph of N vertices numbered 1, 2, ⋯ , N such that `A[i, j]` is `true` if and only if there is an edge from vertex i to vertex j.

adjacent vertices Two vertices of a graph that are joined by an edge. In a directed graph, vertex y is adjacent to vertex x if there is a directed edge from vertex x to vertex y.

ADT See *abstract data type.*

algorithm A step-by-step specification of a method to solve a problem within a finite amount of time.

allocate See *dynamic allocation* and *static allocation.*

analysis of algorithms A branch of computer science that measures the efficiency of algorithms.

ancestor object type An object type that provides all of its data fields and methods to another object. See also *descendent object type, immediate ancestor,* and *inheritance.*

ancestor of a node *N* A node on the path from the root of a tree to *N*.

array A data structure that contains a fixed maximum number of elements of the same data type that are referenced directly by means of an index, or subscript.

array-based implementation An implementation of an ADT or a data structure that uses an array to store the data values.

assertion A statement that describes the state of an algorithm or program at a certain point in its execution.

average-case analysis A determination of the average amount of time that an algorithm requires to solve problems of size *N*.

AVL tree A balanced binary search tree in which rotations restore the tree's balance after each insertion or deletion of a node.

axiom A mathematical rule or relationship. Axioms can be used to specify the behavior of an ADT operation.

backtracking A problem-solving strategy that, when it reaches an impasse, retraces its steps in reverse order before trying a new sequence of steps.

balanced binary tree A binary tree in which the left and right subtrees of any node have heights that differ by at most 1.

base case See *basis.*

base type of a set The data type of permissible elements in a set.

basis The known case in either a recursive definition or an inductive proof. Also called the base case or degenerate case.

best-case analysis A determination of the minimum amount of time that an algorithm requires to solve problems of size *N*.

BFS See *breadth-first search.*

BFS spanning tree A spanning tree formed by using a breadth-first search to traverse a graph's vertices.

Big O notation A notation that uses the capital letter O to specify an algorithm's order. For example, "O(*f*(*N*))" means "order *f*(*N*)". See also *order of an algorithm.*

binary file See *general file.*

binary operator An operator that requires two operands: for example, the * in 3*5.

binary search An algorithm that searches a sorted collection for a particular item by repeatedly halving the collection and determining which half can contain the item.

binary search tree A binary tree where the search key in any node N is greater than the search key in any node in N's left subtree but less than the search key in any node in N's right subtree.

binary tree A tree in which each node has at most two children, the left child and the right child.

binding The association of a name, such as a variable, with a memory address.

black box A device whose method of transforming inputs into outputs or actions is unknown.

block (1) A program section that consists of optional declarations and a group of statements between `begin` and `end`. (2) A group of data records in a file.

block access time The time required to read or write a block of data associated with a file.

bottom-up implementation An implementation method that starts at the submodules that make up larger modules. You implement and debug these submodules before you implement and debug the modules that use them.

box method A systematic way to trace the actions of a recursive function or procedure.

breadth-first search (BFS) A graph-traversal strategy that visits every vertex adjacent to a vertex v that it can before it visits any other vertex. Thus, the traversal will not embark from any of the vertices adjacent to v until it has visited all possible vertices adjacent to v.

breakpoint A point in a Turbo Pascal program that you mark to indicate that execution should halt there. Breakpoints facilitate debugging.

B-tree of degree *m* A search tree whose leaves are at the same level and whose nodes each contain between $m - 1$ and m `div` 2 records. Each internal node has one more child than it has records. The root of the tree can contain as few as one record and can have as few as two children.

bubble sort A sorting algorithm that compares adjacent elements and exchanges them if they are out of order. Comparing the first two elements, the second and third elements, and so on, will move the largest element to the end of the array. Repeating this process will eventually sort the array into ascending order. Also called exchange sort.

bucket A structure associated with a hash address that can accommodate more than one item. An array of buckets can be used as a hash table to resolve collisions.

buffer A location that temporarily stores data as it makes its way from one process or location to another. A buffer enables data to leave one process or location at a different rate than it enters another process or location, thus compensating for the differences in these rates.

Cand See *conditional and.*

chain A linked list used within separate chaining, which is a collision-resolution scheme associated with hashing.

chaining See *separate chaining.*

child of a node *N* A node directly below node N in a tree.

circuit A path in a graph that begins at a vertex *v*, passes through every vertex in the graph exactly once, and terminates at *v*.

circular doubly linked list A doubly linked list whose first node contains a *previous* pointer to the list's last node and whose last node contains a *next* pointer to the list's first node.

circular linked list A linked list whose last node points to the first node on the list.

closed-form formula A nonrecursive algebraic expression.

clustering A difficulty with the linear probing collision-resolution scheme in hashing whereby items tend to map into groups of locations in the hash table, rather than randomly scattered locations. This difficulty can cause lengthy search times.

code Statements in a programming language.

coding Implementing an algorithm in a programming language.

collision A condition that occurs when a hash function maps two or more different search keys into the same location.

collision-resolution scheme The part of hashing that assigns locations in the hash table to items with different search keys when the items are involved in a collision. See also *bucket, chain, clustering, double hashing, folding, linear probing, open addressing, probe sequence,* and *separate chaining.*

compiler A program that translates a program written in a high-level language, such as Pascal, into machine language.

compile time The time during which a compiler translates a program from source form into machine language.

complete binary tree A binary tree of height h that is full to level $h - 1$ and has level h filled from left to right.

complete graph A graph such that there is an edge between every pair of vertices.

completely balanced binary tree A binary tree in which the left and right subtrees of any node have the same height.

conditional and An `and` operator in pseudocode that does not evaluate its second operand if the first operand is false. The default `and` in Turbo Pascal.

conditional or An `or` operator in pseudocode that does not evaluate its second operand if the first operand is true. The default `or` in Turbo Pascal.

connected component For a graph that is not connected, a subset of the graph's vertices that a traversal visits, beginning at a given vertex.

connected graph A graph such that there is a path between every pair of vertices.

constructor An object initialization method that you must call before any virtual method is called. Any object type that contains a virtual method must have a constructor. You denote a constructor by using the reserved word `constructor` instead of `procedure`, and typically you name it `Init`.

Cor See *conditional or.*

cost of a path The sum of the weights of the edges of a path in a weighted graph. Also called the weight or length of a path.

cost of a program Factors such as the computer resources (computing time and memory) that the program consumes, the difficulties encountered by those who use the program, and the consequences when a program does not behave correctly.

cost of a spanning tree The sum of the weights of the edges in a weighted graph's spanning tree.

cycle In a graph, a path that begins and ends at the same vertex, but does not pass through other vertices more than once.

data abstraction A design principle that separates the operations that can be performed on a collection of data from the implementation of the operations.

data flow The flow of data between modules.

data record An element in a file. A data record can be anything from a simple value, such as an integer, to a multifield Pascal-like record, such as an employee record. See also *block*.

data structure A construct that is defined within a programming language to store a collection of data.

degenerate case See *basis*.

depth-first search (DFS) A graph-traversal strategy that goes as deep into the graph as it can before backtracking. That is, after visiting vertex *v*, DFS visits, if possible, an unvisited vertex *u* adjacent to *v*. The algorithm then visits an unvisited vertex adjacent to *u* and continues as far as possible before returning to *v* to visit the next unvisited vertex adjacent to *v*.

descendent object type An object type that inherits all of another object's data fields and methods, usually augmenting or redefining them. See also *ancestor object type, immediate descendent,* and *inheritance*.

descendent of a node *N* A node on a path from *N* to a leaf of a tree.

destructor An object method that performs all tasks necessary to deallocate the object. By convention, you name the destructor `Done`.

DFS See *depth-first search*.

DFS spanning tree A spanning tree formed by using a depth-first search to traverse a graph's vertices.

digraph See *directed graph*.

direct access A process that provides access to any element in a data structure by position without the need to first access other elements in the structure. Also called random access.

direct access file A file whose elements are accessible by position without first accessing preceding elements within the file.

directed edge An edge in a directed graph; that is, an edge that has a direction.

directed graph A graph whose edges indicate a direction. Also called a digraph.

directed path A sequence of directed edges that begins at one vertex and ends at another vertex in a directed graph. See also *path* and *simple path*.

disconnected graph A graph that is not connected; that is, a graph that has at least one pair of vertices without a path between them.

divide and conquer A problem-solving strategy that divides a problem into smaller problems, each of which is solved separately.

double hashing A collision-resolution scheme that uses two hash functions. The hash table is searched for an unoccupied location, starting from the location that one hash function determines and considering every n^{th} location, where n is determined from a second hash function.

doubly linked list A linked list whose nodes each contain two pointers, one to the next node and one to the previous node.

dummy head node In a linked list, a first node that is not used for data but is always present. The item at the first position of the list is thus actually in the second node. See also *head record.*

dynamic allocation The assignment of memory to a variable during program execution, as opposed to during compilation. See also *static allocation.*

dynamic binding See *late binding.*

dynamic object A dynamically allocated object. An object whose memory is allocated at execution time and remains allocated only as long as you want. See also *static object.*

early binding The association of a variable with an object type at compilation time. Also called static binding. See also *late binding, static method,* and *virtual method.*

edge The connection between two vertices of a graph.

empty string A string of length zero.

empty tree A tree with no nodes.

encapsulation An information-hiding technique that combines data and operations to form an object.

event An occurrence, such as an arrival or a departure, in an event-driven simulation. See also *external event* and *internal event.*

event-driven simulation A simulation that uses events generated by a mathematical model that is based on statistics and probability. The times of events are either read as input or computed from other event times. Because only those times at which the events occur are of interest, and because no action is required at times between the occurrence of events, the simulation can advance from the time of one event directly to the time of the next.

event list A data structure within an event-driven simulation that keeps track of arrival and departure events that will occur but have not occurred yet.

exchange sort See *bubble sort.*

exhaustive search A search strategy that must examine every item in a collection of items before it can determine that the item sought does not exist.

extensible The property of an object type that enables you to add capabilities to its descendents without access to its implementation. Extensible object types must define virtual methods.

external event An event that is determined from the input data to an event-driven simulation.

external file A file that exists after program execution.

external methods Algorithms that require external files because the data will not fit entirely into the computer's main memory.

external sorting A sorting algorithm that is used when the collection of data will not fit in the computer's main memory all at once but must reside on secondary storage such as a disk.

fail-safe programming A technique whereby a programmer includes checks within a program for anticipated errors.

Fibonacci sequence A sequence of integers that is defined by a particular recurrence relation and that models many naturally occurring phenomena.

field A component of a record or an object.

field identifier An identifier of a field in a record or an object.

FIFO See *first in, first out.*

file A data structure that contains a sequence of components of the same data type. See also *external file, general file, index file, internal file,* and *textfile.*

file component An indivisible piece of data in a file.

file variable A Pascal identifier that names a file.

file window A marker of the current position in the file.

first in, first out (FIFO) A property of a queue whereby the removal and retrieval operations access the item that was inserted first (earliest).

fixed size A characteristic of a data structure whose memory allocation is determined at compilation time and cannot change during program execution. See *static allocation.*

folding A hashing technique that breaks a search key into parts and combines some or all of those parts, by using an operation such as addition, to form a hash address.

formal parameter An identifier that appears in the heading of a subprogram definition and represents the actual parameter that the calling program will pass to the subprogram. See also *value parameter* and *variable parameter.*

free list A list of available nodes used in an implementation of an ADT or a data structure.

front of a queue The end of a queue at which items are removed.

full binary tree A binary tree of height h whose leaves are all at level h and whose nonleaves each have two children.

general file A file whose elements are in the computer's internal representation. A general file is not organized into lines. Also called a binary file or nontext file.

general tree A set of nodes that is either empty or has a root node and zero or more subtrees of the root.

global identifier (1) An identifier declared in the outermost (main) block of a program; that is, an identifier whose scope is the entire program. (2) An identifier whose scope includes a block that does not define the identifier explicitly.

global variable A variable declared in the outermost (main) block of a program; that is, a variable whose scope is the entire program.

grammar The rules that define a language.

graph A set V of vertices, or nodes, and a set E of edges that connect the vertices.

graph traversal A process that starts at vertex v and visits all vertices w for which there is a path between v and w. A graph traversal visits every vertex in a graph if and only if the graph is connected, regardless of where the traversal starts.

growth-rate function A function of the size of a problem, used to specify an algorithm's order.

hash function A function that maps the search key of a table item into a location that will contain the item.

hashing A method that enables access to table items in time that is relatively constant and independent of the items by using a hash function and a scheme for resolving collisions.

hash table An array that contains table items, as assigned by a hash function.

head pointer A pointer to the first node on a linked list. Also called head.

head record A record that contains the external pointer to the first node on a linked list, along with global information about the list, such as its length. See also *dummy head node*.

heap A complete binary tree whose nodes each contain a priority value that is greater than or equal to the priority values in the node's children.

heapsort A sorting algorithm that first transforms an array into a heap, then removes the heap's root (the largest element) by exchanging it with the heap's last element, and finally transforms the resulting semiheap back into a heap.

height-balanced binary tree See *balanced binary tree*.

height of a tree The number of nodes on the longest path from the root of the tree to a leaf.

hierarchical relationship The "parent-child" relationship between the nodes in a tree.

host type A single ordinal data type from which a subrange type is constructed.

immediate ancestor The nearest ancestor of an object type. An object can have only one immediate ancestor. See also *immediate descendent*.

immediate descendent A nearest descendent of an object type. An object can have many immediate descendents. See also *immediate ancestor*.

implement (1) To create a program for an algorithm. (2) To use a data structure to realize an ADT.

implementation section The private portion of a unit. This section contains the complete definitions of the procedures and functions whose headers appear in the interface section. The implementation section also contains variable declarations and definitions for constants, data types, procedures, and functions that are available only within the unit itself. See also *initialization section* and *interface section*.

index (1) An ordinal value that references the elements of an array. Also called a subscript. (2) Another name for an index file.

index file A data structure whose entries—called index records—are used to locate items in an external file. Also called the index.

index record An entry in an index file that points to a record in the corresponding external data file. This entry contains a key field and a pointer field.

induction See *mathematical induction.*

inductive conclusion See *inductive step.*

inductive hypothesis See *inductive step.*

inductive proof A proof that uses the principle of mathematical induction.

inductive step The step in an inductive proof that begins with an inductive hypothesis ("if $P(k)$ is true for any $k \geqslant 0$") and demonstrates the inductive conclusion ("then $P(k + 1)$ is true").

infix expression An algebraic expression in which every binary operator appears between its two operands.

information hiding A process that hides certain implementation details within a module and makes these details inaccessible from outside the module.

inheritance The ability of an object data type to inherit properties from one or more previously defined object data types. See also *descendent object type.*

initialization section The portion of a unit whose statements are executed before the statements in the main body of the program that uses the unit. See also *implementation section* and *interface section.*

inorder successor of a node *N* The node in a tree that an inorder traversal visits immediately after node *N*. This node is the leftmost node of *N*'s right subtree.

inorder traversal A traversal of a binary tree that processes (visits) a node after it traverses the node's left subtree but before it traverses the node's right subtree.

insertion sort A sorting algorithm that considers items one at a time and inserts each item into its proper sorted position.

instance An object that is the result of either declaring a variable of a particular object type or calling `new` with a pointer to an object type.

interface The communication mechanisms between modules or systems.

interface section The public portion of a unit. This section contains the variable declarations, constant definitions, data type definitions, and headers for procedures and functions that are available to the unit's users. See also *initialization section* and *implementation section.*

internal event An event that is determined by a computation within an event-driven simulation, as opposed to an external event, which is determined by the reading of data.

internal file A file that is temporary and exists only during program execution.

internal sort A sorting algorithm that requires the collection of data to fit entirely in the computer's main memory.

invariant An assertion that is always true at a particular point in an algorithm or program.

iteration (1) A process that is repetitive. (2) A single pass through a loop.

iterative solution A solution that involves loops.

key See *search key.*

key field A field in an index record that contains the same value as the search key in the record in the data file to which the index record points.

language A set of strings of symbols that adhere to the rules of a grammar.

last in, first out (LIFO) A property of a stack whereby the deletion and retrieval operations access the most recently inserted item.

late binding The association of a variable with an object type during program execution. Late binding allows you to write only one version of a method, which you can use with various objects with dramatically different results. Also called dynamic binding. See also *early binding, static method,* and *virtual method.*

leaf A tree node with no children.

left child of a node *N* A node directly below and to the left of node *N* in a tree.

left subtree of a node *N* The left child of node *N* plus its descendents in a binary tree.

length of a path The sum of the weights of the edges of a path in a weighted graph. Also called the weight or cost of a path.

level of a node The root of a tree is at level 1. If a node is not the root, then its level is 1 greater than the level of its parent.

life cycle of software The phases of software development: specification, design, verification, coding, testing, refining, production, and maintenance.

LIFO See *last in, first out.*

linear implementation An array-based implementation or a pointer-based implementation.

linear linked list A linked list that is not circular.

linear probing A collision-resolution scheme that searches the hash table sequentially, starting from the original location specified by the hash function, for an unoccupied location.

linked list A list of elements, or nodes, that are linked to one another such that each element points to the next element.

local environment of a subprogram A subprogram's formal value parameters, its local variables, a return address in the calling routine, and, in the case of functions, the value of the function itself.

local identifier An identifier whose scope is the block that contains its declaration.

local variable A variable declared within a subprogram and available only within that subprogram.

loop invariant An assertion that is true before and after each execution of a loop within an algorithm or program.

machine language A language composed of the fundamental instructions that a computer can execute directly.

mathematical induction A method for proving properties that involve nonnegative integers. Starting from a base case, you show that if a property is true for an arbitrary nonnegative integer k, then the property is true for the integer $k + 1$.

mergesort A sorting algorithm that divides an array into halves, sorts each half, and then merges the sorted halves into one sorted array. Mergesort can also be adapted for sorting an external file.

message A request, in the form of a subprogram call, that an object perform an operation.

method An operation that is defined within an object.

minimum spanning tree A graph's spanning tree for which the sum of its edge weights is minimal among all spanning trees for the graph.

modular program A program that is divided into isolated components, or modules, that have well-specified purposes and interactions.

module An individual component of a program, such as a procedure, function, or other block of code.

multiple indexing A process that uses more than one index file to an external data file.

node An element in a linked list, graph, or tree that usually contains both data and a pointer to the next element in the structure.

nonrecursive shell A nonrecursive subprogram that contains a locally defined recursive subprogram.

nontext file See *general file.*

O($f(N)$) Order $f(N)$. See *order of an algorithm.*

object A data type that combines data and operations on that data. See also *object-oriented programming.*

object-oriented programming (OOP) A software engineering technique that views a program as a collection of components called objects that interact. OOP embodies three fundamental principles: encapsulation, inheritance, and polymorphism.

object type compatible A characteristic of objects that enables the use of an instance of a descendent object type instead of an instance of an ancestor object type, but not the converse.

OOP See *object-oriented programming.*

open A process that prepares a file for either input or output and positions the file window. A state of readiness for I/O.

open addressing A type of collision-resolution scheme in hashing that probes for an empty, or open, location in the hash table in which to place the item. See also *double hashing* and *linear probing.*

ordered list An ADT whose elements are referenced by position number within a list.

order of an algorithm An algorithm's time requirement as a function of the problem size. An algorithm A is order $f(N)$ if, for any implementation of the algorithm and any computer, there is some constant c such that for all but a finite number of values of N, A requires no more than $c * f(N)$ time units to solve a problem of size N. See also *Big O notation.*

order-of-magnitude analysis An analysis of an algorithm's time requirement as a function of the problem size. See also *order of an algorithm.*

owned variable A variable that is declared in the implementation section of a unit.

palindrome A character string that reads the same from left to right as it does from right to left, for example, "deed."

parent of a node N The node directly above node N in a tree.

partition To divide a data structure such as an array into segments.

path A sequence of edges in a graph that begins at one vertex and ends at another vertex. Because a tree is a special graph, you can have a path through a tree. See also *directed path* and *simple path*.

perfect hash function An ideal hash function that maps each search key into a unique location in the hash table. Perfect hash functions exist when all possible search keys are known.

pivot element A central element in an algorithm. For example, the quicksort algorithm partitions an array about a particular element called the pivot.

planar graph A graph that can be drawn in a plane in at least one way so that no two edges cross.

pointer A pointer variable in Pascal. Generically, a dynamic element that references a memory cell. Sometimes an indicator, such as an integer, to an element within a data structure.

pointer-based implementation An implementation of an ADT or a data structure that uses pointers to organize its elements.

pointer field A field in an index record that points to a data record in a data file. This field contains the number of the block that contains the data record.

pointer variable A Pascal variable that references a memory cell. Also called a pointer.

polymorphism The ability of a variable name to represent, during program execution, instances of different but related object types that descend from a common abstract object type.

pop To remove an item from a stack.

position oriented The characteristic of certain ADT's whose operations involve the ith position of a data structure.

postcondition A statement of the conditions that exist at the end of a module.

postfix expression An algebraic expression in which every binary operator follows its two operands.

postorder traversal A traversal of a binary tree that processes (visits) a node after it has traversed both of the node's subtrees.

precondition A statement of the conditions that must exist at the beginning of a module in order for the module to work correctly.

prefix expression An algebraic expression in which every binary operator precedes its two operands.

preorder traversal A traversal of a binary tree that processes (visits) a node before it traverses both of the node's subtrees.

primitive data types A collection of built-in data types provided in high-level programming languages (for example, integers, reals, characters, and arrays in Pascal).

principle of locality A principle that states that the effects of any statement should, as much as possible, be limited to other statements in its immediate vicinity.

priority queue An ADT that orders its items by a priority value. The first item removed is the one having the highest priority value.

priority value A value assigned to the items in a priority queue to indicate the item's priority.

private field A field within the private section of an object definition.

private method A method within the private section of an object definition.

private portion The part of a unit or subprogram that is hidden from the user. That is, the implementation portion of a unit or the body of a subprogram.

private section The portion of an object definition that is accessible only within the unit or program that contains the object type definition. See also *private field* and *private method.*

probe sequence The sequence of locations in the hash table that a collision-resolution scheme examines.

problem solving The entire process of taking the statement of a problem and developing a computer program that solves that problem.

procedural abstraction A design principle that separates the purpose and use of a module from its implementation.

public portion The part of a subprogram or unit that a user can see. What you see when you want to use a subprogram or unit.

push To add an item to a stack.

qualify In Pascal, to relate an item `A` to an item `B` by writing `B.A`, in which case "`B` qualifies `A`" or "`A` is qualified by `B`".

queue An ADT whose first (earliest) inserted item is the first item removed or retrieved. This property is called first in, first out, or simply FIFO. Items enter a queue at its rear and leave at its front.

quicksort A sorting algorithm that partitions an array's elements around a pivot p to generate two smaller sorting problems: Sort the array's left section, whose elements are less than p, and sort the array's right section, whose elements are greater than or equal to p.

radix sort A sorting algorithm that treats each data element as a character string and repeatedly organizes the data into groups.

random access See *direct access.*

range check error An execution-time error that occurs when either a value is not within a certain range or an instance of an object type is not initialized by its constructor before a call to a virtual method occurs.

range query An operation that retrieves all table items whose search keys fall into a given range of values.

rear of a queue The end of a queue at which items are inserted.

recognition algorithm An algorithm, based on a language's grammar, that determines whether a given string is a member of the language.

record A group of related items, called fields, that are not necessarily of the same data type.

recurrence relation A mathematical formula that generates successive terms in a sequence.

recursion A process that solves a problem by solving smaller problems of exactly the same type as the original problem.

recursive call A call within a subprogram to the subprogram itself.

right child of a node *N* A node directly below and to the right of node *N* in a binary tree.

right subtree of a node *N* The right child of node *N* plus its descendents in a binary tree.

rightward drift (1) In an array-based implementation of a queue, the problem of the front of the queue moving toward the end of the array. (2) In a Pascal program, the problem of nested blocks bumping against the right-hand margin of the page.

root The only node in a tree with no parent.

rotation An operation used to maintain an AVL tree.

run time The execution phase of a program. The time during which a program's instructions execute.

scope of an identifier The blocks of a program in which an identifier has meaning.

search A process that locates a certain item in a collection of items.

search key A field that identifies an entire record within a collection of records. A field that a search algorithm uses to locate a record within a collection of records.

selection sort A sorting algorithm that selects the largest item and puts it in its correct place, then selects the next largest item and puts it in its correct place, and so on.

semiheap A complete binary tree in which the root's left and right subtrees are both heaps.

separate chaining A collision-resolution scheme that uses an array of linked lists as a hash table. The ith linked list, or chain, contains all items that hash (map) into location *i*.

sequential access A process that stores or retrieves elements in a data structure one after another starting at the beginning.

sequential access file A file whose elements must be processed sequentially. That is, to process the data stored at a given position, you must advance the file window beyond all the data that precedes it. Textfiles are sequential access files.

sequential search An algorithm that locates an item in a collection of items by examining them in order one at a time, beginning with the first item.

set A collection of distinct elements. In Pascal, the elements must have the same data type.

shortest path The path between two given vertices in a weighted graph that has the smallest sum of its edge weights.

siblings Tree nodes that have a common parent.

side effect (1) A change to a variable that exists outside of the scope of a procedure or function and that is not passed as a parameter. (2) An occurrence that is not specified by a module.

silent program A program that produces no visible output.

simple data type A data type that is not structured, such as integer, real, character, boolean, enumerated, and subrange.

simple path In a graph, a path that does not pass through a vertex more than once. See also *directed path.*

simulation A technique for modeling the behavior of both natural and artificial systems. Generally, its goal is to generate statistics that summarize the performance of an existing system or to predict the performance of a proposed system. A simulation reflects the long-term average behavior of a system rather than predicting occurrences of specific events.

software engineering A branch of computer science that provides techniques to facilitate the development of computer programs.

solution Algorithms and ways to store data that solve a problem.

sorted run Sorted data that is part of an external sort.

sorting A process that organizes a collection of data into either ascending or descending order.

sort key A field that determines the order of entire records within a collection of records. A field that a sorting algorithm uses to order records within a collection of records.

source-inclusion facility A facility that automatically places the contents of a file at a specified point in a program before the program is compiled.

source program A program written in a programming language that needs to be compiled. For example, a Pascal program. Also called source code.

spanning tree A subgraph of a connected, undirected graph *G* that contains all of *G*'s vertices and enough of its edges to form a tree. See also *BFS spanning tree* and *DFS spanning tree.*

stack An ADT whose most recently inserted item is the first item removed or retrieved. This property is called last in, first out, or simply LIFO. Items enter and leave a stack at its top.

standard input file The default file, designated by `input`, from which a Pascal program reads data.

standard output file The default file, designated by `output`, to which a Pascal program writes data.

static allocation The assignment of memory to a variable during compilation, as opposed to during program execution. See also *dynamic allocation.*

static binding See *early binding.*

static method An object method whose body is determined (bound to the object) at compilation time. See also *early binding, late binding,* and *virtual method.*

static object A statically allocated object. An object whose memory is allocated at compilation time and remains allocated for the duration of the program's execution. See also *dynamic object.*

string A Turbo Pascal data structure that contains a sequence of characters that you can manipulate by calling standard procedures and functions. A standard data type in Turbo Pascal. Generically, a sequence of characters.

structure chart An illustration of the hierarchy of modules that solve a problem.

structured data type A data type composed of multiple elements. Some examples of structured data types are arrays, records, files, and sets.

stub A dummy procedure or function that you use during the development and testing of other modules of a program.

subgraph A subset of a graph's vertices and edges.

subrange type A data type whose values are a subset of values of an ordinal data type and are consecutive. See also *host type*.

subscript An ordinal value that references the elements of an array. Also called an index.

subtree Any node in a tree, together with all of the node's descendents.

subtree of a node *N* A tree that consists of a child of *N* and the child's descendents.

successor In a linked list, the successor of node *x* is the node to which *x* points. In a graph, vertex *y* is a successor of vertex *x* if *y* is adjacent to *x*.

symmetric matrix An *N*-by-*N* matrix *A* whose elements satisfy the relationship $A_{ij} = A_{ji}$.

table An ADT whose data items are stored and retrieved according to their search-key values.

tag field A field in a variant record that indicates which fields exist in a particular record.

tail recursion A type of recursion where the recursive call is the last action taken.

textfile A file of characters that are organized into lines.

time-driven simulation A simulation where the time of an event, such as an arrival or departure, is determined randomly and compared to a simulated clock.

time-sharing system An operating system that allows you to share a computer with many other users.

top-down design A process that addresses a task at successively lower levels of detail, producing independent modules.

top of a stack The end of a stack at which items are inserted and deleted.

topological order A list of vertices that occur in a directed graph without cycles such that vertex *x* precedes vertex *y* if there is a directed edge from *x* to *y* in the graph. A topological order is not unique, in general.

topological sorting The process of arranging the vertices that occur in a directed graph without cycles into a topological order.

traversal An operation that accesses (visits) each element in an ADT or data structure.

tree A connected, undirected graph without cycles.

2–3 search tree A type of search tree whose balance is readily maintained. A 2–3 tree in which, if a node has two children and contains one data item, the value of the search key in the node must be greater than the value of the search key in the left child and smaller than the value of the search key in the right child. If a node has three children and contains two data items, the value of the smaller search key in the node must be greater than the value of the search key in the left child and smaller than the value of the search key in the middle child; the value of the larger search key in the node must be greater than the value of the search key in the middle child and smaller than the value of the search key in the right child.

2–3 tree A tree in which each internal node (nonleaf) has either two or three children, and all leaves are at the same level. A node can have a left subtree, a middle subtree, and a right subtree. People often use the term "2–3 tree" to mean "2–3 search tree."

type compatible A characteristic of two or more sets that have the same base type. See also *object type compatible.*

unary operator An operator that requires only one operand: For example, `not` or the − in −5.

undirected graph A graph that has at most one edge between any two vertices and whose edges do not indicate a direction.

unit A collection of subprograms, constant definitions, type definitions, and variable declarations that can be compiled for later use in a program.

user interface The portion of a program that provides for user input.

value oriented The characteristic of certain ADT's whose operations involve data items with given values.

value parameter A formal parameter whose value is initially the value of the corresponding actual parameter. Any change that the subprogram makes to a value parameter is not reflected in the corresponding actual parameter in the calling routine. The default when you do not specify the keyword *`var`*.

variable parameter A formal parameter that represents an actual parameter. Any change that the subprogram makes to a variable parameter changes the corresponding actual parameter in the calling routine. A variable parameter is used when a procedure needs to return a value to the calling routine. You designate a variable parameter in the subprogram heading by writing *`var`* before the parameter.

variant record A record that has both a fixed part, which contains the fields that are common to all records, and a variant part, which contains fields that differ for certain records according to the value of a tag field.

vertex A node in a graph.

virtual method An object method whose body is determined at execution time. That is, the method's body is bound to the object during program execution. See also *early binding, late binding, static method,* and *virtual method table.*

virtual method table (VMT) The table that exists for an object type that defines a virtual method. For every virtual method in the object, the object's VMT contains a pointer to the actual instructions that implement the method. This pointer is established by the constructor during program execution.

visit The act of processing an item during a traversal of an ADT or a data structure.

VMT See *virtual method table.*

watch A Turbo Pascal feature that enables you to examine the current values of variables and expressions during program execution.

weighted graph A graph whose edges are labeled with numeric values.

weight of an edge The numeric label on an edge in a weighted graph.

weight of a path The sum of the weights of the edges of a path in a weighted graph. Also called the length, or cost, of a path.

worst-case analysis A determination of the maximum amount of time that an algorithm requires to solve problems of size *N*.

ANSWERS TO SELF-TEST EXERCISES

Chapter 1

1. $1 \leq$ `Index` $\leq$ `N` and `Sum` = `A[1]` + ⋯ + `A[Index]`.

2. The specifications include type definitions, parameters, and pre- and postconditions.

```
const   MaxSize = 50;
type    elementType = integer;
        arrayType = array[1..MaxSize] of elementType;

procedure ComputeSum(A : arrayType; N : integer;
                     var Sum : elementType);
{ Computes the sum of the first 5 positive elements in an array A.
Precondition: A is an array of N elements, N >= 5, that contains
at least 5 positive elements.
Postcondition: Sum = sum of first 5 positive elements; A and N are
unchanged. }
```

Another solution:

```
procedure ComputeSum(A : arrayType; N : integer;
                var Sum : elementType; var Success : boolean);
{ Computes the sum of the first 5 positive elements in an array A.
Precondition: A is an array of N elements.
Postcondition: If there are at least 5 positive elements in A, then
Sum = sum of first 5 positive elements and Success = true. Otherwise,
Sum = 0 and Success = false. A and N are unchanged. }
```

Chapter 2

1. a.
```
for Day := 1 to DaysPerWeek do
      write(MinTemps(Day, 1):7:1)
```
   b.
```
for Week := 1 to 5 do
      write(MinTemps(1, Week):7:1)
```

c.
```
for Week := 1 to WeeksPerYear do
      begin
         for Day := 1 to DaysPerWeek do
            write(MinTemps(Day, Week):7:1);
         writeln
      end
```

2. `function Average(X : weekType) : real;`

3. a. `Student1.Address.State`; b. `Student1.Address.Zip[1]`; c. `Student1.GPA`; d. `Student1.Name[1]`

4. a. `true`; b. `[1,3,5,9]`; c. `[6,8]`; d. `A`; e. `[9]`; f. `false`; g. `[1..6,8,9]`; h. `[1..5,9..15,20,22]`

5.

OriginalFile	**Ch**	**eoln**	**eof**	**CopyFile**
a b *<eoln>* c d *<eoln>* *<eof>*	?	F	F	_
a b *<eoln>* c d *<eoln>* *<eof>*	a	F	F	a _
a b *<eoln>* c d *<eoln>* *<eof>*	b	T	F	a b _
a b *<eoln>* c d *<eoln>* *<eof>*	*<eoln>*	F	F	a b *<eoln>* _
a b *<eoln>* c d *<eoln>* *<eof>*	c	F	F	a b *<eoln>* c _
a b *<eoln>* c d *<eoln>* *<eof>*	d	T	F	a b *<eoln>* c d _
a b *<eoln>* c d *<eoln>* *<eof>*	*<eoln>*	T	T	a b *<eoln>* c d *<eoln>* _ a b *<eoln>* c d *<eoln>* *<eof>*

(In Turbo Pascal, *<eoln>* consists of a carriage return character and a line feed character. Reading and writing *<eoln>* requires two iterations of *`CopyTextFile`*'s *`while`* loop.)

Chapter 3

1. Incorrect statements:

```
writeln(p, q);       { cannot write addresses (pointer values) }
writeln(p^, pp^);    { pp^ is a pointer; use pp^^ instead }
pp^ := 20;           { cannot assign a value to a pointer }
```

Output from hand trace:

```
7    11
18   18
18   11   26
```

2. a.
```
Prev^.Next := Cur^.Next;
Cur^.Next := nil;
dispose(Cur);
Cur := nil;
```
b.
```
Head := Cur^.Next;
Cur^.Next := nil;
dispose(Cur);
Cur := nil;
```

c.
```
new(p);
p^.Data := 'A';
p^.Next := Head;
Head := p
```

d. The pointer *Head* points to a node that contains *'A'*; this node points to a node that contains *'J'*. The *Next* portion of the last node is *nil*.

3.
```
procedure PrintNodeN(Head : ptrType; N : integer);
var Cur : ptrType; Node : integer;
begin
   Cur := Head;
   for Node := 1 to N-1 do
      Cur := Cur^.Next;
   write(Cur^.Data)
end; { PrintNode }
```

4. *N*, ignoring the assignments to *Node* in the *for* statement.

5. Use *Lists[i]* instead of *Head* in the procedure calls.

Chapter 4

1. A wall is a visualization of abstraction and modularity. Modules should be as independent as possible: Walls prevent other parts of the program from seeing the details of modules. A contract is a specification of what the module, which is behind the wall, is to do. The contract governs the slit in the wall; it specifies what is to be passed to the module and what will be passed out. The contract does not specify how to implement the module.

   These concepts help during the problem-solving process by encouraging you to divide the problem into small parts and to focus first on what you want done rather than on how to do it.

2.
```
OrderedListReplace(OL, Position, NewItem)
{ Replaces the item at position Position in the ordered
  list OL with NewItem. }

   OrderedListDelete(OL, Position)
   OrderedListInsert(OL, Position, NewItem)
```

3. For example, the following specify operations for output:
```
PrepareForOutput(F)
{ Readies a textfile F for output. If F exists, erases its data;
  otherwise creates an empty textfile F. }

Output(F, X)
{ Places X at the end of the file F. }

OutputLine(F, X)
{ Places X at the end of the file F and writes an end-of-line
  symbol. }
```

4.
```
CreateOrderedList(OL)
{ Pre: None.
  Post: The ordered list OL is empty. }

OrderedListLength(OL)
{ Pre: CreateOrderedList(OL) has been called.
  Post: Returns the number of items that are in ordered list OL. }

OrderedListInsert(OL, Position, NewItem)
{ Pre: CreateOrderedList(OL) has been called. Position
  indicates where the insertion should occur. NewItem is the
  item to be inserted.
  Post: If 1 <= Position <= OrderedListLength(OL) + 1 before
  the insertion, NewItem is at position Position in the list
  and other items are renumbered accordingly. }

OrderedListDelete(OL, Position)
{ Pre: CreateOrderedList(OL) has been called. Position
  indicates where the deletion should occur.
  Post: If 1 <= Position <= OrderedListLength(OL) before
  the deletion, the item at position Position in the list
  is deleted and other items are renumbered accordingly. }

OrderedListRetrieve(OL, Position, DataItem)
{ Pre: CreateOrderedList(OL) has been called. Position
  indicates the position of the desired item.
  Post: If 1 <= Position <= OrderedListLength(OL), DataItem
  is the value of the desired item. The list is left
  unchanged by this operation. }
```

5.
```
type cylinderType = object(circleType)
        TheHeight : real; { new field: the cylinder's height }

        procedure Init(R, H : real);
        { Initializes the cylinder, its radius, and height. }
        function Height : real;
        { Returns the cylinder's height. }
        function Volume : real;
        { Returns the cylinder's volume. }
        function SurfaceArea : real;
        { Returns the cylinder's surface area. }
        procedure DisplayStatistics;
        { Displays statistics of the cylinder. }
     end;  { object }
```

6.
```
type squarePtrType = ^squareType;
     squareType = object(genericObjectType)
        TheSide: real; { the side of the square }

        constructor Init(S : real);
        { Initializes the square and its side. }
```

```
      destructor Done; virtual;
      { Deallocates the square. }
      function Side : real;
      { Returns the square's side. }
      function Area : real;
      { Returns the square's area. }
      function Perimeter : real;
      { Returns the square's perimeter. }
      procedure DisplayStatistics;
      { Displays statistics of the square. }
   end;  { object }
```

Chapter 5

1. The product of n numbers is defined in terms of the product of $n-1$ numbers, which is a smaller problem of the same type. When $n = 1$, the product is 1; this occurrence is the degenerate case. Because $n \geq 1$ initially and n decreases by 1 at each recursive call, the degenerate case will be reached.

2.
```
procedure ComputeProduct(A: arrayType; n: integer; var Product: real);
begin
    if n = 1
       then Product := A[1]

       else
       begin
          ComputeProduct(A, n-1, Product);
          Product := A[n] * Product
       end
end;  { ComputeProduct }
```

3.
```
function Product(A : arrayType; First, Last : integer) : real;
{ Pre: A[First..Last] is an array of integers, where First <= Last.
  Post: Returns the product of the integers in A[First..Last]. }
begin
   if First = Last
      then Product := A[First]
      else Product := A[Last] * Product(A, First, Last-1)
end;  { Product }
```

4.
```
procedure PrintIntegers(N : integer);
{ Pre: N > 0.
  Post: Prints N, N - 1, ... , 1. }
begin
   if N > 0
      then
      begin
         writeln(N);
         PrintIntegers(N-1)
      end
end;  { PrintInteger }
```

5. A nonrecursive shell provides a compromise between efficiency and style when a recursive subprogram operates on an array. The shell is a nonrecursive subprogram that contains a locally defined recursive subprogram. You define the array within the shell so that it is global to the recursive subprogram. Thus, you do not pass the array to the recursive subprogram and can avoid copies of the array.

6. `WriteBackward`, `BinSearch`, and `KSmall`.

Chapter 6

1. The three recursive calls result in the following moves: move a disk from *A* to *C*, from *A* to *B*, and then from *C* to *B*.

2.
```
procedure Retrieve(Head:ptrType; i:integer; var DataItem:integer);
begin
   if i = 1
         then DataItem:= Head^.Data
         else Retrieve(Head^.Next, pred(i), DataItem)
end
```

3. The positions of the queens are given as (*row, column*) pairs.

Solution 1: (2, 1), (4, 2), (1, 3), (3, 4)

Solution 2: (3, 1), (1, 2), (4, 3), (2, 4)

4. $-*/ABC*+DEF$

5. $AB*C-D/EF-+$

6. $(A - B/(C + D * E)) - F$

7. <*T*> = $ | cc<*T*>d

Chapter 7

1.

20	80	40	25	60	30
20	30	40	25	60	**80**
20	30	40	25	**60**	**80**
20	30	25	**40**	**60**	**80**
20	25	**30**	**40**	**60**	**80**
20	**25**	**30**	**40**	**60**	**80**

2. Find the smallest instead of the largest element at each pass.

20	80	40	25	60	30
30	80	40	25	60	**20**
30	80	40	60	**25**	**20**
60	80	40	**30**	**25**	**20**
60	80	**40**	**30**	**25**	**20**
80	**60**	**40**	**30**	**25**	**20**

3. **Pass 1**

25	30	20	80	40	60
25	30	20	80	40	60
25	20	30	80	40	60
25	20	30	80	40	60
25	20	30	40	80	60
25	20	30	40	60	**80**

Pass 2

25	20	30	40	60	**80**
20	25	30	40	60	**80**
20	25	30	40	60	**80**
20	25	30	40	60	**80**
20	25	30	40	**60**	**80**

There are no exchanges during pass 3, so the algorithm will terminate.

4.

25	30	20	80	40	60
25	**30**	20	80	40	60
20	**25**	**30**	80	40	60
20	**25**	**30**	**80**	40	60
20	**25**	**30**	**40**	**80**	60
20	**25**	**30**	**40**	**60**	**80**

5. • *Mergesort* sorts an array by sorting each half of the array by using a mergesort.
   • Sorting half of an array is a smaller problem than sorting the entire array.
   • An array of one element is the degenerate case.
   • By halving an array and repeatedly halving the halves, you must reach array segments of one element each.

6.

```
38 | 16   40   39   12   27   Swap 16 with itself
38 | 16 | 40   39   12   27
38 | 16 | 40 | 39   12   27
38 | 16 | 40   39 | 12   27   Swap 12 and 40
38 | 16   12 | 39   40 | 27   Swap 27 and 39
38 | 16   12   27 | 40   39   Swap 38 and 27 to position pivot
27   16   12 | 38 | 40   39
```

7. $(N-1) + (N-2) + \cdots + 1 = N * (N-1)/2$

8. $N + (N-1) + \cdots + 2 = N * (N+1)/2 - 1$

9. **a.** $O(N^3)$; **b.** $O(\log N)$; **c.** $O(N)$

10. **a.** You can stop searching as soon as `SearchValue` is less than a data element, because you will have passed the point where `SearchValue` would have occurred if it was in the data collection.
    b. Sorted data, using the scheme just described in the answer to Part *a:* best case: O(1); worst case: O(*N*); average case: O(*N*).
    Unsorted data: O(*N*) in all cases.
    c. Regardless of whether the data is sorted, the best case is O(1) (you find the item after one comparison) and both the average and worst cases are O(*N*) (you find the item after *N*/2 or *N* comparisons, respectively).

Chapter 8

1. D, C, B, A

2. *S*: 1 4 5; *T*: 3 6 (elements listed bottom to top)

3. Use an array-based implementation if you know the maximum line length in advance and you know that the average line length is not much shorter than the maximum length. Clearly, you would use a pointer-based implementation if you could not predict the maximum line length. In addition, if the maximum line length is 300, for example, but the average line length is 30, a pointer-based implementation would use less storage on average than an array-based implementation.

4. a. The stack is empty when the last close parenthesis is encountered. When the loop ends, `Continue` is *`false`* and `I` equals `length(Str)`.
   b. The stack contains one open parenthesis when the loop ends.
   c. The stack is empty when the loop ends and `I` is greater than `length(Str)`.

5. 2

6. *AB/C**

7. The precedence tests control association. The $\geq$ test enables left-to-right association when operators have the same precedence.

8. a. Stack contains A, then A B, then A B D.
   b. Stack contains A, then A B.
   c. Stack contains C, then C D, then C D H, then C D H G.

Chapter 9

1. A, B, C, D

2. *Q*: 2 3 5; *T*: 4 6 (elements listed front to rear)

3. a. When the *`for`* loop ends, the stack and queue are as follows:

   Stack: a b c d a ← top   Queue: a b c d a ← rear

   The *a* at the top of the stack matches the *a* at the front of the queue. After deleting the *a* from both ADT's, the *d* at the top of the stack does not match the *b* at the front of the queue, so the string is not a palindrome.
   b. The letters that you delete from the stack and the queue are the same, so the string is a palindrome.

4. **a.** 1; **b.** 3; **c.** 3; **d.** 2; **e.** 3; **f.** 1; **g.** 2; **h.** 2; **i.** 1; **j.** 1; **k.** 1; **l.** 2

Chapter 10

1. **a.** 60; **b.** 60, 20, 40; **c.** 20, 70, 10, 40, 30, 50; **d.** 20 and 70, 10 and 40, 30 and 50; **e.** 40, 20, 60; **f.** 10, 40, 30, 50; **g.** 70, 10, 30, 50

2. a. 1: A; 2: B, C; 3: E, D; 4: F; 5: G
   b. 1: A; 2: B; 3: C; 4: D; 5: E; 6: F; 7: G

3. 4

4. Complete: b, c, d, e; Full: e; Balanced: b, c, d, e.

5. Preorder: A, B, D, E, C, F, G; Inorder: D, B, E, A, F, C, G; Postorder: D, E, B, F, G, C, A

6. No. H should be in G's right subtree. U and V should be in T's right subtree.

7.

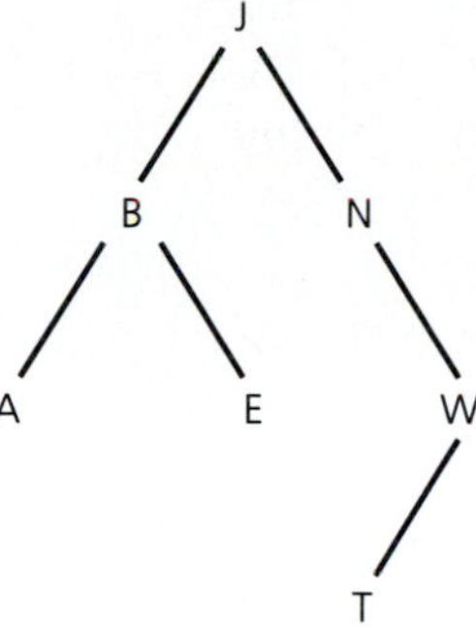

8.
```
TableReplace(T, X, ReplacementItem, Success)

    TableDelete(T, X, Success)
    if Success
       then TableInsert(T, ReplacementItem, Success)
```

9. **a.** 60, 20, 40, 30; **b.** 60, 20, 10

10. **a.**

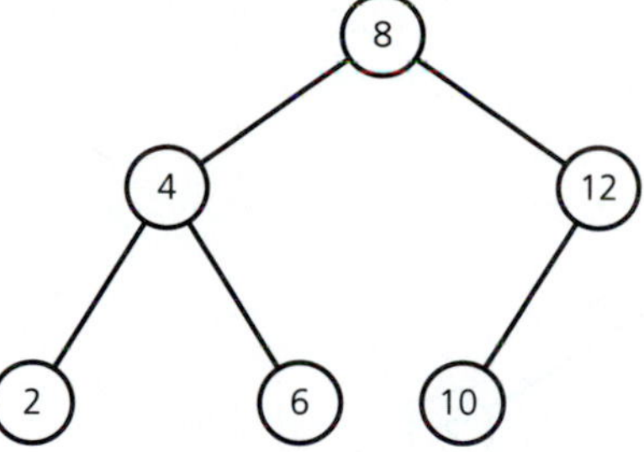

b. The tree has minimum height and is complete but not full.

Chapter 11

1. **a.** Directed, connected; **b.** Undirected, connected

2. DFS: 1 2 3 5 4; BFS: 1 2 3 4 5

3.

	1	2	3	4	5
1	F	T	F	F	F
2	F	F	T	T	F
3	F	F	F	F	T
4	F	T	F	F	F
5	T	F	F	F	F

4. a d b e c

5. No. See Observation 2 on page 572.

6. 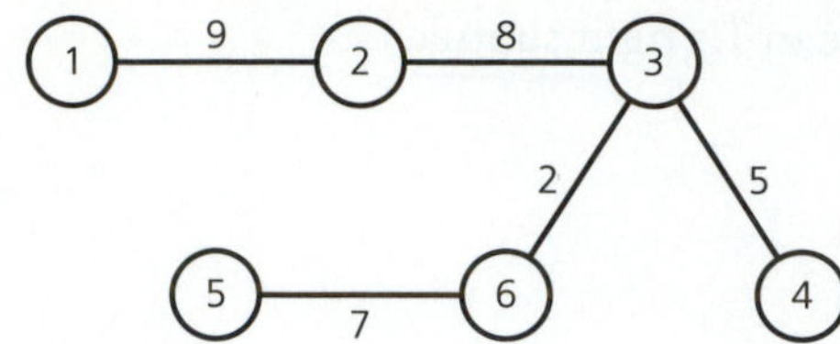

7. 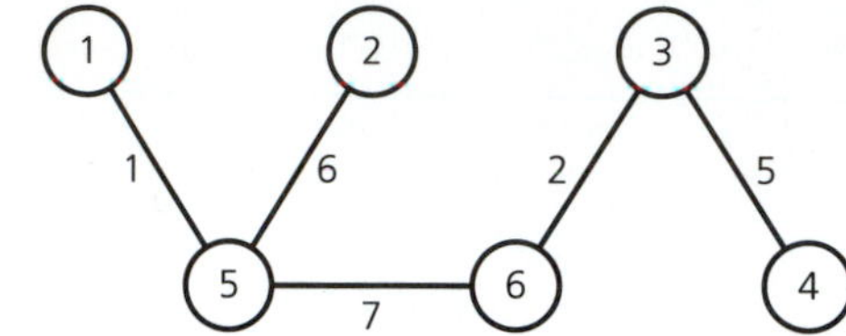

8. Path 1, 5, 3, 2 has weight 7.
Path 1, 5, 3 has weight 5.
Path 1, 5, 3, 4 has weight 8.
Path 1, 5 has weight 4.

Chapter 12

1. The array is 30 20 50 10 25 40 60.
2. This tree is not a heap.

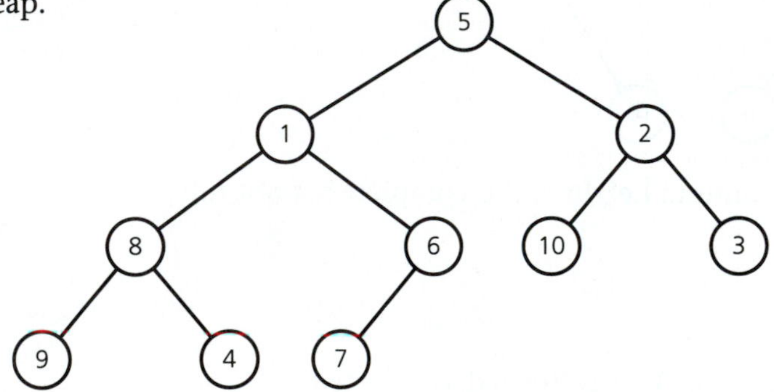

3. It is neither a semiheap nor a heap.
4. After inserting 12:

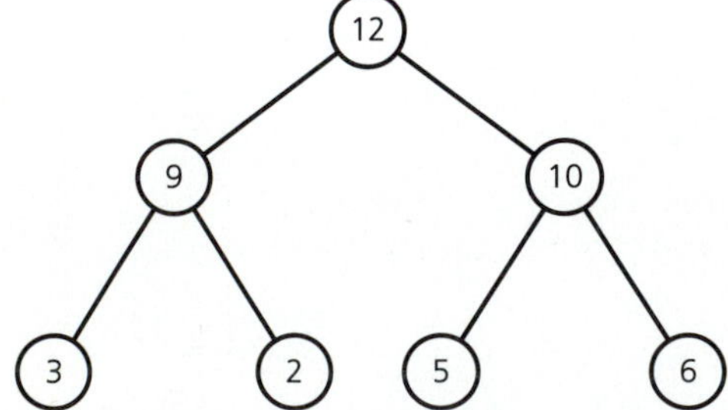

After removing 12:

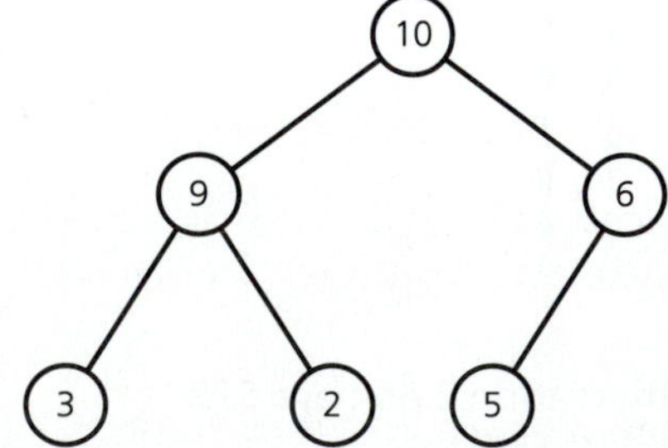

5. The array that represents the heap is 7 5 6 4 3 2.

6. The array is 10 9 5 8 7 2 3 1 4 6.

Chapter 13

1.

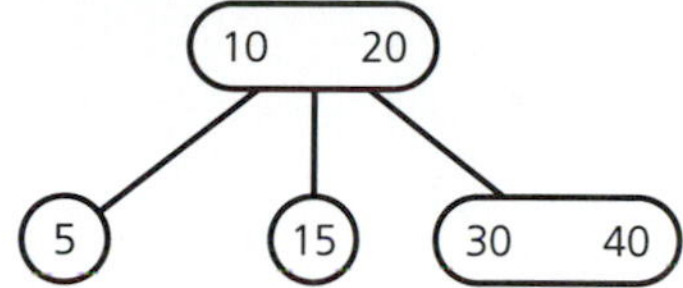

2.

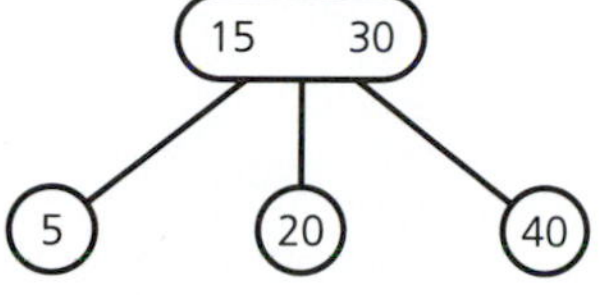

3. *TableDelete(T, SearchKey, Success)*

```
I := h(SearchKey)
while ((T[I] is occupied) and (T[I] <> SearchKey))
      or (T[I] is deleted) do
   I := I + 1
if T[I] is not empty
   then { T[I] = SearchKey }
   begin
      Mark T[I] deleted
      Success := true
   end

   else Success := false
```

4. 8, 2, 7, 1, 6, 0, 5, 10, 4, 9, 3

5. `T[1]` → 15 → 8
`T[2]` is *nil*
`T[3]` → 17 → 24 → 10
`T[4]` → 32

Chapter 14

1. Sequential access: Copy the original file *F1* into the file *F2*. Write a new block containing the desired record and 99 blank records. Copy *F2* to the original file *F1*.

   Direct access: Create a new block containing the desired record and 99 blank records. Write the new block to the file as block 17.

2.
```
ExternalMergesort(UnsortedFileName, SortedFileName)

    Associate UnsortedFileName with the file variable InFile
      and SortedFileName with the file variable OutFile

    Blocksort(InFile, TempFile1, NumBlocks)
    { records in each block are now sorted; NumBlocks = 16 }
    MergeFile(TempFile1, TempFile2, 1, 16)
       MergeRuns(TempFile1, TempFile2, 1, 1)
       MergeRuns(TempFile1, TempFile2, 3, 1)
       MergeRuns(TempFile1, TempFile2, 5, 1)
       MergeRuns(TempFile1, TempFile2, 7, 1)
       MergeRuns(TempFile1, TempFile2, 9, 1)
       MergeRuns(TempFile1, TempFile2, 11, 1)
       MergeRuns(TempFile1, TempFile2, 13, 1)
       MergeRuns(TempFile1, TempFile2, 15, 1)
    MergeFile(TempFile2, TempFile1, 2, 16)
       MergeRuns(TempFile2, TempFile1, 1, 2)
       MergeRuns(TempFile2, TempFile1, 5, 2)
       MergeRuns(TempFile2, TempFile1, 9, 2)
       MergeRuns(TempFile2, TempFile1, 13, 2)
    MergeFile(TempFile1, TempFile2, 4, 16)
       MergeRuns(TempFile1, TempFile2, 1, 4)
       MergeRuns(TempFile1, TempFile2, 9, 4)
    MergeFile(TempFile2, TempFile1, 8, 16)
       MergeRuns(TempFile2, TempFile1, 1, 8)
    CopyFile(TempFile1, OutFile)
```

3.
```
TableRetrieve(TIndex[1..20], TData, SearchKey, TableItem, Success)
  ReadBlock(TIndex[1..20], 10, B)
  TableRetrieve(TIndex[1..9], TData, SearchKey, TableItem, Success)
    ReadBlock(TIndex[1..9], 5, B)
    TableRetrieve(TIndex[1..4], TData, SearchKey, TableItem, Success)
      ReadBlock(TIndex[1..4], 2, B)
      TableRetrieve(TIndex[1..1], TData, SearchKey, TableItem, Success)
        ReadBlock(TIndex[1..1], 1, B)
        Success := false
```

4.
```
TableRetrieve(TIndex[1..20], TData, SearchKey, TableItem, Success)
  ReadBlock(TIndex[1..20], 10, B)
  TableRetrieve(TIndex[11..20], TData, SearchKey, TableItem, Success)
    ReadBlock(TIndex[11..20], 15, B)
    TableRetrieve(TIndex[11..14], TData, SearchKey, TableItem, Success)
      ReadBlock(TIndex[11..14], 12, B)
      j := 26
      BlockNum := 98
      ReadBlock(TData, 98, D)
      Find record D[k] whose search key equals SearchKey
      TableItem := D[k]
      Success := true
```

INDEX

SUMMARY OF TURBO PASCAL STATEMENTS

assignment

```
<variable> := <expression>;
```

compound

```
begin
   <statement_1>;
   <statement_2>;
   .
   .
   .
   <statement_n>
end;
```

if-then

```
if <boolean expression>
   then <statement>;
```

if-then-else

```
if <boolean expression>
   then <statement_1>
   else <statement_2>;
```

case

```
case <expression> of
   <label_1> : <statement_1>;
   <label_2> : <statement_2>;
           .
           .
           .
   <label_n> : <statement_n>;
else
   <statement>
end;  { case }
```

while

```
while <boolean expression> do
   <statement>;
```

repeat

```
repeat
   <statement_1>;
   <statement_2>;
         .
         .
         .
   <statement_n>;
until <boolean expression>;
```

for

```
for <variable> := <expression> to <expression> do
   <statement>;
```

```
for <variable> := <expression> downto <expression> do
   <statement>;
```